PRINCIPLES OF AUDITING

PEARSON
Education

We work with leading authors to develop the strongest
educational materials in business and finance, bringing
cutting-edge thinking and best learning practice to a
global market.

Under a range of well-known imprints, including
Financial Times Prentice Hall, we craft high quality print
and electronic publications which help readers to
understand and apply their content, whether studying
or at work.

To find out more about the complete range of our
publishing please visit us on the World Wide Web at:
www.pearsoned.co.uk

Companion Website resources

Visit the Companion Website at **www.booksites.net/hayes**

For lecturers
- Complete, downloadable Instructor's Manual
- PowerPoint slides that can be downloaded and used as OHTs

Second Edition

PRINCIPLES OF AUDITING
An Introduction to International Standards on Auditing

Rick Hayes
California State University, Los Angeles

Roger Dassen
Deloitte Touche, Amsterdam
International Auditing and Assurance Standards Board (IAASB)
Free University of Amsterdam, University of Maastrict

Arnold Schilder
The Netherlands Central Bank
Basel Committee of Banking Supervisions Accounting Task Force
University of Amsterdam

Philip Wallage
KPMG, Amsterdam
University of Amsterdam

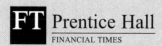

FT Prentice Hall
FINANCIAL TIMES

An imprint of **Pearson Education**
Harlow, England • London • New York • Boston • San Francisco • Toronto • Sydney • Singapore • Hong Kong
Tokyo • Seoul • Taipei • New Delhi • Cape Town • Madrid • Mexico City • Amsterdam • Munich • Paris • Milan

Pearson Education Limited

Edinburgh Gate
Harlow
Essex CM20 2JE
England

and Associated Companies throughout the world

Visit us on the World Wide Web at:
www.pearsoned.co.uk

First published by McGraw-Hill Publishing Company 1999
Second edition published by Pearson Education Limited 2005

Copyright © 1999 by McGraw-Hill International (UK) Limited
© Pearson Education Limited 2005

ISBN 0 273 68410 8

British Library Cataloging-in-Publication Data
A catalogue record for this book is available from the British Library.

Library of Congress Cataloging-in-Publication Data
A catalog record for this book is available from the Library of Congress.

10 9 8 7 6 5 4 3 2 1
08 07 06 05

Typeset in 10.5/12.5 pt Minion by 25.
Printed and bound in Great Britain by Ashford Colour Press Ltd. Gosport.

The publisher's policy is to use paper manufactured from sustainable forests.

Contents

1 International Auditing Overview   1

2 The Audit Market   43

6 Understanding the Entity, Risk Assessment and Materiality 193

7 Internal Control and Control Risk 229

8 Control Risk, Audit Planning and Test of Controls 272

13 Overview of a Group Audit 541

14 Corporate Governance 592

List of Illustrations

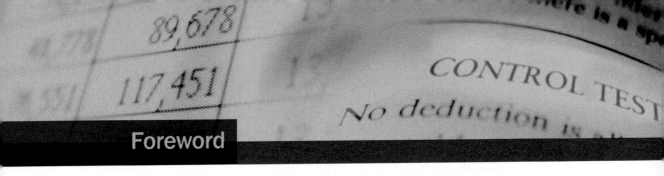

In the last few years the auditing environment has changed dramatically. The failure of Enron was perhaps the biggest single catalyst for change, but other corporate scandals, in the US and in Europe, also led to serious concern about the quality of financial reporting and corporate behavior. Inadequate audits, poor corporate governance, lax standards and insufficient regulatory oversight were, to varying degrees, blamed for the problems. In particular, the regulation of accounting firms and their auditing practices came under intense scrutiny throughout the world, even in those jurisdictions that had not suffered from a serious scandal.

The changes may have been swiftest and most radical in the United States of America, where the Sarbanes-Oxley Act created a new regulatory regime for public company auditing, but in other countries there have also been changes. In Europe, for example, the proposed revisions to the EC's 8th Directive on statutory audit have undoubtedly been influenced by these recent events. Further restrictions have been placed on the ability of auditors to provide non-audit services to their audit clients, standard setting in some jurisdictions has been moved wholly or partly out of the hands of the auditing profession and standard-setters have been looking closely at what can be done to improve the ability of auditors to meet public expectations.

The International Auditing and Assurance Standards Board (IAASB), the independent standards-setter that operates under the auspices of the International Federation of Accountants (IFAC), has sought to respond effectively to the new environment. At the time of the Enron scandal, IAASB was working on revising its core standards for the basis of the audit process (the 'audit risk model' standards dealing with the identification of the risks of error in financial statements and effective audit responses to those risks). The finalization of those standards reflected the lessons learned from the recent scandals. The standard on the auditor's approach to the risk of fraudulent misstatement of financial statements has also been recently revised and strengthened. Included in our current work program are new standards on materiality and group audits.

IAASB has also been reorganized to enhance its independence from the profession and to meet the standards expected today of a public interest body. Amongst other things, its meetings and agendas have been opened to the public; three public interest members have been appointed to the board, together with some non-voting observers; and a public interest oversight board (PIOB) is in the process of being established.

In such an environment, the importance of the education of our auditors cannot be over-emphasized. The scope, applied standards, and even the thinking behind the audit has changed, and these changes need to be reflected in what students learn. Students need a clear understanding of what is important in audits today. They need to learn the principles and to be aware of what audit tools they will be using. A new edition of this book is therefore welcome. It is up to date, and includes relevant standards andregulations, considers the audit tools as they are used and describes the current thinking in the profession.

This book covers the standards set by the IAASB: International Standards on Auditing (ISAs), International Standards on Assurance Engagements (ISAEs), International Standards on Quality Control (ISQCs), and International Standards on Related Services (ISRSs), together with International Auditing Practice Statements (IAPSs). Also discussed are the Sarbanes-Oxley Act, the Public Company Accounting Oversight Board's audit standards, the EC's revised 8th directive, corporate governance best practices, and other standards and regulations that apply in today's global market. In other words, the book contains essential knowledge for today's auditors.

A book of this kind needs to be authoritative, and this and its other qualities usually reflect those of the authors. The co-authors of this book include members of the IAASB and the Basel Committee. The co-authors taken together represent over 80 years experience in the global auditing profession and 70 years in accounting education.

The authors communicate a clear vision of the modern audit environment.

John Kellas
Chairman, International Auditing and Assurance Standards Board

This audit text in all editions is created and written from the point of view of the international student – the world's future audit and accounting professional.

So much has changed in the audit profession since our first edition that this second edition had to be no less than a major revision. The basic audit concepts remain as timeless as ever, but many of the rules have changed.

Oversight and governance issues have moved to the top of an auditor's agenda. The US Public Companies Accounting Standards Board (PCAOB), created by the Sarbanes–Oxley Act of 2002, has become a powerful force in the US and the rest of the world. PCAOB has declared existing US audit standards *temporary* and now set their own standards. Corporate Governance has also become a high-priority concern for world governments (e.g. EU revised 8th Directive, UK Combined Code).

Audit services have undergone extensive change. Ethics standards have been re-conceptualized. What was once considered legitimate services for audit clients are now forbidden. The International Auditing and Assurance Standards Board (IAASB) have revised their International Standards on Auditing (ISAs) extensively, re-categorizing and renumbering standards on review, prospective financial information, compilations and agreed-upon services. The newly revised standards focus on the concept of risk.

There are whole new sets of international standards: International Standards on Quality Control (ISQCs), International Standards on Review Engagements (ISREs), International Standards on Assurance Engagements (ISAEs), and International Standards on Related Services (ISRSs). Auditors are using other standards for their assurance services such as sustainability reporting under Global Reporting Initiative (GRI).

Even before we co-authors began to write the first edition of this book over 10 years ago, we all agreed that our only concern was to produce a high quality audit text for the international student. This meant that it had to be fully up to date, use outstanding material, have a sound balance of audit theory and real practice, and be based on international auditing standards. We were determined that this would be written from a truly global, cross cultural perspective.

In addition to being fully in line with International Standards on Auditing, this text offers many unique features. To make the whole audit process clear, the audit is explained step-by-step using a real-world multinational company group audit. This text explains the widespread use of Computer Aided Audit Techniques (CAAT) (such as generalized audit software (GAS) and embedded audit software) and the extensive use of analytical procedures in today's audits. This text approaches statistical sampling geared specifically to the audit standards on sampling. There is a focus on the audit market and the theory, regulation and liability concerns of auditors. As befits a profession where accepting the right client is the key to avoiding audit failure, the text looks at client acceptance from all sides. There is a chapter on Corporate Governance and appendices on the Combined Code and bank auditing and regulation.

To spotlight the key auditing concepts, we present original thought-provoking audit cases that address the audit problems of Enron, WorldCom, Arthur Andersen, Parmalat, Ahold, Adelphia, Tyco, Vivendi, Resona Bank, HIH Insurance, Hollinger, Waste Management, Xerox, Health South, Citibank, Kmart, and many others throughout.

All the co-authors are professors and as such we have a special place in our hearts for our students. Learning is an almost magical process. People who are highly motivated will learn no matter how the material is presented, but to open their mind, to give them insight, takes a special combination of the practical and philosophical. We have endeavored to mix these elements in the right proportion to produce that magic.

We are also grateful to fellow-teachers and other professionals who provided us with useful comments to improve the book and its accompanying guidance. (An Instructor's Manual and PowerPoint slides that can be downloaded and used as OHTs are available at www.booksites.net/hayes)

Rick Hayes, Roger Dassen,
Arnold Schilder, and Philip Wallage
July 29, 2004

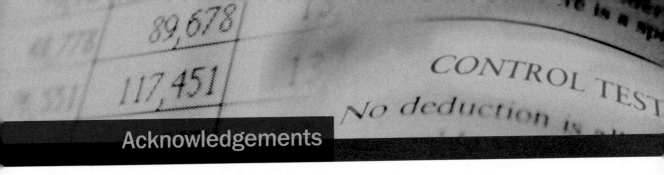

Acknowledgements

This book was not the work of the co-authors alone, but also of the many professionals and students who helped us shape our ideas and give depth to the knowledge contained here.

First we would like to acknowledge the professional accountants who helped us: Lucas Hoogduin, John Kellas, Wendy Kotterer, Herman Brons, and Elvira Könst.

We would like to thank these publishers and professional organizations: American Accounting Association, American Institute of Certified Public Accountants, Canadian Institute of Chartered Accountants, The Chartered Association of Certified Accountants (ACCA), Chartered Institute Of Management Accountants, Institute of Chartered Accountants of England and Wales, International Accounting and Assurance Standards Board, International Federation of Accountants (IFAC), Royal NIvRA, Prentice Hall Publishing Co.

In the writing of the book several individuals helped with the questions: Rong Hu, Dizhou (Daisy) Chen, Stephanie Panzariello, and Ahava Goldman. We would like to also thank the students in Hayes' auditing class at California State University at Los Angeles as well as students at the University of Amsterdam and the University of Maastricht who gave us very helpful comments.

And, of course, who can do any massive undertaking without the support of their families. We thank the Hayeses, Dassens, Schilders, and Wallages.

Publisher's Acknowledgements

We would also like to express our gratitude to the following academics who provided invaluable feedback on this book at various stages during its development:

- Karin Andersson and Thomas Polesie, Göteborg University, Sweden
- Ron Crijns, The Hague University, The Netherlands
- Marcia Halvorsen, Göteborg University, Sweden
- Claus Holm, The Aarhus School of Business, Denmark
- Chris McMahon, Liverpool John Moores University, UK
- Stellan Nilsson, Umeå School of Business & Economics, Sweden

We are grateful to the following for permission to reproduce copyright material:

Deloitte & Touche LLP for extracts adapted from "The History of Deloitte" published at www.deloitte.com; Ernst & Young for extracts adapted from "The History of Ernst & Young" published at www.ey.com; KPMG for extracts from "The History of KPMG" published at www.kpmg.nl: PricewaterhouseCoopers LLP for extracts adapted from

"The History of PricewaterhouseCoopers" published at www.pwcglobal.com: IFAC for extracts from *The Handbook of International Auditing, Assurance and Ethics Pronouncements 2003*, Copyright © International Federation of Accountants (All standards, guidelines, discussion papers and other IFAC documents are the copyright of the International Federation of Accountants (IFAC), 545 Fifth Avenue, 14th Floor, New York, New York, 10017, USA, all rights reserved); Copyright Clearance Center for an extract from "Over the Line" by S. Pulliam published in *The Wall Street Journal Eastern Edition* 23rd June 2003; Public Company Accounting Oversight Board for an extract from *PCAOB Release No. 2003-017 Proposed Auditing Standard*; Shell International BV and PricewaterhouseCoopers LLP for extracts from *The Royal Dutch Shell Report 2002 environmental, economic and social performance sustainability report*; The Financial Reporting Council for extracts from *The Combined Code on Corporate Governance 2003*; the American Institute of Certified Public Accountants (AICPA) for AICPA EPA exam questions. Adapted and reprinted with permission from AICPA. Copyright © 2000 & 1985 by American Institute of Certified Public Accountants; AICPA are not responsible for the suggested answers to the questions. Full responsibility for these is accepted by the authors; and the Canadian Institute of Chartered Accountants, Toronto for CICA questions. Adapted with permission. Copyright © Canadian Institute of Chartered Accountants. Any changes to the original material are the sole responsibility of the author (and/or publisher) and have not been reviewed or endorsed by the CICA.

Illustration 4.1: based on International Auditing and Assurance Standards Board (IAASB), 2003, *Interim Terms of Reference and Preface to the International Standards on Quality Control, Auditing, Assurance and Related Services*, "Appendix", International Federation of Accountants, New York. Copyright © International Federation of Accountants; Illustration 6.2: based on International Auditing and Assurance Standards Board, 2002, *Exposure Draft Audit Risk Proposed International Auditing, Assurance, and Ethics Pronouncements*, Appendix 2: Overview of the proposed ISA, International Federation of Accountants, New York, October. Copyright © International Federation of Accountants; Illustrations 6.3 and 6.6: from Bell, T., *et al.*, 1997, *Auditing Organizations Through a Strategic-Systems Lens: The KPMG Business Measurement Process*, KPMG, p.27 and p.31; Illustration 6.12: from AICPA, 1985, 'Auditing Procedures Study' in *Audits of Small Business*, New York, p. 44; Illustration 7.1: from Committee of Sponsoring Organizations of the Treadway Commission (COSO), 2002, *Internal Control – Integrated Framework*, American Institute of Certified Public Accountants (AICPA), New Jersey.

In some instances we have been unable to trace the owners of copyright material and we would appreciate any information that would enable us to do so.

Chapter 1

INTERNATIONAL AUDITING OVERVIEW

1.1 Learning Objectives

After studying this chapter, you should be able to:

1 Relate some of the early history of auditing.

2 Discuss some of the audit expectations of the general public.

3 Identify organizations that affect international accounting and auditing.

4 Name the standards set by International Auditing and Assurance Standards Board.

5 Give an overview of the IFAC International Standards on Auditing (ISA).

6 Understand the basic definition of auditing in an international context.

7 Distinguish between audit risk and business risk

8 Differentiate the different types of audits.

9 Distinguish between the types of auditors and their training, licensing and authority.

10 Name and categorize the key management assertions.

11 Give the components of the audit process model.

12 Describe how international accountancy firms are organized and the responsibilities of auditors at the various levels of the organization.

1.2 Auditing through World History

Auditing predates the Christian era. Anthropologists have found records of auditing activity dating back to early Babylonian times (around 3000 BC). There was also auditing activity in ancient China, Greece and Rome. The Latin meaning of the word "auditor" was a "hearer or listener" because in Rome auditors heard taxpayers, such as farmers, give their public statements regarding the results of their business and the tax duty due.

■ Scribes of Ancient Times

Auditors existed in ancient China and Egypt. They were supervisors of the accounts of the Chinese Emperor and the Egyptian Pharaoh. The government accounting system of the Zhao dynasty in China included an elaborate budgetary process and audits of all government departments. From the dawn of the dynastic era in Egypt (3000 BC) the scribes (accountants) were among the most esteemed in society and the scribal occupation was one of the most prestigious occupations.

Egyptian Pharaohs were very severe with their auditors. Each royal storehouse used two auditors. One counted the goods when they came in the door and the second counted the goods after they were stored. The supervisor looked at both accounts. If there was a difference, the auditors were both killed.

Bookkeeping as a support mechanism for the determination of profit or wealth, or as a decision support system for achieving profit maximization, was basically unknown in ancient cultures like the Mesopotamian, Egyptian, Greek or Roman. Auditing in English-speaking countries dates to 1130 AD. Then, although they had highly developed economic systems, registration of economic facts or events was limited to the recording of single transactions whose sole purpose was to support the short-term memory of the trading partner.

Rational maximization of wealth or profit did not fit into the systems of these cultures. Wealth was not a function of keen entrepreneurship or of smart cost–benefit trade-offs. It was merely a reward for one's loyalty to the government or for living in accordance with religious and moral principles and rules.

■ Profit Maximization and Double Entry

The attitude of profit maximization emerged at the end of the Middle Ages, with the emergence of large merchant houses in Italy. Trading was no longer the domain of the individual commercial traveler; it was now coordinated centrally at the luxurious desks of the large merchant houses in Venice, Florence or Pisa. As a result, communication became vital. Not unexpectedly, therefore, the system of double entry bookkeeping was first described in Italy, in Luca Pacioli's *Summa de Arithmetica* dated 20 November 1494.

The practice of modern auditing dates back to the beginning of the modern corporation at the dawn of the Industrial Revolution. In 1853, the Society of Accountants was founded in Edinburgh. Several other institutes emerged in Great Britain, merging in 1880 into the Institute of Chartered Accountants in England and Wales. This nationwide institute was a predecessor to institutes that emerged all over the Western world at the end of the nineteenth century, for example, in the USA (in 1886) or in the Netherlands (in 1895).

Further developments of the separation between provision of capital and management and in the complexity of companies, along with the occurrence of several financial scandals (e.g. City of Glasgow Bank, 1883; Afrikaansche Handels-vereeniging, 1879)[1] have led to a steady growth of the audit profession and regulation. The British Companies Acts (1845–62) were models for US auditing. The first US authoritative auditing pronouncement was issued in 1917.

■ Economic Conditions for Audit Reports

At the same time, companies across the world experienced growth in technology, improvement in communications and transportation, and the exploitation of expanding worldwide markets. As a result, the demands of owner-managed enterprises for capital rapidly exceeded the combined resources of the owners' savings and the wealth-creating potential of the enterprises themselves. It became necessary for industry to tap the savings of the community as a whole. The result has been the growth of sophisticated securities markets and credit-granting institutions serving the financial needs of large national, and increasingly international, corporations.

The flow of investor funds to the corporations and the whole process of allocation of financial resources through the securities markets have become dependent to a very large extent on financial reports made by company management. One of the most important characteristics of these corporations is the fact that their ownership is almost totally separated from their management. Management has control over the accounting systems. They are not only responsible for the financial reports to investors, but they also have the authority to determine the way in which the information is presented.

Investors and creditors may have different objectives than management (e.g., management prefers higher salaries and benefits (expenses), whereas investors wish higher profits and dividends). Investors and creditors must depend on fair reporting of the financial statements. To give them confidence in the financial statements, an **auditor**[2] provides an independent and expert opinion on the fairness of the reports, called an **audit opinion**.

1.3 The Auditor, Corporations and Financial Information

■ The Importance of Auditing

It can be said that the function of auditing is to lend credibility to the financial statements. The financial statements are the responsibility of management and the auditor's responsibility is to lend them credibility. By the audit process, the auditor enhances the usefulness and the value of the financial statements, but he also increases the credibility of other non-audited information released by management.[3]

■ The Expectations of Auditors

The importance of the company as a potential generator of wealth is increasingly understood, and so is the impact that a company's activities have on society and the environment. This has led to the expectation by investors that more information than just financial statements should be provided about a company. Public expectations go further and include questions such as:

- Is the company a **going concern**?
- Is it free of fraud?
- Is it managed properly?
- Is there integrity in its **database**?
- Do directors have proper and adequate information to make decisions?
- Are there adequate controls?
- What effect do the company's products and by-products have on the environment?
- Can an "unfortunate mistake" bring this company to its knees?

These are matters of **corporate governance** as well as reporting and are all concerns of the auditor.

The auditors are very important to the directors of these corporations. As Sir Adrian Cadbury commented:[4]

> The external auditors are not part of the company team, but the chairmen (members of a corporate board of directors) have a direct interest in assuring themselves of the effectiveness of the audit approach within their companies. No chairman appreciates surprises, least of all in financial matters. The relationship between auditors and managers should be one where the auditors work with the appropriate people in the company, bur do so on a strictly objective and professional basis, never losing sight of the fact that they are there on the shareholders' behalf. Chairmen need auditors who will stand up to management when necessary and who will unhesitatingly raise any doubts about the people or procedures with the audit committee. Weak auditors expose chairmen to hazards.

◼ Auditing Expertise

Ordinarily, considerable expertise is needed to perform the auditing function. The auditor must be as competent in financial accounting as the most competent of his clients. He must be an expert in deciding what evidence is necessary to satisfy the assertions of the financial statements.

With the explosion in the use of **information technology** the auditor needs sufficient expertise, coupled with the knowledge of his client's affairs, to enable him to obtain and interpret all the evidence needed to provide **reasonable assurance** that the financial statements are fairly presented. The new auditing environment will demand new skills of auditors if they are to be reporters and assessors of governance and measurements. They must have a questioning mind and be able to analyze and critically assess evidence.

Certification Exam Question 1.1[5]

An attitude that includes a questioning mind and a critical assessment of audit evidence is referred to as:

(A) Due professional care.
(B) Professional skepticism.
(C) Reasonable assurance.
(D) Supervision.

■ Future of Auditing

In the future, as is the case today, the annual report, financial statements, notes and auditors' reports will be required. In addition to these, however, there will also be a **management report**,[6] a director's report on corporate governance[7] (including effectiveness of **internal control systems**,[8] going concern, and adherence to Codes of Best Practice), and presumably an environmental management report.[9] These new reports come from the widespread concern about corporate governance resulting from major accounting scandals in the beginning of the twenty-first century. (See Chapters 2 and 14 for further discussion.)

Professor P. Percy, a partner in Grant Thornton and professor at Aberdeen University, outlined a perspective on the auditor's future.[10] He predicted that auditors will account for information not only in financial but also non-financial terms. Furthermore, only retrospective, but more and more prospective information will be in the annual report. The public desire will be for external and internal assessors on the board of directors. External assessors will appraise the integrity of information and business conduct, and internal assessors will appraise the efficiency and effectiveness of systems and their adequacy. Independent directors or assessors working on behalf of the shareholders within the board will ensure proper governance is being observed. (See Chapter 4 for further discussion of assurance services.)

1.4 International Accounting and Auditing Standards

■ International Financial Reporting Standards (IFRS)

Financial accounting standards are unique and separate from audit standards. By its nature, auditing requires that the real-world evidence of financial transactions be compared to financial standards. The standards to which an international auditor compares financial statements are generally standards in the reporting country (e.g. FAS in the USA, or national standards in European Union (EU) Member States which are based on EU Directives. In the future, companies and auditors in the EU and other countries will use International Financial Reporting Standards (IFRS), formerly called International Accounting Standards (IAS), which are set by the International Accounting Standards Board (IASB).

In March 2001, the IASC Foundation was formed as a not-for-profit corporation. The IASC Foundation is the parent entity of the International Accounting Standards Board, an independent accounting standard setter based in London, UK. In April 2001, the International Accounting Standards Board (IASB) assumed accounting standard setting responsibilities from its predecessor body, the International Accounting Standards Committee.[11] New standards issued by the IASB will be called International Financial Reporting Standards (IFRS). The EU has agreed to apply most of the IFRS from 2005 onwards.

The EU, formed in 1970, has issued a series of accounting standards for Member States. The European Commission (EC) achieves its law objectives through two instruments: Directives which must be incorporated into the laws of Member States; and Regulations, which become law throughout the EU without the need to pass through national legislatures.

Although all the EU Directives influence international accounting, the Eighth Company Law Directive is especially applicable to auditing. The Eighth Directive sets the minimum requirements for accounting training and experience for the community.

■ Auditing Standards Become International

As international accounting standards acquired more authority, logic dictated a set of international auditing standards collateral to them. Auditing standards were required by multinational corporations that wanted consistent auditing throughout the world.

With a set of international standards adopted for the world, international investors can be more confident in financial statements prepared in another country. The non-domestic auditor's opinion will lend as much credibility as a domestic auditor's opinion.

In the Peoples' Republic of China, Chinese Accounting Standards (CAS) are becoming more and more in line with IFRS. While CAS are needed for specific Chinese circumstances, convergence with IRFS is seen as equally important to reach international harmonization.

Developing Nations Adopt International Auditing Standards

International auditing standards encourage and assist developing nations to adopt codified sets of national auditing standards. The evolution of domestic accounting standards in developing nations can be expected to flow from the work of the IASB. Many developing countries rely to a large extent on foreign investment. Foreign investors are more likely to channel funds into a developing country if they have confidence in the accounting and auditing standards in that country. Audit has played a very important role in maintaining state financial and economic order, promoting the development of China's socialist economy and strengthening the construction of clean governments. The promulgation of the 1994 Audit Law symbolizes that auditing in China has entered a new phase of development.[12] It is expected that many developing nations will adopt IASs.

■ IAASB Auditing Standards

The International Auditing and Assurance Standards Board (IAASB) is a standing committee of the Council of IFAC which sets the international standards on auditing. Their objective is to improve the degree of uniformity of auditing practices and related services throughout the world by issuing pronouncements on a variety of audit and attest functions. The member bodies in the countries selected by the IFAC Council to serve on IAASB nominate the members of IAASB.

IAASB issues several sets of standards to be applied to international auditing and assurance services. IAASB Standards contain basic principles and essential procedures together with related guidance in the form of explanatory and other material. IAASB issues:

- International Standards on Auditing (ISAs) as the standards to be applied by auditors in reporting on historical financial information;
- International Standards on Assurance Engagements (ISAEs) as the standards to be

applied by practitioners in assurance engagements dealing with information other than historical financial information;

- International Standards on Quality Control (ISQCs) as the standards to be applied for all services falling under the standards of the IAASB; and
- International Standards on Related Services (ISRSs) as the standards to be applied on related services, as it considers appropriate
- International Standards on Review Engagements (ISREs) as the standards to be applied to the review of historical financial information. Developed by the IAASB.

The International Auditing and Assurance Standards Board aims for voluntary international acceptance of its guidelines. Therefore, the International Standards on Auditing (ISAs) are not intended to override national regulations or pronouncements relating to audits of financial information. These ISAs are not yet authoritative in the way that pronouncements of, say, the Public Company Accounting Oversight Board (PCAOB) are to determine **Generally Accepted Audit Standards (GAAS)** in the USA. ISAs will be mandatory in Europe in 2005, and other regions in the world including the USA [13] may follow.

■ International Standards on Auditing (ISA)

International Standards on Auditing (ISAs) are developed by the International Federation of Accountants (IFAC) through its International Auditing and Assurance Standards Board (IAASB). The efforts of IFAC, founded in 1977, are directed towards developing international technical, ethical and educational guidelines for auditors, and reciprocal recognition of practitioners' qualifications. The membership of IFAC member bodies represents several million accountants in public and private practice, education, academe and government service.

There are several important groups within IFAC. The IFAC Council is responsible for overall governance of IFAC. The IFAC Board oversees the management of the organization, takes action to enhance the transparency of certain IFAC activities, and overseas expansion of its size to include more member bodies. The standard-setting activities of the IFAC are carried out by the International Auditing and Assurance Standards Board (IAASB), the Ethics Committee, the Education Committee, and the Public Sector Committee with an interest in governmental financial reporting.

New IFAC Reform Proposals [14]

These provide for more transparent standard-setting processes; greater public and regulatory input into those processes; regulatory monitoring; and public interest oversight. Key features of the reform proposals include provision for the establishment of the following groups: the Public Interest Oversight Board (PIOB), Monitoring Group (MG), and IFAC Leadership Group.

The Public Interest Oversight Board (PIOB) will oversee IFAC standard-setting activities in the areas of audit performance standards, independence, other ethical standards for auditors, audit quality control, and assurance standards. The PIOB will decide other areas that might fall within the scope of its oversight after consulting with the Monitoring Group (MG) and the IFAC Leadership Group (ILG) (see below). The composition of the PIOB will be selected by the MG. It will be made up of members of the organizations within the MG or their representatives.

ILLUSTRATION 1.1

List of 2004 International Standards on Auditing

AUDITING AND ASSURANCE

CONTENTS

Structure of Pronouncements Issued by the International Auditing and Assurance Standards Board
International Auditing and Assurance Standards Board—Interim Terms of Reference
Preface to the International Standards on Quality Control, Auditing, Assurance and Related Services
Glossary of Terms
International Framework for Assurance Engagements

AUDITS AND REVIEWS OF HISTORICAL FINANCIAL INFORMATION

100–999 International Standards on Auditing (ISAs)

100–199 INTRODUCTORY MATTERS
120 Framework of International Standards on Auditing

200–299 GENERAL PRINCIPLES AND RESPONSIBILITIES
200 Objective and General Principles Governing an Audit of Financial Statements
210 Terms of Audit Engagements
220 Quality Control for Audit Work
230 Documentation
240 The Auditor's Responsibility to Consider Fraud and Error in an Audit of Financial Statements
250 Consideration of Laws and Regulations in an Audit of Financial Statements
260 Communications of Audit Matters with Those Charged With Governance

300–499 RISK ASSESSMENT AND RESPONSE TO ASSESSED RISKS
300 Planning
310 Knowledge of the Business
315 Understanding the Entity and Its Environment and Assessing the Risks of Material Misstatement
320 Audit Materiality
330 The Auditor's Procedures in Response to Assessed Risks
400 Risk Assessments and Internal Control
401 Auditing in a Computer Information Systems Environment
402 Audit Considerations Relating to Entities Using Service Organizations

500–599 AUDIT EVIDENCE
500 Audit Evidence
501 Audit Evidence—Additional Considerations for Specific Items
505 External Confirmations
510 Initial Engagements—Opening Balances
520 Analytical Procedures
530 Audit Sampling and Other Selective Testing Procedures
540 Audit of Accounting Estimates
545 Auditing Fair Value Measurements and Disclosures
550 Related Parties
560 Subsequent Events
570 Going Concerns
580 Management Representations

Illustration 1.1 (continued)

600–699 USING THE WORK OF OTHERS
600 Using the Work of Another Auditor
610 Considering the Work of Internal Auditing
620 Using the Work of an Expert

700–799 AUDIT CONCLUSIONS AND REPORTING
700 The Auditor's Report on Financial Statements
710 Comparatives
720 Other Information in Documents Containing Audited Financial Statements

800–899 SPECIALIZED AREAS
800 The Auditor's Report on Special Purpose Audit Engagements

1000–1100 International Auditing Practice Statements (IAPSs)

1000 Inter-Bank Confirmation Procedures
1001 IT Environments—Stand-alone Personal Computers
1002 IT Environments—On-line Computer Systems
1003 IT Environments—Database Systems
1004 The Relationship Between Bank Supervisors and Banks' External Auditors
1005 The Special Considerations in the Audit of Small Entities
1006 Audits of the Financial Statements of Banks
1007 Communications With Management—Withdrawn June 2001
1008 Risk Assessments and Internal Control—CIS Characteristics and Considerations
1009 Computer-assisted Audit Techniques
1010 The Consideration of Environmental Matters in the Audit of Financial Statements
1011 Implications for Management and Auditors of the Year 2000 Issue—Withdrawn June 2001
1012 Auditing Derivative Financial Instruments
1013 Electronic Commerce—Effect on the Audit of Financial Statements
1014 Reporting by Auditors on Compliance With International Financial Reporting Standards

2000–2699 International Standards on Review Engagements (ISREs)

2400 Engagements to Review Financial Statements (Previously ISA 910)

ASSURANCE ENGAGEMENTS OTHER THAN AUDITS OR REVIEWS OF HISTORICAL FINANCIAL INFORMATION

3000–3699 International Standards on Assurance Engagements (ISAEs)

3000–3399 APPLICABLE TO ALL ASSURANCE ENGAGEMENTS
3000   Assurance Engagements (Previously ISAE 100)
3000R Assurance Engagements Other Than Audits or Reviews of Historical Financial Information

3400–3699 SUBJECT SPECIFIC STANDARDS
3400 The Examination of Prospective Financial Information (Previously ISA 810)

RELATED SERVICES

4000–4699 International Standards on Related Services (ISRSs)

4400 Engagements to Perform Agreed-upon Procedures Regarding Financial Information (Previously ISA 920)
4410 Engagements to Compile Financial Information (Previously ISA 930)

The Monitoring Group (MG) will comprise international regulators and related organizations including representatives of the International Organization of Securities Commissions, the Basel Committee on Banking Supervision, the European Commission, the International Association of Insurance Supervisors and the World Bank. The MG will update the PIOB regarding significant events in the regulatory environment, and among other things, will be the vehicle for dialogue between regulators and the international accountancy profession.

The IFAC Leadership Group (ILG) includes the IFAC President, Deputy President, Chief Executive, the Chairs of the IAASB, the Transnational Auditors Committee, the Forum of Firms, and up to four other members designated by the IFAC Board. It will work with the MG and address issues related to the regulation of the profession.

ISAs as Harmonization Standards

International Standards on Auditing (ISAs) are the standards that are of most interest to auditors because they are the standards for the most frequent work of auditors, that is, **financial statement audits** and special purpose engagements. Although not all countries require ISAs, they will be used as the basic standards throughout this book because they represent the highest and best international representation of **generally accepted auditing standards (GAAS)**.

ISAs are harmonization standards, the application of which promotes consistent auditing across the world. The practice and theory of international auditing includes, in addition to knowledge of ISAs, consideration of quality control standards, allocating materiality, performing the audit, coordinating international reports and personnel, etc.

A listing of the International Standards on Auditing and International Auditing Practice Statements is given in Illustration 1.1.

Certification Exam Question 1.2[15]

Which of the following elements underlies the application of generally accepted auditing standards, particularly the standards of fieldwork and reporting?

(A) Internal control.
(B) Corroborating evidence.
(C) Quality control.
(D) Materiality and relative risk.

1.5 An Audit Defined

International auditing education starts with a thorough understanding of what we mean by an audit. There is no definition of an audit, *per se*, in the International Standards on Auditing. The definition given in ISA 200 states the **objective of an audit**[16] of financial statements is to enable the auditor to express an opinion whether the financial statements are prepared, in all material respects, in accordance with an identified financial reporting framework. The phrases used to express an auditor's opinion are "give a true and fair view" or "present fairly, in all material respects", which are equivalent terms.

Two problems with the ISA 200 definition are that it restricts an audit to examination of the financial statements and some auditors believe that the terms "present fairly" and "true and fair view" are not equivalent. Although the great majority of audit work today is financial auditing, **operational auditing** and **compliance auditing** are becoming more and more important. Some auditors say "present fairly," means in accordance with laws and regulations. "True and fair", they say, includes the possibility of deviating from law and regulation when that deviation provides a "true" view.

A better, more general, definition of auditing is:[17]

> An audit is a systematic process of objectively obtaining and evaluating evidence regarding assertions about economic actions and events to ascertain the degree of correspondence between these assertions and established criteria, and communicating the results to interested users.

■ Components of the Audit Definition

An audit is a **systematic** approach. The audit follows a structured, documented plan (audit plan). In the process of the audit, accounting records are analyzed by the auditors using a variety of generally accepted techniques. The audit must be planned and structured in such a way that those carrying out the audit can fully examine and analyze all-important evidence.

An audit is conducted **objectively**. An audit is an independent, objective and expert examination and evaluation of evidence. Auditors are fair and do not allow prejudice or bias to override their **objectivity**. They maintain an impartial attitude.

The auditor **obtains** and **evaluates evidence**. The auditor assesses the reliability and sufficiency of the information contained in the underlying accounting records and other source data by:

- studying and evaluating accounting systems and internal controls on which he wishes to rely and testing those internal controls to determine the **nature, extent** and **timing** of other auditing procedures; and
- carrying out such other tests, inquiries and other verification procedures of accounting transactions and account balances, as he considers appropriate in the particular circumstances.

The evidence obtained and evaluated by the auditor concerns **assertions** about economic actions and events. The basis of evidence-gathering objectives, what the evidence must prove, are the **assertions of management.** Assertions are representations by management, explicit or otherwise, that are embodied in the financial statements. One assertion of management about economic actions is that all the assets reported on the balance sheet actually exist at the balance sheet date. The assets are real, not fictitious. This is the existence assertion. Furthermore, management asserts that the company owns all these assets. They do not belong to anyone else. This is the rights and obligations assertion.

The auditor **ascertains the degree of correspondence** between assertions and established criteria. The audit program tests most assertions by examining the physical evidence of documents, confirmation, inquiry, and observation. The auditor examines the evidence for the assertion presentation and disclosure to determine if the accounts are described in accordance with the applicable financial reporting framework, such as IFRS, local standards or regulations and laws.

Certification Exam Question 1.3

In designing written audit programs, an auditor should establish specific audit objectives that relate primarily to the:

(A) Timing of audit procedures.
(B) Cost–benefit of gathering evidence.
(C) Selected audit techniques.
(D) Financial statement assertions.

The goal, or objective, of the audit is **communicating the results to interested users**. The audit is conducted with the aim of expressing an informed and credible opinion in a written report. If the item audited is the financial statements, the auditors must state that in their opinion the statements "give a true and fair view" or "present fairly, in all material respects" the financial position of the company. The purpose of the independent expert opinion is to lend credibility to the financial statements. The communication of the auditor's opinion is called **attestation**, or the attest function. In an audit this attestation is called the "audit report" (see Chapter 12).

Certification Exam Question 1.4

Which of the following is a conceptual difference between the attestation standards and International Standards on Auditing?

(A) The attestation standards provide a framework for the attest function beyond historical financial statements.
(B) The requirement that the practitioner be independent in mental attitude is omitted from the attestation standards.
(C) The attestation standards do not permit an attest engagement to be part of a business acquisition study or a feasibility study.
(D) None of the standards of audit planning are included in the attestation standards.

■ General Principles Governing an Audit of Financial Statements

Although a public auditor can also examine non-financial information, such as compliance with company policies or environmental regulations, the majority of audit work is concerned with the financial statements. The financial statements audited under international standards are the balance sheets, income statements and cash flow statements and the notes thereto. The first International Standard on Auditing, ISA 1 (ISA 200)[18] discusses the principles governing an audit of financial statements.

General Principles Standard ISA 200

ISA 200 states that an auditor should comply with the *Code of Ethics for Professional Accountants* issued by IFAC (see Chapter 3). The ethical principles governing the auditor's professional responsibilities are: independence, integrity, objectivity, professional **competence** and due care, confidentiality, professional behavior, and technical standards.

ISA 200 further states that the auditor should conduct an International Standards on Auditing. The auditor would plan a an attitude of **professional skepticism** recognizing that circu cause the financial statements to be **materially misstated**.

The term **scope of an audit** refers to the audit procedur circumstances to achieve the objective of the audit. ISA 200

> The procedures required to conduct an audit in accordance with ISAs and by the auditor having regard to the requirements of ISAs, relevant professional bodies, lation, regulation and, where appropriate, the terms of the audit engagement and reporting requirements.

An audit in accordance is designed to provide reasonable assurance that the financial statements taken as a whole are free from material misstatement. Reasonable assurance relates to the fairness of the financial statements.

Limitations of the Audit

There are certain **inherent limitations in an audit** that affect the auditor's ability to detect material misstatements. These limitations result from such factors as the use of testing, the inherent limitations of any accounting and internal control system and the fact that most audit evidence is persuasive rather than conclusive. Furthermore, the work performed by an auditor to form an opinion is permeated by judgment. Judgment is required to determine the nature and extent of audit evidence and the drawing of conclusions based on the audit evidence gathered. Because of these factors, an audit is no guarantee that the financial statements are free of material misstatement.

Business Risk and Audit Risk

Companies face a variety of **business risks**. Management is responsible for identifying such risks and responding to them. The auditor is concerned primarily with risks that may affect the financial statements.

The risk that causes the greatest concern by the auditor is the risk that the auditor gives a clean audit opinion when the financial statements are materially misstated (known as **audit risk**). The newest revision of ISA 200[20] states, "The auditor should plan and perform the audit to reduce audit risk to an acceptably low level that is consistent with the objective of an audit." The components of audit risk are **inherent risk**, **control risk**, and **detection risk** which we will discuss in detail in Chapters 6, 7, and 8.

Risk in Financial Statements, Transactions, Account Balances and Disclosures

In order to design audit procedures to determine whether financial statements are materially misstated, the auditor considers the risk at two levels. One level of risk is that the overall financial statements may be misstated. The second risk is misstatement in relation to classes of transactions, account balances, and disclosures.

The risk of material misstatement at the overall financial statement level often relate to the entity's **control environment** (although these risks may also relate to other factors, such as declining economic conditions). This overall risk may be especially relevant to the auditor's consideration of fraud. The auditor also considers the risk of material misstatement at the class of transactions, account balance, and disclosure level. These considerations directly assist in determining the nature, timing, and extent of further audit procedures.

While the auditor is responsible for forming and expressing an opinion on the financial statements, the responsibility for preparing and presenting the financial statements is that of the management of the entity. However, the audit of the financial statements does not relieve management of its responsibilities.

Certification Exam Question 1.5

Which of the following statements is correct concerning an auditor's responsibilities regarding financial statements?

(A) Making suggestions that are adopted about the form and content of an entity's financial statements impairs an auditor's independence.
(B) An auditor may draft an entity's financial statements based on information from management's accounting system.
(C) The fair presentation of audited financial statements in conformity with GAAP is an implicit part of the auditor's responsibilities.
(D) An auditor's responsibilities for audited financial statements are not confined to the expression of the auditor's opinion.

1.6 Types of Audits

Audits are typically classified into three types: audits of financial statements, operational audits, and compliance audits.

■ Audits of Financial Statements

Audits of financial statements examine financial statements to determine if they give a true and fair view or fairly present the financial statements in conformity with specified criteria. The criteria may be International Financial Reporting Standards (IFRS), generally accepted accounting principles (GAAP) as in the USA, national company laws as in Northern Europe, or the tax code in South America. This book primarily discusses audits of financial statements.

■ Operational Audits

An **operational audit** is a study of a specific unit of an organization for the purpose of measuring its performance. Operational audits review all or part of the organization's operating procedures to evaluate effectiveness and efficiency of the operation. Effectiveness is a measure of whether an organization achieves its goals and objectives. Efficiency shows how well an organization uses its resources to achieve its goals. Operational reviews may not be limited to accounting. They may include the evaluation of organizational structure, marketing, production methods, computer operations or whatever area the organization feels evaluation is needed. Recommendations are normally made to management for improving operations.

The operations of the receiving department of a manufacturing company, for example, may be evaluated in terms of its effectiveness. Performance is also judged in terms of efficiency on how well it uses the resources available to the department. Because the criteria for effectiveness and efficiency are not as clearly established as accepted accounting principles and laws, an operational audit tends to require more subjective judgment than audits of financial statements or compliance audits.

■ Compliance Audits

A **compliance audit** is a review of an organization's procedures to determine whether the organization is following specific procedures, rules or regulations set out by some higher authority. A compliance audit measures the compliance of an entity with established criteria. The performance of a compliance audit is dependent upon the existence of verifiable data and of recognized criteria or standards, such as established laws and regulations, or an organization's policies and procedures. Accounting personnel, for example, may be evaluated to determine if they are following the procedures prescribed by the company controller. Other personnel may be evaluated to determine if they follow policies and procedures established by management. Results of compliance audits are generally reported to management within the organizational unit being audited.

Compliance audits are usually associated with government auditors – for example, the tax authority, the government **internal auditing** arm, or audit of a bank by banking regulators. An example of a compliance audit is an audit of a bank to determine if they comply with capital reserve requirements. Another example would be an audit of taxpayers to see if they comply with national tax law, for example, the audit of an income tax return by an auditor of the government tax agency such as the Internal Revenue Service (IRS) in the USA.

Compliance audits are quite common in not-for-profit organizations funded at least in part by government. Many government entities and non-profit organizations that receive financial assistance from the federal government must arrange for compliance audits. Such audits are designed to determine whether the financial assistance is spent in accordance with applicable laws and regulations.

Illustration 1.2 summarizes the three types of audit.

ILLUSTRATION 1.2

Types of Adult

Audits of financial statements	Operational audits	Compliance audits
Examine financial statements, determine if they give a true and fair view or fairly present the financial position, results, and cash flows.	A study of a specific unit of an organization for the purpose of measuring its performance.	A review of an organization's procedures and financial records performed to determine whether the organization is following specific procedures, rules or regulations set out by some higher authority.

Each of these types of audit has a specialist auditor, namely the independent auditor, internal auditor, and governmental auditor. The independent auditor is mainly concerned with financial statement audits, the internal auditor concentrates on operational audits, and the governmental auditor is most likely to determine compliance. However, given information technology developments, the different processes are becoming more and more integrated, and as a consequence the split between these categories may become theoretical.

1.7   Types of Auditors

There are two basic types of auditors: independent external auditors and internal auditors. Governmental auditors take both the functions of internal and external auditor. The independent auditor and his qualifications will be discussed in the next section.

■ Internal Auditors

Many large companies and organizations maintain an internal auditing staff. Internal auditors are employed by individual companies to investigate and appraise the effectiveness of company operations for management. Much of their attention is often given to the appraisal of internal controls. A large part of their work consists of operational audits; in addition, they may conduct compliance audits. In many countries internal auditors are heavily involved in financial audits. In these circumstances the external auditor should review the work performed by the internal auditor.

The internal audit department reports directly to the president or board of directors. An internal auditor must be independent of the department heads and other executives whose work he reviews. Internal auditors, however, can never be independent in the same sense as the independent auditors because they are employees of the company they are examining.

Internal auditors have two primary effects on a financial statement audit:

1 Their existence and work may affect the nature, timing, and extent of audit procedures.
2 External auditors may use internal auditors to provide direct assistance in performing the audit. If this is the case the external auditor must assess internal auditor competence (education, experience, professional certification, etc.) and objectivity (organizational status within the company).

Concept and a Company 1.1

WorldCom Internal Auditor Discovers Misstatements

Concept	The work of internal auditors in review of financial statements.
Story	To illustrate the importance of internal auditors to companies we can look at what happened at WorldCom (now called MCI). Everyone knows about Enron. It was the $9

billion fraud that was perpetrated at WorldCom, at the time the Number 2 long-distance telephone carrier in the USA, that formed the motivation to pass the first US accounting law since 1934. At the time the fraud was disclosed, US President George W. Bush said, "I'm deeply concerned ... There is a need for renewed corporate responsibility in America." (Wolffe 2002). One month later Bush signed the Sarbanes-Oxley Act.

The fraud that created the largest bankruptcy in US history and resulted in the payment of the largest fine ever imposed by the Securities and Exchange Commission ($500 million (Larson and Michaels 2003)) involved transferring on the corporate books some $9 billion of telephone line leases and other expenses to capital investments, an asset. This allowed the expenses to be spread over 40 years. The accounting effect was to increase four crucial financial numbers: operating profit, cash flow from operations, total assets, and retained earnings. This, in turn, increased WorldCom's share price and made those who exercised low cost stock options rich. Chief Executive Officer (CEO) Bernard Ebbers, made $35 million in June 1999, Chief Executive Officer Scott D. Sullivan made $18 million in August 2000, and chairman of the audit committee, Max Bobbitt, made $1.8 million in 1999 (Romeo and Norris 2002).

Cynthia Cooper, vice president for internal auditing, was the one who discovered the fraud at WorldCom and reported it to the board of directors. She may be the only internal auditor in history to be named *Time* magazine's person of the year (2002).

The story begins when a worried executive in the wireless division told Cooper in March 2002 that corporate accounting had taken $400 million out of his reserve account and used it to boost WorldCom's income. Cooper went to Arthur Andersen, the CPA firm. They told her it was not a problem. When she didn't relent, CFO Sullivan told Cooper that everything was fine and she should back off. Cooper, concerned that her job might be in jeopardy, cleaned out personal items from her office. Cooper told *Time* magazine, "when someone is hostile, my instinct is to find out why" (Ripley, 2002).

As the weeks went on, Cooper directed her team members to widen their net. Having watched the Enron implosion and Andersen's role in it, she was worried they could not necessarily rely on the accounting firm's audits. So they decided to do part of Andersen's job over again. She and her team began working late into the night, keeping their project secret. And they had no allies. At one point, one of Cooper's employees bought a CD burner and started copying data, concerned that the information might be destroyed before they could finish.

In late May, Cooper and her group discovered a gaping hole in the books. In public reports the company had categorized billions of dollars as capital expenditures in 2001, meaning the costs could be stretched out over a number of years into the future. But in fact the expenditures were for regular fees WorldCom paid to local telephone companies to complete calls and therefore were not capital outlays but operating costs, which should be expensed in full each year. The trick allowed WorldCom to turn a $662 million loss into a $2.4 billion profit in 2001.

On June 11, Sullivan called Cooper and gave her ten minutes to come to his office and describe what her team was up to, says a source involved with the case. She did, and Sullivan asked her to delay the audit. She told him that would not happen. The next day, Cooper told the head of the audit committee about her findings. On June 25, after firing Sullivan, the board revealed the fraud to the public.

| Discussion Questions | ■ What advantages does an internal auditor have over an external auditor in discovering fraud? |
| | ■ And what disadvantages? |

▶

References Ripley, Amanda, 2002, "The Night Detective," *Time* magazine, Vol. 160, Iss. 27, p. 58, December 30.

Larsen, Peter and Adrian Michaels, 2003, "MCI fined $500m over fraud charges," *Financial Times*, p. 1, May 20.

Romeo, Simon and Floyd Norris, 2002, "New Bookkeeping Problems Disclosed by WorldCom," *New York Times*, pp. A1–C8, 2 July.

Spiegel, Peter, 2003, "WorldCom finance chief 'tried to delay inquiry'," *Financial Times*, p. 1. July 9.

Wolffe, Richard, 2002, "Bush condemns new scandal as outrageous," *Financial Times*, p. 1, June 27.

■ The Independent External Auditor: Training, Licensing and Authority

Independent auditors have primary responsibility to the performance of the audit function on published financial statements of publicly traded companies and non-public companies. Some countries have several classes of auditors who have different functions. Independent auditors are typically certified either by a professional organization or a government agency.

ILLUSTRATION 1.3

Auditor Certification Designations Around the World

Certified Public Accountants (CPA)	Australia, Belize, El Salvador, Guatemala, Hong Kong, Israel, Japan, Kenya (CPA (K)), Korea, Malaysia, Malawi, Myanmar, Philippines, Singapore, Taiwan, Western Samoa, and the USA.
Chartered Accountants (CA)	Australia (ACA), Bahamas, Bermuda, Botswana, Canada, Cayman Islands, Channel Islands, Cyprus, Fiji, Guyana, Hungary, India, Jamaica, Nigeria, Trinidad, New Zealand, Papua New Guinea, Saudi Arabia, South Africa (CA-SA), Swaziland (CA (SD)), United Arab Emirates, the UK and Zimbabwe.
Contador Publico (CP)	Argentina, Brazil (Contador), Chile, Columbia (CP Titulado), Costa Rica (CP Autorizado -CPA), Dominican Republic (CPA), Ecuador (CPA), Mexico, Panama (CPA) and Peru.
Expert Comptable	France (or Commissaire aux comptes), Luxembourg and Senegal.
Auditors	Bahrain, Czech Republic, Qatar and Solomon Islands.
Other titles	Registeraccountants (RA) and Accountants Administratie-Consulenten (AC) in the Netherlands and Netherlands Antilles; Wirtschaftsprufer in Austria and Germany; Statautoriseret Revisor in Denmark and Norway; Dottore Commercialista in Italy; Revisor Official de Contas (ROC) in Portugal; Auktoriserad Revisor (AR) in Sweden; Wirtschaftsprufer and Expert Comptable in Switzerland; Reviseur d'Entreprises in Belgium; KHT or CGR in Finland; Soma Orkoton Logiston (SOL) in Greece; Licenciado en Contaduria Publico in Venezuela; Akuntan Publik in Indonesia; Loggilturendurskodandi in Iceland; Licensed Accountant (LA) in Iraq; Technician Superior in Lebanon; and Sworn Financial Advisor (SFA) in Turkey.

The source of authority for the attest function comes from national commercial or company law in most countries, but in some cases (e.g. the USA and Canada) the individual provinces or states exercise considerable control over who the auditor is and how he becomes qualified. All CPAs in the USA are licensed by the individual states. Most countries have strong professional accountant organizations which may also influence who becomes an auditor.

Certified designations for auditors in different countries are listed in Illustration 1.3.

Licensing Requirements

The auditor is someone who is trained in an academic program and who meets certain licensing requirements. Countries may have requirements for minimum age, citizenship, university degree and completion of a qualifying examination. The Eighth European Union (EU) Directive[21] has a minimum experience requirement of three years, whereas the USA only requires one or two years. It is common for people in the USA and Canada to become professional accountants in their early twenties, but in Germany and Japan many people do not attain their credentials until their mid-thirties.

The EU Eighth Company Law Directive[22] sets minimum qualifications for statutory auditors. This directive specifies that an individual must attain at least entrance-level qualifications at university level, engage in a program of theoretical instruction, receive at least three years' practical training and pass an examination of professional competence, Furthermore, the Eighth Directive puts an obligation on Member States to ensure that statutory audits are carried out with professional integrity and that there are appropriate safeguards in national law to protect the independence of auditors.

1.8 Setting Audit Objectives Based on *Management Assertions*

Conceptually, where does the audit start? It starts with the financial statements prepared by the client and the claims that the client makes about these numbers. These claims by management are called "assertions". For example, management claims (asserts) that sales exist, i.e. sales are not fiction created by management. Management claims that the expenses and liabilities are complete, i.e. they did not leave out any expenses to make net income look better. Management claims that they have disclosed all that should be disclosed. Inventory is properly valued and it belongs to the company, not some other company who put it there on consignment. And so on.

The Auditor's Process

Where it is management's responsibility to prepare the financial statements, it is the auditor's job to verify whether the financial statements are true and fair. Put differently, it is the auditor's job to validate management's assertions. In order to do so, the auditor will identify **audit objectives**, which can be regarded as the auditor's counterpart of management assertions. The auditor will define audit objectives for **existence** of sales, **completeness** of expenses, **presentation and disclosure** (based on IFRS) and **valuation** and **rights and obligations** of inventory. The auditor will develop these specific audit objectives for which they must test for evidence as proof.

After the identification of accounts, classes of transactions and the related management assertions and audit objectives, the auditor will determine the nature, amount and timing of the audit procedures to be carried out. In order to do so, he will perform risk analysis for each audit objective, i.e. he will determine the susceptibility of account balances and transactions to misstatement.

Further, the auditor will have to determine the exactness with which he will perform his audit. It is reasonable to suppose that the auditor will accept a greater tolerance in the audit of a large, multinational enterprise than in the audit of a small, local company. This raises the issue of materiality and of **tolerable errors** in the audit process.

In designing an audit program for a specific account, the auditor starts by developing general objectives from the financial statement assertions of management. Then, specific objectives are developed for each account under audit, and finally, audit procedures are designed to accomplish each specific audit objective.

■ Management Assertions and Audit Objectives

Audit procedures are designed to obtain evidence about the assertions of management that are embodied in the financial statements. **Management assertions** are implied or expressed representations by management about classes of transactions (e.g. sales transactions) and related accounts (e.g. revenue, accounts receivable) in the financial statements. When the auditors have gathered sufficient evidence to support each management assertion, they have sufficient evidence to support the audit opinion.

An example of a management assertion is that "the company's financial statements are prepared based on international accounting standards". This assertion is one of presentation and disclosure. The auditor must obtain sufficient evidence that this assertion is materially true. He must gather evidence that accounts are classified correctly and the proper disclosures have been made based on international standards.

Assertions Categorized

According to ISA 500, financial statement assertions are assertions by management, explicit or otherwise, that are embodied in the financial statements. They can be categorized as follows:[23]

(1) Assertions about classes of transactions and events for the period under audit

- **Occurrence** – transaction and events that have been recorded have occurred and pertain to the entity. For example, management asserts that a recorded sales transaction was effective during the year under audit.
- **Completeness** – all transactions and events that should have been recorded have been recorded. For example, management asserts that all expense transactions are recorded, none were excluded.
- **Accuracy** – amounts and other data relating to recorded transactions and events have been recorded appropriately. For example, management asserts that sales invoices were properly extended and the total amounts that were thus calculated were input into the system exactly.
- **Cutoff** – transactions and events have been recorded in the correct accounting period. For example, management asserts that expenses for the period are recorded in that period and not in the next accounting period.

■ **Classification** – transactions and events have been recorded in the proper accounts. For example, management asserts that expenses are not recorded as assets.

(2) Assertions about account balances at the period end

■ **Existence** – assets, liabilities and equity interests exist. For example, management asserts that inventory in the amount given exists, ready for sale, at the balance sheet date.

■ **Rights and obligations** – an entity holds or controls the rights to assets, and liabilities are the obligations of the entity. For example, management asserts that the company has the legal rights to ownership of the equipment they use and that they have an obligation to pay the notes that finance the equipment.

■ **Completeness** – all assets, liabilities and equity interests that should have been recorded have been recorded. For example, management asserts that all liabilities are recorded and included in the financial statements, that no liabilities were "off the books".

■ **Valuation and allocation** – assets, liabilities, and equity interests are included in the financial statements at appropriate amounts and any resulting valuation or allocation adjustments are appropriately recorded. For example, management asserts that their accounts receivable are stated at face value, less an allowance for doubtful accounts.

(3) Assertions about presentation and disclosure

■ **Occurrence and rights and obligations** – disclosed events, transactions, and other matters have occurred and pertain to the entity. For example, management asserts that events that did not occur have not been included in the disclosures.

■ **Completeness** – all disclosures that should have been included in the financial statements have been included. For example, management asserts that all disclosures that are required by IFRS are made.

■ **Classification and understandability** – financial information is appropriately presented and described, and disclosures are clearly expressed. For example, management asserts that all long-term liabilities listed on the balance sheet mature after one operating cycle or one year and that any special conditions pertaining to the liabilities are clearly disclosed.

■ **Accuracy and valuation** – financial and other information are disclosed fairly and at appropriate amounts. For example, management asserts that account balances are not materially misstated.

Illustration 1.4 gives some management assertions/audit objectives, their definitions and an example of the type of audit procedures that may be required for that assertion based on the audit of marketable securities.

Certification Exam Question 1.6

An auditor tests an entity's control of obtaining credit approval before shipping goods to customers in support of management's financial statement assertion of

(A) Valuation or allocation.
(B) Completeness.
(C) Existence or occurrence.
(D) Rights and obligations.

ILLUSTRATION 1.4

Financial Statement Assertions, Definitions and Procedures for Auditing Receivables

Assertion	Definition	Procedures
Existence	Assets, liabilities and equity interests exist.	✓ Confirm customer account balances ✓ Inspect shipping documents
Rights and obligations	An entity holds or controls the rights to assets, and liabilities are the obligations of the entity.	✓ Inquire about factoring of receivables ✓ Inspect cash receipts
Occurrence	Transaction and events that have been recorded have occurred and pertain to the entity.	✓ Inspect notes receivable ✓ Inspect sales invoices
Completeness	All transactions, events, assets, liabilities and equity interests that should have been recorded have been recorded.	✓ Perform analytical procedures ✓ Inspect inter-company sales invoices
Valuation and allocation	Assets, liabilities, and equity interests are included in the financial statements at appropriate amounts and any resulting valuation or allocation adjustments are appropriately recorded.	✓ Reconcile subsidiary ledger to general ledger ✓ Age receivables to test adequacy of allowance for doubtful accounts
Accuracy	Amounts and other data relating to recorded transactions and events have been recorded appropriately.	✓ Recalculate sales invoices ✓ Reperform sales transactions
Classification	Transactions and events have been recorded in the proper accounts.	✓ Inquire about revenue recognition policies
Cutoff	Transactions and events have been recorded in the correct accounting period.	✓ Inspect next period bank statements for cash receipts ✓ Inspect credit memos for sales returns
Presentation and disclosure	An item is disclosed, classified, and described in accordance with acceptable accounting reporting framework.	✓ Review disclosures for compliance with IFRS and applicable regulation ✓ Inspect loan documents for pledging or discounting of accounts receivable

1.9 The Audit Process Model

In the international environment today, the professional auditor audits financial statements, internal control, compliance with policies, compliance with laws and regulations, and codes of best practice. However, no matter what subject matter the audit is designed to evaluate, the audit process is a well-defined methodology to help the auditor accumulate sufficient competent evidence.

■ Empirical Scientific Cycle and the Audit

The audit process may be compared to the empirical scientific cycle.[24] The empirical scientific cycle is a systematic process of experimenting that starts with a research question, then a plan for an empirical test of the question is made, the test is done, feedback is analyzed, and the scientist makes a judgment. The scientist's opinion is that the experimental hypothesis is false or not false, or perhaps that the test is inconclusive.

Although the numerous judgments made during a financial audit (about audit approach, sampling, audit risk, etc.) make it more of an art than a science, the audit process follows a systematic process. The audit process begins with a client's request for an audit of financial statements, which is followed by a plan of the audit and tests of evidence, culminating in a judgment or opinion. The auditor's judgment is whether the financial statements are unqualified as to their fairness, **qualified** or disclaimed.

A scientist poses a question; this is similar to the client asking an auditor to audit a set of financial statements. A plan is drawn up for the experiment (an audit plan). The scientist tests his theory and evaluates the evidence and an auditor tests the assertions made in the financial statements. The scientist writes up a report on the experiment and an auditor writes a report on the representational quality of the financial statements based on the underlying accounting evidence.

Assessing risk is the core of the audit. The rest of the audit is designed to provide a response to these identified risks. In 2002 and 2003, the IAASB published an exposure draft[25] and new standards.[26] In this book, we will provide this new "**business risk**" oriented approach. Business risks result from significant conditions, events, circumstances, actions, or inactions that could adversely affect a company's ability to execute its strategies, for example, changes in customer demand, government regulations, etc. Most business risks will eventually have financial consequences and, therefore, an effect on the financial statements. As such, the auditors are required to discuss business risks as part of the planning process

Standard Audit Process Model in Four Phases

In this book, a four-phase standard audit process model is used, based on the scientific empirical cycle. The phases of the audit are:

1 client acceptance (pre-planning)
2 planning and design of an audit approach
3 tests for evidence
4 completion of the audit and issuance of an audit report.

Illustration 1.5 shows the four-phase audit process model and its major sub-components.

ILLUSTRATION 1.5

Audit Process Model

Phase I: Client Acceptance

Objective: Determine both acceptance of a client and acceptance by a client. Decide on acquiring a new client or continuation of relationship with an existing one and the type and amount of staff required.

Procedures: (1) Evaluate the client's background and reasons for the audit
(2) Determine whether the auditor is able to meet the ethical requirements regarding the client
(3) Determine need for other professionals
(4) Communicate with predecessor auditor
(5) Prepare client proposal
(6) Select staff to perform the audit
(7) Obtain an engagement letter

Phase II: Planning

Objective: Determine the amount and type of evidence and review required to give the auditor assurance that there is no material misstatement of the financial statements.

Procedures: (1) Perform audit procedures to understand the entity and its environment, including the entity's internal controls
(2) Assess the risks of material misstatements of the financial statements
(3) Determine materiality; and
(4) Prepare the planning memorandum and audit program, containing the auditor's response to the identified risks

Phase III: Testing and Evidence

Objective: Test for evidence supporting internal controls and the fairness of the financial statements.

Procedures: (1) Tests of controls
(2) Substantive tests of transactions
(3) Analytical procedures
(4) Tests of details of balances
(5) Search for unrecorded liabilities

Phase IV: Evaluation and Reporting

Objective: Complete the audit procedures and issue an opinion.

Procedures: (1) Evaluate governance evidence
(2) Perform procedures to identify subsequent events
(3) Review financial statements and other report material
(4) Perform wrap-up procedures
(5) Prepare Matters for Attention of Partners
(6) Report to the board of directors
(7) Prepare Audit report

■ Phase I: Client Acceptance

An audit firm carries out audits for both existing clients and new clients. For existing clients, there is not much activity involved in accepting the client for another year's audit. The audit firm is familiar with the company and has a great deal of information for making an acceptable decision. However, in the case that it is concluded that the auditor's business risk is unacceptably high (client is a fraudster or acts illegally) the auditor reconsiders continuation of the agreement. Accountancy firms have strict procedures for reconsidering high-risk engagements.

When prospective clients approach the audit firm with a request to bid on their financial audits, audit firms must investigate the business background, financial statements, and industry of the client. The firm must also convince the client to accept them. The process of client acceptance involves evaluation of the client's background, selecting personnel for the audit, and evaluating the need and requirements for using the work of other professionals.

The client acceptance phase of the auditing methodology is discussed in detail in Chapter 5 Client Acceptance.

■ Phase II: Planning

The audit firm must plan its work to enable it to conduct an effective audit in an efficient and timely manner. Plans should be based on knowledge of the client's business. Plans are developed after obtaining a basic understanding of the business background, **control environment, control procedures,** the client's accounting system, and after performing **analytical procedures.** The second part of the planning process is to determine the riskiness of the engagement and set materiality levels. Finally, the auditor prepares an **audit program** which outlines the nature, timing and extent of audit procedures required to gather evidence.

One of the most widely accepted concepts on auditing is the importance of the client's **internal control structure** to reliable financial information. If the client has adequate internal control for proving reliable data and safeguarding assets and records, the amount of audit evidence required, and planned for, is significantly less than where internal controls are inadequate. Therefore, assessing internal controls is a very important part of the planning process.

An entity's internal control structure includes five basic categories of policies and procedures. Management designs and implements this in order to provide reasonable assurance that its control objectives will be met. These components of internal control are:[27]

1 the control environment
2 risk assessment
3 control procedures
4 information and communication
5 monitoring.

Certification Exam Question 1.7

Which of the following is **not** a component of an entity's internal control?

(A) Control risk.
(B) Control activities.
(C) Monitoring.
(D) Control environment.

Planning concepts are discussed in Chapter 6 Planning, Chapter 7 Internal Control and Risk, Chapter 8 Responses to risk and Chapter 9 Analytical Procedures. Illustration 1.6 shows a diagrammatic view of the result of planning – devising the audit program from an understanding of the company, internal control analysis, and analysis of assertions.

ILLUSTRATION 1.6

Developing an Audit Program

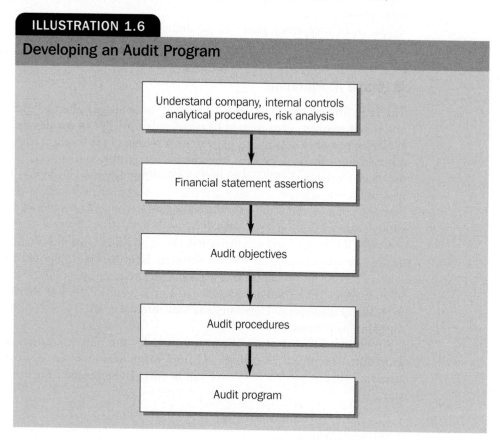

■ Phase III: Testing and Evidence

The audit should be performed and the report prepared with due professional care by persons who have adequate training, experience, and competence in auditing. The auditor should also be independent of the audit and keep the results of the audit confidential, as required by international ethics. "Due professional care" means that the auditor is a professional responsible for fulfilling his duties diligently and carefully. Due care includes the completeness of the working papers, the sufficiency of the audit evidence and the appropriateness of the audit report.

The testing and evidence-gathering phase of the audit requires first testing any controls that the auditor expects to rely upon. Once the controls are tested, the auditor must decide on additional, substantive, tests. The understanding of controls is needed to determine what kind of tests (the nature), when they should be done (timing), and what the number (extent) of the tests should be.

Gathering Evidence

The auditor should obtain sufficient appropriate audit evidence through the performance of control and **substantive procedures** to enable him to draw reasonable conclusions on which to base his audit opinion. **Tests of controls** are tests designed to obtain reasonable assurance that financial information system controls are in place and effective. Substantive procedures are designed to obtain evidence as to the completeness, accuracy, and validity of the data produced by the accounting system. They are of three types: tests of details of transactions, account balances, and analysis of significant ratios and trends. Audit evidence is discussed in Chapter 10 Substantive Testing and Evidence.

■ Phase IV: Evaluation and Reporting

The auditor should review and assess the conclusions drawn from audit evidence on which he will base his opinion on the financial information. This review and assessment involves forming an overall conclusion as to whether:

■ the financial information has been prepared using acceptable accounting policies, consistently applied;
■ the financial information complies with relevant regulations and statutory requirements;
■ the view presented by the financial information as a whole is consistent with the auditor's knowledge of the business of the entity; and
■ there is adequate disclosure of all material matters relevant to the proper presentation of the financial information.

The auditor must perform final audit procedures before the audit report can be written. The auditor must:

■ obtain legal letters,
■ identify subsequent events,
■ carry out an overall review,
■ review all material that goes into the annual report, report to the board of directors,
■ obtain a **management representations letter**,
■ carry out final analytical and other procedures, and
■ prepare **matters for attention of partners**.

The Audit Opinion

The audit report should contain a clear written expression of opinion on the financial information. An **unqualified opinion** indicates the auditor's satisfaction in all material respects with the matters. When a qualified opinion, **adverse opinion** or **disclaimer of opinion** is given, the audit report should state the reasons in a clear and informative manner.

Completing the audit is discussed in Chapter 11 Completing the Audit. Audit reports are discussed in detail in Chapter 12.

1.10 International Public Accountancy Firms

The four largest accountancy firms in the world (known as "the Big Four") influence international auditing because of their day-to-day operations in many countries and their membership in most of the world's professional accounting organizations. All of these firms have revenues of billions of dollars. The Big Four are: Deloitte, Ernst & Young, KPMG, and PricewaterhouseCoopers.

In the earliest days of multinational accountancy firms, the organizational form of audit firms was a partnership or professional corporation. This legal form still predominates, but legal forms vary around the world between countries as well as between firms. Recently the limited liability forms of organization, such as Limited Liability Partnership (LLP), have come into widespread use.

■ Professional Staff

The partners hire professional staff to assist them in their work. The organizational hierarchy in a typical international auditing firm (shown in Illustration 1.7) includes

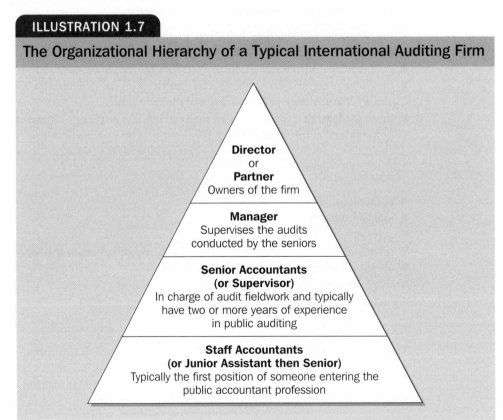

ILLUSTRATION 1.7

The Organizational Hierarchy of a Typical International Auditing Firm

Director
or
Partner
Owners of the firm

Manager
Supervises the audits
conducted by the seniors

**Senior Accountants
(or Supervisor)**
In charge of audit fieldwork and typically
have two or more years of experience
in public auditing

**Staff Accountants
(or Junior Assistant then Senior)**
Typically the first position of someone entering the
public accountant profession

partners, managers, supervisors, seniors or in-charge auditors, and staff accountants. A new employee usually starts as a staff accountant and spends several years at each classification before eventually achieving partner status.

In the remainder of this section the allocation of personnel to an audit is discussed. However, it must be remembered that human resource models will vary between auditing firms. The following describes the common threads of work.

Staff Accountants (or Junior Assistants then Senior)

The first position when someone enters the public accounting profession is that of staff accountant (also called assistant or junior accountant). The staff accountant often performs the more detailed routine audit tasks.

Senior Accountants (or Supervisor)

The senior ("in-charge") auditor or "supervisor" is in charge of audit fieldwork and typically has two or more years' experience in public auditing. The senior takes a major part in planning the audit and is primarily responsible for conducting the audit engagement at the client's place of business. Planning and supervision of more complex audits may involve the partner or director in planning and the manager in supervising the engagement.

The senior supervises the work of the audit staff, reviews working papers and time budgets, and assists in drafting the audit report. The senior maintains a continuous record of staff hours in each phase of the audit examination and maintains professional standards of fieldwork. This work is subject to review and approval by the manager and partner.

Managers

The manager supervises the audits conducted by the seniors. The manager helps the seniors plan their audit programs, reviews working papers periodically, and provides other guidance. The manager is responsible for determining the audit procedures applicable to specific audits and for maintaining uniform standards of fieldwork. Often managers have the responsibility of compiling and collecting the firm's billings to the audit client. The manager, who typically has at least five years' experience, needs a broad and current knowledge of tax laws, accounting standards and government regulations. A manager is likely to specialize in accounting requirements of a specific industry.

Partners/Directors

Partners are the owners of the auditing firm. The change in legal structure means that in some countries those formerly known as partners are directors. They are heavily involved in the planning of the audit, evaluation of the results and determination of the audit opinion. The degree to which they are involved in the audit will vary between firms and assignments because firms have to ensure that partners allocate their time in an appropriate way. Partners will delegate as much of the work as possible to experienced managers and seniors. Moreover, the larger the accountancy firm the more variation there is likely to be in practice depending on the nature of the engagement.

Other partner or director duties include maintaining contacts with clients, resolving controversies that may arise, and attendance at the client's stockholders' meetings to answer any questions regarding the financial statements or the auditor's report. They may also recruit new staff members, review audit working papers, supervise staff and sign the audit reports, depending on the complexity of the engagements. Partners may specialize in a particular area such as tax laws or a specific industry. The partner is the person who must make the final decisions involving complex judgments.

Concept and a Company 1.2

History of Deloitte

Concept	Founding fathers and international mergers of Big Four audit firms.
Story	In 1990 Deloitte Touche Tohmatsu was created following a number of earlier mergers. In 2003 the names of Touche and Tohmatsu were dropped, leaving Deloitte as the firm's full name. Deloitte was established by three founders: William Welch Deloitte, George Touche and Admiral Nobuzo Tohmatsu.

In 1845, at the age of 25, W.W. Deloitte opened his own office opposite the Bankruptcy Court in Basinghall Street, London. At that time three Companies Acts created joint-stock companies, laying the foundation for modern company structures. Deloitte made his name with the industry of the day – the railways – and in 1849 the Great Western Railway appointed Deloitte the first independent auditor in that industry. He discovered frauds on the Great North Railway, invented a system for railway accounts that protected investors from mismanagement of funds, and was to become the grand old man of the profession. As president of the newly created Institute of Chartered Accountants, Deloitte found a site for its headquarters in 1888. In 1893 he opened offices in the USA.

Financial disasters in the new and booming investment trust business in the England gave George Touche his business opportunity. His reputation for flair, integrity, and expertise brought him a huge amount of work setting these trusts on the straight and narrow. A similar flair for saving doomed businesses from disaster and restructuring them led to the formation of George A. Touche & Co. in 1899. In 1900, along with John Niven, the son of his original Edinburgh accounting mentor, Touche set up the firm of Touche, Niven & Co. in New York. Offices spread across the USA and Canada and were soon attracting clients like R.H. Macy, a large US nationwide department store. In the UK, General Electric Company was an important client and still is. Meanwhile Touche himself took his reputation for probity and ran for public election in England and became MP for North Islington, England in 1910, and was knighted in 1917. He died in 1935.

After Tohmatsu qualified as a certified public accountant at the age of 57 in 1952, he became a partner in a foreign-affiliated accounting firm and a director of a private corporation. In 1967, he became president of the Japanese Institute of Certified Public Accountants. In the 1960s, the Japanese government wanted to see national audit corporations established, and Tohmatsu asked Iwao Tomita, a former student and a graduate of the Wharton School in Chicago, to respond to that challenge. In May of 1968, Tohmatsu & Co. (formerly Tohmatsu Awoki & Co.) was incorporated.

Discussion Question	■ What events and circumstances contributed to the growth and international scope of Deloitte's operations?
References	www.Deloitte.com

Concept and a Company 1.3

A History of Ernst & Young

Concept	Founding fathers and international mergers of Big Four audit firms.
Story	The founders of Ernst & Young were Arthur Young who had an interest in investments and banking which led to the foundation in 1906 of Arthur Young & Co. in Chicago, USA and A.C. Ernst, who was a bookkeeper while still in high school, joined his brother and started Ernst & Ernst in 1903.

Ernst pioneered the idea that accounting information could be used to make business decisions – the forerunner of management consulting. He also was the first to advertise professional services. Young was profoundly interested in the development of young professionals. In the 1920s he originated a staff school; in the 1930s, his firm was the first to recruit from university campuses.

Both firms were quick to enter the global marketplace. As early as 1924, they allied with prominent British firms – Young with Broads Paterson & Co. and Ernst with Whinney Smith & Whinney. In 1979, Ernst's original agreement led to the formation of Ernst & Whinney. These alliances were the first of many for both firms throughout the world – and they are the roots of the global firm today.

Young and Ernst, never having met, both died in 1948 within only a few days of each other. In 1989, the firms they started combined to create Ernst & Young. |
| Discussion Questions | ■ What is the impact today of Ernst's innovation of advertising professional services?
■ What do you think Young's staff school taught to professional accountants in 1920?
■ What do you think Ernst & Young teach today in their staff school? |
| References | www.Ernst&Young.com |

Concept and a Company 1.4

History of KPMG

Concept	Founding fathers and international mergers of Big Four audit firms.
Story	KPMG was formed in 1987 with the merger of Peat Marwick International (PMI) and Klynveld Main Goerdeler (KMG) and their individual member firms. Spanning three centuries, the organization's history can be traced through the names of its principal founding members – whose initials form the name "KPMG."

K stands for Klynveld. Piet Klijnveld founded the accounting firm Klynveld Kraayenhof & Co. in Amsterdam in 1917.
P is for Peat. William Barclay Peat founded the accounting firm William Barclay Peat & Co. in London in 1870.
M stands for Marwick. James Marwick founded the accounting firm Marwick, Mitchell & Co. with Roger Mitchell in New York City in 1897. |

▶

History of KPMG (continued)

G is for Goerdeler. Dr. Reinhardt Goerdeler was for many years chairman of Deutsche Treuhand-Gesellschaft and later chairman of KPMG. He is credited with laying much of the groundwork for the KMG merger.

In 1911, William Barclay Peat & Co. and Marwick Mitchell & Co. joined forces to form what would later be known as Peat Marwick International (PMI), a worldwide network of accounting and consulting firms. William Barclay Peat & Co. was founded in 1870 in London, Marwick Mitchell & Co. was founded in 1897 in New York City.

Klynveld Kraayenhof & Co. was founded in Amsterdam in 1917. In 1979, Klynveld Kraayenhof & Co. joined forces with Deutsche Treuhand-Gesellschaft and the international professional services firm McLintock Main Lafrentz & Co. to form Klynveld Main Goerdeler (KMG). Goerdeler was Dr. Reinhard Goerdeler, the chairman of Deutsche Treuhand-Gesellschaft.

In 1987, PMI and KMG and their member firms joined forces. Today, all member firms throughout the world carry the KPMG name exclusively or include it in their national firm names.

Discussion Question	▪ What types of problems could result from combining four firms from different nations with different cultures into a working environment?

References	www.KPMG.nl

Concept and a Company 1.5

History of PricewaterhouseCoopers

Concept	Founding fathers and international mergers of Big Four Audit firms.
Story	A merger in 1998 of Coopers & Lybrand and Price Waterhouse created Pricewaterhouse-Coopers. These two firms have historical roots going back some 150 years. Pricewater-houseCoopers employs about 125,000 people in more than 142 countries throughout the world.

In 1850, Samuel Lowell Price started an accounting business in London. In 1865, William H. Holyland and Edwin Waterhouse joined him in partnership, and by 1874 the company name changes to Price, Waterhouse & Co. (or PW for short). In 1873, the firm conducted their first US project. The growing US practice lead to the establishment of permanent PW presence in the Western hemisphere, which began with the opening of the office in New York City in 1890. By the turn of the century, it had a roster of clients that covered a wide range of industrial and commercial fields in most sections of the USA. Branch offices began to open throughout the USA and then in other parts of the world. In 1982 Price Waterhouse World Firm was formed.

In 1854, William Cooper established his own practice in London, which seven years later became Cooper Brothers. The firm's history in the USA began in 1898, when Robert H. Montgomery, William M. Lybrand, Adam A. Ross Jr., and his brother T. Edward Ross formed Lybrand Ross Brothers and Montgomery in Philadelphia. During the early twentieth century their offices spread around the country and then in Europe.

From 1953, the firm experienced a major transformation from a medium-size company, focused on auditing and primarily national in scope, into a multinational player with a growing mix of consulting services. The boldest step was a 1957 merger between Cooper Brothers & Co. (UK), McDonald, Currie and Co. (Canada), and Lybrand, Ross Bros, & Montgomery (US), forming Coopers & Lybrand, which had 79 offices in 19 countries. In 1990, Coopers & Lybrand merged with Deloitte Haskins & Sells in a number of countries around the world. Finally, in 1998 Price Waterhouse and Coopers & Lybrand merged worldwide to become PricewaterhouseCoopers.

Discussion Question	■ Why did the Western hemisphere operations of Price and Coopers grow rapidly in the twentieth century?
References	www.columbia.edu/cu/libraries/indiv/rare/guides/PWC/main www.pwcglobal.com

1.11 Summary

Anthropologists have found records of auditing activity dating back to early Babylonian times (around 3000 BC). There was also auditing activity in ancient China, Greece and Rome. Auditors existed in ancient China and Egypt. They were supervisors of the accounts of the Chinese Emperor and the Egyptian Pharaoh. From the dawn of the dynastic era in Egypt (3000 BC) the scribes (accountants) were among the most esteemed in society and the scribal occupation was one of the most prestigious occupations. The practice of modern auditing dates back to the beginning of the modern corporation at the dawn of the Industrial Revolution. In 1853, the Society of Accountants was founded in Edinburgh. Several other institutes emerged in Great Britain, merging in 1880 into the Institute of Chartered Accountants in England and Wales.

Auditors today are responsible for adding credibility to international corporate financial statements and annual reports. In addition to financial information, an auditor may be required to attest to the representational quality of non-financial information such as footnote disclosures, management's report, the directors' report, codes of best practice and internal controls. By the audit process, the auditor enhances the usefulness and the value of the financial statements, but he also increases the credibility of other non-audited information released by management.

Organizations that affect international auditing today are primarily the International Accounting Standards Board (IASB) and the International Federation of Accountants (IFAC) who set the International Standards on Auditing (ISAs). Increasingly, oversight bodies such as the Public Company Accounting Oversight Board (PCAOB) and the Public Interest Oversight Board (PIOB), and national regulators emerge.

The International Auditing and Assurances Standards Board (IAASB) of the International Federation of Accountants (IFAC) issues international auditing standards (International Standards on Auditing (ISAs)). IAASB issues several sets of standards to be applied to international auditing and assurance services. IAASB issues:

1 International Standards on Auditing (ISAs) as the standards to be applied by auditors in reporting on historical financial information.

2 International Standards on Assurance Engagements (ISAEs) as the standards to be applied by practitioners in assurance engagements dealing with information other than historical financial information.

3 International Standards on Quality Control (ISQCs) as the standards to be applied for all services falling under the Standards of the IAASB.

4 International Standards on Related Services (ISRSs) as the standards to be applied on related services, as it considers appropriate

An audit may be defined as a systematic process of objectively obtaining and evaluating evidence regarding assertions about economic actions and events to ascertain the degree of correspondence between these assertions and established criteria and communicating the results to interested users.

Although an auditor may examine more than financial information such as company policies and the environment, the majority of audit work concerns financial statements. The financial statements audited under international standards are the income statement, balance sheet and statement of cash flows. The first International Standard on Auditing, ISA 200, discusses the principles governing an audit of financial statements.

Audits are classified into three types: audits of financial statements, operational audits and compliance audits. There are two basic types of auditors: independent external auditors and internal auditors.

Management makes representations and assertions about the financial statements. Their assertions are about classes of transactions and related accounts in the financial statements and are used to set objectives for obtaining audit evidence. The assertions about financial statements fall into three categories:

1 assertions about classes of transactions and events for the period under audit;
2 assertions about account balances at the period end;
3 assertions about presentation and disclosure.

The individual assertions are occurrence, completeness, accuracy, cutoff, classification, existence, rights and obligations, valuation and allocation, and understandability. The auditor must systematically check these "management assertions" because they form the basis of the audit process.

The audit process is a well-defined methodology to help the auditor accumulate sufficient competent evidence. In this book a four phase standard audit process model is: (1) client acceptance (pre-planning); (2) planning and design of an audit approach; (3) tests for evidence; and (4) completion of the audit and issuance of an audit report.

The four largest accountancy firms in the world (known as "the Big Four") influence international auditing because of their day-to-day operations in many countries and their membership in most of the world's professional accounting organizations. Each of these firms has revenues of billions of dollars. The Big Four are: Deloitte, Ernst & Young, KPMG, and PricewaterhouseCoopers.

The organizational hierarchy in a typical international auditing firm includes partners, managers, supervisors, seniors or in-charge auditors, and staff accountants. A new employee usually starts as a staff accountant and spends several years at each classification before eventually achieving partner status.

1.12 Answers to Certification Exam Questions

1.1 (B) The requirement is to determine which concept requires an attitude that includes a questioning mind and a critical assessment of audit evidence. Answer (B) is correct because ISA 100 (paragraph 42) states professional skepticism is an attitude that includes a questioning mind and a critical assessment of evidence.

1.2 (B) The requirement is to identify a reason why audits cannot reasonably be expected to bring all illegal acts to the auditor's attention. Answer (B) is correct because illegal acts relating to the operating aspects of an entity are often highly specialized and complex and often are far removed from the events and transactions reflected in financial statements.

1.3 (D) Financial statement assertions. Answer (D) is correct because in obtaining evidential matter in support of financial statement assertions, the auditor develops specific audit objectives in the light of those assertions.

1.4 (A) The requirement is to express the differences between ISA and attestation standards. Answer (A) is correct because attestation standards cover all engagements that exhibit five characteristics: (1) a three-party relationship involving a practitioner (a *responsible party*) and the intended users; (2) a subject matter; (3) suitable criteria; (4) evidence; and (5) an assurance report. An attestation includes examination of historical financial statements

1.5 (B) The requirement is to identify the correct statement concerning an auditor's responsibilities regarding financial statements. Answer (B) is correct because an auditor may draft an entity's financial statements based on information from management's accounting system.

1.6 (A) The requirement is to identify the assertion used to develop audit objectives regarding an entity's control of obtaining credit approval before shipping goods. Answer (A) is correct because the auditor wishes to determine if accounts receivable are properly valued. If credit is not checked, the collectability of accounts receivable is brought into question.

1.7 (A) The requirement is to identify the reply that is **not** component of an entity's internal control. Answer (A) is correct because while auditors assess control risk as a part of their consideration of internal control, it is not a component of an entity's internal control.

1.13 Notes

1 The Afrikaansche Handels-vereeniging was a company controlled by a very reputable citizen of Rotterdam, the Netherlands. He managed to conceal important losses of his company to bankers, creditors and stockholders by providing false balance sheets.
2 As important audit terms are first introduced in a chapter they are set in colored type. If you see a word in color, the definition will be given in the glossary.
3 Such non-financial information might include footnote disclosures, the management's report, the report of the directors, or even the whole annual report.
4 Adrian Cadbury, 1995, *The Company Chairman*, 2nd ed. Prentice Hall, Hemel Hempstead, England, p. 116.
5 Adapted and reprinted with permission from AICPA. Copyright © 2000 & 1985 by American Institute of Certified Public Accountants.
6 A management report is required for publicly traded companies in the USA.

7 Required of companies listed on the London Stock Exchange. Recommended in 1992 by the Committee on the Financial Aspects of Corporate Governance (the Cadbury Report). At the heart of the Cadbury Report is a Code of Best Practice designed to achieve the necessary high standards of corporate behavior.

8 The Committee of Sponsoring Organizations of the Treadway Commission (COSO) recommended a management report on internal control in 1992. In 1989, one public company in four reported in some way on internal controls. For Fortune 500 companies, the number was about 60 percent. Now internal control is required for all companies listed on the US Stock Exchange or otherwise reporting to the SEC under the Sarbanes-Oxley Act.

9 European Community Commission EMS Regulation (Environmental Management and Audit Scheme) recommends an environmental report on a voluntary basis. The International Standards Organization (ISO) has formed the Technical Committee TC 207 to develop a new standard series ISO numbered 14000–14999 for the regulation of environmental management. ISO 14001, 14000 and 14010–12 could be directly binding under the EMAS Regulation.

10 J. P. Percy, "The Relevance of Research in the Development of Interpersonal Skills for Accountants," FEE/IFAC 1995 International Accountancy Conference, 12 May 1995, Amsterdam and Breukelen, the Netherlands.

11 This was the culmination of a restructuring based on the recommendations of the report *Recommendations on Shaping IASC for the Future.*

12 Guo Zhenqian, February 1998, "National Audit Office of the People's Republic in China," *Auditor General.*

13 SEC, 2003, *Study Report: Study Pursuant to Section 108(d) of the Sarbanes-Oxley Act of 2002 on the Adoption by the United States Financial Reporting System of a Principles-Based Accounting System,* Securities and Exchange Commission. **http://www.sec.gov**. 25 July.

14 IFAC, 2003, *Reform Proposals,* International Federation Of Accountants, New York, **http://www. IFAC.org**, 10 September.

15 Adapted and reprinted with permission from AICPA. Copyright © 2000 & 1985 by American Institute of Certified Public Accountants.

16 IFAC, 2004, *Handbook of International Auditing, Assurance, and Ethics Pronouncements,* International Standards on Auditing 200 (ISA 200), "Objective and General Principles Governing an Audit of Financial Statements", para. 2, International Federation of Accountants, New York.

17 American Accounting Association, *A Statement of Basic Auditing Concepts,* American Accounting Association, Sarasota, Florida, 1971, p. 2.

18 IFAC, 2004, *Handbook of International Auditing, Assurance, and Ethics Pronouncements,* International Standards on Auditing 200 (ISA 200), "Objective and General Principles Governing an Audit of Financial Statements", International Federation of Accountants, New York.

19 IFAC, 2004, *Handbook of International Auditing, Assurance, and Ethics Pronouncements,* International Standards on Auditing 200 (ISA 200), "Objective and General Principles Governing an Audit of Financial Statements", para. 7, International Federation of Accountants, New York.

20 International Auditing and Assurance Standards Board (IAASB), 2003, *International Standard on Auditing 200,* "Objective and General Principles Governing and Audit of Financial Statements," para. 15. International Federation of Accountants, New York, October.

21 Council of European Communities, Eighth Council Directive of 10 April 1994, Article 24, *Official Journal of the European Communities,* No. L 126, 1994.

22 Ibid.

23 IFAC, 2004, *Handbook of International Auditing, Assurance, and Ethics Pronouncements,* International Standards on Auditing 500 (ISA 500), "Audit Evidence," para. 17, International Federation of Accountants, New York.

24 Philip Wallage, 1993, "Internationalizing Audit: A study of audit approaches in the Netherlands," *European Accounting Review,* 1993, No. 3, pp. 555–578.

25 IFAC International Auditing and Assurance Standards Board, 2002, *Exposure Draft Audit Risk Proposed International Standards on Auditing,* Explanatory Memorandum to Exposure Drafts, International Federation of Accountants, New York, October.

26 An extended version of ISA 200, "Objective and General Principles Governing an Audit of Financial Statements," The New ISA 315 "Understanding the Entity and Its Environment and Assessing the Risks of Material Misstatement" replaces ISA 310, "Knowledge of the Business;" ISA 400, "Risk Assessments and Internal Control;" and ISA 401, "Auditing in a Computer Information Systems Environment." The new ISA 330, "The Auditor's Procedures in Response to Assessed Risks," also replaces ISA 400 and ISA 401. A new ISA 500, "Audit Evidence," replaces the old ISA 500.

27 Committee of Sponsoring Organizations of the Treadway Commission (COSO), 1992, *Internal Control Integrated Framework: Framework*, Chapter 1 Definition, American Institute of Certified Public Accountants. Jersey City, New Jersey, 1992.

1.14   Questions, Exercises and Cases

QUESTIONS

1.2 Auditing through World History

1.1 Identify and briefly discuss factors that have created the demand for international auditing.

1.2 What characteristics of the Industrial Revolution were essential for the enhanced development of the audit profession?

1.3 The Auditor, Corporations and Financial Information

1.3 Evaluate this quote: "Every international business, large or small, should have an annual audit by an independent auditor." Why should an auditor review the financial statements of a company each year?

1.4 International Accounting and Auditing Standards

1.4 How do International Financial Reporting Standards (IFRS) differ from International Standards on Auditing (ISA)?

1.5 What are the ISA standards that are used by an auditor to guide him through the first phase of an audit?

1.5 An Audit Defined

1.6 What is the objective of an audit?

1.7 What is the general definition of an audit? Briefly discuss the key component parts of the definition.

1.8 Name two types of risk in the audit process? Briefly discuss each.

1.6 Types of Audits

1.9 How many types of audits are there? Name each and briefly define them?

1.10 What are the differences and similarities in audits of financial statements, compliance audits, and operational audits?

1.7 Types of Auditors

1.11 What are the three types of auditors? Briefly define them.

1.8 Setting Audit Objectives Based on Management Assertions

1.12 What are the financial statement assertions made by management according to ISA 500?

1.13 What is the existence assertion? The rights and obligation assertion? The completeness assetion?

1.9 The Audit Process Model

1.14 How can one compare the empirical scientific cycle to the financial audit process?

1.15 What are the four phases of an audit process model? Briefly describe each.

1.16 Based on the Evaluation and Judgment Phase (IV) of the audit process model the overall conclusions are formed on what judgments?

1.10 International Public Accountancy Firms

1.17 List the four basic positions within the organizational structure of an audit firm and describe the duties of each position.

1.18 Name the Big Four international audit firms and give a brief history of each.

PROBLEMS AND EXERCISES

1.2 Auditing through World History

1.19 History of Auditing. In this chapter, the history of auditing has been briefly described, from an international perspective.

Required:

Identify the major differences with the developments specific for your country and try to explain these based on differences in the economic system or development.

1.3 The Auditor, Corporations and Financial Information

1.20 Expectations Gap. The general public thinks that an auditor guarantees the accuracy of financial statements. Is this true? Why? What other things does the public believe about audited financial statements?

1.4 International Accounting and Auditing Standards

1.21 International Auditing Standards. The London, Tokyo and New York Stock Exchanges, among others, require an annual audit of the financial statements of companies whose securities are listed on it. What are the possible reasons for this?

1.22 Describe the Public Interest Oversight Board. Discuss what you think their impact will be on worldwide auditing

1.5 An Audit Defined

1.23 Objectives of an Audit. Tracy Keulen, the sole owner of a small bakery, has been told that the business should have financial statements reported on by an independent Registeraccountant (RA). Keulen, having some bookkeeping experience, has personally prepared the company's financial statements and does not understand why such statements should be examined by a RA. Keulen discussed the matter with Petra Dassen (a RA), and asked Dassen to explain why an audit is considered important.

Required:
A. Describe the objectives of the independent audit.
B. Identify five ways in which an independent audit may be beneficial to Keulen.

1.24 Based on ISA 200 what are the general principles governing an audit of financial statements. Discuss ethics, professional skepticism, audit scope, business risk and audit risk.

1.6 Types of Audits

1.25 Operational Audits. List four examples of specific operational audits that could be conducted by an internal audit in a manufacturing company. Describe how you would conduct each

1.26 Auditing Tasks. Each of the following represents tasks that auditors frequently perform:
1 Compilation of quarterly financial statements for a small business that does not have any accounting personnel capable of preparing financial statements.
2 Review of tax return of corporate president to determine whether she has included all taxable income.
3 Review of the activities of the receiving department of a large manufacturing company, with special attention to the efficiency of the materials inspection.

4   Evaluation of a company's computer system to determine whether the computer is being used effectively.

5   Examination on a surprise basis of Topanga Bank. Emphasis placed on verification of cash and loans receivable and observation of the California banking code.

6   Examination of vacation records to determine whether employees followed company policy of two weeks' paid vacation annually.

7   Audit of a small college to determine that the college had followed requirements of a bond indenture agreement.

8   Examination of financial statements for use by stockholders when there is an internal audit staff.

9   Audit of a German government agency to determine if the agency has followed policies of the German government.

10 Audit of annual financial statements to be filed with the SEC.

11 Examination of a French government grant to a private company to determine whether it would have been feasible to accomplish the same objective at less cost elsewhere.

12 Audit of a statement of cash receipts and disbursements to be used by a creditor.

Required:

For each of the above, identify the most likely type of auditor (independent, government, or internal) and the most likely type of audit (financial, compliance, or operational).

1.7 Types of Auditors

1.27 Independent External Auditor. Give reasons why the following organizations should have annual audits by an independent external auditor:

(a) The US Federal Reserve Board

(b) A retail company traded on the London Stock Exchange

(c) Walt Disney Company

(d) Amnesty International

(e) A small grocery store in Ponta Grossa, Brazil

(f)   A local Baptist church in Lubbock, Texas.

1.8 Setting Audit Objectives Based on Management Assertions

1.28 Management Assertions and Audit Objectives. The following are management assertions (1 through 9) and audit objectives applied to the audit of accounts payable ((a) through (h)).

Management Assertion:

1   Existence

2   Rights and obligations

3   Occurrence

4   Completeness

5   Valuation and allocation

6   Accuracy

7   Cutoff

8   Classification

9   Understandibility

Specific Audit Objective:

(a) Existing accounts payable are included in the accounts payable balance on the balance sheet date.

(b) Accounts payable are recorded in the proper account.

(c) Acquisition transactions in the acquisition and payment cycle are recorded in the proper period.

(d) Accounts payable representing the accounts payable balance on the balance sheet date agree with related subsidiary ledger amounts, and the total is correctly added and agrees with the general ledger.

(e) Accounts in the acquisition and payment cycle are properly disclosed according to IASs.

(f) Accounts payable representing the accounts payable balance on the balance sheet date are valued at the correct amount.

(g) Accounts payable exist.

(h) Any allowances for accounts payable discounts is taken.

Required:

A. Explain the differences among management assertions and specific audit objectives and their relationships to each other.

B. For each specific audit objective, identify the appropriate management assertion.

1.9 The Audit Process Model

1.29 Audit Process Model. What are the four Phases of an Audit? Discuss each. Determine which is the most important of the four and explain why.

1.30 Audit Process Model. Based on the standard Audit Process Model, trace the procedures an auditor would use to audit a retail clothing business (continuing client) from the initial client contact to the audit opinion.

1.10 International Public Accountancy Firms

1.31 Auditor Responsibility. Four friends who are auditing students have a discussion. Jon says that the primary responsibility for the adequacy of disclosure in the financial statements and footnotes rests with the auditor in charge of the audit field work. Mai-ling says that the partner in charge of the engagement has the primary responsibility. Abdul says the staff person who drafts the statements and footnotes has the primary responsibility. Yalanda contends that it is the client's responsibility.

Required:

Which student is correct and why?

CASES

1.32 Audit Objectives and Financial Statement Accounts. Look at the financial statements of a major public company. Pick three accounts and discuss the financial statement assertions that might be associated with those accounts. For example, the financial statement assertions that might be associated with "Accrued Product Liability" are valuation, existence, completeness, and understandability. Valuation relates to product liability because a judgment (estimate) must be made regarding the expected cost of defective products.

1.33 International Standards on Auditing (ISA). Download the latest version of *Handbook Of International Auditing, Assurance, And Ethics Pronouncements* from the IFAC website **www.IFAC.org**. Pick one ISA and discuss how that standard would influence the work of an auditor.

1.34 Qualifications of Auditors. From the library get a copy of the EC Eighth Company Law Directive which is about the qualifications and work of auditors.

Required:
Based on the Eighth Directive, answer the following questions.
A. How many years of work experience must an auditor have before he can receive an auditing credential?
B. How many years of education must an auditor have before certification?
C. Name some of the requirements for the work of auditors.

1.35 Due Professional Care. Discuss lawsuits resulting from negligence of "Due professional Care."

Required:
A. Consult the library, a database like Lexis-Nexis or the internet for lawsuits resulting from negligence of "Due Professional Care." Discuss at least two.
B. Describe briefly the courts final conclusion and results from the court decision.
(Written by Thai Silver and Shirlene Xicotencatl)

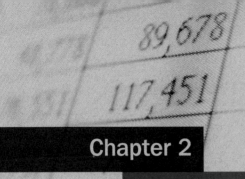

Chapter 2

THE AUDIT MARKET

2.1 Learning Objectives

After studying this chapter, you should be able to:

1 Distinguish between different theories on the demand and supply of audit services.

2 Understand drivers for audit regulation.

3 Understand the role of public oversight.

4 Distinguish between different audit firms.

5 Describe the elements of audit quality an audit fee.

6 Identify auditor's liability issues.

7 Know the auditor's responsibilities with regard to the detection of fraud and illegal acts.

8 Identify some current developments in the audit market.

9 Portray the series of codes of conduct and guidance at the London Stock Exchange from the Cadbury Report to the Turnbull Report.

10 Be acquainted with the Sarbanes-Oxley Act of 2002.

2.2 Introduction

The emergence of today's auditors happened during the Industrial Revolution that started in Great Britain around 1780. This revolution led to the emergence of large industrial companies with complex bureaucratic structures and, gradually, the need to look for external funds in order to finance further expansion: the separation between capital provision and management. Both developments resulted in demand for the services of specialists in bookkeeping and in auditing internal and external financial representations. The institutionalization of the audit profession was then merely a matter of time.

■ Management Controls Operations and Communications

Management has control over the accounting systems of the enterprises that auditors audit. Management is not only responsible for the financial reports to investors, but also has the authority to determine the precise nature of the representations that go into those reports. However, management can scarcely be expected to take an impartial view of this process.

■ Communications to Stakeholders – the Financial Statements

The financial reports measure the effectiveness of management's performance of its duties. They have an important influence on management's salaries, on the value of managers' shareholdings in the enterprise and even on their continued employment with the company. To increase the confidence of investors and creditors in these financial statements, they are provided with an independent and expert opinion on the fairness of the reports. An auditor provides this opinion.

2.3 Theories on the Demand and Supply of Audit Services

The demand for audit services may be explained by several different theories. Some theories like the **Theory of Inspired Confidence** and **Agency Theory** have been well researched and reported on. Other theories based on public perceptions such as the **Policeman Theory** and the **Lending Credibility Theory** serve more as a point of reference than a researched construct.

These four audit theories are shown in Illustration 2.1.

■ The *Policeman Theory*

Is an auditor responsible for discovering fraud, like a policeman? Think of this idea as the Policeman Theory. Up until the 1940s it was widely held that an auditor's job was to focus on arithmetical accuracy and on prevention and detection of fraud. However, from the 1940s until the turn of the century there was a shift of auditing to mean verification of truth and fairness of the financial statements. Recent financial statement frauds such as

ILLUSTRATION 2.1

An Illustration of Four Theories of Auditing

Policeman Theory

An auditor's job is to focus on arithmetical accuracy and on the prevention and detection of fraud.

Lending Credibility Theory

Audited financial statements are used by management to enhance the stakeholders' faith in management's stewardship.

Theory of Inspired Confidence

The demand for audit services is the direct consequence of the participation of outside stakeholders (third parties) in the company. These stakeholders demand accountability from the management, in return for their contribution to the company. Since information provided by management might be biased, because of a possible divergence between the interests of management and outside stakeholders, an audit of this information is required.

Agency Theory

A company is viewed as the result of more or less formal contracts, in which several groups make some kind of contribution to the company, given a certain price. A reputable auditor is appointed not only in the interest of third parties, but also in the interest of management.

those at Ahold, Xerox, Enron, Tyco, etc. have resulted in careful reconsideration of this theory. There now is an ongoing public debate on the auditor's responsibility for detection and disclosure of **fraud** returning us to the basic public perceptions on which this theory derives.

■ The *Lending Credibility Theory*

Another public perception is that the primary function of auditing is the addition of credibility to the financial statements. We may think of this as the Lending Credibility Theory. Audited financial statements are used by management to enhance the stakeholders' faith in management's stewardship. If **stakeholders** such as stockholders, government, or creditors have to make their judgments based on the information they receive, they must have faith that this is a fair representation of the economic value of the firm. In audit research terms this reduces the "**information asymmetry**". However, there is an efficient markets theory that holds that audited information does not form the primary basis for investors' investment decisions. [1]

■ The Theory of Inspired Confidence

This theory was developed in the late 1920s by the Dutch professor Theodore Limperg. [2] In contrast to the preceding theories, Limperg's theory addresses both the demand and the supply of audit services. According to Limperg, the demand for audit services is the direct consequence of the participation of outside stakeholders (**third parties**) in the company. These stakeholders demand accountability from the management, in return for their contribution to the company. Since information provided by management might be biased, because of a possible divergence between the interests of management and outside stakeholders, an audit of this information is required. With regard to the level of **audit assurance** that the auditor should provide (the supply side), Limperg adopts a normative approach. The auditor should act in such a way that he does not disappoint the expectations of a "rational outsider", while, on the other hand, he should not arouse greater expectations in his report than his examination justifies. So, given the possibilities of audit technology, the auditor should do everything to meet reasonable public expectations.

■ Agency Theory

In the agency theory, originally proposed by Watts and Zimmerman, [3] a reputable auditor – an auditor who is perceived to meet expectations – is appointed not only in the interest of third parties, but also in the interest of management. A company is viewed as the result of more or less formal "contracts", in which several groups make some kind of contribution to the company, given a certain "price". Company management tries to get these contributions under optimum conditions for management: low interest rates from bankers, high share prices for stockholders, low wages for employees.

In these relationships, management is seen as the "agent," trying to obtain contributions from "principals" such as bankers, stockholders and employees. Costs of an agency relationship are monitoring costs (the cost of monitoring the agents), bonding costs (the costs, incurred by an agent, of insuring that agents will not take adverse actions against the principals), and residual loss (effective loss that results despite the bonding and monitoring costs incurred).

Management Knows More – Information Asymmetry

Several types of complexities arise in these agent–principal relationships, such as information asymmetry. The agent (management) has a considerable advantage over the principals regarding information about the company. Basically, management knows more about the company's ability to repay loans than the banker does, and it knows better than the stockholders what the actual profit is, or whether it enjoys excessive perquisites. Furthermore, management knows better than the employees whether the company's financial condition is such that everybody will still be employed next year. However, management needs the principals to look favorably on them, because they ultimately depend on principals for the financial structuring of the business that management supervises.

In order for the principals (who buy shares in the company, loan the company money, or work for them) to have faith in the information given by management, it must be reliable. This means that there is an incentive for both managers and outside investors to engage reputable auditors.

Supply Side of Agency Theory

Agency theory can also be used to explain the supply side[4] of the audit market. The contribution of an audit to third parties is basically determined by the probability that the auditor will detect errors in the financial statements (or other irregularities, such as fraud or illegal acts) and the auditor's willingness to report these errors (e.g. by qualifying the auditor's report), even against the wish of the auditee (auditor independence). Costs as a result of reputation damage have been demonstrated in several empirical studies, which showed that audit firms, having suffered a public rebuke, were confronted with a decline in their market share.

2.4 Audit Regulation

In the previous section, the demand for audit has been described. In most countries, this demand has long been on a voluntary basis, i.e. it was left to the companies to decide whether they had their financial statements audited or not. As for the supply side, the provision of audit services has been left open to the free market in some countries, without any official legal requirements for auditors. Although regulation and legislation differ, both the demand and the supply of audit services are currently regulated to some degree in most countries. Recent accounting and finance research suggests that national legal environments are among the key determinants of financial market development, corporate ownership structures, corporate policies, and the properties of accounting information around the world.[5]

In most countries, audits are now legally required for some types of companies. For example, in the USA and the European Union, large, and in some cases medium-sized enterprises, are required by law to provide audited financial statements. The European Union audit rules apply to all companies that are required to be audited by the individual Member States. The requirements may vary from state to state. For example, in the Netherlands, companies with more than 50 employees, and/or assets greater than Euro 3.1 million, and/or net sales greater than Euro 6.2 million must be audited. The major bourses (including NYSE, NASDAQ, London Stock Exchange, Tokyo NIKKEI, and Frankfurt DAX) have listing rules that require all listed companies to have their annual report audited.

The supply of audit services is currently also regulated in most countries. In the European Union, **statutory audits**, i.e. audits required by law, can only be performed by auditors who have met specific technical requirements with regard to education and experience.

■ Public Oversight Board

There is a recent growth in accounting oversight boards – government or professional committees to review the work of auditors and take an active part in setting and enforcing standards. Three such boards are in the USA (the Public Company Accounting Oversight Board), Australia (Financial Reporting Council), and the UK (The Review Board).

The Sarbanes-Oxley Act of 2002 required the US Securities and Exchange Commission (SEC) to create a Public Company Accounting Oversight Board (PCAOB). The Board oversees and investigates the audits and auditors of public companies, and sanctions both firms and individuals for violations of laws, regulations, and rules. The Board, at this point, has decided the generally accepted auditing standards (GAAS) set by the American Institute of Certified Public Accountants (AICPA) will only be used temporarily.[6] The PCAOB is empowered to regularly inspect registered accounting firms' operations and will investigate potential violations of securities laws, standards, consistency, and conduct. Accounting firms headquartered outside the USA that "prepare and furnish" an audit report involving US firms registered with the SEC are subject to the authority of the PCAOB.

Concept and a Company 2.1

The Basic Theory

Concept	Auditor's search for materiality.
Story	There was once a group of very famous accountants and auditors who joined together as a mutual study group. They determined that they could find the basic truths of auditing. They read all manner of philosophical, scientific, and religious works and discussed those theories amongst themselves. They felt that knowledge of the pure truths of auditing would form a basis for discovering the core truths of business and, indeed, life itself.
	They studied the great works of accounting for many years, but felt that they were getting nowhere. Finally, they decided to take leave of their day jobs and search the world to find the answer. They sought the advice of great teachers the world over. They would ask each great teacher to recommend one who was even wiser. Thus, they collected these recommendations until their search pointed to one man – a teacher of teachers.
	The group journeyed to an isolated area in the great dessert wastes of Africa. There they met the great man, and paying their respects, they told him of their heart-felt desire and long suffering to find the pure truths of auditing. He said, "I cannot give you the answers. These you must find yourself." He instructed them to collect all the world's accounting knowledge, encompassing everything from the Sarbanes-Oxley Act 2002 back to cuneiform tablets of 3400 BCE. Then they were to condense all that knowledge to ten volumes.
	The group went away and gathered and summarized knowledge for all the ages. After years of work, they again sat at the feet of the teacher of teachers and presented their ten volumes. The sage picked up the volumes and thumbed through them. He handed the volumes back to the group and then said, "Go and make this into one volume."
	After years of toil, the group, whose membership was now thinning appreciably, returned with their one volume of the world's audit truths. The teacher of teachers said, "Make this into one sentence."

Taking on this almost impossible task, the remaining members of the group locked themselves into a cave and ate nothing but soup made of nettles to sustain them until they came up with the one true answer. When they returned to the guru with this sentence, he smiled and said to them, "You got it." This was the sentence.

"There is no such thing as a free lunch."

Discussion Questions	■ Why can we expect that a fraud that works now may not work in the future? ■ Why can a company not continue to grow indefinitely at 15 percent per year? ■ Why can a management who make up fictitious sales not profit in the long run? ■ Why does every form of earnings manipulation have its cost? ■ Based on this one sentence, how would you justify the existence of ethics?
References	The great audit works.

Sparked by the Enron and WorldCom debacles and other widely publicized corporate and accounting scandals, the Sarbanes-Oxley Act of 2002 was passed almost unanimously by Congress and signed into law by President George W. Bush on July 30, 2002. The Act, described by the President as incorporating "the most far-reaching reforms of American business practices since the time of Franklin Delano Roosevelt," is intended to establish investor confidence by improving the quality of corporate disclosure and financial reporting, strengthen the independence of accounting firms, and increase the role and responsibility of corporate officers and directors in financial statements and corporate disclosures.

In Australia, the Corporate Law Economic Reform Program Act 1999 established a new body, the **Financial Reporting Council** (**FRC**), with the responsibility for the broad oversight of the accounting standard-setting process for the private, public and not-for-profit sectors. The FRC has an obligation to monitor the development of international accounting standards and accounting standards that apply in major international financial centers. It sets the broad strategic direction for the Australian Accounting Standards Board (AASB), approves and monitors its priorities and business plan, and oversees its operations.

The **Review Board** in the UK is funded by the Accountancy Foundation Limited. The Review Board's task is to monitor the operation of the regulatory system to confirm that it is fully meeting the public interest. In carrying out this function the Review Board's remit covers the work of the three associated bodies – the Ethics Standards Board, the Auditing Practices Board and the Investigation and Discipline Board. It also has limited scrutiny over the UK accounting professional bodies' authority for investigation and discipline, monitoring, training, qualification, and registration of their members from the accounting profession

Chapter 14 Corporate Governance and the Future of Auditing will discuss public oversight boards in some detail.

Certification Exam Question 2.1

A group that was established in 2002 by the US Congress to oversee and investigate the audits and auditors of public companies and sanction both firms and individuals for violations of laws, regulations, and rules is:

(A) The Public Interest Oversight Board.
(B) The Review Board.
(C) The Public Company Accounting Oversight Board.
(D) The Financial Reporting Council.

2.5 Audit Firms

In previous sections we have extensively discussed the demand side of the audit market and its ideas of what auditors should provide. But what about the supply side? How is it structured? Usually, audit firms are classified into two distinct categories:

- the Big Four firms;
- the Non-Big Four firms.

■ The Big Four Firms

These firms resulted partially from several major mergers in the late 1980s. This group is made up of Deloitte, Ernst & Young, KPMG and PricewaterhouseCoopers. These audit firms have a global network of affiliated firms. Actually, there were the Big Five firms after a series of mergers, including Arthur Andersen. However, as a result of the Enron accounting scandal, the market lost its confidence in Arthur Andersen and this firm had to forfeit its business in 2002 after almost 90 years of having been a highly respected firm (see Concept and a Company 2.2.). This case study demonstrates how important it is for auditors to fully respond to the inspired confidence of their stakeholders. We discuss these ethics issues in Chapter 3.

Although most of these firms are still structured as national partnerships with national instead of international profit sharing, these national member firms participate in an international head office, in which global technologies, procedures, and directives are developed. In addition to sharing the methodology, the networks are also used for the co-ordination of international audit engagements. The group auditor of a worldwide operating company uses the services of auditors of the member firms in the countries where the client has subsidiaries. As a result of the developments in communications technology, the effectiveness of these networks and the efficiency of the co-ordination of international engagements have increased significantly.

For the Big Four firms, audit and accounting services represent approximately half of the firms' total fee income.

■ The Non-Big Four Firms

These firms can hardly be treated as a homogeneous group. At one extreme there is a very large number of small local firms, with only a handful of professionals. At the other extreme there is a small number of **second tier** firms, which also have an international network, although not quite as extensive as the Big Four network. In between, there is a large number of medium-sized national or regional audit firms, with several offices.

It has often been suggested that Big Four audit firms perform higher quality audits – both in detection and independence – than non-Big Four firms, because they have a technological edge and because a given client will represent a smaller amount of their aggregate fee income. In line with this argument, it is often suggested that audit firms are more independent towards small than towards big clients. Losing a small client due to a technical discussion with client management is considered less harmful than losing a big one. Further, it is assumed that clients in financial trouble are audited more thoroughly (higher audit quality) than well-performing clients, because the risk of litigation due to an audit error is perceived as higher in case of a company failure.

2.6 Audit Quality and Audit Fee Determination

How is the auditor evaluated in the market place? In line with other service providers, auditors are evaluated based on **technical and functional quality** elements. Technical audit quality is defined[7] as the degree to which an audit meets a consumer's expectations with regard to the detection and reporting of errors and irregularities regarding the audited company and its financial statements. Hence, technical audit quality addresses the quality of the **outcome** of the audit process: how good is the auditor at finding errors in the financial statements, or at detecting fraud or going concern problems?

Functional audit quality is defined as the degree to which the process of carrying out the audit and communicating its results meets a consumer's expectations. This aspect of audit quality represents not the outcome, but the process itself. Dassen found, in his study of the Dutch audit market,[8] that clients do not just appreciate the detection ability of auditors (technical quality), but also the auditor's ability to identify points of interest to management regarding corporate finance, internal control, or general business management, as a by-product to giving their opinion on the accuracy of the financial statements. Furthermore, they appreciate an auditor's empathy (does the auditor understand the client's business and language, does he know his client's needs?) and communication skills.

Quality and Length of Tenure

An interesting engagement characteristic is the length of tenure. Mostly, first-year audit engagements are perceived as less thorough, since it takes some time to identify all potential audit risks for a new client. However, after a long period, the auditor might lose his professional skepticism if the length of tenure exceeds 10 to 15 years. The abovementioned relationships have been subjected to many different research techniques with mixed results.

Fee Determination

As is very often the case, quality represents just one side of the coin. The other side is fee level. Fee setting by auditors has often been studied in audit research. Important determinants of audit fees are:

- the size of the auditee and the geographical dispersion;
- the size of the audit firm (Big Four firms seem to demand a fee premium);
- the level of consulting services;
- the quality of the auditee's internal control system;
- the type of fee contract (fixed fee versus variable fee).

Certification Exam Question 2.2

The nature and extent of a CPA firm's quality control policies and procedures depend on:

	The audit firm's size	The nature of the audit firm's practice	Cost–benefit considerations
(A)	Yes	Yes	Yes
(B)	Yes	Yes	No
(C)	Yes	No	No
(D)	No	Yes	Yes

2.7 Legal Liability

There are many stakeholders who rely on audited financial statements: the client (with which there is a **privity** relationship), actual and potential stockholders, vendors, bankers and other creditors, employees, customers, and the government. Legal liability of the auditor to each stakeholder varies from country to country, district to district. This liability can generally be classified as based on one or more of the following: common law, civil liability under statutory law, criminal liability under statutory law, and liability as members of professional accounting organizations.

■ Liability Under Common Law

Liability for auditors under common law generally falls in two categories: liabilities to clients and third party liability.

Liability to Clients

Breach of contract

A typical civil lawsuit filed by a client involves a claim that the auditor did not discover financial statement fraud or employee fraud (defalcation) because the auditors showed negligence in the conduct of an audit. The legal action can be for **breach of contract**, or more likely, a **tort** action for negligence. Tort actions are the most common, for generally they generate larger monetary judgments than breach of contract.

Liabilities to Third Parties

Third parties include all stakeholders in an audit other than the audit client. An audit firm may be liable to third parties such as banks who have incurred a loss due to reliance on misleading financial statements.

Ultramares

The most famous US audit case in third party liabilities happened in the 1931 *Ultramares–Touche* case (*Ultramares Corporation* v *Touche et al.*).[9] In this case, the court held that although the accountants were negligent in not finding that a material amount of accounts receivable had been falsified when careful investigation would have shown the amount to be fraudulent, they were not liable to a third party bank because the creditors were not a primary beneficiary, or known party, with whom the auditor was informed before conducting the audit. This precedent is called the Ultramares doctrine, that ordinary negligence is not sufficient for a liability to a third party because of lack of privity of contract between the third party and the auditor.

Caparo

In the famous 1990 *Caparo* case (*Caparo Industries, PLC* v *Dickman* and *Others*),[10] the British House of Lords reached a verdict that the key determinant for the duty of care criterion was the purpose for which the auditor's service was performed. In the case of annual accounts, this purpose was to give the shareholders the information necessary to enable them to question the past management of the company, to exercise their voting rights and to influence future policy and management.

German Liability   → Liability is caped in Germany

In Germany, auditors have an unlimited liability to the client if there is an intentional violation of duties, but the liability is capped by law at Euro 1,000,000 to 4,000,000, depending on circumstances, for negligent violation of duties. Liability to third parties as described by the Tort Law (§§ 823–826 BGB) is restricted to certain prerequisites such as intent and violation of morality. There is also liability to third parties under Contract Law, which has less restrictive prerequisites than Tort Law.

■ Civil Liability Under Statutory Law

Most countries have laws that affect the civil liabilities of auditors. Securities laws, for example, may impose strict standards on professional accountants. In the USA, the Securities Act of 1933 not only created the Securities and Exchange Commission (SEC), it established the first statutory civil recovery rules for third parties against auditors. Original purchasers of securities of a firm newly registered to make a public offering have recourse against the auditor for up to the original purchase price if the financial statements are false or misleading.

Anyone who purchased securities described in the registration statement (S1) may sue the auditor for material misrepresentations or omissions in financial statements published in the S1. The auditor has the burden of demonstrating that reasonable investigation was conducted or all that the loss of the purchaser of securities (plaintiff) was caused by factors other than the misleading financial statements. If the auditor cannot prove this, the plaintiff wins the case.

■ Criminal Liability Under Statutory Law

A professional accountant may be held criminally liable under the laws of a country or district that make it a criminal offense to defraud another person through knowingly being involved with false financial statements.

US Securities and Exchange Act of 1934

The Securities an Exchange Act of 1934 in the USA requires every company with securities traded on national and over-the-counter exchanges to submit audited financial statements annually (10-K) as well as other reports for quarterly financials (10-Q), unusual events (8-K) and other events. The Act also sets out (Rule 10b-5) criminal liability conditions if the auditor employs any device, scheme or artifice to defraud or make any untrue statement of a material fact or omits to state a material fact, i.e. the auditor intentionally or recklessly misrepresents information for third party use. The SEC also has authority to sanction or suspend an auditor from doing audits for SEC-registered companies.[11]

Several court cases have been subjected to an application of the Act's criminal liability section. In *United States* v *Natelli (1975)* two auditors were convicted of criminal liability for certifying financial statements of National Student Marketing Corporation that contained inadequate disclosures pertaining to accounts receivable. In *United States* v *Weiner (1975)* three auditors were convicted of securities fraud in connection with their audit of Equity Funding Corporation of America. The fraud the company perpetrated was so massive and the audit work so sub-standard that the court concluded that the auditors must have been aware of the fraud. Management revealed to the audit partner that the prior years' financials were misstated and the partner agreed to say nothing in *ESM Government Securities* v *Alexander Grant & Co. (1986)*. The partner was convicted of criminal charges for his role in sustaining the fraud and was sentenced to a 12-year prison term.

Concept and a Company 2.2

Arthur Andersen and Obstruction of Justice

Concept	Auditor statutory legal liability – illegal acts.
Story	Arthur Andersen, LLP, one of the former Big Five audit firms with 2,311 public company clients and 28,000 US employees, was found guilty of "obstruction of justice." The obstruction of justice statute, 18 USC. § 1512(b), makes it a crime for anyone to "corruptly persuade" "another person" to destroy documents "with intent to impair" the use of the documents "in an official proceeding." The US District Court for the Southern District of Texas sentenced Andersen to pay a $500,000 fine and serve five years of probation. (WSJ 2002)
	The charge resulted from Andersen's destruction of thousands of documents and e-mail messages relating to work performed for Enron. The court found that Andersen illegally destroyed the documents with the intent of thwarting an investigation by the US Securities and Exchange Commission. On June 15, 2002, the tenth day of deliberations, the jury met for only 30 minutes, and then delivered its fatal verdict. This was the first time a major accounting firm had ever been convicted of a criminal charge. (Manor 2002)

Andersen contended that the document destruction was done in the standard course of business and was not illegal. The prosecution introduced evidence that Andersen billed Enron about $720,000 for consultation services relating to "SEC Inquiry" at the same time the firm was destroying documents relating to the Enron audit. The Department of Justice said that the Andersen billing records presented strong evidence that the firm knew about the SEC investigation at the same time they were shredding documents that might have been subpoenaed in that investigation. This establishes that many people at Andersen who were involved in the document destruction had direct, personal knowledge of the investigation. (Fowler 2002)

The document destruction was precipitated by a memo from Nancy Temple in Andersen's legal department which stated that, under the Andersen document retention policy, superseded drafts of memos should be discarded. David Duncan, the Andersen lead audit partner on the Enron account, ordered employees to adhere to the firm's guidelines on "document retention" and destroy irrelevant documents. In the trial, prosecution produced a binder of handwritten notes from Temple, taken from numerous conference calls with Andersen executives, to show that the attorney realized that the SEC would probably open an investigation into Enron. (Beltran *et al.* 2002)

Andersen appealed the judgment on several grounds. Andersen complained that the judge allowed the government to tell jurors about SEC actions against Andersen for faulty audits of Waste Management and Sunbeam, thereby prejudicing the jury. They also said that the judge gave improper instructions to the jury. The jury gave a message to the judge asking for guidance on making their decision. The question they asked was: "If each of us believes that one Andersen agent acted knowingly and with a corrupt intent, is it for all of us to believe it was the same agent? Can one believe it was agent A, another believe it was agent B, and another believe it agent C?" (*Houston Chronicle* 2003)

Over strenuous objections from the prosecution, Judge Harmon returned a message to the jury, telling them they could find Andersen guilty of obstructing justice even if they could not agree on which employee committed the crime. (McNulty 2002)

Discussion Questions	■ Should the whole audit firm be charged with an offense by a few of its auditors? ■ In what ways can auditor workpapers (correspondence, plans and audit notes) be beneficial to an investigation of company fraudulent practices?

References	Beltran, L.J. Rogers, and P. Viles, 2002, "U.S. Closes in Andersen Trial," *CNNMoney*, June 5. Fowler, Tom, 2002, "Soul searching led to plea, Duncan says," *Houston Chronicle*, May 16. Manor, R., 2002, "Andersen Finally Admits Demise," *Chicago Tribune*, June 17. McNulty, S., 2002, "Andersen guilty in Enron obstruction case," *Financial Times*, June 16. WSJ, 2002, "Andersen Sentenced To 5 Years Probation," *Wall Street Journal*, October 17.

Concept and a Company 2.3

US SEC Response to WorldCom Illegal Acts

Concept	Liability under statutory law – involving auditors in the disciplinary process.
Story	WorldCom's illegal activities, which included providing falsified financial information to the public, led to the company's downfall in 2002.

▶

US SEC Response to WorldCom Illegal Acts (continued)

WorldCom misled investors from at least as early as 1999 through the first quarter of 2002, and during that period, as a result of undisclosed and improper accounting, WorldCom materially overstated the income it reported on its financial statements by approximately $9 billion. (SEC *Litigation Release* 2002)

WorldCom was ordered to hire a qualified consultant, acceptable to the SEC, to review the effectiveness of its material internal accounting control structure and policies, including those related to line costs, reserves, and capital expenditures, as well as the effectiveness and propriety of WorldCom's processes, practices and policies to ensure that the company's financial data was accurately reported in its public financial statements. The company hired KPMG to launch a comprehensive audit of its financial statements for 2001 and 2002. (Ulick 2002)

WorldCom was also ordered to provide reasonable training and education to certain officers and employees to minimize the possibility of future violations of federal securities laws.

The SEC proposed a settlement in its civil action against WorldCom Inc. in a federal district court. The proposed settlement was for WorldCom to pay a civil penalty of $1.5 billion. As a result of the company's pending bankruptcy case, the proposed settlement provides for satisfaction of the Commission's judgment by WorldCom's payment, after review and approval of the terms of the settlement by the bankruptcy court, of $500 million. (SEC *Litigation Release* 2003)

Discussion Questions	■ What security procedures should WorldCom have had taken overall in order to prevent these illegal acts from happening? ■ What steps should innocent middle management have taken in order to stop or prevent top executives who performed the illegal acts? ■ Should they have reported to officials at the first sign of improper accounting? Or should they have just quit the company immediately.
References	SEC, 2002, *Litigation Release* 17866, "In SEC v WorldCom, Court Imposes Full Injunctive Relief, Orders Extensive Reviews of Corporate Governance Systems and Internal Accounting Controls," US Securities and Exchange Commission, November, 2002. SEC, 2003, *Litigation Release* 18147, "In WorldCom Case, SEC Files Proposed Settlement of Claim for Civil Penalty," US Securities and Exchange Commission, May 2003. Ulick, Jake, 2002, "WorldCom's Financial Bomb," *CNN/Money*, June 26.

■ Liabilities as Members of Professional Accounting Organizations

Nearly all national audit professions have some sort of disciplinary court. In most countries, anyone can lodge a complaint against an auditor, regardless of one's involvement with the auditor. The disciplinary court typically consists of representatives of the audit and legal professions, and sometimes representatives of the general public. Having heard the arguments of the plaintiff and the defendant, the court makes its judgment and determines the sanction – if any – against the auditor. The sanction may vary. It may be:

■ a fine;
■ a reprimand (either oral or written);
■ a suspension for a limited period of time (e.g. six months); or
■ a lifetime ban from the profession.

In some countries, the trials of these disciplinary courts are public. In most countries, the verdicts are made public, in particular if the verdict is either a suspension or a lifetime ban. Appeal against the verdict of the disciplinary court is usually possible. Suppose the auditor is condemned by the disciplinary court for an audit failure. Is that enough for a civil suit against an auditor? No. In order to hold the auditor legally liable successfully in a civil suit, the following conditions have to be met:

- An audit failure/neglect has to be proven (*negligence* issue). A verdict by the disciplinary court is often the basis for meeting this condition.
- The auditor should owe a duty of care to the plaintiff (**due professional care** issue).
- The plaintiff has to prove a causal relationship between his losses and the alleged audit failure (causation issue).
- The plaintiff must quantify his losses (quantum issue).

■ Suggested Solutions to Auditor Liability

In the 1980s and 1990s, several auditor litigation cases have resulted in multimillion dollar claims to be paid by auditors. For example, some Big Four audit firms made settlements with the US government for more than US $500 million, because of audit failures regarding several US savings and loans banks. Insurance against litigation is now common for audit firms. Even though the premium rates for these insurance policies have risen dramatically over the last decade, these policies only cover damage to a certain amount. Claims paid above this "cap" are not covered and have to be paid by the audit firm itself.

It is widely acknowledged that the financial risks resulting from litigation for audit firms and partners might be a threat to the viability of the audit profession. In order to reduce these risks several measures are considered:

- In some countries, a system of **proportionate liability** is under study. In such a system, an audit firm is not liable for the entire loss incurred by plaintiffs (as is the case under **joint and several liability**), but only to the extent to which the loss is attributable to the auditor. The US has a system of proportionate liability, but only under the federal acts.
- Some countries (e.g. Germany) have put a legally determined cap on the liability of auditors (to the client in the case of Germany).
- In order to protect the personal wealth of audit partners, some audit firms are structured as a limited liability partnership (e.g. in the UK).

2.8 Some Developments in the Audit Market

In our discussion of audit theories, the policeman theory was mentioned and its inability to explain the historic shift (from around 1940 to 2002) from prevention and detection of fraud to verification of truth and fairness of the financial statements. The development of the auditor's duties, linked to changes in the audit market, is still an object of public debate, often referred to as the **audit expectation gap** debate. This gap results from the fact that users of audit services have expectations regarding the duties of auditors that exceed the current practice in the profession.

Auditors Duties and the Expectations of Audit Services Users

The users of audit services can broadly be classified as **auditees** (the board of directors of the company) and third parties (shareholders, bankers, creditors, employees, customers, and other groups). Each of these groups has its own set of expectations with regard to an auditor's duties. Expectations were found with regard to the following duties of auditors:

- giving an opinion on the fairness of financial statements;
- giving an opinion on the company's ability to continue as a going concern;
- giving an opinion on the company's internal control system;
- giving an opinion on the occurrence of fraud;
- giving an opinion on the occurrence of illegal acts.

Current developments in each of these duties will be described in the remainder of this section.

■ Opinion on The Fairness of Financial Statements

Giving an opinion on the fairness of the financial statements is generally regarded as the auditor's core business. Most of the national and international auditing guidelines are concerned with this particular duty. Expectation gap studies demonstrate that public expectations are high. Basically, it seems that a large part of the financial community (users of audit services) expects that financial statements with an **unqualified audit opinion** are completely free from error. Companies like Enron, Parmalat, and WorldCom who reported fraudulent financial statements had financial statements that did not fairly reflect the underlying financial condition of those companies. The inherent limitations of auditing, expressed in materiality and audit risk (see Chapter 6 Understanding the Entity, Risk Assessment and Materiality) are not entirely accepted and/or understood by all groups of users.

ISA 700[12] discusses the consideration of fairness in reporting:

> The financial reporting framework is determined by International Financial Reporting Standards, rules issued by recognized standard setting bodies, and the development of general practice within a country, with an appropriate consideration of fairness and with due regard to local legislation.

■ Opinion on the Company's Ability to Continue as a Going Concern

Perhaps the most disturbing events for the public's trust in the audit profession are cases where an unqualified audit report has been issued shortly before a company's bankruptcy. Under ISA 570[13] and most national regulations, auditors need to determine whether the audited entity is able to continue as a **going concern**. If there are serious doubts about this ability, both the financial statements and the auditor's opinion need to express these doubts. However, it is generally felt that auditors face a dilemma in this regard. Although warning the users of financial statements of any threatening financial distress is appropriate, the disclosure of the indications of a possible future bankruptcy – especially when the future course of events is hard to predict – may prove to be a self-fulfilling prophecy which deprives management of its remaining means to save the company.

US Airline Bankruptcies

The US airline industry in the first few years of the twenty-first century experienced great operating difficulties caused by reduced travel brought on by the bursting of the tech and telecom bubbles, the terrorist attacks on the USA of September 11, 2001, volatility in world oil prices, the worldwide business recession, and the war in Iraq. The industry lost control of costs in the 1990s with overcapacity (too many airplanes) and high labor costs (about 40 percent of total operating costs). All of these factors resulted in bankruptcies for US Air in August 2002 and United Air Lines, Inc. in December 2002 (which was the largest bankruptcy in US airline industry history). In both cases, the auditors did not issue a going concern opinion until after the companies' bankruptcy filings.

The expectations of some groups within the financial community clearly exceed the auditor's current duties under the prevailing international and national audit guidelines. If there is a possibility of bankruptcy, auditors issue an unqualified report (because, even though financial statements show problems, the financial statements fairly represent the underlying finances) with modification paragraphs.

Certification Exam Question 2.3[14]

An auditor concludes that there is substantial doubt about an entity's ability to continue as a going concern for a reasonable period of time. If the entity's financial statements adequately disclose its financial difficulties, the auditor's report is required to include an explanatory paragraph that specifically uses the phrase(s)

	"Reasonable period of time, not to exceed one year"	"Going concern"
(A)	Yes	Yes
(B)	Yes	No
(C)	No	Yes
(D)	No	No

■ Opinion on the Company's Internal Control System

The issue of testing and reporting on the quality of a company's internal control system has been recognized as one of the focal issues in auditing. Currently, ISA 400[15] requires the auditor to obtain an understanding of a company's accounting and internal control systems, sufficient to plan the audit and develop an effective audit approach. However, testing the adequacy of the internal controls is not required. If the audit objectives can be met more efficiently by substantive testing, it is acceptable not to examine the internal control structure. Nonetheless, reliance on the firm's internal controls in performing an audit became a major pillar in auditing during the1980s, whereas the reporting on the effectiveness of (part of the) internal controls has become a predominant item in management letters.

Expectation gap surveys show high expectations of the auditor's role in testing whether a satisfactory system of internal control is being operated. These expectations clearly exceed the auditor's current duties.

Barings Bank Example

Barings Bank is an example of a company whose breakdown in internal controls, specifically segregation of duties, led to the ultimate destruction of the company. In 1995 Nicholas Leeson, manager of the Singapore Branch of Barings, not only made investments in the Nikkei exchange index derivatives, but also was able to authorize and account for his investment. This ultimately led to the multi-billion dollar collapse of Barings and a jail sentence for Leeson.

Reporting on Effectiveness of Internal Control

There has been much discussion in Europe, Canada and the USA about reporting on the effectiveness and functioning of internal controls. The Sarbanes-Oxley Act requires auditors to report on internal control[16] and the AICPA Auditing Standards Board (ASB) released an exposure draft on Internal Control Reporting.[17] Support for reporting lies in the belief that users of financial information have a legitimate interest in the condition of the controls over the accounting system and management's response to the suggestions of the auditors for correction of weaknesses. Those who argue against reporting on controls say that such reporting would increase the cost of audits, increase auditor (and director) liability and is not relevant information.

Section 404 of the Sarbanes-Oxley Act and PCAB Audit Standard #2 requires each annual report of a company to contain an "internal control report" which should:

1 state the responsibility of management for establishing and maintaining an adequate internal control structure and procedures for financial reporting
2 contain an assessment, as of the end of the fiscal year, of the effectiveness of the internal control structure and procedures for financial reporting
3 contain an 'attestation' to management's assessment by the company's independent, outside auditors.

The Combined Code of the Committee on Corporate Governance,[18] which represents the Code of Best Practice of the London Stock Exchange, states in Principle D.2 that: "The board should maintain a sound system of internal control to safeguard shareholders' investment and the company's assets." Provision D.2.1 states that: "The directors should, at least annually, conduct a review of the effectiveness of the group's system of internal control and should report to shareholders that they have done so. The review should cover all controls, including financial, operational and compliance controls and risk management."

■ Opinion on The Occurrence of Fraud

The audit expectation gap is frequently associated with the **fraud** issue. Both governments and the financial community expect the auditor to find existing fraud cases and report them. The fact that this part of the expectation gap has attracted so much attention is partly attributable to the evolution of auditing. As stated in our brief description of the history of auditing, the detection of fraud has been one of the profession's cornerstones during the first decades of its existence.

Famous Frauds

There are many examples of fraud from before the Enron collapse in 2001 up until today. Other major companies who issued fraudulent financial statements after Enron included:

US companies WorldCom, Xerox, Tyco, Health South, Bristol Myers, Citibank, KMart and NextCard; European firms Ahold, Parmalat and Comroad; Japanese bank Resona; and Australian insurance company HIH. Famous frauds before Enron include: Lincoln Savings and Loan, Penn Square, Sunbeam, Regina, ZZZZ Best, Crazy Eddy, Waste Management, Cendant, Livent, and Mattel. These cases are discussed in "Concept and a Company" cases throughout this book.

Object of an Audit One Hundred Years Ago

In their review of the historical development of the audit profession's views regarding the issue of fraud, Humphrey *et al.* (1991)[19] cite from Dicksee's 1900 edition *of Auditing – A Practical Manual for Auditors*, which states:

> The object of an audit may be said to be threefold:
>
> 1 The detection of fraud.
> 2 The detection of technical errors.
> 3 The detection of errors of principle.
>
> The detection of fraud is a most important portion of the auditor's duties. Auditors, therefore, should assiduously cultivate this branch of their activities.

Fraud – A Responsibility Not Assumed

Gradually, the auditor's responsibilities began to change, with fraud no longer being a key priority. Some researchers have demonstrated this by the changing priority of the fraud issue in Montgomery's *Auditing*. In its first three editions, fraud was labeled as a chief audit objective but its priority was gradually eroded until, in the 1957 Eighth Edition, it was described as "a responsibility not assumed."

What was the reason of this development "away from fraud?" Several reasons have been given for this phenomenon, but the most important reasons are:

- the acceptance that the audit of the financial statements on behalf of the third parties is an art of its own and justifies the existence of auditors; and
- the acceptance that an investigation aimed at finding any kind of fraud is extremely laborios, expensive and not practical, considering the increases in size and complexity of the companies, as well as their improved self or internal controls.

Fraud Back in the Spotlight

However, this "total" rejection of responsibility for fraud, which is evident from this historical outline, gave way to renewed discussion in the 1980s. Under public pressure to investigate the reasonableness of the auditors' position regarding fraud, the profession was forced to reconsider its total rejection stance that culminated in the installation of several committees such as the Cohen Commission (1978), the Treadway Commission (1987) and the Dingell Committee (1988) in the USA, and the Davison and Benson Committees (1985) in the UK.

The current position of the audit profession is described in ISA 240.[20] According to ISA 240, the responsibility for the prevention and detection of fraud and error rests with both those charged with the governance and the management of an entity. Fraud may involve sophisticated and carefully organized schemes designed to conceal it, such as forgery, deliberate failure to record transactions, or intentional misrepresentations being made to the auditor.

Concept and a Company 2.4

Trading Fraud Early on at Enron

Concept   Investigation of fraudulent acts.

Story   The first sign of fraud at Enron goes back to a trading division called Enron Oil in January 1987.

David Woyek, the head of Enron's internal audit department, received a call from Apple Bank in New York. He was told that wire transfers amounting to about $5 million had been flowing in from a bank in the Channel Islands, and over $2 million went into an account of Tom Masteroeni, treasurer of Enron Oil. The Apple Bank account could not be found anywhere on Enron's books. Masteroeni admitted that he had diverted funds to his account, but insisted that it was a profit-sharing tactic and that he always intended to repay the money. After a preliminary investigation, Woyek's deputy, John Beard wrote on his working papers "misstatement of records, deliberate manipulation of records, impact on financials for the year ending 12/31/86." (McLean and Elkin 2003)

Louis Borget, CEO of Enron Oil, explained that the Apple account was used to move profits from one quarter to another for Enron management. From 1985, the oil trader had been doing deals with companies Isla, Southwest, Petropol and other entities that allowed Enron Oil to generate the loss on one contract then have the loss cancelled out by a second contract to generate a gain of the same amount. Borget described Enron Oil as "the swing entry to meet objectives each month." Woyek wrote in a memo the process was a creation of "fictitious losses." (McLean and Elkin 2003). The management of Enron Oil were not even reprimanded. Instead, Borget received a thank you note saying, "keep making millions for us."

The internal auditors continued their investigation. They consulted directories of trading organizations, but could not find Isla, Southwest, or Petropol. They discovered other irregularities in the Apple account amounting to hundreds of thousands of dollars. Before they completed their fieldwork, management told them to stop and let the work be done by Enron's outside auditor, Arthur Andersen.

Andersen presented their findings to the Enron audit committee of the board of directors some months later. They told the board that they "were unable to verify ownership or any other details" regarding Enron Oil's supposed trading partners. They also found that Enron Oil was supposed to have strict controls on trading – their open position was never supposed to exceed 8 million barrels, and when the losses reached $4 million, the traders were required to liquidate their position. Andersen could not test the controls because Borget and Masteroeni destroyed daily position reports.

But even so, Andersen would not give an opinion on these unusual transactions or whether the profit shifting had a material impact on the financial statements. Andersen claimed that it was beyond their professional competence and that they would rely on Enron itself to make that determination. Andersen got a letter from Rich Kidder, Enron CEO, and another Enron lawyer saying, "the unusual transactions would not have a material effect on the financial statements. and that no disclosure of these transactions is necessary."

In October 1997, it was discovered that the management at Enron Oil had been losing on their trades and they were $1.5 billion short. Enron fired Borget and Masteroeni and brought in traders who were able to reduce the position to a $85 million charge which Enron announced for the third quarter of 1987. (Bryce 2002)

Discussion Questions	■ Was Andersen fulfilling its responsibility to consider fraud and risk? ■ Whose responsibility is it to determine the materiality of fraud on the financial statements: Enron management or Andersen?
References	Bryce, Robert, 2002, *Pipe Dreams: greed, ego and the death of Enron*, Public Affairs, New York. McLean, Bethany and Peter Elkind, 2003, *The Smartest Guys in The Room: the amazing rise and scandalous fall of Enron*, Portfolio, New York.

Fraud in Planning, Evaluating and Reporting

ISA 210A states that when planning and performing audit procedures and in evaluating and reporting the results, auditors should consider the risk of misstatements in financial statements resulting in fraud. In planning the audit, the auditor must assess the risk that material fraud or error has occurred. The auditor plans and performs an audit with an attitude of professional skepticism, recognizing that conditions or events may be found that indicate that fraud or error may exist in accordance with ISA 200, "Objective and General Principles Governing an Audit of Financial Statements" (paragraph 6).

In performing substantive tests, the audit procedures may indicate the possible existence of fraud or error. If the auditor believes the indicated fraud or error could have a material effect on the financial statements he should perform appropriate modified or additional procedures. When suspicion of fraud or error is not dispelled by the results of these procedures, the auditor must discuss the matter with management. The auditor should consider the possible impact on the auditor's report and the implications of fraud and significant error in relation to other aspects of the audit. In some countries (such as France and the Netherlands) laws exist that require the auditor to inform government authorities of material fraud under specific circumstances. ISA 240 suggests that the auditor should communicate his fraud findings to management on a timely basis if:

■ it is believed fraud may exist even if the potential effect on the financial information may be immaterial; or
■ fraud or significant error has been found.

US Fraud Standard

The AICPA in 2002 released Statement on Auditing Standards No. 99 (SAS 99).[21] The standard requires that as part of the planning process the audit team must consider how and where the entity's financial statements might be susceptible to fraud. It requires that auditors gather information necessary to identify risks of material misstatement due to fraud, by:

■ inquiring of management and others within the entity about the risks of fraud; and
■ considering fraud risk factors.

Auditors use the information found about risk to determine if proper controls are in place and the nature, timing and extent of certain fraud-focussed procedures.

Certification Exam Question 2.4[22]

Which of the following statements best describes an auditor's responsibility to detect errors and fraud?

(A) An auditor should design an audit to provide reasonable assurance of detecting errors and fraud that are material to the financial statements.

(B) An auditor is responsible to detect material errors, but has no responsibility to detect fraud that is concealed through employee collusion or management override of internal control.

(C) An auditor has no responsibility to detect errors and fraud unless analytical procedures or tests of transactions identify conditions causing a reasonably prudent auditor to suspect that the financial statements were materially misstated.

(D) An auditor has no responsibility to detect errors and fraud because an auditor is not an insurer and an audit does not constitute a guarantee.

▓ Opinion on The Occurrence of Illegal Acts

Closely related to the subject of fraud is the auditor's reaction to the occurrence of **illegal acts** in a company. Both ISA 250[23] and most national regulators state that the auditor's responsibility in this area is restricted to designing and executing the audit in such a way that there is a reasonable expectation of detecting material illegal acts which have a direct impact on the form and content of the financial statements. In reporting illegal acts most national regulators require the auditor to assess the potential impact on the financial statements and determine the consequences of the uncertainty or error in the financial statements for the nature of the opinion.

Apart from reporting the acts through the report, the professional regulations in some countries require the auditor to inform members of the audit committee or board of directors. Informing third parties is not allowed, except for some very special, narrowly defined circumstances.

Most expectation gap studies reveal that respondents expect the auditor to detect and report illegal acts that have a significant impact on the financial statements. With regard to the auditor's responsibility for detecting and reporting other types of illegal acts, the answers found in expectation gap studies were inconclusive.

2.9 Examples of Landmark Studies and Legislation that Influenced the International Audit Market

Partly as a response to some of the expectation gap issues, there have been two landmark studies (the COSO Report and the Cadbury Report which lead to the Combined Code and the Turnbull Report) and most recently responses have been legislated into the US accounting profession by the Sarbanes-Oxley Act of 2002.

ILLUSTRATION 2.2

Objectives of the COSO Report

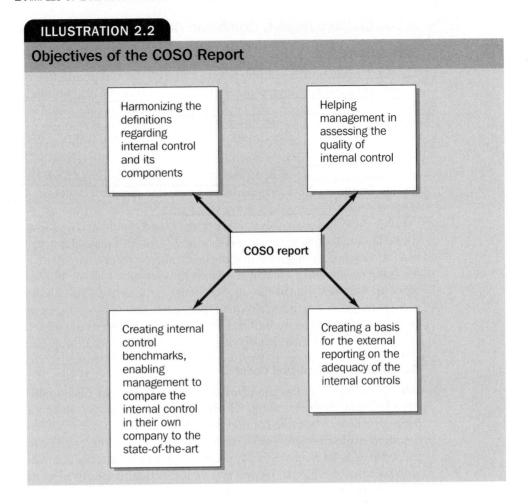

■ The COSO Report

The COSO report was published by the Committee of Sponsoring Organizations of the Treadway Commission. The COSO report envisaged (see Illustration 2.2):

- ■ harmonizing the definitions regarding internal control and its components;
- ■ helping management in assessing the quality of internal control;
- ■ creating internal control benchmarks, enabling management to compare the internal control in their own company to the state-of-the-art; and
- ■ creating a basis for the external reporting on the adequacy of the internal controls.

Although all of these objectives might have an influence on the audit service, the latter subject is particularly relevant, because it might lead to certification by the auditor of management's assertions regarding the quality of a company's internal control system. The COSO report is discussed extensively in Chapter 7 on internal control components.

■ The Cadbury Report, Combined Code, and Turnbull Report

Cadbury Report

The Cadbury Report[24] was published in the UK by the Committee on the Financial Aspects of Corporate Governance. Cadbury deals with the responsibilities and duties of the executive and non-executive members of the board of directors. The report suggests that companies listed on the London Stock Exchange should adhere to a Code of Best Practice, in which these responsibilities and duties are listed. In June 1998 the London Stock Exchange published a new Listing Rule together with related Principles of Good Governance and Code of Best Practice (called "the Combined Code"). The Combined Code[25] combines the recommendations of the so-called Cadbury, Greenbury, and Hampel committees on corporate governance.

In the published financial statements, the board should declare the adherence to this code and should explicitly assume responsibility for the financial statements. In addition, the Cadbury Report suggested that the board should report that it tested the adequacy of the company's internal control as well as the company's ability to continue as a going concern. Amongst the changes in Combined Code versus the Cadbury Best Practices, perhaps the greatest is the extension of the requirement to report on the review of internal controls beyond financial controls. The Cadbury Report originally suggested reporting on all controls, but had subsequently modified its stance to include only financial controls.

Turnbull Report/Combined Code

Internal Control: Guidance for Directors on the Combined Code, called the "Turnbull Report"[26] after Nigel Turnbull, Chairman of the Committee which wrote the Report, provides guidance to assist London Stock Exchange listed companies to implement the requirements in the Combined Code relating to internal control. The Report states that the board of directors should set appropriate policies on internal control and seek regular assurance that the internal control system is functioning effectively in managing risks in the manner that the board has approved.

■ The Sarbanes-Oxley Act of 2002

The accounting scandals begun by the Enron collapse and extending to such giant companies as WorldCom, Xerox, and Tyco, caused a backlash in the USA, resulting in legislation being signed into law by the US President in July 2002. The Sarbanes-Oxley Act[27] is the first accounting law passed by the US since the Securities and Exchange Act of 1934.

New Requirements for Audit Firms and Audit Committees

The Act has new requirements for audit firms and audit committees. Auditors must report to the audit committee,[28] not management. The lead audit partner and audit review partner must be rotated every five years. A second partner must review and approve audit reports. It is a felony with penalties of up to ten years in jail to willfully fail to maintain "all audit or review work papers" for at least five years. Destruction of documents carries penalties of up to 20 years in jail. The Act lists eight types of services that are "unlawful" if provided to a publicly held company by its auditor: bookkeeping, information systems design and implementation, appraisals or valuation services, actuarial services, internal audits, management and human resources services, broker/dealer and investment banking, and legal or expert services related to audit service. The Public Company Accounting Oversight Board (PCAOB), created by the Act, may also determine by regulation other services it wishes to prohibit. Non-audit services not banned by the Act must be pre-approved by the audit committee. Management must assess and make representations about the effectiveness of the internal control structure and their auditor will be required to attest to the assessment and describe the tests used.

2.10 Summary

The Industrial Revolution, which started in Great Britain around 1780, resulted in demand for the services of specialists in bookkeeping and in auditing internal and external financial representations. The institutionalization of the audit profession followed shortly thereafter.

The demand for audit services may be explained by several different theories. Some theories like the Theory of Inspired Confidence and Agency Theory have been well researched and reported on. Other theories based on public perceptions such as the Policeman Theory and the Lending Credibility Theory serve more as a point of reference than a researched construct.

Although regulation and legislation differ, both the demand and the supply of audit services are currently regulated to some degree in most countries. Recent accounting and finance research suggests that national legal environments are among the key determinants of financial market development, corporate ownership structures, corporate policies, and the properties of accounting information around the world. There is a recent growth in accounting oversight boards – government or professional committees to review the work of auditors and take an active part in setting and enforcing standards. Three such boards are in the US (the Public Company Accounting Oversight Board), Australia (Financial Reporting Council) and the UK (The Review Board Limited).

Audit firms are classified into two distinct categories: Big Four firms and non-Big Four firms. Big Four firms participate in an international head office, in which global technologies, procedures and directives are developed. The non-Big Four firms include a range of firms from small local firms, with only a handful of professionals, to second tier firms that also have an international network.

The auditor is evaluated by the market place based on technical and functional quality elements. Technical audit quality is defined as the degree to which an audit meets a consumer's expectations with regard to the detection and reporting of errors and irregularities regarding the audited company. Functional audit quality is defined as the degree to which the process of carrying out the audit and communicating its results meets a consumer's expectations. The functional aspect of audit quality represents not the outcome, but the process itself.

There are many stakeholders who rely on audited financial statements: the client (with which there is a privity relationship), actual and potential stockholders, vendors, bankers and other creditors, employees, customers and the government. Legal liability of the auditor to each stakeholder varies from country to country, district to district. This liability can generally be classified as based on one or more of the following: common law, civil liability under statutory law, criminal liability under statutory law, and liability for members of professional accounting organizations.

The users of audit services can broadly be classified as auditees (the board of directors of the company) and third parties (shareholders, bankers, creditors, employees, customers and other groups). Each of these groups has its own set of expectations with regard to an auditor's duties. Expectations were found with regard to the following duties of auditors:

- the fairness of financial statements,
- the company's ability to continue as a going concern,
- the company's internal control system,
- the occurrence of fraud,
- the occurrence of illegal acts.

In response to the controversies there have been in two landmark studies (the COSO Report and the Cadbury Report which lead to the Combined Code and the Turnbull Report) and most recently have been legislated into the US accounting profession by the Sarbanes-Oxley Act of 2002.

2.11 Answers to Certification Exam Questions

2.1 (C) The requirement is to identify the organization established in 2002 by the US congress. Answer (C) is correct because the organization set up by the Sarbanes-Oxley Act of 2002 was the Public Company Accounting Oversight Board. The Public Interest Oversight Board (A) was set up by IFAC and several international organizations. The Review Board (B) is the oversight board in the UK. The Financial Reporting Council (D) is an Australian entity.

2.2 (A) The requirement is to determine the dependency of quality control standards on two audit firm criteria – size and nature of business – and cost of the control versus its benefit. Answer (A) is correct, because the nature and extent of quality controls depend on all these factors.

2.3 (C) The requirement is to determine the wording in the explanatory paragraph if there is substantial doubt about the entity's ability to continue as a going concern. Answer (C) is correct because if the auditor concludes that there is substantial doubt, the auditor should include an explanatory paragraph following the opinion paragraph and should include the phrase, "substantial doubt about its ability to continue as a going concern." The time period is not mentioned in the audit report.

2.4 (A) The requirement is about the auditor's responsibility to detect errors and fraud. Answer (A) is correct because the auditor should design the audit to provide reasonable assurance of detecting errors and fraud. Choice (B) is incorrect. The auditor is not "responsible for" detecting all material errors, but is responsible for designing an audit to provide reasonable assurance of detecting material misstatements. Due to the fact that fraudulent activity is frequently concealed, even a properly planned and performed audit may not detect a material misstatement resulting from fraud. Choice (C) is incorrect. The auditor should specifically assess the risk of material misstatement of the financial statements due to fraud and consider that assessment in designing the audit, regardless of whether analytical procedures or tests of transactions identify specific conditions. Choice (D) is incorrect. The auditor does have some responsibility for detecting errors and fraud.

2.12 Notes

1 Porter, B.A., 1990, *The Audit Expectations Gap and the Role of External Auditors in Society*, Ph.D. Thesis, Massey University, p. 50.

2 Limperg, Th., 1932, *Theory of Inspired Confidence*, University of Amsterdam, Amsterdam, 1932/1933.

3 See Watts, R.L., Zimmerman J.L., 1978, "Towards a positive theory of the determination of Accounting standards," *The Accounting Review*, (January): 112–134; and Watts, R.L., Zimmerman J.L., 1979, "The demand for and supply of accounting theories: The market for excuses," *The Accounting Review*, (April): 273–305.

4 The supply side of the audit market is concerned with the determination of the level of audit labor and independence.

5 See Ball, R., S. Kothari, A. Robin, 2000, "The effect of international institutional factors on Properties of accounting earnings," *Journal of Accounting and Economics*, 29 (February): 1–52; and Shleifer, A., and R. Vishny, 1997, A survey of corporate governance, *Journal of Finance*, 52 (July): 737–783.

6 As of June 2004 there were only two permanent audit standards in the US: PCAOB Audit Standard #1, *References in Auditor's Reports to the Standards of the Public Company Accounting Oversight Board*, Release 2003-025 and PCAOB Audit Standard #2, *An Audit of Internal Control over Financial Reporting Performed in Conjunction with an Audit of Financial Statements*, Release 2004-0308-1a.

7 Dassen, R.J.M., *Audit Quality: An empirical study of the Attributes and Determinants of Audit Quality Perceptions*, University of Maastricht, 1995.

8 Ibid.

9 255 NY 170, 174 NE 441 (1930); see also Knapp, Michael C., *Contemporary Auditing Issues and Cases*, 2002.

10 *Caparo Industries PLC v Dickman and Others*, 1990, 1 All ER 568. See Cooper, B.J. and M.L. Barkoczy, 1994, "Third party liability: The auditor's lament", *Managerial Auditing Journal*, Bradford, Vol. 9. Iss. 5. p. 31.

11 Rule 3(e) of the SEC's *Rules of Practice* states: The commission can deny, temporarily or permanently, the privilege of appearing or practicing before it in any way to any person who is found by the commission ... (1) not to possess the requisite qualifications to represent others, or (2) to be lacking in character of integrity or to have engaged in unethical or improper professional conduct."

12 IFAC, 2004, *Handbook of International Auditing, Assurance, and Ethics Pronouncements*, ISA 700, "The Auditor's Report On Financial Statements", para. 19, International Federation of Accountants, New York.

13 IFAC, 2004, *Handbook of International Auditing, Assurance, and Ethics Pronouncements*, International Standards on Auditing 570 (ISA 570), "Going Concern", International Federation of Accountants, New York.

14 Adapted and reprinted with permission from AICPA. Copyright © 2000 & 1985 by American Institute of Certified Public Accountants.

15 IFAC, 2004, *Handbook of International Auditing, Assurance, and Ethics Pronouncements*, International Standards on Auditing 400 (ISA 400), "Risk Assessments and Internal Control", International Federation of Accountants, New York.

16 Sarbanes-Oxley Act of 2002, addresses internal control reporting in Section 404, "Management Assessment of Internal Controls."

17 AICPA, Reporting on an Entities Internal Control Over Financial Reporting," March 2003, American Institute of Certified Public Accountants.

18 The Committee on Corporate Governance, 1998, *The Combined Code*, London Stock Exchange, London, January.

19 Humphrey, C., Turley, S., Moizer, P., *Protecting Against Detection: The Case of Auditors and Fraud*, unpublished paper, University of Manchester, 1991.

20 IFAC, 2004, *Handbook of International Auditing, Assurance, and Ethics Pronouncements*, International Standards on Auditing 240 (ISA 240), "The Auditor's Responsibility to Consider

Fraud and Error in an Audit of Financial Statements", International Federation of Accountants, New York.

21 AICPA, Consideration of Fraud in a Financial Statement Audit, Statement on Auditing Standards No. 99, American Institute of Certified Public Accountants, November 2002.

22 Adapted and reprinted with permission from AICPA. Copyright © 2000 & 1985 by American Institute of Certified Public Accountants.

23 13 IFAC, 2004, *Handbook of International Auditing, Assurance and Ethics Pronouncements*, International Standards on Auditing 250 (ISA 250), "Consideration of Laws and Regulations in an Audit of Financial Statements", International Federation of Accountants, New York.

24 Committee on the Financial Aspects of Corporate Governance, *Report of the Committee on the Financial Aspects of Corporate Governance* (The Cadbury Report), Gee and Co. Ltd, London, December 1992.

25 KPMG Review, 1999, *The Combined Code: A Practical Guide*, KPMG. UK, January.

26 Internal Control Working Party, 1999, *Internal Control: Guidance for Directors on the Combined Code*, published by the Institute of Chartered Accountants in England & Wales, London, September.

27 107th US Congress, 2002, *Sarbanes-Oxley Act of 2002*, Public Law 107–204, Senate and House of Representatives of the United States of America in Congress Assembled, Washington, DC, July 30.

28 An audit committee is made up of selected members of the company's outside directors who take an active role in overseeing the company's accounting and auditing policies and practices.

2.13 Questions, Exercises and Cases

QUESTIONS

2.3 Theories on the Demand and Supply of Audit Services

2.1 What are the most important theories on the demand of audit services?

2.2 Give a brief description of the agency theory as applied to both the demand and the supply of audit services.

2.4 Audit Regulation

2.3 Name the three public oversight boards discussed in the chapter. Discuss their similarities and dissimilarities.

2.5 Audit Firms

2.4 What is the theoretical basis for the assumption that Big Four firms provide higher technical audit quality than non-Big Four firms?

2.5 What is meant by second tier firms?

2.6 Audit Quality and Audit Fee Determination

2.6 Identify and define the two components of audit quality.

2.7 Briefly discuss the determinants of the audit fee level.

2.7 Legal Liability

2.8 What are four major sources of auditors legal liability? Briefly discuss them.

2.9 Discuss the conditions that have to be met in order to hold an auditor successfully liable.

2.8 Some Developments in the Audit Market

2.10 Describe the historical shift in the audit profession's attitude towards the auditor's responsibilities regarding fraud.

2.11 Discuss the following statement: "Auditors perform extensive tests on a company's internal control system, in order to determine whether they can rely on that system in the course of their audit. Therefore, auditors can express an opinion on the adequacy of the audited company's internal control system."

2.9 Examples of Landmark Studies and Legislation that Influenced the International Audit Market

2.12 Discuss the potential impact of the Cadbury and COSO report on the audit profession.

2.13 Discuss the following statement: "Auditors should not be allowed to combine an audit for one client with advisory services to that client."

PROBLEMS AND EXERCISES

2.2 Theories on the Demand and Supply of Audit Services

2.14 **Agency Theory.** Identify principals and agents in the cases mentioned below. Describe the contributions and "prices" associated with these relationships, identify potential risks for the principal and give suggestions for limiting these risks.

A.   The Pasadena Bank lends money to the Alhambra Construction Company.

B.   Employee Mario Auditorio considers leaving his current job and starting a new career with Instituto Milanese.

71

C.   Manager Yu-Chang receives an annual bonus, based on last year's profit of company Shang-Zu.
D.   Supplier "Vite et Juste" delivers goods to company "Merci." Payment is due 60 days after the date of the invoice.

2.3 Audit Regulation

2.15 Audit Regulation. Comment on the following statements:
A.   In most countries audits are legally required for every type of company.
B.   The PCAOB sanctions firms but not individuals for violations of laws, regulations, and rules.
C.   The PCAOB inspects all US audit firms.
D.   The FRC has broad oversight for setting accounting standards in the public and private sectors.
E.   The Review Board is responsible for training the members of UK accounting professional bodies.

2.4 Audit Firms

2.16 How do the markets for the Big Four differ from second tier firms? Describe a typical audit client for each group including average revenue, global nature, number of employees, government regulation, and governance mechanism.

2.5 Audit Quality and Audit Fee Determination

2.17 Audit Quality and Audit Fee Determination. Company Hochbau, a construction company, has decided to change auditors, as a result of continuous communication problems with the existing auditors. As the chief financial officer, you have made a schedule for the audit tender.

Required:
Give a brief outline of how you would organize the tender. Make a list of 15 criteria on which you would rate the tendering audit firms.

2.6 Legal Liability

2.18 Legal Liability to Third Parties. Suppose you are a judge in the following civil case.
Plaintiff Sue Bank, a banker, accuses auditor Big Zero of having performed a negligent audit in the financial statements of company "Trouble." Five months after the financial statements (with an unqualified opinion) were published, "Trouble" filed for bankruptcy, leaving the bank with unrecovered loans amounting to $20 million.

Required:
Describe the relevant issues to be addressed in this case.

2.7 Some Developments in the Audit Market

2.19 Auditor's Opinion on the Occurrence of Fraud. Sundback, CGR, is the auditor for Upseerin Manufacturing, a privately owned company in Espoo, Finland, which has a June 30 fiscal year. Upseerin arranged for a substantial bank loan which was dependent upon the bank receiving, by September 30, audited financial statements which showed a current ratio of at least 2 to 1. On September 25, just before the audit report was to be issued, Sundback received an anonymous letter on Upseerin's stationery indicating that a five-year lease by Upseerin, as lessee, of a factory building which was accounted for in the financial statements as an operating lease was in fact a capital lease. The letter stated that there was a secret written agreement with the lessor modifying the lease and creating a capital lease.

Sundback confronted the president of Upseerin who admitted that a secret agreement existed but said it was necessary to treat the lease as an operating lease to meet the current ratio requirement of the pending loan and that nobody would ever discover the secret agreement with the lessor. The president said that if Sundback did not issue its report by September 30, Upseerin would sue Sundback for substantial damages which would result from not getting the loan. Under this pressure and because the work papers contained a copy of the five-year lease agreement which supported the operating lease treatment, Sundback issued its report with an unqualified opinion on September 29.

In spite of the fact the loan was received, Upseerin went bankrupt within two years. The bank is suing Sundback to recover its losses on the loan and the lessor is suing Sundback to recover uncollected rents.

Required:

Answer the following, setting forth reasons for any conclusions stated.
A. Is Sundback liable to the bank?
B. Is Sundback liable to the lessor?

2.20 Opinion on the Occurrence of Illegal Acts. Ostling, Auktoriserad Revisor, accepted an engagement to audit the financial statements of Sandnes Company of Göteborg, Sweden. Ostling's discussions with Sandnes's new management and the predecessor auditor indicated the possibility that Sandnes's financial statements may be misstated due to the possible occurrence of errors, irregularities, and illegal acts.

Required:

A. Identify and describe Ostling's responsibilities to detect Sandnes's errors and irregularities. Do not identify specific audit procedures.
B. Identify and describe Ostling's responsibilities to report Sandnes's errors and irregularities.
C. Describe Ostling's responsibilities to detect Sandnes's material illegal acts. Do not identify specific audit procedures.

[Adapted and reprinted with permission from AICPA. Copyright © 2000 & 1985 by American Institute of Certified Accountants]

2.8 Examples of Landmark Studies and Legislation that Influenced the International Audit Market

2.21 Compare the Combined Code and the Sarbanes-Oxley Act on what each says about the following:
A. Corporate governance
B. Audit firms
C. Internal controls.

CASES

2.22 Legal Responsibilities of Auditors. Pick five countries. Assume that you are the head of an international commission to determine legal responsibilities of accountants in various countries. Use your university library and the internet to research accounting in these five countries.

Required:

A. List the country, concept of independence and functions generally not allowed.
B. List the ethical standards, enforcement, legal liabilities and responsibility for the detection of fraud.
C. Using the library, Lexis-Nexis, or internet, find one recent legal case in each country that impacts auditor independence or resulted from fraud. Summarize each case.
D. Write a brief comparing the recent legal case and auditor ethical standards in each country.

Chapter 3

ETHICS FOR PROFESSIONAL ACCOUNTANTS

3.1 Learning Objectives

After studying this chapter, you should be able to:

1 Explain what ethics means to an accountant.

2 State the purpose for a professional code of ethics.

3 Explain purpose and content of the IFAC *Code of Ethics for Professional Accountants*.

4 Identify and discuss the fundamental principles of ethics as described by the IFAC Guideline.

5 Explain the concept of independence and identify the principles-based approach for resolving the attendant issues.

6 Describe non-audit services prohibited by the Code of Ethics.

7 Discuss the responsibilities of an accountant in public practice, other than independence, that apply to his clients and colleagues.

8 State the topics of guidance that are particularly relevant to professional accountants working in industry, commerce, the public sector or education.

9 Summarize the possible disciplinary actions for violation of the Code of Ethics.

3.2 What Are Ethics?

Ethics represent a set of moral principles, rules of conduct, or values. Ethics apply when an individual has to make a decision from various alternatives regarding moral principles. All individuals and societies possess a sense of ethics in that they have some sort of agreement as to what right and wrong are.

Illustration 3.1 incorporates the characteristics most people associate with ethical behavior.[1]

ILLUSTRATION 3.1

Ethical Principles

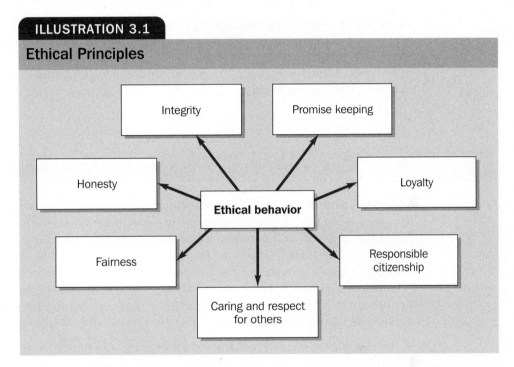

Ethical behavior is necessary for society to function in an orderly manner. The need for ethics in society is sufficiently important that many commonly held ethical values are incorporated into laws. However, a considerable portion of the ethical values of a society such as integrity, loyalty, and pursuit of excellence cannot be incorporated into law. By establishing a code of ethics, a profession assumes self-discipline beyond the requirements of the law.

■ Ethics in the Accounting Profession

The attitude and behavior of professional accountants in providing auditing and assurance services have an impact on the economic well-being of their community and country. Accountants can remain in this advantageous position only by continuing to provide the public with these unique services at a level that demonstrates that the public confidence is well founded.

The distinguishing mark of the profession is acceptance of its responsibility to the public. Therefore the standards of the accountancy profession are heavily determined by the public interest. One could say in accountancy "the public and the auditee are our clients and our main product is credibility."

■ Objectives of Accountancy

It is in this context that the International Federation of Accountants (IFAC) *Code of Ethics for Professional Accountants*[2] states:

> Objectives of the accountancy profession are to work to the highest standards of professionalism, to attain the highest levels of performance and generally to meet the public interest.[3]

To achieve these objectives, the Code of Ethics suggests several fundamental principles for professional accountants and for those who are undertaking reporting assignments, which is discussed in the balance of this chapter. Due to the importance of the Code, it will be quoted extensively in this chapter. When a direct quote is taken from the Code, that quote will be given in **bold**.

3.3 The IFAC Code of Ethics for Professional Accountants

The ethical guidance set out by the International Federation of Accountants (IFAC) is developed by the IFAC Ethics Committee who report their recommendations to the IFAC Board after a research and appropriate exposure of draft guidance. The guidance is incorporated into the *Code of Ethics for Professional Accountants* (the Code). The Code is intended to serve as a model on which to base national ethical guidance. It sets standards of conduct for professional accountants and states the fundamental principles that should be observed by professional accountants in order to achieve common objectives.

The Code is divided into three parts: Illustration 3.2 gives the overall contents by section.

- Part A applies to all professional accountants unless otherwise specified.
- Part B applies only to those professional accountants in public practice.
- Part C applies to **employed professional accountants**, and may also apply, in appropriate circumstances, to accountants employed in public practice.

3.4 Ethics Guidelines Applicable to All Accountants (Part A)

The process of establishing ethical principles is complicated. In France and Japan, the ethical code is a matter of law. In the USA, Singapore, Mexico, and the UK, the standards are developed and regulated by professional bodies. The IFAC *Code of Ethics for Professional Accountants* offers fundamental principles that are of a general nature and not intended to be used to solve a professional accountant's ethical problems in a specific case. However, it provides detailed guidance as to the application in practice of the objectives and the fundamental principles with regard to a number of typical situations occurring in the accounting profession.

ILLUSTRATION 3.2

Three-Part Framework of IFAC Ethics Code

PART A – Applicable To All Professional Accountants	PART B – Applicable To Professional Accountants In The Public Practice	PART C – Applicable To Employed Professional Accountants
Integrity and Objectivity	Independence for Assurance Engagements	Conflict of Loyalties
Resolution of Ethical Conflicts	Professional Competence and Responsibilities Regarding the Use of Non-Accountants	Support for Professional Colleagues
Professional Competence	Fees and Commissions	Professional Competence
Confidentiality	Activities Incompatible with the Practice of Public Accountancy	Presentation of Information
Tax Practice	Clients' Monies	
Cross-Border Activities	Relations with Other Professional Accountants in Public Practice	
Publicity	Advertising and Solicitation	

There are six fundamental principles of ethics applicable to ALL accountants. They are

- integrity,
- objectivity,
- professional competence and due care,
- confidentiality,
- professional behavior,
- technical standards.

The Proposed Revised Code includes a paragraph regarding the professional accountant's obligation to evaluate any threat to complying with the fundamental principles when the accountant "knows or could reasonably be expected to know of the circumstances that might compromise compliance."

The IFAC guideline offers further discussion on these principles. Each concept is the topic of subsequent Sections (1–7) in the Code.

■ Integrity and Objectivity (Sec. 1)

A professional accountant should be straightforward and honest in performing professional services. A professional service is any service requiring accountancy or related skills performed by a professional accountant including accounting, auditing, taxation, management consulting and financial management services.

No Conflicts of Interest

The principle of objectivity imposes the obligation on all professional accountants to be fair, intellectually honest, and free of conflicts of interest. Professional accountants will be exposed to many situations where they are under pressure from employers, colleagues or clients. Situations and relationships should be avoided in which bias or influences of others might override auditor objectivity. Professionals involved in assurance services should neither accept nor offer gifts or entertainment that might appear to have a significant improper influence on their professional judgment.

■ Resolution of Ethical Conflicts (Sec. 2)

From time to time accountants encounter situations when the responsibilities of the accountant may conflict with internal or external demands. There may be pressure from an overbearing supervisor, manager, director or partner, or family member. For example, the accountant may be asked to act contrary to technical or professional standards, there may be divided loyalty between the accountant's superior and accepted professional standards, or misleading information may be published.

Steps to Resolving a Conflict

The IFAC *Code of Ethics for Professional Accountants*[4] includes the following process in case the policies of the accountant's employing organization do not resolve the ethical conflict:

1 **Review the conflict problem with the immediate superior.** If there is no resolution, he should go to the next higher managerial level. If that higher level of management is involved in the conflict problem, the accountant should raise the issue with the next higher level of management, etc.
2 **Seek counseling and advice on a confidential basis with an independent adviser or the applicable accountancy body to obtain an understanding of possible courses of action.**
3 If the ethical conflict still exists after fully exhausting all levels of internal review, **the accountant, as a last resort, may have to resign from the employing organization and submit an information memorandum to an appropriate representative of that organization.**

Certification Exam Question 3.1

The auditor with final responsibility for an engagement and one of the assistants has a difference of opinion about the client's application of an accounting method. If the assistant believes it is necessary to be disassociated with the matter's resolution, the audit firm's procedures should enable the assistant to

(A) Refer the disagreement to IFAC's Quality Review Committee.
(B) Review the conflict with a senior partner in the audit firm.
(C) Discuss the disagreement with the entity's management or its audit committee.
(D) Report the disagreement to an impartial peer review monitoring team.

■ Professional Competence and Due Care (Sec. 3)

A professional accountant, in agreeing to provide professional services, implies that he is competent to perform the services.

Professional competence requires a high standard of general education followed by specific education, training, examination in relevant subjects, and work experience. Competence also requires continuing awareness by the professional accountants of developments in the accountancy profession and adoption of a quality control program.

Accountants should refrain from agreeing to perform professional services which they are not competent to carry out unless competent advice and assistance are obtained. The accountant should perform all services with due care, competence and diligence and has a continuing duty to maintain professional knowledge and skill. That knowledge and skill should be sufficient to ensure that work performed is based on up-to-date developments in practice, legislation and techniques.

■ Confidentiality (Sec. 4)

Professional accountants have an obligation to respect the confidentiality of information about a client's (or employer's) affairs acquired in the course of professional services.

Accountants should respect the confidentiality of information acquired during the course of performing professional services. They should not use or disclose any such information without proper and specific authority. There exists a responsibility to keep the information discovered in the course of an assurance service confidential and thus continues even after the accountant–client or the accountant–employer relationship ends.

Accountants must also ensure that in addition to themselves, staff and outside advisers under their control understand and follow the principle of confidentiality. Information acquired during the engagement should not be used by those involved in the service for personal advantage or for the advantage of a third party.

Permitted Disclosure of Confidential Information

Confidential information may be disclosed when disclosure is authorized by the client, required by law, or where there is a professional duty or right to disclose (such as in a peer review quality control program). When disclosure is authorized by the employer or client, the accountants should consider the interests of all the parties, including third parties, who might be affected.

Concept and a Company 3.1

Confidentiality – Deloitte, Reliance, and KKR

Concept	Professional accountants have an obligation to respect the confidentiality of information about a client's (or employer's) affairs acquired in the course of professional services.
Story	According to a court filing by the US State of Pennsylvania Insurance Department, within days of Deloitte signing off on an audit of Reliance Insurance Co. indicating sufficient cash reserves in February 2000, the firm told another client, the Kohlberg Kravis & Roberts (KKR) investment partnership, that Reliance was suffering a "seriously deficient" $350 million shortfall in its reserves. (WSJ 2003)

▶

Confidentiality – Deloitte, Reliance, and KKR (continued)

Deloitte told the investment company about the shortfall "in exchange for millions of dollars" in accounting fees, according to the state. Deloitte "exploited the competing interests of [the investment company] and Reliance and benefited financially by receiving payments from clients on opposite sides" of the proposed deal, according to the state. KKR also got another opinion from Am-Re Consultants, of Princeton, an affiliate of American Reinsurance Co. Am-Re estimated Reliance's reserve shortfall at $500 million, the state reported. (DiStefano 2003)

In 2001 Reliance Insurance Company, an auto and workman's compensation insurer, defaulted on its stock, bonds and loans, and left policyholders and industry bailout funds with more than $2 billion in unpaid losses. The Pennsylvania Insurance Department was charged with liquidating the assets of the company.

Deloitte issued a short written statement accusing the state of "serious distortion of the facts." According to Deloitte, Pennsylvania Insurance Commissioner E. Diane Koken was trying to "improperly" fault Reliance's ex-auditors "for a business and regulatory failure that largely rests with [Koken] herself." (DiStefano 2003)

| Discussion Questions | ■ Does an auditor violate the confidentially of their client by revealing the client's financial condition to another client? |
| | ■ Why would an auditor report sufficient cash reserves in their audit report and then tell another client that the audited company had a shortfall cash position? |

| References | DiStefano, J.N. 2003, "Insurance regulators say the accounting firm called the company healthy shortly before its $2 billion collapse, while revealing a bleak picture to a potential investor," *Philadelphia Inquirer*, October 12. |
| | WSJ, 2003, "Pennsylvania Charges Deloitte Contributed to Insurer's Failure," *Wall Street Journal*, October 20. |

Examples of Disclosure

One example of when disclosure to client information is required by law is when the accountant produces documents or gives evidence in legal proceedings. Another example is disclosure of infringements of the law to appropriate public authorities. In the USA, accountants may be required to give evidence in court and in the Netherlands and UK auditors may be required to disclose fraud to government-appointed authorities.

Confidentiality of information is part of statute or common law and therefore requirements of confidentiality will depend on the law of the home country of each accountant.

■ Professional Behavior

An accountant should act in a manner consistent with the good reputation of the profession and should refrain from any conduct that might bring discredit to the profession regarding responsibilities to clients, third parties, other members of the accountancy profession, staff, employers and the general public.

Specific guidance to the professional accountant regarding professional behavior is provided in three areas: tax practice (Section 5 of the Code), cross-border activities (Section 6), and publicity (Section 7).

■ Tax Practice (Sec. 5)

An accountant performing tax services may put forward the best position in favor of a client or employer, provided the service is done with professional competence, does not in any way impair integrity and objectivity, and is consistent with the law.

An accountant should not represent to a client or an employer that the tax return prepared and the tax advice given is above challenge. He should make sure that the client or employer is aware of the limitations involved in interpretation of tax law and tax reporting. The accountant's client or employer should be advised that they, not the accountant, have the responsibility for the content of the tax return.

Misleading Tax Returns

The accountant should not be associated with any tax return if he has reason to believe that it contains a false or misleading statement or omits important information. When estimates are used in the tax return, they should not be presented in a manner that implies greater accuracy than exists. The tax preparer usually relies on information furnished by the client but should consider whether supporting data needs to be provided. If the accountant discovers a material error or omission in a tax return of a prior year, he should advise his client.

■ Cross-Border Activities (Sec. 6)

An accountant may perform services in a country other than his home country. If differences exist between ethical requirements of the two countries the following provisions should be applied:

1　When the ethical requirements of the country in which the services are being performed are less strict than the IFAC Code of Ethics, then the ethical guidance of IFAC should be applied.
2　When the ethical requirements of the country in which the services are being performed are stricter than the IFAC ethical guidance then the ethical requirements of the country where the services are being performed should be applied.
3　When the ethical requirements of the home country are mandatory for services performed outside that country and are stricter than set out in (1) and (2) above, then the ethical requirements of the home country should be applied.

■ Publicity (Sec. 7)

Publicity is the communication to the public of facts about a professional accountant which are not designated for the deliberate promotion of that professional accountant.

When accountants market themselves and their work, they should:

- Not use means which brings the profession into disrepute;
- Not make exaggerated claims for the services they are able to offer, the qualifications they possess, or the experience they have gained; and
- Not denigrate the work of other accountants.

For more discussion see "Advertising and Solicitation" later in this chapter.

■ Technical Standards

Professional services should always be carried out in accordance with the relevant technical and professional standards. These services should follow the technical standards such as International Standards on Auditing; International Financial Reporting Standards, rules of the accountant's professional body, and relevant legislation.

3.5 Ethics Applicable to Professional Accountants in Public Practice (Part B)

Whereas the ethics guidance discussed above is applicable to all professional accountants. Part B of IFAC's Code of Ethics is only applicable to accountants in public practice. A **professional accountant in public practice** refers to each partner or person occupying a position similar to that of a partner, and each employee in a practice providing professional services to a client irrespective of their functional classification (e.g. audit, tax or consulting), and professional accountants in a practice having managerial responsibility.

Ethical guidance for accountants in public practice is offered in the areas of: **independence**; responsibilities to clients such as fees, commissions, and clients' monies; and responsibilities to colleagues such as relations to other professionals, advertising and activities incompatible with practice.

Concept and a Company 3.2

Lincoln Savings and Loan – Employment of a Former Auditor

Concept	Independence in Fact and Appearance
Story	Upon completion of the 1987 Arthur Young (later Ernst & Young) audit of Lincoln Savings & Loan Association (Lincoln) which resulted in an unqualified opinion, the engagement audit partner, Jack Atchison, resigned from Arthur Young and was hired by Lincoln's parent American Continental Corporation (ACC) for approximately $930,000 annual salary. His prior annual earnings as a partner at Arthur Young was approximately $225,000 (Knapp 2001)
	Charles Keating, Jr. siphoned money out of Lincoln Savings and Loan for his own benefit from the day he acquired Lincoln in 1984 until the Federal Home Loan Bank Board (FHLBB) seized control on April 14, 1989. At the time of the seizure nearly two-thirds of Lincoln's asset portfolio was invested in high-risk land ventures and Keating had used fraudulent accounting methods to create net income. In the end, Lincoln's demise involved investors' losses of $200 million and its closure cost US taxpayers $3.4 billion in guaranteed deposit insurance and legal, making it the most costly savings and loan failure in US history. For their part in the Lincoln failure, Ernst & Young paid the California State Board of Accountancy (the state agency which registers California CPAs) $1.5 million in 1991 to settle negligence complaints and in 1992 paid the US Government $400 million to settle four lawsuits. (Knapp 2001)

In the court case *of Lincoln S&L v Wall*, it was suggested that Atchison might have known about the financial statement problems during his audit of Lincoln. ACC was in dire need of obtaining $10 million because of an agreement with the Bank Board to infuse an additional $10 million into Lincoln. Thus, Lincoln was actually the source of its own $10 million cash infusion. Ernst & Young LLC learned of these facts from Jack Atchison after Atchison had become a top official at Lincoln. (USDC – DC 1990)

At the time Atchison made his move, the practice of "changing sides" was not against the AICPA's ethics standards; however, the Securities and Exchange Commission (SEC) stated that Atchison's should certainly be examined by the accounting profession's standard setting authorities as to the impact such a practice has on an accountant's independence. Furthermore, they stated that it would seem that a "cooling-off period" of one to two years would not be unreasonable before the client can employ a senior official on an audit. (SEC 1990)

Ultimately, the Sarbanes-Oxley Act of 2002 required a cooling-off period of one year after a company's last audit before clients can hire as an officer any member of the audit team.

Discussion Questions	■ What impact does employment of former independent auditors by an audit client have on that auditor's independence during the audit? ■ Were Atchison's actions ethical?

References	Knapp, M., 2001, "Lincoln Savings and Loan Association," *Contemporary Auditing Real Issues & Cases*, South Western College Publishing, Cincinnati, Ohio, pp. 57–70. SEC, 1990, Final rule release 33-7919, *Final Rule: Revision of the Commission's Auditor Independence Requirements*, Securities and Exchange Commission, February, 5. USDC – DC, 1990, *Lincoln Savings & Loan Association v Wall*, "Consolidated Civil Action Nos. 89-1318, 89-1323," 743 F. Supp. 901; 1990 US Dist. LEXIS 11178, United States District Court for the District of Columbia, August 22, 1990; Decided, August 22, 1990, Filed.

3.6 Independence Requirements

The independence of the auditor from the firm that he is auditing is one of the basic requirements to keep public confidence in the reliability of the audit report. Independence adds credibility to the audit report on which investors, creditors, employees, government and other stakeholders depend to make decisions about a company. The benefits of safeguarding an auditors' independence extend so far as to the overall efficiency of the capital markets.

Across the world, national rules on auditors' independence differ in several respects such as: the scope of persons to whom independence rules should apply; the kind of financial, business or other relationships that an auditor may have with an audit client; the type of non-audit services that can and cannot be provided to an audit client; and the safeguards which should be used. The European Commission has issued independence standards to be applied throughout the European Union (EU). The USA enacted the Sarbanes-Oxley Act of 2002, which describes independence requirements of US auditors.

The European Commission Council Directive 84/253/EEC (EU Eighth Company Law Directive), gives discretionary power to Member States to determine the conditions of independence for a statutory auditor. Article 24 says[5] that Member States shall prescribe that auditors shall not carry out **statutory audits**[6] if they are not independent in accordance with the law of the Member State which requires the audit.

To provide each EU country with a common understanding of this independence requirement, the European Union Committee on Auditing developed a set of fundamental principles set out in a Commission Recommendation called *Statutory Auditors' Independence in the EU: A Set of Fundamental Principles.*[7] The principles based approach was considered "preferable to one based on detailed rules because it creates a robust structure within which statutory auditors have to justify their actions."[8]

The EU framework, which parallels the threat and safeguard approach of IFAC, is based on the requirement that an auditor must be independent from his audit client both in mind and appearance. The auditor should not audit a client if there are any financial, business, employment or other relationships between them that a "reasonable and informed third party" would conclude compromised independence.

US based firms and firms that audit US publicly traded firms must adhere to the regulations of the Sarbanes-Oxley Act,[9] Title II, *Auditor Independence*, as interpreted by the Public Company Accounting Oversight Board (PCAOB).[10] The Independence sections and the prohibited services are listed in Illustration 3.3.

ILLUSTRATION 3.3

Independence in the Sarbanes-Oxley Act of 2002

TITLE II – AUDITOR INDEPENDENCE
Sec. 201. Services outside the scope of practice of auditors.
Sec. 202. Pre-approval requirements.
Sec. 203. Audit partner rotation.
Sec. 204. Auditor reports to audit committees.
Sec. 205. Conforming amendments.
Sec. 206. Conflicts of interest.
Sec. 207. Study of mandatory rotation of registered public accounting firms.
Sec. 208. Commission authority.
Sec. 209. Considerations by appropriate State regulatory authorities.

Prohibited non-audit service contemporaneously with the audit include:
(1) bookkeeping or other services related to the accounting records or financial statements of the audit client;
(2) financial information systems design and implementation;
(3) appraisal or valuation services, fairness opinions, or contribution-in-kind reports;
(4) actuarial services;
(5) internal audit outsourcing services;
(6) management functions or human resources;
(7) broker or dealer, investment adviser, or investment banking services;
(8) legal services and expert services unrelated to the audit; and
(9) any other service that the Board determines, by regulation, is impermissible.

Under PCAOB rules all non-audit services to clients, which are not specifically prohibited, must be pre-approved by the Audit Committee and disclosed to the shareholders. Audit partners must be rotated every five years. Clients cannot hire as an officer any member of the audit team within one year after their last audit. Determination of independence of auditors who audit non-publicly traded firms is left up to the regulatory authorities of the 50 states of the USA.

■ Independence as Defined in the Code (Sec. 8)

Independence is described as:

- having a position to take an unbiased viewpoint in the performance of audit tests, analysis of results, and attestation in the audit report;
- independent in fact: accountant's ability to maintain an unbiased attitude throughout the audit, so being objective and impartial;
- independent in appearance: the result of others' interpretations of this independence.

The *Code of Ethics for Professional Accountants*, Section 8 discusses independence in assurance services in terms of a principles-based approach that takes into account threats to independence, accepted safeguards and the public interest.

Principles Based (Conceptual) Approach

IFAC Ethics Committee strongly believes that a high-quality principles based approach to independence will best serve the public interest by eliciting thoughtful auditor assessment of the particular circumstances of each engagement.[11] However, the Code gives related guidance and explanatory material as well. The section on independence discusses the application of the conceptual approach to specific situations such as financial interest, loans, fees and others listed in Illustration 3.4.

The Code states: **It is in the public interest and, therefore, required by this Code of Ethics, that members of assurance teams, firms and, when applicable, network firms be independent of assurance clients.**

Independence in auditing means having a position to take an unbiased viewpoint in the performance of audit tests, analysis of results, and **attestation** in the audit report. Since the main product of attestation is the credibility added to financial information by the audit report, it is essential that the auditor be independent and is perceived as such by the users of audited financial statements.

Independence in Fact and Appearance

Accountants must not only maintain an independent attitude in fulfilling their responsibilities, but the users of financial statements must have confidence in that independence. These two objectives are frequently identified as "independence in fact" and "independence in appearance." Independence in fact exists when the accountant is able to maintain an unbiased attitude throughout the audit, so being objective and impartial, whereas independence in appearance is the result of others' interpretations of this independence.

The IFAC ethics guideline states that independence requires:[12]

(a) **Independence of mind: The state of mind that permits the provision of an opinion without being affected by influences that compromise professional judgment, allowing an individual to act with integrity, and exercise objectivity and professional skepticism.**

(b) **Independence in appearance: The avoidance of facts and circumstances that are so significant that a reasonable and informed third party, having knowledge of all relevant information, including safeguards applied, would reasonably conclude a firm's, or a member of the assurance team's, integrity, objectivity or professional skepticism had been compromised.**

ILLUSTRATION 3.4

Application of Ethics to Specific Situations (Topic and Applicable Paragraph in the Code of Ethics for Professional Accountants)[13]

Topic	Paragraph
Financial Interests	8.102
Provisions Applicable to all Assurance Clients	8.104
Provisions Applicable to Audit Clients	8.111
Provisions Applicable to Non-Audit Assurance Client	8.120
Loans and Guarantees	8.124
Close Business Relationships with Assurance Clients	8.130
Family and Personal Relationships	8.133
Employment with Assurance Clients	8.140
Recent Service with Assurance Clients	8.143
Serving as an Officer or Director on the Board of Assurance Clients	8.146
Long Association of Senior Personnel with Assurance Clients	
General Provisions	8.150
Audit Clients that are Listed Entities	8.151
Provision of Non-Assurance Services to Assurance Clients	8.155
Preparing Accounting Records and Financial Statements	8.163
General Provisions	8.166
Audit Clients that are not Listed Entities	8.167
Audit Clients that are Listed Entities	8.168
Emergency Situations	8.170
Valuation Services	8.171
Provision of Taxation Services to Audit Clients	8.177
Provision of Internal Audit Services to Audit Clients	8.178
Provision of IT Systems Services to Audit Clients	8.184
Temporary Staff Assignments to Audit Clients	8.189
Provision of Litigation Support Services to Audit Clients	8.190
Provision of Legal Services to Audit Clients	8.193
Recruiting Senior Management	8.200
Corporate Finance and Similar Activities	8.201
Fees and Pricing	
Fees – Relative Size	8.203
Fees – Overdue	8.205
Pricing	8.206
Contingent Fees	8.207
Gifts and Hospitality	8.210
Actual or Threatened Litigation	8.211

Identify Threats, Evaluate, and Apply Safeguards

Section 8 of the Code of Ethics, the Independence section, provides a principles based framework for identifying, evaluating and responding to threats to independence. The framework establishes principles to identify threats to independence, determine the significance of those threats, and, if they are significant, identify and apply safeguards to reduce or eliminate the threats.

The independence section of the Code outlines the threats to independence (paragraphs 8.28 through 8.33), safeguards for reducing threats to an acceptable level (paragraphs 8.34

through 8.47), and concludes with some examples of how this conceptual approach is to be applied (paragraphs 8.100 onwards).

■ Threats to Independence

Independence is potentially affected by self-interest, self-review, advocacy, familiarity and intimidation threats. The independence recommendations of the European Commission discuss the same types of threats.[14] (See Illustration 3.5.)

ILLUSTRATION 3.5

Identification of Potential Threats to Auditors Independence

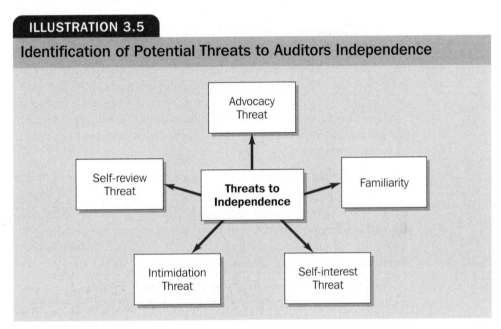

Self-Interest Threats

"Self-Interest Threat" occurs when an auditor could benefit from a financial interest in, or other self-interest conflict with, an assurance client. Examples are as follows.

(a) A **direct** financial interest or material **indirect** financial interest in an assurance client

- **Direct** financial interest in a client might include ownership of client equities or financial instruments; financial interest in a joint venture with a client or employee(s) of a client; and financial interest in a non-client as an investor or investee.
- **Indirect** material financial interest results from being an administrator of any trust or estate with a financial interest in the client company.

Certification Exam Question 3.2

Which of the following statements is correct about independence?

(A) Independence is potentially affected by self-interest, self-review, advocacy, familiarity and intimidation threats.
(B) Independence is not an element that is considered in the audit process.
(C) Independence is immaterial to the financial statements.
(D) Independence is not a requirement of IFAC's Code of Ethics.

Certification Exam Question 3.3

An auditor strives to achieve independence in appearance to

(A) Appear to an independent third party not to have compromised their integrity.
(B) Become independent in fact.
(C) Comply with the international auditing standards of fieldwork.
(D) Evaluation of all matters of continuing accounting significance.

(b) **Ability to influence** client

The IFAC Code of Ethics prohibits individuals with the ability to influence the audit engagement to have ownership interest in the client company. For example a secretary of KPMG could own common shares in a client company if the secretary does not participate in the audit process. However, if the secretary becomes a partner of the engagement while obtaining ownership, all the information regarding his ownership status would have to be disclosed. Otherwise his action could be perceived as a threat to independence in fact and in appearance with respect to that client.

(c) A **loan or guarantee** to or from an assurance client or any of its directors or officers

If members of the assurance team receive a loan from, or a loan guarantee by, an assurance client whose business is making such loans (e.g. a bank) and the loan is made under normal lending procedures, terms and requirements, independence is not jeopardized. Loans that would ordinarily not affect independence include home mortgages, bank overdrafts, car loans and credit card balances.

(d) **Undue dependence** on total fees from an assurance client

The compromise or appearance of compromise of independence may arise if fees from an assurance client are a large proportion of the revenue of an individual partner. Furthermore, if fees due from a client for professional services remain unpaid for an extended period of time, especially if a substantial part is not paid before the issue of the audit report or attestation, a threat to independence may occur.

(e) **Concern** about the possibility of **losing** the engagement

(f) Having a **close business relationship** with an assurance client

(g) **Potential employment** with an assurance client

(h) **Contingent fees** relating to assurance engagements.

Contingent fees are fees calculated on a predetermined basis relating to the outcome or result of a transaction or the result of the work performed. That is, a contingent fee is an arrangement whereby no fee will be charged unless a specified finding or result is obtained or when the fee is otherwise contingent upon the findings or results of services. Fees charged on a percentage or similar basis may also be considered contingent fees. Fees are not contingent fees if fixed by a court or other public authority.

Self-Review Threat

"**Self-Review Threat**" occurs when (1) results of a previous engagement needs to be re-evaluated in reaching conclusions on the present assurance engagement or (2) when a member of the assurance team previously was an employee of the client (especially a director or officer) in a position to exert significant influence over the subject matter of the assurance engagement. For example, assisting an audit client in matters such as preparing accounting records or financial statements may create a self-review threat when the firm subsequently audits the financial statements.

Advocacy Threat

"Advocacy Threat" occurs when a member of the assurance team promotes, or seems to promote, an assurance client's position or opinion. That is, the auditor subordinates his judgment to that of the client. Examples of circumstances that may create this threat include:

- selling, underwriting or otherwise dealing in financial securities or shares of an assurance client;
- acting as the client's advocate in a legal proceeding.

Familiarity Threat

"Familiarity Threat" occurs when an auditor becomes too sympathetic to the client's interests because he has a close relationship with an assurance client, its directors, officers or employees. Examples of circumstances that may create this threat include:

- a member of the assurance team having an immediate family member or close family member who is a director or officer of the assurance client;
- a member of the assurance team having a close family member who is an employee of the assurance client and in a position to significantly influence the subject matter of the assurance engagement;

In some countries, the range of relationship may be wider that a spouse or dependant (e.g. the child, or its spouse, the parent or grandparent, parent-in-law, brother, sister, or brother-in-law or sister-in-law of the client). For example, a CPA firm that prepares a tax return for a client who is an immediate family member, for example, a spouse or a sister, and gives a tax deduction in which adequate evidence for the deduction is not provided, could be in violation of independency law. Violations of independence include;

- a former partner of the firm being a director, officer of the assurance client or an employee in a position of significant influence;
- long association of a senior member of the assurance team with the assurance client; and
- acceptance of gifts or hospitality, unless the value is clearly insignificant, from the assurance client, its directors, officers or employees.

Concept and a Company 3.3

Independence of Audit and Consulting – PeopleSoft and E&Y

Concept	Auditor independence – auditors should be aware of significant threats to independence that may arise and the appropriate safeguards to apply in an attempt to eliminate those threats.
Story	In 2002, the Securities and Exchange Commission (SEC) announced proceedings against Big Four audit firm Ernst & Young (E&Y). The case involved alleged independence ▶

Independence of Audit and Consulting – PeopleSoft and E&Y (continued)

violations due to product sales and consulting fees related to PeopleSoft software, while PeopleSoft was an E&Y audit client. SEC suggested a sanction be imposed against Ernst & Young, which would not allow the firm to provide audit services to publicly traded companies for a period of six months. (SEC 2002a)

The SEC alleged that E&Y and PeopleSoft co-developed and co-marketed a software product called "EY/GEMS for PeopleSoft." These allegations focus on E&Y's use of components of PeopleSoft's proprietary source code in software previously developed and marketed by the accounting firm's tax department. In return for the code, SEC says E&Y agreed to pay royalties ranging from 15 percent to 30 percent from each sale of the resulting product.

Additionally, the SEC finds fault with hundreds of millions of dollars in consulting revenues from implementing PeopleSoft software for clients. The SEC says the revenues were derived from close coordination and co-marketing. As evidence, it cites reciprocal endorsements, links to each other's websites, holding themselves out as "business partners" of one another, and sharing customer information, customer leads, and "target accounts." (SEC 2002b)

In response to SEC's announcement, Ernst & Young released this statement (Schlank 2002):

"Our conduct was entirely appropriate and permissible under the profession's rules. It did not affect our client, its shareholders, or the investing public, nor is the SEC claiming any error in our audits or our client's financial statements as a result of them. Moreover, the issues the SEC has raised are purely technical and relate to judgments we made and actions we took in good faith years ago.

"The SEC's main focus is on the activities of our former consultants in implementing PeopleSoft software for third parties. These occurred between 1994 and 1999 and have no bearing on our current business. In fact, we sold our consulting business to Cap Gemini in May 2000. The SEC's other focus is on a software license agreement between Ernst & Young and PeopleSoft entered into when the parties were making an EY software product compatible with PeopleSoft. This issue is also purely historical. The license agreement terminated years ago and the PeopleSoft-compatible version of the product is no longer sold.

"For the record, we did carefully consider the potential independence implications of our consultants' actions before they undertook them. We correctly concluded at the time that the actions were permissible under the profession's rules and that they were commonplace."

Discussion Questions

- Why would selling and servicing the product of an audit client for significant revenue be considered a threat to independence?
- What safeguards could E&Y have put in place to compensate for this threat?
- Would the relationship between E&Y and PeopleSoft be viewed differently if it happened after the Sarbanes-Oxley Act was passed?

References

Schlank, R., 2002, "SEC Reaches Way Back for EY Independence Case," *Accountingweb.com*, May 21.

SEC, 2002a, *Litigation release 8146*, "SEC Institutes Proceedings Against Ernst & Young To Resolve Auditor Independence Allegations," US Securities and Exchange Commission, November 13.

SEC, 2002b "SEC Institutes Proceedings Against Ernst & Young To Resolve Auditor Independence Allegations Stemming From Joint Business Relationships With Audit Client," *SEC News Digest*, Issue 2002–97, May 20.

Intimidation Threat

"Intimidation Threat" occurs when a member of the assurance team may be deterred from acting objectively and exercising professional skepticism by threats, actual or perceived, from the directors, officers or employees of an assurance client. Two examples of intimidation threats are when an auditor is told he will be replaced based on a disagreement over application of an accounting principle and pressure to reduce the scope of the audit in order to reduce fees.

■ Safeguards

When threats are identified, other than those that are clearly insignificant, appropriate safeguards should be identified and applied to eliminate the threats or reduce them to an acceptable level. The safeguards chosen should be documented. When deciding the nature of the safeguards to be applied consideration should be given to what would be unacceptable to an informed third party having knowledge of all relevant information, including safeguards applied.

Safeguards fall into three broad categories:

1 safeguards created by the profession, legislation or regulation;
2 safeguards within the assurance client; and
3 safeguards within the audit firm's own systems and procedures.

Safeguards Created by the Profession, Legislation or Regulation: Examples

Safeguards created by the profession, legislation or regulation, may include: educational, training and experience requirements to become a certified member of the profession; continuing education requirements; professional accounting, auditing and ethics standards and monitoring and disciplinary processes; peer review of quality control; and professional rules or legislation governing the independence requirements of the firm.

Safeguards Within The Assurance Client: Examples

Safeguards within the assurance client include: ratification by an audit committee of the assurance client's management appointment of the audit firm; the assurance client has competent employees; the assurance client is committed to fair financial reporting; the client has internal procedures that ensure objective choices in commissioning non-assurance engagements; and the client has a corporate governance structure, such as an audit committee, that provides appropriate oversight of an assurance firm's services.

Safeguards Within The Audit Firm: Examples

Safeguards within the audit firm's own systems and procedures may include firm-wide safeguards such as the following (see Illustration 3.6):

- leadership stressing the importance of independence;
- designation of a member of senior management to oversee the adequate functioning of the safeguarding system;
- policies and procedures to assure quality control of assurance engagements;
- written independence policies;
- internal policies to monitor compliance with independence ethics;

ILLUSTRATION 3.6

Examples of Safeguards Within Audit Firms[15]

1 Leadership stressing the importance of independence and the expectation that members of assurance teams will act in the public interest.

2 Designation of a member of **senior management** to **oversee** the adequate functioning of the safeguarding system.

3 Policies and procedures to assure quality control of assurance engagements.

4 Written independence policies on how to identify threats to independence, how to evaluate the significance of these threats and how to identify safeguards to eliminate or reduce the threats.

5 Internal policies to **monitor compliance** with independence ethics.

6 Policies and procedures that will **identify relationships** between the firm or members of the assurance team and assurance clients.

7 Policies and procedures to manage the **reliance on revenue** received from a **single** assurance **client**.

- policies and procedures that will identify relationships between the firm or members of the assurance team and assurance clients;[15]
- policies and procedures to manage the reliance on revenue received from a single assurance client.

Safeguards within the firm's own systems and procedures may also include **engagement specific** safeguards such as:

- using an additional professional accountant not on the assurance team to review the work done;
- consulting an outside third party (e.g. a committee of independent directors or a professional regulatory body);

- rotation of senior personnel;
- communicating to the audit committee the nature of services provided and fees charged;
- involving another audit firm to perform or re-perform part of the assurance engagement; and
- removing an individual from the assurance team, when his relationships or interests indicate a threat to independence.

■ Non-Audit Services to Audit Clients in IFAC Ethics Code (Sec. 8)

For audit clients, the IFAC code generally prohibits bookkeeping services, **valuation services**, managerial decision-making functions (such as expert services), broker-dealer or investment advisor services, and **litigation support** to audit clients. Financial information systems design and implementation as well as internal audit outsourcing is permitted where specified safeguards are in place.

Services Audit Firms Cannot Offer Audit Clients

The IFAC Code prohibits the following non-audit services for audit clients:

- Bookkeeping services, including payroll services and the preparation of financial statements or financial information, which forms the basis of the financial statements on which the audit report is provided for audit clients;
- Valuation services for audit clients that involve the valuation of matters material to the financial statements and where the valuation involves a significant degree of subjectivity (paragraph 8.173);
- Management decision-making functions (paragraph 8.156) including the following examples: (a) Authorizing, executing or consummating a transaction, or exercising authority on behalf of the assurance client (b) **Determining which recommendation of the firm should be implemented; and** (c) **Reporting, in a management role, to those charged with governance;**
- Corporate finance and similar activities including the following examples: (a) **Promoting, dealing in, or underwriting of a client's shares;** (b) **Committing the client to the terms of a transaction; and** (c) **Consummating a transaction on behalf of the client** (paragraph 8.201).
- Litigation support role. Conflicts of interest will arise if the auditor is engaged in both auditing and litigation services because the litigation function requires the auditor to be an advocate for the client, whereas the auditing function requires the auditor to practice with professional skepticism.

Information Technology System and Internal Audit Advice OK with Safeguards

Financial information systems design and implementation as well as internal audit outsourcing is permitted where specified safeguards are in place.

- The IFAC Code currently permits the provision of information technology systems services to audit clients where certain safeguards are in place. These safeguards should ensure that the audit client accepts all responsibility for: establishing and monitoring internal controls; all management decisions with respect to the design and implementation; operating the system; and the data used or generated by the system.

■ Where the auditor is undertaking the outsourcing of internal audit function, the Code provides that **any self-review threat created may be reduced to an acceptable level by ensuring that there is a clear separation between control of the internal audit by audit client management and the internal audit activities themselves.** Where the auditor is performing a significant portion of the internal audit activities, the auditor should consider the threats and proceed with caution. Appropriate safeguards should be put in place. (Paragraphs 8.178–8.183)

3.7 Other Topics Applicable To Professional Accountants in Public Practice

Other sections in the Code that apply specifically to professional accountants in public practice include: professional competence and use of non-accountants (Section 9), fees and commissions (Section 10), incompatible activities (Section 11), clients' monies (Section 12), relations with others in public accountancy (Section 13), and advertising and solicitation (Section 14).

■ Professional Competence and Responsibilities Regarding the Use of Non-Accountants (Sec. 9)

If an auditor does not have the competence to perform a specific part of the professional service, technical help may be had from experts such as other accountants, lawyers, actuaries, engineers, geologists, and evaluators. However, since the auditors have ultimate responsibility for the service, it is their responsibility to see that the requirements of ethical behavior are followed. For example, Section 8 of the Code requires all professionals participating in the assurance engagement to be independent of the assurance client.

Responsibility for non-accountants might be undertaken by asking non-accountants involved in the assurance service to read the appropriate ethical codes. The auditor might also require written confirmation that the non-accountant has an understanding of the ethical requirements. The auditor should be ready to provide advice and judgment if conflicts arise.

■ Fees and Commissions (Sec. 10)

Section 10[16] of the Ethics Code discusses the responsibilities to clients in pricing auditing services via fees and commissions.

Professional fees should be a fair reflection of the value of the professional service performed for the client, taking into account the skill and knowledge required, the level of training and experience of the persons performing the services, the time necessary for the services and the degree of responsibility that performing those services entails.

Sections 10.3 through 10.7 of the Code discuss appropriate fees. Generally, professional fees should reflect rates per hour or per day for the time of each person involved in the services. It is okay for an auditor to charge a client a lower fee than has previously been charged for similar services, as long as the fee was calculated based on Sections 10.3–10.7.

The Code warns that a **self-interest threat may be created if fees due from an assurance client for professional services remain unpaid for a long time**, especially if a significant part is not paid before the issue of the assurance report for the following year. **Generally the payment of such fees should be required before the report is issued. The firm should also consider whether the overdue fees might be regarded as being equivalent to a loan to the client and whether, because of the significance of the overdue fees, it is appropriate for the firm to be re-appointed.** [17]

Fees are distinct from reimbursement of expenses. **Out-of-pocket expenses, in particular traveling expenses, attributable directly to the professional services performed for a particular client would normally be charged in addition to the professional fees.**

Contingent Fees and Commissions

An assurance engagement should not be performed for a fee that is contingent on the result of the assurance work or on items that are the subject matter of the assurance engagement. The accountant should not pay a commission to obtain a client nor should a commission be accepted for referral of a client or products or services of others to a third party. In those countries where payment and receipt of commissions are permitted, the accountant should disclose the commission arrangements to the client. [18]

Illustration 3.7 gives some illustrations of fee responsibility.

ILLUSTRATION 3.7

Considerations of Fees Charged to Clients

- Professional fees should be a fair reflection of the value of the professional service performed for the client.

- Professional fees should be computed on the basis of appropriate rates per hour or per day for the time of each person involved in the services.

- It is not improper for an auditor to charge a client a lower fee than has previously been charged for similar services.

- Out-of-pocket expenses, in particular traveling expenses, attributable directly to the professional services performed for a particular client would normally be charged in addition to the professional fees.

- The basis on which the fees are computed and any billing arrangements should be clearly defined, preferably in writing, to the client before the commencement of the engagement to avoid misunderstandings.

- The accountant should not pay a commission to obtain a client nor should a commission be accepted for referral of a client or products or services of others to a third party.

■ Activities Incompatible with Practice (Sec. 11)

Section 11 [19] of the Code details some activities incompatible with practice. **A professional accountant in public practice should not concurrently engage in any business, occupation or activity that impairs or might impair integrity, objectivity or independence, or the good reputation of the profession.** The simultaneous engagement in another activity unrelated to assurance or accounting services, which reduces the accountant's ability to conduct his accounting practice according to ethical principles, is inconsistent with public practice. Illustration 3.8 shows some professional accountants' acts inconsistent with practice.

ILLUSTRATION 3.8

Considerations Concerning Incompatible Activities and Advertising

Activities incompatible with practice for a professional accountant in public practice are:

- any business, occupation or activity that impairs or might impair integrity, objectivity or independence, or the good reputation of the profession;
- the simultaneous engagement in another business, occupation or activity unrelated to professional services that has the effect of preventing the accountant from conducting a public practice in accordance with ethical principles.

Advertising activities that are not permitted to accountants are those which:

- create false, deceptive or unjustified expectations of favorable results;
- imply the ability to influence any court, tribunal or regulatory agency;
- consist of self-laudatory statements that are not based on verifiable facts;
- make comparisons with other professional accountants in public practice;
- certain testimonials or endorsements;
- contain any other representations that would be likely to cause a reasonable person to misunderstand or be deceived;
- make unjustified claims to be an expert or specialist in a particular field of accountancy.

Clients' Monies (Sec. 12)

Section 12[20] of the Ethics Code discusses **clients' monies**. Clients' monies are any monies, including documents of title to money, for example, bills of exchange, promissory notes and documents of title which can be converted into money. One example is bearer bonds received by a professional accountant in public practice to be held or paid out on the instruction of the person from whom or on whose behalf they are received.

In some countries, the law or professional organization does not permit an accountant in public practice to hold clients' monies. In other countries, there may be legal duties imposed on accountants who hold client monies. In any case, the accountant in public practice should not hold clients' monies if there is reason to believe that the funds were obtained from or used for illegal activities.

Illustration 3.9 illustrates requirements given in paragraphs 12.2 to 12.10 of the Code.

Relations with Other Professional Accountants (Sec. 13)

Section 13 of the *Code of Ethics for Professional Accountants* describes relations with other professional accountants in public practice.[21]

Existing Accountant Requests Assistance from Another Accountant

Sometimes the extension of operations of a company results in creation or purchase of branches or subsidiary companies at locations, or in areas of expertise, where the company's **existing accountant** does not practice. In these instances the client or the

ILLUSTRATION 3.9

Considerations for Handling Clients' Monies

- The auditor should not hold clients' monies if there is reason to believe that they were obtained from, or are to be used for, illegal activities.

- Monies belonging to others should be kept separate from firm or personal monies, used only for the purpose intended, and accounted for to any person entitled to know.

- One or more bank accounts should be maintained for clients' monies. Such bank accounts may include a general **client account**[20] into which the monies of a number of clients may be paid.

- Clients' monies received should be deposited without delay to the credit of a client account, or – if in the form of documents of title to money and documents of title which can be converted into money – be safeguarded against unauthorized use.

- Monies may only be drawn from the client account on the instructions of the client.

- Fees due from a client may be drawn from client's monies provided the client, after being notified of the amount of such fees, has agreed to such withdrawal.

- Payments from a client account shall not exceed the balance standing to the credit of the client.

- When it seems likely that the client's monies remain on client account for a significant period of time, the professional accountant in public practice should, with the concurrence of the client, place such monies in an interest bearing account within a reasonable time.

- All interest earned on clients' monies should be credited to the client account.

- Books of account should be kept in a way that will enable the accountant, at any time, to establish clearly their dealings with clients' monies in general and the monies of each individual client in particular. A statement of account should be provided to the client at least once a year.

existing accountant may request a **receiving accountant** practicing at those locations to perform services necessary to complete the assignment. Auditors should only undertake services that they can expect to complete with professional competence.

An existing accountant without a specific skill, fearing that he might lose his existing business, may be reluctant to refer a client to another accountant who has that skill, but he must always consider the interest of the client. The relationship between the receiving accountant and the existing auditor is discussed in greater detail in Chapter 5 Client Acceptance. Illustration 3.10 shows the key points that auditors must consider concerning relations with other accountants.

Existing Auditor is Superseded by Another

In cases when the appointment will result in another professional accountant in public practice being superseded, the Code advises the following:[22]

1 A proposed accountant who is asked to replace another accountant must determine if there are any professional reasons why the appointment would not be accepted.

ILLUSTRATION 3.10

Considerations Concerning Relations with Other Professional Accountants

Procedures to be observed in cases where there is an existing accountant who will continue to provide professional services:

1 The receiving accountant should limit the services provided to the specific assignment received, take reasonable steps to support the existing accountant's current relationship with the client, and should generally not express criticism of the services of the existing accountant.

2 Before accepting to undertake an assignment of a type which is clearly distinct from that being carried out by the existing accountant, the receiving accountant should advise the client and communicate with the existing accountant, preferably in writing, advising of the general nature of the request.

3 The receiving accountant should ensure that the existing accountant is kept informed of the general nature of the services performed.

4 When the opinion of a professional accountant, other than the existing accountant, is sought on the application of accounting, auditing, reporting or other standards or principles to specific circumstances or transactions, it is required that there be communication with the existing accountant. With the permission of the client, the receiving accountant should also provide a copy of the final report to the existing accountant.

This cannot effectively be done without direct communication with the existing accountant. Communication between the parties serves to protect the accountant from accepting an appointment in circumstances where pertinent facts are not known. It also protects the interests of the existing accountant when the proposed change is an attempt to interfere with the exercise of the existing accountant's independence.

2 The extent to which an existing accountant can discuss the affairs of the client with the proposed accountant will depend on receipt of the client's permission and/or the legal or ethical requirements relating to this disclosure.

It can be questioned, however, whether it is sufficiently effective that engagement acceptance information exchange with the previous accountant only takes place with the client's permission. A preferred standard procedure might be to inform the client about the exchange of information, but not to seek his permission.

3 **The proposed accountant in public practice should treat in the strictest confidence and give due weight to any information provided by the existing accountant.**

4 Before accepting an appointment involving services that were carried out by another accountant, the proposed accountant should determine if the existing accountant has been notified by the client and given permission to discuss the client's affairs fully and freely. The proposed accountant should then request permission from the client to communicate with the existing accountant. If such permission is refused, the auditor may decline the engagement.

On receipt of permission, the accountant should ask the existing accountant to provide information on anything about the client that should be known before deciding whether or not to accept the appointment.

5 When the existing accountant receives the communication referred to above, he should reply, preferably in writing, advising of any reasons why the proposed accountant should not accept the appointment. If there are such reasons, the existing accountant should ensure that the client has given permission to disclose details. If no permission is given, this should be reported to the proposed accountant.

6 If the proposed accountant does not receive a reply from the existing accountant within a reasonable period of time, further communication should be attempted. If unable to obtain a satisfactory outcome, the proposed accountant should send a letter

ILLUSTRATION 3.11

Procedures to Change Auditors

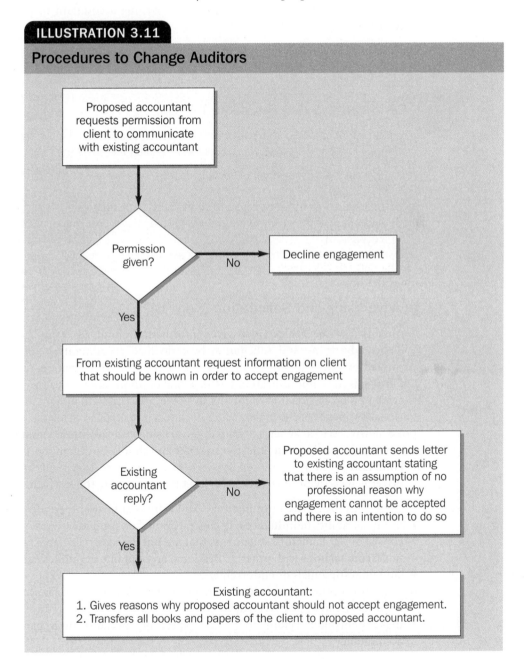

to the existing accountant **stating that there is an assumption that there is no professional reason why the appointment should not be accepted and that there is an intention to do so.**

7 The existing accountant should promptly transfer to the new accountant all books and papers of the client which are or may be held after the change in appointment.

8 Certain organizations request competitive bids for employment of assurance services. In reply to a request for a proposal, the accountant should, if the appointment may result in the replacement of an existing accountant, state in the submission that before acceptance the opportunity to contact the existing accountant in public practice is required.

Illustration 3.11 shows a diagram of the procedures auditors follow when one auditor is superseded by another auditor.

Certification Exam Question 3.4

Before accepting an audit engagement a proposed (successor) auditor should make specific inquiries of the existing (predecessor) auditor regarding the existing auditor's:

(A) Opinion of any subsequent events occurring since the existing auditor's audit report was issued.
(B) Understanding as to the reasons for the change of auditors.
(C) Awareness of the consistency in the application of accounting principles between periods.
(D) Evaluation of all matters of continuing accounting significance.

■ Advertising and Solicitation (Sec. 14)

Section 14[23] of the Ethics Code gives information about advertising and **solicitation**. Whether advertising and solicitation by individual accountants in public practice is permitted or not is up to the professional accounting organizations in each country. **Advertising** is the communication to the public of information as to the services or skills provided by professional accountants in public practice with a view to procuring professional business. **Solicitation** is an approach to a potential client for the purpose offering professional services. **When permitted, advertising and solicitation should be aimed at informing the public in an objective manner and should be decent, honest, truthful and in good taste.**[24]

Advertising activities that DO NOT meet this criteria are those which:[25]

■ create false, deceptive or unjustified expectations of favorable results;
■ imply the ability to influence any court, tribunal or regulatory agency;
■ consist of self-laudatory statements that are not based on verifiable facts;
■ make comparisons with other professional accountants in public practice;
■ contain testimonials or endorsements;
■ contain any other representations that would be likely to cause a reasonable person to misunderstand or be deceived;
■ make unjustified claims to be an expert or specialist in a particular field of accountancy.

Accountants in a country where advertising is permitted should not seek to obtain an advantage by advertising in newspapers or magazines published or distributed in a country where advertising is prohibited, or vice versa.[26]

When advertising is not permitted, publicity is acceptable, provided it:

- is not misleading or deceptive,
- is in good taste,
- is professionally dignified,
- avoids giving undue prominence to the name of the accountant.

Publicity is acceptable[27] for:

- announcement of appointments and rewards,
- staff recruitment,
- non-promotional directories,
- booklets containing technical information,
- publicity on behalf of clients,
- stationery and name-plates,
- in newspaper announcements of a new practice, changes in a partnership public practice, change of address,
- a document issued by a client.

It is possible for professional accountants to author books or articles on professional subjects, or participate in a lecture, interview or a radio or television program on a professional subject. What professional accountants write or say, however, should not be promotional of themselves or their firm.

Illustration 3.8, earlier in this chapter, shows the major prohibitions for advertising and promotion.

3.8 Applicable to Employed Professional Accountants (Part C)

The last part, Part C, of the Code contains guidance that is particularly relevant to professional accountants working in industry, commerce, the public sector or education.

The topics in Part C:

- conflict of loyalties (Section 15),
- support for professional colleagues (Section 16),
- professional competence (Section 17),
- presentation of information (Section 18).

Concept and a Company 3.4

Accountant Falsifies Accounts for Bosses at WorldCom

Concept	Ethics and the employed accountant – caving in to pressure from your bosses
Story	On October 10, 2002 the US attorney's office announced that Betty Vinson, former Director of Management Reporting at WorldCom, had pleaded guilty to two criminal counts of

Accountant Falsifies Accounts for Bosses at WorldCom (continued)

conspiracy and securities fraud, charges that carry a maximum sentence of 15 years in prison. One year later, October 10, 2003, she was charged with breaking Oklahoma securities laws by entering false information on company documents a charge that potentially carries a ten-year prison sentence. (English 2003)

Over the course of six quarters Vinson made illegal entries to bolster WorldCom's profits at the request of her superiors. Each time she worried. Each time she hoped it was the last time. At the end of 18 months she had helped falsify at least $3.7 billion in profits. (Lacter 2003)

In 1996, Ms. Vinson got a job in the international accounting division at WorldCom making $50,000 a year. Ms. Vinson developed a reputation for being hardworking and diligent. Within two years Ms. Vinson was promoted to be a senior manager in WorldCom's corporate accounting division where she helped compile quarterly results and analyzed the company's operating expenses and loss reserves. Ten employees reported to her. (Pulliam 2003)

Work began to change in mid-2000. WorldCom had a looming problem: its huge line costs – fees paid to lease portions of other companies' telephone networks – were rising as a percentage of the company's revenue. Chief Executive Bernard Ebbers and Chief Financial Officer Scott Sullivan informed Wall Street in July that the company's results for the second half of the year would fall below expectations.

A scramble ensued to try to reduce expenses on the company's financial statements enough to meet Wall Street's expectations for the quarter. But the accounting department was able to scrape together only $50 million, far from the hundreds of millions it would take to hit the company's profit target. In October, her boss told Vinson to dip into a reserve account set aside to cover line costs and other items for WorldCom's telecommunications unit and use $828 million to reduce expenses, thereby increasing profits. (Pulliam 2003)

Ms. Vinson was shocked by her bosses' proposal and the huge sum involved. She worried that the adjustment wasn't proper. She agreed to go along. But afterward Ms. Vinson suffered pangs of guilt. On October, 26, the same day the company publicly reported its third-quarter results, she told her colleagues who were also involved that she was planning to resign. A few suggested that they, too, would quit.

CFO Sullivan heard of the mutiny in accounting and called Vinson and other employees into his office. He explained that he was trying to fix the company's financial problems. Think of it as an aircraft carrier, he said, We have planes in the air. Let's get the planes landed. Once they are landed, if you still want to leave, then leave. But not while the planes are in the air. Mr. Sullivan assured them that nothing they had done was illegal and that he would assume all responsibility. He noted that the accounting switch wouldn't be repeated. (Pulliam 2003)

That night, she told her husband about the meeting and her worries over the accounting. Mr. Vinson urged her to quit. But in the end, she decided not to quit. She was the family's chief support, earning more than her husband. She, her husband and daughter depended on her health insurance. She was anxious about entering the job market as a middle-aged worker.

By the end of the first quarter of 2001, it was clear Ms. Vinson could find no large pools of reserves to transfer to solve the profit shortfall. Sullivan suggested that rather than count line costs as part of operating expenses in the quarterly report, they would shift $771 million in line costs to capital-expenditure accounts which would result in decreased expenses and increased assets and retained earnings. Accounting rules make it clear that line costs are to be counted as operating leases, not capital assets.

Accountant Falsifies Accounts for Bosses at WorldCom (continued)

Ms. Vinson felt trapped. That night she reviewed her options with her husband and decided to put together a resume and begin looking for a job. Nevertheless, she made the entries transferring the $771 million, backdating the entries to February by changing the dates in the computer for the quarter. She faced the same dilemma in the second, third and fourth quarters of 2001. Each subsequent quarter she made more fraudulent entries. (Pulliam 2003)

Ms. Vinson began waking up in the middle of the night, unable to go back to sleep because of her anxiety. Her family and friends began to notice she was losing weight and her face took on a slightly gaunt look. At work she withdrew from co-workers, afraid she might let something slip. In early 2002, she received a promotion, from senior manager to director, along with a raise that brought her annual salary to about $80,000. (Pulliam 2003)

In March 2002 the SEC made requests for information from WorldCom and Cynthia Cooper, head of internal auditing (see Chapter 1) started asking questions. Ms. Vinson and two other accountants hired an attorney and told their story to federal officials from the FBI, SEC and US attorney, hoping to get immunity from prosecution for their testimony.

On August 1, 2002, Ms. Vinson received a call from her attorney telling her that the prosecutors in New York would probably indict her. In the end, they viewed the information Ms. Vinson had supplied at the meeting with federal officials as more of a confession than a tip-off to wrongdoing. Within hours, WorldCom fired her because of the expected indictment. The only thing she was allowed to take with her was a plant from her desk. (Pulliam 2003)

Two of her colleagues pleaded guilty to securities fraud. Unable to afford the legal bill that would result from a lengthy trial, Betty Vinson decided to negotiate a guilty plea as well.

| Discussion Questions | ■ Was Betty Vinson justified in her actions because there were at the request of her superiors? Why? |
| | ■ If you were in Ms. Vinson's situation, what would you have done? |

References English, S., 2003, "City – WorldCom boss on fraud charges," *The Daily Telegraph*, September 4.

Lacter, M., 2003, "Looking the other way (Comment) (Editorial)," *Los Angeles Business Journal*, June 30.

Pulliam, S., 2003, "Over the Line: A Staffer Ordered To Commit Fraud Balked, Then Caved – Pushed by WorldCom Bosses, Accountant Betty Vinson Helped Cook the Books – A Confession at the Marriott," *The Wall Street Journal*, June 23, p. 1.

■ Conflict of Loyalties (Sec. 15)

Accountants who are employed by non-audit firms owe loyalty to their employer as well as to their profession, but there may be times when the two are in conflict. An employee's normal priority should be to support his or her organization. However, an employee cannot legitimately be required to break the law, breach the ethics, rules, and standards of the accounting profession, lie to their employer's auditors, or be associated with a statement that materially misrepresents the facts.

Differences in view about the correct judgment on accounting or ethical matters should normally be raised and resolved within the employee's organization, initially with the employee's immediate superior and possibly with higher levels of management or non-executive directors. If employed accountants cannot resolve any material issue involving a conflict between their employers and their professional requirements they may have no other recourse but to resign. Employees should state their reasons for resigning to their employer but their duty of confidentiality normally precludes them from communicating the issue to others (unless legally or professionally required to do so).

■ Support For Professional Colleagues (Sec. 16)

An accountant, particularly one in a management position, should develop and hold his own judgment in accounting matters, but should deal with differences of opinion between him and his colleagues in a professional way.

■ Professional Competence (Sec. 17)

An accountant employed in industry, commerce, the public sector or education may be asked to undertake important tasks for which he has not had sufficient specific training or experience. When undertaking these tasks, an accountant should not mislead his employer as to his degree of expertise. Where it is appropriate, expert advice and assistance should be requested from the employer.

■ Presentation Of Information (Sec. 18)

A professional accountant is expected to present financial information fully, honestly and professionally and so that it will be understood in its context. Financial and non-financial information should be kept describing clearly the true nature of business transactions, assets or liabilities and whether transactions are recorded in a timely and proper manner.

3.9   Enforcement of Ethical Requirements

The effectiveness of enforcing ethical standards varies from country to country. In many countries an auditor who violates the ethical standard may be disciplined by law or by the professional organization. The penalties range from a reprimand to expulsion or fine. In the USA expulsion from a state society or the American Institute of Certified Public Accountants (AICPA) does not mean that the expelled member cannot practice public accounting because only the state boards of public accountancy have the authority to revoke a license. As illustrated in the case of Arthur Andersen,[28] if a company is convicted of a felony, the US Security and Exchange Commission (SEC) prohibits them from auditing publicly traded companies. In other countries such as Japan, France and Germany government often takes a formal role in the enforcement of the standards.

IFAC has no authority to require disciplinary action for violation of the Code of Ethics. IFAC relies on legislation or the constitution of professional bodies in each country. However, Attachment B to the Code offers guidance.

Attachment B to the IFAC Ethics Code – Guidance on Disciplinary Action

Attachment B to the Code[29] discusses the causes of disciplinary action and common sanctions.

- Disciplinary action ordinarily arises from such issues as: failure to observe the required standard of professional care, skills or competence; non-compliance with rules of ethics and discreditable or dishonorable conduct.
- Sanctions commonly imposed by disciplinary bodies include: reprimand, fine, payment of costs, withdrawal of practicing rights, suspension, and expulsion from membership. Other sanctions can include a warning, the refund of the fee charged to the client, additional education, and the work to be completed by another member at the disciplined member's expense.

Attachment B advises that the disciplinary committee or similar tribunal will ordinarily carry out disciplinary proceedings. The proceedings should be held in a manner that is consistent with the legal requirements of the country concerned. This will ordinarily involve legal representation, taking evidence and keeping records of the proceedings. A lawyer, a representative of the investigation committee, or the secretariat of the member body may present the case against the defendant. Ordinarily there is a right to appeal by both sides within fixed time limits. Such a right of appeal may be to a body not connected with the member body.

3.10 Future Developments

First, a new Companies Bill is being developed in the UK. The focus of this bill will be to shed more light on directors' responsibilities. This new bill will hold directors' accountable if they abuse their position. Large companies will be required to undergo a complete review of their operating and financial section, which will increase investors' confidence in the financial statements.

Secondly, International Financial Reporting Standards and International Standards on Auditing will be adopted throughout the EU by 2005. The European Commission goal is to bring about uniformity in the accounting and auditing standards employed throughout capital markets in the EU. This will also help professional accountants who are engaged in cross-border activities.

France is also setting forth new legislation that will prevent audit firms from providing non-assurance services to audit clients. Small business owners who are being driven off the market because of big audit firms favor this legislation. The French are developing this legislation in response to the concerns regarding auditor independence after the Enron and WorldCom scandals. By preventing audit firms from undertaking work in corporate finance, insolvency, legal and tax services, and consulting services, the French hope to reinstall investors' confidence in the financial statements.

3.11 Summary

The attitude and behavior of professional accountants in providing auditing and assurance services have an impact on the economic well-being of their community and country. Accountants can remain in this advantageous position only by continuing to provide the public with these unique services at a level that demonstrates that the public confidence is well-founded. The standards of the accountancy profession are heavily determined by the public interest. Therefore, the objectives of the accountancy profession are to work to the highest standards of professionalism, to attain the highest levels of performance and generally to meet the public interest.

The IFAC Ethics Committee who report recommendations to the IFAC Board after research and appropriate exposure of draft guidance develops the ethical guidance incorporated into the Code of Ethics for Professional Accountants (the Code). The Code sets standards of conduct for professional accountants and states the fundamental principles that should be observed by professional accountants. The Code is divided into three parts:

- Part A applies to all professional accountants unless otherwise specified;
- Part B applies only to those professional accountants in public practice; and
- Part C applies to employed professional accountants.

The fundamental principles of ethics are described in Part A of the Code. They are: integrity, objectivity, professional competence and due care, confidentiality, professional behavior, and technical standards. Part A of the Code offers further discussion on integrity and objectivity, resolution of ethical conflicts, professional competence, confidentiality, and professional behavior (tax, cross-border activities, and publicity). Each concept is the topic of subsequent Sections (1–7) in the Code.

Part B of IFAC's Code of Ethics is only applicable to accountants in public practice. A professional accountant in public practice refers to each partner or person occupying a position similar to that of a partner, and each employee in a practice providing professional services to a client irrespective of their functional classification (e.g. audit, tax, or consulting) and professional accountants in a practice having managerial responsibility. Ethical guidance for accountants in public practice is offered in the areas of: independence; responsibilities to clients such as fees, commissions, and clients' monies; and responsibilities to colleagues such as relations to other professionals, advertising and activities incompatible with practice.

Across the world, national rules on auditors' independence differ in several respects such as: the scope of persons to whom independence rules should apply; the kind of financial, business or other relationships that an auditor may have with an audit client; the type of non-audit services that can and cannot be provided to an audit client; and the safeguards which should be used. The European Commission has issued independence standards to be applied throughout the EU. The USA enacted the Sarbanes-Oxley Act of 2002 that describes independence requirements of US auditors.

Accountants must not only maintain an independent attitude in fulfilling their responsibilities, but the users of financial statements must have confidence in that independence. These two objectives are frequently identified as "independence in fact" and "independence in appearance." Independence in fact exists when the accountant is able to maintain an unbiased attitude throughout the audit, so being objective and impartial, whereas independence in appearance is the result of others' interpretations of this independence.

Section 8 of the Code discusses independence in assurance services in terms of a principles-based approach that takes into account threats to independence, accepted safeguards and the public interest. The Section states principles that members of assurance teams should use to identify threats to independence (self-interest, self-review, advocacy, familiarity and intimidation threats), evaluate the significance of those threats, and, if the threats are other than clearly insignificant, identify and apply safeguards created by the profession, legislation or regulation, safeguards within the assurance client, and safeguards within the firm's own systems and procedures to eliminate the threats or reduce them to an acceptable level.

Concerning non-assurance services for audit clients, the IFAC code generally prohibits bookkeeping services, valuation services, managerial decision-making functions (such as expert services), broker-dealer or investment advisor services, and litigation support to audit clients. Financial information systems design and implementation as well as internal audit outsourcing is permitted where specified safeguards are in place.

Other sections in the Code that apply specifically to professional accountants in public practice include: professional competence and use of non-accountants (Section 9), fees and commissions (Section 10), incompatible activities (Section 11), clients' monies (Section 12), relations with others in public accountancy (Section 13), and advertising and solicitation (Section 14).

The last part, Part C, of the Code contains guidance that is particularly relevant to professional accountants working in industry, commerce, the public sector, or education. The topics in Part C concern conflict of loyalties (Section 15), support for professional colleagues (Section 16), professional competence (Section 17), and presentation of information (Section 18).

IFAC has no authority to require disciplinary action for violation of the Code of Ethics. IFAC relies on legislation or the constitution of professional bodies in each country. However, Attachment B to the Code offers guidance regarding the causes of disciplinary action and common sanctions.

3.12 Answers to Certification Exam Questions

3.1 (B) the requirement is to determine the proper method for handling a difference of opinion between auditors over a technical matter. Answer (B) is correct because Section 2 of the IFAC Code of Ethics for Professional Accountants suggests a three-step approach to resolving ethical conflicts, the first of which is to contact an immediate superior (which presumably the assistant has done). If there is no resolution, the assistant is to go to the next higher level of management in the firm. The senior partner is a higher level of management. Answer (A) is incorrect because there is no IFAC's Quality Review Committee. Answer (C) is incorrect because an assistant auditor should never approach client management or audit committee. Answer (D) is incorrect because going to an independent committee should only be done after senior management in the firm is contacted.

3.2 (A) The requirement is to identify one of the four statements that is true about independence. Answer (A) is the only true statement. Independence is affected by all the threats mentioned.

3.3 (A) The requirement is to list a reason why an auditor will try to achieve independence in appearance. Answer (A) is correct because independence in appearance is defined in the Code as the avoidance of facts and circumstances so that a third party would conclude an auditor's integrity, objectivity or professional skepticism had been compromised.

3.4 (B) The requirement is to identify the correct statement regarding a proposed auditor's inquiries of the existing auditor. Answer (B) is correct because the proposed auditor is required to ask reasons for the change in auditors and any information that may have a bearing on the audit. Answers (A), (C) and (D) related to matters not required to be discussed prior to accepting an audit engagement.

3.13 Notes

1 Developed by the Josephson Institute for the Advancement of Ethics, a US not-for-profit foundation to encourage ethical conduct of professionals in the fields of government, law, medicine, business, accounting and journalism.

2 IFAC, 2003, Introduction – Objectives, para. 14, *Code of Ethics for Professional Accountants*, International Federation of Accountants, New York.

3 Please note, the *Code of Ethics for Professional Accountants* is so clear that this chapter will use several direct quotes from the Code. To distinguish the direct quotes from the authors' discussion, **the direct quotes will be in bold font.**

4 IFAC, 2004, *Handbook of International Auditing, Assurance, and Ethics Pronouncements*, Resolutions of Ethical Conflicts, Section 2, International Federation of Accountants, New York.

5 Council of European Communities, Eighth Council Directive of 10 April 1994, Article 24, *Official Journal of the European Communities*, No. L 126, 12.5.1984, pp. 20–26.

6 *Statutory audits* are audits established by law.

7 European Union Committee on Auditing, 2002, Commission Recommendation, *Statutory Auditors' Independence in the EU: A Set of Fundamental Principles*, 2002/590/EC, *Official Journal of the European Communities*, 19.7.2002, pp. L 191/22–L 191/97.

8 See para. 11 of the above Commission Recommendation.

9 The Senate and House of Representatives of the United States of America, Sarbanes-Oxley Act of 2002, Public Law 107–204, July 30, 2002.

10 SEC, 2003, *Final Rule: Strengthening the Commission's Requirements Regarding Auditor Independence*; Rel. Nos. 33-8183, 34-47265; 35-27642; IC-25915; IA-2103; File No. S7-49-02, Securities and Exchange Commission, January 28.

11 Pendergast, Marilyn A., "Strengthening the Commission's Requirements Regarding Auditor Independence: file s7-49-02," International Federation of Accountants, New York, January 10, 2003.

12 IFAC, 2004, *Handbook of International Auditing, Assurance, and Ethics Pronouncements*, Independence, Section 8, para 8.8, International Federation of Accountants, New York.

13 IFAC, 2003, *Handbook of International Auditing, Assurance, and Ethics Pronouncements*, International Standards on Auditing 910, Table of Contents, International Federation of Accountants, New York.

14 See para. A.3.1 of the Commission Recommendation given in note 7.

15 All the Big Four and most large firms use compliance tools such as an automated tracking system, which require that partners and staff track their investments and relationships on a periodic, at least annual, basis. The data in the tracking system is matched to a restricted entity list. Those staff who do not enter their data in the system will nevertheless receive an independence compliance letter indicating the list of audit clients.

16 IFAC, 2004, *Handbook of International Auditing, Assurance, and Ethics Pronouncements*, Fees and Commissions, Section 10, International Federation of Accountants, New York.

17 IFAC, 2004, *Handbook of International Auditing, Assurance, and Ethics Pronouncements*, Fees Overdue, Section 8, paragraph 8.205, International Federation of Accountants, New York.

18 IFAC, 2004, *Handbook of International Auditing, Assurance, and Ethics Pronouncements*, Commissions, Section 10, paragraphs 10.11–10.13, International Federation of Accountants, New York.

19 IFAC, 2004, *Handbook of International Auditing, Assurance, and Ethics Pronouncements*, Activities Incompatible With the Practice of Public Accountancy, Section 11, International Federation of Accountants, New York.

20 IFAC, 2004, *Handbook of International Auditing, Assurance, and Ethics Pronouncements*, Clients' Monies, Section 12, International Federation of Accountants, New York.

21 IFAC, 2004, *Handbook of International Auditing, Assurance, and Ethics Pronouncements*, Relationships With Other Professional Accountants in Public Practice, Section 13, International Federation of Accountants, New York.

22 IFAC, 2004, *Handbook of International Auditing, Assurance, and Ethics Pronouncements*, Superseding Another Professional Accountants in Public Practice, Section 13, paras. 13.15–13.18, 13.20–13.23, International Federation of Accountants, New York.

23 IFAC, 2004, *Handbook of International Auditing, Assurance, and Ethics Pronouncements*, Advertising and Solicitation, Section 14, International Federation of Accountants, New York.

24 IFAC, 2004, *Handbook of International Auditing, Assurance, and Ethics Pronouncements*, Advertising and Solicitation, Section 14, para. 14.2, International Federation of Accountants, New York.

25 IFAC, 2004, *Handbook of International Auditing, Assurance, and Ethics Pronouncements*, Advertising and Solicitation, Section 14, para. 14.3, International Federation of Accountants, New York.

26 IFAC, 2004, *Handbook of International Auditing, Assurance, and Ethics Pronouncements*, Advertising and Solicitation, Section 14, paras. 14.4–14.5, International Federation of Accountants, New York.

27 IFAC, 2004, *Handbook of International Auditing, Assurance, and Ethics Pronouncements*, Advertising and Solicitation, Section 14, para. 14.8, International Federation of Accountants, New York.

28 Arthur Andersen was one of the largest auditing firms in the world (one of the Big Five) when they were convicted by the US Department of Justice of obstruction of justice (a felony) when in 2001, the Houston, Texas, branch shredded documents relating to their audit client, Enron Corporation. See Concept and a Company 2.2 in Chapter 2.

29 IFAC, 2003, Statement of Policy of Council, Implementation and Enforcement of Ethical Requirements, Attachment B, *Code of Ethics for Professional Accountants*, International Federation of Accountants, New York.

3.14 Questions, Exercises and Cases

QUESTIONS

3.2 What Are Ethics?

3.1 What are ethics?

3.2 What ethical principles incorporate characteristics used by society as good moral behavior?

3.4 Ethics Guidelines Applicable to All Accountants (Part A)

3.3 What are the Fundamental Principles an accountant must observe to achieve the objectives of the accounting profession according the to IFAC ethics guidelines? Briefly discuss them.

3.4 Confidential client information may generally be disclosed only with the permission of the client. What are the exceptions to this rule?

3.5 Can an accountant claim that the returns he prepares are always acceptable to the taxing authorities? Why?

3.6 Independence Requirements

3.6 Discuss the differences between the European Commission Council Directive on independence and the Sarbanes-Oxley Act's view of auditor independence.

3.7 What is the difference between independence in fact and independence in appearance? State two activities that may not affect independence in fact but are likely to affect independence in appearance.

3.8 Define the five types of threats listed in the Code of Ethics for Professional Accountants. Give one example and one safeguard for each type of threat.

3.9 Name some forms of financial involvement with a client that may affect independence.

3.7 Other Topics Applicable To Professional Accountants in Public Practice

3.10 What are contingent fees? Give two examples and explain why accountants in public practice should or should not take them.

3.11 Give an example of a professional accountant in public practice engaging in activities incompatible with practice.

3.12 What steps must an exiting auditor take if he is going to audit a company now audited by another firm?

3.8 Applicable To Employed Professional Accountants (Part C)

3.13 What should employed accountants do if they feel they are being asked to so something that is contradictory to accounting standards?

3.9 Enforcement of Ethical Requirements

3.14 Can IFAC discipline an accountant for violation of the Code of Ethics? What common sanctions does IFAC suggest?

PROBLEMS AND EXERCISES

3.2 What Are Ethics?

3.15 Ethics Guidelines. Why is there a need for an ethics guideline for professional accountants? Explain. In what ways should the ethics code for accountants be different from that of other groups such as physicians or attorneys?

3.4 Ethics Guidelines Applicable to All Accountants (Part A)

3.16 Violations of Code of Ethics. For each of the following situations involving relations between auditors and the companies they audit indicate whether it violates IFAC's *Code of Ethics for Professional Accountants* and the rationale for the applicable guideline.

A. Yaping Lei, CPA, discloses confidential information in a peer review of the firm's quality control procedures.

B. Frank Smith, CPA, prepares and submits a tax return to the Internal Revenue Service which he believes omits income his client receives from trading goods on eBay.com.

C. El-Hussein El-Masery, CA, is auditing a company in Nigeria that has offered to send him and his wife on a holiday in Hawaii for two weeks.

D. Tabula Gonzales, CP, says in an interview in the local paper that Emilio Rios, CP, misleads his clients about the quality of his audit work.

3.6 Independence Requirements

3.17 Independence in Fact and Appearance. Auditors must not only appear to be independent; they must also be independent in fact.

Required:

A. Explain the concept of auditor's independence as it applies to third-party reliance upon financial statements.

B. (1) What determines whether or not an auditor is independent in fact?
    (2) What determines whether or not an auditor appears to be independent?

C. Explain how an auditor may be independent in fact but not appear to be independent.

D. Would an accountant in public practice be considered independent for a review of the financial statement of a: (1) a church in which the accountant is serving as treasurer without compensation?; (2) a club for which the accountant's spouse is serving as a treasurer-bookkeeper if the accountant is not to receive a fee for the review.

3.18 Independence and Gifts. Samantha Seekineau, Soma Orkoton Logiston (SOL), is in charge of the audit of Olympic Fashions. Five young assistant accountants are working with Seekineau on the engagement, and several are avid wind-surfers. Olympic Fashions owns two villas on Mikonos, which it uses to entertain clients. The comptroller of Olympic Fashions has told Seekineau that she and her audit staff are welcome to use the villas at no charge any time they are not already in use. How should Seekineau respond to this offer? Explain.

3.7 Other Topics Applicable To Professional Accountants in Public Practice

3.19 Professional Accountants in Public Practice. Galati and Brambila formed a corporation called Financial Fitness Systems, each woman taking 50 percent of the authorized common stock. Galati is a Dottore Commercialista (CONSOB), a public accountant, and Brambila is an insurance underwriter. The corporation provides auditing and tax services under Galati's direction and insurance services under Branbila's direction. The opening of the corporation's office was announced by a 15 cm, two-column announcement in the local newspaper.

One of the corporation's first audit clients was the Galore Company. Galore had total assets of €923,820 and total liabilities of €415,719. In the course of her examination, Galati found that Galore's building with a book value of €369,528 was pledged as security for a ten-year term note in the amount of €307,940. Galore's statements did not mention that the building was pledged as security for the ten-year term note. However, as the failure to disclose the lien did not affect either the value of the assets or the amount of the liabilities and her examination was satisfactory in all other respects, Galati rendered an unqualified opinion on Galore's financial statements. About two months after the date of her opinion, Galati learned that an insurance company was planning to loan Galore €230,955 in the form of a first mortgage note on the building. Galati had Brambila notify the insurance company of the fact that Galore's building was pledged as security for the term note.

Shortly after the events described above, Galati was charged with a violation of professional ethics.

Required:

Identify and discuss the ethical implications of those acts by Galati that were in violation of IFAC's *Code of Ethics for Professional Accountants*.

CASES

3.20 Ethical Issues. The following situation involves Kevin Smith, staff accountant with the local CPA firm of Hobb, Mary, and Khang (HM&K). The bookkeeper of Mirage Manufacturing Company resigned three months ago and has not yet been replaced. As a result, Mirage's transactions have not been recorded and the books are not up to date. Mirage must prepare interim financial statements to comply with terms of a loan agreement, but cannot do so until the books are posted. To help them with this matter, Mirage turns to HM&K, their independent auditors. Mirage wants Kevin Smith to update their books because Kevin had audited them last year.

Required:
A. Identify the ethical issues that are involved.
B. Discuss whether there has or has not been any violation of ethical conduct.
(Written by Khang Tran, Mary Horton, and Hob Chen)

Chapter 4

AN AUDITOR'S SERVICES

4.1 Learning Objectives

After studying this chapter, you should be able to:

1 Understand the general definition of assurance services.

2 Identify the assurance and non-assurance services normally performed by auditors.

3 Explain what an assurance engagement entails.

4 Describe the five elements exhibited by all assurance engagements.

5 Know the various subject matters that can be covered in an assurance engagement.

6 Distinguish between the different suitable criteria applicable to an assurance service.

7 Understand what distinguishes a review from a compilation.

8 Give the distinguishing characteristics of the six special purpose reports.

9 Describe the key uses of reports on prospective financial information.

10 Explain the requirements of the Sarbanes-Oxley internal control reporting standards.

11 State the components of a triple bottom-line report based on the Global Reporting Initiative.

12 Discuss agreed-upon procedures and accounting compilation.

4.2 International Framework for Auditor Services

Auditor services are work that an audit firm performs for their clients. Except for consulting services, the work that auditors do is under the guidance of engagement standards set by the International Auditing and Assurance Standards Board (IAASB). Consulting services engagements will not be discussed in this chapter.[1]

■ IAASB'S Technical Pronouncements

Illustration 4.1 shows the general structure of IAASB's technical pronouncements.

Code of Ethics and ISQC

All auditor services standards have as their basis the *IFAC Code of Ethics*[2] (discussed in Chapter 3 Ethics for Professional Accountants) and *International Standards on Quality Control*[3] (ISQC) (see Chapter 1 International Auditing Overview). The Code has been employed by IFAC from the early days, but has been recently revised. Quality control standards are currently being created by the IAASB.

Two Audit Services Frameworks – "Assurance" and "Related Services"

Some engagement standards are based on "International Framework for Assurance Engagements" (assurance engagements), and others result from the "Related Services Framework" (related services engagements). Three sets of standards (ISAs, ISREs and ISAEs) share the assurance engagement framework and one standard set (ISRS) is based on the related services framework. ISAs, ISREs, ISAEs and ISRSs are collectively referred to as the IAASB's Engagement Standards.

IAASB's Engagement Standards

The IAASB engagement standards encompass the following:[4]

- International Standards on Auditing (ISAs) are to be applied, as appropriate, in the audit of historical financial information.
- International Standards on Review Engagements (ISREs) are to be applied in the review of historical financial information.
- International Standards on Assurance Engagements (ISAEs) are to be applied in assurance engagements dealing with subject matters other than historical financial information.
- International Standards on Related Services (ISRSs) are to be applied to compilation engagements, engagements to apply agreed upon procedures to information, and other related services engagements as specified by the IAASB.

Assurance Engagements for Audits and Reviews for Historical Financial Information (ISAs and ISREs)

International Standards on Auditing (ISA) 100[5] "Audits and Reviews of Historical Financial Information" describes the main concepts applicable to audit, review or special purpose engagements. Audit standards are described in ISA 200–799.[6] Special Purpose Engagement and other examinations of historical financial information is ISA 800-899.[7] Review standards are ISREs 2000-2699.

ILLUSTRATION 4.1

Assurance Engagements and Related Services[2]

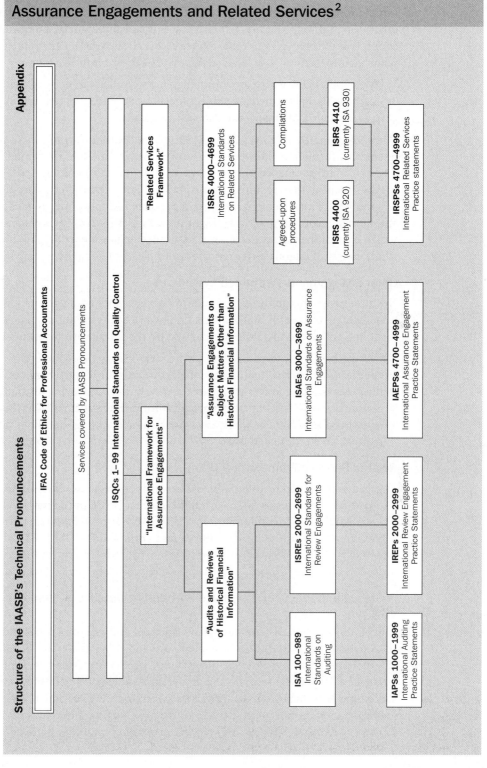

Assurance Engagements on Subject Matters Other than Historical Financial Information (ISAEs)

International Standards on Assurance Engagements (ISAE) 3000R[9] "Assurance Engagements on Subject Matters Other than Historical Financial Information" describes concepts applicable to assurance services whose subject matter are not related to historical financial information. The ISAE standards are divided into two parts:

1 ISAEs 3000–3399 which are topics that apply to all assurance engagements.
2 ISAEs 3400–3699 which are subject specific standards, for example standards relating to examination of **prospective financial information**.[10]

The subject matter of ISAEs 3400–3699 now includes only examination of prospective financial information. However, in future it might include non-financial information (e.g. **corporate governance**, statistical, environmental), systems and processes (e.g. **internal control** (such as that required under the Sarbanes-Oxley Act), corporate governance, environmental management systems), and behavior (corporate governance, compliance, and human resources practices). Right now, as IAASB does not set standards, reports of social, environmental and economic assurance engagements are commonly based on a whole variety of established criteria, for example, the Global Reporting Initiative (GRI).[11]

Other Engagements Performed by Auditors

Not all engagements performed by auditors are assurance engagements. Other engagements frequently performed by auditors that do not meet the definition of an assurance engagement and which are therefore not covered by the framework for assurance engagements include:

- engagements covered by International Standards for Related Services (ISRSs);
- the preparation of tax returns where no conclusion conveying assurance is expressed;
- consulting engagements such as tax consulting, or engagements in which a practitioner is engaged to testify as an expert witness in accounting, auditing, taxation or other matters, given stipulated facts.

Related Services Framework (ISRSs)

Engagements covered by International Standards on Related Services ISRS are based on the "Related Services Framework" – a framework that is still in the development stage at the IAASB. Standards under this framework (ISRSs) are applied currently to two audit services: agreed-upon procedures (ISRS 4400[12]) and compilations (ISRS 4410[13]). Compilations offer no assurance whatsoever. Agreed-upon procedures are assurance based on audit procedures in a very limited "agreed upon" area with a proscribed set of users.

Guidance and Practical Assistance Provided by Practice Statements (IAPS, IAEPs, IRSPSs)

The IAASB's Standards contain basic principles and essential procedures together with related guidance in the form of explanatory and other material, including appendices. International Auditing Practice Statements (IAPSs) are issued to provide interpretive guidance and practical assistance to auditors in implementing ISAs for audit, review, and special purpose engagements. International Assurance Engagement Practice Statements (IAEPSs) provide interpretive guidance for ISAEs, and International Related Services Practice Statements (IRSPSs) will provide assistance for auditors implementing ISRSs.

Certification Exam Question 4.1

Which of the following is a conceptual difference between the International Standards for Assurance Engagements (ISAE) and International Auditing Standards (ISA)?

(A) ISAEs provide a framework for the attest function beyond historical financial statements.

(B) The requirement that the practitioner be independent in mental attitude is omitted from the ISAEs.

(C) The ISAEs do **not** permit an attest engagement to be part of a business acquisition study or a feasibility study.

(D) Internal control is important in ISAs but not ISAEs.

4.3 Elements of an Assurance Engagement

Assurance engagements are performed by a **professional accountant** and are intended to enhance the credibility of information about the subject matter. The subject matter of an assurance engagement is the topic about which the assurance engagement is conducted. Subject matter could be financial statements, statistical information, non-financial performance indicators, capacity of a facility, etc. The subject matter could also be systems and processes (e.g. internal controls, environment, IT systems) or behavior (e.g. corporate governance, compliance with regulation, human resource practices). The assurance engagement evaluates whether the subject matter conforms to suitable criteria that will meet the needs of an intended user. (See Illustration 4.1 "International Framework for Assurance Engagements.")

■ Assurance Engagement Defined

Assurance engagement means an engagement in which a **practitioner** (professional accountant or auditor) expresses a conclusion (in report form) that is designed to enhance the degree of confidence users have about the evaluation of the subject matter against identified criteria.

Common examples of assurance engagements include: financial statement audits and reviews, independent assurance on sustainability reports (such as "**triple bottom line**" reports based on GRI Guidelines), and opinions on the effectiveness of internal controls.

Assurance engagements may be distinguished from other engagements performed by auditors, such as consulting engagements. When performing consulting for an audit client, the auditor may compromise auditor **independence**.

■ Five Elements Exhibited by all Assurance Engagements

The International Framework for Assurance Engagements describes five elements[14] that all assurance engagements exhibit:

1 a three party relationship involving a practitioner, a **responsible party**, and the intended users;

2 a subject matter;

3 suitable criteria;

4 **evidence**; and

5 an assurance report.

Illustration 4.2 is a context data flow diagram of the engagement process. Illustration 4.3 shows a more in depth (zero level) data flow diagram of the relations between the five elements during an engagement process.

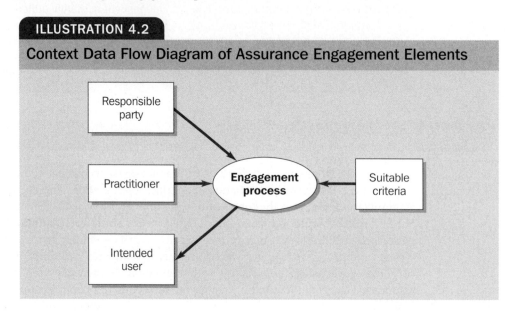

ILLUSTRATION 4.2

Context Data Flow Diagram of Assurance Engagement Elements

■ Three Party Relationship – Practitioner, Responsible Party and User

Assurance engagements always involve three separate parties: a practitioner, a responsible party, and the intended users. The practitioner (e.g. auditor, accountant, expert) gathers evidence to provide a conclusion to the intended users about whether a subject matter (e.g. financial statements) conforms, in all material respects, to identified criteria. The responsible party (usually management or the board of directors) is the one who is responsible for the subject matter, choosing the criteria and typically engaging the practitioner. The responsible party should not be the intended user. In some circumstances the intended users are identified by the responsible party or by law. Often the intended users are the addressees of the assurance report.

The responsible party is responsible for maintaining the accounting, computer and operation systems and determining accounting and internal control methods. As you can see from Illustration 4.3, the responsible party selects criteria (e.g. the tax code), determines the subject matter (financial statements) and engages the practitioner (public accountant). The subject matter and criteria taken together generates the subject matter information. For example, the tax code criteria and financial statements subject matter combine to make the company income tax returns. In an audit, the criteria could be IFRS, the subject matter is financial performance and position of the company, and subject matter information would be the income statement and balance sheet. In preparing internal control assurances, the criteria could be the COSO criteria, subject matter

ILLUSTRATION 4.3

Data Flow Diagram Assurance Engagement Elements and Engagement Sub-Processes

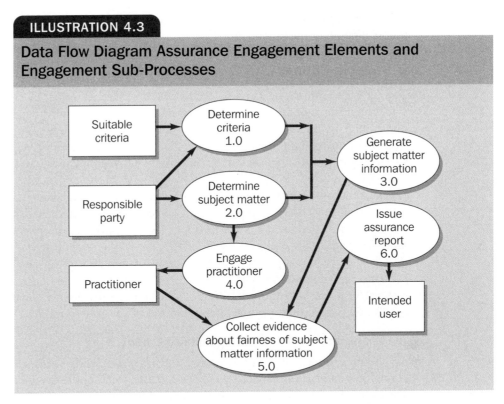

internal controls, and the subject matter information could be a measure of effectiveness of internal control.

The practitioner determines if the criteria is suitable, collects evidence about the subject matter information and issues an assurance report. For example, the auditor determines if the proper income tax codes are being used, evaluates the income tax information provided by the company by seeking evidence that the information is complete and all transactions from which the data were derived exist. Put another way – a responsible party **measures**, the auditor **re-measures**.

■ Subject Matter

The subject matter of an assurance engagement can take many forms, such as:

- information or data about historical or prospective financial performance or physical characteristics (e.g. statistical information, non-financial performance indicators, capacity of a facility).
- systems and processes (e.g. internal controls, IT systems).
- Behavior (e.g. corporate governance, compliance with regulation, human resource practices).

The auditor should accept an assurance engagement only if the subject matter is the responsibility of a party other than the intended users or the auditor. That generally means that the intended user is not management or the auditor. The subject matter must be identifiable and capable of consistent evaluation or measurement against identified, suitable criteria (such as International Financial Reporting Standards (IFRS)). It must also be in a form that can be subjected to procedures for gathering evidence to support that evaluation or measurement.

■ Suitable Criteria

Suitable criteria are the benchmarks (standards, objectives, or set of rules) used to evaluate evidence or measure the subject matter of an assurance engagement. For example, in the preparation of financial statements, the suitable criteria may be IFRS, US Generally Accepted Accounting Principles (US GAAP), or national standards. When reporting on social or environmental aspects of the company an auditor might use the Global Reporting Initiative.

Several standards may guide the report, depending on the assurance service. When using accounting criteria to report on internal control, the criteria may be an established internal control framework, such as the COSO[15] report criteria, or individual control objectives specifically designed for the engagement. When reporting on compliance, the criteria may be the applicable law, regulation or contract, or an agreed level of performance (for instance, the number of times a company's board of directors is expected to meet in a year). Without the frame of reference provided by suitable criteria, any conclusion is open to individual interpretation and misunderstanding.

The Characteristics for Assessing Suitable Criteria

An auditor cannot evaluate or measure a subject matter on the basis of his own expectations, judgments and individual experience. That would not constitute suitable criteria. The characteristics for assessing whether criteria are suitable are as follows:[16]

- **Relevance**: relevant criteria contribute to conclusions that meet the objectives of the engagement, and assist decision making by the intended users.
- **Completeness**: criteria are sufficiently complete when relevant factors that could affect the conclusions in the context of the engagement objectives are not omitted. Complete criteria include, where relevant, benchmarks for presentation and disclosure of the subject matter.
- **Reliability**: reliable criteria result in reasonably consistent evaluation or measurement including, where relevant, presentation and disclosure of the subject matter, when used in similar circumstances by similarly qualified practitioners.
- **Neutrality**: neutral criteria are free from bias.
- **Understandability**: understandable criteria are clear and comprehensive and are not subject to significantly different interpretation.

Criteria Established or Specifically Developed

Criteria can be either established or specifically developed. Established criteria are those embodied in laws or regulations, or issued by recognized bodies of experts that follow due process. Examples of established criteria are GAAP, IFRS, the national tax code, etc. Specifically developed criteria are those identified for the purpose of the engagement and which are consistent with the engagement objective. Examples of specifically developed criteria are criteria generally understood by the intended users (e.g. the criterion for measuring time in hours and minutes is generally understood); or criteria available only to specific intended users (e.g. the terms of a contract, or criteria issued by an industry association that are available only to those in the industry).

Concept and a Company 4.1

A "Clean Audit" for HealthSouth

Concept	What is an assurance service? What is an audit-related service?

Story	Ernst & Young (E&Y) were the independent auditors of HealthSouth between 2000 and 2002. They also conducted janitorial inspections of the company's facilities. These inspections were called "pristine audits." E&Y advised HealthSouth to classify the payments for "pristine audits" as "audit-related fees."

HealthSouth, headquartered in Birmingham, Alabama, USA, is the largest provider of outpatient surgery, diagnostic and rehabilitative healthcare services in the USA with approximately 1,800 worldwide facilities in the USA, Australia, Puerto Rico, and the UK. Its former CEO, Richard M. Scrushy, is under an 85-count federal indictment, accused of conspiracy, securities fraud, mail and wire fraud, and money laundering. (SEC 2003)

A US government indictment charged that between 1996 and 2002 HealthSouth managers, at the insistence of Scrushy, inflated profits by $2.74 billion. Scrushy certified the HealthSouth financial statements when he knew that they were materially false and misleading. On November 4, 2003, he became the first CEO of a major company to be indicted for violating the Sarbanes-Oxley Act, which holds executives personally accountable for their companies' financial reporting. (*Business Week* 2003).

Six months elapsed from the start of the SEC's investigation to the filing of its fraud suit against Scrushy in March 2003. It took just seven weeks, from March 19 to May 5, for the US Justice Department to accumulate 11 guilty pleas from Scrushy aides. All five CFOs in the company's history have admitted to cooking the books. (Helyar 2003)

Pristine Audits

Scrushy devised a facilities inspection program called "Pristine Audits" and hired E&Y to do the work. The primary purpose of the inspections was to check the cleanliness and physical appearance of HealthSouth's surgical and rehabilitation facilities. Under the program, E&Y made unannounced visits to each facility once a year, using dozens of junior-level accountants who were trained for the inspections at HealthSouth's headquarters. For the most part E&Y used audit personnel who were not members of the HealthSouth audit-engagement team to conduct the pristine audits.

The accountants carried out the reviews using as criteria a 50-point checklist designed by Mr. Scrushy. The checklist included procedures such as seeing if magazines in waiting rooms were orderly, the toilets and ceilings were free of stains, and the trash receptacles all had liners. Other items on the checklist included: check the walls, furniture, floors and whirlpool areas for stains; check that the heating and cooling vents "are free of dust accumulation;" that the "floors are free of trash;" and that the "overall appearance is sanitary." A small portion of the checklist pertained to money matters, though none of it pertained to accounting. Assignments included checking if petty-cash drawers were secure and company equipment was properly tagged. The checklists did not cover insurance-billing procedures or the quality of the medical treatment. (Weil 2003a)

In 2002 E&Y ended their relationship with HealthSouth, and HealthSouth discontinued the pristine audits.

▶

Describing the pristine audits, Mr. Scrushy told an investor group: "We believe one of the reasons that we have done so well has to do with the fact that we do audit all of our facilities, 100 percent, annually. And we use an outside audit firm, our auditors, Ernst & Young. They visit all our facilities, 100 percent." On its website, HealthSouth said the pristine audit, "administered independently by Ernst & Young LLP ... ensures that all of our patients enjoy a truly pristine experience during their time at HealthSouth. The average score was 98 percent, with more than half of our facilities scoring a perfect 100 percent."

E&Y Fees Charged HealthSouth

HealthSouth's April 2001 proxy (form DEF14A), filed with the SEC, said the company paid E&Y $1.03 million to audit its 2000 financial statements and $2.65 million of "all other fees." The proxy said the other fees included $2.58 million of "audit-related fees," and $66,107 of "non-audit-related fees." In its April 2002 proxy, HealthSouth said it paid E&Y $1.16 million for its 2001 audit and $2.51 million for "all other fees." The proxy said the other fees included $2.39 million for "audit-related fees" and $121,580 for "non-audit-related fees."

Neither proxy described in any detail the audit-related or non-audit-related services for which E&Y was paid. Andrew Brimmer, a HealthSouth spokesman, was quoted as saying the "audit-related-fee" figures for each year included about $1.3 million for the pristine audits. Mr. Brimmer said HealthSouth paid E&Y $5.4 million for 2002, including $1.1 million for financial-statement audit services and $1.4 million for the pristine audits. (Weil 2003a)

Pristine Audits as "Audit-Related Fees"

A March 2002 E&Y report to HealthSouth's Board of Directors included an attachment that summarized E&Y's fees and provided a suggested "Proxy Disclosure Format." The attachment classified the pristine audits as "audit-related services" and the fees for them as "audit-related fees." (Weil 2003a)

David Howarth, a spokesman for E&Y is quoted as saying: "The audit-related category is not limited to services related to the financial statement audit per se. At the time of HealthSouth's disclosures, there were no SEC rules that defined audit-related services. Describing operational audit procedures as audit-related services was reasonable." Howarth claimed that SEC ruled that audit-related fees would include assurance services traditionally performed by the independent auditor, including "internal-control reviews." He maintained the pristine audit was an internal control review. "Under the new SEC rules adopted in response to the Sarbanes-Oxley Act, these (internal control review) fees are specifically mentioned as ones that should be included in audit-related fees." (Weil 2003b)

After the Weil 2003b article appeared, Scott A. Taub, the Deputy Chief Accountant of the SEC wrote a letter to E&Y partner Ed Caulson. Taub wrote: "The Commission's current rules state that registrants are to "disclose, under the caption *Audit-Related Fees*, the aggregate fees billed in each of the last two fiscal years for assurance and related services by the principal accountant that are reasonably related to the performance of the audit or review of the registrant's financial statements." (emphasis added) It is clear from a reading of the release text and related rules that the Commission's intent is that only fees for services that are reasonably related to the performance of an audit or review of the financial statements and that traditionally have been performed by the independent accountant should be classified as audit-related."(Taub 2003)

A "Clean Audit" for HealthSouth (continued)

Discussion Questions	■ What criteria would the pristine audits have to meet to be considered an audit engagement? ■ What criteria would the pristine audits have to meet to be considered "audit-related"? ■ Can the pristine audits be considered an assurance service? How does the pristine audit meet the five criteria required to qualify an engagement as an assurance service?
References	*Business Week*, 2003, "Sarbanes-Oxley's First," p. 52, November 17. Helyar, J., 2003, "The Insatiable King Richard; He started as a nobody. He became a hotshot CEO. He tried to be a country star. Then it all came crashing down. The bizarre rise and fall of HealthSouth's Richard Scrushy," *Fortune*, p. 76. July 7. SEC, 2003, *Litigation Release 18044*, "SEC charges HealthSouth Corp., CEO Richard Scrushy with $1.4 Billion Accounting Fraud," US Security and Exchange Commission, March 20. Taub, S., 2003, *Letter to Ed Coulson, Partner Ernst & Young*, Office of Chief Accountant, US Security and Exchange Commission, July 8. Weil, J., 2003a, "What Ernst Did for HealthSouth – Proxy Document Says Company Performed Janitorial Inspections Misclassified as Audit-Related," *Wall Street Journal*, June 11. Weil, J., 2003b, "HealthSouth and Ernst Renew Flap Over Fee Disclosures," *Wall Street Journal*, July 1.

■ Evidence

In general, the same evidence gathering procedures, quality control and planning process apply to assurance services as applies to audits. The quantity or quality of evidence available will be affected by:

■ The characteristics of the subject matter. For example, when the subject matter is future oriented, less objective evidence might be expected to exist than when the subject matter is historical.

■ Other non-subject matter characteristics. When evidence that could reasonably be expected to exist is not available to the practitioner. Such reasons might be the timing of the practitioner's appointment, an entity's document retention policy or some restriction imposed by the responsible party.

Evidence is discussed in Chapter 10 Substantive Procedures and Evidence. Risk is discussed in Chapters 6, 7 and 8.

■ Assurance Report

The auditor provides a written report containing a conclusion that conveys the assurance obtained as to whether the subject matter conforms, in all material respects, to the identified criteria. For instance, an audit of financial statements provides an opinion on conformity with IFRS.

The assurance report may be in "short-form" or "long-form." "Short-form" reports ordinarily include only the basic elements identified in appropriate ISAs and International Standards on Assurance Engagements (ISAEs). "Long-form" not only gives the auditor's conclusion on compliance ISAs and ISAEs, but also reports in detail the terms of the engagement, the criteria being used, findings relating to particular aspects of the engagement and related recommendations.

Reasonable Assurance

In most assurance services the audit conclusion is expressed in the positive form, for example, "in our opinion [subject matter] conforms, in all material respects, with [criteria]." This form of expression conveys "reasonable assurance," which indicates that, given the evidence gathering procedures and the characteristics of the subject matter, the auditor has obtained **sufficient appropriate** evidence. (See Chapter 12 Audit Reporting and Communications.) The opinion on an audit of financial statements and a report on internal controls for the Sarbanes-Oxley Act are both examples of opinions with positive assurance.

Limited Assurance

There are some exceptions to using the positive form of assurance. In a review of historical financial statements, the conclusion is expressed in the negative form, for example, "nothing has come to our attention that causes us to believe that [subject matter] does not conform, in all material respects, with [criteria]." This form of expression conveys "limited assurance," which indicates that the auditor has obtained sufficient appropriate evidence to reduce assurance engagement risk to a moderate level. Prospective financial reports give a disclaimer that "actual results are likely to be different from forecast (projection)."

4.4 General Considerations in An Assurance Engagement

The assurance engagement calls for planning, gathering evidence, and reporting. The extent of planning, the sufficiency of evidence, acceptable engagement risk, and the level of assurance of the opinion will depend on the type of assurance engagement. An assurance engagement based on historical financial information requires more intensive planning and evidence gathering than a related services engagement. The auditor should reduce assurance engagement risk to an acceptably low level in the case of a historical financial information engagement. It is also possible to conduct an assurance engagement that provides a reasonable level of assurance on a subject matter other than historical financial information (e.g. the subject matter of a sustainability report or internal control report).

■ Procedures in the Assurance Engagements

In the planning phase of the assurance engagement, the auditor should obtain an understanding of the subject matter and other engagement circumstances in order to assess risks. He should document matters that are significant in providing evidence to support the assurance report and to show that the engagement was performed in accordance with ISAEs.

■ Assurance Report Basic Elements

The assurance report should be in writing and should contain a clear expression of the practitioner's conclusion about the subject matter. International Standards on Assurance

Engagements 3000R does not require a standardized format for reporting on all assurance engagements, but rather identifies the basic elements required to be included in the assurance report:[17]

ILLUSTRATION 4.4

Assurance Report Basic Elements

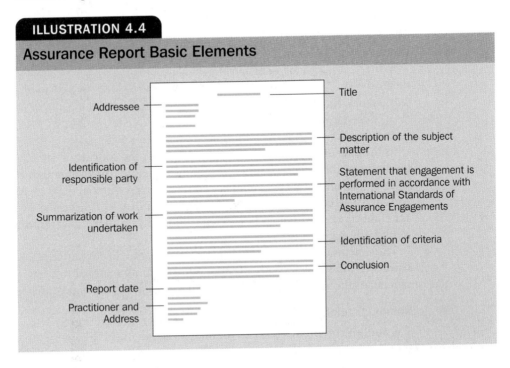

The standard elements of the report include the title, addressee, report date, and practitioner's name and specific location. The title indicates this is an independent assurance report. The addressee is the party or parties to whom the report is directed.

Subject Matter

In the body of the report is a description of the subject matter, for example, identification of the subject matter and explanation of the subject matter characteristics. The subject matter description gives the name of the entity to which the subject matter relates and the period of time covered. Are characteristics of the subject matter qualitative, quantitative, objective, subjective, historical, or prospective? Are there inherent limitations such as the imprecision of the measurement techniques being applied?

Assurance Engagement Criteria

Criteria by which the evidence is measured or evaluated can be either established or specifically developed. To illustrate, International Financial Reporting Standards are established criteria for the preparation and presentation of financial statements in the private sector, but specific users may decide to specify some other comprehensive basis of accounting (OCBOA) such as cash accounting, rules of a regulatory authority, or income tax basis that meets their specific information. When users of the report have agreed to criteria other than established criteria, then the assurance report states that it is only for the use of identified users and for the purposes they have specified.

The assurance report identifies the criteria so the intended users can understand the basis for the auditor's conclusion. Disclosure of the source of the criteria, measurement methods used, and significant interpretations made are important for that understanding.

Practitioner's Conclusion

The practitioner's conclusion is expressed in positive form, negative form or as a reservation or denial of conclusion.

In the case of an audit of financial statements or Sarbanes-Oxley internal control engagement, the conclusion should be expressed in the positive form. The practitioner's conclusion may, for example, be worded as follows: "in our opinion [subject matter] conforms, in all material respects, with [criteria]" or "the responsible party's assertion concerning [subject matter's] conformity, in all material respects, with [criteria] is fairly stated."

In the case of a review of financial statements, the conclusion should be expressed in the negative form. For example, "nothing has come to our attention that causes us to believe that [subject matter] does not conform, in all material respects, with [criteria]" or "nothing has come to our attention that causes us to believe the responsible party's assertion concerning [subject matter's] conformity, in all material respects, with [criteria] is not fairly stated."

The conclusion should clearly express a reservation in circumstances where some or all aspects of the subject matter do not conform, in all material respects, to the identified criteria; or the auditor is unable to obtain sufficient appropriate evidence.

Communications with the Audit Committee

The auditor communicates relevant matters arising from the assurance engagement with those charged with governance (such as the audit committee). Relevant matters of governance interest include only information that has come to the attention of the auditor as a result of performing the assurance engagement. He is not required to design procedures for the specific purpose of identifying matters of governance interest.

An auditor who, before the completion of an assurance engagement, is requested to change the engagement to a non-assurance engagement or from an audit-level engagement to a review-level engagement should consider if that is appropriate. He should not agree to a change where there is no reasonable justification for the change. Examples of a reasonable basis for requesting a change in the engagement are a change in circumstances that affects the intended users' requirements or a misunderstanding concerning the nature of the engagement.

4.5 Audits and Reviews of Historical Financial Information

Audits, reviews and examination (special purpose engagements) of historical financial information are assurance engagements that have as their subject matter historical financial information.

■ Engagements to Audit Financial Statements

The objective of an audit of financial statements is to enable the auditor to express an opinion whether the financial statements are prepared, in all material respects, in accordance with an identified financial reporting framework. The expression of a conclusion by an auditor is designed to enhance the degree of confidence intended users can have about historical financial statements. Audit engagements standards include ISA 120 to ISA 300. The rest of this book is about audit engagements, so these will not be discussed here.

■ Engagements to Review Financial Statements (ISRE 2000–2699)[18]

A review of financial statements is similar to an audit in the way it requires terms of an engagement, planning, consideration of work performed by others, documentation, and paying attention to **subsequent events.** These concerns are discussed throughout this book, especially Chapter 5 on client acceptance, Chapter 6 on planning, Chapter 11 on completing the audit, and Chapter 11 which considers the appendix on documentation. Where reviews of financial statements differ most from a financial statement audit is that in a review report only limited procedures are performed (primarily inquiry of management and analytical procedures).

The objective of a review of financial statements is to enable an auditor to state whether (based on procedures that are not as extensive as would be required in an audit) anything has "come to the auditor's attention that causes the auditor to believe that the financial statements are not prepared, in all material respects, in accordance with an identified financial reporting framework." This way of expressing an opinion is called negative assurance.

Limited Audit Procedures

Sufficient appropriate evidence for a financial statement review is limited to inquiry, analytical procedures, limited inspection and, in certain cases only, additional evidence gathering procedures. **Inquiry** (discussed in Chapter 10 on substantive procedures) consists of seeking information of knowledgeable persons inside or outside the entity. **Analytical procedures** (discussed in Chapter 9) consist of the analysis of significant ratios and trends including the resulting investigation of fluctuations and relationships that are inconsistent with other relevant information or deviate from predictable amounts. **Inspection** (in Chapter 10), which consists of examining records, documents, or tangible assets, is carried out on a limited basis.

A review of financial statement engagement, unlike an audit, usually does not involve collecting evidence about the design and operation of internal control, or obtaining evidence to back up the findings from inquiries or analytical procedures (i.e. corroborating evidence). Review engagements do not employ the evidence gathering techniques used in a financial statement audit such as observation, confirmation, recalculation, reperformance or extensive inspection.

Review of Financial Statements Report

The report on a review of financial statements should contain the following basic elements, ordinarily in the following layout[19] (see Illustration 4.5 for a sample unqualified review report):

(a) Title;
(b) Addressee;

    (c) Opening or introductory paragraph including:
        (i) Identification of the financial statements on which the review has been performed; and
        (ii) A statement of the responsibility of the entity's management and the responsibility of the auditor;
    (d) Scope paragraph, describing the nature of a review, including:
        (i) A reference to the International Standard on Auditing applicable to review engagements, or to relevant national standards or practices;
        (ii) A statement that a review is limited primarily to inquiries and analytical procedures; and
        (iii) A statement that an audit has not been performed, that the procedures undertaken provide less assurance than an audit, and that an audit opinion is not expressed;
    (e) Statement of negative assurance;
    (f) Date of the report;
    (g) Auditor's address; and
    (h) Auditor's signature.

ILLUSTRATION 4.5

Form of Unqualified Review Report[20]

REVIEW REPORT TO ...

We have reviewed the accompanying balance sheet of ABC Company at December 31, 20XX, and the related statements of income and cash flows for the year then ended. These financial statements are the responsibility of the Company's management. Our responsibility is to issue a report on these financial statements based on our review.

We conducted our review in accordance with the International Standard on Auditing (or refer to relevant national standards or practices) applicable to review engagements. This Standard requires that we plan and perform the review to obtain moderate assurance as to whether the financial statements are free of material misstatement. A review is limited primarily to inquiries of company personnel and analytical procedures applied to financial data and thus provides less assurance than an audit. We have not performed an audit and, accordingly, we do not express an audit opinion.

Based on our review, nothing has come to our attention that causes us to believe that the accompanying financial statements do not give a true and fair view (or "are not presented fairly, in all material respects") in accordance with International Accounting Standards [or indicate the relevant national accounting standards].

Date

                                                   AUDITOR

Address

Review Conclusion

The review conclusion will be either an **unqualified**, **qualified** or **adverse** opinion. The **unqualified opinion** offers negative assurance, as we have discussed. If matters that impair a true and fair view in accordance with the identified financial reporting framework have come to the auditor's attention, the auditor may express a **qualification** of the negative assurance provided; or give an adverse opinion. When the effect of the matter is so material and pervasive to the financial statements that a qualification is not adequate an **adverse** statement states that the financial statements do not give a true and fair view (or "are not presented fairly, in all material respects") in accordance with the identified financial reporting framework.

Certification Exam Question 4.2

Financial statements of a non-public entity that have been reviewed by an accountant should be accompanied by a report stating that a review:

(A) Provides only limited assurance that the financial statements are fairly presented.
(B) Includes examining, on a test basis, information that is the representation of management.
(C) Consists principally of inquiries of company personnel and analytical procedures applied to financial data.
(D) Does not contemplate obtaining corroborating evidential matter or applying certain other procedures ordinarily performed during an audit.

The auditor should date the review report as of the date the review is completed, which includes performing procedures relating to events occurring up to the date of the report. However, the auditor should not date the review report earlier than the date on which the financial statements were approved by management.

■ Examination of Historical Financial Information such as Special Purpose Engagements (ISA 800[21])

Standard audit reports are based on the financial statements "taken as a whole." However, sometimes the auditor may have a request for a financial statement based on historical financial information, but which is not based on the financial statements as a whole or on IFRS or the requisite national standard. This is called examination of historical financial information, the prime example being special purpose engagements.

Auditors may examine historical financial information for special purpose reports. An auditor may be called upon to report on components of the financial statements, such as when a bank requests an audit of accounts receivable in anticipation of financing. Sometimes there are audits that give an opinion on compliance with legal agreements required of a company. For instance, a subcontractor may ask for an audit to give comfort to a main contractor. Management or the board of directors may request a summarized financial statement. Small businesses are generally not required to comply with IFRS or a national standard. Small businesses may want to have financial statements based on the cash basis, an income tax basis, or a basis required by regulatory agencies.

List of Special Purpose Engagement Reports

The special purpose engagements reports[22] include:

1 Reports on Financial Statements Prepared in Accordance with a Comprehensive Basis of Accounting other than International Accounting Standards or National Standards such as:
  (a) That used by an entity to prepare its income tax return.

(b) The cash receipts and disbursements basis of accounting.

(c) The financial reporting provisions of a government regulatory agency.

2 Reports on a Component of Financial Statements.

3 Reports on Compliance with Contractual Agreements.

4 Reports on Summarized Financial Statements.

Illustration 4.6 gives the relationships of these reports to financial statement information and contractual or government standards.

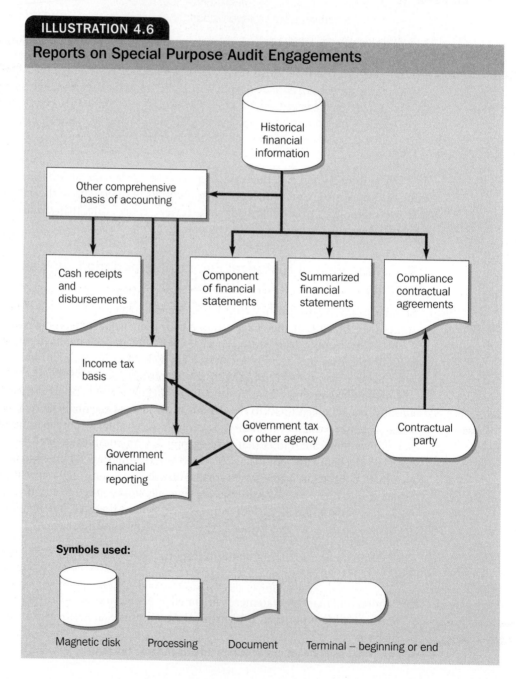

ILLUSTRATION 4.6

Reports on Special Purpose Audit Engagements

The auditor's report on a special purpose audit engagement, except for a report on summarized financial statements, should include the following basic elements.[23] Like the audit review engagement described above, the report would include a title; addressee; opening or introductory paragraph; date of the report; auditor's address; and auditor's signature. The scope paragraph (describing the nature of an audit) and the opinion paragraph are different than that of a review. The scope paragraph describes the work the auditor performed, but does not say it is limited to inquiries and analytical procedures. The opinion paragraph contains a positive expression of opinion (not a negative assurance as in the review of financial statements) on the financial information.

Reports on Financial Statements Prepared in Accordance with OCBA other than International Accounting Standards or National Standards

Financial statements may be prepared for a special purpose in accordance with a comprehensive basis of accounting that is different to International Accounting Standards or relevant national standards. This is called an "other comprehensive basis of accounting" (OCBA). A comprehensive basis of accounting comprises a set of criteria used in preparing financial statements which applies to all material items and which has substantial support.

Other comprehensive financial reporting frameworks may include:

- that used by an entity to prepare its income tax return;
- the cash receipts and disbursements basis of accounting;
- the financial reporting provisions of a government regulatory agency.

The auditor's report on financial statements prepared in accordance with another comprehensive basis of accounting should include a statement that indicates the basis of accounting used. The opinion paragraph of the report should state whether the financial statements are prepared, in all material respects, in accordance with the identified basis of accounting. Illustration 4.7-A gives a sample report for a statement of Cash Receipts and Disbursements (cash basis accounting). Illustration 4.7-B gives a sample report for financial reports prepared on the Income Tax Basis.

Reports on a Component of Financial Statements

The auditor may be requested to express an opinion on one or more components of financial statements, for example, accounts receivable, inventory, an employee's bonus calculation, or a provision for income taxes. This type of engagement may be done as a separate engagement or in conjunction with an audit of the entity's financial statements. However, this type of engagement does not result in a report on the financial statements taken as a whole and, accordingly, the auditor would express an opinion only as to whether that specific component audited is prepared in accordance with the accounting standards.

The auditor's report on a component of financial statements should include a statement that indicates the basis of accounting in accordance with which the component is presented or refers to an agreement that specifies the basis.

The opinion should state whether the component is prepared, in all material respects, in accordance with the identified basis of accounting. Illustration 4.8 gives an example of a report on the Account Receivable component.

ILLUSTRATION 4.7

Form of Examples of Reports on Financial Statements Prepared in Accordance with a Comprehensive Basis of Accounting Other than International Accounting Standards or National Standards[24]

(A) A Statement of Cash Receipts and Disbursements

AUDITOR'S REPORT TO ...

We have audited the accompanying statement of ABC Company's cash receipts and disbursements for the year ended December 31, 20X1. This statement is the responsibility of ABC Company's management. Our responsibility is to express an opinion on the accompanying statement based on our audit.

We conducted our audit in accordance with International Standards on Auditing (or refer to relevant national standards or practices). Those Standards require that we plan and perform the audit to obtain reasonable assurance about whether the financial statement is free of material misstatement. An audit includes examining, on a test basis, evidence supporting the amounts and disclosures in the financial statement. An audit also includes assessing the accounting principles used and significant estimates made by management as well as evaluating the overall statement presentation. We believe that our audit provides a reasonable basis for our opinion. The Company's policy is to prepare the accompanying statement on the cash receipts and disbursements basis. On this basis revenue is recognized when received rather than when earned, and expenses are recognized when paid rather than when incurred.

In our opinion, the accompanying statement gives a true and fair view of (or "presents fairly, in all material respects") the revenue collected and expenses paid by the Company during the year ended December 31, 20X1 in accordance with the cash receipts and disbursements basis as described in Note X.

Date

AUDITOR

Address

(B) Financial Statements Prepared on the Entity's Income Tax Basis

AUDITOR'S REPORT TO ...

We have audited the accompanying income tax basis financial statements of ABC Company for the year ended December 31, 20X1. These statements are the responsibility of ABC Company's management. Our responsibility is to express an opinion on the financial statements based on our audit.

We conducted our audit in accordance with International Standards on Auditing (or refer to relevant national standards or practices). Those Standards require that we plan and perform the audit to obtain reasonable assurance about whether the financial statements are free of material misstatement. An audit includes examining, on a test basis, evidence supporting the amounts and disclosures in the financial statements. An audit also includes assessing the accounting principles used and significant estimates made by management, as well as evaluating the overall financial statement presentation. We believe that our audit provides a reasonable basis for our opinion.

In our opinion, the financial statements give a true and fair view of (or "present fairly, in all material respects") the financial position of the Company as of December 31, 20X1 and its revenues and expenses for the year then ended, in accordance with the basis of accounting used for income tax purposes as described in Note X.

Date

AUDITOR

Address

Certification Exam Question 4.3[25]

An auditor's report on financial statements prepared on the cash receipts and disbursements basis of accounting should include all of the following **except**:

(A) A reference to the note to the financial statements that describes the cash receipts and disbursements basis of accounting.

(B) A statement that the cash receipts and disbursements basis of accounting is **not** a comprehensive basis of accounting.

(C) An opinion as to whether the financial statements are presented fairly in conformity with the cash receipts and disbursements basis of accounting.

(D) A statement that the audit was conducted in accordance with ISAs.

Certification Exam Question 4.4

An auditor may express an opinion on an entity's accounts receivable balance even if the auditor has disclaimed an opinion on the financial statements taken as a whole provided the:

(A) Report on the accounts receivable discloses the reason for the disclaimer of opinion on the financial statements.

(B) Distribution of the report on the accounts receivable is restricted to internal use only.

(C) Auditor also reports on the current asset portion of the entity's balance sheet.

(D) Report on the accounts receivable is presented separately from the disclaimer of opinion on the financial statements.

ILLUSTRATION 4.8

Report on Components of Financial Statements – Schedule of Accounts Receivable[26]

AUDITOR'S REPORT TO ...

We have audited the accompanying schedule of accounts receivable of ABC Company for the year ended December 31, 20X1. This schedule is the responsibility of ABC Company's management. Our responsibility is to express an opinion on the schedule based on our audit.

We conducted our audit in accordance with International Standards on Auditing (or refer to relevant national standards or practices). Those Standards require that we plan and perform the audit to obtain reasonable assurance about whether the schedule is free of material misstatement. An audit includes examining, on a test basis, evidence supporting the amounts and disclosures in the schedule. An audit also includes assessing the accounting principles used and significant estimates made by management, as well as evaluating the overall presentation of the schedule. We believe that our audit provides a reasonable basis for our opinion.

In our opinion, the schedule of accounts receivable gives a true and fair view of (or "presents fairly, in all material respects") the accounts receivable of the Company as of December 31, 20X1 in accordance with ... .

Date   AUDITOR

Address

ILLUSTRATION 4.9

Report on Compliance[27]

(a) Separate Report

AUDITOR'S REPORT TO ...

We have audited ABC Company's compliance with the accounting and financial reporting matters of sections XX to XX inclusive of the Indenture dated May 15, 20X1 with DEF Bank.

We conducted our audit in accordance with International Standards on Auditing applicable to compliance auditing (or refer to relevant national standards or practices). Those Standards require that we plan and perform the audit to obtain reasonable assurance about whether ABC Company has complied with the relevant sections of the Indenture. An audit includes examining appropriate evidence on a test basis. We believe that our audit provides a reasonable basis for our opinion.

In our opinion, the Company was, in all material respects, in compliance with the accounting and financial reporting matters of the sections of the Indenture referred to in the preceding paragraphs as of December 31, 20X1.

Date

Address

AUDITOR

(b) Report Accompanying Financial Statements

AUDITOR'S REPORT TO ...

We have audited the accompanying balance sheet of the ABC Company as of December 31, 20X1, and the related statements of income, and cash flows for the year then ended (the reference can be by page numbers). These financial statements are the responsibility of the Company's management. Our responsibility is to express an opinion on these financial statements based on our audit.

We have also audited ABC Company's compliance with the accounting and financial reporting matters of sections XX to XX inclusive of the Indenture dated May 15, 20X1 with DEF Bank. We conducted our audits in accordance with International Standards on Auditing (or refer to relevant national standards or practices) applicable to the audit of financial statements and to compliance auditing. Those Standards require that we plan and perform the audits to obtain reasonable assurance about whether the financial statements are free of material misstatement and about whether ABC Company has complied with the relevant sections of the Indenture. An audit includes examining, on a test basis, evidence supporting the amounts and disclosures in the financial statements. An audit also includes assessing the accounting principles used and significant estimates made by management, as well as evaluating the overall financial statement presentation.

We believe that our audits provide a reasonable basis for our opinion. In our opinion:
(a) the financial statements give a true and fair view of (or "present fairly, in all material respects") the financial position of the Company as of December 31, 20X1, and of the results of its operations and its cash flows for the year then ended in accordance with ... (and comply with ...); and
(b) the Company was, in all material respects, in compliance with the accounting and financial reporting matters of the sections of the Indenture referred to in the preceding paragraphs as of December 31, 20X1.

Date

Address

AUDITOR

When an adverse opinion or disclaimer of opinion on the entire financial statements has been expressed, the auditor should report on components of the financial statements only if those components are not so extensive as to constitute a major portion of the financial statements. To do otherwise may overshadow the report on the entire financial statements.

Reports on Compliance with Contractual Agreements

An auditor may undertake an engagement to report on a company's compliance with contractual agreements, such as bond indentures or loan agreements. Usually these agreements require a company to comply with a variety of conditions (covenants) written into the contracts. These covenants may involve restrictions of company actions such as payments of interest, maintenance of predetermined financial ratios, restriction of dividend payments and the use of the proceeds of sales of property.

The report should state whether, in the auditor's opinion, the company has complied with the particular provisions of the agreement. Illustration 4.9 gives examples of auditor's reports on compliance given in a separate report and in a report accompanying financial statements.

Reports on Summarized Financial Statements

Some financial statement users may only be interested in the highlights of a company's financial position. Therefore, a company may only require statements summarizing its annual audited financial statements. An auditor should only take an engagement to report on summarized financial statements if he has expressed an audit opinion on the financial statements from which the summary is made.

Summarized financial statements are much less detailed than annual audited financial statements. Therefore, the summarized nature of the information reported needs to be clearly indicated. The report must caution the reader that summarized financial statements should be read in conjunction with the company's most recent audited financial statements.

What sets the summarized financial statements apart from the other reports in this section is that they include the following basic elements:

- an identification of the audited financial statements from which the summarized financial statements were derived;
- a reference to the date of the audit report on the unabridged financial statements and the type of opinion given in that report;
- an opinion as to whether the information in the summarized financial statements is consistent with the audited financial statements from which it was derived;
- a statement, or reference to the note within the summarized financial statements, which indicates the summarized financial statements should be read in conjunction with the unabridged financial statements and the accompanying audit report.

Illustration 4.10 gives an example of an auditor's reports on summarized financial statements when an unqualified audit opinion has been expressed on the company's annual financial statements.

ILLUSTRATION 4.10

Report on Summarized Financial Statements when an Unqualified Opinion was Expressed on the Annual Audited Financial Statements[27]

AUDITOR'S REPORT TO ...

We have audited the financial statements of ABC Company for the year ended December 31, 20X0, from which the summarized financial statements were derived, in accordance with International Standards on Auditing (or refer to relevant national standards or practices). In our report dated March 10, 20X1 we expressed an unqualified opinion on the financial statements from which the summarized financial statements were derived.

In our opinion, the accompanying summarized financial statements are consistent, in all material respects, with the financial statements from which they were derived.

For a better understanding of the Company's financial position and the results of its operations for the period and of the scope of our audit, the summarized financial statements should be read in conjunction with the financial statements from which the summarized financial statements were derived and our audit report thereon.

Date

AUDITOR

Address

4.6 Assurance Engagements Other than Historical Financial Information

The International Standard on Assurance Engagements (ISAE) 3000R establishes basic principles and essential procedures for professional accountants in public practice for the performance of assurance engagements on subject matters other than historical financial information. Assurance engagements other than historical financial information have two main components:

1 topics that apply to all assurance engagements (ISAEs 3000–3399); and
2 subject specific standards (ISAEs 3400–3699).

The only subject specific standard currently is for prospective financial statements.[29]

Currently there are no standards other than the framework standard ISAE 3000 on topics that apply to all subject matters (ISAEs 3000–3399). These will be added by the IAASB as needed. (See Illustration 4.1 "ISAE 3000R 'Assurance Engagements on Subject Matters Other than Historical Financial Information.'")

■ Subject Specific Standards

Subject specific standards for assurance services on other than historical financial information may be thought of as falling into four subject matter groups:

1 subject matter related to prospective financial statements;

2 subject mater related to non-financial information (e.g. corporate governance, statistical, environmental);

3 subject matter related to systems and processes (e.g. corporate governance, environmental management systems, and internal control such as that required under the Sarbanes-Oxley Act);

4 subject matter about behavior (corporate governance, compliance, and human resources practices).

The only subject matter currently covered by IAASB's technical pronouncements is prospective financial statements. There are currently **no** ISAEs related to the subject matters of non-financial information, systems, and process and behavior.

Example Existing Standards Other Than IFAC Used in an Assurance Engagement

Examples of existing standards that may be considered in systems and processes, non-financial information, or behavior assurance engagements are:

- Sarbanes-Oxley Section 404 internal control audit standard,[30]
- Global Reporting Initiative (GRI) *Sustainability Reporting Guidelines*,[31]
- SA8000 standards for social accountability towards employees,[32]
- International Labour Organization (ILO) conventions for social accountability towards employees,[33],
- World Business Council for Sustainable Development (WBCSD) social and eco-efficiency indicators,[34]
- European Union Eco-management and Audit scheme (EMAS) standard for environmental management systems,[35] and
- ISO14001 standard for environmental management systems.[36]

In this section we will discuss prospective financial statement engagements. We will also discuss the Sarbanes-Oxley internal control audit standard and the GRI *Sustainability Reporting Guidelines*, as these are the most influential non-IFAC standards currently.

Considerations When Providing Assurance Services on Subject Matters Other than Historical Financial

Several things must be considered when providing assurance services other than those based on historical financial information. Some of the considerations are similar to those of a financial statement audit including ethics, quality control, terms of engagement, planning, materiality, using the work of an expert, subsequent events, and documentation. These topics are discussed throughout this book. The primary considerations of an assurance report that differ from an audit of financial statements is client acceptance, subject matter, and reporting.

■ The Examination of Prospective Financial Information

"Prospective financial information" means financial information based on assumptions about events that may occur in the future. Prospective financial information can be in the form of a forecast, a projection or a combination of both. A "forecast" is prospective financial information prepared on the basis of management's assumptions as to future events (best-estimate assumptions). A "projection" means prospective financial information prepared on the basis of hypothetical assumptions about future events and management actions which may or may not take place, such as a possible merger of two companies. A projection is a "what-if" scenario.

A report on an examination of prospective financial information may take several forms. It may be a prospectus to provide potential investors with information about future expectations. The report may take the form of an annual report to provide information to shareholders, regulatory bodies, and other interested parties. It might be a report to lenders of cash flow forecasts.

Prospective Financial Information Offers Moderate Level of Assurance

Reporting on prospective financial information is highly subjective. Prospective financial information relates to events and actions that have not yet occurred and may not occur. While evidence may be available to support the assumptions, the evidence is future oriented and, therefore, speculative in nature. This means that this evidence does not offer the same level of assurance as historical financial information. The auditor is, therefore, not in a position to express an opinion as to whether the results shown in the prospective financial information will be achieved.

Given the types of evidence available, it may be difficult for the auditor to obtain a level of satisfaction sufficient to provide a positive expression of opinion. The auditor can generally only provide a moderate level of assurance.

Report on Examination of Prospective Financial Information

The report by an auditor on an examination of prospective financial information differs from the reports on historical financial information in that it contains the following: [37]

- identification of the prospective financial information;
- a statement that management is responsible for the prospective financial information including the assumptions on which it is based;
- when applicable, a reference to the purpose and/or restricted distribution of the prospective financial information;
- a statement of negative assurance as to whether the assumptions provide a reasonable basis for the prospective financial information;
- appropriate warnings to the reader concerning the achievability of the results indicated by the prospective financial information.

The warnings in the report on prospective financial statements should be clear. They would state that actual results are likely to be different from the prospective financial information since anticipated events frequently do not occur as expected and the variation could be material. In the case of a projection, the caveat would be that "the prospective financial information has been prepared for [state purpose], using a set of assumptions that include hypothetical assumptions about future events and management's actions that are not necessarily expected to occur."

Illustration 4.11 shows examples of extracts from both an unmodified report on a forecast and unmodified report on a projection.

ILLUSTRATION 4.11

Prospective Financial Report Examples[38]

(a) Extract From An Unmodified Report On A Forecast

AUDITOR'S REPORT TO ...

We have examined the forecast 1 in accordance with International Standards on Auditing applicable to the examination of prospective financial information. Management is responsible for the forecast including the assumptions set out in Note X on which it is based.

Based on our examination of the evidence supporting the assumptions, nothing has come to our attention that causes us to believe that these assumptions do not provide a reasonable basis for the forecast. Further, in our opinion the forecast is properly prepared on the basis of the assumptions and is presented in accordance with [name of standard].

Actual results are likely to be different from the forecast since anticipated events frequently do not occur as expected and the variation may be material.

Date   AUDITOR

Address

(b) Extract From An Unmodified Report On A Projection

AUDITOR'S REPORT TO ...

We have examined the projection in accordance with International Standards on Auditing applicable to the examination of prospective financial information. Management is responsible for the projection including the assumptions set out in Note X on which it is based.

This projection has been prepared for (describe purpose). As the entity is in a start-up phase the projection has been prepared using a set of assumptions that include hypothetical assumptions about future events and management's actions that are not necessarily expected to occur. Consequently, readers are cautioned that this projection may not be appropriate for purposes other than that described above.

Based on our examination of the evidence supporting the assumptions, nothing has come to our attention that causes us to believe that these assumptions do not provide a reasonable basis for the projection, assuming that (state or refer to the hypothetical assumptions). Further, in our opinion the projection is properly prepared on the basis of the assumptions and is presented in accordance with [standards].

Even if the events anticipated under the hypothetical assumptions described above occur, actual results are still likely to be different from the projection since other anticipated events frequently do not occur as expected and the variation may be material.

Date   AUDITOR

Address

Certification Exam Question 4.5[39]

An examination of a financial forecast is a professional service that involves:

(A) Compiling or assembling a financial forecast that is based on management's assumptions.

(B) Limiting the distribution of the accountant's report to management and the board of directors.

(C) Assuming responsibility to update management on key events for one year after the report's date.

(D) Evaluating the preparation of a financial forecast and the support underlying management's assumptions.

■ Internal Control Reporting and SOX 404 reporting

The Sarbanes-Oxley Act of 2002 (SOX) requires certification of internal control by the Chief Executive Officer (CEO) and Chief Financial Officer (CFO) of all companies that trade on the stock exchanges in the USA including companies headquartered outside the USA. SOX also requires that the company's auditor give an opinion on management's report on internal control.

The rules on internal control reporting published by the SEC[40] require a company's annual report to include an internal control report of management that contains:[41]

■ a statement of management's responsibility for establishing and maintaining adequate internal control over financial reporting for the company;

■ a statement identifying the framework used by management to evaluate the effectiveness of the company's internal control over financial reporting;

■ Management's assessment of the effectiveness of the company's internal control over financial reporting, including a statement as to whether or not the company's internal control over financial reporting is effective.[42] The assessment must include disclosure of any "material weaknesses"[43] in the company's internal control over financial reporting identified by management.

■ A statement that the registered public accounting firm that audited the financial statements included in the annual report has issued an attestation report on management's assessment of the registrant's internal control over financial reporting.[44]

Standards for Preparation and Issuance of Audit Reports

The US Public Company Accounting Oversight Board (PCAOB) established an internal control audit standard (Audit Standard #2)[45] required by US publicly traded companies. The PCAOB rules require that public accounting firms describe in the audit report the scope of its testing of the company's internal control structure and procedures performed in its internal control evaluation under SOX Section 404(b). In the audit report, the registered public accounting firm also must describe, at a minimum, material weaknesses in company internal controls and any material noncompliance found.[46]

ILLUSTRATION 4.12

Illustrative Report Expressing An Unqualified Opinion on Management's Assessment of the Effectiveness of Internal Control Over Financial Reporting (Separate Report)[47]

Independent Auditor's Report

[Introductory paragraph]

We have audited management's assessment, included in the accompanying [*title of management's report*], that W Company maintained effective internal control over financial reporting as of December 31, 20X3, based on [*Identify criteria, for example, "criteria established in Internal Control – Integrated Framework issued by the Committee of Sponsoring Organizations of the Treadway Commission (COSO)"*]. W Company's management is responsible for its assessment about the effectiveness of internal control over financial reporting. Our responsibility is to express an opinion on management's assessment based on our audit.

[Definition paragraph]

A company's internal control over financial reporting is a process designed to provide reasonable assurance regarding the reliability of financial reporting and the preparation of financial statements for external purposes in accordance with generally accepted accounting principles. A company's internal control over financial reporting includes those policies and procedures that (1) pertain to the maintenance of records that in reasonable detail accurately and fairly reflect the transactions and dispositions of the assets of the company; (2) provide reasonable assurance that transactions are recorded as necessary to permit preparation of financial statements in accordance with generally accepted accounting principles, and that receipts and expenditures of the company are being made only in accordance with authorizations of management and directors of the company; and (3) provide reasonable assurance regarding prevention or timely detection of unauthorized acquisition, use, or disposition of the company's assets that could have a material effect on the financial statements.

[Scope paragraph]

We conducted our audit in accordance with auditing and related professional practice standards established by the Public Company Accounting Oversight Board. Those standards require that we plan and perform our audit to obtain reasonable assurance about whether effective internal control over financial reporting was maintained in all material respects. Our audit included obtaining an understanding of internal control over financial reporting, testing and evaluating the design and operating effectiveness of internal control, and performing such other procedures as we considered necessary in the circumstances. We believe that our audit provides a reasonable basis for our opinion.

[Inherent limitations paragraph]

Because of its inherent limitations, internal control over financial reporting may not prevent or detect misstatements. Also, projections of any evaluation of effectiveness to future periods are subject to the risk that controls may become inadequate because of changes in conditions, or that the degree of compliance with the policies or procedures may deteriorate.

[Opinion paragraph]

In our opinion, management's assessment that W Company maintained effective internal control over financial reporting as of December 31, 20X3, is fairly stated, in all material respects, based on [*Identify criteria, for example, "criteria established in Internal Control – Integrated Framework issued by the Committee of Sponsoring Organizations of the Treadway Commission (COSO)"*].

[Signature]

[Date]

Management's Assertions on Internal Control over Financial Reporting

Management provides a written report of their assertions similar to this:

> Management assessed the Company's internal control over financial reporting as of December 31, 200X. Based on this assessment, **management believes** that, as of December 31, 200X, the Company maintained **effective internal control over financial reporting** including **maintenance of records** that in reasonable detail accurately and fairly reflect the transactions and dispositions of the assets of the Company, and policies and procedures that provide reasonable assurance that (a) transactions are **recorded** as necessary to permit preparation of financial statements in accordance with accounting principles generally accepted in the United States of America and (b) receipts and expenditures of the Company are being made only in accordance with **authorizations** of management and directors of the Company based on the criteria for effective internal control over financial reporting established in Internal Control – Integrated Framework issued by the **Committee of Sponsoring Organizations** of the Treadway Commission.

Illustrative Report on an Unqualified Opinion on the Effectiveness of Internal Control

Auditors must report on management's assertions. Illustration 4.12 gives a sample auditor's report on internal control. The introductory paragraph says the practitioner audited management's assertions that it maintained effective internal control over financial reporting. It also gives the responsibilities of management and auditor. The definition paragraph gives the company's internal control policies and procedures. The scope paragraph tells how the auditor followed PCAOB standards in its audit, which serves as a reasonable basis for its opinion. The inherent limitations paragraph is a disclaimer that internal controls may not detect or prevent misstatements.

■ Sustainability Reporting

The verification of sustainability reports providing assertions regarding financial, environmental and social issues is a fast-growing assurance service. An important driver of this demand is the legal requirement to report on environmental issues in several countries. In Denmark and the Netherlands special environmental reporting is legally required, while in Norway and Sweden environmental issues have to be included in the annual report. In Australia, Canada and the USA, specific environmental output and related financial risks have to be reported.[48]

Economic Sustainability

The economic dimension of sustainability concerns an organization's impact on the economic circumstances of its stakeholders and on economic systems at the local, national and global levels. Economic indicators in the sustainability-reporting context focus on the manner in which an organization affects the stakeholders with whom it has direct and indirect economic interactions.

Environmental Sustainability

The environmental dimension of sustainability concerns an organization's impact on living and non-living natural systems, including ecosystems, land, air and water. The reporting organization provides both normalized (e.g. resource use per unit of output)

ILLUSTRATION 4.13

"Year at a Glance" from the Shell Report[49]

The year at a glance

The year at a glance

Performance

Economic performance
- Earnings of $9.2 billion
- Return on average capital employed (ROACE) of 14%
- $25 billion of capital investment, including $11 billion in key acquisitions
- Highest hydrocarbon production in recent history of 4 million barrels of oil equivalent per day
- Motorists rank Shell top brand for sixth year running

Environmental performance
- 2002 greenhouse gas emissions reduction target met
- Phase out of continuous gas venting nearly completed
- Improved spills performance

Social performance
- Mixed performance on safety
- Highest overall reputation within the energy sector
- Increasing involvement in international public-private partnerships
- More staff feel respected by Shell
- Progress towards senior leadership gender target

Highlights and lowlights

Global sustainable development awards
Shell was ranked top of the energy sector in the **Dow Jones Sustainability Index**. The index tracks the financial performance of companies that have made sustainability a key driver of business strategy.

The Malampaya Deepwater Gas-to-Power project in the Philippines won a **Partnerships Award** – sponsored by the UN Environment Programme and the International Chamber of Commerce – for its approach to sustainable development.

World Summit on Sustainable Development
The business community was a full participant at the World Summit on Sustainable Development (WSSD) in South Africa. Shell was well represented and helped to launch **several new public-private partnerships** (page 43).

Building capacity
The Shell Foundation and World Resources Institute established the **WRI Center for Transport and the Environment** (called EMBARQ) to encourage sustainable solutions to urban transport (page 29).

The **Shell Center for Sustainability** was established at Houston's Rice University and Shell companies in Norway and the UK established **sustainable development professorships** at local universities (page 9).

Resolving differences at Norco
A Joint Statement of Success was signed by the **Norco** refinery and petrochemical plant in Louisiana, USA and the local community. It recognised the steps taken to meet concerns about the plant's environmental and social performance (page 37).

Loss of life
Fifty-three Shell employees and contractors lost their lives at work during 2002. Eleven died when a helicopter crashed in the North Sea (page 33).

Security
Shell companies in 13 countries experienced significant security incidents, including war, civil unrest or violent crimes. In particular, security incidents at operations in the **Niger Delta** remain a concern (page 33). Significant efforts continue to protect Shell people and assets against potential threats, including terrorism.

Dealing with legacies
Plans were progressed with local authorities to clean up two sites contaminated with pesticides from previous operations – **Paulinia and Ipiranga** in Brazil (page 29).

External criticism and protests
Shell was the subject of criticism and received a "**Greenwash award**" from pressure groups at the WSSD (page 43).

There were local community protests about the environmental performance of the **SAPREF refinery** in South Africa, a Shell joint venture (Group interest 50%) (page 27).

and absolute figures. Organizations are encouraged to relate their individual performance to the broader ecological systems within which they operate. For example, organizations could seek to report their pollution output in terms of the ability of the environment (local, regional, or global) to absorb the pollutants.

Social Sustainability

The social dimension of sustainability concerns an organization's impact on the social systems within which it operates. Social performance can be gauged through an analysis of the organization's impact on stakeholders at the local, national, and global levels. In some cases, social indicators influence the organization's intangible assets, such as its human capital and reputation. GRI has selected indicators by identifying key performance aspects surrounding labor practices, human rights, and broader issues affecting consumers, community, and other stakeholders in society.

The assurance report by Shell is a very good example of this type of reporting. Illustration 4.13 is a "Year at a Glance" page from the Royal Dutch Shell 2002 environmental, economic and social performance sustainability report, called "The Shell Report", available on the **www.Shell.com** website. Illustration 4.14, also from the Shell Report, gives the auditor's assurance on the report of Shell management.

GRI Sustainability Reporting Guidelines

There are no specific auditing or assurance standards for environmental, economic or social reporting. However, most environmental and social reporting by large corporations follows the guidelines of the Global Reporting Initiative (GRI) *Sustainability Reporting Guidelines.*[50] These Guidelines are for voluntary use by organizations for reporting on the economic, environmental, and social dimensions of their activities, products, and services.[51]

Company Report Under GRI Guidelines

A report under the GRI Guidelines comprises of five sections:

1 **Vision and Strategy** – a description of the reporting organization's strategy with regard to sustainability, including a statement from the CEO.
2 **Profile** – an overview of the reporting organization's structure and operations and of the scope of the report.
3 **Governance Structure and Management Systems** – a description of organizational structure, policies, and management systems, including stakeholder engagement efforts.
4 **GRI Content Index** – a table supplied by the reporting organization identifying where the information listed in Part C of the Guidelines is located within the organization's report.
5 **Performance Indicators** – measures of the impact or effect of the reporting organization divided into integrated, economic, environmental, and social performance indicators.

ILLUSTRATION 4.14

Auditor's assurance on the Shell's Sustainability Report[52]

Assurance

Message from the Independent Auditors

Over the five years we have provided assurance over information in the Shell Report, we have aligned our approach with emerging standards. In 2002, building on our work to provide a high level of assurance on certain information, we have developed an approach to enable us to provide assurance over Shell's reporting on "hot spots". Next year, evolution of the overall assurance approach will continue to further integrate the input of external experts and panels.

Three symbols have been used to describe the scope of our work:

⊕ At Group, Business and Operating Company (OC) level we obtained an understanding of the systems used to generate, aggregate and report the data for these parameters. We assessed the completeness and accuracy of the data reported by visiting OCs to test systems and data, performed a review of all data reported and assessed data trends in discussion with management. We tested the calculations made at Group level. We did not obtain assurance over Safety and Environmental (SE) data

reported by OCs acquired during 2002, for the reasons set out in the report. Our SE work was therefore only completed for the Shell portfolio as at 31 December 2001. For the economic parameters, we also checked that they are properly derived from the audited Financial Statements of the Royal Dutch/Shell Group of Companies.

↻ We determined that the statements marked with this symbol are supported by underlying evidence at Group and/or local level. Our work included interviewing Shell people as well as external panels where these have been established, reviewing systems and documentation and confirming the accurate use of information derived from external sources. We also checked that panel comments, where presented, were derived from and reflect full reported findings.

⊕ At Group level we tested the accuracy of the data aggregation process for data received from a complete set of responses from countries in which Shell operates. We did not provide assurance over the reliability of the data reported by those countries.

Assurance Report

To: Royal Dutch Petroleum Company and The "Shell" Transport and Trading Company, p.l.c.

Introduction

We have been asked to provide assurance over selected data, graphs and statements of the Royal Dutch/Shell Group of Companies reported in this year's Shell Report. We have marked these statements with the symbols below. This Report is the responsibility of management. Our responsibility is to express an opinion on the data, graphs and statements indicated, based on work referred to above in "Message from the Independent Auditors".

In our opinion:

⊕ The data and graphs (together with the notes), properly reflect the performance of the reporting entities for each parameter (SE – for portfolio as at 31 December 2001) marked with this symbol.

↻ The statements marked with this symbol are supported by underlying evidence.

In addition the data for each parameter marked ⊕ are properly aggregated at Group level.

Basis of opinion

There are no generally accepted international environmental, social and economic reporting standards. This engagement was conducted in accordance with the International Standards for Assurance Engagements. Therefore, we planned and carried out our work to provide reasonable, rather than absolute, assurance on the reliability of the data and statements marked with the symbols ⊕ and ↻ and on the accuracy of the Group level aggregation process for data marked ⊕ . We believe our work provides a reasonable basis for our opinion.

Assurance work performed

In forming our opinion, we carried out the work summarised above in "Message from the Independent Auditors." We used a multi-disciplinary team, comprising financial auditors and environmental and social specialists. We also examined the whole Report to confirm consistency of the information reported with our findings.

Considerations and limitations

It is important to read the data and statements in the context of the reporting policies and limitations and the notes to the graphs. Environmental and social data are subject to many more inherent limitations than financial data given both their nature and the methods used for determining, calculating or estimating such data.

We have not provided assurance over all contents of this report, nor have we undertaken work to confirm that all relevant issues are included.

We have not carried out any work on data reported in respect of future projections and targets. Where we have not provided assurance over previous years' data it is clearly shown.

We have not carried out any work to provide assurance over the completeness and accuracy of the underlying data for the parameters aggregated at Group level, and marked with ⊕ .

It is also important that, in order to obtain a thorough understanding of the financial results and financial position of the Group, the reader should consult the Royal Dutch/Shell Group of Companies Financial Statements for the year ended 31 December 2002.

5 March 2003

KPMG
PRICEWATERHOUSECOOPER

Not all engagements performed by auditors are assurance engagements based on the Assurance Framework.[53] Some audit services are based on the Related Services Framework. International Standards on Related Services (ISRS) Engagements that use ISRS are Agreed-upon Procedures (ISRS 4400)[54] and Compilation of Financial or Other Information (ISRS 4410).[55] (See Illustration 4.1 "Related Services Framework.")

A report issued by a auditor in connection with an engagement that does not exhibit all of the elements described in the Assurance Framework,[56] such as a compilation or engagement to perform agreed-upon procedures, should specifically state it does not offer assurance nor does it make any claim about compliance with the Assurance Framework, ISAs or ISAEs. Furthermore, it does not purport to enhance the degree of confidence intended users can have.

A related service engagement is generally an examination of historical financial statements to develop a conclusion based on the criteria, but no audit opinion. In some instances, this kind of engagement could also be linked to information in other historical financial statements.

■ Engagements to Perform Agreed-Upon Procedures Regarding Financial Information (ISRS 4400)[57]

An agreed-upon procedures engagement is an engagement in which the party engaging the professional accountant or the intended user determines the procedures to be performed and the auditor provides a report of factual findings as a result of undertaking those procedures.

Agreed-upon procedures are not considered an assurance engagement. While the intended user of the report may derive some assurance from the report of factual findings, the engagement is not intended to provide, nor does the auditor express, a conclusion that provides a level of assurance. Rather, the intended user assesses the procedures and findings and draws his own conclusions.[58] (See Illustration 4.1 "Agreed-upon Procedures.")

Matters to Be Agreed

The auditor should ensure that all involved parties have a clear understanding regarding the agreed procedures and the conditions of the engagement. Matters to be agreed between auditor and management include the:[59]

■ nature of the engagement including the fact that no assurance will be expressed on the procedures performed;
■ identification of the financial information to which the agreed-upon procedures will be applied;
■ nature, timing, and extent of the specific procedures to be applied.

Procedures Performed

An engagement to perform agreed-upon procedures may involve the auditor in performing certain procedures on subject matter information like financial data (e.g.

accounts payable, accounts receivable, purchases from related parties, and sales and profits of a segment of an entity), a financial statement (e.g. a balance sheet) or even a complete set of financial statements.

The procedures applied in an engagement to perform agreed-upon procedures may include: inquiry and analysis, recompilation, comparison and other clerical accuracy checks, observation, inspection, and obtaining confirmations (these are discussed in Chapter 10 Substantive Testing and Evidence).

Objective

The objective of an agreed-upon procedures engagement is for the auditor to carry out procedures of an audit nature to which the auditor, the company, and some third party have agreed and to report on factual findings. The report is restricted to those parties that have agreed to the procedures since others, unaware of the reasons for the procedures, may misinterpret the results.

Report

The report on an agreed-upon procedures engagement needs to describe the purpose and the agreed-upon procedures of the engagement in sufficient detail to enable the reader to understand the nature and the extent of the work performed. The report of factual findings should contain,[60] among other things, a description of the auditor's factual findings including sufficient details of errors and exceptions found and a statement that the report is restricted to those parties that have agreed to the procedures to be performed.

Illustration 4.15 contains an example of a report of factual findings issued in connection with an engagement to perform agreed-upon procedures regarding financial information.

Independence Not Required

Independence is not a requirement for agreed-upon procedures engagements; however, the terms or objectives of an engagement or national standards may require the auditor to comply with the independence requirements of IFAC's Code of Ethics. Where the auditor is not independent, a statement to that effect would be made in the report of factual findings.[61]

Certification Exam Question 4.6[62]

A certified accountant's report on agreed-upon procedures related to management's assertion about an entity's compliance with specified requirements should contain:

(A) A statement of limitations on the use of the report.
(B) An opinion about whether management's assertion is fairly stated.
(C) Negative assurance that control risk has **not** been assessed.
(D) An acknowledgement of responsibility for the sufficiency of the procedures.

ILLUSTRATION 4.15

Example of a Report of Factual Findings in Connection with Accounts Payable[63]

REPORT OF FACTUAL FINDINGS

To (those who engaged the auditor)

We have performed the procedures agreed with you and enumerated below with respect to the accounts payable of ABC Company as at (date), set forth in the accompanying schedules (not shown in this example). Our engagement was undertaken in accordance with the International Standard on Auditing (or refer to relevant national standards or practices) applicable to agreed-upon procedures engagements. The procedures were performed solely to assist you in evaluating the validity of the accounts payable and are summarized as follows:

1. We obtained and checked the addition of the trial balance of accounts payable as at (date) prepared by ABC Company, and we compared the total to the balance in the related general ledger account.

2 We compared the attached list (not shown in this example) of major suppliers and the amounts owing at (date) to the related names and amounts in the trial balance.

3 We obtained suppliers' statements or requested suppliers to confirm balances owing at (date).

4 We compared such statements or confirmations to the amounts referred to in 2. For amounts which did not agree, we obtained reconciliations from ABC Company. For reconciliations obtained, we identified and listed outstanding invoices, credit notes and outstanding checks, each of which was greater than €xxx. We located and examined such invoices and credit notes subsequently received and checks subsequently paid and we ascertained that they should in fact have been listed as outstanding on the reconciliations.

We report our findings below:
(a) With respect to item 1 we found the addition to be correct and the total amount to be in agreement.
(b) With respect to item 2 we found the amounts compared to be in agreement.
(c) With respect to item 3 we found there were suppliers' statements for all such suppliers.
(d) With respect to item 4 we found the amounts agreed, or with respect to amounts which did not agree, we found ABC Company had prepared reconciliations and that the credit notes, invoices and outstanding checks over €xxx were appropriately listed as reconciling items with the following exceptions:

(Detail the exceptions)

Because the above procedures do not constitute either an audit or a review made in accordance with International Standards on Auditing (or relevant national standards or practices), we do not express any assurance on the accounts payable as of (date).

Had we performed additional procedures or had we performed an audit or review of the financial statements in accordance with International Standards on Auditing (or relevant national standards or practices), other matters might have come to our attention that would have been reported to you.

Our report is solely for the purpose set forth in the first paragraph of this report and for your information and is not to be used for any other purpose or to be distributed to any other parties. This report relates only to the accounts and items specified above and does not extend to any financial statements of ABC Company, taken as a whole.

Date   AUDITOR

Address

■ Engagements to Compile Financial Information (ISRS 4410)[64]

The objective of a compilation engagement is for the accountant to use accounting expertise, as opposed to auditing expertise, to collect, classify and summarize financial information. This ordinarily entails reducing detailed data to a manageable and understandable form without a requirement to test the assertions underlying that information. The procedures employed do not enable the accountant to express any assurance on the financial information. (See Illustration 4.1 "Compilations.")

Independence

Unlike assurance engagements, independence is not a requirement for a compilation engagement. However, where the accountant is not independent, a statement to that effect would be made in the accountant's report.

Understanding Terms of the Engagement

The accountant should ensure that there is a clear understanding between the client and the accountant regarding the terms of the engagement. Matters to be considered, among other things, include:[65]

- the nature of the engagement including the fact that neither an audit nor a review will be carried out and that accordingly no assurance will be expressed;
- the basis of accounting on which the financial information is to be compiled and the fact that it, and any known departures therefrom, will be disclosed;
- the intended use and distribution of the information, once compiled.

Compilation Procedures

A compilation engagement would ordinarily include the preparation of financial statements (which may or may not be a complete set of financial statements) but may also include the collection, classification, and summarization of other financial information.

The accountant should read the compiled information and consider whether it appears to be appropriate in form and free from obvious material misstatements. The accountant is **not ordinarily** required to: assess internal controls; verify any matters or explanations; or make any inquiries of management to assess the reliability and completeness of the information provided.

Reporting on a Compilation Engagement

Reports on compilation engagements should contain, among other requirements:[66]

- identification of the financial information noting that it is based on information provided by management;
- a statement that neither an audit nor a review has been carried out and that accordingly no assurance is expressed on the financial information;
- a paragraph, when considered necessary, drawing attention to the disclosure of material departures from the identified financial reporting framework.

Illustration 4.16 contains examples of compilation reports.

The financial information compiled by the accountant should contain a reference such as "Unaudited," "Compiled without Audit or Review," or "Refer to Compilation Report" on each page of the financial information or on the front of the complete set of financial statements.

ILLUSTRATION 4.16

Examples of Compilation Reports[67]

(a) Example of a Report on an Engagement to Compile Financial Statements

COMPILATION REPORT TO ...

On the basis of information provided by management we have compiled, in accordance with the International Standards on Related Services (or refer to relevant national standards or practices) applicable to compilation engagements, the balance sheet of ABC Company as of December 31, 19XX and statements of income and cash flows for the year then ended. Management is responsible for these financial statements. We have not audited or reviewed these financial statements and accordingly express no assurance thereon.

Date   ACCOUNTANT

Address

(b) Example of a Report on an Engagement to Compile Financial Statements with an Additional Paragraph that Draws Attention to a Departure from the Identified Financial Reporting Framework

COMPILATION REPORT TO ...

On the basis of information provided by management we have compiled, in accordance with the International Standards on Related Services (or refer to relevant national standards or practices) applicable to compilation engagements, the balance sheet of XYZ Company as of December 31, 19XX and the related statements of income and cash flows for the year then ended. Management is responsible for these financial statements. We have not audited or reviewed these financial statements and accordingly express no assurance thereon.

We draw attention to Note X to the financial statements because management has elected not to capitalize the leases on plant and machinery which is a departure from the identified financial reporting framework.

Date   ACCOUNTANT

Address

Certification Exam Question 4.7[68]

Financial statements of a non-public entity compiled without audit or review by an accountant, which are expected to be used by a third party, should be accompanied by a report stating that:

(A) The scope of the accountant's procedures has **not** been restricted in testing the financial information that is the representation of management.
(B) The accountant assessed the accounting principles used and significant estimates made by management.
(C) The accountant does **not** express an opinion or any other form of assurance on the financial statements.
(D) A compilation consists principally of inquiries of entity personnel and analytical procedures applied to financial data.

4.8 Summary

Auditor services are work that an audit firm performs for their clients. Except for consulting services, the work that auditors do is under the guidance of engagement standards set by the International Auditing and Assurance Standards Board (IAASB). All auditor services standards have as their basis the *IFAC Code of Ethics* and *International Standards on Quality Control* (ISQC).

Some engagement standards are based on "International Framework for Assurance Engagements" (assurance engagements), and others result from the "Related Services Framework" (related services engagements). Three sets of standards (ISAs, ISREs and ISAEs) share the assurance engagement framework and one standard set (ISRS) is based on the related services framework. ISAs, ISAEs, ISREs and ISRSs are collectively referred to as the IAASB's Engagement Standards.

The three sets of standard based on the assurance framework are ISA, ISRE and ISAE. International Standards on Auditing (ISA) 100 "Audits and Reviews of Historical Financial Information" describes the main concepts applicable to audit, review or special purpose engagements. International Standards on Assurance Engagements (ISAE) 3000R "Assurance Engagements on Subject Matter Other than Historical Financial Information" describes concepts applicable to assurance services whose subject matter is not related to historical financial information. The ISAE standards are divided into two parts: (1) ISAEs 3000–3399 which are topics that apply to all assurance engagements (2) ISAEs 3400–3699 which are subject specific standards, for example, standards relating to examination of prospective financial information.

Engagements covered by International Standards on Related Services ISRS are based on the "Related Services Framework" – a framework that is still in the development stage at the IAASB. Standards under this framework (ISRSs) are applied currently to two related services: agreed-upon procedures (ISRS 4400) and compilations (ISRS 4410).

Assurance engagements are performed by a professional accountant and are intended to enhance the credibility of information about a subject matter. The subject matter of an assurance is the topic about which the assurance is conducted. Assurance engagement means an engagement in which a practitioner (professional accountant or auditor) expresses a conclusion (in report form) that is designed to enhance the degree of confidence of users.

The International Framework for Assurance Engagements describes five elements that all assurance engagements exhibit: (1) a three party relationship involving a practitioner, a responsible party, and the intended users; (2) a subject matter; (3) suitable criteria; (4) evidence; and (5) an assurance report.

Assurance engagements always involve three separate parties: a practitioner, a responsible party and the intended users. The subject matter of an assurance is the topic about which the assurance is conducted. Subject matter could be financial statements, statistical information, non-financial performance indicators, systems and processes (e.g. internal controls, environment, IT systems) or behavior (e.g. corporate governance, compliance with regulation, human resource practices). Suitable criteria, which can either be established or specifically developed, are the benchmarks (standards, objectives, or set of rules) used to evaluate evidence or measure the subject matter of an assurance engagement. In general, the same evidence gathering procedures, quality control and planning process apply to assurance services as applies to audits. The auditor provides a written report containing a conclusion that conveys the assurance obtained as to whether the subject matter conforms, in all material respects, to the identified criteria.

Where reviews of financial statements differ most from audits is in the limited procedures performed (limited in inquiry of management and analytical procedures) and the review report. The objective of a review of financial statements is to enable an auditor to state whether anything has "come to the auditor's attention that causes the auditor to believe that the financial statements are not prepared, in all material respects, in accordance with an identified financial reporting framework (negative assurance)."

Sometimes the auditor may have a request for a financial statement audit based on historical financial information, but which is not based on the financial statements as a whole or on IFRS or the requisite national standard. An auditor may be called upon to do special purpose reports. Sometimes there are audits that give an opinion on compliance with legal agreements required of a company. Management or the board of directors may request a summarized financial statement. Small businesses, which generally are not required to comply with IFRS or a national standard required of publicly traded companies, may feel that an audit based on the cash basis, an income tax basis, or a basis required by regulatory agencies is needed.

The special purpose reports include:

1 Reports on Financial Statements Prepared in Accordance with a Comprehensive Basis of Accounting other than International Accounting Standards or National Standards such as:
   (a) That used by an entity to prepare its income tax return.
   (b) The cash receipts and disbursements basis of accounting.
   (c) The financial reporting provisions of a government regulatory agency.
2 Reports on a Component of Financial Statements.
3 Reports on Compliance with Contractual Agreements.
4 Reports on Summarized Financial Statements.

The International Standard on Assurance Engagements (ISAE) 3000R establishes basic principles and essential procedures for professional accountants in public practice for the performance of assurance engagements on subject matters other than historical financial information. Assurance engagements other than historical financial information have two main components: (1) topics that apply to all assurance engagements (ISAEs 3000–3399) and (2) subject specific standards (ISAEs 3400–3699). The only subject specific standard currently is for prospective financial statements.

Subject specific standards for assurance services on other than historical financial information may be thought of as falling into four subject matter groups:

1 subject matter related to prospective financial statements;
2 subject mater related to non-financial information (e.g. corporate governance, statistical, environmental);
3 subject matter related to systems and processes (e.g. corporate governance, environmental management systems, and internal control (such as that required under the Sarbanes-Oxley Act));
4 subject matter about behavior (corporate governance, compliance, and human resources practices).

Prospective financial information means financial information based on assumptions about events that may occur in the future. Prospective financial information can be in the form of a forecast, a projection, or a combination of both. A "forecast" is prospective financial information prepared on the basis of management's best-estimate assumptions about future events. A "projection" means prospective financial information prepared on the basis of hypothetical assumptions about future events and management actions which may or may not take place, such as a possible merger of two companies.

Standards that apply in all these subject matter areas are just being developed. The most influential standards in this specific subject matter area are the Global Reporting Initiative and the Sarbanes-Oxley internal control reporting standards. The Sarbanes-Oxley Act of 2002 (SOX) and PCAOB Audit Standard #2 require certification of internal control by the CEO and CFO of all companies that trade on the stock exchanges in the USA including companies headquartered outside the USA. SOX also requires that the company's auditor give an opinion on management's report on internal control. Most environmental and social reporting by large corporations follows the guidelines of the Global Reporting Initiative (GRI) Sustainability Reporting Guidelines. These Guidelines are for voluntary use by organizations for reporting on the economic, environmental, and social dimensions of their activities, products, and services.

An accounting-related service engagement is an examination of historical financial statements to develop a conclusion based on the criteria, but no audit opinion. The most common of the accounting-related services non-assurance report are agreed-upon procedures (ISRS 4400) and accounting compilation (ISRS 4410). An agreed-upon procedures engagement is an engagement in which the party engaging the professional accountant or the intended user determines the procedures to be performed and the professional accountant provides a report of factual findings as a result of undertaking those procedures. The objective of a compilation engagement is for the accountant to use accounting expertise, as opposed to auditing expertise, to collect, classify, and summarize financial information. This ordinarily entails reducing detailed data to a manageable and understandable form without a requirement to test the assertions underlying that information.

4.9 Answers to Certification Exam Questions

4.1 (A) The requirement is to explain the conceptual difference between the International Standards for Assurance Engagements (ISAE) and International Auditing Standards (ISA). Answer (A) is correct because assurance standards provide a framework for the attest function beyond historical financial information. Choice (B) is incorrect. The independence standard is almost the same for both assurances and audits. Choice (C) is incorrect. An attest engagement may be part of a larger engagement (such as a business acquisition study or a feasibility study) where "investment performance statistics" are prepared. Choice (D) is incorrect. Internal control standards apply to all assurances.

4.2 (C) The requirement is to determine what is stated in a review report. Answer (C) is correct because financial statements reviewed by an accountant should be accompanied by a report stating that a review consists principally of inquiries of company personnel and analytical procedures applied to financial data. Choice (A) is incorrect. While a review does provide only limited (negative) assurance, this statement is implicit in the accountant's review report. Choice (B) is incorrect. Examination of client information is part of an audit engagement, not a review engagement. Choice (D) is incorrect. While this statement is true, this is not stated in the accountant's review report.

4.3 (B) The requirement is to review the answers and find what statement or opinion is NOT in a special purpose engagement based on Cash Receipts and Disbursements (another comprehensive basis of accounting). Answer (B) is correct because the auditor's report on financial statements prepared in conformity with a comprehensive basis of accounting other than IFRS or a national standard would include a statement that the basis is a comprehensive basis of accounting other than IFRS or a national standard. It would **not** state that the cash receipts and disbursements basis is **not** a comprehensive basis of accounting. Choice (A) is incorrect. The auditor's report should include a paragraph that states the basis and refers to the note to the financial statements that describes the basis. Choice (C) is incorrect. The auditor's report should include a paragraph that expresses the auditor's opinion on whether the financial statements are presented fairly, in all material respects, in conformity with the basis described. Choice (D) is incorrect. The auditor's report should state that the audit was conducted in accordance with ISAs.

4.4 (D) The requirement is the provision that allows an auditor to express an opinion on accounts receivable (Component of Financial Statement engagement) even though the auditor has disclaimed an opinion on the financial statements taken as a whole. Answer (D) is correct because even though the auditor has disclaimed an opinion on the financial statements taken as a whole, the auditor may express an opinion on an entity's accounts receivable balance **only** if the special report on the accounts receivable is presented separately from the disclaimer of opinion on the financial statements. Choice (A) is incorrect. The report on the accounts receivable balance should **not** refer to the disclaimer of opinion on the financial statements. Choice (B) is incorrect. A special purpose engagement report expresses an opinion on the accounts receivable balance based on an audit of this specified element of the balance sheet. The report need not be restricted to internal use only. Choice (C) is incorrect. A special purpose engagement report expresses an opinion on the accounts receivable balance based on an audit of this specified element. The auditor need not also report on the current asset portion of the entity's balance sheet.

4.5 (D) The requirement is to state what is involved in an examination of a financial forecast (an examination of Prospective Financial Information). Answer (D) is correct because an examination of a financial forecast is a professional service that involves: evaluating the preparation of the prospective financial statements and the support underlying the assumptions. Choice (A) is incorrect. Compiling or assembling a financial forecast based on management's assumptions is a compilation rather than an examination. Choice (B) is incorrect. A financial forecast may be issued for general use. Choice (C) is incorrect. Generally the engagement is a one-time service and the accountant assumes no responsibility to update the report for events and circumstances occurring after the date of the report.

4.6 (A) The requirement is to find among the answers a component of an agreed-upon procedures engagement. Answer (A) is correct because the practitioner's report on agreed-upon procedures related to management's assertion about the entity's compliance with specified requirements is intended solely for the use of specified parties. Thus, the report should include a statement of limitations on the use of the report. Choice (B) is incorrect. The report is in the form of procedures and findings. Since the work performed is less in scope than an examination, the accountant disclaims any opinion. Choice (C) is incorrect. The auditor does not provide any negative assurance relative to assessment of control risk or to compliance with the specified requirements. Choice (D) is incorrect. The report contains a statement that the sufficiency of the procedures is solely the responsibility of the parties specifying the procedures and a disclaimer of responsibility on the part of the accountant.

4.7 (C) The requirement is to give the verbiage of a compilation report. Answer (C) is correct because financial statements compiled without audit or review by an accountant, which are expected to be used by a third party, should be accompanied by a report stating that the financial statements have not been audited or reviewed and, accordingly, the accountant does not express an opinion or any other form of assurance on them. Choice (A) is incorrect. The appropriate reference to the representation of management is that a compilation is "limited to presenting in the form of financial statements information that is the representation of management." Choice (B) is incorrect. This statement is part of the standard audit report; it is not applicable to an accountant's compilation report. Choice (D) is incorrect. It is a review, not a compilation that consists principally of inquiries of company personnel and analytical procedures applied to financial data.

4.10 Notes

1 "Consulting engagements employ a professional accountant's technical skills, education, observations, experiences, and knowledge of the consulting process. The consulting process is an analytical process that typically involves some combination of activities relating to objective-setting, fact-finding, definition of problems or opportunities, evaluation of alternatives, development of recommendations including actions, communication of results and sometimes implementation and follow-up. Where a report is issued, it is generally in a narrative (or "long-form") style. Generally the work performed is only for the use and benefit of the client. The nature and scope of work is determined by agreement between the professional accountant and the client. Any service that meets the definition of an assurance engagement is not a consulting engagement but an assurance engagement." Footnote 7 IAASB, 2003, *Proposed International Framework for Assurance Engagements*, International Auditing and Assurance Standards Board, International Federation of Accountants, New York, June 30.

2 Based on International Auditing and Assurance Standards Board (IAASB), 2003, *Interim Terms of Reference and Preface to the International Standards on Quality Control, Auditing, Assurance and Related Services*, "Appendix", International Federation of Accountants, New York.

3 IAASB, 2004, "Ethics" part of the 2004 IFAC *Handbook of International Auditing, Assurance, and Ethics Pronouncements*, International Federation of Accountants, New York.

4 International Audit and Assurance Standards Board (IAASB), 2003, *Proposed International Standard On Quality Control #1*, "Quality Control For Audit, Assurance And Related Services Practices Contents," International Federation of Accountants (IFAC), New York, May.

5 International Auditing and Assurance Standards Board (IAASB), 2003, *Interim Terms of Reference and Preface to the International Standards on Quality Control, Auditing, Assurance and Related Services*, International Federation of Accountants, New York, Approved July, Revised November.

6 The new ISA 100 is derived from two standards applicable in 2003: ISA 120 "Framework of International Standards on Auditing" and ISA 200 "Objective and General Principles Governing an Audit of Financial Statements," from 2004 *IFAC Handbook of International Auditing, Assurance, and Ethics Pronouncements*, International Federation of Accountants, New York.

7 In the 2003 edition of the *Handbook of International Auditing, Assurance, and Ethics Pronouncements*, ISA 910 was the review standard.

8 In the 2003 edition of the *Handbook of International Auditing, Assurance, and Ethics Pronouncements*, ISA 800 was the standard on special purpose audit engagements.

9 IAASB, 2004, *International Standard On Assurance Engagements 3000R* (ISAE 3000R), "Assurance Engagements On Subject Matters Other Than Audits Of Reviews Of Historical Financial Information," part of the 2004 IFAC *Handbook of International Auditing, Assurance, and Ethics Pronouncements*, International Auditing and Assurance Standards Board, International Federation of Accountants, New York.

10 In the 2003 edition of the *Handbook of International Auditing, Assurance, and Ethics Pronouncements*, ISA 810 was the standard on examination of prospective financial information.

11 Global Reporting Initiative, 2002, *Sustainability Reporting Guidelines*, GRI Secretariat, www.global reporting.org, Amsterdam, Netherlands.

12 In the 2003 IFAC *Handbook of International Auditing, Assurance, and Ethics Pronouncements*, agreed-upon procedures standards were known as ISA 920.

13 In the 2003 IFAC *Handbook of International Auditing, Assurance, and Ethics Pronouncements*, compilation standards were known as ISA 930.

14 IFAC, 2004, *Handbook of International Auditing, Assurance, and Ethics Pronouncements*, International Framework for Assurance Engagements, para. 11, International Auditing and Assurance Standards Board, International Federation of Accountants, New York.

15 Committee of Sponsoring Organizations of the Treadway Commission (COSO), 1992, *Internal Control – Integrated Framework*, American Institute of Certified Public Accountants, Jersey City, New Jersey.

16 IFAC, 2004, *Handbook of International Auditing, Assurance, and Ethics Pronouncements*, International Framework for Assurance Engagements, para. 27, International Auditing and Assurance Standards Board, International Federation of Accountants, New York.

17 IFAC, 2004, *Handbook of International Auditing, Assurance, and Ethics Pronouncements*, International Standard On Assurance Engagements 3000R (ISAE 3000R), "Assurance Engagements On Subject Matters Other Than Historical Financial Information," para. 49, International Auditing and Assurance Standards Board, International Federation of Accountants, New York, November.

18 In the 2003 edition of the *Handbook of International Auditing, Assurance, and Ethics Pronouncements*, ISA 910 was the review standard.

19 IFAC, 2004, *Handbook of International Auditing, Assurance, and Ethics Pronouncements*, International Standards on Review Engagements 2400, "Engagements to Review Financial Statements," para. 26, International Federation of Accountants, New York.

20 IFAC, 2004, *Handbook of International Auditing, Assurance, and Ethics Pronouncements*, International Standards on Review Engagements 2400, "Engagements to Review Financial Statements," Appendix 1, International Federation of Accountants, New York.

21 In the 2003 edition of the *Handbook of International Auditing, Assurance, and Ethics Pronouncements*, ISA 800 was the special purpose engagement standard.

22 Special purpose engagements are presently based on standards in the 2004 IFAC *Handbook Of International Auditing, Assurance, and Ethics Pronouncements*, International Standards on Auditing 800, "The Auditor's Report on Special Purpose Engagements," para. 1, International Federation of Accountants, New York.

23 IFAC, 2004, *Handbook of International Auditing, Assurance, and Ethics Pronouncements*, International Standards on Auditing 800, "The Auditor's Report on Special Purpose Engagements," para. 5, International Federation of Accountants, New York.

24 Illustrations 4.7 A and B are from 2004 IFAC, *Handbook of International Auditing, Assurance, and Ethics Pronouncements*, International Standards on Auditing 800, "The Auditor's Report on Special Purpose Engagements," Appendix 1, International Federation of Accountants, New York.

25 Adapted and reprinted with permission from AICPA. Copyright © 2000 & 1985 by American Institute of Certified Public Accountants.

26 Illustration 4.8 is from 2004 IFAC, *Handbook of International Auditing, Assurance, and Ethics Pronouncements*, International Standards on Auditing 800, "The Auditor's Report on Special Purpose Engagements," Appendix 2, International Federation of Accountants, New York.

27 Illustration 4.9 is from 2004 IFAC, *Handbook of International Auditing, Assurance, and Ethics Pronouncements*, International Standards on Auditing 800, "The Auditor's Report on Special Purpose Engagements," Appendix 3, International Federation of Accountants, New York.

28 Illustration 4.10 is from 2004 IFAC, *Handbook of International Auditing, Assurance, and Ethics Pronouncements*, International Standards on Auditing 800, "The Auditor's Report on Special Purpose Engagements," Appendix 4, International Federation of Accountants, New York.

29 Prospective financial information is presently based on standards in 2004 IFAC, *Handbook of International Auditing, Assurance, and Ethics Pronouncements*, International Standards on Auditing

810, "Examination of Prospective Financial Information," International Federation of Accountants, New York.

30 Public Company Accounting Oversight Board (PCAOB), 2003, *PCAOB Release No. 2003-017*, "Proposed Auditing Standard – An Audit Of Internal Control Over Financial Reporting Performed In Conjunction With An Audit Of Financial Statements," PCAOB, Washington, DC, October 7.

31 Global Reporting Initiative, 2002, *Sustainability Reporting Guidelines*, GRI Secretariat, www.global reporting.org, Amsterdam, Netherlands.

32 Social Accountability 8000 has been developed under the auspices of the Council on Economic Priorities Accreditation Agency (CEPAA) to promote socially responsible production. The CEPAA developed SA 8000 in 1998 in accordance with 12 International Labor Organization conventions and UN human rights treaties. CEPAA accredits independent audit firms to monitor conformity to the SA 8000 Standard (www.cepaa.org).

33 International Labor Organization, C138, Minimum Age Convention, 1973, Art. 2 paragraph 4.

34 WBCSD is a coalition of some 140 international companies united by a shared commitment to sustainable development, i.e. environmental protection, social equity and economic growth (www.wbcsd.ch).

35 Eco-Management and Audit Scheme was adopted by the European Council on June 29, 1993 and allows voluntary participation by companies in the industrial sector. The aim of the scheme is to promote continuous environmental performance improvements of industrial activities by committing sites to evaluate and improve their own environmental performance (www.europe.eu.int/ comm/environment/emas/intro_en.htm.

36 ISO 14001, published in 1996, offers a common, harmonized approach for organizations to achieve and demonstrate sound environmental performance. The main objective of ISO 14001 is to help organizations manage the environmental aspects and impacts of their operations while working toward continual improvement.

37 IFAC, 2004, *Handbook of International Auditing, Assurance, and Ethics Pronouncements*, International Standards on Assurance Engagements 3400 (ISAE 3400), "The Examination of Prospective Financial Information," para. 27, International Federation of Accountants, New York.

38 Illustration 4.7 is from 2004 IFAC, *Handbook of International Auditing, Assurance, and Ethics Pronouncements*, International Standards on Assurance Engagements 3400 (ISAE 3400), "The Examination of Prospective Financial Information," paras. 29 and 30, International Federation of Accountants. New York.

39 Adapted and reprinted with permission from AICPA. Copyright © 2000 & 1985 by American Institute of Certified Public Accountants.

40 US Securities and Exchange Commission (SEC), 2003, Rel. No. 33-8238, Section II. A (1), *Final Rule: Management's Reports on Internal Control Over Financial Reporting and Certification of Disclosure in Exchange Act Periodic Reports*, SEC, June 5.

41 US Securities and Exchange Commission (SEC), 2003, *Final Rule: Management's Reports on Internal Control Over Financial Reporting and Certification of Disclosure in Exchange Act Periodic Reports*, Rel. No. 33-8238, Section II. B (3), SEC, June 5.

42 Management must state whether or not the company's internal control over financial reporting is effective. A negative assurance statement indicating that nothing has come to management's attention to suggest that the company's internal control over financial reporting is not effective will not be acceptable.

43 For the purposes of these standards, a "material weakness" is defined the same as in US GAAS Statement on Auditing Standards No. 60 (codified in Codification of Statements on Auditing Standards AU §325) as a reportable condition in which the design or operation of one or more of the internal control components does not reduce to a relatively low level the risk that misstatements caused by errors or fraud in amounts that would be material in relation to the financial statements being audited may occur and not be detected within a timely period by employees in the normal course of performing their assigned functions.

44 Final rules also require a company to file, as part of the company's annual report, the attestation report of the registered public accounting firm that audited the company's financial statements.

45 Public Company Accounting Oversight Board (PCAOB), 2004, *PCAOB Release No. 2004-001*, "Auditing Standard #2 – An Audit Of Internal Control Over Financial Reporting Performed In Conjunction With An Audit Of Financial Statements," PCAOB, Washington, DC, March 9.

46 See Sections 103(a)(2)(A)(iii)(I), (II) and (III) of the Sarbanes-Oxley Act.

47 PCAOB, 2003, *PCAOB Release No. 2003-017*, "Proposed Auditing Standard – An Audit of Internal Control over Financial Reporting Performed in Conjunction with an Audit of Financial Statements", p. A-65 – standard, example A-1, PCAOB, Washington DC, October 7.

48 Kolk, A., 2000, "Verificatie van milieuverslagen (Verification of Environmental Reports)," *Maandblad voor Accountancy en Bedrijfseconomie*, pp. 363–375, September.

49 Extract from the Royal Dutch Shell Report, 2002, *Environment, Economic and Social Performance Report*. Used with permission from Shell International BV and PricewaterhouseCoopers LLP.

50 Global Reporting Initiative, 2002, *Sustainability Reporting Guidelines*, GRI Secretariat, www.global reporting.org, Amsterdam, Netherlands.

51 GRI uses the term "sustainability reporting" synonymously with citizenship reporting, social reporting, triple-bottom line reporting and other terms that encompass the economic, environmental, and social aspects of an organization's performance.

52 Extract from the Royal Dutch Shell Report, 2002, *Environment, Economic and Social Performance Report*. Used with permission from Shell International BV and PricewaterhouseCoopers LLP.

53 IFAC, 2004, *Handbook of International Auditing, Assurance, and Ethics Pronouncements*, International Framework for Assurance Engagements, International Auditing and Assurance Standards Board, International Federation of Accountants, New York.

54 In the 2003 edition of the *Handbook of International Auditing, Assurance, and Ethics Pronouncements* ISA 930 was the standard on compilations.

55 In the 2003 edition of the *Handbook of International Auditing, Assurance, and Ethics Pronouncements* ISA 920 was the standard on agreed-upon procedures.

56 According to Paragraph 11 of the Assurance Framework: An assurance engagement performed by a practitioner must exhibit all of the following elements, (1) A three party relationship involving: a practitioner, a responsible party; and the intended users; (2) A subject matter; (3) Suitable criteria; (4) Evidence; and (5) An assurance report.

57 Based on 2004 IFAC, *Handbook of International Auditing, Assurance, and Ethics Pronouncements*, International Standards on Related Services 4400 (ISRS 4400), "Engagements To Perform Agreed-Upon Procedures Regarding Financial Information", International Federation of Accountants, New York.

58 However, if, in the judgment of the professional accountant, the procedures agreed to be performed are appropriate to support the expression of a conclusion that provides a level of assurance on the subject matter, then that engagement becomes an assurance engagement governed by the International Standards on Assurance Engagements and the Assurance Framework.

59 IFAC, 2004, *Handbook of International Auditing, Assurance, and Ethics Pronouncements*, International Standards on Related Services 4400 (ISRS 4400), "Engagements To Perform Agreed-Upon Procedures Regarding Financial Information", para. 9, International Federation of Accountants, New York.

60 IFAC, 2004, *Handbook of International Auditing, Assurance, and Ethics Pronouncements*, International Standards on Related Services 4400 (ISRS 4400), "Engagements To Perform Agreed-Upon Procedures Regarding Financial Information", para. 18, International Federation of Accountants, New York.

61 IFAC, 2004, *Handbook of International Auditing, Assurance, and Ethics Pronouncements*, International Standards on Related Services 4400 (ISRS 4400), "Engagements To Perform Agreed-Upon Procedures Regarding Financial Information", para. 7, International Federation of Accountants, New York.

62 Adapted and reprinted with permission from AICPA. Copyright © 2000 & 1985 by American Institute of Certified Public Accountants.

63 IFAC, 2003, *Handbook of International Auditing, Assurance, and Ethics Pronouncements*, International Standards on Auditing 920, "Engagements To Perform Agreed-Upon Procedures", Appendix 2, International Federation of Accountants, New York.

64 Based on 2004 IFAC, *Handbook of International Auditing, Assurance, and Ethics Pronouncements*, International Standards on Related Services 4410 (ISRS 4410), "Engagements To Compile Financial Statements," International Federation of Accountants, New York.

65 IFAC, 2004, *Handbook of International Auditing, Assurance, and Ethics Pronouncements*, International Standards on Related Services 4410 (ISRS 4410), "Engagements To Compile Financial Statements," para. 7, International Federation of Accountants, New York.

66 IFAC, 2004, *Handbook of International Auditing, Assurance, and Ethics Pronouncements*, International Standards on Related Services 4410 (ISRS 4410), "Engagements To Compile Financial Statements", para. 18, International Federation of Accountants, New York.

67 IFAC, 2003, *Handbook of International Auditing, Assurance, and Ethics Pronouncements*, International Standards on Auditing 930, "Engagements To Compile Financial Statements", Appendix 2, International Federation of Accountants, New York.

68 Adapted and reprinted with permission from AICPA. Copyright © 2000 & 1985 by American Institute of Certified Public Accountants.

4.11 Questions, Exercises and Cases

QUESTIONS

4.2 International Framework for Auditor Services

4.1 What are audit related services? List the major categories (except for consulting) of auditor's services.

4.2 Name IAASB's two engagement frameworks and the audit and practice standards that apply to these two frameworks.

4.3 Elements of an Assurance Engagement

4.3 Define subject matter. Give some examples of common subject matter in assurance and related service engagements.

4.4 What is an assurance engagement? Name the five elements exhibited by all assurance engagements.

4.4 General Considerations in An Assurance Engagement

4.5 What are the basic elements required to be included in the assurance report according to International Standards on Assurance Engagements 2000?

4.6 Are the criteria given in the assurance report always based on established criteria? Explain.

4.5 Audits and Reviews of Historical Financial Information

4.7 What are the assurance engagements that have as their subject matter historical financial information? Discuss the differences between these assurance engagements.

4.8 Discuss the three basic opinions an auditor can have on a review engagement.

4.6 Assurance Engagements Other than Historical Financial Information

4.9 Describe what is meant by "prospective financial information." Give some examples of when a prospective financial information report might be used.

4.10 What must auditors cover in their internal control report under the PCAOB standards?

4.7 Related Services

4.11 How does the related services framework differ from the assurance framework?

4.12 In an agreed-upon procedures engagement what matters generally have to be agreed between auditor and management?

PROBLEMS AND EXERCISES

4.2 International Framework for Auditor Services

4.13 Summarize in your own words Illustration 4.1. The Structure of IAASB's Technical Pronouncements.

4.14 Halmtorvet, a Copenhagen, Denmark, company that manufactures security devices, has contacted Christian Jespersen, Statautoriseret Revisor, to submit a proposal to do a financial statement audit. Halmtorvet was a bit taken aback when they saw the cost of the financial statement audit, even though the fees were about average for an audit of a company Halmtorvet's size. Halmtorvet's board of directors determined that the company could not afford to pay that price.

Required:

A. Discuss the alternatives to having a financial statement audit.
B. What should Halmtorvet consider when choosing the assurance service?

4.3 Elements of an Assurance Engagement

4.15 Kolitar Corporation offers a unique service to telecommunication companies in South America. For a fee they will review the telecom's telephone transactions for calls from outside their country that might originate illegally from inside their country.

Required:

Use the five elements exhibited by all assurance engagements to prove that Kolitar's work is an assurance engagement.

4.4 General Considerations in An Assurance Engagement

4.16 Discuss the differences between assurance conclusions expressed in the positive (reasonable assurance) form, versus the negative (limited assurance) form. Give examples of assurance engagements that generally use the positive form; and then examples that use the negative form.

4.5 Audits and Reviews of Historical Financial Information

4.17 List the four special purpose engagements and give some examples of each.

4.18 Using Illustrations 4.7 through 4.10, compare Reports on Financial Statements Prepared in Accordance with a Comprehensive Basis of Accounting other than International Accounting Standards or National Standards, Reports on a Component of Financial Statements, Reports on Compliance with Contractual Agreements, and Reports on Summarized Financial Statements:

A. Using the first (introductory) paragraph as the basis of comparison.
B. Using the second (scope) paragraph as the basis of comparison.
C. Using the third (opinion) paragraph as the basis of comparison.

4.6 Assurance Engagements Other than Historical Financial Information

4.19 Haruspex is a new consulting company. They specialize in analysis of the market and process of producing sellable products from industrial waste. They have asked Sophia Coronis, SOL, to prepare an examination of prospective financial information report of the prospective company financial statements for the first two years. This will be presented to Apollo Bank as part of a loan request.

Required:

A. What type of report would Coronis prepare – forecast or projection?
B. Draft the report for Apollo Bank.

4.20 Diamond Jousts, a UK Limited Company, is traded on the American Stock Exchange as American Depository Receipts (ADRs). They hire Lancelot, Elaine, and Guinevere, Chartered Accountants, to prepare an internal control report to meet Sarbanes-Oxley requirements.

Required:

A. What should the report of management contain?
B. Draft an unqualified opinion on management's assessment of the effectiveness of internal control for the CA firm.

4.7 Related Services

4.21 Da Xing Fan, CPA, is engaged by the management of Ky-lin, a non-public company, to review the company's financial statements for the year ended February 28, 20XX.

Required:

A. Discuss the content of the report on a review of financial statements.

B. Summarize Fan's responsibilities if she finds the financial statements contain a material departure from IFRS.

4.22 The following list describes seven situations certified accountants may encounter, or contentions they may have to deal with, in their association with and preparation of *unaudited* financial statements. Briefly discuss the extent of the certified accountant's responsibilities and, if appropriate, the actions they should take to minimize any misunderstandings. Mark your answers to correspond to the letters in the following list.

A. Armando Almonza, CP, was engaged by telephone to perform accounting work including the compilation of financial statements. The client believes that the Almonza has been engaged to audit the financial statements and examine the records accordingly.

B. A group of investors who own a farm that is managed by an independent agent engage An Nguyen, CPA to compile quarterly unaudited financial statements for them. Nguyen prepares the financial statements from information given to her by the independent agent. Subsequently, the investors find the statements were inaccurate because their independent agent was embezzling funds. They refuse to pay the Nguyen's fees and blame her for allowing the situation to go undetected, contending that the CPAs should not have relied on representations from the independent agent.

C. In comparing the trial balance with the general ledger, Thynie Pukprayura, CPA, finds an account labeled Audit Fees in which the client has accumulated the his CPA firm's quarterly billings for accounting services including the compilation of quarterly unaudited financial statements.

D. Unaudited financial statements for a public company were accompanied by the following letter of transmittal from Franz Ravel, Expert Comptable:

> We are enclosing your company's balance sheet as of June 30, 20X1, and the related statements of income and retained earnings and cash flows for the six months then ended to which we have performed certain auditing procedures.

E. To determine appropriate account classification, Jose Torres, CP Titulado, examined a number of the client's invoices. He noted in his working papers that some invoices were missing, but did nothing further because it was felt that the invoices did not affect the unaudited financial statements he was compiling. When the client subsequently discovered that invoices were missing, he contended that the Torres should not have ignored the missing invoices when compiling the financial statements and had a responsibility to at least inform him that they were missing.

F. Omar El Qasaria, CA compiled a draft of unaudited financial statements from the client's records. While reviewing this draft with their client, El Qasaria learned that the land and building were recorded at appraisal value.

G. Tomoko Nakagawa, CPA, is engaged to compile the financial statements of a non-public company. During the engagement, Nakagawa learns of several items for which IFRS would require adjustments of the statements and note disclosure. The controller agrees to make the recommended adjustments to the statements, but says that she is not going to add the notes because the statements are unaudited.

CASE

4.23 British Airways, ENI, ING, Novartis, Norsk Hydro, Shell, Statoil, Volkswagen, Body Shop, and Novo Nordisk are companies that produce annual sustainability verification statements.

Required:
A. Chose two of the companies listed above.
B. Download a copy of their sustainability verification statements from their websites.
C. Compare the two reports on the basis of GRI guidelines:
1. Vision and Strategy
2. Profile
3. Governance Structure and Management Systems
4. GRI Content Index
5. Performance Indicators.

Chapter 5

CLIENT ACCEPTANCE

5.1 Learning Objectives

After studying this chapter, you should be able to:

1 Explain what is meant by client acceptance.

2 Describe the seven primary procedures involved in the client acceptance process.

3 Understand the main reasons for obtaining an understanding of client's business and industry.

4 Know the sources of client information and the methods for gathering the information.

5 Discuss the ethical and competency requirements of the audit team.

6 Know what is required in using the work of another auditor.

7 Understand the auditor's responsibility in using the work of an expert.

8 Describe the procedures for communicating with an existing (predecessor) auditor.

9 Know the contents of a client audit engagement proposal.

10 Express the differences between items covered in an audit engagement proposal to existing clients and one for new clients.

11 Explain on what basis audit fees are negotiated.

12 Understand what an audit engagement letter includes and why its contents are important.

13 Describe the differences between items covered in an audit engagement proposal to existing clients and one for new clients.

5.2 Client Acceptance: the First Step on the Journey to an Opinion

The client acceptance phase of the audit has two objectives:

1 examination of the proposed client to determine if there is any reason to reject the engagement (acceptance of the client);
2 convincing the client to hire the auditor (acceptance by the client).

The procedures to acceptance of the client are: acquiring knowledge of the client's business; examination the audit firm's ethical requirements and technical competence; possible use of other professionals (including outside specialist) in the audit; communication with the **predecessor auditor**; preparation of client proposal; assignment of staff and the submission of the **terms of the engagement** in the form of an **audit engagement letter**. See Illustration 5.1.

ILLUSTRATION 5.1

Standard Audit Process Model – Phase I Client Acceptance

Objective	Determine both acceptance of a client and acceptance by a client. Decide on acquiring a new client or continuation of relationship with an existing one and the type and amount of staff required.
Procedures	1 Evaluate the client's background and reasons for the audit [sec. 5.3]. 2 Determine whether the auditor is able to meet the ethical requirements regarding the client [sec. 5.4]. 3 Determine need for other professionals [sec. 5.5]. 4 Communicate with predecessor auditor [sec. 5.6]. 5 Prepare client proposal [sec. 5.7]. 6 Select staff to perform the audit. 7 Obtain an engagement letter [sec. 5.8].

An auditor must exercise care in deciding which clients are acceptable. An accounting firm's legal and professional responsibilities are such that clients who lack integrity can cause serious and expensive problems. Some auditing firms refuse to accept clients in certain high-risk industries. For example, when the USA and Northern Europe in the 1990s many large auditing firms were very careful when accepting audit engagements of financial institutions after the legal judgments and fines resulting from audits of Lincoln Savings, Standard Charter Bank, and International Bank of Credit and Commerce (BCCI). At the beginning of the twenty-first century, there were great problems in the energy business (Enron, Dynergy, Pacific Gas and Electric, the State of California), the telecommunications industry (WorldCom, Global Crossing, Qwest), and health care (Health South, ImClone), and even in old-line industries such as retailing (K-mart, Ahold) and food products (Parmalat).

■ Audit Clients

The client – audit firm relationship is **not** a one-way street where the audit firm evaluates the client and then, judging the client "acceptable,", sends out an engagement letter closing the deal. The market for audit services is competitive and, just like in any other business, there are highly desirable clients with whom any audit firm would like to have an audit relationship. Although not always the case, audit firms prepare and submit **engagement proposals** to many of their (potential) clients, especially the large ones.

■ Steps in the Client Acceptance Process

The next section in this chapter discusses the importance of obtaining a preliminary understanding of the client, in order to both evaluate the client's background and the risks associated with accepting the engagement. There must also be an understanding of the auditors' relationship to the client to enable the auditor to consider if the ethical and professional requirements (**independence**, competence, etc.) typical to the specific engagement can be met. That is the second step in the client acceptance process.

The balance of the chapter concerns acceptance by the client (called **responsible party** in assurance services terms). Here we discuss competition and audit market; cost considerations; and quality of audit services. The audit firm must write and present to the client an engagement proposal (some auditors consider this a beauty contest). The chapter also discusses the components of a client engagement proposal for existing and new clients; and briefly discusses the International Standard Organization (ISO) quality control standard 9000 and how that applies to an auditing firm and its engagement services.

5.3 Evaluate the Client's Background

The auditor should obtain a knowledge of the client's business that is sufficient to enable him to identify and understand the events, transactions, and practices that may have a significant effect on the financial statements or on the **audit report**.[1] Main reasons for obtaining this understanding are (1) to evaluate the engagement risks associated with accepting the specific engagement and (2) to help the auditor in determining whether all professional and ethical requirements (including independence, competence, etc.) regarding this client can be met.

Auditors do not just obtain knowledge of the client preliminary to the engagement, during the client acceptance phase (Phase I of the audit process model). Once the engagement has been accepted, auditors will do a more extensive search for knowledge of the client, its business and industry in the planning phase (Phase II of the model – see Chapter 6 Understanding the Entity, Risk Assessment and Materiality).

Auditors may do a preliminary examination of both new and existing clients by visiting their premises, reviewing annual reports, having discussions with client's management and staff, and accessing public news and public information databases, usually via the internet. If the client is an existing one, prior years' working papers should be reviewed.

If the client is new, the auditor should consult prior auditors and increase the preliminary information search. (See Illustration 5.2.)

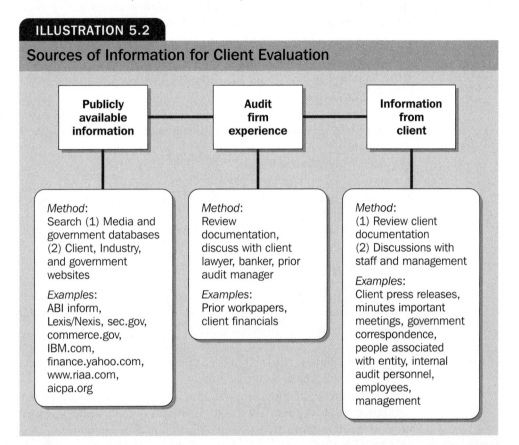

ILLUSTRATION 5.2

Sources of Information for Client Evaluation

Publicly available information	**Audit firm experience**	**Information from client**
Method: Search (1) Media and government databases (2) Client, Industry, and government websites	*Method*: Review documentation, discuss with client lawyer, banker, prior audit manager	*Method*: (1) Review client documentation (2) Discussions with staff and management
Examples: ABI inform, Lexis/Nexis, sec.gov, commerce.gov, IBM.com, finance.yahoo.com, www.riaa.com, aicpa.org	*Examples*: Prior workpapers, client financials	*Examples*: Client press releases, minutes important meetings, government correspondence, people associated with entity, internal audit personnel, employees, management

Certification Exam Question 5.1[2]

Which of the following factors would be most likely to cause a professional auditor in public practice to decline a new audit engagement?

(A) The prospective client has already completed its physical inventory count.
(B) The auditor lacks an understanding of the prospective client's operations and industry.
(C) The auditor is unable to review the predecessor auditor's working papers.
(D) The prospective client is unwilling to make all financial records available to the auditor.

Auditors get their information about an audit client from three basic sources: their experience with the client, publicly available information, and from the client themselves. Methods used to assess the information varies from database search for public information to discussions with staff and management at the client entity. (See Illustration 5.2.)

■ Topics of Discussion

Discussions with client's management and staff is important to evaluate **governance**, **internal controls** and possible risks. These discussions might include such subjects as:

- changes in management, organizational structure, and activities of the client;
- current government regulations affecting the client;
- current business developments affecting the client such as social, technical and economic factors;
- current or impending financial difficulties or accounting problems;
- susceptibility of the entity's financial statements to material misstatement due to error or fraud;
- existence of **related parties**;
- new or closed premises and plant facilities;
- recent or impending changes in technology, types of products or services and production or distribution methods;
- changes in the accounting system and the system of internal control.

■ New Client Investigation

Before accepting a new client an audit firm will do a thorough investigation to determine if the client is acceptable and if the auditor can meet the ethical requirements of independence, specific competence, etc.

Other sources of information include interviews with local lawyers, other CPAs, banks and other businesses, although many of them, depending on local circumstances, might be bound by obligations of confidentiality. Sometimes the auditor may hire a professional investigator or use its forensic accounting department to obtain information about the reputation and background of the key members of management. If there has not been a previous auditor, more extensive investigation may be undertaken.

■ Continuing Clients

Many auditing firms evaluate existing clients every year. In addition to the research discussed above, the auditor will consider any previous conflicts over scope of the audit, type of opinion and fees, pending litigation between the audit firm and client, and management integrity. (See Illustration 5.3.) These three factors strongly influence whether the relationship will continue. For continuing engagements, the auditor would update and re-evaluate information gathered from the prior years' working papers. The auditor should also perform procedures designed to identify significant changes that have taken place since the last audit.

The auditor may also choose not to continue conducting audits for a client because he feels excessive risk is involved. For example, there may be regulatory conflict between a governmental agency and a client which could result in financial failure of the client and perhaps ultimately lawsuits against the auditor. It may be that the auditor feels that the industry (such as financial services) offers more risk than is acceptable to the specific auditor.

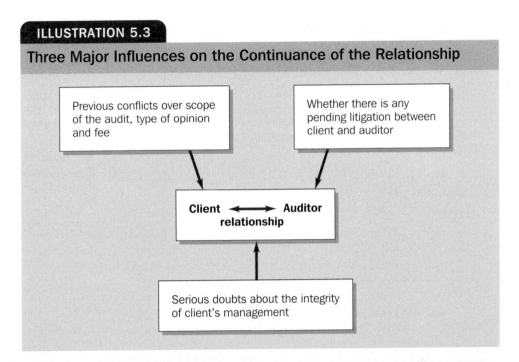

ILLUSTRATION 5.3

Three Major Influences on the Continuance of the Relationship

Previous conflicts over scope of the audit, type of opinion and fee

Whether there is any pending litigation between client and auditor

Client ←——→ Auditor relationship

Serious doubts about the integrity of client's management

Concept and a Company 5.1

Resona, the Auditor, and Japan's Banking Industry

Concept   An auditor must consider company and industry background before accepting an audit client.

Story   "Auditors shouldn't be allowed to act like God," said Hideyuki Aizawa, a senior member of Japan's major political party the LDP. "Resona should be the first and last time this happens." Mr. Aizawa's comments came in reaction to the government's decision to inject Y2,000 billion ($17 billion, £10.4 billion) into Resona after auditors found that Japan's fifth largest bank was badly undercapitalized. (Pilling 2003)

The Resona filing was the first-ever test of emergency assistance under the Deposit Insurance Law. Resona had already received around Y1,000bn ($8.5bn) from the government in two previous rounds of fund injections. (*Nikkei Weekly* 2003)

Auditor Says No

Shin Nihon, one of Japan's Big Four accounting firms, in effect forced Resona to seek government help by refusing to accept the bank's estimate of how much deferred tax assets it should be allowed to include as capital. This was after co-auditor Asahi & Co refused to sign off on the banks accounts. Shin Nihon's move stunned the Japanese business community, which had been accustomed to more lenient treatment from auditors.

Troubles at Resona

Resona Bank was created after the integration of Daiwa Bank and Asahi Bank, and began operating March 3, 2003. Neither bank wanted to merge, but both were forced to do so by

▶

Resona, the Auditor, and Japan's Banking Industry (continued)

the combined efforts of the Ministry of Finance and the Financial Services Agency, which were overseeing the consolidation of Japan's banking industry from 13 large lenders to five mega-lenders. (Ibison 2003)

Resona admitted that its capital-adequacy ratio (i.e. its capital divided by its assets, weighted by risk) had fallen to around 2 percent, half the required minimum for domestic banks that do not have international operations.

Resona's Tier 1 capital comprised 70 percent deferred tax assets (DTAs) according to Moody's Investors Service, the credit rating company. This compares with about 40 percent at Japan's four other largest banks – Mizuho, SMFG, MTFG and UFJ – and is enormous compared with US regulations, which limit banks to using DTAs of just 10 percent of their capital. (Ibison 2003)

Deferred tax assets are generated through the losses from taxable bad-loan write-offs by entities such as banks. The losses can be set off against future taxable income. Since the tax burden on the bank is effectively reduced, the deferred amount is counted toward the entity's shareholders' equity.

Combined with the dual pressures of a more strict calculation of its non-performing loans and exposure to a declining stock market, the circumstances for Resona's bailout were created. Their solvency was also affected by participation in government development schemes.

Japan's Banking Industry in Early 2004

Resona is an example of the problems that are occurring in the Japanese banking industry. Other major banks staved off a crisis in March 2003 by procuring more than 2 trillion yen in capital from the government, but by year end 2003, they still needed to bolster their capital bases.

At that time Japan's seven biggest banks held around Y6,510 billion ($60.5 billion) as deferred tax assets. Mizuho Holdings held over Y1,500 billion in net deferred tax assets – accounting for over 41 percent of its tier 1 capital – even though it reduced them by 22 percent in March and December 2003. Bank of Mitsubishi-Tokyo Group and Sumitomo Trust Bank have made similar-sized efforts to reduce their deferred tax assets, which at the beginning of 2004 accounted for 30 percent and 26 percent of their tier 1 capital, respectively. Mitsui-Sumitomo Banking Group, Mitsui Trust and UFJ Holdings made virtually no effort to reduce their deferred tax asset levels, cutting them by just single-digit percentage amounts. The most worrying in early 2004 was Mitsui Trust, with deferred tax assets accounting for 77 percent of its capital. (Accountant 2003)

Discussion Questions	■ If Shin Nihon will not audit Resona in 2004, what concerns would a replacement auditor have?
	■ What kind of industry risks would be encountered by audit firms wishing to audit a Japanese bank in 2004?

References	*The Accountant*, 2003, "Japan's top seven banks slash deferred tax assets by 18 percent," December 31.
	Ibison, D., 2003, "Unholy Japanese alliance ends in tears," *Financial Times*, May 19, p. 23.
	Nikkei Weekly, 2003, "Resona accepts 2 trillion yen bailout," Nihon Keizai Shimbun, May 19.
	Pilling, D., 2003, "Japanese bailout prompts political backlash,'. *Financial Times*, May 22.

5.4 Ability to Meet Ethical and Specific Competence Requirements

Based on the evaluation obtained regarding the background of the client, the auditor should determine whether all ethical requirements, as discussed in Chapter 3, Ethics for Professional Accountants can be met with regard to the specific engagement. Probably the most important procedure in this step of the engagement acceptance process is verification of the auditor's independence. Given the facts and circumstances identified in the client evaluation phase, a determination is made whether the auditor and the audit team collectively possess the specific competence required to deal with the issues that the auditor is likely to encounter in the audit.

This audit team evaluation is also important for step six in the client acceptance process – selecting staff to perform the audit.

Concept and a Company 5.2

New Client Acceptance – Penn State Bank

Concept	Evaluation of a client and the audit firm for client acceptance.
Story	In late November 1981, without prior warning, B.P "Beep" Jennings, CEO of Penn Square Bank notified Harold Russell, managing partner of audit firm Arthur Young Oklahoma City, that Peat Marwick would be the new auditor for the bank's 1981 financial statements. For the years ending December 31, 1976, through December 31, 1979, Penn received unqualified (clean) opinions from Arthur Young (predecessor of Ernst & Young). In 1980, Arthur Young issued a qualified opinion on Penn Square's financial statements stating that the auditors were unable to satisfy themselves "as to the adequacy of the reserve for possible loan losses."

Penn Square Bank – Loans to Wildcatters

Penn Square Bank, an Oklahoma City, USA, bank named after a shopping mall, served small business and residents of the surrounding community until 1974 when the bank was acquired by Jennings. From that date onward, the bank expanded its deposit base by offering interest rate premiums on "jumbo" bank certificates of deposit that carried interest rates 25 to 150 basis points above prevailing market rates.

The money deposited was loaned to the highest risk oil and gas speculators ("wildcatters"). Because of the rapid growth in their loan portfolio that doubled the bank's assets every two years from 1976 to 1982, they joint-ventured the loans with major metropolitan banks around the country. Penn Square performed all necessary administrative functions for these loans, including obtaining appraisals and engineering estimates of oil reserves.

Oil and gas prices worldwide plummeted in 1980. Many of the Penn Square-backed exploration ventures were aimed at recovering oil and gas from the deepest reservoirs, which, because of large exploration costs, were economically feasible when the price of crude oil dropped.

Also in 1980, the bank's large profits and rapidly increasing high-risk loan volume caused an investigation by the US Office of the Comptroller of the Currency (OCC) federal bank examiners. The investigation uncovered numerous violations of banking laws by Penn

▶

Square, including insufficient liquidity, inadequate capital, and poor loan documentation. In late 1980, the OCC forced the bank's directors to sign an "administrative agreement" that required them to take remedial measures to correct these problems. (Knapp 2001)

Qualified Opinion – Management Not Pleased

Russell reported (US Congress 1982) that there were loan considerations that led to the qualification of the 1980 audit opinion. The bank's loan documentation practices had deteriorated between 1979 and 1980. Many loans did not have current engineering reports documenting oil reserves. Other loans had engineering reports that did not include an opinion of the engineer or did not list the assumptions used in estimating the reserves. When Russell discussed these problems with client management they were "not pleased."

Peat Marwick Steps In

Peat Marwick officials testified (US Congress 1982) that their firm made the standard inquiries required of predecessor auditor Arthur Young. Arthur Young responded to these inquiries by stating that its relationship with Penn Square Bank had been "free of significant problems." However, Arthur Young did bring to Peat Marwick's attention the qualified opinion that it had issued on Penn Square's 1980 financial statements.

Jim Blanton, the managing partner of Peat Marwick's Oklahoma City office, told the US Congress committee (US Congress 1982) that several members of his firm were well-acquainted with Penn Square's top executives. Peat Marwick disclosed that several Oklahoma City partners had previously obtained more than $2 million in loans and a $1 million line of credit from Penn Square. To resolve a possible independence problem an agreement reached between the two parties required Penn Square to "fully participate out" (sell) the loans and the line of credit to other banks.

The results of the Peat Marwick's 1981 Penn Square audit were an unqualified (clean) opinion. On July 5,1982, bank examiners from the Federal Deposit Insurance Corporation (FDIC) locked the doors of the Penn Square Bank. The more than $2 billion in losses suffered by Penn Square, its affiliated banks, uninsured depositors, and the FDIC insurance fund made this bank failure the most costly in US history at the time.

Discussion Questions	■ When Penn Square Bank replaced Arthur Young in late 1980, what concerns should have been apparent to any proposed new auditor? ■ What independence issues were at stake for the new auditor Peat Marwick?

References	Knapp, M., 2001, "Penn State Bank," *Contemporary Auditing Real Issues & Cases*, South Western College Publishing, Cincinnati, Ohio. US Congress, 1982, House Committee on Banking, Finance and Urban Affairs, *Penn Square Bank Failure, Part 1*, US Government Printing Office, Washington, DC.

■ Independence

The auditor will ensure that the members of the auditor team as well as the entire audit firm meet the relevant independence requirements (see Chapter 3 Ethics for Professional Accountants). This will require procedures to check personal financial investments of partners and employees and the business relationships with the potential audit client.

He should review the non-audit services his audit firm are providing or have recently been providing to this potential client.

IFAC's *Code of Ethics for Professional Accountants* in a commentary on fees[3] suggests independence is jeopardized if fees due from a client for professional services remain unpaid for an extended period of time. There is a threat to independence if a substantial part of what is owed is not paid before the issue of the report of the auditor for the following year.

Litigation and Independence

Another influence on the continuance of the relationship is whether there is any pending litigation between client and auditor. If the client is involved in litigation with the auditor, to continue to audit the client could jeopardize independence.[4] The commencement by a client or other third party of proceedings against the auditor would compromise independence. The commencement of litigation by the auditor alleging, for example, fraud or deceit by the officers of a company, or substandard performance of the client's audit by the accountant, would also impair independence. On the other side of the legal fence, acting as an advocate on behalf of an assurance client in litigation or in resolving disputes with third parties is an "advocacy threat" to independence.[5]

Specific Competencies

The issue of specific competence needs specific consideration in the light of client evaluation in the previous step of the engagement process. On the basis of the specific circumstances of the client and its industry, the auditor should determine if the necessary expertise regarding the industry, specific GAAP issues, or certain non-audit skills are available to the audit team.

Audit team members must have a degree of technical training and proficiency required in the circumstances. There should be sufficient direction, supervision and review of work at all levels in order to provide reasonable assurance that the work performed meets appropriate standards of quality. There is a preference for year-to-year continuity in staffing.

Consideration of whether the firm has the competencies and resources to undertake a new engagement includes reviewing existing partner and staff competencies, for:[6]

- knowledge of relevant industries or subject matters;
- experience with relevant regulatory or reporting requirements, or the ability to gain the necessary skills and knowledge in an effective manner;
- ability to complete the engagement within the reporting deadline;
- understanding and practical experience of similar engagements;
- appropriate technical knowledge, including relevant information technology knowledge;
- ability to apply professional judgment.

Partner Rotation

In some countries audit partners must be rotated every specified number of years. In the European Union Guideline (see Chapter 3 Ethics for Professional Accountants) audit partners should rotate once every seven years. The Sarbanes-Oxley Act of the USA requires that audit partners rotate at least every five years.

■ IAPS on Group Audit

An International Auditing Practice Statement (IAPS), "The Audit of Group Financial Statements"[7] provides practical assistance to auditors in applying ISAs to the audit of group financial statements.

Finally, on the basis of the competence analysis, the auditor might conclude that the audit team should rely on the work of other auditors or other experts.

Concept and a Company 5.3

SureBeam Not Sure of its Auditor

Concept	Client acceptance.

Story

SureBeam Corporation makes systems that irradiate food to remove harmful bacteria. Using SureBeam's system, a food company can scan a food product and break down the DNA chains of bacteria that can cause illnesses such as E. coli, Listeria Monocytogenes, Salmonella, and Campylobacter. (PR Newswire 2003)

In 2003, Big Four firm Deloitte & Touche was dismissed from its role as auditor for SureBeam Corporation after expressing concern over SureBeam's compliance with generally accepted accounting principles. Before they hired Deloitte, the company discharged Andersen and KPMG in the span of less than a year. As they were publicly traded, SureBeam needed audited financial statements. (Wallmeyer 2003)

After Andersen was prohibited from auditing listed firms in 2002, SureBeam hired KPMG to carry on its audit work, but in June 2003 KPMG was fired for charging too much for the audit work. Deloitte was hired to replace KPMG. (Freeman 2004)

After a preliminary examination of SureBeam's accounting records, Deloitte questioned SureBeam's accounting treatment of the sale of equipment to an international company in 2000. Millions of dollars of revenue were recognized on the sale, but the money was ultimately not recovered. According to SureBeam's chief executive officer, John C. Arme, Deloitte "said they could not come to a conclusion as to whether accounting for that contract was proper." Deloitte also questioned the accounting treatment of a barter transaction where by SureBeam recognized revenue from the exchange of equipment for services with Texas A&M University. (AcccountingWeb.com 2003)

Some of SureBeam's accounting practices have been questioned by the Securities and Exchange Commission, but no request for a change in the company's accounting methods has been issued to date. (Norris 2003)

Discussion Question

■ SureBeam has approached your audit firm to do their current audit. What client acceptance procedures should be carried out? What risks are involved in taking on this client?

References

AccountingWeb.com, 2003, "Deloitte Relieved of Duties After Questioning Accounting Methods," AccountingWeb.com, September 4.

Freeman, M., 2004, "Accounting dispute led to demise of SureBeam," *San Diego Union-Tribune*, January 14.

Norris, F. 2003, "Don't like the audit? Then fire the auditor; SureBeam searches for accountant No. 4," *International Herald Tribune*, August 23, p. 13.

PR Newswire, 2003, "SureBeam Corporation Appoints Peterson & Co., LLP as Independent Auditor," PR Newswire Association LLC, December 3.

Wallmeyer, A., 2003, "SureBeam Says It Won't Meet Targets for Revenue and Profit," *Wall Street Journal*, (Eastern edition), New York, N.Y., September 17, p. A.22.

5.5 Use of Other Professionals in the Audit

The auditor may discover in doing the search for background information that another auditor will audit a portion of the client's financial statements or that an outside specialist such as IT, environmental or tax specialist, may be needed to properly audit the client. International standards dictate certain procedures in these cases.

■ Using the Work of Another Auditor

Part of the search for background information includes considering if another auditor will be required to audit a component of the business such as a division in another country. If another auditor is auditing part of the financial statements, the auditor should consider the impact of using the work of another auditor on the combined financial statements.

The purpose of ISA 600,[8] the standard about the work of another auditor, is to establish standards and provide guidance when an auditor, acting as a **group auditor**, decides to use the work of a **related auditor** or **other auditor** in the audit of **group financial statements**. A related auditor is an auditor from the group auditor's firm, a network firm, or other firm operating under common quality control policies and procedures. Any auditor who is not the group auditor or a related auditor is an "other auditor."

Group Auditor

The group auditor is responsible for expressing an audit opinion on whether the group financial statements give a true and fair view (or are presented fairly, in all material respects) in accordance with the applicable financial reporting framework. The group auditor is responsible for determining the work to be performed on the **components'** financial information and on the consolidation in order to obtain sufficient appropriate audit evidence to be able to express an opinion on the group financial statements. If the group auditor uses a related auditor or other auditor to work on the audit, the group auditor determines the scope of work to be performed and communicates the plan to the related auditor or other auditor.

Audit Responsibility

Unless national standards enable, and national law or regulation permits, the group auditor to divide responsibility for the audit opinion on the group financial statements (referred to as "division of responsibility") and the group auditor decides to do so, the group auditor should take sole responsibility for the audit opinion on the group financial statements. When the group auditor takes sole responsibility for the audit opinion on the group financial statements, the group auditor should not refer to the other auditor in the auditor's report on the group financial statements.[9]

National standards differ as to whether division of responsibility is allowed. No divided responsibility is allowed in Australia,[10] Japan,[11] and the UK.[12] The Canadian standards allow division of responsibility only when expressing an opinion with reservation. The auditor may refer to his inability to rely on the work of the secondary auditor in his report if such a disclosure explains the reason for his or her reservation.

When the group auditor decides to use the work of another auditor, he should consider the professional qualifications, independence, professional competence, and resources of the other auditor, and the quality control process of the other auditor's firm in the context of the work to be performed by the other auditor.

Documentation

The group auditor should document in the audit working papers the following:[13]

- The group auditor's conclusion with regard to the professional qualifications, independence, professional competence and resources of the other auditor, and of the quality control process of the other auditor's firm.
- The assessment of significant risks of material misstatement of the group financial statements that may arise from components, individually or together, and the group auditor's response to such risks.
- The scope of work performed on the components' financial information.
- The group auditor's conclusion as to whether the group auditor has obtained sufficient appropriate audit evidence that the work of the related auditor and other auditor is adequate for the group auditor's purposes, as well as any additional procedures performed by the group auditor on the component's financial information.
- The group auditor's conclusion with regard to the significant findings arising from the work of the related auditor or other auditor.
- Discussions of significant accounting, auditing and financial reporting matters with **group management, component management**, related auditors or other auditors.

When the group auditor concludes that the work of the related auditor or other auditor cannot be used and the group auditor has not been able to perform sufficient additional procedures, the group auditor should express a qualified opinion because there is a limitation in the scope of the audit. In some countries, like the Netherlands, the group auditor may only refer to the use made of other auditors to motivate a qualified, disclaimer of adverse audit opinion. This is to emphasize the undivided responsibility of the group auditor. In other countries (e.g. the USA) it is possible to assume divided responsibility, which is expressed by referring in the audit opinion to the fact that the financial statements include numbers that have been audited by another auditor, without affecting the unqualified nature of the opinion.

Certification Exam Question 5.2

A group auditor decides not to refer to the audit of another auditor who audited a subsidiary of the group auditor's client. After making inquires about the other auditor's professional reputation and independence, the group auditor most likely would:

(A) Add an explanatory paragraph to the auditor's report indicating that the subsidiary's financial statements are not material to the consolidated financial statements.
(B) Document in the engagement letter that the group auditor assumes no responsibility for the other auditor's work and opinion.
(C) Obtain written permission from the other auditor to omit the reference in the group auditor's report.
(D) Contact the other auditor and review the audit program and working papers pertaining to the subsidiary.

■ Using the Work of an Expert

The auditor's education and experience enable him to be knowledgeable about business matters in general, but he is not expected to have the expertise of a person trained for another profession such as an actuary or engineer. If the auditor requires special expertise, the auditor should consider hiring an **expert** to assist in gathering the necessary evidence.[14] ISA 620[15] defines an expert as a person or firm possessing special skill, knowledge, and experience in a particular field other than accounting and auditing.

Situations where an auditor might use an expert are valuations of certain types of assets (land and building, works of art, precious stones, etc.); determination of physical condition of assets; actuarial valuation; value of contracts in progress; specific IT expertise (e.g. in the audit of a telecommunications company); and legal opinions.

Expert's Competence, Objectivity

If an expert's work is to be used as audit evidence, the auditor should determine the expert's skills and competence by considering professional certifications, experience and reputation. The expert's objectivity should be evaluated. Objectivity is impaired when the expert is employed by the client or related in some manner to the client (i.e. a **related entity** or "related party"). The auditor should obtain sufficient appropriate audit evidence that the scope of the expert's work is adequate for the purposes of the audit.

Communications to Expert

The client should write instructions to the expert which cover:

■ scope of the expert's work,
■ coverage of the expert's report,
■ intended use by the auditor of the expert's work,
■ access of the expert to files and records of the client.

When issuing an unqualified and unmodified auditor's report, the auditor should not refer to the work of the expert. Such a reference might be misunderstood to be a qualification of the auditor's opinion or division of responsibility, neither of which is intended.

If, as a result of the work of an expert, the auditor decides to issue a modified auditor's report, in some circumstances when explaining the nature of the modification it may be appropriate to refer to the expert by name and the extent of his involvement. This disclosure requires the permission of the expert.

5.6 Communicating With the Predecessor (Existing) Auditor

If there is an existing auditor, the IFAC *Code of Ethics for Professional Accountants* (discussed in Chapter 3 Ethics for Professional Accountants) requires the new auditor to communicate directly with the predecessor auditor.[16] In cases when a new auditor will replace an existing auditor, the code of ethics advises the new, proposed auditor to communicate with the **existing accountant**. The extent to which an existing accountant can discuss the affairs of the client with the **proposed accountant** will depend on receipt of the client's permission and the legal or ethical requirements relating to this disclosure. The purpose of this communication is to determine whether there are technical or ethical facts, or circumstances the new auditor should be aware of, prior to accepting the audit. This requirement is an important measure to prevent "opinion shopping," or to notify the new auditor of the circumstances under which the predecessor auditor has ended the relationship with the client.

As stated in the *Code of Ethics for Professional Accountants* (the Code), on receipt of an inquiry from a proposed successor auditor, the existing auditor should advise whether there are any professional reasons why the proposed successor auditor should not accept the appointment. If the client denies the existing auditor permission to discuss its affairs with the proposed successor auditor or limits what the existing auditor may say, that fact should be disclosed to the proposed successor auditor.

■ Request Permission of Client

Before accepting an appointment to audit a company that has been using another accountant, the new auditor should determine if the existing accountant has been notified by the client and given permission to discuss the client's affairs fully and freely. The proposed accountant should then request permission from the client to communicate with the existing accountant.

When the predecessor (existing) auditor receives the communication of the newly proposed auditor, he should reply, preferably in writing, advising of any professional reasons why the proposed accountant should not accept the appointment. The proposed accountant should receive a satisfactory reply from the existing accountant within a reasonable period of time. If a reply is not received, the proposed accountant should send a letter to the existing accountant stating that there is an assumption that there is no professional reason why the appointment should not be accepted and that the new auditor is going to proceed with the engagement, if accepted.

For first-time engagements, ISA 510 suggests:[17]

The auditor should obtain sufficient appropriate audit evidence that: (a) the opening balances do not contain misstatements that materially affect the current period's financial statements;

(b) the prior period's closing balances have been correctly brought forward to the current period or, when appropriate, have been restated; and (c) appropriate accounting policies are consistently applied or changes in accounting policies have been properly accounted for and adequately disclosed.

Of course, one of the best ways to be assured that the opening balances and accounting policies are correct when the prior period financial statements were audited by another auditor, is to review the predecessor auditor's working papers. This should allow the new auditor to obtain sufficient appropriate evidence. The new auditor should also consider the professional competence and independence of the predecessor auditor. If the prior period's auditor's report was not the standard **unqualified opinion**, the new auditor should pay particular attention in the current period to the matter which resulted in the modification.

Certification Exam Question 5.3[18]

Before accepting an audit engagement, a successor (proposed) auditor should make specific inquiries of the predecessor (existing) auditor regarding:

(A) Disagreements the predecessor had with the client concerning auditing procedures and accounting principles.
(B) The predecessor"s evaluation of matters of continuing accounting significance.
(C) Opinion of any subsequent events occurring since the predecessor's audit report was issued.
(D) The predecessor's assessments of inherent risk and judgments about materiality.

5.7 Acceptance by the Client – The Engagement Proposal

The auditor has determined that the client is acceptable from a risk and ethics perspective, and has concluded that the ethical requirements regarding the specific client engagement can be met. Then, typically, significant effort will be devoted to gaining the auditee as a client, given the competitive pressure that exists in the current audit environment (see Chapter 2 The Audit Environment). This requires a carefully prepared engagement proposal.

Aspects of the procedures for the engagement proposal may be found in ISA 210, "Terms of Audit Engagement."[19] The auditor and the client should have a mutual understanding of the nature of the audit services to be performed, the timing of those services, the expected fees, audit team, audit approach, audit quality, use of client's internal auditors, and the transition needs.

References to the quality aspects of the client proposal may be found in ISO 9001,[20] which suggests that the auditing firm should define and document its policy and objectives for, and commitment to, quality. The auditor should ensure that this policy is understood, implemented, and maintained at all levels in the organization.

There are two basic types of audit engagement proposals: those to continuing clients and those for new clients.

■ Continuing Client Audit Proposal

The continuing client proposal will differ between firms, but generally it discusses the following:

■ a review of how the auditing firm can add value, both to the company in general and to those directly responsible for the engagement of the auditor, for example the Audit Committee;
■ plans for further improvement in value added including discussion of present regulatory trends, audit scope, and any recent changes in the company that may affect the audit;
■ a description of the audit team and any changes in the audit team from the previous year;
■ a detailed fee proposal.

A Review of How the Auditing Firm Can Add Value

The introductory part of the client proposal is a discussion of how the proposing firm can benefit (*add value* to) the client firm. There is a discussion of the focus of the firm, its management philosophy, and quality control policies. The relationship with the client's internal audit department and accounting department may be discussed.

This section on plans for *further improvement in value added* might identify the client's requirements and discuss how the audit firm meets these requirements. The audit scope and materiality limits may also be discussed. Reliance on audit regulatory requirements – local, national, and international – should also be discussed. The extent of reliance on the client's internal audit staff should be spelled out. Finally, it is important to review any changes in client company management, new projects undertaken, and the general regulatory environment. Especially important are those changes that affect the audit.

Audit Team

An important part of the proposal is a description of members of the **audit team** and summary of their work experience. Special emphasis may be placed on the members of the team returning from previous engagements. Selecting the audit team is Step 6 in the client acceptance process (see Illustration 5.1).

Fee Proposal

The detailed description of the proposed *fee* is traditionally a separate part of the proposal, presented as a separate document. The fee proposal may involve several levels of detail or a few depending on type. The core audit requires the most time and detail. It will show costs for operation audits including, perhaps, audits of subsidiaries and quarterly audits. Less level of detail would be required for statutory audits and potential future developments.

■ New Client Audit Proposal

A proposal to audit a new client is very important to audit firms because new clients are the primary growth engine for firms. Obtaining more prestigious clients is the desire of most firms. A proposal to a large, solid client may be very complex, requiring many hours of staff time to prepare, especially if it is a competitive situation. A sample table of contents for a new client proposal is shown in Illustration 5.4.

ILLUSTRATION 5.4

Sample Table of Contents of New Client Proposal

ABC Company Engagement Proposal

- Executive summary
- ABC Company business and audit expectations
- Strengths of Big One, LLP
- The audit team
- The audit approach
- ABC Company internal auditors
- ABC Company transition needs and management
- After service monitoring
- Fee details
- Appendix

Big One, LLP CPAs

The **executive summary** gives a brief summary of the proposal with special emphasis on client expectation, audit approach, firm selling points and co-ordination of the audit with staff internal auditors.

The general proposal may begin with a description of client business sectors, technology, financial strengths and divisions. The client's objectives as the basis of the audit strategy[21] could be outlined. It may point out audit requirements relating to securities exchange, environmental, governmental and other regulations, including items in the company's policies that go beyond existing statutory requirements.

Strengths of the audit firm may explore client service attitudes, technical competency, experience, desire to exceed expectations, and advice and assistance. This section might also emphasize report quality, continuity of audit teams, worldwide service, cost effectiveness of audits, and audit firm's quality standards.

The **audit team** section includes a description of members of the team and a summary of their work experience. This section might also detail how the team will communicate with management, the role of the team and supervisors, and team meetings and communications. Choosing the audit team is Step 6 in the client acceptance process and is generally done well ahead of writing the client proposal.

The **audit approach** is an important section because it allows a discussion of how the audit is tailored to this one, specific client. The section could explain audit emphasis or concentration on specific audit risks, the use of information technology on the audit, the involvement of other auditors or experts, and the number of locations or components reviewed. The section could address terms of the engagement, any statutory responsibilities, and internal control and client systems. The nature and timing of reports or other communications (e.g., audit opinion, review, special procedures, governmental reporting, oral and written reports to the audit committee) expected under the engagement is also important.

The client's **internal auditors' work**[22] must be relied upon to a certain extent in all audits. This section may include reference to the internal auditors' work and production, supplier selection, and supplier failure. Other issues explored may include safeguarding of assets, internal controls, management information systems, systems security, adherence to corporate policy, due diligence reviews, and opportunities for improvement.

A discussion of the **transition needs of the company** in terms of accommodating the new auditor may be very important in convincing a new client to switch auditors. This section of the proposal might include a transition schedule detailing meetings with management and former auditors. Other areas addressed might include permanent file documentation, understanding of internal control, and benefits of the change.

After the audit is complete there are still opportunities for the auditor to offer **service to the client**. These after-service monitoring activities may include monitoring the audit performance, audit firm self-evaluation (usually at closing meetings), questionnaires for management to evaluate the audit performance, and written summaries of what was done in the audit (i.e. audit and satisfaction survey) can be given to the client.

An **appendix** might include further information about the audit team, an outline of the audit plan and a list of representative publications. The outline of the audit plan usually shows the degree of audit time required for fieldwork, confirmation of controls, validation of balances and transactions. In particular, the outline of the audit plan will provide an overview of the audit risks, and the auditor's suggested response to those risks, in the form of detailed audit procedures.

■ Establishing and Negotiating Audit Fees

According to the Code of Ethics,[23] professional fees should be a fair reflection of the value of the professional services performed for the client, taking into account:

- the skill and knowledge required for the type of professional services involved;
- the level of training and experience of the persons necessarily engaged in performing the professional services;
- the time required by each person engaged in performing the professional services;
- the degree of responsibility that performing those services entails.

These factors can be influenced by the legal, social, and economic conditions of each country.

Sometimes an auditing firm charges a lower fee when a client is first signed up. This is called "low balling". The Code of Ethics states[24] that it is only proper for a professional accountant to charge a client a lower fee than has previously been charged for similar services, provided the fee has been calculated in accordance with certain factors referred to in Chapter 3 Ethics for Professional Accountants (paragraphs 10.2 through 10.4, Section 10 of the Code).

Contingency Fees

Professional services should not be offered or rendered to a client under a contingency fee. A **contingency fee** is an arrangement whereby no fee will be charged unless a specified finding or result is obtained, or when the fee is otherwise contingent on the findings or results of these services. Furthermore, fees charged on a percentage or similar basis, should be regarded as contingent fees. It is easy to see that a contingency fee can jeopardize the auditor's independence. Imagine what impact it could have on an auditor's independence and objectivity if the audit fee were a percentage of the net profit.

There are two exceptions to the prohibition of contingency fees. First, fees are not considered contingent if fixed by a court or other public authority. Secondly, in those countries where charging contingent fees is permitted either by statute or by a professional member body, such engagements are permitted, but should be limited to those for which independence is not required (e.g. services other than assurance services).

Commissions

The auditor also should not take or pay commissions. The payment or receipt of a commission by a professional accountant could impair objectivity and independence. Nor should the auditor accept a commission for the referral of the products or services of others.

5.8 The Audit Engagement Letter

It is in the interests of both client and auditor that the auditor sends an engagement letter,[25] preferably before the commencement of the engagement, to help in avoiding misunderstandings with respect to the engagement. An engagement letter is an agreement between the accounting firm and the client for the conduct of the audit and related services. An auditor's engagement letter documents and confirms his acceptance of the appointment, the objective and scope of the audit, the extent of auditor responsibilities to the client, and the form of any reports.

The engagement letter may affect legal responsibilities to the client. In litigation, the auditor may use an engagement letter as a contract stating its scope, responsibilities, and limitations. The letter describes the auditor's purpose, that the audit entails study of internal control, the time schedule of the engagement, and fees.

■ Contents of the Engagement Letter

The form and content of the audit engagement letter may vary for each client, but they should generally include reference to:[26]

- the objective of the audit of financial information;
- management's responsibility for the financial information as described in ISA 200;
- the applicable financial reporting framework;
- the scope of the audit, including reference to applicable legislation such as related to fraud (ISA 240) or money laundering, regulations or pronouncements of professional bodies to which the auditor adheres;
- the form of any reports or other communication of results of the engagement, including with those charged with governance (ISA 260);
- the fact that because of the test nature and other inherent limitations of an audit, together with the inherent limitations of any system of internal control, there is an unavoidable risk that even some material misstatement may remain undiscovered;

■ unrestricted access to whatever records, documentation and other information requested in connection with the audit.

The auditor may also wish to include in the letter:

■ arrangements regarding the planning of the audit;
■ an applicable code of ethics;
■ an expectation of receiving from management written confirmation concerning representations made in connection with the audit (ISA 580);
■ a request for the client to confirm the terms of the engagement by acknowledging receipt of the engagement letter;
■ a description of any other letters or reports the auditor expects to issue to the client;
■ the basis on which fees are computed and any billing arrangements.

When relevant, the following points could also be made:

■ arrangements concerning the involvement of other auditors and experts in some aspects of the audit;
■ arrangements concerning the involvement of internal auditors and other client staff;
■ arrangements to be made with the predecessor auditor, if any, in the case of an initial audit;
■ any restriction of the auditor's liability;
■ a reference to any further agreements between the auditor and the client.

On recurring audits, the auditor may decide not to send a new engagement letter each year. However, he should consider sending a letter in any of the following circumstances:

■ where there is an indication that the client misunderstands the objective and scope of the audit;
■ where the terms of the engagement are revised;
■ where there has been a recent change in management;
■ where the size or nature of the business has changed;
■ where there are legal requirements that an engagement letter be written.

If the auditor reviews both the parent and a subsidiary, branch or division of the company, he may consider sending a separate engagement letter to that component business. The factors that the auditor should consider are who appoints the auditor of the component, legal requirements, degree of ownership by parent and the extent of any work performed by the auditors.

Illustration 5.5 shows a sample engagement letter.

Certification Exam Question 5.4

Which of the following matters is generally included in an auditor's engagement letter?

(A) Management's liability for illegal acts.
(B) The factors to be considered in setting judgments about audit risk.
(C) Management's responsibility for the entity's financial statements.
(D) Management's responsibility to investigate internal control deficiencies.

ILLUSTRATION 5.5

Sample Audit Engagement Letter

The following is an example of an engagement letter for an audit of general purpose financial statements prepared in accordance with International Financial Reporting Standards. This letter is to be used as a guide in conjunction with the considerations outlined in this ISA and will need to be varied according to individual requirements and circumstances.

To the Board of Directors or the appropriate representative of senior management:

You have requested that we audit the financial statements of ..., which comprise the balance sheet as at ..., and the related income statement, statement of changes in equity and cash flow statements for the year then ending, and the related notes. We are pleased to confirm our acceptance and our understanding of this engagement by means of this letter. Our audit will be conducted with the objective of our expressing an opinion on the financial statements.

We will conduct our audit in accordance with International Standards on Auditing. Those Standards require that we plan and perform the audit to obtain reasonable, but not absolute, assurance about whether the financial statements are free from material misstatements, whether due to fraud or error. An audit involves performing procedures to obtain audit evidence about the amounts and disclosures in the financial statements. The audit procedures selected depend on the auditor's assessment of the risks of material misstatement of the financial statements. An audit also includes evaluating the appropriateness of accounting policies used and the reasonableness of significant estimates made by management, as well as evaluating the overall financial statement presentation and disclosures.

Because of the test nature and other inherent limitations of an audit, together with the inherent limitations of any accounting and internal control system, there is an unavoidable risk that even some material misstatements may remain undiscovered.

In making our risk assessments, we consider internal control relevant to the entity's preparation of the financial statements as a basis for designing audit procedures that are appropriate in the circumstances, but not for the purpose of expressing an opinion on the effectiveness of the entity's internal control. However, we expect to provide you with a separate letter concerning any material weaknesses in the design or implementation of internal control over financial reporting that come to our attention during the audit of the financial statements.*

We remind you that the responsibility for the preparation of financial statements that present fairly the financial position, financial performance and cash flows of the company in accordance with International Financial Reporting Standards is that of the management of the company. Our auditors' report will explain that management's responsibility for the preparation of the financial statements also includes:

- maintaining internal control relevant to the preparation of financial statements that are free from misstatement, whether due to fraud or error;
- selecting and applying appropriate accounting policies that are consistent with International Financial Reporting Standards; and
- making accounting estimates that are appropriate in the circumstances.

As part of our audit process, we will request from management written confirmation concerning representations made to us in connection with the audit.

We look forward to full co-operation from your staff and we trust that they will make available to us whatever records, documentation and other information are requested in connection with our audit.

[*Insert additional information here regarding fee arrangements and billings, as appropriate.*]

Please sign and return the attached copy of this letter to indicate that it is in accordance with your understanding of the arrangements for our audit of the financial statements.

HDSW, Auditors
Acknowledged on behalf of Werwater Company by
(signed)
Name and Title
Date

* In some jurisdictions, the auditor may have responsibilities to report separately on the entity's internal control. In such circumstances, the auditor reports on that responsibility as required in that jurisdiction. The reference in the auditor's report on the financial statements to the fact that the auditor's consideration of internal control is not for the purpose of expressing an opinion on the effectiveness of the entity's internal control may not be appropriate in such circumstances.

■ Financial Reporting Framework

ISA 200 describes the financial reporting frameworks that are acceptable for general purpose financial statements. Legislative and regulatory requirements often identify the applicable financial reporting framework for general purpose financial statements. In most cases, the applicable financial reporting framework will be established by a national standards setting organization that is recognized to promulgate standards in the jurisdiction in which the entity is registered or operates. The auditor should not accept an engagement for an audit of financial statements when the auditor concludes that the financial reporting framework identified by management is not acceptable.

5.9 Summary

The Client Acceptance phase of the audit has two objectives:

1 examination of the proposed client to determine if there is any reason to reject the engagement (acceptance **of** the client and consideration whether the auditor is able to meet the ethical requirements vis-à-vis the particular client engagement);
2 convincing the client to hire the auditor (acceptance **by** the client).

In the client acceptance phase of the audit, the auditor is primarily concerned with the riskiness of his client and the complexities that can be expected when an audit is performed. The audit firm is also interested in preparing a client proposal to convince the acceptable client to develop a relationship.

Components of acceptance of the client are: acquiring knowledge of the client's business; examination of the audit firm's ethical requirements and technical competence, possible use of other professionals (including outside specialists) in the audit; communication with the predecessor auditor; preparation of client proposal; assignment of staff; and the submission of the terms of the engagement in the form of an audit engagement letter.

The auditor must develop a preliminary understanding of the client in order to both evaluate the client's background and the risks associated with accepting the engagement. There must also be an understanding of the auditors' relationship to the client to enable the auditor to consider if the ethical and professional requirements (independence, competence, etc.) typical to the specific engagement can be met.

Based on the evaluation obtained regarding the background of the client, the auditor should determine whether all ethical requirements could be met with regard to the specific engagement. Probably the most important procedure in this step of the engagement acceptance process is verification of the auditor's independence. Given the facts and circumstances identified in the client evaluation phase, a determination is made whether the auditor and the audit team collectively possess the specific competence required to deal with the issues that the auditor is likely to encounter in the audit.

The auditor may discover in doing the search for background information that another auditor will audit a portion of the client's financial statements or that an outside specialist such as IT, environmental or tax specialist, may be needed to properly audit the client. International standards dictate certain procedures in these cases. If the auditor uses related auditors or other auditors, he becomes the "group auditor." The group auditor is responsible for expressing an audit opinion on whether the group financial statements give a true and fair view (or are presented fairly, in all material respects) in accordance with the applicable financial reporting framework.

If there is an existing auditor, the IFAC *Code of Ethics for Professional Accountants* requires the new auditor to communicate directly with the predecessor auditor. In cases when a new auditor will replace an existing auditor, the code of ethics advises the new, proposed auditor to communicate with the existing accountant. The extent to which an existing accountant can discuss the affairs of the client with the proposed accountant will depend on receipt of the client's permission and the legal or ethical requirements relating to this disclosure. The purpose of this communication is to determine whether there are technical or ethical facts or circumstances the new auditor should be aware of, prior to accepting the audit.

There are two basic types of audit engagement proposals:

1 those to continuing clients;
2 those to new clients.

The continuing client proposal discusses how the auditing firm can add value, plans for further improvement in the client relationship, and provides a description of the audit team and a detailed fee proposal. The new client proposal discusses business and audit expectations, audit firm strengths, audit team, audit approach, reliance on internal auditors, transition needs and management, after-service monitoring, and fee details.

It is in the interests of both client and auditor that the auditor sends an engagement letter, preferably before the commencement of the engagement, to help in avoiding misunderstandings with respect to the engagement. An engagement letter is an agreement between the accounting firm and the client for the conduct of the audit and related services. An auditor's engagement letter documents and confirms his acceptance of the appointment, the objective and scope of the audit, the extent of auditor responsibilities to the client, and the form of any reports. ISA 210 shows the principal contents of an engagement letter, what to do in recurring audits, and when there is an audit of components.

5.10 Answers to Certification Exam Questions

5.1 (D) The requirement is to identify reasons why a professional accountant in public practice to reject a new audit engagement. Answer (D) is correct because the auditor must have available financial records to conduct an audit. If the prospective client refused to provide records, the auditor might have serious doubts about his integrity. Answer (A) is incorrect because alternative procedures may be performed to validate the inventory count. Answer (B) is incorrect because the auditor can learn about the industry and operations and/or hire expert help. Answer (C) is incorrect because there are occasions when the predecessor auditor may refuse turning over working papers.

5.2 (D) The requirement is to what a group auditor would consider, apart from reputation and independence, about another auditor who audited a subsidiary of the group auditor's client. Answer (D) is correct because the group auditor should want to check the quality of the subsidiary's audit by discussing audit procedures with the other auditor and/or reviewing the audit programs and working papers. Answer (A) is incorrect because the group auditor may not make reference to the other auditor even though the part he audited is material. Answer (B) is wrong because the engagement letter does not usually discuss the work of the other auditor. Answer (C) is incorrect because permission is only needed when the group auditor refers to the other auditor by name.

5.3 (A) The requirement is to determine the nature of the inquiries that a successor auditor should make of the predecessor auditor prior to accepting an audit engagement. Answer (A) is correct because the inquiries should include specific questions to management on: (1) disagreements with management as to auditing procedures and accounting principles; (2) facts that might bear on the integrity of management; and (3) the predecessor's understanding as to the reasons for the change of auditors. Answers (B), (C), and (D) are incorrect because they are not areas that the predecessor auditor are required to divulge.

5.4 (C) The requirement is to identify what is generally included in an auditor's engagement letter. Answer (C) is correct because ISA 210 "Terms of Engagements," paragraph 6, suggests that management responsibilities for the financial statements be made clear. None of answers (A), (B) or (D) include material that would ordinarily appear in the engagement letter.

5.11 Notes

1 IFAC, 2004, *Handbook of International Auditing, Assurance, and Ethics Pronouncements*, International Standards on Auditing 310 (ISA 310), "Knowledge of the Business," para. 2, International Federation of Accountants, New York.

2 Adapted and reprinted with permission from AICPA. Copyright © 2000 & 1985 by American Institute of Certified Public Accountants.

3 IFAC Ethics Committee, *Code of Ethics for Professional Accountants*, Independence, Section 8, para. 8.205 commentary, International Federation of Accountants, New York, July 2003.

4 AICPA, 2002, *Code of Professional Conduct*, Section 101, "Independence," para. 8, American Institute of Certified Public Accountants, New York, states: "Independence may be impaired whenever the member and the member's client company or its management are in threatened or actual positions of material adverse interest by reason of threatened or actual litigation."

5 IFAC, 2004, *Handbook of International Auditing, Assurance, and Ethics Pronouncements*, Ethics, para. 8.31, International Federation of Accountants, New York.

6 IAASB, 2003, *Exposure Draft Proposed International Standard On Quality Control 1 (ISQC 1)*, "Quality Control for Audit, Assurance and Related Services Practices," para. 30, 42, International Federation of Accountants, New York, May.

7 IAASB, 2003, Proposed International Auditing Practice Statement, "The Audit of Group Financial Statements," International Federation of Accountants, New York, December.

8 IAASB, 2003, ISA 600 (Revised), "The Work of Related Auditors and Other Auditors in the Audit of Group Financial Statements," International Federation of Accountants, New York, December.

9 The group auditor will mention the related or other auditor if his work does not provide sufficient appropriate audit evidence. See para. 31 of ISA 600.

10 AUS 602 (October 1995), *Using the work of another auditor*, "The auditor should not refer to the work of another auditor in an audit report unless required by legislation or as part of a qualification."

11 The "Implementation Guidance" issued by the JICPA provides that while the principal auditor may use the work of the other auditor, the principal auditor should express an opinion based on his own judgment and does not make reference to the work of the other auditor in the auditor's report.

12 SAS 510, which is the UK equivalent of ISA 600, states: "When the principal auditors are not satisfied that the work of the other auditors is adequate for the purposes of their audit, no reference to the other auditors is made in the principal auditors' report. The principal auditors have sole responsibility for their audit opinion and a reference to the other auditors in the principal auditors' report may be misunderstood and interpreted as a qualification of their opinion or a division of responsibility, neither of which is appropriate."

13 IAASB, 2003, ISA 600 (Revised), "The Work of Related Auditors and Other Auditors in the Audit of Group Financial Statements," para. 34, International Federation of Accountants, New York, December.

14 In the ISA context the expert is considered a specialist employed by the auditor, whereas in the USA and other countries the expert is considered to be an assistant rather than a specialist.

15 IFAC, 2004, *Handbook of International Auditing, Assurance, and Ethics Pronouncements*, International Standards on Auditing 620 (ISA 620), "Using the Work of an Expert," para. 3, International Federation of Accountants, New York, 2003.

16 IFAC, 2004, *Handbook of International Auditing, Assurance, and Ethics Pronouncements*, Ethics, para. 13.21, International Federation of Accountants, New York.

17 IFAC, 2004, *Handbook of International Auditing, Assurance, and Ethics Pronouncements*, International Standards on Auditing 510 (ISA 510), "Initial Engagements – Opening Balances," para. 2, International Federation of Accountants, New York.

18 Adapted and reprinted with permission from AICPA. Copyright © 2000 & 1985 by American Institute of Certified Public Accountants.

19 IFAC, 2004, *Handbook of International Auditing, Assurance, and Ethics Pronouncements*, International Standard on Auditing No. 2 (ISA 210), "Terms of Audit Engagements," International Federation of Accountants, New York.

20 American National Standard, 1987, ANSI/ASQC Q91–1987, "Quality Systems – Model for Quality Assurance in Design/Development, Production, Installation and Servicing," American Society for Quality Control (ASQC), 19 June.

21 *Audit strategy* is the design of an optimized audit approach that seeks to achieve the necessary audit assurance at the lowest cost within the constraints of the information available.

22 IFAC, 2004, *Handbook of International Auditing, Assurance, and Ethics Pronouncements*, International Standards on Auditing 610 (ISA 610), "Considering the Work of Internal Auditing," International Federation of Accountants, New York.

23 IFAC, 2004, *Handbook of International Auditing, Assurance, and Ethics Pronouncements*, Ethics, para. 10.2, International Federation of Accountants, New York.

24 IFAC Ethics Committee, *Code of Ethics for Professional Accountants*, 2003, "Fees and Commissions," Section 10, para. 10.6, International Federation of Accountants, New York, July.

25 In the USA and other national contexts, an engagement letter is not required, although it is usually recommended.

26 IFAC, 2004, *Handbook of International Auditing, Assurance, and Ethics Pronouncements*, International Standards on Auditing 210 (ISA 210), "Terms of Audit Engagements," paras. 6 to 8, International Federation of Accountants, New York.

5.12 Questions, Exercises and Cases

QUESTIONS

5.2 Client Acceptance: The First Step on the Journey to an Opinion

5.1 What is the difference between acceptance of the client and acceptance by the client?

5.3 Evaluate the Client's Background

5.2 What are the major sources of client information auditors have available? Which source would prove the best for new businesses? Why?

5.4 Ability to Meet Ethical and Specific Competence Requirements

5.3 If money is owed by a client to the auditor and it is overdue, what can an auditor do to collect it and what risks are involved?

5.5 Use of Other Professionals in the Audit

5.4 What is a group auditor? What must he consider when the work of another auditor is used?

5.5 How is an "expert" defined according to ISA 620? When should an auditor bring in an expert?

5.6 Communicating With the Predecessor (Existing) Auditor

5.6 To what extent can an existing auditor discuss the affairs of his client with a new auditor?

5.7 Acceptance by the Client – the Engagement Proposal

5.7 List four things an auditor must consider when establishing professional fees. What is meant by "lowballing?"

5.8 Define a contingency fee. Why should a contingency fee not be used? What are the two exceptions for using contingency fees?

5.9 Briefly list the four items found in a continuing client audit proposal. List and define the items that may be found in an audit proposal for a new client.

5.8 The Audit Engagement Letter

5.10 What should be included in an engagement letter? What are some reasons a client might change the terms of the engagement?

5.11 Under what circumstances will an auditor send a new engagement letter each year to an continuing client?

5.12 List the ISAs used in this chapter and briefly define them.

PROBLEMS AND EXERCISES

5.3 Evaluate the Client's Background

5.13 Client Evaluation. The audit firm of F.A. Bloch and Co. has been approached by the following companies who wish to retain Bloch for audit work:

1   Interlewd, an internet company, whose website features explicit images of male nudes and which operates male strip clubs on the west coast of Australia.

2   Dreamtime, a company that operates gambling casino boats off shore and video game machines in major Australian cities.

3   Bernadette, an entertainment company, whose chief executive officer has been investigated by the Italian government for taking bribes, violating public securities laws,
conspiring to commit bodily harm, and issuing bad checks. The CEO has not been
convicted of any of these charges. The board of directors claim that this happened many
years ago, and he has since run several companies successfully.

Required:

A.   What procedures should F.A. Bloch and Co. use to investigate these potential clients?

B.   What would F.A. Bloch and Co. consider in determining whether to accept these clients?

5.4 Ability to Meet Ethical and Specific Competence Requirements

5.14 The audit firm of Guiseppe Mulciber, Dottore Commercialista, has been asked to bid on an
annual audit of the financial statements Mammon, a publicly traded gold jewelry
manufacturer. The Mulciber firm has been performing assurance services for Mammon
over the past there years. Almost everyone on the audit team has investments in stocks
and mutual funds. Mammon and the Mulciber had disputes in the past about the extent of
assurance services provided. One of the members of the proposed audit staff was an
employee of Mammon until 14 months ago. Only one person on the proposed audit team
has audited a jewelry manufacturer.

Required:

A.   What procedures would Mulciber conduct to determine independence of the firm and
audit team?

B.   Does the Mulciber audit team have the proper competencies? Explain.

C.   What circumstances might disqualify Mulciber from serving as an auditor for Mannon?

5.5 Use of Other Professionals in the Audit

5.15 Use of Other Auditor. Rene Lodeve, Reviseur d'Entreprises, has been hired by BelleRei,
N.V., a Liege, Belgium, company. Lodeve will audit all accounts except those of a
subsidiary in Spain, which represents 15 percent of the total sales of BelleRei, which is
audited by an "other accountant," Jeme Indigena.

Required:

A.   What procedures would Lodeve perform to determine whether Indigena has sufficient
professional competence to perform the work?

B.   If Lodeve concludes that he cannot depend on the work of Indigena, and he cannot
perform additional procedures, what sort of audit opinion should Lodeve give?

5.6 Communicating With the Predecessor (Existing) Auditor

5.16 Preparation and Planning. Roger Buckland was recently appointed auditor of Waterfield
Ltd., a public company. He had communicated with the company's previous auditor before
accepting the audit. Buckland attended the company's shareholders meeting at which he
was appointed but he has not yet visited the company's offices.

Required:

List the matters that Buckland should attend to between the time of his appointment and
the commencement of his audit work in order to effectively plan the audit.
[CICA adapted]

5.7 Acceptance by the Client – The Engagement Proposal

5.17 Audit Proposal. Juao Castelo, Revisor Oficial de Contas (ROC), is required to write a client
audit proposal for two clients, one continuing (Jinne) and one new (Autodafe).

Required:

A. Based on the proposal for a continuing client and a new client discussed in this chapter, list the contents of the proposal to Jinne and Autodafe.

B. What do the two proposals have in common? What is different?

C. Describe what is discussed in each section of the proposal to Autodafe.

5.18 Audit Fees. Ursula Chona, Contador Publico (CP Titulado), an auditor from Medellin, Columbia, was referred a client by a local attorney and she has agreed to accept the client for a financial statements audit. She must now determine what fee she will charge.

Required:

A. According to international ethics, the fee should be a fair reflection of effort, taking what conditions into account?

B. On what basis should the fee be calculated? Should out-of-pocket expenses be included or listed separately?

C. What are the circumstances under which Chona can ask for a contingency fee?

D. Can Chona pay a "finder's fee" to the attorney who referred the client to her?

5.8 The Audit Engagement Letter

5.19 Engagement Letter. Stephen Hu, CPA, from Taipei, Taiwan, has just accepted a new client, Kiwan Xou. The company will be audited under the ISA and IAS standards. The client will be given an audit opinion and a management letter. The fees are based on hourly fees, the audit will take 125 hours, and will involve one senior (TD3,500 per hour), two staff auditors (TD2,800 per hour), and a partner (TD5,000 per hour). Out-of-pocket expenses are estimated at TD65,000. The payments will be 33 percent at the beginning of the audit with the balance at the end of the audit.

Required:

Based on the above information, write an engagement letter to Kiwan Xou from Steven Hu.

CASE

5.20 Description of the Business. Compu Group Corporation designs, develops, manufactures, and markets a wide range of personal computing products, including desktop personal computers, portable computers, network servers, and peripheral products that store and manage data in network environments. The company markets its products primarily to business, home, government, and education customers. The company operates in one principal industry segment across geographically diverse markets.

The company is subject to legal proceedings and claims which arise in the ordinary course of its business. Management does not believe that the outcome of any of those matters will have a material adverse effect on the company's consolidated financial position or operating results.

Required:

A. Based on the information presented evaluate the company for acceptance. List criteria that must be reviewed in order to determine acceptability.

B. Make a checklist for areas covered.

C. Outline your audit approach.

(Adopted from idea by Phoong Ngo, Qiang Hsing, and Chi-hui Lee)

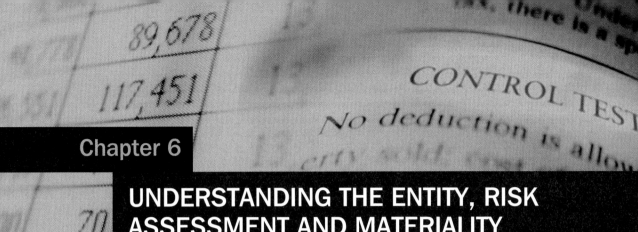

Chapter 6

UNDERSTANDING THE ENTITY, RISK ASSESSMENT AND MATERIALITY

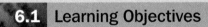

6.1 Learning Objectives

After studying this chapter, you should be able to:

1 State what is the general objective in planning an audit.

2 Give the standard planning procedures.

3 Understand the knowledge of a client's business required to plan the audit.

4 Identify the differences between obtaining company knowledge and industry knowledge.

5 Describe what is done during initial interviews, discussions and site visits with the client.

6 Know how legal obligations of the client are investigated.

7 Describe when analytical procedures are used and why they are important at the planning stage.

8 List the different types of risk that auditors must assess in planning.

9 Define each type of risk.

10 Give examples of a management objective, the related strategy, and the resultant business risk.

11 Discuss four tasks followed to assess risk.

12 Understand inherent risk factors at the financial statement and the account balance, and class of transaction levels.

13 Know the meaning of detection risk and its relationship to evidence.

14 Understand the conditions commonly resulting in greater levels of risk.

15 Illustrate the conditions that determine materiality.

16 Identify the areas involved in the development of the audit planning memorandum.

6.2 Planning – Phase II of the Audit Process Model

International Standards on Auditing (ISA) 300, "Planning," states,[1] "The auditor should plan the audit work so that the audit will be performed in an effective manner. Planning means developing a general strategy and a detailed approach for the expected nature, timing and extent of the audit."

■ Planning Objective and Procedures

Hence, the objective of planning is to determine the amount and type of evidence and review required to assure the auditor that there is no material misstatement of the financial statements. This is Phase II in the Audit Process Model (see Illustration 6.1).

The planning procedures are:

1 Perform audit procedures to understand the entity and its environment, including the entity's internal control.
2 Assess the risks of material misstatements of the financial statements.
3 Determine materiality.
4 Prepare the planning memorandum and audit program containing the auditor's response to the identified risks.

This chapter will primarily deal with the first three steps of the planning procedures, with the exception of the internal control considerations, which will be dealt with in Chapter 7 Internal Control and Control Risk. Chapter 8 Control Risk, Audit Planning and Test of Controls will cover step 4 of the planning procedures.

Before an audit program can be written for the audit, the audit planning process should include procedures to: acquire an understanding of the entity and its environment by reviewing financial (e.g. going concern, analytical procedures) and non-financial (e.g. industry, company, legal, related party, statutory) information; understand the accounting and internal control systems; and assess risk and materiality. Other issues such as the nature and timing of the engagement, involvement of other auditors, involvement of experts, staffing requirements, and reports usually receive preliminary attention at the client acceptance phase (Phase I in the model in Chapter 5 Client Acceptance), but might require follow-up in the planning phase and subsequent phases. The auditor determines the nature, timing, and extent of audit procedures as well as the form of supervision and review, and incorporates that into an audit program (discussed in Chapter 8 Control Risk, Audit Planning and Test of Controls).

■ New ISAs on Audit Risk

Assessing risk is the core of the audit. The rest of the audit is designed to provide a response to these identified risks. Because of the importance to the audit of risk analysis and the response, the IFAC International Auditing and Assurance Standards Board (IAASB) conducted a joint audit risk project with the US Auditing Standards Board (ASB) to reexamine existing audit standards in this area. In 2003, the IAASB published ISAs 315[2] (Understanding the Entity and its Environment and Assessing the Risks of Material Misstatement), 330[3] (The Auditor's Procedures in Response to Assessed Risks), and 500[4] (Audit Evidence).[5]

ILLUSTRATION 6.1

Audit Process Model

Phase I: Client Acceptance

Objective	Determine both acceptance of a client and acceptance by a client. Decide on acquiring a new client or continuation of relationship with an existing one and the type and amount of staff required.
Procedures	1 Evaluate the client's background and reasons for the audit 2 Determine whether the auditor is able to meet the ethical requirements regarding the client 3 Determine need for other professionals 4 Communicate with predecessor auditor 5 Prepare client proposal 6 Select staff to perform the audit 7 Obtain an engagement letter

Phase II: Planning the Audit

Objective	Determine the amount and type of evidence and review required to give the auditor assurance that there is no material misstatement of the financial statements.
Procedures	1 Perform audit procedures to understand the entity and its environment, including the entity's internal control 2 Assess the risks of material misstatements of the financial statements 3 Determine materiality 4 Prepare the planning memorandum and audit program containing the auditor's response to the identified risks

Phase III: Testing and Evidence

Objective	Test for evidence supporting internal controls and the fairness of the financial statements.
Procedures	1 Tests of controls 2 Substantive tests of transactions 3 Analytical procedures 4 Tests of details of balances 5 Search for unrecorded liabilities

Phase IV: Evaluation and Reporting

Objective	Complete the audit procedures and issue an opinion.
Procedures	1 Evaluate governance evidence 2 Perform procedures to identify subsequent events 3 Review financial statements and other report material 4 Perform wrap-up procedures 5 Prepare Matters for Attention of Partners 6 Report to the board of directors 7 Prepare Audit report

ILLUSTRATION 6.2

Overview of the Proposed ISA 315 and ISA 330[6]

Perform risk assessment procedures
Perform audit procedures to understand the entity and its environment:

- Industry, regulatory, and other external factors including applicable financial reporting framework
- Nature of the entity
- Objectives and strategies and related business risks
- Measurement and review of the entity's financial performance
- Internal control

See paragraphs 7 to 99 of ISA 315 "Understanding the Entity and Its Environment and Assessing the Risks of Material Misstatement"

Assess the risks of material misstatement
Assess the risks of material misstatement at the financial statement level and the assertion level by:

- Identifying risks through considering
  - the entity and its environment, including its internal control
  - classes of transactions, account balances and disclosures
- Relating the identified risks to what can go wrong at the assertion level
- Considering the significance and likelihood of the risks

See paragraphs 100 to 114 of ISA 315 "Understanding the Entity and Its Environment and Assessing the Risks of Material Misstatement"

Respond to assessed risks
Respond to the risks at the financial statement level and assertion level by:

- Developing overall responses to the assessed risks at the financial statement level; and
- Determining the nature, timing and extent of further audit procedures at the assertion level

See paragraphs 5 to 21 of ISA 330 "The Auditor's Procedures in Response to Assessed Risks"

Perform further audit procedures
Perform further audit procedures that are clearly linked to risks at the assertion level by:

- Performing tests of the operating effectiveness of controls
- Performing substantive procedures

See paragraphs 22 to 65 of ISA 330 "The Auditor's Procedures in Response to Assessed Risks"

Evaluate audit evidence obtained
Evaluate whether sufficient and appropriate audit evidence has been obtained.

See paragraphs 66 to 72 of ISA 330 "The Auditor's Procedures in Response to Assessed Risks"

The new standards specify and expand upon what the auditor must understand about the entity whose financial statements are being audited. In particular, the standard introduces the concept that the auditor is required to obtain an understanding of **business risks** and **significant risks** to the extent that they are relevant to the financial statements. In understanding the entity's internal control, the auditor is required to evaluate the design of controls and determine whether they have been implemented. The new standard requires a level of understanding controls greater than that previously required. Evaluation of the design and implementation of controls that address significant risks is emphasized.

We will discuss these new standards throughout this chapter, Chapter 7 Internal Control and Control Risk, and Chapter 8 Control Risk, Audit Planning and Test of Controls. Illustration 6.2 gives an overview of these new ISAs. The standards describe procedures for identifying, assessing, and responding to audit risk – activities that encompass the client acceptance, planning and testing/evidence phase of the audit.

6.3 Understanding the Entity and its Environment

In the client acceptance phase (Phase I of the audit process model), the auditors review material that is readily available about the entity and the entity's environment (annual reports, public news, and public information databases). However, in the planning phase the auditor's understanding of the entity and its environment should grow significantly. As ISA 315 points out, this understanding is an essential aspect of carrying out an ISA audit. It establishes a frame of reference within which the auditor plans the audit and exercises professional judgment about assessing risks of material misstatement of the financial statements and responding to those risks.

■ Procedures to Obtain an Understanding

ISA 315 provides an overview of the procedures that the auditor should follow in order to obtain an understanding sufficient to assess the risks and consider these risks in designing the audit plans. The risk assessment procedures should, at a minimum, be a combination of the following:

- **Inquiries of management** and others within the entity. It is important to have discussions with the client's management about its objectives and expectations, and its plans for achieving these goals. The discussions may encompass short-term management objectives such as increasing profit, reducing investment in working capital, introducing new product lines, reducing taxes, or reducing selling and distribution expenses. Expectations should be explored concerning the company's external agents such as customers, suppliers, shareholders, financial institutions, government, etc. However, although management will typically be the most effective and efficient information source, it might be worthwhile to obtain information from others, in order to reduce the potential for bias.
- **Analytical procedures**. These may help the auditor in identifying unusual transactions or positions. Analytical procedures usually involve a comparison of company results to

that of the industry. There are publications of major industry ratios and trends that might be helpful to the auditor doing analytical procedures (see Chapter 7 Internal Control and Control Risk).

■ **Observation and inspection.** These procedures may cover a broad area, ranging from the observation of an entity's core activities, the reading of management reports or internal control manuals to the inspection of documents. A visit to, and tour of, the company premises will help the auditor develop a better understanding of the client's business and operations. Viewing the facilities helps to identify some internal control safeguards. Seeing the production process will help the auditor assess the inventory movement and the use of fixed assets. Observations of the orderliness, cleanliness, and physical layout of facilities and of the employees' routine functions and work habits can often tell the auditor more about the client than can be learned from studying the accounting records. A knowledge of the physical facilities and plant layout may point to the right questions to ask during the planning phase, or getting the right answers to questions later in the audit. Knowing the layout will assist in planning how many audit staff members will be needed to participate in observing the physical inventory. On the site visit, the auditor may see signs of potential problems. Rust on equipment may indicate that plant assets have been idle. Excessive dust on raw materials or finished goods may indicate a problem of obsolescence. The auditors can see the physical extent of segregation of duties within the client organization by observing the number of office employees.

Other Information Sources

In addition to these procedures, the auditor might consider obtaining information from others sources, for example, the entity's external legal counsel, or externally available data sources, including analysts' reports, industry journals, government statistics, surveys, texts, financial newspapers, etc. Professional organizations like the American Institute of Certified Public Accountants (AICPA) distribute industry audit guides and most industries have trade magazines and books describing their business. Most large audit firms also have industry groups following the developments in those industries and creating newsletters on industry-specific items.

■ Audit Team Discussion

Finally, ISA 315 requires a team-wide discussion of the susceptibility of the financial statements to fraud or error. An important reason for this requirement is the consideration that the team members collectively have a broader access to people within the organization and their insights. As they say, the most interesting information may typically be obtained in elevators and on the parking lot, and, again, there might be a better balance in the team's insights if the perspectives on the entity are not just confined to those conveyed by top management.

■ Continuing Client

If the client is a continuing one, prior year's working papers are reviewed and reliance can be placed on the observations from prior periods. The client's **permanent audit file** frequently contains information on company history, records of most important accounting policies in previous years and lists However, before relying on existing working papers, the auditor needs to make sure that there have been no significant changes in the relevant aspects of the client's entity or environment.

■ Understanding the Entity and its Environment

ISA 315 distinguishes the following relevant aspects in the understanding of the entity and its environment:

- industry, regulatory and other external factors, including the applicable financial reporting framework;
- nature of the entity, including the entity's selection and application of accounting policies;
- objectives and strategies, and the related business risks that may result in a material misstatement of the financial statements;
- measurement and review of the entity's financial performance;
- internal control (discussed in Chapter 7 Internal Control and Control Risk).

In the remainder of this chapter, these aspects will be discussed in more detail.
Illustration 6.3 gives a global systems perspective of client business risk.

ILLUSTRATION 6.3

Global Systems Perspective on Client Business Risk. [7]

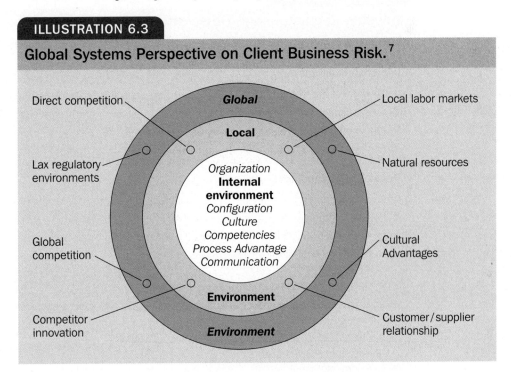

■ Industry, Regulatory And Other External Factors

It is important to understand the client's industry because their industry has specific risks created by the nature of the business, accounting conventions, and industry regulation. Understanding inherent risks common to all companies in a certain industry helps the auditor identify the inherent risks of the individual company. For example, the telecommunications industry has certain risks because it is globally competitive, technological changes may render certain assets obsolete at a quicker pace than anticipated, and telecommunication laws control a client's base and service fees. In other words, the industry gives rise to risks that may result in material **misstatement** of the financial statements of an individual company.

One of the relevant factors in this regard is the financial reporting framework (e.g. International Financial Reporting Standards (IFRS)) that is applicable to the jurisdiction in which the company operates. Other factors relevant to the industry understanding could be the competition, supplier and customer relationships, technological developments, and energy costs. The regulatory environment issues relevant to understanding the industry are: accounting principles (and their industry specific application), taxation, environmental requirements, and the laws and government policies affecting the industry. Industries are also affected by external factors such as general economic conditions, interest rates, and availability of capital and debt. A list of matters that an auditor might consider when obtaining an understanding of the industry, regulatory, and other external factors affecting an entity is given in Illustration 6.4.

ILLUSTRATION 6.4

Industry, Regulatory and Other External Factors, Including the Applicable Financial Reporting Framework Auditors Should Consider

Industry conditions

- The market and competition, including demand, capacity, and price competition
- Cyclical or seasonal activity
- Product technology relating to the entity's products
- Energy supply and cost

Regulatory environment

- Accounting principles and industry specific practices
- Regulatory framework for a regulated industry
- Legislation and regulation that significantly affect the entity's operations
  - Regulatory requirements
  - Direct supervisory activities
- Taxation (corporate and other)
- Government policies currently affecting the conduct of the entity's business
  - Monetary, including foreign exchange controls
  - Financial incentives (e.g. government aid programs)
  - Tariffs, trade restrictions
- Environmental requirements affecting the industry and the entity's business

Other external factors currently affecting the entity's business

- General level of economic activity (e.g. recession, growth)
- Interest rates and availability of financing
- Inflation, currency revaluation

Certification Exam Question 6.1[8]

In obtaining an understanding of an entity's internal controls that are relevant to audit planning, an auditor is required to obtain knowledge about the:

(A) Design of relevant internal controls pertaining to financial reporting in each of the five internal control components.

(B) Effectiveness of the internal controls that have been placed in operation.

(C) Consistency with which the internal controls are currently being applied.

(D) Controls related to each principal transaction class and account balance.

■ Nature of the entity

This aspect of the understanding phase deals with the entity's core, i.e. its operations, types of investments, its financing/ownership, and how management applies and discloses accounting policies.

■ Information acquired about **business operations** may include nature of revenue sources (retailer, manufacturer, and professional services); products and services (e.g. pricing policies, locations and quantities of inventory, profit margins, warranties, order book); market (exports, contracts, terms of payment, market share, franchises, licenses, patents, composition of customer group), location of company facilities (warehouses, offices); employment (wage levels, supply, union contracts, pensions), key suppliers, and customers.

■ *Investments* that have reduced in value have been the downfall of as diverse a group of entities as Metallgesellschaft, a German manufacturer who lost a large amount on the derivatives market,[9] and Orange County, California, which was forced into bankruptcy by speculation on their municipal bonds.[10] Important transactions for which information should be gathered include: acquisitions, mergers and disposals of business divisions; use of derivative financial instruments; type of major investments by the company; capital investment activities (in plant and equipment, technology, etc.) and investment in non-consolidated entities such as joint ventures, **special purpose entities**,[11] and partnerships.

■ A company's **capital structure** and *financing* activities (sources and methods of financing currently and historically) are very important when determining its ability to continue as a **going concern**, a key consideration in determining the type of audit opinion. Companies may use financing arrangements with subsidiaries, spin-offs, transfer of sales contracts to SPEs, and other off-balance sheet financing. Off-balance sheet deals caused Enron to overstate 1998 profits by $113 million; the 1999 profits were too high by $250 million and the 2000 profits by $132 million. Enron used six complex accounting maneuvers including non-economic hedges, tax transactions, and SPEs to make its financial picture more attractive. Such techniques accounted for 96 percent of Enron's reported $979 million net income for 2000.[12] The auditor needs information on debt structure (especially guarantees and off-balance sheet financing), leases, beneficial owners, and related parties (discussed in more detail later in this section).

■ The entity's choice and application of **financial reporting policies** is one of the core considerations of the auditor, because this is the *criteria* on which the auditor gives his assurance. The auditor should review company accounting policies including revenue recognition, inventories, research and development, important expense categories, judgmental accounting valuations, and financial statement **presentation and disclosure.** Foreign currency assets, liabilities, and transactions require special attention.

A list of matters that an auditor might consider when obtaining an understanding of the nature of the entity is given in Illustration 6.5.

There are models, such as in an Entity Level Business Model (see Illustration 6.6), which allows an auditor to organize all information gathered about industry, company, strategic audit, and related party transactions. The entity level business model may be pre-

---

ILLUSTRATION 6.5

Considerations When Obtaining an Understanding of the Nature of the Entity[13]

Business operations

■ Nature of revenue sources (e.g. manufacturer, wholesaler, banking, insurance or other financial services, import/export trading, utility, transportation and technology products and services)

■ Products or services and markets (e.g. major customers and contracts, terms of payment, profit margins, market share, competitors, exports, pricing policies, reputation of products, warranties, order book, trends, marketing strategy and objectives, manufacturing processes)

■ Conduct of operations (e.g. stages and methods of production, business segments, delivery or products and services, details of declining or expanding operations)

■ Alliances, joint ventures, and outsourcing activities

■ Involvement in e-commerce, including Internet sales and marketing activities

■ Geographic dispersion and industry segmentation

■ Location of production facilities, warehouses, and offices

■ Key customers

■ Important suppliers of goods and services (e.g. long-term contracts, stability of supply, terms of payment, imports, methods of delivery such as "just-in-time")

■ Employment (e.g. by location, supply, wage levels, union contracts, pension and other post employment benefits, stock option or incentive bonus arrangements, and government regulation related to employment matters)

■ Research and development activities and expenditures

■ Transactions with related parties

Investments

■ Acquisitions, mergers or disposals of business activities (planned or recently executed)

■ Investments and dispositions of securities and loans

■ Capital investment activities, including investments in plant and equipment and technology, and any recent or planned changes

■ Investments in non-consolidated entities, including partnerships, joint ventures and special-purpose entities

Illustration 6.5 (continued)

Financing and capital structure

- Group structure – major subsidiaries and associated entities, including consolidated and non-consolidated structures
- Debt structure, including covenants, restrictions, guarantees, and off-balance-sheet financing arrangements
- Leasing of property, plant or equipment for use in the business
- Beneficial owners (local, foreign, business reputation, and experience)
- Related parties
- Use of derivative financial instruments

Financial reporting

- Accounting principles and industry specific practices
- Revenue recognition practices
- Accounting for fair values
- Inventories (e.g. locations, quantities)
- Foreign currency assets, liabilities and transactions
- Industry specific significant categories (e.g. loans and investments for banks, accounts receivable and inventory for manufacturers, research and development for pharmaceuticals)
- Accounting for unusual or complex transactions including those in controversial or emerging areas (e.g. accounting for stock-based compensation)
- Financial statement presentation and disclosure

ILLUSTRATION 6.6

Entity Level Business Model[14]

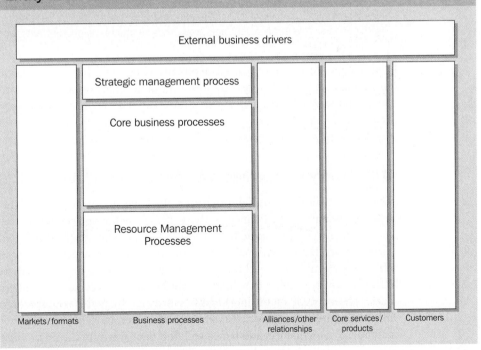

pared to provide a pictorial summary of the entity's business to the entity's management, Audit Committee, Board of Directors, etc., or to facilitate communication within the engagement team.

Legal Documents

Many of these aspects of the nature of the entity can be affected by legal considerations. Therefore, it is important to, at an early stage, consider specific legal documents, including corporate charter and bylaws, minutes of the board of directors and stockholders' meetings, and contracts. Local standards may require disclosure of contracts in the financial statements. Examples are listed in Illustration 6.7.

ILLUSTRATION 6.7

Examples of Legal Documents and Records to Consider in the Context of Understanding the Entity's Nature

Corporate charter – generally gives the name of the corporation, the date of incorporation, the kinds and amounts of capital stock the corporation is authorized to issue, and the types of business activities the corporation is authorized to conduct.

Bylaws – includes rules and procedures of the corporation including fiscal year, frequency of stockholder meetings, method of voting for Board of Directors, and the duties and powers of the corporate officer.

Corporate minutes – official record of the meetings of the board of directors and stockholders. Include authorization of compensation of officers, new contracts, acquisition of fixed assets, loans and dividends payments.

Contracts – include long-term notes and payables, stock options, pension plans, contracts with vendors, government contracts, royalty agreements, union contracts, and leases.

Auditors are interested in all **contracts**. Contracts that are of particular interest to auditors are long-term notes and bonds payable, stock options, pension plans, contracts with vendors for future delivery of supplies, government contracts for completion and delivery of manufactured products, royalty agreements, union contracts, and leases. Contracts may affect the assessed inherent risk.

■ The Entity's Objectives, Strategies and Related Business Risks

The auditor will also consider the entity's objectives and strategies, and the related business risks that may affect the financial statements. The **entity's objectives** are the overall plans for the company as determined by those charged with **governance**[15] and management. *Strategies* are the operational approaches by which management intends to achieve its objectives. Significant conditions, events, circumstances or actions that could adversely affect the entity's ability to achieve its objectives and execute its strategies create **business risks**. The concept of business risks is broader than the concept of risks of material misstatements in the financial statements. However, most business risks will typically have a financial consequence, and hence will find their way into the financial statements.

One could compare a business entity to a living system. The communications network (formal and informal) is like a central nervous system where important direction is given from the brain to the body to perform work. In an organization, management or those responsible for governance (e.g. the board of directors) formulate a strategy which, in turn, influences how employees perform work. Any living organism has a symbiotic relationship with the environment. Events such as severe weather may engender survival risks for an entity. Searching for food in the environment modifies the work an organism does and shapes its survival strategy. Similarly, in business organizations there exists a symbiotic alliance between the business processes of the organization and external economic agents. Customers, suppliers, shareholders, and the general public are external economic agents who impact on a company's profitability and ultimate survival. Financial statements are the communications that describe, on a monetary level, the company's dynamic interrelationship with external agents.

■ Strategic Framework

An interesting interpretation of this part of the "understanding and risk assessment" phase is taken in a strategy-oriented framework,[16] which involves the following steps:

1 Understand the client's strategic advantage. What are the entity's plans? What market niches do they control?
2 Understand the risks that threaten the client's business objectives. What forces are challenging the entity's competitive advantages?
3 Understand the key processes and related competencies to realize strategic advantage. What advantages and competencies are needed to increase market share in their business area? What are the risks and safeguards?
4 Measure and benchmark process performance. What is the evidence that the expected value is being created by the strategy?
5 Document the understanding of the client's ability to create value and generate future cash flows using a client business model, process analysis, **key performance indicators**, and a business risk profile.
6 Use the comprehensive business knowledge decision frame to develop expectations about key **assertions** embodied in the overall financial statements.
7 Compare reported financial results to expectations and design additional audit test work to address any gaps between expectations.

This method uses the models given in Illustrations 6.3 and 6.6.

Illustration 6.8 shows what an auditor might consider in determining objectives, strategies and risks of the firm.

■ Measurement and Review of the Entity's Financial Performance

In order to assess the risk of material misstatements in the financial statements, an auditor should examine internally generated information used by management and external (third party) evaluations of the company. Internal measures provide management with information about progress towards meeting the entity's objectives. Internal information may include key performance indicators, budgets, variance analysis, segment information, and divisional, departmental or other level performance reports, and comparisons

ILLUSTRATION 6.8

Considerations Concerning Entity Objectives, Strategies and Related Business Risks

Existence of objectives (i.e., how the entity addresses industry, regulatory, and other external factors) relating to, for example, the following:

■ Industry developments (potential related business risk – entity does not have the personnel or expertise to deal with the changes in the industry)

■ New products and services (potential related business risk – increased product liability)

■ Expansion of the business (potential related business risk – demand has not been accurately estimated)

■ New accounting requirements (potential related business risk – incomplete or improper implementation, increased costs)

■ Regulatory requirements (potential related business risk – increased legal exposure)

■ Current and prospective financing requirements (potential related business risk – loss of financing due to inability to meet requirements)

■ Use of IT (potential related business risk – systems and processes not compatible).

Effects of implementing a strategy, particularly any effects that will lead to new accounting requirements (potential related business risk – incomplete or improper implementation).

of an entity's performance with that of competitors. External information, such as analysts' reports and credit rating agency reports, may be useful to the auditor. Internal or external performance measures may create pressures on management to misstate the financial statements. A deviation in the performance measures may indicate a risk of misstatement of related financial statement information. See Illustration 6.9.

ILLUSTRATION 6.9

Measurement and Review of the Entity's Financial Performance

The following are matters that an auditor might consider before performing analytical procedures during the planning phase:[19]

■ Key ratios and operating statistics

■ Key performance indicators

■ Employee performance measures and incentive compensation policies

■ Use of forecasts, budgets and variance analysis

■ Analyst reports and credit rating reports

■ Competitor analysis

■ Period-on-period financial performance (revenue growth, profitability, leverage)

■ Trends.

Analytical procedures are so important to the audit and so universally employed, that a separate chapter is needed to describe them (Chapter 9 Analytical Procedures). Analytical procedures[17] are performed at least twice in an audit. ISA 520 states,[18] "The auditor should apply analytical procedures at the planning and overall review stages of the audit." In addition, most practicing accountants recommend analytical procedures also be applied during Phase III (testing and evidence). However, in this section we will only discuss the analytical procedures in the planning stage. Illustration 6.10 summarizes some important characteristics of analytical procedures performed at the three stages of an audit.

ILLUSTRATION 6.10

Important Characteristics of Analytical Procedures at Three Audit Stages

Stage of an Audit	Required?	Purpose	Comment
Planning	Yes	To assist in planning the nature, timing and extent of other auditing procedures.	Level of aggregation can vary and will have impact on effectiveness.
Substantive testing	No	To obtain evidential matter about particular assertions related to account balances or classes of transactions.	Effectiveness depends upon: ■ nature of assertion, ■ plausibility and predictability of relations, ■ reliability of data, ■ precision of expectation.
Overall review	Yes	To assist in assessing the conclusions reached and in the evaluation of the overall financial statement presentation.	Includes reading financial statements to consider: ■ accuracy of evidence gathered for unusual or unexpected balances identified during planning or during course of audit, ■ unusual or unexpected balances or relationships previously identified.

The auditor should apply analytical procedures at the planning stage to assist in understanding the business and in identifying areas of potential risk. Application of analytical procedures may indicate aspects of the business of which the auditor was unaware. Analytical procedures in planning the audit use information that is both financial and non-financial (e.g. the relationship between sales and square footage of selling space or volume of goods sold).

In order to better understand the client's business and industry, the auditor will calculate typical ratios and compare the company ratios to those of the industry. If the auditor is concerned about possible misstatements the ratios like repair and maintenance expenses can be compared to prior years and looked at for fluctuations. To learn about liquidity or going concern, the auditor may compare the current or quick ratio to previous years and to the industry.

When analytical procedures identify significant fluctuations or relationships that are inconsistent with other relevant information or that deviate from predicted amounts, the auditor should increase procedures to obtain adequate explanations and appropriate corroborative evidence.

■ Internal Control

As addressed before, internal control – the final aspect to consider in understanding the entity and its environment – will be dealt with separately in Chapter 7 Internal Control and Control Risk, given the complexity and extent of this topic. However, it should be borne in mind that the auditor needs to obtain a level of understanding of an entity's internal control that is sufficient for a proper understanding of the entity. A good understanding of internal control is required for an appropriate assessment of the risk of material misstatement in the financial statements.

6.4 Based on the Evidence, Assess Risk; Types of Risk

■ The Risk Assessment Process

Before risk can be assessed, the auditor must perform procedures to obtain an understanding of accounting and internal control systems (see Chapter 7 Internal Control and Control Risk). Audit procedures to obtain an understanding are referred to as "risk assessment procedures"[20] because some of the results may be used by the auditor as audit evidence to support the assessments of the risks of material misstatement of the financial statements. The audit evidence obtained might also apply to transactions, account balances, disclosures, and the operating effectiveness of controls.

The auditor examines the risks of material misstatement at the financial statement level and at the **financial statement assertion** level for **classes of transactions**, account balances, and disclosures. Risks that exist at the financial statement level are pervasive, i.e. they have a potential impact on a large number of items in the financial statements. An example is the risk that a company is unable to continue as a going concern. This risk would not just have an impact on one item of the financial statements, but would be of importance on the recognition and valuation of many items. Other risks are confined to one or only a few assertions in the financial statements, e.g. the risk of theft from a specific warehouse A could have an impact on the **existence** of the items recorded on account balance "Inventory warehouse A". "Inventory" is the financial statement element and the related class of transaction would be "Goods in" or "Goods out."

Assessment Tasks

To assess the misstatement risks, the auditor performs four tasks.

1 Identify risks by developing an understanding of the entity and its environment, including relevant controls that relate to the risks. Analyze the strategic risks and the significant classes of transactions.

2 Relate the identified risks to what could go wrong in management's assertions about completeness, existence, valuation, occurrence, and measurement of transactions or assertions about rights, obligations, presentation, and disclosure.

3 Determine whether the risks are of a magnitude that could result in a material misstatement of the financial statements.

4 Consider the likelihood that the risks will result in a material misstatement of the financial statements and their impact on classes of transactions, account balances and disclosures.

Illustration 6.11 gives some guidance on how these four tasks can be documented in terms of strategic risk on significant classes of transactions.

ILLUSTRATION 6.11

Documentation Formats for Strategic Risk and Significant Classes of Transactions

Strategic risk(s)

W/P ref	Description	Significance		Potential FS effect (including assertion)
		Magnitude of impact	Likelihood of occurrence	
	[Enter description here]			

Significant classes of transactions

W/P ref	Description	FS assertion
	[Enter description here]	

■ Business Risk, Audit Risk and its Components

As discussed before, business risks result from significant conditions, events, circumstances, or actions that could adversely affect the entity's ability to achieve its objectives and execute its strategies. Even though such risks are likely to eventually have an impact on an entity's financial statements, not every business risk will translate directly in a risk of a material misstatement in the financial statements, which is often referred to as audit risk. For example, the fact that an engineering company has difficulty finding sufficient engineers is clearly a business risk, without there being an obvious direct link to an audit risk.

Audit Risk

Audit risk is the risk that the auditor gives an inappropriate audit opinion when the financial statements are materially misstated. Audit risk is a measure of how reliable the information used by the accounting system is, i.e. how much reliance can be put on it. The higher the audit risk, the more evidence must be gathered in order for the auditor to obtain sufficient assurance as a basis for expressing an opinion on the financial statements.

Audit risk has three components: inherent risk, control risk and detection risk.[21] Even though the new ISAs make only scarce reference to these components, we believe that they are illustrative in understanding how the risk assessment process works. The three components are traditionally defined as follows:

1 **Inherent risk** is the susceptibility of an account balance or class of transactions to misstatements that could be material, individually or when aggregated with misstatements in other balances or classes, assuming that there were no related internal controls.

2 **Control risk** is the risk that a misstatement that could occur in an account balance or class of transactions and that could be material – individually or when aggregated with misstatements in other balances or classes – will not be prevented or detected and corrected on a timely basis by accounting and internal control systems.

3 **Detection risk** is the risk that an auditor's substantive procedures[22] will not detect a misstatement that exists in an account balance or class of transactions that could be material, individually or when aggregated with misstatements in other balances or classes.

When inherent and control risks are high, acceptable detection risk needs to be low to reduce audit risk to an acceptably low level. For example, if the internal control structure is effective in preventing and/or detecting errors (i.e. control risk is low), the auditor is able to perform less effective substantive tests (detection risk is high). Alternatively, if the account balance is more susceptible to misstatement (inherent risk is higher), the auditor must apply more effective substantive testing procedures (detection risk is lower). In short, the higher the assessment of inherent and control risk, the more audit evidence the auditor should obtain from the performance of substantive procedures.

Concept and a Company 6.1

Bristol-Myers Squibb 2001–03 – Business Risk and Significant Risk

Concept	What is business risk? What is significant risk?
Story	During the period 2001 through 2003, Bristol-Myers Squibb, a large New York-based pharmaceutical company, lost about 11 percent of its sales and saw its stock value decrease by about 50 percent due to business and significant risks.

Major events triggering Bristol's problems included the following:

1 Sales losses for 2002 of about $2 billion (11 percent) to generic manufacturers resulting from expiration of patents on three key drugs – cancer medicine Taxol, diabetes drug Glucophage, and anti-anxiety medicine BuSpar. (Revell 2003)
2 Investment loss of about two-thirds of its stake in biotech company ImClone Systems acquired in late 2001 for $1.2 billion, due to delays in FDA approval of ImClone's intended blockbuster cancer drug Erbitux, and compounded by well-publicized insider-trading scandals (Anand 2002) centering around ImClone's founder Samuel Waksal who was sentenced to 87 months in prison for his role in the scandal.
3 Between 1999 and 2001, the company acknowledged it had overstated revenue by $2.5 billion by improperly recording sales to wholesales, generally towards the end of the quarter, in order to meet quarterly sales projections established by senior management. (Landers 2003) This practice (called "channel stuffing") involved the company persuading its wholesale customers to buy about $2 billion more of drugs than they actually needed so that Bristol could meet its earnings targets for that year. The SEC and the Justice Department launched an investigation into inventory and accounting practices.

Discussion Questions	■ Discuss of the events given – which were significant risks and which were business risks. ■ How could Bristol Myers have avoided these risks?

References	Anand, G., 2002, "Focus of Furor, ImClone's CEO Calls It Quits," *Wall Street Journal*, May 23, p. B.I. Landers, Peter, 2003, "Bristol-Myers Launches Review Into Sales, Marketing Practices," *The Wall Street Journal*, July 26. Revell, J., 2003, "Bristol-Myers Cleans Up Its Mess," *Fortune*, February 17, p. 136.

Illustration 6.12 shows a symbolic graphic used by AICPA to illustrate how audit risk works. The potential pool of material errors is represented by the *tap*[23] at the top of the illustration. The *sieves*[24] represent the means by which the client and the auditor attempt to remove material errors from the financial statements. The auditor has no way of knowing how many errors exist.

Components of Audit Risk Illustration

In Illustration 6.12, the first sieve represents the internal control system. The client may install a system of internal accounting control to detect material errors and correct them. Ideally, the control system should detect any material errors before they enter the financial statements. However, there is some risk that errors will either pass undetected through the control system (perhaps as a result of a breakdown or weakness) or will bypass the control system altogether (e.g. where there are no controls in place such as an unusual exchange of non-monetary assets). The liquid falling through the sieve represents the errors not detected and the spillover represents those errors that bypass the control system. If the internal control system does not detect and correct the errors, they will be included in the financial statements. The auditor must design audit procedures that will provide reasonable assurance that material errors will be detected and removed from the financial statements. In Illustration 6.12, the second sieve represents the auditor's procedures. Despite internal controls and auditors' procedures to detect misstatement, there will always be the possibility that some misstatements will be undetected. This is audit risk.

> **ILLUSTRATION 6.12**
>
> ## Components of Audit Risk[25]
>
>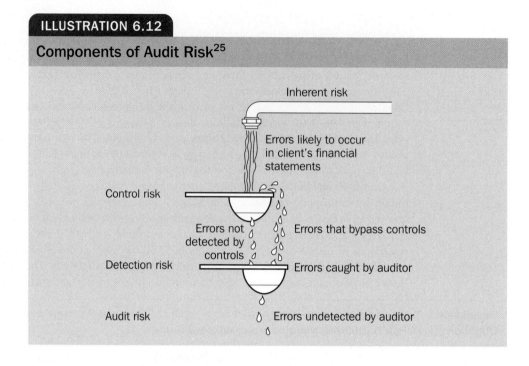

Illustrations 6.13 and 6.14 show the relationship between inherent, control and detection risks.

> **ILLUSTRATION 6.13**
>
> ## Interrelationship of the Components of Audit Risk
>
> The following table shows how the acceptable level of detection risk may vary based on assessments of inherent and control risks, based on the Appendix to International Standard on Auditing 400.
>
> | | | Auditor's assessment of control | | |
> | --- | --- | --- | --- | --- |
> | | | High | Medium | Low |
> | Auditor's assessment of inherent risk | High | Lowest | Lower | Medium |
> | | Medium | Lower | Medium | Higher |
> | | Low | Medium | Higher | Highest |
>
> The darker shaded areas in this table relate to detection risk.
>
> There is an inverse relationship between detection risk and the combined level of inherent and control risks. For example, when inherent and control risks are high, acceptable levels of detection risk need to be low to reduce audit risk to an acceptably low level. On the other hand, when inherent and control risks are low, an auditor can accept a higher detection risk and still reduce audit risk to an acceptably low level.

ILLUSTRATION 6.14

Relationship between Inherent, Control and Detection Risk

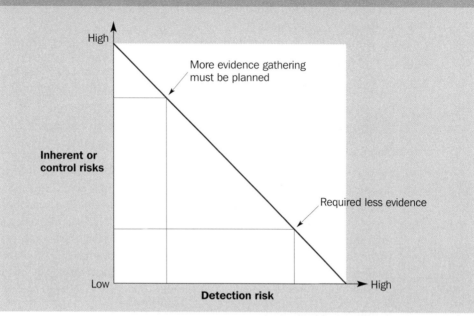

 ## Certification Exam Question 6.2[26]

The risk that an auditor will conclude, based on substantive tests, that a material misstatement does not exist in an account balance when, in fact, such misstatement does exist is referred to as:

(A) Sampling Risk.
(B) Detection Risk.
(C) Nonsampling Risk.
(D) Inherent Risk.

 ## Certification Exam Question 6.3

Relationship between control risk and detection risk is ordinarily:

(A) Parallel.
(B) Inverse.
(C) Direct.
(D) Equal.

■ Significant Risks

Significant risks are audit risks that require special audit consideration. Significant risks generally relate to judgmental matters and significant non-routine transactions. Judgment is used, for example, in the development of significant accounting or **fair value**

213

estimates. Non-routine transactions are transactions that are unusual, either due to size or nature, and that therefore occur infrequently. Risks of material misstatement may be greater for significant judgmental matters requiring accounting estimates or revenue recognition, and for assumptions about the effects of future events (e.g. fair value) than for ordinary transactions.

Significant non-routine transactions may arise from management intervention in specifying the accounting treatment for a transaction, manual intervention for data collection and processing, complex calculations or accounting principles, transactions for which there is difficulty in implementing effective controls, and significant related party transactions. These risks are less likely to be subjected to routine control systems and so a more in-depth understanding helps the auditor develop an effective audit approach.

Special Audit Consideration

As part of risk assessment, the auditor may determine some of the risks identified are significant risks that require special audit consideration. Classification of a risk as requiring special consideration is important in the context of the auditor's response to the risk (see Chapter 8 Control Risk, Audit Planning and Test of Controls). In particular, it is even more important for significant than for non-significant risks that the auditor evaluates the design of the entity's controls, including relevant control procedures, and obtains contemporaneous evidence as to whether or not they have been implemented. Further, it is required that the auditor performs substantive procedures[27] that are specifically responsive to the risks.

Is the Risk Significant?

Significant risks arise on most audits, but their determination is a matter for the auditor's professional judgment. In determining what is a significant risk the auditor considers a number of matters, including the following:[28]

- Whether the risk is a risk of fraud.
- The likelihood of the occurrence of the risk.
- The likely magnitude of the potential misstatement and the possibility that the risk may give rise to multiple misstatements.
- Whether the risk is related to recent significant economic, accounting, or other developments and, therefore, requires specific attention.
- The complexity of transactions that may give rise to the risk.
- Whether the risk involves significant transactions with related parties.
- The degree of subjectivity in the measurement of financial information related to the risk.
- Whether the risk involves significant transactions that are outside the normal course of business for the entity, or that otherwise appear to be unusual given the auditor's understanding of the entity and its environment.

Certification Exam Question 6.4[29]

The audit program usually cannot be finalized until the:

(A) Consideration of the entity's internal control has been completed.
(B) Engagement letter has been signed by the auditor and the client.
(C) Audit findings have been communicated to the audit committee of the board of directors.
(D) Search for unrecorded liabilities has been performed and documented.

6.5 Planning Materiality

Materiality is defined in IFAC's *Glossary Of Terms*:[30]

> "Information is material if its omission or misstatement could influence the economic decisions of users taken on the basis of the financial statements. Materiality depends on the size of the item or error judged in the particular circumstances of its omission or misstatement. Thus, materiality provides a threshold or cutoff point rather than being a primary qualitative characteristic which information must have if it is to be useful."

The auditor's responsibility is to express an opinion on whether the financial statements are prepared, in all material respects, in accordance with financial accounting standards. Materiality is the degree of inaccuracy or imprecision that is still considered acceptable given the purpose of the financial statements.

■ Materiality Level

Planning materiality is a concept that is used to design the audit such that the auditor can obtain reasonable assurance that any error of a relevant (material) size or nature will be identified. There are additional costs for an auditor to audit with a lower materiality. The lower the materiality, the more costly is the audit. If any error of whatever small size needs to be found in the audit, the auditor would spend significantly more time than when a certain level of imprecision (higher materiality level) is considered acceptable.

What is material is often difficult to determine in practice. However, four factors are generally considered: size of item; nature of item; the circumstances; and the cost and benefit of auditing the item.

■ Size of the Item

The most common application of materiality concerns the *size of the item* considered. A large dollar amount item omitted from the financial statements is generally material. Size must be considered in relative terms, for example, as a percentage of the relevant base (net income, total assets, sales, etc.) rather than an absolute amount. The view that size is an essential determinant of materiality means that, for financial reporting purposes, materiality can only be judged in relation to items or errors which are quantifiable in monetary terms.

■ Nature of the Item

The *nature of an item* is a qualitative characteristic. An auditor cannot quantify the materiality decision in all cases; certain items may have significance even though the dollar amount may not be quite as large as the auditor would typically consider material. For example, a political bribe by a client, even though immaterial in size, may nevertheless be of such a sensitive nature and have such an effect on the company financial statement that users would need to be told. It has been suggested[31] that in making judgments about materiality, the following aspects of the nature of a misstatement should be considered:

■ the events or transactions giving rise to the misstatement;

■ the legality, sensitivity, normality, and potential circumstances of the event or transaction;
■ the identity of any other parties involved; and
■ the accounts and disclosure notes affected.

■ Circumstances of Occurrence

The materiality of an error depends upon the *circumstances of its occurrence*. There are two types of relevant circumstances:

1 the users of the accounting information's economic decision-making process;
2 the context of the accounting information in which an item or error occurs.

Since materiality means the impact on the decisions of the user, the auditor must have knowledge of the likely users of the financial statements and those users' decisions process. If a company is being audited prior to listing on a national stock exchange or a large loan or merger, the users will be of one type. If statements of a closely held partnership are being audited, users will be of a different type.

   For example, if the primary users of the financial statements are creditors, the auditor may assign a low materiality threshold to those items on financial statements that affect **liquidity**[32] such as current assets and current liabilities. On the other hand, if the primary users are investors or potential investors, the auditor may assign a low materiality threshold to income. Secondly, a misstatement may be in the context of comparative figures and trends, financial statements of comparable entities, and management or stakeholder expectations.

Certification Exam Question 6.5[33]

Which of the following relatively small misstatements most likely could have a material effect on an entity's financial statements?

(A) An illegal payment to a foreign official that was not recorded.
(B) A piece of obsolete office equipment that was not retired.
(C) A petty cash fund disbursement that was not properly authorized.
(D) An uncollectible account receivable that was not written off.

■ Reliability, Precision and Amount of Evidence

The auditor should consider materiality and its relationship with audit risk when conducting an audit, according to ISA 320.[34] What does this mean? In statistical sampling, there is a fixed relationship between:

■ the reliability of an assertion based on the sampling (in auditing this is determined by audit risk);
■ the precision of this statement (in auditing it is determined by materiality);
■ the amount of evidence that should be gathered in order to make this assertion.

Changes in one of these three items have implications for (one of) the other two.

■ Example: Three Assumptions in the Same Circumstance

A real-life example might illustrate this relationship between reliability, precision, and amount of evidence. Suppose you are asked to make an assertion about the average taxable income of randomly selected people, shopping at the Kurfurstendamm in Berlin. Also suppose that gathering information regarding the taxable income of these people is costly. Consider the following three situations:

1 You are asked to make, with a high degree of reliability (you were asked to bet quite some money on the correctness of your assertion), the assertion that the average annual taxable income of ten people will be between minus and plus €300,000,000. Even though a high degree of reliability is requested (i.e. a lot is at stake for you), you will probably do little or no investigative work because you were allowed to make a very imprecise statement (i.e. a very high level of tolerance is allowed).

2 You are asked to make, with a low degree of reliability (you were asked to bet only a symbolic €1 on the correctness of your assertion), the assertion that the average annual taxable income of these random ten people will be between 0 and €70,000. Even though this time a high degree of precision is requested, you will probably only do little or no (costly) investigative work, since you were only asked to make your assertion with a low degree of reliability (not a lot at stake for you).

3 You are asked to make, with a high degree of reliability (again, you were asked to bet quite some money on the correctness of your assertion), the assertion that the average annual taxable income of these ten people will be between 0 and €70,000. Because of the high degree of reliability and precision requested (i.e. a lot is at stake for you and only a relatively low degree of tolerance is accepted in your statement), you will probably do extensive investigative work.

These examples might clarify how there is an inverse relationship between audit risk (as a measure of reliability) and materiality (as a measure of precision). (See also Illustration 6.15).

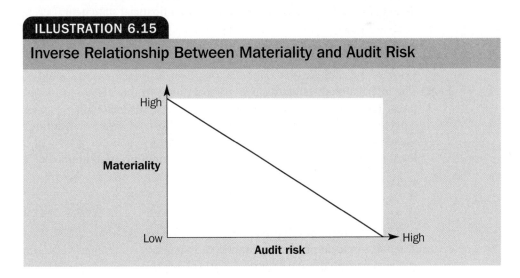

ILLUSTRATION 6.15

Inverse Relationship Between Materiality and Audit Risk

What degree of imprecision or materiality is acceptable in auditing financial statements? In order to decide this, the imprecision tolerated should be related to the size of the audited company's business and its profitability. Try to determine how much error or misstatement auditors would be willing to tolerate and still render an opinion that the financial statements were not materially misleading in Case One and Case Two, following.

■ Materially Misstated or Not?

Case One

A few days before the end of 20X1, a $1,000 expenditure for the repair of equipment was incorrectly charged to the equipment account in the balance sheet rather than to operating expenses in the income statement. As a result (ignoring depreciation), total assets should be stated at $1,589,000 instead of $1,590,000 and income before taxes should be stated at $107,000 instead of $108,000. Are the financial statements still fairly presented and not materially misleading?

Case Two

A few days before the end of 20X1, $50,000 expenditure for the repair of equipment was incorrectly charged to the equipment account rather than to operating expenses. As a result (ignoring depreciation), total assets should be stated at $1,490,000 rather than $1,540,000 and income before taxes should be stated at $58,000 rather than $108,000? Are the financial statements fairly presented and not materially misleading?

Analysis

In Case One the financial statements are fairly presented and not materially misstated because the $1,000 difference in assets and net income will not make a difference to the financial statement user, i.e. it is not material. Case Two is different. The financial statements are materially misstated, primarily because net income, an important basis of materiality, is overstated by 86 percent. This overstatement of net income is something that could definitely change the decisions of a financial statement user, i.e. it is material.

■ Where to Set Materiality?

Considering all these materiality factors, then, at what amount should materiality be set? The international standards give no guidelines. In the USA only 10 percent of authoritative accounting pronouncements contain specific materiality percentages, and only 6 percent give judgment items.[33] In practice, however, every accounting firm has its own set of guidelines or "rules of thumb" related to a financial statement base such as net income, total revenues, etc. Rules of thumb commonly used in practice include:

- 5 to 10 percent of net income before taxes;
- 5 to 10 percent of current assets;
- 5 to 10 percent of current liabilities;
- 0.5 to 2 percent of total assets;
- 0.5 to 2 percent of total revenues;
- 1 to 5 percent of total equity.

The appropriate financial statement base for computing materiality will vary based on the nature of the client's business. For example, if a company is near break even, net income for the year will be much too small to use as the financial statement base. In that case the auditors will often choose another financial statement base or use an average of net income over a number of prior years.

Concept and a Company 6.2

Arthur Andersen, Waste Management and Materiality

Concept	What is material and how is materiality determined?

Story

In 1993 and early 1994, Arthur Andersen audited Waste Management's 1993 financial statements. By February 1, 1994, the engagement team quantified current and prior period misstatements totaling $128 million, which, if recorded, would have reduced net income before special items by 12 percent.

The engagement team prepared Proposed Adjusting Journal Entries (PAJEs) in that amount for Waste Management to record in 1993. A PAJE is an adjustment proposed by the auditor to the company during the audit that, if accepted by the company, would correct a misstatement in the books.

The engagement team also identified "accounting practices that gave rise to other known and likely misstatements" involving understatements of operating expenses for which **no** PAJEs were prepared. These misstatements included, among other things:

1 amounts for deferred costs of impaired projects that should have been written off;
2 land carrying values in excess of net realizable value;
3 improper purchase acquisition accruals in connection with the establishment of environmental remediation reserves (liabilities);
4 reversals of the environmental remediation reserves (liabilities) to income; and
5 unsupported changes to the salvage values of waste vehicles and containers.

The engagement team also knew of the company's capitalized interest methodology, which Andersen knew did not conform to GAAP but which it had determined was "not materially inaccurate."

Waste Management refused to record the PAJEs or to correct the accounting practices giving rise to the PAJEs and other misstatements and likely misstatements.

The engagement team informed Andersen's risk management partner of the PAJEs and questionable accounting practices. Andersen's Audit Objectives and Procedures Manual required that risk management partners consult with senior partners when cumulative PAJEs exceeded 8 percent of net income from continuing operations. These partners reviewed and discussed the unrecorded PAJEs as well as "continuing audit issues." They determined that Andersen would nonetheless issue an **unqualified** audit report on Waste Management's 1993 financial statements.

Applying an analytical procedure for evaluating the materiality of audit findings referred to as the "roll-forward" method, these partners determined that, because the majority of PAJEs concerned prior period misstatements, the impact of the PAJEs relating to current period misstatements on Waste Management's 1993 income statement was **not material**. They would issue an unqualified audit report. But they also warned Waste Management that Andersen expected the company to change its accounting practices and to reduce the cumulative amount of the PAJEs in the future.

Arthur Andersen, Waste Management and Materiality (continued)

Discussion Questions	■ What analysis do you think the engagement team did to determine the amount of the PAJEs?
	■ By what reasoning did the audit team determine the accounting practices that gave rise to other known and likely misstatements mentioned that did not need adjustment?
	■ What items do you think the senior partners discussed when determining that Andersen would issue an unqualified opinion?
References	SEC, 2001, Release No. 44444, *Accounting And Auditing Enforcement Release No. 1405*, "In the Matter of Arthur Andersen LLP Respondent," Securities and Exchange Commission, June 19.

6.6 Summary

The auditor should plan the audit work so that the audit will be performed in an effective manner. Planning means developing a general strategy and a detailed approach for the expected nature, timing, and extent of the audit. The objective of planning is to determine the amount and type of evidence and review required to give the auditor assurance that there is no material misstatement of the financial statements.

The planning procedures are:

■ perform audit procedures to understand the entity and its environment, including the entity's internal control;
■ assess the risks of material misstatements of the financial statements;
■ determine materiality;
■ prepare the planning memorandum and audit program, containing the auditor's response to the identified risks.

This chapter has covered the first three steps in the planning process, with the exception of the internal control considerations, which are dealt with in Chapter 7 Internal Control and Control Risk.

In performing an audit of financial statements, the auditor should have or obtain an understanding of the entity and its environment sufficient to enable the auditor to identify and understand the events, transactions, practices, and risks that, in the auditor's judgment, may have a significant effect on the financial statements or on the examination or audit report. This business knowledge requires knowledge of the industry and company (including finances, internal controls, legal issues, and related party information). It is important to understand the client's industry because its industry has specific risks created by the nature of the business, accounting conventions, and industry regulation. Understanding inherent risks common to all companies in a certain industry helps the auditor identify the inherent risks of the individual company.

Crucial information about a company starts with management's attitudes, organization, and direction. Initial interviews with client's management and other personnel are key procedures. A visit to, and tour of, the company premises will help the auditor develop a better understanding of the client's business and operations. Certain documents and records should be collected and examined early in the engagement. Analytical procedures are performed at least twice in an audit: at the planning and overall review stages of the audit.

ISA 315 distinguishes the following relevant aspects in the understanding of the entity and its environment:

- industry, regulatory and other external factors, including the applicable financial reporting framework;
- nature of the entity, including the entity's selection and application of accounting policies;
- objectives and strategies and the related business risks that may result in a material misstatement of the financial statements;
- measurement and review of the entity's financial performance;
- internal control (discussed in Chapter 7 Internal Control and Control Risk).

There are primarily two categories of risk of concern to an auditor: business risk and audit risk. Business risks result from significant conditions, events, circumstances or actions that could adversely affect the entity's ability to achieve its objectives and execute its strategies. Even though such risks are likely eventually to have an impact on an entity's financial statements, not every business risk will translate directly in a risk of a material misstatement in the financial statements, which is often referred to as audit risk. Significant risks are audit risks that require specific audit consideration. Significant risks generally relate to judgmental matters and significant non-routine transactions. Classification of a risk as a significant risk might have an impact on the auditor's response to that risk. This will be dealt with in Chapter 8 Control Risk, Audit Planning and Test of Controls.

Audit risk has three components: inherent risk, control risk, and detection risk. Inherent risk is the susceptibility of an account balance or class of transactions to misstatements that could be material (individually or when aggregated with misstatements in other balances or classes), assuming that there were no related internal controls. Control risk is the risk that a material misstatement that could occur will not be prevented or detected and corrected on a timely basis by accounting and internal control systems. Detection risk is the risk that an auditor's substantive procedures will not detect a misstatement that exists in an account balance or class of transactions that could be material.

The auditor assesses the risks of material misstatement at the financial statement level, and at the assertion level for classes of transactions, account balances, and disclosures. The higher the audit risk, the more evidence must be collected to reduce the risk to an acceptable level. To assess the audit risk, the auditor performs four tasks.

1 Identify risks by developing an understanding of the company environment, including relevant controls that relate to the risks, key transactions, fairness of account balances, and key financial statement disclosures.
2 Relate the identified risks to what could make management's assertions go wrong about completeness, existence, valuation, occurrence, and measurement of transactions or assertions about rights, obligations, presentation, and disclosure.
3 Determine whether the risks are of a magnitude that could result in a material misstatement of the financial statements.
4 Consider the likelihood that the risks will result in a material misstatement of the financial statements.

The auditor should consider materiality and its relationship with audit risk when conducting an audit. It is the auditor's responsibility to determine whether financial statements are materially misstated. The auditor considers materiality at both the overall financial statement level and in relation to individual account balances, classes of transactions, and disclosures.

6.7 Answers to Certification Exam Questions

6.1 (A) The requirement is to obtain an understanding of the entity's internal controls for audit planning. Answer (A) is correct because the auditor should obtain an understanding of the design of relevant internal controls for financial reporting and each of the five internal control components. Answers (B) and (C) are not correct because the auditor is not required as part of obtaining an understanding of internal control to determine the operating effectiveness of internal control or the consistency with which the controls are applied. Answer (D) is incorrect because not all transaction classes and account balances have controls, and some account balances may not be material.

6.2 (B) The requirement is to assess the risk that an auditor will find no misstatements but they do, in fact, exist. Answer (B) is correct because the part of the audit risk that is under the auditor's control is detection risk – and that risk is that misstatement will not be detected by the auditor's procedures. Answer (A) is wrong because sampling risk arises from the possibility that the auditor's conclusion, based on a sample, may be different from the conclusion reached if the entire population were subjected to the same audit procedure. Answer (C) is wrong because non-sampling risk arises from factors that cause the auditor to reach an erroneous conclusion for any reason not related to the size of the sample. For example, most audit evidence is persuasive rather than conclusive, the auditor might use inappropriate procedures, or the auditor might misinterpret evidence and fail to recognize an error. Answer (D) is incorrect because inherent risk is something over which the auditor has no control.

6.3 (B) The requirement is to state the relationship between control risk and detection risk. Answer (B) is correct because as control risk increases, the risk of not detecting misstatement should be set low. The two do not move in parallel (answer (A)) nor in an equal direction (answer (D)). Control risk and detection risk are not directly related.

6.4 (A) The requirement is to determine what must occur before an audit program may be finalized. Answer (A) is correct because no audit program can be written without first determining what information is reliable or not because of internal controls or lack thereof. The engagement is not required in all countries and even when it is, it may not necessarily be signed by the client, so answer (B) is incorrect. Audit findings cannot be reported before an audit program is written and the audit has occurred, so answer (C) is incorrect. Search for unrecorded liabilities is part of the audit that occurs after the audit program has be drawn up. Answer (D) is wrong.

6.5 (A) The requirement is what type of small misstatements may have a material effect. Answer (A) is correct because illegal payments, once they are found out, could harm the company's stock price and operations. Small misstatements brought about by a piece of obsolete office equipment (B) or petty cash disbursements (C) are not material. An uncollectable receivable would only be material if it was a small amount such as we are talking about here.

6.9 Notes

1 IFAC, 2003, *Handbook of International Auditing, Assurance, and Ethics Pronouncements*, International Standards on Auditing 300 (ISA 300), "Planning", para. 2, International Federation of Accountants, New York.

2 IAASB, 2003, *International Standard on Auditing 315 (ISA 315)*, "Understanding the Entity and Its Environment and Assessing the Risks of Material Misstatement," International Federation of Accountants, New York, October 2003.

3 IFAC, 2004, *Handbook of International Auditing, Assurance, and Ethics Pronouncements*, International Standard on Auditing 330 (ISA 330), "The Auditor's Procedures In Response to Assessed Risks," International Federation of Accountants, New York.

4 IFAC, 2004, *Handbook of International Auditing, Assurance, and Ethics Pronouncements*, International Standard on Auditing 500R (ISA 500), "Audit Evidence," International Federation of Accountants, New York.

5 Part of the new risk standard suite is an amendment to ISA 200, "Objective and General Principles Governing an Audit of Financial Statements." ISA 315, "Understanding the Entity and Its Environment and Assessing the Risks of Material Misstatement" will replace ISA 310, "Knowledge of the Business"; ISA 400, "Risk Assessments and Internal Control"; and ISA 401, "Auditing in a Computer Information Systems Environment". ISA 330, "The Auditor's Procedures in Response to Assessed Risks" also replaces ISA 400 and ISA 401. New ISA 500, "Audit Evidence" replaces the old ISA 500, "Audit Evidence."

6 Update and Modification of International Auditing and Assurance Standards Board, 2002, *Exposure Draft Audit Risk Proposed International Standards on Auditing*, Appendix 2: Overview of the Proposed ISAs, International Federation of Accountants, New York, October.

7 Bell, T., *et al.*, 1997, *Auditing Organizations Through a Strategic-Systems Lens: The KPMG Business Measurement Process*, KPMG, p. 27.

8 Adapted and reprinted with permission from AICPA. Copyright © 2000 & 1985 by American Institute of Certified Public Accountants.

9 See Degenan, J.D. *et al.*, 1995, "Metallgesellschaft AG: A Case Study," *The FMT Review*, Illinois Institute of Technology; and Lowenstein, R., 1995, "Is Corporate Hedging Really Speculation?" *Wall Street Journal*, July 20.

10 See Jorion, P., 1995, *Big Bets Gone Bad: Derivatives and Bankruptcy in Orange County*, Academic Press, September.

11 *Special Purpose Entity (SPEs)* is defined as an entity (e.g. corporation, partnership, trust, joint venture) created for a specific purpose or activity. SPEs may be used to transfer assets and liabilities from an entity – accounted for as a gain for that entity. Between 1993 and 2001, Enron created over 3000 SPEs.

12 See Batson, N., 2000, *Second Interim Report of Neal Batson Court-Appointed Examiner* (for Enron Chapter 11 Corporate Bankruptcy), Case Number 01-16034 (AGJ), United States Bankruptcy Court Southern District of New York, January 21.

13 Adapted from 2004 IFAC, *Handbook of International Auditing, Assurance, and Ethics Pronouncements*, International Standard on Auditing 315 (ISA 315), "Understanding the Entity and Its Environment and Assessing the Risks of Material Misstatement," Appendix 1, International Federation of Accountants, New York.

14 For an entity level model of a retail client see Bell, T., *et al.*, 1997, *Auditing Organizations Through a Strategic-Systems Lens The KPMG Business Measurement Process*, KPMG, p. 41.

15 *Governance* – the term "governance" describes the role of persons entrusted with the supervision, control and direction of an entity. Those charged with governance ordinarily are accountable for ensuring that the entity achieves its objectives, financial reporting, and reporting to interested parties. Those charged with governance include management only when it performs such functions.

16 Bell, T., *et al.*, 1997, *Auditing Organizations Through a Strategic-Systems Lens The KPMG Business Measurement Process*, KPMG, p. 31.

17 According to ISA 520, para. 3, "*Analytical procedures* means the analysis of significant ratios and trends including the resulting investigation of fluctuations and relationships that are inconsistent with other relevant information or which deviate from predicted amounts."

18 IFAC, 2003, *Handbook of International Auditing, Assurance, and Ethics Pronouncements*, International Standards on Auditing 520 (ISA 520), "Analytical Procedures," para. 2, International Federation of Accountants, New York.

19 IFAC International Auditing and Assurance Standards Board, 2002, *Exposure Draft Understanding the Entity and Its Environment and Assessing the Risks of Material Misstatement*, Appendix 1, International Federation of Accountants, New York, October.

20 IFAC, 2004, *Handbook of International Auditing, Assurance, and Ethics Pronouncements*, International Standard on Auditing 500 (ISA 500), "Audit Evidence," International Federation of Accountants, New York.

21 IFAC, 2004, *Handbook of International Auditing, Assurance, and Ethics Pronouncements*, Glossary Of Terms At December 2002, International Federation of Accountants, New York.

22 *Substantive procedures* are tests performed to obtain audit evidence to detect material misstatements in the financial statements, and are of three types: tests of details of transactions, tests of details of balances, and analytical procedures.

23 *Tap* – an apparatus used for controlling the flow of liquid or gas from a pipe: *Oxford Student's Dictionary*, 2003.

24 *Sieve* – utensil with wire network, used for separate small and large lumps, etc.: *Oxford Student's Dictionary*, 2003.

25 AICPA, 1985, Auditing Procedures Study *Audits of Small Business*, AICPA, New York, p. 44.

26 Adapted and reprinted with permission from AICPA. Copyright © 2000 & 1985 by American Institute of Certified Public Accountants.

27 *Substantive procedures* – Substantive procedures are tests performed to obtain audit evidence to detect material misstatements in the financial statements, and are of two types: (a) Tests of details of transactions and balances; and (b) Analytical procedures.

28 IFAC, 2004, *Handbook of International Auditing, Assurance, and Ethics Pronouncements*, International Standard on Auditing 315 (ISA 315), "Understanding the Entity and Its Environment and Assessing the Risks of Material Misstatement," International Federation of Accountants, New York.

29 Adapted and reprinted with permission from AICPA. Copyright © 2000 & 1985 by American Institute of Certified Public Accountants.

30 IFAC, 2004, *Handbook of International Auditing, Assurance, and Ethics Pronouncements*, Glossary Of Terms At December 2002, International Federation of Accountants, New York.

31 Financial Reporting & Auditing Group, *Of International Auditing, Assurance and Ethics Release FRAG 1/9*, Materiality in Financial Reporting – A Discussion Paper, para. 27, the Institute of Chartered Accountants in England and Wales, January 1995.

32 A liquid company has less risk of being able to meet debt than an illiquid one. Also, a liquid business generally has more financial flexibility to take on new investment opportunities.

33 Adapted and reprinted with permission from AICPA. Copyright © 2000 & 1985 by American Institute of Certified Public Accountants.

34 IFAC, 2004, *Handbook of International Auditing, Assurance, and Ethics Pronouncements*, International Standards on Auditing 320 (ISA 320), Audit Materiality (AU 8025), para. 2, International Federation of Accountants, New York.

35 Worthington, J.S., 1990, An inventory of materiality guidelines in accounting literature, *CPA Journal Online*, New York Society of CPAs, July.

6.9 Questions, Exercises and Cases

QUESTIONS

6.2 Planning – Phase II of the Audit Process Model

6.1 What is the objective of audit planning?

6.2 List the planning procedures.

6.3 Describe the approach to auditing risk given in ISAs 315, 330, and 500.

6.3 Understanding The Entity And Its Environment

6.4 When obtaining knowledge of a company what type of material can auditors use? What ISA concept discusses this issue? Briefly discuss the standard.

6.5 How can understanding a certain industry help an auditor?

6.4 Based on the Evidence, Assess Risk; Types of Risk

6.6 What are the definitions of the three audit risk components?

6.7 What components of the audit risk exist independently of the audit? What does an auditor do in this situation?

6.8 Distinguish between Business Risk and Significant Risk.

6.5 Planning Materiality

6.9 How is materiality defined in IFAC's Glossary of Terms?

6.10 What four factors are generally considered in determining materiality? Briefly discuss them.

6.11 What guidelines or "rules of thumb" related to a financial statement base such as net income, total revenues, etc. are commonly used in practice?

PROBLEMS AND EXERCISES

6.2 Planning – Phase II of the Audit Process Model

6.12 Planning Procedures. Constantijn & Nianias, Soma Orkaton Logistons (SOLs), have been hired to audit Eidola Company, a biochemical company listed on the Athens Stock Exchange. Constantijn & Nianias is auditing the client for the first time in the current year as a result of a dispute between Eidola and the previous auditor over the proper booking of sales and accounts receivable for sales of inventory that has not been delivered but has for practical purposes been completed and sold.

Eidola has been grown from a small startup to a highly successful company in the industry in the past seven years, primarily as a result of many successful mergers negotiated by George Panis, the president and chairman of the board. Although other biotech firms have had difficulty in recent years, Eidola continues to prosper, as shown by its constantly increasing earnings and growth. Bayer, the large German chemical company, has a special discount contract with them and represents 15 percent of their sales. In the last year, however, the company's profits turned downward.

His board of directors, that include many of his old university classmates, generally supports Panis. The board, which meets twice annually, recently issued a policy on corporate ethics conduct. Panis says he owes much of his success to the hiring of aggressive young executives paid relatively low salaries combined with an unusually generous profit-sharing plan. The corporate structure is very informal, as Panis does not believe than any employee should have a title or a specific job description as it "gives people airs." Panis's only corporate objective is "to make large profits so our stock price will increase and our shareholders will be happy."

225

The management information system at Eidola is very limited and they lack sophisticated accounting records for a company that size. The information system will be updated this year. The personnel in the accounting department are competent but somewhat overworked and underpaid relative to the other employees, and therefore turnover is high. The most comprehensive records are for production and marketing because Panis believes these areas are more essential to operations than accounting. There are only four internal auditors and they spend the majority of their time taking inventories, which is time consuming because inventories are located at 11 facilities in four countries.

The financial statements for the current year include a profit 20 percent less than the previous year, but the auditors feel it should be a larger decrease because of the reduced volume and the disposal of a segment of the business, Kata-Karpos. The disposal of this segment was considered necessary because it had become increasingly unprofitable over the past three years. When it was acquired from Christopher Panis, George Panis's brother, it was considered profitable even though its largest customer was Kata-Klino, also owned by Christopher Panis.

Eidola is considered under-financed by market analysts. There is excessive current debt and management is reluctant to sell equity on the capital markets because increasing the number of shares will decrease share price. George Panis is now talking to several large companies with hopes of a merger.

Required:

A. Briefly discuss which matters Constantijn & Nianias, SOLs should consider for each of the first three planning procedures.

B. What techniques should the auditors use to gather the necessary information?

6.3 Understanding The Entity And Its Environment

6.13 Nature of the Entity. To get information about the core processes of the entity an auditor examines its business operations, investments, capital structure and financing activities, and financial reporting policies.

Required:

A. Explain the problems an auditor may incur in each of these four areas.

B. What would be the characteristics of a company that had low risk in each of these areas?

C. You are assigned to evaluate on general economic and industry characteristics Eikon Elektronik, AS, a small, but fast-growing Turkish company that manufactures chip memories for personal computers. What business operations, investments, capital structure and financing activities, and financial reporting policies factors do you believe will be important in this evaluation?

6.14 Client Facilities Tour. When an auditor has accepted an engagement from a new client who is a manufacturer, it is customary for the auditor to tour the client's plant facilities. Discuss the ways in which the auditor's observations made during the course of the plant tour would be of help in planning and conducting the audit.

6.15 Risk assessment procedures should, at a minimum, be a combination of inquires of management and others within the entity, analytical procedures, and observation and inspection.

Required:

Give the advantages and disadvantages for each of these assessment procedures.

6.4 Based on the Evidence, Assess Risk; Types of Risk

6.16 Risk Analysis. Four tasks are required to assess the risk of misstatement. They are:

1 Identify risk by developing an understanding of the entity and its environment.
2 Relate the risk to what could go wrong in management's assertion.
3 Determine whether risks could result in material misstatement of the financial statements.
4 Consider that risks will result in material misstatement.

Required:

Using these tasks, analyze the following risks:

A. Cash receipts from sales in an office supply store are not recorded.
B. Investment in securities by the treasury department of a small manufacturing firm result in large losses.
C. Financial statement disclosures do not comply with IASs.
D. Pollution equipment in a large international steel refinery does not comply with local pollution control laws.
E. Bank statements do not correlate with cash receipts and disbursements.

6.5 Planning Materiality

6.17 Materiality and Risk. Dag Nilsson, Auktoriserad Revisor (AR), considers the audit risk at the financial statement level in the planning of the audit of the financial statements of Lycksele Lappmark Bank (LLB) in Storuman, Sweden, for the year ended December 31, 20X5. Audit risk at the financial statement level is influenced by the risk of material misstatements, which may be indicated by a combination of factors related to management, the industry, and the entity. In assessing such factors, Nilsson has gathered the following information concerning LLB's environment.

LLB is a nationally insured bank and has been consistently more profitable than the industry average by making mortgages on properties in a prosperous rural area, which has experienced considerable growth in recent years. LLB packages its mortgages and sells them to large mortgage investment trusts. Despite recent volatility of interest rates, LLB has been able to continue selling its mortgages as a source of new lendable funds.

LLB's board of directors is controlled by Kjell Stensaker, the majority stockholder, who is also the chief executive officer (CEO). Management at the bank's branch offices has authority for directing and controlling LLB's operations and is compensated based on branch profitability. The internal auditor reports directly to Hakon Helvik, a minority stockholder, who is chairman of the board's audit committee.

The accounting department has experienced little turnover in personnel during the five years Nilsson has audited LLB. LLB's formula consistently underestimates the allowance for loan losses, but its controller has always been receptive to Nilsson's suggestions to increase the allowance during each engagement.

During 20X5, LLB opened a branch office in Ostersund, 300km from its principal place of business. Although this branch is not yet profitable due to competition from several well-established regional banks, management believes that the branch will be profitable by 20X7.

Also during 20X5 LLB increased the efficiency of its accounting operations by installing a new computer system.

Required:

Based only on the information above, describe the factors that would most likely have an effect on the risk of material misstatement. Indicate whether each factor increases or decreases the risk. Use the format illustrated below:

Environmental factor	Effect on risk of material misstatements
Branch management has authority for directing and controlling operations	Increase

CASES

6.18 Materiality. Via the internet, get the latest balance sheet and income statement of Nokia, an international manufacturer of portable telephones headquartered in Finland. At the **www.Nokia.com** website click investors, click reports, click financial reports, finally click annual information or use the site search box using the terms Nokia's financial statements.

Required:

A. Use professional judgment in deciding on the initial judgment about materiality for the basis of net income, current assets, current liabilities, and total assets. State materiality in both percentages of the basis and monetary amounts.

B. Assume materiality for this audit is 7 percent of earnings from operations before income taxes. Furthermore, assume that every account in the financial statements may be misstated by 7 percent and each misstatement is likely to result in an overstatement of earnings. Allocate materiality to these financial statements.

C. Now, assume that you have decided to allocate 80 percent of your preliminary judgment (on the basis of earnings from operations before taxes) to accounts receivable, inventories, and accounts payable. Other accounts on the balance sheet are low in inherent and control risk. How does this allocation of materiality impact on evidence gathering?

D. After completing the audit you determine that your initial judgment about materiality for current assets, current liabilities, and total assets has been met. The actual estimate of misstatements in earnings exceeds your preliminary judgment. What should you do?

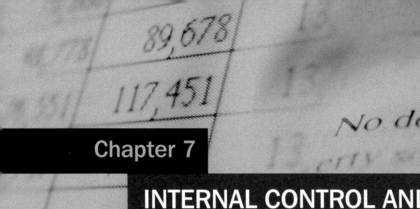

Chapter 7

INTERNAL CONTROL AND CONTROL RISK

After studying this chapter, you should be able to:

1 Understand the basic definition of internal control.

2 Discuss why internal controls are important.

3 Distinguish between the different components of internal control.

4 Describe the elements of the control environment.

5 Evaluate how management's objectives are related to risk assessment.

6 Explain the effects of information and communication on the internal control system.

7 Distinguish between the major types of control activities.

8 Give examples of major types of control activities.

9 Identify monitoring controls.

10 Know what is meant by design of controls.

7.2 Introduction

Internal control is not only essential to maintaining the accounting and financial records of an organization, it is essential to managing the entity. Everyone from the external auditors to management to the board of directors to the stockholders of large public companies to government, have an interest in internal controls. In many parts of the world, regulators have emphasized the importance of internal control by requiring management to make annual public statements about the effectiveness of internal controls.

Reinforcing internal controls is generally seen as one of the most important steps in avoiding negative surprises. Even a company that is considered "in control" will face risks. Effective internal controls will ensure that risks are identified at an early stage. Company risk management procedures will identify ways to deal with these risks, to the extent possible.

As we discussed in Chapter 6 Understanding the Entity, Risk Assessment and Materiality, the consideration of internal control is an important part of Phase II (Planning) of the Audit Process Model. In Chapter 6, it was also stated that the first two steps in the planning procedures are:

1 perform audit procedures to understand the entity and its environment, including the entity's internal control;
2 assess the risks of material misstatements of the financial statements

For both steps, the consideration of internal control and **control risk** is essential.

This chapter will concentrate on the importance of internal control, on general concepts in internal control, and on its components (the control environment, risk assessment, control activities, information and communication, and monitoring). In Chapter 8 Control Risk, Audit Planning and Test of Controls, assessment of control risk and the techniques for testing internal control as part of the audit will be discussed.

7.3 Internal Control Defined

Internal control, according to the Committee of Sponsoring Organizations of the Treadway Commission (COSO), is a process, effected by an entity's board of directors, management and other personnel, designed to provide **reasonable assurance** regarding the achievement of objectives in the following categories: effectiveness and efficiency of operations, reliability of financial reporting, compliance with applicable laws and regulations, and safeguarding of assets against unauthorized acquisition, use or disposition.[1]

This definition reflects certain fundamental concepts:

■ **Internal control is a "process."** Internal control is not one event or circumstance, but a series of actions that permeate an entity's activities. These actions are persuasive and are inherent in the way management runs the business.
■ Internal control is **effected by people.** A board of directors, management, and other personnel in an entity effect internal control. The people of an organization

accomplish it, by what they do and say. People establish the entity's objectives and put control mechanisms in place.

■ Internal control can be **expected to provide only reasonable assurance**, not absolute assurance, to an entity's management and board that the company's objectives are achieved. The likelihood of achievement is affected by limitations inherent in all internal control systems. These limitations include the realities that human judgment can be faulty, breakdowns may occur because of human failures such as simple error, and controls may be circumvented by **collusion** of two or more people. Finally, management has the ability to override the internal control system.

■ Internal control is geared to the **achievement of objectives** in one or more separate overlapping categories:

   1 **operations** – relating to effective and efficient use of the entity's resources;
   2 **financial reporting** – relating to preparation of reliable published financial statements;
   3 **compliance** – relating to the entity's compliance with applicable laws and regulations;
   4 **safeguarding of assets**.

■ Components of Internal Control

International standards require that the auditor performs risk assessment procedures (see Chapter 6) to gather knowledge of the **components of internal control**.[2] Both COSO and ISA 315[2] distinguish the following components of internal control:

■ the **control environment**;
■ the entity's risk assessment process;
■ the information system and related business processes relevant to financial reporting and communication;
■ control procedures;
■ monitoring of controls.

Illustration 7.1 shows internal control components from the most recent COSO report.

Certification Exam Question 7.1

When considering internal control, an auditor should be aware of the concept of reasonable assurance, which recognizes that:

(A) Internal control may be ineffective due to mistakes in judgment and personal carelessness.
(B) Adequate safeguards over access to assets and records should permit an entity to maintain proper accountability.
(C) Establishing and maintaining internal control is an important responsibility of management.
(D) The cost of an entity's internal control should not exceed the benefits expected to be derived.

ILLUSTRATION 7.1

Components of Internal Control – COSO Report[4]

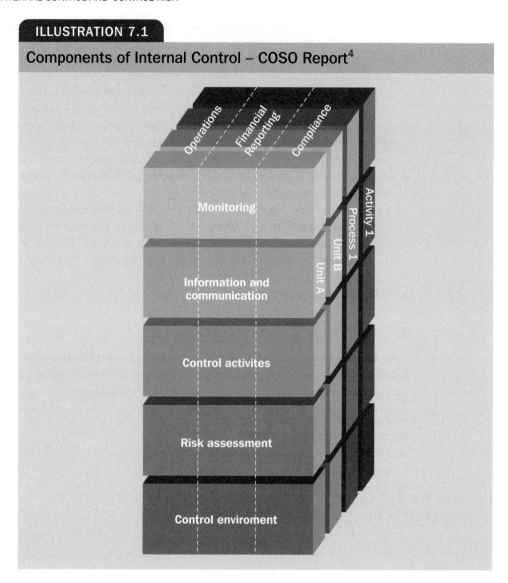

7.4 The Importance of Internal Control

The reason a company establishes a system of control is to help achieve its performance and profitability goals and prevent loss of resources by fraud and other means. Internal control can also help to ensure reliable financial reporting and compliance with laws and regulations. The entity's internal control system consists of many specific policies and procedures designed to provide management with reasonable assurance that the goals and objectives it believes important to the company will be met.

Everyone in the organization has responsibility for internal controls: management, board of directors, internal auditors, and other personnel. The chief executive officer is ultimately responsible and should assume ownership of the internal control system, providing leadership and direction to senior managers. Of particular significance are financial officers and their staff. The board of directors provides governance, guidance, and oversight. A strong, active board is best able to identify and correct management attempts to override controls and ignore or stifle communications from subordinates. Internal control should be an explicit or implicit part of everyone's job description.

■ Fraud Surveys

The annual fraud survey by KPMG[5] (a Big Four international accounting firm) showed that 75 percent of respondents report they had uncovered fraud in their organizations in the last year, compared with 62 percent of executives responding to a similar survey in 1998. Employee fraud occurred the most frequently, although financial reporting and medical/insurance fraud were much more costly. KPMG's 2003 report surveyed executives at 459 US public companies, with revenues of more than $250 million, and at state and federal government agencies. The 2003 survey showed a dramatic rise in internal controls as the chief means for detecting fraud from 51 percent to 77 percent.

A survey by KPMG in Singapore[6] reported that 43 percent of 1,500 companies surveyed said fraud was a major problem. Poor internal controls, override of internal controls, and collusion between employees and third parties were the top three reasons cited as to why frauds took place. The survey also found that management investigation, informant notification, and good internal controls rate highly as methods of detecting fraud increased.

■ Management Control Objectives

The three major categories of management objectives are effective operations, financial reporting, and compliance. An important goal of effective operations is safeguarding of assets. The physical assets (e.g. cash), non-physical assets (e.g. accounts receivable), important documents, and records (e.g. journals) of a company can be stolen, misused, or accidentally destroyed unless they are protected by adequate controls. The goal of financial controls requires accurate information for internal decision because management has a legal and professional responsibility to be sure that information is prepared fairly in accordance with accounting standards. Organizations are required to comply with many laws and regulations including company law,[7] tax law and environmental protection regulations.

A company's management sets objectives and then implements controls to assure the achievement of these objectives. For example, management requires that all order dates and delivery dates for all products be recorded as a control to monitor the CEO's strategic objective of "all deliveries on time." But not all of these objectives and their corresponding controls are relevant to the audit of the entity's financial statements.

■ Financial Reporting Controls

The auditor is interested primarily in controls that relate to reliability of financial reporting – accounting and internal control systems. These controls pertain to the entity's objective of preparing financial statements for external purposes that give a true and fair view in accordance with the applicable financial accounting standards.

Why internal control matters to the auditor is quite obvious. If the auditor is able to assess the quality of accounting and internal control systems and to verify their proper operation throughout the year under audit, the auditor might be able to rely heavily on these systems for sufficient audit evidence.

The rationale for relying on a company's accounting and internal control systems is twofold. First, reliance on accounting and **control procedures** will enhance the efficiency of the external audit. If inherent risks are mitigated by effective internal control procedures, less **substantive** testing is required to gather sufficient audit evidence. Further, by testing accounting and internal control procedures, the auditor is able to add value to the client by assessing the quality of the internal control system and giving recommendations for further improvement.

The auditor's primary consideration is whether, and how, a specific control prevents, or detects and corrects, **material misstatements** in **classes of transactions**, account balances or disclosures.[8]

■ Controls Over Transactions

Emphasis by auditors is placed on understanding controls over classes of transactions rather than account balances or disclosures. The reason is that the accuracy of the output of the accounting system (account balances) is dependent upon the accuracy of the inputs and processing (transactions). If, for example, controls are adequate to ensure all billings, cash receipts, charge-offs, and returns and allowances are correct, then the ending balance in accounts receivable is likely to be correct. Disclosures are generally dependent on the account balances.

■ Management Information System, Operations and Compliance Controls

Auditors primarily rely on financial controls, but controls affecting internal management information, such as budgets and internal performance reports, controls relating to operations, and controls for compliance objectives may also be relevant to an audit. Auditors have significant responsibility for the discovery of management and employee fraud and, to a lesser degree, certain types of illegal acts. Controls over non-financial data that the auditor uses in analytical procedures or controls over compliance with income tax laws may be relevant to an audit. The extensive use of general information system controls like restricted access (i.e. password controls) that limit access to the data are relevant to a financial statement audit. Conversely, controls to prevent the excessive use of materials in production generally are not relevant to a financial statement audit.

■ Design and Implementation of Controls

To understand the entity's internal control the auditor will evaluate the design of a control and judge whether it has been implemented. He determines if the control is designed to prevent, detect, or correct transactions that misstate the account balances.[9] Implementation of a control means that the control exists and that the entity is using it.

As is stated in ISA 315, internal control, no matter how well designed and operated, can only provide an entity with reasonable assurance about achieving the entity's objectives.

For example, human judgment can be faulty and breakdowns in internal control can occur because of human error. Also, controls can be circumvented by the collusion of two or more people or management override of internal control. For example, management may enter into **side agreements** with customers that alter the terms and conditions of the entity's standard sales contract in ways that would preclude revenue recognition.

Certification Exam Question 7.2[10]

During the consideration of internal control in a financial statement audit, an auditor is not obligated to:

(A) Search for significant deficiencies in the operation of the internal control.
(B) Understand the internal control and the information system.
(C) Determine whether the control activities relevant to audit planning have been placed in operation.
(D) Perform procedures to understand the design of internal control.

7.5 Components of Internal Control

Internal control consists of five interrelated components:

1 control environment;
2 risk assessment process;
3 the information system, communication, and related business processes;
4 control procedures;
5 monitoring of controls.

Illustration 7.2 gives more detail on each component including a description. Risk assessment should not be treated as a strictly separate component, for risk is assessed in all the other components – control environment risk, information system risk, risk of lack of control procedures, and risk from absence of adequate monitoring.

Certification Exam Question 7.3

Which of the following is not a component of an entity's internal control?

(A) Control risk.
(B) Control activities.
(C) Monitoring.
(D) Control environment.

ILLUSTRATION 7.2

Components of Internal Control Structure

Components	Description of component	Component elements
Control environment	Actions, policies and procedures that reflect the overall attitude of top management, directors, and owners of an entity about controls and its importance	▪ Integrity and ethical values ▪ Commitment to competence ▪ Those charged with governance (board of directors or audit committee) ▪ Management's philosophy and operating style ▪ Organizational structure ▪ Assignment of authority and responsibility ▪ Human resource polices and practice
Management's risk assessment	Management's identification and analysis of risks relevant to the preparation of financial statements in accordance with IFRS	Management's assertions: existence, completeness, valuation, presentation and disclosure, measurement, occurrence
Accounting information systems and communication	Methods used to identify, assemble, classify, record, and report an entity's transactions and to maintain accountability for related assets	Transaction-related audit objectives: existence, completeness, accuracy, classification, timing, posting, and summarization
Control activities (control procedures)	Policies and procedures that management established to meet its objectives for financial reporting	▪ Adequate segregation of duties ▪ Proper authorization of transactions and activities (specific computer controls) ▪ Adequate documents and records (general computer controls) ▪ Physical control over assets and records ▪ Independent checks on performance
Monitoring	Management's ongoing and periodic assessment of the effectiveness of the design and operation of an internal control structure to determine if it is operating as intended and modified when needed	Not applicable

7.6 Control Environment

The control environment means the overall attitude, awareness, and actions of directors and management regarding the internal control system and its importance in the entity. The control environment has a pervasive influence on the way business activities are structured, the way objectives are established, and the way risks are assessed. The control environment is influenced by the entity's history and culture. It influences the control consciousness of its people. Effectively controlled companies set a positive "tone at the top" and establish appropriate policies and procedures.

■ Organization's Management

The attitude of an organization's management, its management style, corporate culture, and values are the essence of an efficient control. If management believes control is important, others in the company will observe the control policies and procedures. If employees in the organization feel control is not important to top management, it will not be important to them. The control environment consists of the actions, policies and procedures that reflect the overall attitudes of top management, directors, and owners.

■ Elements Contributing to a Successful Control Environment

There are a number of specific elements that usually contribute to a successful control environment and which may be used as indicators of the quality of the control environment of a particular organization. These elements are:[11]

- communication and enforcement of integrity and ethical values;
- commitment to competence;
- participation by those charged with governance – independence and integrity of the board of directors;
- management's philosophy and operating style – leadership via control by example;
- organizational structure;
- assignment of authority and responsibility;
- human resource policies and practices.

■ Integrity and Ethical Values

The integrity and ethical values of the people who create, administer, and monitor controls determines their effectiveness. The communication of company integrity and ethical values to employees and reinforcement in practice affects the way in which employees view their work. Setting a good example is not enough. Top management should verbally communicate the entity's values and behavioral standards to employees.

Concept and a Company 7.1

Weaknesses in the Control Environment – The Case of Xerox (1997–2000)

Concept	A control environment in which there is motivation to misstate financial statements may lead to problems.
Story	Xerox is a US copy machine manufacturing company that saw its market share eroded in the USA in the 1990s because of foreign competition. The management, in order to cash in on a compensation scheme that would net them $35 million if Xerox's stock price rose to more than $60 per share, developed a scheme to artificially increase revenue.
To settle charges that included fraud, the Securities and Exchange Commission (SEC) required that Xerox pay a $10 million civil penalty – at that time, the largest ever by a company for financial-reporting violations. The SEC also required that Xerox restate its financial statements for the years 1997 to 2000. (SEC *Litigation release* 2002)

▶

Weaknesses in the Control Environment – The Case of Xerox (1997–2000) (continued)

Most of the improper accounting – involving $2.8 billion in equipment revenue and $660 million in pretax earnings – resulted from improper accounting for revenue. On some sales, service revenue was immediately recognized, in violation of GAAP. The revenue associated with the servicing component of multi-year lease contracts was recognized during the first year, instead of recognized over the life of the lease. To increase revenue, Xerox increasingly booked more revenue associated with the equipment.

Xerox also increased earnings by nearly $500 million by improperly setting aside various reserves, then gradually adding them back as gains to make up for profit shortfalls. In one instance Xerox changed its vacation policy by limiting the amount of time off employees could carry over from one period to the next, saving $120 million. But instead of taking the gain immediately as required by US GAAP, Xerox systematically and improperly released the money at a rate of $30 million per year. (Bandler & Hechinger 2002)

Discussion Questions	▪ What impact does this weakness in the control environment have on Xerox, its auditors, its management, and its shareholders? ▪ What audit procedures in this case should the auditor perform to reduce the risk of misstatement?
References	Bandler, J. and Hechinger, J., 2001, "Fired Executive Questioned Xerox's Acccounting Practices," *The Wall Street Journal*, February 6. SEC, 2002, *Litigation release 17465*, "Xerox Settles SEC Enforcement Action Charging Company With Fraud," US Securities and Exchange Comission, April 11.

Management can act to maximize control integrity and reduce misstatement. Management might remove incentives and temptations that prompt personnel to engage in fraudulent or unethical behavior. Incentives for unethical behavior include pressure to meet unrealistic performance targets, high performance-dependent rewards, and upper and lower cutoffs on bonus plans. Temptations for employees to engage in improper acts include: non-existent or ineffective controls; top management who are unaware of actions taken at lower organizational levels; ineffective board of directors; and insignificant penalties for improper behavior.

Communication and enforcement of integrity and ethical values are essential elements which influence the effectiveness of the design, administration, and monitoring of internal controls. The auditor uses information gathered by performing risk assessment procedures to obtain an understanding of the design of controls as audit evidence to support the risk assessment. The effectiveness of controls cannot rise above the integrity and ethical values of the people who create, administer, and monitor them. Integrity and ethical values are essential elements of the control environment that influence the design of other components.

■ Commitment to Competence

A company's control environment will be more effective if its culture is one in which quality and competence are openly valued. **Competence** is the knowledge and skills necessary to accomplish tasks that define the individual's job. Management needs to specify the competence levels for particular jobs and make sure those possessing the necessary training, experience, and intelligence perform the job.

■ Participation of Those Charged with Governance

The participation of those charged with governance, especially, the entity's board of directors and audit committee, significantly influences the control environment and "tone at the top." The guidance and oversight responsibilities of an active and involved board of directors who possess an appropriate degree of management, technical, and other expertise is critical to effective internal control.

Because the board must be prepared to question and scrutinize management's activities, present alternative views and have the courage to act in the face of obvious wrongdoing, it is necessary that the board contain at least a critical mass of independent (non-executive) directors.[12] For instance, the Sarbanes-Oxley Act requires that members of the audit committee be independent. In order to be considered to be independent, a member of an audit committee may not accept any consulting, advisory, or other compensatory fee from the company they govern or be affiliated with any company subsidiary.[13]

The responsibilities of those charged with governance are of considerable importance for publicly traded companies. This is recognized in codes of practice such as the London Stock Exchange Combined Code and other regulations such as the Sarbanes-Oxley Act. The board of directors usually has a compensation committee charged with executive and management compensation. If the compensation is performance-related the board must counterbalance the pressures for management to manipulate financial reporting.

■ Auditor Evaluation of Those Charged with Governance

Important factors to consider in evaluating a board of directors, board of trustees, or comparable body is experience and stature of its members, extent of its involvement, scrutiny of activities, and the appropriateness of its action. Another factor is the degree to which difficult questions are raised and pursued with management regarding plans or performance. Interaction of the audit committee with internal and external auditors, existence of a written audit committee charter, and regularity of meetings are other factors affecting the control environment.

■ Management's Philosophy and Operating Style

Management's philosophy and operating style is their attitude about, and approach to, financial reporting, accounting issues, and to taking and managing business risk. A personal example set by top management and the board provides a clear signal to employees about the company's culture and about the importance of control. In particular, the chief executive plays a key role in determining whether subordinates decide to obey, bend, or ignore company rules, and the kinds of business risks accepted.

Management philosophy may create significant risk. A key element of risk is dominance of management by a few individuals. Auditors may consider key questions, such as: Does management take significant risk or are they risk adverse? and What is management's attitude towards monitoring of business risk?

■ Organizational Structure

The entity's organizational structure provides the framework within which business activities are planned, executed, controlled, and monitored. Important considerations are clarity of lines of authority and responsibility; the level at which policies and procedures are established; adherence to these policies and procedures; adequacy of supervision and monitoring of decentralized operations; and appropriateness of organizational structure for size and complexity of the entity. By understanding the entity's organizational structure, the auditor can discover the management and functional elements of the business and how control policies are carried out.

■ Assignment of Authority and Responsibility

How authority and responsibility are assigned throughout the organization and the associated lines of reporting has an impact on controls. For example, a bank may require that two officers sign all checks written for more than a certain amount. Computer users are only allowed to access certain parts of the accounting system. Responsibility and delegation of authority should be clearly assigned. How responsibility is distributed is usually spelled out in formal company policy manuals.

Certification Exam Question 7.4

The overall attitude and awareness of an entity's board of directors concerning the importance of internal control usually is reflected in its:

(A) Computer-based controls.
(B) System of segregation of duties.
(C) Control environment.
(D) Safeguards over access to assets.

Certification Exam Question 7.5

In assessing control risk, an auditor ordinarily selects from a variety of techniques, including:

(A) Inquiry and analytical procedures.
(B) Re-performance and observation.
(C) Comparison and confirmation.
(D) Inspection and verification.

These manuals describe policies such as business practice, employee job responsibilities, duties and constraints (including written job descriptions). The auditor should consider whether management may have established a formal code of conduct but nevertheless acts in a manner that condones violations of that code or authorizes exceptions to it.

Illustration 7.3 gives a company organization that demonstrates a good organizational segregation of duties and assignment of authority and responsibility of accounting personnel.

ILLUSTRATION 7.3

Organizational Chart Segregation of Duties and Assignment of Authority and Responsibility

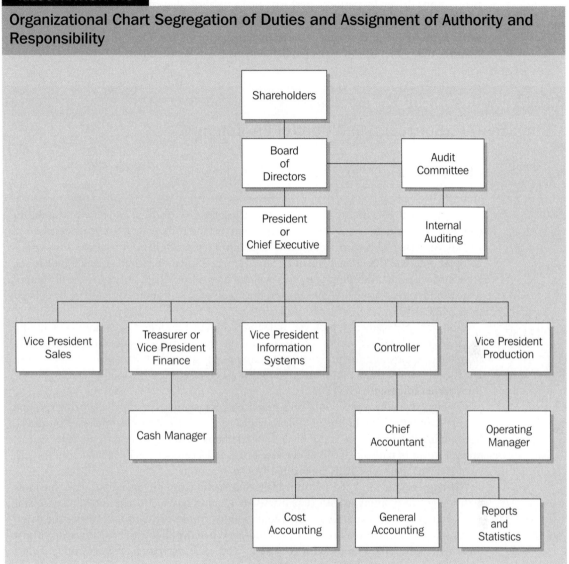

■ Human Resource Policies and Practices

The most important element of the control environment is personnel, which is why human resource policies and practices are essential. With trustworthy and competent employees, weaknesses in other controls can be compensated and reliable financial statements might still result. Honest, efficient people are able to perform at a high level even when there are few other controls to support them.

A company should take care in hiring, orientation, training, evaluation, counseling, promoting, compensating, and remedial actions. Recruiting practices that include formal, in-depth employment interviews and evidence of integrity and ethical behavior result in hiring high-quality employees. Training improves employee technical skills and

241

communicates their prospective roles in the enterprise. Rotation of personnel and promotions driven by periodic performance appraisals demonstrate the entity's commitment to its people. Competitive compensation programs that include bonus incentives serve to motivate and reinforce outstanding performance. Disciplinary actions send a message that violations of expected behavior will not be tolerated.

Concept and a Company 7.2

"Chainsaw Al", Sunbeam, and Control Environment

Concept	"Tone at the top" sets the control environment. Big egos and greed can destroy a company.
Story	The SEC filed a civil injunctive action charging five former officers of Sunbeam Corporation, including CEO "Chainsaw Al" Dunlop, and the former engagement partner of Arthur Andersen LLP with fraud, resulting in billions of dollars of investor losses. The complaint alleged that management of Sunbeam, a US manufacturer of small appliances, security devices, and camping gear, engaged in a fraudulent scheme to create the illusion of a successful restructuring of Sunbeam and thus facilitate a sale of the company at an inflated price. (SEC 2001)

Sunbeam management employed a laundry list of fraudulent techniques, including creating "cookie jar" revenues, recording revenue on contingent sales, accelerating sales from later periods into the present quarter, and using improper bill and hold transactions. For fiscal 1997, at least $60 million of Sunbeam's record setting $189 million earnings came from accounting fraud. (SEC 2001)

The biggest problem was Sunbeam's practice of overstating sales by recognizing revenue in improper periods, including its "bill and hold" practice of billing customers for products, but holding the goods for later delivery. One famous example was Sunbeam sales of $58 million worth of barbecue grills at cut-rate prices in December (giving stores until June to pay for them). Barbecue grills are ordinarily sold in summer.

When he became CEO of Sunbeam, a faltering manufacturer in an overcrowded business with low profit margins, Albert (Chainsaw Al) Dunlop had just orchestrated a successful turn-around of Scott Paper and had a reputation for ruthless cost cutting (hence the name "chainsaw"). He was also a tireless self-promoter. When the Sunbeam board awarded him a three-year, $70 million contract, he boasted, "You can't overpay a great executive. Don't you think I'm a bargain?" (Harrop 1998)

At his first press conference Dunlop announced that he had already begun firing executives. (Schifrin 1996) Three months later, Dunlop said he would fire half of Sunbeam's 12,000 employees, sell or consolidate 39 of the company's 53 facilities, divest the company of several business lines, eliminate six regional headquarters in favor of a single office in Florida, and scrap 87 percent of Sunbeam's products. In July 1996 when Dunlop became CEO, Sunbeam had already been through a bankruptcy and years of cost cutting. In October 1997, Dunlap hired Morgan Stanley to find potential suitors or takeover targets. (*Weekly Corporate Growth Report* 1998)

Dunlap believed in carrots and sticks. Dunlop preached sales at any cost and in any way. He gave people great incentives to perform and fired them when they did not. The need to overpower was also present in the executive suite. In fact, as a biographer puts it, "working with Al Dunlap was a lot like going to war ... The pressure was brutal, the hours exhausting, and the casualties high ... At Sunbeam, Dunlap created a culture of misery, an environment of moral ambiguity, indifferent to everything except the stock price. He would throw papers or furniture, bang his hands on his desk, knock glasses of water off a table, and shout so ferociously that a manager's hair could lift from his head by the stream of air that rushed from Dunlap's screaming mouth." (Byrne 1999)

The bullying and outrageous sales targets left Sunbeam with no idea of what its real inventory was. Divisional managers would report sales that met the targets, whether they had been effected or not. By early 1998, routine operational functions within the company were breaking down. Assembly lines were not working at peak efficiency. Supplies were not arriving on time. Maintenance was not being performed when it was needed. So goods were not getting shipped to the shops. (Uren 1998)

Discussion Questions	■ When Dunlop became CEO of Sunbeam in 1996, the share price shot up from \$12.12 to \$18.58 in a day. What aspect of Dunlop's management style could have caused this? ■ If you were auditing Sunbeam in 1996, what financial statement accounts do you believe world be susceptible to misstatement?

References	Byrne, J.A., 1999, *Chainsaw: The Notorious Career of Al Dunlap in the Era of Profit-at-Any-Price*, HarperCollins Publishing Inc., New York. Harrop, F., 1998, "Dunlap Backers Had It Coming," *Rocky Mountain News*, June 22, p. 35A. Schifrin, M., 1996, "Chain Saw Al to the rescue? (Corporate turn-around expert Albert Dunlop hired to help Sunbeam Corp.)," *Forbes*, Vol. 158, No. 5, August 26, p. 42. SEC, 2001, *Litigation news release 2001–49*, "SEC Sues Former CEO, CFO, Other Top Former Officers of Sunbeam Corporation in Massive Financial Fraud," Securities and Exchange Commission, May 15. Uren, D., 1998, "Dunlap style no match for tough times," *The Australian*, June 20, p. 57. "Sunbeam to acquire Coleman Co. for 1.3 times revenue," *Weekly Corporate Growth Report*, March 9, 1998.

■ Cumulative Effect of Controls

When analyzing the control environment, the auditor must think about the collective effect of various control environment elements. Strengths in one of the elements might mitigate weaknesses in another element. For example, an active and independent board of directors may influence the philosophy and operating style of senior management. Alternatively, human resource policies directed toward hiring competent accounting personnel might not mitigate a strong bias by top management to overstate earnings.

■ Factors on Which to Assess Internal Control

Illustration 7.4 lists issues that might be focussed on to assess the internal control environment, based on the COSO report. These elements are cited as factors to consider when doing a control environment assessment to determine whether a positive control environment exists, but the absence or opposite of these factors indicate negative control environment. Elements of a negative control environment such as unethical management, management with low integrity, incompetent management, or governance

ILLUSTRATION 7.4

Factors on Which to Assess Internal Control Environment[14]

Integrity and Ethical Values
(Communication and enforcement of integrity and ethical values)

- Existence and implementation of codes of conduct and other policies regarding acceptable business practice, conflicts of interest, or expected standards of ethical and moral behavior.
- Dealings with employees, suppliers, customers, investors, creditors, insurers, competitors, and auditors, etc. (e.g. whether management conducts business on a high ethical plane, and insists that others do so, or pays little attention to ethical issues).
- Pressure to meet unrealistic performance targets – particularly for short-term results – and extent to which compensation is based on achieving those performance targets.

Commitment to Competence

- Formal or informal job descriptions or other means of defining tasks that comprise particular jobs.
- Analysis of the knowledge and skills needed to perform jobs adequately.

Board of Directors or Audit Committee
(Participation by those charged with governance)

- Independence from management, such that necessary, even if difficult and probing, questions are raised.
- Frequency and timeliness with which meetings are held with chief financial and/or accounting officers, internal auditors, and external auditors.
- Sufficiency and timeliness with which information is provided to board or committee members, to allow monitoring of management's objectives and strategies, the entity's financial position and operating results, and terms of significant agreements.
- Sufficiency and timeliness with which the board or audit committee is apprised of sensitive information, investigation, and improper acts (e.g. travel expenses of senior officers, significant litigation, investigations of regulatory agencies, defalcations, embezzlement or misuse of corporate assets, violations of insider trading rules, political payments, illegal payments).

Management's Philosophy and Operating Style

- Nature of business risks accepted, for example, whether management often enters into particularly high-risk ventures, or is extremely conservative in accepting risks.
- Frequency of interaction between senior management and operating management, particularly when operating from geographically removed locations.
- Attitudes and actions towards financial reporting, including disputes over application of accounting treatments (e.g. selection of conservative versus liberal accounting policies, whether accounting principles have been misapplied, important financial information not disclosed, or records manipulated or falsified).

Organizational Structure

- Appropriateness of the entity's organizational structure and its ability to provide the necessary information flow to manage its activities.
- Adequacy of definition of key managers' responsibilities and their understanding of these responsibilities.

Assignment of Authority and Responsibility

- Assignment of responsibility and delegation of authority to deal with organizational goals and objectives, operating functions and regulatory requirements, including responsibility for information systems and authorizations for changes.
- Appropriateness of control-related standards and procedures, including employee job descriptions.
- Appropriate numbers of people, particularly with respect to data processing and accounting functions, with the requisite skill levels related to the size of the entity and nature and complexity of activities and systems.

Human Resource Policies and Practices

- Extent to which policies and procedures for hiring, training, promoting, and compensating employees are in place.
- Appropriateness of remedial action taken in response to departures from approved policies and procedures.
- Adequacy of employee candidate background checks, particularly with regard to prior actions and activities considered to be unacceptable by the entity.
- Adequacy of employee retention and promotion criteria and information-gathering techniques (e.g. performance evaluations) and relation to the code of conduct or other behavioral guidelines.

promoting a "cowboy culture" in the company increase the risk of financial misstatement as well as the risk of business sustainability. If the board of directors seldom meet or are lax in their oversight responsibility, risk increases. Poor training, retention, or morale of employees increases the risk that controls will not be implemented.

7.7 Risk Assessment

All components of internal control, from control environment to monitoring, should be assessed for risk. Managements risk assessment differs from, but is closely related to, the auditor's risk assessment discussed in Chapter 6 Audit Planning and Risk Analysis. Management assesses risks as part of designing and operating the internal control system to minimize errors and irregularities. Auditors assess risks to decide the evidence needed in the audit. The two risk assessment approaches are related in that if management effectively assesses and responds to risks, the auditor will typically need to accumulate less audit evidence than when management fails to, because control risk is lower.

■ Internal and External Business Risk

Risks to the organization may arise from external or internal factors. Externally, technological developments can affect the nature or timing of research and development, or lead to changes in procurement. Changing customer needs affect product development, pricing, warranties, and service. New legislation and regulation can force changes in operating policies and strategies. Economic changes have an impact on decisions relating to financing, capital expenditures, and expansion. Risks arising from internal factors might include a disruption of information systems processing; the quality of personnel and training; changes in management responsibilities; misappropriation opportunities because of the nature of the entity's activities or employee accessibility to assets; and an ineffective audit committee.

■ Identify Risks of a Business

Many techniques have been developed to identify general risks to a business. The majority involves identifying and prioritizing high-risk activities. One method[15] follows this procedure:

- identify the essential resources of the business and determine which are most at risk;
- identify possible liabilities that may arise;
- review the risks that have arisen in the past;
- consider any additional risks imposed by new objectives or new external factors;
- seek to anticipate change by considering problems and opportunities on a continuing basis.

To illustrate, let us take as an example. Feats, an importer of apparel and footwear, established an objective of becoming an industry leader in high-quality fashion merchandise. Entity-wide risks are: supply sources (including quality, stability and number of foreign

ILLUSTRATION 7.5

Risk Assessment Blank Evaluation Tool[16]

Considerations	Comments Yes/No
Entity-Wide Objectives Describe the entity-wide objectives and key strategies that have been established.	Attached comments
1 Management has established entity-wide objectives.	1
2 Information on the entity-wide objectives is disseminated to employees and the board of directors.	2
3 Management obtains feedback from key managers, other employees, and the board signifying that communication to employees is effective.	3
Strategies	
4 Are strategies related to and consistent with entity-wide objectives?	4
5 The strategic plan supports the entity-wide objectives.	5
6 The strategic plan addresses high-level resource allocations and priorities.	6
Plans and Budgets	
7 Are business plans and budgets consistent with entity-wide objectives, strategic plans and current conditions?	7
8 Assumptions inherent in the plans and budgets reflect the entity's historical experience and current conditions.	8
9 Plans and budgets are at an appropriate level of detail for each management level.	9
Activity-Level Objectives Are objectives established for each of the following activities?	
10 Operations	10
11 Marketing and Sales	11
12 Service,	12
13 Process Accounts Receivable	13
14 Procurement,	14
15 Process Accounts Payable	15
16 Process Funds,	16
17 Fixed Assets,	17
18 Benefits and Retiree Information,	18
19 Payroll	19
20 Product Costs	20
21 Tax Compliance	21
22 Financial and Management Reporting	22
23 Human Resources and Administrative Services	23
24 External Relations,	24
25 Information Technology	25
26 Technology Development	26
27 Legal Affairs	27
28 Are those activity-level objectives consistent with each other?	28
29 Are activity-level objectives linked with entity-wide objectives and strategic plans?	29
30 Activity-level objectives are reviewed from time to time for continued relevance.	30
31 Are activity-level objectives complementary and reinforcing within activities?	31

suppliers); currency rate fluctuations; timeliness of receiving shipments (including customs delays); availability, reliability and costs of shipping; and likelihood of trade embargoes caused by political instability. Other more generic business risks such as economic conditions, market acceptance, competitors, and changes in regulations also have to be considered.

■ Conditions That May Increase Risk

Certain conditions may increase risk and deserve special consideration. These conditions are: changed operating environment; new personnel; new or revamped information systems; rapid growth; new technology; new lines, products and activities; corporate restructuring; and foreign operations.

A sample blank risk assessment internal control questionnaire is shown in Illustration 7.5.

Certification Exam Question 7.6[17]

Which of the following statements is correct concerning an auditor's assessment of control risk?

(A) Assessing control risk may be performed concurrently during an audit with obtaining an understanding of the entity's internal control.
(B) Evidence about the operation of internal control in prior audits may not be considered during the current year's assessment of control risk.
(C) The basis for an auditor's conclusions about the assessed level of control risk need not be documented unless control risk is assessed at the maximum.
(D) The lower the assessed level of control risk, the less assurance the evidence must provide that the control procedures are operating effectively.

7.8 Information Systems, Communication, and Related Business Processes

Every enterprise must capture pertinent information related to both internal and external events and activities in both financial and non-financial forms. The information must be identified by management as relevant and then communicated to people who need it in a form and time frame that allows them to do their jobs.

The information relevant to financial reporting is recorded in the accounting system and is subjected to procedures that initiate, record, process, and report entity transactions. The quality of information generated by the system affects management's ability to make appropriate decisions in controlling the entity's activities and preparing reliable financial reports.

Not just a matter of reporting, communication occurs in a broader sense, flowing down, across, and up the organization. All personnel must receive a clear message from top management that control responsibilities must be taken seriously. Employees must understand their own role in the internal control system, as well as how individual activities relate to the work of others, and how to report significant information to senior management. There also needs to be effective communication with external parties such as customers, suppliers, and regulators.

■ Information System Includes

An organization uses an array of information. The information systems used by companies include the accounting system; production system; budget information; personnel system; systems software; applications software for word-processing, calculating, presentations, communications, and databases; and all the records and files generated by this software such as customer and vendor records. The information system also includes information about external events, activities, and conditions necessary to make informed business decisions and comply with external reporting.

Illustration 7.6 shows the typical input, subsystems and output of an information system.

ILLUSTRATION 7.6

Typical Input, Subsystems and Output of an Information System

Input

- accounting transactions
- correspondence
- personnel information
- customer and vendor information
- entity objectives and standards
- procedure manuals
- information about external events, activities, and conditions

Subsystems

- accounting system
- customer and vendor records
- production system
- budget system
- personnel system
- computer systems software
- computer applications software (word processing, spreadsheet, presentation, communication, computer languages and database)

Output

- accounting reports
- budget reports
- production reports
- operating reports
- correspondence
- all the records and files generated by applications software

■ Financial Reporting Information System and Processes

For an audit, the auditor should obtain an understanding of the information system and the related business processes relevant to financial reporting in the following areas: [18]

- the classes of transactions in the entity's operations that are significant to the financial statements;
- the procedures, within both IT and manual systems, by which those transactions are initiated, recorded, processed, and reported from their occurrence to their inclusion in the financial statements;
- the related accounting records, supporting information, and specific accounts in the financial statements and how they initiate, record, process, and report transactions;
- how the information system captures events and conditions, other than transactions, that are significant to the financial statements;
- the financial reporting process used to prepare the entity's financial statements, including significant accounting estimates and disclosures.

■ IT Transaction Procedures

The procedures by which transactions are initiated, recorded, processed, and reported from their occurrence to their inclusion in the financial statements include entries of transaction totals into the general ledger (or equivalent records) and to initiate, record, and process journal entries. Especially important is understanding recurring and infrequent or unusual adjustments to the financial statements.

IT may be used to transfer information automatically from transaction processing systems to general ledger to financial reporting. The automated processes and controls in such systems may reduce the risk of inadvertent error but creates new risk. When IT is used to transfer information automatically, there may be little or no visible evidence of unauthorized intervention in the information systems if it occurs.

The auditor should also understand how the incorrect processing of transactions is resolved. For example, is there an automated **suspense file** and, if so, how are suspense items cleared out on a timely basis? How are system overrides or bypasses to controls accounted for?

■ IT Risks

The auditor should be aware that IT poses specific risks to an entity's internal control including:

- Reliance on systems or programs that are inaccurately processing data, processing inaccurate data, or both.
- Unauthorized access to data that may result in destruction of data or improper changes to data, including the recording of unauthorized or non-existent transactions or inaccurate recording of transactions.
- Unauthorized changes to data in master files.
- Unauthorized changes to systems or programs.
- Failure to make necessary changes to systems or programs.
- Inappropriate manual intervention.
- Potential loss of data or inability to access data as required.

■ Input Risks

Risk exists at all levels of the information system, but especially related to input. Input should be only by those people and systems with authorized access. Data entry should be secure from unauthorized access. Input should be accurate (correct data is entered correctly), valid (transaction is approved or authorized), and complete (all valid transactions should be entered and captured by the system). Sub-systems should process transactions completely (all data that should be transacted into the general ledger is there) and accurately (data that is entered is reflected in the general ledger). Lack of controls or insufficient controls on authorization, data input and processing by sub-systems increases risk.

■ Accounting System

For internal control and documentation purposes the auditor may view an **accounting system** as a series of steps by which economic events are captured by the enterprise, recorded, and assembled in a normal ledger and ultimately reflected in the financial statements. Controls are needed to ensure that all the relevant economic events are captured by the accounting system, and that processes that modify and summarize financial information do not introduce errors.

To understand the accounting system sufficiently, the auditor should identify major classes of transactions in the client's operations and understand the accounting and financial reporting process thoroughly: from how the transactions are initiated to their inclusion in the financial statements. The auditor should identify significant accounting records, supporting documents and accounts in the financial statements. The critical points of interest for an auditor are where financial information *changes* along the path of recording and assembling a ledger.

■ Financial Reporting Process

The auditor should know how the company communicates significant matters relating to financial reporting. Open communication channels help ensure that exceptions are reported and acted on. When evaluating the communication system, the auditor will consider:

- effectiveness with which employees' duties and control responsibilities are communicated;
- establishment of channels of communication for people to report suspected improprieties;
- receptivity of management to employee suggestions of ways to enhance productivity, quality, or other similar improvements;
- adequacy of communication across the organization (e.g. between procurement and production activities), and the completeness and timeliness of information and its sufficiency to enable people to discharge their responsibilities effectively.
- openness and effectiveness of channels with customers, suppliers, and other external parties for communicating information on changing customer needs.
- timely and appropriate follow-up action by management resulting from communications received from customers, vendors, regulators, or other external parties.

7.9 Control Activities (Control Procedures)

Control procedures (sometimes called "control activities")[19] are policies and procedures that help ensure management directives are carried out. They help ensure that necessary actions are taken to address risks to the achievement of the entity's objectives for operations, financial reporting, or compliance. Generally, control procedures fall into four broad categories: performance reviews, information processing, physical controls, and segregation of duties.

■ Two Elements of Control Procedures

Control procedures may be divided into two elements: a **policy** establishing what should be done and **procedures to effect that policy**. A policy, for example, might be that a securities dealer retail branch manager must monitor customer trades. The control procedure is a review of a computer printout of daily trade activities by the customer, performed in a timely manner and with attention given to the nature and volume of securities traded. Control procedures implement the control policies by specific routine tasks, performed at particular times by designated people, held accountable by adequate supervision and evidence of performance.

The categories of control activities given in ISA 315[20] are:

- *performance reviews,*
- *information processing,*
- *physical controls,*
- *segregation of duties,*
- *authorization.*

The first four categories of control activities will be discussed in this section. **Authorization**, not discussed in detail in the standard, is the delegation of initiation of transactions and obligations on the company's behalf. Management should restrict authorization of personnel to access assets and records.

■ Performance Reviews

Performance reviews are independent checks on performance by a third party not directly involved in the activity. Sometimes called internal verification, these reviews include reviews of actual performance versus budgets; surprise checks of procedures; periodic comparisons of accounting records and physical assets; and a review of functional or activity performance. An example of surprise check would be to pull the time cards at the beginning of a shift and see that everyone who is "punched in" is present. A routine comparison of accounting records and physical assets is a bank reconciliation performed by a person independent of the accounting records and handling of cash. A review of functional or activity performance would be a bank's consumer loan manager's review of reports by branch, region, and loan type for loan.

■ Information Processing

Information processing control procedures are primarily of two types: application controls and general controls. **Application controls** are controls that apply to applications that initiate, record, process, and report transactions (such as MS Office, SAP, QuickBooks), rather than the computer system in general. Examples of application controls are **edit checks** of input data, numerical **sequence checks**, and manual follow-up of exception reports. In manual systems applications controls may be referred to as adequate document and record controls.

General controls are policies and procedures that relate to many applications and support the effective functioning of application controls by helping to ensure the continued proper operation of information systems. Some examples of general controls are controls over data center and **network** operations, controls over system software acquisition, controls over access to the computer software (password controls), change and maintenance controls, access security, and application system acquisition and development controls. A good example of a general control in accounting software is an error message if there is a problem in using the operating system (e.g. "Please insert a CD-ROM in Drive D"). In manual systems, general controls are controls over proper authorization of transactions and activities.

Transaction Records

The company should maintain a set of records on which transactions are recorded and summarized. In a manual system these records include sales invoices, shipping documents, purchase orders, subsidiary records, journals, ledgers, and employee time cards. In a computer system, these records are all represented in the **database** maintained by an accounting application program (such as QuickBooks, SAP, Oracle Financials).

These records must be adequate to provide good assurance that all assets are properly controlled and all transactions correctly recorded. Well-designed documents in a manual system and **preformatted** input screens in a computer system should be pre-numbered consecutively, prepared at the time a transaction takes place, simple enough to be clearly understood, designed for multiple use to minimize the number of different forms, and constructed in a manner that encourages correct preparation.

Application Controls

There are several standard application controls. The chart of accounts is an important application control because it provides the framework for determining the information presented on to financial statements and budgets. The most widely applicable control device is the use of serial numbers on documents and input transactions. Serial numbers provide control over the number of documents issued. Checks, tickets, sales invoices, purchase orders, stock certificates, and many other business papers use this control. Documents should be recorded immediately because long periods between transaction and recording increase the chance of misstatement. Systems manuals for computer accounting software should provide sufficient information to make the accounting functions clear.

General Controls

General IT controls assure that access to the computer system is limited to people who have a right to the information. Appropriate delegation of authority sets limits on what levels of risk are acceptable and these limits determine the discretion of the employees delegated to authorize the main types of business transactions. Authorization may be general or specific. An example of general limits set by policy is product price lists, inventory reorder points, and customer credit limits. Specific authorization may be made on a case-by-case basis such as authorization of reduction in the price of a dress with buttons missing in a retail-clothing store.

Computer Facility Controls

Computer facilities may have several types of controls. Access controls are general or application controls such as passwords that allow only authorized people admittance to the computer software on line. A very important general control is back-up and recovery procedures, as anyone who has had a system go down without current records being adequately backed up will tell you. Physical controls such as locks on the doors to the computer room and locked cabinets for software and back-up tapes protect the tangible components of a computer system.

■ Physical Controls

Physical controls are procedures to ensure the physical security of assets. Assets and records that are not adequately protected can be stolen, damaged, or lost. In highly computerized companies damaged data files could be costly or even impossible to replace. For these reasons only individuals who are properly authorized should be allowed access to the company's assets. Direct physical access to assets may be controlled through physical precautions, for example: storerooms guard inventory against pilferage; locks, fences and guards protect other assets such as equipment; and fireproof safes and safety deposit vaults protect assets such as currency and securities.

■ Segregation of Duties

Segregation of duties seeks to prevent persons with access to readily realizable assets from being able to adjust the records that record and thereby control those assets. Duties are divided, or segregated, among different people to reduce the risks of error or inappropriate actions. For instance, responsibilities for authorizing transactions, recording them, and handling the related assets (called custody of assets) are divided.

Segregation of duties entails three fundamental functions that must be separated and adequately supervised:

1 **Authorization** is the delegation of initiation of transactions and obligations on the company's behalf.
2 **Custody** is physical control over assets or records.
3 **Recording** is the creation of documentary evidence of a transaction and its entry into the accounting records.

A separation of these three functions is an essential element of control. Let us use the example of wages. Authorization is required for hiring of staff and is a function of the personnel department. The receipt of paychecks and issuance of them to the employees is handled by work supervisors. The accounting department handles the recording of the time records and the payroll in the payroll journals.

Illustration 7.7 shows an overview of segregation of duties.

ILLUSTRATION 7.7

Overview of Segregation of Duties

Transaction type	Controls
Authorization	Controls that ensure that only necessary transactions based on the entity's objectives are undertaken. They prevent unnecessary and fraudulent transactions. Examples: organizational chart, accounting procedures manual, chart of accounts, conflict of interest policy, signatures on checks limited to that of president, etc.
Recording	Controls which ensure that all authorized transactions are allowed in the accounting records, they are properly entered, and are not deleted or amended without proper authorization. Examples: entries in journals then ledgers, posting reference in journals, rotation of accounting personnel, listing of mail receipts, cash register tapes, reconciliation of bank statements, etc.
Custody	Controls that ensure that assets cannot be misused. Examples: pre-numbered forms, access to records (computer or manual) limited to authorized personnel, individuals handling cash do not keep the accounting records of cash, bonding of employees, locked storage, people responsible for assets should not be authorized to sell them, daily deposits of cash, etc.

People who authorize transactions should not have control over the related asset. In 1995 Barings, a 300 year-old British bank, was forced into insolvency by hundreds of millions of US dollar losses. Nicholas Leeson, the manager of the Singapore branch, not only made investments in Nikkei exchange indexed derivatives, but also was able to authorize his own investments.[21] The authorization of a transaction and the handling of the related asset by the same person increase the possibility of **defalcation** within the organization.

Another example of when duties were not separated with a disastrous result was the bond trading loss in the New York Office of Daiwa Bank in 1995. Over 11 years, 30,000 unauthorized trades were made resulting in a $1.1 billion loss (an average of $400,000 in losses for every trading day). Daiwa allowed Toshihide Iguchi, a bond trader, to authorize sales, have custody of the bond assets and record these transactions.[22] Daiwa Bank paid fines of $340 million, and closed its American operations, after being sued by US authorities. Mr. Iguchi was convicted and jailed for four years and paid $2.5 million in fines in 1996.[23] Four years later, in 2000, a court in Osaka, Japan ordered 11 senior executives at the bank to repay a total of $775 million in damages to their own bank.

Custody and Recording

If an individual has custody of assets and also accounts for them, there is a high risk of that person dispensing of the asset for personal gain and adjusting the records to cover the theft. The basic control imposed by the double-entry bookkeeping means that, to conceal the theft or fraudulent use of an asset, the perpetrator must be able to prevent the asset being recorded in the first place or to write it off. If the theft cannot be permanently written off, it may still be temporarily concealed by being carried forward in preparing stock sheets, in performing the bank reconciliation, or in reconciling the debtor or creditor control accounts.

IT Segregation of Duties

Operations responsibility and record keeping and the information technology (IT) duties should be separate. Information systems are crucially important to control, so it is suggested that those duties be segregated for programmer, computer operator, librarian, and data reviewer. A programmer wrote (or configured) the software. Giving him access to input data creates temptation. The computer operator (who inputs the accounting data) should not be able to modify the program. A librarian maintains and is custodian of the records and files that should only be released to authorized personnel. The person who tests the efficiency of all aspects of the system should be independent of the other computer jobs.

Concept and a Company 7.3

Citibank Global Private Banking – Significant weaknesses in Internal Control (1990–2000)

Concept	Weakness in Internal Control.
Story	Fraudsters, criminals, drug dealers, dictators, and greedy politicians all use the international global bank network to move their ill-gotten gains around the world. There are agreements between banking authorities in every country to reduce this illegal traffic in funds. Banks are required to set up internal controls, fill out "suspicious activity reports," and report all transactions above a certain monetary amount to bring compliance with anti-money laundering laws.

In 1999, a report by the US Senate Select Subcommittee on Investigations, faulted the global private banking business of Citigroup Inc., the largest US financial services company, for poor due diligence and lax controls. Private-banking officers helped clients such as the president of Gabon, the husband of former Pakistan Prime Minister Benazir Bhutto and Raul Salinas, the brother of Mexican President Carlos Salinas de Gortari, to hide tens of millions of dollars in suspected corruption proceeds from the authorities in their home countries. (Allen 1999a)

Raul Salinas, brother of then Mexican President Carlos Salinas, was-arrested in early 1995 for the suspected murder of a prominent Mexican politician and suspicion of influence peddling. (In Mexico, Salinas had earned the nickname "Mr. 10 Percent" for his reputed habit of skimming off the top of government contracts with which he was even tangentially involved.) Swiss authorities froze his accounts in that country and seized the money on the grounds that it came from drug-trafficking activities.

Salinas was the client of Amy Elliott, a Citibank executive specializing in banking services for rich Mexicans. Over the three prior years, Salinas had transferred more than $100 million from Mexico into his Citibank account in New York. Yet Elliot had never seriously questioned the source of the funds nor even completed the paperwork required to open such an account. (Lozada 2002)

Illustration 2.3 (continued)

In the wake of Mr. Salinas's arrest, Ms. Elliott says she was "mortified and dismayed" to discover that she had not filled out required background information on her client's source of funds, despite a series of memos from private-bank executives entreating everyone to comply with such internal procedures. (Allen 1999a)

An internal Citibank audit of the private-banking department in 1996 determined that the department's priorities centered on serving clients, even if it meant compromising the bank's internal controls. (Lozada 2002) "It appears that there are no consequences for bad audits – as long as the private bank meets their financial goals," wrote a Federal Reserve examiner in 1997. (Allen 1999b)

Discussion Questions	■ Why did Citibank's non-compliance with banking laws represent a weakness in internal control? ■ What controls were in place, but not operating? ■ Why were established control procedures not followed?
References	Allen, M., 1999a, "Citigroup's Reed Concedes Bank Moved Slowly," *Wall Street Journal*, New York, November 10, p. A.2. Allen, M., 1999b, "Citibank Managers Criticized in Probe of Private-Banking Unit," *Wall Street Journal*, New York, November 8, p. A.4. Lozada, C., 2002, "Corruption's true face," *Foreign Policy*, Washington, May/June, Iss. 130. p. 82.

Control Procedures Risk

All control procedures should be analyzed for risk. The main risk is that a control procedure has not been set up to ensure a policy is carried out. In other words, a policy has been identified, but there are no control activities to support the policy. If there is no control activity in place to ensure the achievement and monitoring of that objective, it is considered a weakness in internal control. Risk is also increased if a control procedure is designed, but has not been operating. Also, because of changes in business, product or industry, there may be control activities in place that are no longer pertinent.

Certification Exam Question 7.7

Proper segregation of functional responsibilities calls for separation of the functions of:

(A) Authorization, execution, and payment.
(B) Authorization, recording, and custody.
(C) Custody, execution, and reporting.
(D) Authorization, payment, and recording.

7.10 Monitoring of Controls

Internal control systems need to be monitored. Monitoring is a process that deals with ongoing assessment of the quality of internal control performance. The process involves assessing the design of controls and their operation on a timely basis and taking necessary corrective actions. By monitoring, management can determine that internal controls are operating as intended and that they are modified as appropriate for changes in conditions.

Ongoing monitoring information comes from several sources: exception reporting on control activities, reports by government regulators, feedback from employees, complaints from customers, and most importantly from internal auditor reports. For large companies, an internal audit department is essential to effective monitoring.[24] This feedback from the internal auditors may also help external auditors reduce evidence requirements.

Management's monitoring activities may include using information from communications from external parties such as customer complaints and regulator comments that may indicate problems or highlight areas in need of improvement. Two more examples of monitoring activities are management's review of **bank reconciliations**, and an internal auditors' evaluation of sales personnel's compliance with the company's human resource policies.

■ Internal Controls Over Time

Internal control systems change over time. The way controls are applied may evolve. Some procedures can become less effective or perhaps are no longer performed. This can be due to the arrival of new personnel, the varying effectiveness of training and supervision, time and resource constraints, or additional pressures. Furthermore, circumstances for which the internal control system originally was designed also may change, causing it to be less able to warn of the risks brought by new conditions. Accordingly, management needs to determine whether the internal control system continues to be relevant and able to address new risks. This is the monitoring function.

■ Evaluation of Monitoring Activities

When evaluating the ongoing monitoring the following issues might be considered:[25]

- periodic comparisons of amounts recorded with the accounting system with physical assets;
- responsiveness to internal and external auditor recommendations on means to strengthen internal controls;
- extent to which training seminars, planning sessions, and other meetings provide management with information on the effective operation of controls;
- whether personnel are asked periodically to state whether they understand and comply with the entity's code of conduct and regularly perform critical control activities;
- effectiveness of internal audit activities;
- extent to which personnel, in carrying out their regular activities, obtain evidence as to whether the system of internal control continues to function.

Evaluations of all the components are taken together for an overall evaluation and a sample blank evaluation form is shown in Illustration 7.8.

ILLUSTRATION 7.8

Overall Internal Control Evaluation Tool[26]

This exhibit is a blank tool (work paper) for the evaluation of an entity's control environment. This form is to be filled in after the detailed forms such as that shown in Illustration 7.5 are complete.

Internal Control Components	Comments Yes/No
Control Environment	
1 Does management adequately convey the message that integrity cannot be compromised?	1
2 Does a positive control environment exist, whereby there is an attitude of control consciousness throughout the organization and a positive "tone at the top?"	2
3 Is the competence of the entity's people commensurate with their responsibilities?	3
4 Is management's operating style, the way it assigns authority and responsibility, and organizes and develops its people appropriate?	4
5 Does the board provide the right level of attention?	5
Risk Assessment	
6 Are entity-wide objectives and supporting activity-level objectives established and linked?	6
7 Are the internal and external risks that influence the success or failure of the achievement of the objectives identified and assessed?	7
8 Are mechanisms in place to identify changes affecting the entity's ability to achieve its objectives?	8
9 Are policies and procedures modified as needed?	9
Control Activities	
10 Are control activities in place to ensure adherence to established policy and the carrying out of actions to address the related risks?	10
11 Are there appropriate control activities for each of the entity's activities?	11
Information and Communication	
12 Are information systems in place to identify and capture pertinent information – financial and non-financial, relating to external and internal events – and bring it to personnel in a form that enables them to carry out their responsibilities?	12
13 Does communication of relevant information take place?	13
14 Is information communicated clear with respect to expectations and responsibilities of individuals and groups, and reporting of results?	14
15 And does communication occur down, across and upward in the entity, as well as between the entity and other parties?	15
Monitoring	
16 Are appropriate procedures in place to monitor on an ongoing basis, or to periodically evaluate the functioning of the other components of internal control?	16
17 Are deficiencies reported to the right people?	17
18 Are policies and procedures modified as needed?	18
Overall Conclusion	See attached

Certification Exam Question 7.8[27]

Which of the following procedures most likely would provide an auditor with evidence about whether an entity's internal control activities are suitably designed to prevent or detect material misstatements?

(A) Re-performing the activities for a sample of transactions.
(B) Performing analytical procedures using data aggregated at a high level.
(C) Vouching a sample of transactions directly related to the activities.
(D) Observing the entity's personnel applying the activities.

7.11 Design of Internal Controls

Today, careful evaluation of internal control design and how it is operating in practice is stimulated by regulatory requirements, such as the Sarbanes-Oxley Act[28] (in which internal control statements are required), and the SEC.[29] The internal control report is to contain a statement of management's responsibility for establishing and maintaining adequate control over financial reporting, and a description of the framework management uses to evaluate the effectiveness of controls. Management must give their assessment of the effectiveness of internal controls and the auditor is asked for an attestation report on management's assessment. Reporting on internal controls is discussed in Chapter 4 An Auditor's Services and Chapter 12 Completing the audit.

To gain an understanding of the entity's internal control, the auditor is required to evaluate the design of controls and determine whether they have been implemented. Evaluating the design of a control involves considering whether the control is capable of effectively preventing, or detecting and correcting, material misstatements.

Errors in design occur when crucial internal control activities are designed by individuals with limited knowledge of accounting. For instance, if an entity's IT personnel do not completely understand how an order entry system processes sales transactions, they may erroneously design changes to the system. On the other hand, good designs may be poorly implemented. An IT controls change may be correctly designed but misunderstood by individuals who translate the design into program code. IT controls may be designed to report transactions over a predetermined dollar amount to management, but individuals responsible for conducting the review may not understand the purpose of such reports and, accordingly, may fail to review them or investigate unusual items.[30]

■ Controls Addressing Significant Risk

It is especially important to evaluate the design of controls that address **significant risks** and controls for which substantive procedures alone is not sufficient. For significant risks, the auditor should evaluate the design of the entity's controls, including relevant control procedures. Implementation of a control means that the control exists and that the entity is using it. We will discuss tests of implementation of controls in Chapter 8 Control Risk, Audit Planning and Test of Controls.

■ Control Risk

Control risk is a function of the effectiveness of the design and operation of internal control in achieving the entity's objectives relevant to preparation of the entity's financial statements.[31] Some control risk will always exist because of the inherent limitations of internal control. Internal control, no matter how well designed and operated, can provide only reasonable assurance of achieving the entity's objectives. Limitations inherent to internal control include the faultiness of human judgment in decision making and simple human failures such as errors or mistakes.

■ Assessing Control Design

There are no standard procedures for assessing the design of internal controls, but all controls are created to assure that an objective be met. When assessing control design, the auditor will start with the objective. Then he will ask himself what controls should and could be in place to assure that this objective is met and in what way these controls may be implemented. This is the design of the control.

■ Financial Statement Assertions and Controls

There are standard financial statement objectives, or **assertions**, that are assumed to be in place for a financial statement that fairly represents the underlying financial condition of the entity. For example, the assertion **existence** may be applied to sales, i.e. "revenue exists." The objective is that all sales that sum to the revenue account balance actually exist – each sales transaction composing the revenue meets the definition of "revenue" and actually occurred (sales were not factious). Controls such as cash registers, restricted access for recording sales in the general ledger, and control activities such as segregation of duties and monitoring of unusual transactions should be designed and implemented to assure that the revenue account balance is correct. Are revenue transactions input through the cash register? That is a design to assure revenue exists. In addition to using a cash register, an additional part of the design of the control is that all employees are trained to use the cash register.

■ Methods for Obtaining Controls Audit Evidence

Obtaining audit evidence about the design and implementation of relevant controls may involve:[32]

- **Inquiring of entity personnel.** Inquiries directed toward internal audit personnel may relate to their activities concerning the design and effectiveness of the entity's internal control. Ordinarily, only inquiring of entity personnel will not be sufficient to evaluate the design of a control or to determine whether a control has been implemented.
- **Observing and re-performing the application of a specific control.** The auditors may observe the application of the control or reperform the application themselves.
- **Inspecting documents and reports.**
- **Tracing transactions through the information system** relevant to financial reporting.

■ Control Tests of Design

Tests of the operating effectiveness of controls may be performed on controls that the auditor has determined are suitably designed to prevent, or detect and correct, a material misstatement. Some control design risk assessment procedures may provide audit evidence and, consequently, serve as tests of controls. For instance, in obtaining an understanding of the control environment, the auditor may make inquiries about management's use of budgets, observe management's comparison of monthly budgeted and actual expenses, and inspect reports pertaining to the investigation of variances between budgeted and actual amounts. These procedures provide knowledge about the design of the entity's budgeting policies and may also provide audit evidence about the effectiveness of the operation of budgeting policies in preventing or detecting material misstatements.

The result of testing the design may reveal **weaknesses in internal control**, which must be reported to management. "The auditor should make those charged with governance or management aware, as soon as practicable, and at an appropriate level of responsibility, of material weaknesses in the design or implementation of internal control which have come to the auditor's attention."[33] Reports of weaknesses in internal control will be discussed in Chapter 12 Completing the Audit.

Certification Exam Question 7.9

Control risk should be assessed in terms of:

(A) Special controls.
(B) Types of potential fraud.
(C) Financial statement assertions.
(D) Control environment factors.

7.12 Summary

Internal control is not only essential to maintaining the accounting and financial records of an organization, it is essential to managing the entity. For that reason everyone from the external auditors to management to the board of directors to the stockholders of large public companies to government has an interest in internal controls. In many parts of the world, regulators have emphasized the importance of internal control by requiring management to make annual public statements about the effectiveness of internal controls.

Internal control, according to the Committee of Sponsoring Organizations of the Treadway Commission (COSO), is a process, effected by an entity's board of directors, management and other personnel, designed to provide reasonable assurance regarding the achievement of objectives in the following categories: effectiveness and efficiency of operations, reliability of financial reporting, compliance with applicable laws and regulations, and safeguarding of assets against unauthorized acquisition, use or disposition.

The reason a company establishes a system of control is to help achieve its performance and profitability goals and prevent loss of resources by fraud and other means. Internal control can also help to ensure reliable financial reporting and compliance with laws and regulations. The entity's internal control system consists of many specific policies and procedures designed to provide management with reasonable assurance that the goals and objectives it believes important to the company will be met. Controls are especially important in preventing fraud, supporting management objectives, insuring accuracy of transactions, and supporting assessment of the financial statements.

The internal control components are: the control environment, risk assessment, control activities, information, and communication, and monitoring.

The control environment consists of the actions, policies, and procedures that reflect the overall attitudes of top management, directors, and owners. The control environment has a pervasive influence on the way business activities are structured, the way objectives are established, and the way risks are assessed. The control environment is influenced by the entity's history and culture. Effectively controlled companies set a positive "tone at the top" and establish appropriate policies and procedures.

Elements of the control environment are: communication and enforcement of integrity and ethical values; commitment to competence; participation by those charged with governance – independence and integrity of the board of directors; management's philosophy and operating style – leadership via control by example; organizational structure; assignment of authority and responsibility; and human resource policies and practices.

All components of internal control, from control environment to monitoring, should be assessed for risk.

Management's risk assessment differs from, but is closely related to, the auditor's risk assessment. Management assesses risks as part of designing and operating the internal control system to minimize errors and irregularities. Auditors assess risks to decide the evidence needed in the audit. The two risk assessment approaches are related in that if management effectively assesses and responds to risks, the auditor will typically need to accumulate less audit evidence than when management fails to, because control risk is lower.

Information is needed at all levels of the organization: financial information; operating information; compliance information; and information about external events, activities, and conditions. This information must be identified, captured, and communicated in a form and time frame that enables people to carry out their responsibilities. The information system controls should be tested because there are general IT and input risks that the accounting system does not produce sufficient audit evidence.

For an audit, the auditor should obtain an understanding of the information system and the related business processes relevant to:

- the classes of transactions in the entity's operations that are significant to the financial statements;
- the procedures by which those transactions are initiated, recorded, processed and reported;
- the related accounting records, supporting information, and specific accounts in the financial statements and how they initiate, record, process, and report transactions;
- how the information system captures events and conditions;
- the financial reporting process used to prepare the entity's financial statements.

Control procedures (sometimes called "control activities") are policies and procedures that help ensure management directives are carried out. They help ensure that necessary actions are taken to address risks to the achievement of the entity's objectives for operations, financial reporting, or compliance. Generally, control procedures fall into four broad categories: performance reviews, information processing, physical controls, and segregation of duties.

Internal control systems need to be monitored. Monitoring is a process that deals with ongoing assessment of the quality of internal control performance over time. The process involves assessing the design of controls and their operation on a timely basis and taking necessary corrective actions. By monitoring, management can determine that internal controls are operating as intended and that they are modified as appropriate for changes in conditions.

To gain an understanding of the entity's internal control, the auditor is required to evaluate the design of controls and determine whether they have been implemented. Evaluating the design of a control involves considering whether the control is capable of effectively preventing, or detecting and correcting, material misstatements. It is especially important to evaluate the design of controls that address significant risks and controls for which substantive procedures alone are not sufficient.

7.13 Answers to Certification Exam Questions

7.1 (D) The requirement is to associate the meaning of reasonable assurance with one of the statements. Answer (D) is correct because in accounting terms reasonable is a term that reflects the cost–benefit concept, i.e. that the cost of internal control should not exceed the benefits expected to be derived from its operation. Answers (A), (B), and (C), while they are correct statements about internal control, have nothing to do with "reasonable assurance."

7.2 (A) The requirement is to identify the procedure that is **not** required to be included in an auditor's consideration of internal control. Answer (A) is correct because although the Sabanes-Oxley Act and other national acts require **management** to point out deficiencies in internal control, verified by the auditor, the auditor is not required to search for deficiencies in the operation of controls. Answers (B), (C) and (D) are incorrect because an auditor must obtain an understanding of the internal control environment and the information system required to obtain information on the design of internal control and in whether control activities have been placed in operation.

7.3 (A) The requirement is to find the answer that is **not** a component of an entity's internal control. Answer (A) is correct because while auditors assess control risk as a part of their consideration of internal control, it is not a component of an entity's internal control. Answers (B), (C), and (D) are incorrect because, according to ISA 315 and COSO, the control environment, risk assessment, control activities, information and communication, and monitoring are the five components of an entity's internal control.

7.4 (C) The requirement is to determine where the overall attitude and awareness of an entity's board of directors concerning the importance of internal control is normally reflected. Answer (C) is correct because the control environment reflects the overall attitude, awareness, and others concerning the importance of control and its emphasis. Answers computer based controls (A), segregation of duties systems (B), and safeguards over access to assets (D) are implementations of controls, rarely done by member of the board of directors.

7.5 (B) The job is to give the best procedures for assessing control risk. Answer (B) is correct because tests of controls include inquiries of appropriate entity personnel, inspection of documents and reports, observation of the application of the policy or procedure, and re-performance of the application of the policy or procedure. One cannot assess control risk by analytical procedures (A), confirmation (C) or verification (D).

7.6 (A) The requirement is to find the best statement concerning an auditor's assessment of control risk. Answer (A) is correct because assessing control risk may be performed concurrently during an audit with obtaining an understanding if internal control. Answer (B) is incorrect because evidence about the operation of internal control from prior audits is useful in planning and executing the current year's assessment of control risk. Answer (C) is incorrect because the basis for an auditor's conclusions about the level of control risk must be documented when at any time control risk is assessed below maximum. Answer (D) is incorrect because a lower level of control risk requires **more** assurance, not less, that the controls are operating effectively.

7.7 (B) The requirement is to distinguish the functions that should be segregated for effective internal control. Answer (B) is correct because authorizing transactions, recording transactions, and maintaining custody of assets should be segregated. The concept of execution – fulfilling one's work duties – given in (A) and (C) is not related to segregation of duties. The physical act of payment, given in (A) and (D), must be authorized, but is an act and not a conceptual component of segregation of duties.

7.8 (D) The requirement is to give a procedure an auditor would perform to provide evidence about whether an entity's internal control activities are designed to prevent or detect material misstatements. Answer (D) is correct because observing the entity's personnel applying the procedures is a good way to determine whether controls have been placed in operation. Furthermore, ISA 500 says audit evidence obtained directly by the auditor (e.g. observation of the application of a control) is more reliable than audit evidence obtained indirectly or by inference (e.g. inquiry about the application of a control). Answer (A) is not the answer because reperforming the activities is a test of control to assess the effectiveness of a control in operation, not its design. Answer (B) is incorrect because analytical procedures cannot provide evidence of control design. Answer (C) is wrong because vouching a sample of transactions is a substantive test not directly aimed at determining whether controls are suitably designed.

7.9 (C) The requirement is to identify the terms in which control risk should be assessed. Answer (C) is right because ISA 315 states that control risk be assessed in terms of financial statement assertions. Answer (A) does not make sense in the context. Fraud (answer (B)) may result from weaknesses in controls, but controls are not assessed in terms of fraud. Control environment factors (D) influence controls, not the other way around.

7.14 Notes

1 Committee of Sponsoring Organizations of the Treadway Commission (COSO), 1992, Chapter 1 Definition, *Internal Control – Integrated Framework*, American Institute of Certified Public Accountants, Jersey City, New Jersey, p. 9.

2 IAASB, 2004, *International Standards on Auditing, Assurance, and Ethics Pronouncements*, International Standard on Auditing 315 (ISA 315), "Understanding the Entity and Its Environment and Assessing the Risks of Material Misstatement," para. 67–99, International Federation of Accountants, New York.

3 IAASB, 2004, *International Standards on Auditing, Assurance, and Ethics Pronouncements*, International Standard on Auditing 315 (ISA 315), "Understanding the Entity and Its Environment and Assessing the Risks of Material Misstatement," para. 43, International Federation of Accountants, New York.

4 Committee of Sponsoring Organizations of the Treadway Commission (COSO), 2002, *Internal Control – Integrated Framework*, American Institute of Certified Public Accountants, New Jersey.

5 KPMG, LLP, 2003, *Fraud Survey 2003*, KPMG Forensic, USA.

6 KPMG Forensic Consulting, 2002, *KPMG Singapore Fraud Survey Report 2002*, KPMG, Singapore.

7 Examples of the laws requiring "proper record-keeping systems" or "proper accounting records" are the Foreign Corrupt Practices Act of 1977 in the USA and the UK Companies Act 1985.

8 Disclosure is typically required when accounts of interest (revenue, joint venture accounts) exceed certain amounts or have certain characteristics (revenue segments amounts are disclosed if they exceed 10 percent of total revenue and joint venture amounts, and consolidated if the company has effective control).

9 IAASB, 2004, *International Standards on Auditing, Assurance, and Ethics Pronouncements*, International Standard on Auditing 315 (ISA 315), "Understanding the Entity and Its Environment and Assessing the Risks of Material Misstatement," para. 54, International Federation of Accountants, New York.

10 Adapted and reprinted with permission from AICPA. Copyright © 2000 & 1985 by American Institute of Certified Public Accountants.

11 IAASB, 2004, *International Standards on Auditing, Assurance, and Ethics Pronouncements*, International Standard on Auditing 315 (ISA 315), "Understanding the Entity and Its Environment and Assessing the Risks of Material Misstatement," para. 69, International Federation of Accountants, New York.

12 All companies traded on the New York Stock Exchange are required to have an audit committee composed of outside (non-executive) directors. The Code of Best Practice of the London Stock Exchange emphasizes that the independence and integrity of the board as a whole is enhanced by having non-executive (outside) directors and recommends their use on the audit committee.

13 107th US Congress, 2002, "Sec. 301. Public Company Audit Committees," para. 3, Sarbanes-Oxley Act of 2002, Public Law 107–204, Senate and House of Representatives of the United States of America in Congress assembled, Washington, DC, July 30.

14 Committee of Sponsoring Organizations of the Treadway Commission (COSO), 1992, "Chapter 2 Control Environment," *Internal Control – Integrated Framework*, American Institute of Certified Public Accountants, Jersey City, New Jersey, pp. 27–28.

15 From: Internal Control Working Group, 1993, *Internal Control and Financial Reporting: Draft guidance for directors of listed companies registered in the UK in response to the recommendations of the Cadbury Committee*, Institute of Chartered Accountants in England and Wales, London, October, p. 19.

16 Based on the Committee of Sponsoring Organizations of the Treadway Commission (COSO), *Blank Tools – Control Environment, Internal Control – Evaluation Tools*, American Institute of Certified Public Accountants, Jersey City, New Jersey, 1992, pp. 19–28.

17 Adapted and reprinted with permission from AICPA. Copyright © 2000 & 1985 by American Institute of Certified Public Accountants.

18 IAASB, 2003, *International Standards on Auditing, Assurance, and Ethics Pronouncements*, International Standard on Auditing 315 (ISA 315), "Understanding the Entity and Its Environment and Assessing the Risks of Material Misstatement," para. 81, International Federation of Accountants, New York.

19 There is sometimes confusion between "control activities" and "control procedures." ISA and US Generally Accepted Auditing Standards do not define "control activities," but defined "control procedures" as the policies and procedures that management installs to meet objectives. The COSO Report uses the term "control activities" and gives it virtually the same definition.

20 IAASB, 2004, *International Standards on Auditing, Assurance, and Ethics Pronouncements*, International Standard on Auditing 315 (ISA 315), "Understanding the Entity and Its Environment

and Assessing the Risks of Material Misstatement," para. 90, International Federation of Accountants, New York.

21 Bank of England, 1995, *Report Of The Board Of Banking Supervision Inquiry Into The Circumstances Of The Collapse Of Barings*, July 18.

22 Mary Jo White, United States Attorney, 1996, *Complaint against Masaxiro Tsuda* (along with Daiwa Bank and Toshihide Iguchi), US Supreme Court Southern District Of New York.

23 "Daiwa Bank ex-trader fined and sent to prison," *The Wall Street Journal*, December 17, 1996, p. B5.

24 See for additional guidance 2004 IFAC, *Handbook of International Auditing, Assurance, and Ethics Pronouncements*, International Standards on Auditing 610 (ISA 610), "Considering the Work of Internal Auditing," International Federation of Accountants, New York.

25 Committee of Sponsoring Organizations of the Treadway Commission (COSO), 1992, "Chapter 6, Monitoring," *Internal Control – Integrated Framework*, American Institute of Certified Public Accountants, Jersey City, New Jersey, pp. 73–74.

26 Based on the Committee of Sponsoring Organizations of the Treadway Commission (COSO), 1992. Blank Tools – Control Environment, Internal Control – Evaluation Tool, AICPA, New Jersey, pp. 45–47.

27 Adapted and reprinted with permission from AICPA. Copyright © 2000 & 1985 by American Institute of Certified Public Accountants.

28 107th US Congress, 2002, "Sec. 404. Management Assessment of Internal Controls," Sarbanes-Oxley Act of 2002, Public Law 107-204, Senate and House of Representatives of the United States of America in Congress assembled, Washington, DC, July 30.

29 SEC, 2003, "SEC Implements Internal Control Provisions of Sarbanes-Oxley Act; Adopts Investment Company R&D Safe Harbor," www.sec.gov/news/press/2003-66.htm, Washington, DC, May 27.

30 Examples of limitations of internal control from IAASB, 2003, *International Standard on Auditing 315 (ISA 315)*, "Understanding the Entity and Its Environment and Assessing the Risks of Material Misstatement," para. 64. International Federation of Accountants, New York.

31 IAASB, 2004, *Handbook of International Auditing, Assurance, and Ethics Pronouncements*, International Standard on Auditing 315 (ISA 315), "Understanding the Entity and Its Environment and Assessing the Risks of Material Misstatement," para. 55, International Federation of Accountants, New York.

32 Ibid.

33 IAASB, 2004, *Handbook of International Auditing, Assurance, and Ethics Pronouncements*, International Standard on Auditing 315 (ISA 315), "Understanding the Entity and Its Environment and Assessing the Risks of Material Misstatement," para. 120, International Federation of Accountants, New York.

7.15 Questions, Exercises and Cases

QUESTIONS

7.3 Internal Control Defined

7.1 Define internal control. Discuss the fundamental concepts in the definition: process, people, reasonable assurance, and objectives.

7.2 Describe the four objectives of internal control.

7.4 The Importance of Internal Control

7.3 Do corporations believe fraud a problem according to KPMG reports? Explain.

7.4 Why is the auditor interested primarily in controls that relate to reliability of financial reporting, accounting and internal control systems?

7.5 Components of Internal Control

7.5 What are the five interrelated components of internal control? Briefly discuss them.

7.6 Control Environment

7.6 Define control environment. Why is it important to an entity?

7.7 Can evaluation of the control environment be a key element in determining the nature of the audit work? Why or why not?

7.8 What is meant by "tone at the top?"

7.7 Risk Assessment

7.9 What is the difference between management risk assessment and auditor's risk assessment?

7.10 Name and discuss one technique that has been developed to identify risk.

7.8 Information Systems, Communication, and Related Business Processes

7.11 What things might an auditor consider when evaluating the information system of an entity?

7.12 What is the accounting system designed to do? What should be documented about an accounting system as part of the procedures to understand the internal control system?

7.9 Control Activities (Control Procedures)

7.13 Into what five categories do control activities fall?

7.14 Discuss the *Barings* case and the *Daiwa Bank* case. How could similar problems be prevented in the future? What is your opinion of these cases?

7.10 Monitoring of Controls

7.15 Why should an internal control system be monitored over time? What issues are considered when evaluating the ongoing monitoring for internal control?

7.11 Design of Internal Controls

7.16 Discuss the four methods of obtaining audit evidence about the design and implementation of relevant controls.

PROBLEMS AND EXERCISES

7.3 Internal Control Defined

7.17 Internal control is geared to the achievement of objectives in one or more separate overlapping categories.

Required:
A.   Define these four categories of objectives.
B.   For each objective give an example of internal control goals for three industries: retail, manufacturing, and services.

7.4 The Importance of Internal Control

7.18 Obtain Understanding of Internal Control. Johannes Mullauer, Wirtschaftsprufer, who has been engaged to audit the financial statements of Ais, GmbH, is about to start obtaining an understanding of the internal control structure and is aware of the inherent limitations that should be considered.

Required:
A.   What are the reasons for establishing objectives of internal control?
B.   What are the reasonable assurances that are intended to be provided by the accounting internal control structure?
C.   When considering the potential effectiveness of any internal control structure, what are the inherent limitations that should be recognized?

7.5 Components of Internal Control

7.19 Components of Internal Control. Internal control consists of five interrelated components. These are derived from the way management runs a business, and are integrated with the management process.

Required:
A.   Name and define the components of internal control.
B.   How do the components of internal control affect each other?
C.   Discuss the interrelationship of components using as an example a retail clothing store.

7.6 Control Environment

7.20 Assess Internal Control Environment. Using the COSO criteria for assessing the internal control environment (Illustration 7.4) describe a company with an effective control environment.

7.21 Control Environment. Hasse Nilsson, Statautoriseret, is in charge of the audit of a new client, US Clothing Store. It is owned by three men, Messrs. Simpson, Andersson, and Ding. Only one of the owners, Mr. Simpson, is active in the business – the other two live and work in another city. Mr. Simpson operated the business as a proprietorship until a few years ago, when he incorporated it and obtained additional capital for store improvements by selling to Ding and Andersson 24 percent of his equity. In addition to Mr. Simpson, the store employs three sales clerks and Miss Tearsson, the cashier-book-keeper. Miss Tearsson has worked for Mr. Simpson for many years. Nilsson and the partner in his firm responsible for the US Clothing Store audit have agreed that one of the first things Nilsson should do when he starts work on the audit is to consider the internal control environment.

Required:

A. Why is it important to consider the internal control environment of even a small company such as US Clothing Store?

B. What particular features of the internal control environment would Nilsson inquire into in the circumstances described above?

[CICA adapted]

7.7 Risk Assessment

7.22 Risk Assessment. OK Yen, Ltd. is a Japanese electronics games and amusements company specializing in pachinko games. Pachinko parlors are a big industry in Japan, whose 18,000 pachinko parlors in 1996 accounted for a quarter of the country's civil sector and are thought to produce ¥30 trillion per year in revenue – more than Japan's auto industry. Customers who play pachinko buy a supply of pinballs costing around ¥4 and cash in the balls they win back for prizes equivalent to ¥2.5 each. Although it is illegal to give cash to winners, the customers may go to nearby shops and sell their prizes for cash. Recently a new form of pachinko has been developed that gives very large prizes to winners, but decreases the chances of winning. Although the number of players have decreased over the last four years, the gross sales have doubled. Locations of the stores is not crucial, so OK Yen can locate in low rent areas.

Government authorities have recently given much attention to pachinko gaming. Operations featuring the game have been associated with the yacuza, the Japanese criminal organization. Some people in Japan are concerned that pachinko is really addictive gambling. There are complaints to authorities over children being left to play on busy streets or locked up in parked automobiles while their parents go to play pachinko.

Required:

Following the five step procedure outlined in the chapter, identify the risks associated with OK Yen's business.

7.8 Information Systems, Communication, and Related Business Processes

7.23 Information and Communications. The firm of Hayes & Hu, Ltd., personal financial advisors in the Notting Hill area of London, has asked Joseph Smallman, Chartered Accountant (CA), to recommend a computer information system. Hayes & Hu advise individuals on equity investments, manage finances for individuals who are outside the country and develop family budgets.

Required:

A. What type of inputs (information transactions) are Hayes & Hu likely to make?

B. What information subsystems are Hayes & Hu likely to need?

C. What sort of outputs in the form of reports and documents will Hayes & Hu require?

7.9 Control Activities (Control Procedures)

7.24 Separation of Duties. Aurello Pellegrini, Dottore Commercialista (CONSOB), is approached by his client who has just reorganized his medium-sized manufacturing company to make it more structured by giving responsibilities in related areas to one employee. The "supervisor for customers" is responsible for both collection of accounts receivable and maintenance of accounts receivable records. The "inventory coordinator" is responsible for purchasing, receiving, and storing inventory. The "payroll agent" handles all payroll matters including personnel records, keeping time cards, preparation of payrolls, and distribution of payroll checks.

Required:

Consider each of these new positions and discuss the implications of their duties on the internal control system. Discuss what sorts of problems could arise if these positions are created.

7.10 Monitoring of Controls

7.25 Monitoring. Monitoring is done in two ways: through ongoing activities and individual evaluations.

Required:

A. From what sources does ongoing monitoring come? What issues might be considered?
B. When doing individual evaluations what should the auditor consider?
C. What type of reports on monitoring should management receive?

7.11 Design of Internal Controls

7.26 Control Design. Luxury Auto Leases, Inc. of New Mexico, USA, has offices in Tucumcari, Santa Fe, and Albuquerque. Lisa Dockery, the company president has an office in Santa Fe and visits the other offices periodically for internal audits.

Ms. Dockery is concerned about the honesty of her employees. She contacted Back & Front, CPAs, and informed them that she wanted them to recommend a computer system that would prohibit employees from embezzling cash. She also told Back & Front that before starting her own business she managed a nationwide auto leasing company with over 200 offices and was familiar with their accounting and internal control systems. She suggested that Back & Front could base her requested system on the nationwide one.

Required:

A. How should Back & Front advise Ms. Dockery regarding the installation of a system similar to the nationwide one? Explain.
B. What should Back & Front advise Ms. Dockery regarding a system that will absolutely prevent theft? Discuss.
C. If Back & Front takes Luxury Auto Leasing as an audit client, what procedures should they perform to detect fraud? Would they guarantee that their audit could discover fraud? Why?

CASES

7.27 Internal Control Activities. An example of a lack of internal controls with a disastrous result was the bond trading loss in the New York Office of Daiwa Bank in 1995. Over 11 years 30,000 unauthorized trades were made resulting in a $1.1 billion loss (an average of $400,000 in losses for every trading day). Daiwa allowed Toshihide Iguchi, a bond trader, to authorize sales, have custody of the bond assets, and record these transactions.

As a novice trader, Iguchi misjudged the bond market, racking up a $200,000 loss. To raise cash to pay Daiwa's brokers, Iguchi would order Bankers Trust New York to sell bonds held in Daiwa's account. The statements from Banker's Trust came to Iguchi who forged duplicates, complete with bond numbers and maturity dates, to make it look as if Banker's Trust still held the bonds he had sold. When he confessed to his misdeeds, the Daiwa thought their bond account was $4.6 billion when in fact only $3.5 billion was left.

Inadequate review of internal controls was also to blame. Daiwa's internal auditors had reviewed the New York branch several times since the fraud began, but Banker's Trust was never contacted for confirmation of Daiwa's bank statements. If they had, Iguchi's fraud would have been exposed. Diawa's external auditor never audited the New York branch.

Required:

A. What type of control procedures were ignored at Daiwa?

B. For each internal control procedure missing, what damage was caused?

C. What kind of controls could have been instituted that would have prevented the problems at Daiwa?

D. For each of the five internal control procedures discussed above, applying each to a bank trading operation, identify a specific error that is likely to be prevented if the procedure exists and is effective.

E. For each of the five internal control procedures discussed in this chapter, applying each to a bank trading operation, list a specific intentional or unintentional error that might result from the absence of the control.

CONTROL RISK, AUDIT PLANNING AND TEST OF CONTROLS

8.1 Learning Objectives

After studying this chapter you should be able to:

1 Describe the basic approach to planning an audit based on an understanding of internal control.

2 State the methods of obtaining an understanding of the internal control.

3 Be familiar with what documentation requirements are considered important as a means of ensuring that auditors comply with significant requirements of the standards.

4 Know the types of documentation that may be used to describe the entity's internal control structure.

5 Understand how control risk is assessed and why.

6 Describe a weakness in internal control and how it is determined.

7 List four overall responses to risk assessment.

8 Differentiate between the nature, timing and extent of audit procedures.

9 Express what is contained in a planning memorandum.

10 Illustrate what an audit plan is.

11 Define tests of controls and give examples.

12 Describe the four evidence gathering techniques used in tests of controls.

13 Demonstrate the importance of timing in tests of controls.

14 Explain how to evaluate sufficiency and appropriateness of audit evidence.

8.2 Understanding, Assessing and Testing Internal Controls

The nature, extent and timing of the audit procedures take their most significant impetus from a thorough understanding of design and operating effectiveness of internal control. Assessment of control risk includes three steps (see Illustration 8.1):

1 obtaining an understanding of internal controls culminating in documentation of the controls;
2 an initial assessment and response to assessed risk based on the design of internal controls culminating in an **audit planning memorandum** and **audit plan (audit program)**;
3 a final assessment based upon **test of controls** of operating effectiveness.

Internal control documentation, therefore, becomes a "blueprint" for the audit procedures. It serves as a basis for assessing initial control risk. The auditor brings this "blueprint" and his own judgment and an understanding of the company, industry, and economy in the control environment to bear on what audit procedures are set in the audit plan. The tests of controls determine if the design of internal controls operates effectively and if there is a need to rethink or revise the audit plan based upon the auditor's final control risk assessment. Sufficiency and appropriateness of evidence relates to the quality of the control risk assessments.

Certification Exam Question 8.1

Which of the following is **not** a component of an entity's internal control?

(A) Control risk.
(B) Control activities.
(C) Monitoring.
(D) Control environment.

8.3 Understanding of Internal Controls and Documentation

Audit risk, the risk that the auditor gives a wrong opinion based on the evidence, has three components: **inherent risk, detection risk,** and **control risk** (see Chapter 6 Understanding the Entity, Risk Assessment and Materiality). Inherent risk exists in the business environment and increases the likelihood that accounts will be misstated. An inherent risk in a heavily regulated industry is that the company will not follow the regulations. Detection risk is that the auditor will not catch a material misstatement. Detection risk is the only component of audit risk that can be influenced by the auditor. Partially as a reaction against inherent risks, entities set up controls such as a cash register (to reduce the risk of theft of cash and inaccuracy of recorded transactions). Control risk is the risk that these controls will not prevent, detect, or correct possible misstatements (the cash register is not used or malfunctions).

Controls are set up to reduce inherent risk

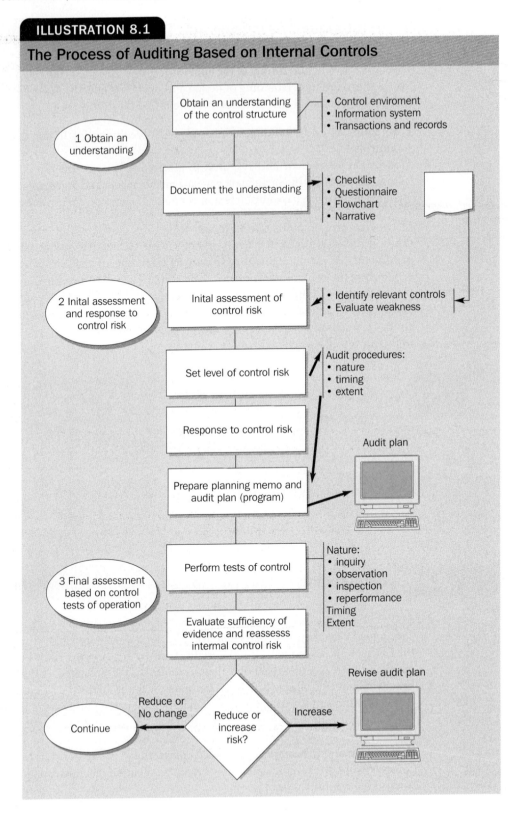

ILLUSTRATION 8.1

The Process of Auditing Based on Internal Controls

■ Control Risk

Control risk may be defined as the risk that a misstatement that could occur in an account balance or class of transactions and that could be material, individually or when aggregated with misstatements in other balances or classes, will not be prevented or detected and corrected on a timely basis by the accounting and internal control systems.[1]

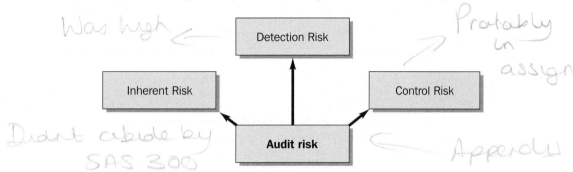

[Handwritten annotations: "Was high", "Didn't abide by SAS 300", "Probably in assign", "Appendix"]

The auditor's first job is to obtain an understanding of the components of the internal control (environment, control activities, etc.) of the entity. Based on this, the auditor makes a preliminary assessment of control risk, at the assertion level (e.g. existence of revenue) for each material account balance (accounts receivable) or transaction cycle (sales and collection).

The auditor assesses control risk based on the perceived effectiveness of the entity's internal control system in preventing and/or detecting material misstatement. As the organization's internal control becomes more effective, the auditor's assessment of level of control risk should decrease (the control risk is assessed to be low).

■ Audit Approach

The auditor first evaluates the internal control environment as well as the accounting and internal control systems because the audit approach relies heavily on internal control. Generally, if an auditor can rely on internal controls, he can reduce substantive tests. If internal controls are weak or non-existent, the auditor becomes dependent on substantive tests to provide audit evidence.

[Handwritten annotation: "IMPORTANT"]

■ Procedures to Obtain an Understanding

Procedures to obtain an understanding are procedures used by the auditor to gather evidence about the design and placement in operation of specific control policies and procedures. Procedures to obtain an understanding focus attention on both the design of relevant policies, procedures, and records, and whether they have been placed in operation by the entity. For example, an effective control environment enables the auditor to have more confidence in internal control and the reliability of audit evidence generated internally within the entity. Illustration 8.2 shows some factors considered in making a judgment about the nature and extent of these procedures in obtaining an understanding of the internal control system.

Examples of Factors that Affect the Nature and Extent of Procedures for an Understanding Sufficient to Plan the Audit[2]

Example factors	Effect on the nature of procedures	Effect on the extent of procedures
Previous experience with the entity		
Knowledge of prior misstatements	Procedures focus on changes, if any, in the internal control structure to correct problems	Focus procedures to limit their extent
Prior permanent file documentation of the understanding	Inquiries about changes in the internal control structure	Reduce extent of procedures to understand the design of the internal control structure
Nature of the entity's specific internal control structure, policies or procedures		
Documentation of extensive client accounting manuals, flow charts, or other internal control structure documentation	Focus on whether relevant internal control structure policies or procedures are placed in operation	Less extensive inquiry and observation to understand design and placed in operation
Nature of the particular policy or procedure		
Internal auditors perform duties relevant to the internal control structure	Procedures should be appropriate to understand the relevant work performed by internal auditor	More extensive procedures may be necessary to understand work performed by functions within internal audit
Size and complexity of the entity		
Complex organization structure	Focus attention on methods of assigning authority and responsibility	More extensive procedures performed through the organization, such as inquiry of more personnel
Complex computer systems Multiple locations	May need to understand computer general control procedures	May perform more extensive procedures to assure systems at multiple locations have not changed

A company's accounting system and control activities are designed to address specific account balances and classes of transactions. Illustration 8.3 presents several accounts for a typical manufacturer: the account characteristics and the resulting difference in the extent of understanding that may be needed are shown.

ILLUSTRATION 8.3

Effect of Account Characteristics on the Auditor's Understanding of the Internal Control System[3]

Example account characteristics	Extent of understanding that may be needed to plan the audit
Large balance relative to total assets	Entity control environment factors
Large number of customer accounts and transactions	Significant classes of transactions
Several significant inherent risks associated with revenue recognition policies, completeness and cutoffs, and realization	■ Revenue recognition policies ■ Significant activities in the initiation, processing, and reporting of transactions (e.g. order entry, shipping, billing, cash receipts)
Complex and detailed computer systems for processing transactions and maintaining records	Selected control procedures (e.g. completeness controls, reconciliations of control account to detail, evaluation of past-due accounts)
Complexity of inventory and number of items in inventory, depending on the nature of the business	■ Significant classes of transactions (particularly in manufacturing entities) ■ Inventory pricing policies
Significant inherent risks associated with complex pricing, receiving and shipping, cutoffs, and product obsolescence	■ Significant activities in the initiation, processing and reporting of transactions (e.g. accumulation of costs, inventory movement, inventory relief)
Accounting system based on periodic physical inventory counts	Selected control procedures (e.g. completeness controls, cutoff procedures, physical counts, including compilation and pricing)
Small number of debt instruments and new transactions during the year	Significant classes of transactions
Inherent risks associated with appropriateness of accounting principles (off balance sheet financing) and compliance with debt covenants	Significant activities in the initiation, processing and reporting of transactions (e.g. approval of debt, review of journal entries, and disclosure)
Simple accounting records (general ledger accounts supported by legal documents, journal entries, and other source documents)	Significant accounting records (legal documents, general ledger accounts)
Small balance relative to total assets	Entity control environment factors
Small number of account balances and transactions	Nature of the account balance
No significant risks	

A starting point for an auditor's understanding of the accounting process might be the general ledger. The main application systems (both computer-based and manual) that feed into, and have a material effect on, the general ledger would be identified.

■ Information System

The auditor should obtain an understanding of the information system, including the related business processes, relevant to financial reporting, including the following areas:[4]

- the classes of transactions in the entity's operations that are significant to the financial statements;
- the procedures, within both IT and manual systems, by which those transactions are initiated, recorded, processed, and reported in the financial statements;
- the related accounting records, whether electronic or manual, supporting information, and specific accounts in the financial statements, in respect of initiating, recording, processing and reporting transactions;
- how the information system captures events and conditions, other than classes of transactions that are significant to the financial statements;
- the financial reporting process used to prepare the entity's financial statements, including significant accounting estimates and disclosures.

■ Examination of Transactions and Records

The understanding involves knowledge of the ways in which transactions are valued, classified, recorded, and summarized in data files, journals, or ledgers. An auditor will want to identify: source documents; accounts (subsidiary or general ledger master files) affected by the transaction; and the nature of the computer files, documents, and relevant accounting reports produced and processed in the general flow of information to the general ledger and financial statements. The auditor may also examine valuation models used to prepare accounting estimates.

It is impractical to describe all systems for processing transactions, so the auditor normally identifies and gains a high level of understanding only of those transactions that are likely to be of greatest importance to the financial statements. High on the auditor's list of important transactions are those with the highest materiality, those related to the client's business operations and those with increased risk of misstatement.

Risk of misstatement is increased when the transaction system initiates and executes transactions (e.g. automatic check printing or funds' transfers), processes complex transactions, or controls the movement of assets. Risk is higher if there are changes in key personnel operating a system or there is a history of processing errors.

■ Accounting System

Understanding the overall flow of transactions through the accounting system involves consideration of the nature and sources of principal inputs, key outputs, important master files and interchange of information throughout the system. Understanding the accounting system reliability requires assessment of the apparent quality of processing, including any history of misstatement. Whether the system is now or has been significantly changed, the experience and competence of staff operating the system, and the complexity of transactions processed by the system are also important considerations.

■ Computer Environment

Auditors obtain a high-level (not detailed) understanding of the computer environment. They look at the principal elements of the computer environment and the computer control structure. This information is gathered by interviewing various management personnel responsible for the systems. To understand the computer environment, the degree of centralized or decentralized control and the relationships between various important processing locations is examined. The auditors also consider the principal types of systems software including access control or security software, program change and library control software, principal programming languages, data retrieval/reporting languages, database managers, communications, and operating systems.

The auditors also consider the principal types of systems software including access control or security software, program change and library control software, principal programming languages, data retrieval/reporting languages, database managers, communications, and operating systems.

■ Documentation of the Understanding of Internal Control

In ISA 315 documentation requirements are considered important as a means of ensuring that auditors comply with significant requirements of the standards.[5] The following audit processes require documentation:

- the discussion among the engagement team regarding the susceptibility of the entity's financial statements to material misstatement due to error or fraud, and the significant decisions reached;
- the understanding obtained regarding each of the aspects of the entity and its environment,[6] and each of the five internal control components[7] discussed in Chapter 7 Internal Control and Control Risk (control environment, risk assessment, etc.) in order to assess both the sources of information from which the understanding was obtained and several risks. The several risks assessed are those of material misstatement of the financial statements, those associated with management objectives and strategies, those related to the nature of the entity, and risks based on the entities' financial performance;
- the identified and assessed risks of material misstatement at the financial statement level and at the assertion level;[8]
- the risks identified and related controls evaluated as a result of *significant risks*[9] and risks for which it is not possible to reduce risks of material misstatement.[10]

Documentation of Internal Control Structure

To comply with the second requirement, how should the auditor document his understanding of the company's internal control structure? The auditor will usually only document the aspects of the control environment that he believes are relevant to the financial statement audit. An auditor is not required to document procedures performed to obtain the understanding unless they also help reduce the level of control risk.

A proper description of the internal control system includes the following four characteristics:

1 the origin of every document and record in the system;
2 all processing that takes place;
3 the disposition of every document and record in the system;
4 indication of the control procedures relevant to the assessment of control risk.

Certification Exam Question 8.2

Which of the following questions would an auditor most likely include on an internal control questionnaire for notes payable?

(A) Are assets that collateralize notes payable critically needed for the entity's continued existence?
(B) Are two or more authorized signatures required on checks that repay notes payable?
(C) Are the proceeds from notes payable used for the purchase of noncurrent assets?
(D) Does the board of directors authorize direct borrowings on notes payable?

■ Types of Documentation

The documentation technique may vary according to the auditor's professional judgment. Common documentation techniques are narrative descriptions, question-naires, checklists and flow charts.

- An **internal control narrative** is a written description of a client's internal control structure.
- An **internal control questionnaire** asks a series of questions about the controls in each audit area as a means of indicating to the auditor aspects of the internal control structure that may be inadequate. In most instances, it is designed to require a "yes" or "no" response, with "no" responses indicating potential internal control difficulties.
- A **checklist** is a list of considerations or procedures that are followed by the auditor. In the case of internal controls it is a list of controls that should normally be in place.
- An **internal control flow chart** is a symbolic, diagrammatic representation of the client's documents and their sequential flow in the organization. For most users, flowcharting is superior to narratives.

The extent of the documentation and its form will depend on the nature, size, and complexity of the organization and its internal control. Generally, the more complex the entity's accounting and internal control systems, and the more extensive the auditor's procedures, the more extensive the auditor's documentation.

Illustrations 8.4 and 8.5 are examples of the narrative description. Illustration 8.4 is a narrative description of the internal control environment whereas Illustration 8.5 is a table illustrating the revenue cycle. Illustration 8.6 is an internal control questionnaire. For another illustration of a questionnaire see Chapter 7 Internal Control and Control Risk and Illustrations 7.5 and 7.8. Illustration 8.6 is a checklist. Illustration 8.7 is a flow chart.

ILLUSTRATION 8.4

Narrative Description of the Control Environment[11]

Client **Ownco. Inc.** Balance Sheet date 12/31

Completed by: **mlw**	Date: 30/9/X5	Reviewed by: **jp**	Date: 02/11/X5
Updated by: **mlw**	Date: 15/9/X6	Reviewed by: **jp**	Date: 29/10/X6
Updated by: ____	Date: _____	Reviewed by: __	Date: _____

The company manufactures plastic fishing worms at one location and is managed by its sole owner, Ed Jones. Jones, who is responsible for marketing, purchasing, hiring, and approving major transactions, dominates management of the company. He has a good understanding of the business and the industry in which it operates. Jones believes that hiring experienced personnel is particularly important because there are no layers of supervisory personnel and thus, because of limited segregation of duties, few independent checks of employees' work. Jones has a moderate-to-conservative attitude toward business risks. The business has demonstrated consistent profitability, and because Jones considers lower taxes to be as important as financial results, he has a conservative attitude towards accounting estimates.

Jones and Pat Willis, the bookkeeper, readily consult with our firm on routine accounting questions, including the preparation of accounting estimates (tax accrual, inventory obsolescence, or bad debts). Our firm also assists in assembling the financial statements.

The company's board of directors is composed of family members. The board is not expected to monitor the business or the owner-manager's activities.

Willis, the bookkeeper, and Jones' secretary, Chris Ross, perform most of the significant accounting functions. Willis was hired by the company in 20X0, has a working knowledge of accounting fundamentals, and we have no reason to question her competence. Willis regularly consults with our firm on unusual transactions, and past history indicates that it is rare for adjustments to arise from errors in the processing of routine transactions.

The company's accounting system runs consists of an off-the-shelf accounting software package. The source code is not available for this software. Access to the computer and computer files is limited to Willis, Ross and Jones, who effectively have access to all computer files.

The owner-manager carefully reviews computer-generated financial reports, such as reports on receivable aging, and compares revenues and expenses with prior years' performance. He also monitors the terms of the long-term debt agreement that requires certain ratios and compensating balances.

ILLUSTRATION 8.5

Internal Control Narrative (Table) Documentation

REVENUE CYCLE

	Contact Customer	Customer agrees to sale	Approve credit	Goods shipment	Bill customer	Receive remittance	Credit accounts receivable	Deposit cash
Accounting transaction				Sale		Cash receipt		
Journal entry					Dr. A/R Cr. Sales		Dr. Cash Cr. A/R	
Documents	Call sheet	Purchase order from customer	Sales order; picking list	Packing slip, shipping advice	Invoice	Remittance advice; remittance list	– Remittance Advice	Deposit slip
Data collected	– Name – Address – Contact person salesperson	All items needed to complete the order or the sales contract	– Current balance – Credit limit	– Date – Carrier – Items shipped – Quantity	Amount due	– Name – Type of payment – Amount	– Name – Invoice – Amount	Total deposit
Department	Sales	Sales	Credit	Shipping	Accounting	Mail room	Accounting	Cashier
Control issues	Follow company policy and strategy	Do not violate laws or company policy	Only approved customers get credit	Ship only what was ordered; document all shipments	Bill for every shipment; bill accurately	Prevent theft of checks or cash	Prevent lapping; properly credit customer accounts	Theft

ILLUSTRATION 8.6

Internal Control Questionnaire Documentation

Question	Comments	
1 When does the company recognize a sale?		
2 When are collections considered to engender an increase in cash?		
3 At what point in the revenue cycle is the sale recorded?		
4 At what point in the revenue cycle is cash credited for the collection of accounts receivable?		
5 For each of the following steps in the revenue cycle what documents are initiated or used and what data is collected?	**Documents**	**Data collected**
Contact customer		
Customer agrees sale		
Approve credit limits		
Goods shipment		
Bill customer		
Receive remittance		
Credit accounts receivable		
Deposit cash		
6 For each of the following steps in the revenue cycle to which department do they pertain and what are the control issues?	**Department**	**Control issues**
Contact customer		
Customer agrees sale		
Approve credit limits		
Goods shipment		
Bill customer		
Receive remittance		
Credit accounts receivable		
Deposit cash		

ILLUSTRATION 8.7

Checklist Documentation

Question	Yes	No
1 Is revenue recognized when goods are transferred?		
2 Is cash recognized when the client pays a remittance?		
3 Are revenue and accounts receivable recorded when the customer is billed?		
4 Is a call sheet or similar document used when a customer is contacted?		
5 Are customer sales agreements evidenced by a purchase order from the customer?		
6 Is a credit approval indicated on the sales order and picking list?		
7 Are packing slips and shipping advises used when goods are shipped?		
8 Is the customer sent an invoice and remittance advice?		
9 When payment is received, are remittance advices listed?		
10 Is a remittance advice used as evidence for crediting accounts receivable?		
11 Are deposit slips collected as evidence of cash deposits?		
12 Is the name, address, and contact person recorded when the customer is contacted?		
13 When credit is approved are current balance and credit limit information available?		
14 When goods are shipped is the carrier, items and quantity recorded?		
15 Does the sales department handle both customer contact and customer agreements?		
16 Is there a credit authority separate from the sales department?		
17 Are remittances counted in the mailroom?		

ILLUSTRATION 8.8

Internal Control Flow Chart Revenue Cycle

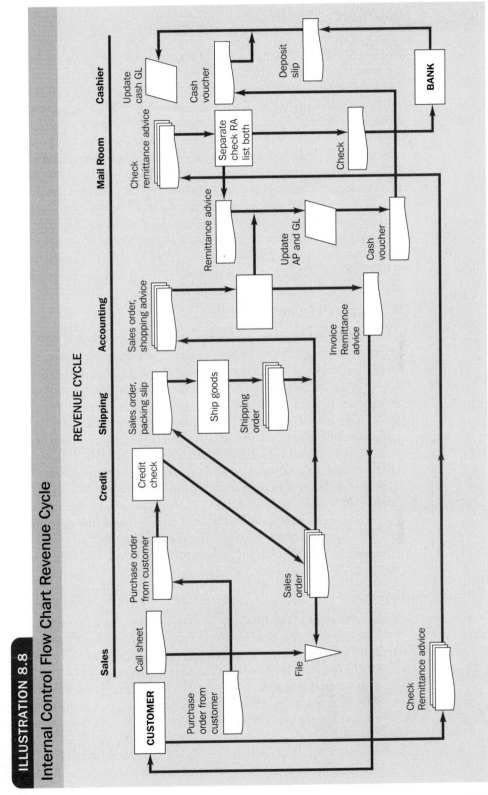

8.4 Assessing Control Risk

Assessing control risk is the process of evaluating the design and operating effectiveness of a company's internal controls as to how it prevents or detects material misstatements in the financial statement assertions. The conclusion reached as a result of assessing control risk is referred to as the assessed level of control risk. The combined aspects of the five **components of internal control**[12] are considered when assessing control risk. In this section, we will discuss how the level of control risk is assessed.

Assessing control risks starts with the financial statement assertion (e.g. completeness) about significant account balances (e.g. accounts payable) and transactions. Based on the assertions, **audit objectives** are set (to determine if all accounts payable are recorded). For each of these audit objectives, the auditor should determine whether he intends to rely on internal controls for achieving the desired level of acceptable audit risk (see Chapter 6 Understanding the Entity, Risk Assessment and Materiality). The auditor then decides whether to identify the relevant internal controls. He will identify controls for the most material financial statement assertion or audit objective.

■ Identify Relevant Controls

After determining the assertions and the related audit objectives, the next step is to identify controls that contribute to each assertion. The auditor identifies important controls by referring to the types of control activities that might exist, and asking if they do exist (as part of understanding the internal controls). For example, for **segregation of duties** in the treasury department of a company there must be separation between the person who performs a trade and the persons who account for that trade (the "back office" activities).

This identification of relevant control procedures and monitoring activities is typically done by inquiring of senior management how it controls business operations that are reflected in the accounting records. This is a "top-down approach." This approach helps to ensure that the auditor does not test controls at a level of detail greater than that needed to meet audit objectives. Generally, controls performed by senior managers tend to involve delegation of responsibilities and monitoring activities using both financial and non-financial data. Lower-level controls may include control procedures that address the processing of transactions, the safeguarding of assets, and direct monitoring of those procedures.

Examples

Using the example of the objective "all accounts payable are recorded," if the auditor feels that the control procedure of reviewing the initial recording of payments to vendors is not operating effectively (there have not been reviews in several months), he may judge the controls to be weak. If the controls are weak, the control risk will be assessed as high. Using this example again, if there are regular reviews of the procedures for initial recording of accounts payable and the company has a past history of good recording, the auditor may feel the control is strong and assesses the control risk for this assertion and objective as low.

The more direct the relationship between an assertion and the controls, the more effective the procedure may be in reducing control risk. For example, a company may have two controls for inventory: (1) management closely monitors gross profit percentage from month to month; and (2) the company maintains perpetual inventory records and carries out physical inventory counts at the end of every quarter. The physical inventory count and perpetual inventory systems are more directly related to the assertion of completeness and existence than monitoring of gross profit percentage because they are more likely to detect and correct misstatements.

■ Evaluate Weaknesses in Internal Control and Set Control Risk Level

When assessing controls the auditor looks for weaknesses in the controls for two reasons: to determine the nature and extent of the substantive tests he will perform and to formulate constructive suggestions for improvements. The constructive suggestions will be presented to management in the **management letter**. A management letter can contain communications of reportable conditions that are significant deficiencies in the internal control. **Reportable conditions** are matters that auditors believe should be communicated to the client's audit committee because they represent significant deficiencies in the design or operation of the internal controls that could adversely affect the organization's ability to record, process, summarize, and report financial data in the financial statements. The auditor should make management aware, as soon as practical and at an appropriate level of responsibility, of material weaknesses in the design or operation of the accounting and internal control systems, which have come to the auditor's attention. [13]

Concept and a Company 8.1

Enron's PRC and RAC – Loose and Tight

Concept	How some controls are effectively designed, in place, but not operating while others may be co-opted to serve destructive ends.
Story	Enron's traders risked losing money every time they made a trade, especially in unpredictable areas like weather and broadband futures. Signing long-term contracts to provide gas and electricity, a market they pioneered, required an understanding of all kinds of risks – pricing, delivery, credit, etc. – and knowing how to hedge those risks. Since all their long-term deals were marked to market, the credibility of their revenue figures were directly related to risk and interest components over time. It is hard to image a more important concept for Enron than managing risk. Controls are management's best resource for managing risk.
	Jeffery Skilling, who served as Enron president and COO from 1996 to early 2001, was widely quoted as saying that Enron had "one of the best control systems in the world," with hundreds of lawyers and accountants vigilant against financial risk. When analysts inquired about the company's risk-management abilities Skilling had a ready answer: he pointed to Enron's Risk Assessment and Control (RAC) department. Skilling knew Wall Street wanted to see a strong system of internal controls, and he made RAC a centerpiece of management presentations to Wall Street analysts, investors, and credit-rating agencies.

▶

Enron's PRC and RAC – Loose and Tight (continued)

Thanks to RAC, Enron was able to portray itself as a company that could safely take *more* risk than other companies, precisely because it had the right controls in place. Skilling often described the minimal risk trading culture of Enron under his charge as "loose and tight," one of the eight attributes of the successful companies profiled by Peters and Waterman Jr. in their best-selling book, *In Search of Excellence*. The idea is to combine tight controls with maximum individual authority to allow entrepreneurship to flourish without the culture edging into chaos. (Byrne 2002)

Risk Assessment and Control RAC

Skilling imposed a requirement that Risk Assessment and Control had to review virtually all Enron deals – even international ones – and he bragged constantly about the sophisticated oversight that RAC provided. RAC would look at issues like currency devaluation, interest rate projections, commodity price projections, and other elements that might factor into a given deal. RAC employed former bankers, accountants, statisticians, and MBAs – experts in every aspect of a commercial transaction. RAC had resources – by the late 1990s it had 150 professionals, a $30 million budget, and access to a $600 million computer system. RAC had a director (Rick Buy) who reported directly to Skilling and Skilling characterized him as Enron's "top cop." (McLean 2003)

RAC failure

Unfortunately, even though Skilling bragged about Enron's sophisticated controls, they were undermined at every turn. As one director put it, RAC "was a façade for Skilling to point to when he wanted to impress the rating agencies and outside investors." (Bryce 2002) The analysis and recommendations of the RAC was undermined by their director, control and subversion by the deal makers whose deals they reviewed, and by another control at Enron, the personnel evaluation system run by the Performance Review Committee (PRC).

Rick Buy, the RAC director, was a man uncomfortable with confrontation. The corporate culture was such that you never said no to a deal. In interviews after the fall, Buy insisted that saying no wasn't even part of his job description. He told his staff that RAC's charge was simply to describe a transaction, analyze its risk and possible returns, and tell senior management "you guys make up your mind." (McLean 2003)

After completing its analysis, RAC had to circulate its draft comments on a transaction to the deal makers who had the right to edit the comments. Entire deals went to RAC just a few days before the close of the quarter, leaving little time to scrutinize transactions involving hundreds of millions of dollars, and putting enormous pressure on RAC to sign off, because the company needed to deal to hit its numbers. (McLean 2003)

Dr. Vince Kaminski, head of the risk control part of RAC, told of how his own mounting worries last fall caused him to refuse to let his research team do further work on partnership-related transactions. Dr. Kaminski said that when he tried to pass along his concerns to Enron's outside auditor, Arthur Andersen LLP, he was told by a senior Enron official to stop such communications. He said that in response to his criticisms, he and his research group were for a time cut off from certain financial information about the partnerships by top management, including Enron's then-president, Jeffrey Skilling. (Emshwiller 2002)

The performance review process by the PRC was another way to beat RAC. One employee commented, "No one would stand in front of a deal because you could get killed in the PRC. People who questioned deals would get attacked by the business units because they weren't as cooperative on a deal as the developers wanted." Members of the RAC feared retribution if they ever wanted to work in other parts of Enron after leaving RAC. (McLean 2003)

Performance Review Committee (PRC)

Under Enron's peer-review process, a select group of 20 people were named to a performance review committee (PRC) to rank more than 400 vice-presidents, then all the directors, and finally all of Enron's managers. The stakes were high because all the rewards were linked to ranking decisions by the PRC which had to unanimously agree on each person. Managers judged "superior" – the top 5 percent – got bonuses 66 percent higher than those who got an "excellent" rating, the next 30 percent. They also got much larger stock option grants. (Byrne 2002) Enron's Performance Review Committee created a highly politicized work environment.

Traders and originators sat on panels that ranked the same RAC executives who reviewed their transactions. The process made honest evaluations virtually impossible. One Enron RAC employee commented, "Once you get there and you realized how it was, do you stand up and lose your job? It was scary. It was easy to get into 'Well, everybody else is doing it, so maybe it isn't so bad.' " (Byrne 2002) Another said "It didn't matter how good you were. It only mattered who you knew." (Bryce 2002) Every employee had to be graded – on paper – by several peers. Skilling told one reporter, "The performance evaluation was the most important thing for forging a new strategy and culture at Enron – the glue that holds the company together." (Durgin 2000)

Two Things Not Subject to Negotiation

Skilling was quoted in a financial journal as saying, "Only two things at Enron are not subject to negotiation: the firm's personnel evaluation policy and its company-wide risk management program." (McLean 2003)

Discussion Questions

- How would you assess the RAC control and the PRC control: weak or strong? Why?
- Why would the RAC control be considered material to the financial statements?
- What tests of control would you recommend to determine if the RAC was effective in operation?

References

Bryce, Robert, 2002, *Pipe Dreams: greed, ego and the death of Enron*, Public Affairs, New York.

Byrne, J.A., France, M., and Zellner, W., 2002, " 'The Environment Was Ripe For Abuse' Enron's unrelenting stress on growth and its absence of controls helped push execs into unethical behavior," *Business Week*, February 25, p. 118.

Durgin, H. and Skinner, R., 2000, "Inside Track: The Guru of Decentralization," *Financial Times*, June 26.

Emshwiller, J.R., 2002, "Companies: Enron Official Warned Management Of Partnership Risks as Early as 1999 – Kaminski Says He Believed Off-Balance-Sheet Deals Were Fraudulent," *Wall Street Journal*, March 19, A4.

McLean, Bethany and Elkind, Peter, 2003, *The Smartest Guys in The Room: the amazing rise and scandalous fall of Enron*, Portfilio, New York.

Weaknesses in internal control are the absence of adequate controls, which increases the risk of misstatements existing in the financial statements. The auditor may find upon examining internal controls that controls do not exist at all where there should be controls or that controls are not operating properly. As a result, the risk increases that financial statement balances will be wrong. In some cases, the presence of the weakness might be so important or pervasive that it may materially affect the financial statements. This is called a **material weakness** in internal control.

A four-step approach to identify significant weaknesses is sometimes recommended:[14]

1 Identify existing controls.
2 Identify the absence of key controls (where controls are lacking).
3 Determine potential material misstatements that could result.
4 Consider the possibility of compensating controls. A compensating control is one elsewhere in the system that offsets a weakness.

For example, in payroll accounting, the auditor flowcharts the existing system to identify key controls. Studying the flowchart he finds that the time cards are given directly to the accounting department and no-one checks the time cards for validity. The potential misstatements that might result are that employees are paid for time that they do not work (an employee's friend punches in their clock-card before the employee arrives at work). The auditor considers offsetting controls and finds that once or twice a year the plant manager stages a surprise inspection minutes after "clock in" time.

Certification Exam Question 8.3

Control risk should be assessed in terms of:

(A) Specific controls.
(B) Types of potential fraud.
(C) Financial statement assertions.
(D) Control environment factors.

Control Risk Assessed at Maximum

Control risk should be assessed *at the maximum* (the greatest risk that a material misstatement that could occur will not be prevented or detected on a timely basis by the internal control structure) for some or all assertions if:

- policies and procedures are unlikely to pertain to an assertion;
- policies and procedures are unlikely to be effective;
- obtaining enough or proper evidence is not efficient.

8.5 Overall Responses to Assessed Risk

The auditor's selection of audit procedures is based upon the assessment of risk. The auditor should develop an overall audit strategy describing the scope and conduct of the audit in order to reduce audit risk to an acceptably low level.[15]

Certification Exam Question 8.4

An auditor is most likely to assess control risk at the maximum if the payroll department supervisor is responsible for:

(A) Examining authorization forms for new employees.
(B) Comparing payroll registers with original batch transmittal data.
(C) Authorizing payroll rate changes for all employees.
(D) Hiring all subordinate payroll departments.

■ Audit Strategy

The auditor plans and performs an audit so that audit risk is reduced to a low level. The overall audit strategy sets the direction of the audit. The purpose of the overall audit strategy is to develop an effective response to the risk of material. The auditor considers what he found in preliminary planning activities such as client acceptance, ethical position of the audit firm and his understanding of the entity and its environment, including its internal control, to develop an effective and efficient overall audit strategy that will appropriately respond to assessed risks.

The overall audit strategy includes consideration of planned audit responses to specific risks through the development of the audit plan. The overall audit strategy also encompasses the approach to organizing the conduct and management of the audit engagement (e.g. staffing requirements and locations to be included in the audit scope) and the relative emphasis to be placed on tests of controls and substantive procedures.

The auditor typically summarizes the overall audit strategy in the form of a planning memorandum (see the next section of this chapter).

■ Overall Responses to Address Risks

The auditor should determine overall responses to address the risks of material misstatement at the financial statement level.[16] Overall response to assessed risk may include

■ emphasizing to the audit team the need to maintain professional skepticism in gathering and evaluating audit evidence;
■ assigning more experienced staff or those with special skills or using experts;
■ providing more supervision;
■ incorporating additional elements of unpredictability in the selection of further audit procedures to be performed.

■ Audit Procedures Responsive to Risks

The auditor should design and perform further audit procedures whose nature, timing and extent are responsive to the assessed risks of material misstatement.[17] There should be a clear link between the nature, timing and extent of the auditor's audit procedures and the risk assessments. For example, the assessment of the risks of material misstatement at the financial statement is directly related to assessment of the control environment. If there are weaknesses in the control environment, the auditor may alter the timing of the procedures (conduct more audit procedures as of the period end rather than at an interim date), increase the extent (seek more extensive audit evidence or increase the number of locations to be included in the audit scope), and change the type of audit evidence (less analytical procedures and more details of balances procedures).

■ Nature of Audit Procedures

The nature of the audit procedures is of most importance in responding to the assessed risks. The nature of audit procedures refers to both their purpose (tests of controls or substantive procedures) and their type (inspection, observation, inquiry, confirmation, recalculation, reperformance, or analytical procedures).

■ Financial Statement Assertions

Financial controls are based on financial statement assertions. Assertions may determine the purpose of audit procedure. The **completeness** assertion in relation to payables suggests tests of controls. Substantive procedures may be the best way to test the **occurrence** assertion. If the entity's information system produced the evidence on which audit procedures are performed, control tests at the assertion level for **accuracy** and completeness should be performed.

■ Timing of Audit Procedures

Timing refers to when audit procedures are performed or the period or date to which the audit evidence applies. The auditor may perform tests at an interim date or at period end. For practical purposes it is generally necessary that an auditor performs audit procedures at a time other than year-end and calculate the year-end results by analytical procedures. Evidence gathered at the period end is more accurate and complete than interim evidence. Therefore, the higher the risk of material misstatement, the more likely the auditor is to perform substantive procedures nearer to, or at, the period end rather than at an earlier date. Audit procedures performed unannounced or at unpredictable times may also mitigate misstatement risk.

In determining the time of the audit procedures, the auditor also considers such matters as:[18]

- ■ the control environment;
- ■ when relevant information is available (e.g. electronic files may require testing at a specific time because they will subsequently be overwritten, or procedures to be observed may occur only at certain times);
- ■ the nature of the risk (e.g. if there is a risk of inflated revenues to meet earnings expectations by subsequent creation of false sales agreements, the auditor may wish to examine contracts available on the date of the period end);
- ■ the period or date to which the audit evidence relates.

■ Extent of Audit Procedures

Extent generally means the quantity of an audit procedure to be performed (e.g. the size of an **audit sample** or the number of observations). The extent of an audit procedure is determined by the assessment of risk. Ordinarily, the auditor increases the extent of audit procedures as the risk of material misstatement increases.

■ Audit Sampling

Audit sampling (see the Appendix to Chapter 10) is the key area in which extent is an important consideration. The auditor may choose to examine more of a particular sample (shipping notices) or sample more related items (sales orders, shipping notices, sales invoices). Valid conclusions may ordinarily be drawn using sampling approaches. However, if the quantity of selections made from a population is too small, the sampling approach selected is not appropriate to the circumstances, or if exceptions are not appropriately followed up on, there will be an unacceptable risk that the auditor's conclusion based on a sample may be different from the conclusion reached if the entire population was subjected to the same audit procedure.

Certification Exam Question 8.5[19]

In determining the effectiveness of an entity's internal controls relating to the existence or occurrence assertion for payroll transactions, an auditor most likely would inquire about and:

(A) Observe the segregation of duties concerning personnel responsibilities and payroll disbursement.
(B) Inspect evidence of accounting for prenumbered payroll checks.
(C) Recompute the payroll deductions for employee fringe benefits.
(D) Verify the preparation of the monthly payroll account bank reconciliation.

8.6 Prepare Planning Memorandum and Audit Plan

The final step in the planning process is to prepare an audit planning memorandum and an audit plan. The audit planning memorandum summarizes the overall audit strategy and contains the decisions regarding the overall scope, emphasis, and conduct of the audit, planned audit responses at the overall financial statement level, along with a summarization of significant matters documented in the audit plan.

Typically, an audit planning memorandum would contain the following sections:

■ **Background information describing the client company's structure, business, and organization**. This should include significant matters affecting the client, cross-referenced as required to the audit files to enable a member of the audit team to gain an overview of the client.

■ The **objectives of the audit** showing whether it is an audit for stockholders, the national government filings, or some special purpose audit.

■ The **assessment of engagement risk** and potential follow-up on identified increased engagement risks, as identified during the client acceptance phase.

■ An identification of **other auditors or experts** that will be relied upon in the audit and a recap of the instructions provided to them.

■ An assessment of **materiality.**

■ **Inherent risks,** emerging from insight into the client's industry and business, specified for each important combination of financial statement account and audit objective.

■ **Conclusions regarding the control environment,** including the possible reliance on internal auditors.

■ Classification of the client's CIS environment and the **level of reliance on the client's CIS systems.**

■ An evaluation of the **quality of the accounting and internal control systems,** in particular an identification of internal control procedures mitigating the identified inherent risks.

■ Summary of the **audit approach** for addressing each account balance and related audit objective for which an inherent risk has been identified.

■ The **timing and scheduling of audit work,** including determining which procedures may be performed before the balance sheet date. Also considered is what audit work must be done on or after the balance sheet date. Dates are shown for such critical procedures as cash counts, accounts receivable confirmations, and inventory observation.

■ **Audit budget,** detailed for each level of expertise available in the audit team.

The audit planning memorandum is normally completed before starting work at the client's offices. It is typically reviewed and approved by both the audit manager and the audit partner before the field work is commenced. It may be modified throughout the engagement as special problems are encountered and as the auditors' consideration of internal control leads to identification of areas requiring more or less audit work.

■ Audit Plan (Audit Program)

Audit plan is the term used by the new ISAs, but in the prior standards the audit plan was referred to as the "audit program." According the ISA 300,[20] "The auditor should develop an audit plan in order to implement the overall audit strategy."

The audit plan (audit program) sets out the nature, timing and extent of planned audit procedures required to implement the overall audit strategy into a comprehensive description of the work to be performed. It serves as a set of instructions to staff involved in the audit and as a means to control and record the proper execution of the work. Illustration 8.9 gives a detail of a sample audit plan for accounts receivable.

The audit plan includes the details of the nature, timing, and extent of planned audit procedures for material classes of transactions, account balances, and disclosures. It includes performance of risk-assessment procedures. The auditor uses the information obtained from the risk-assessment procedures to plan further audit procedures. As the auditor performs audit procedures outlined in the audit plan, the audit plan is updated and changed to reflect the further audit procedures considered necessary given the circumstances.

The demand for audit evidence can be derived from the planning stage. The combination of materiality (precision) and audit risk (reliability) determines for each account balance and audit objective, how much evidence should be gathered. Audit procedures should be selected to ensure that the combined evidence provides adequate assurance.

ILLUSTRATION 8.9

Sample Audit Plan (Audit Program) – Accounts Receivable

Objectives:

1 Recorded sales are for shipments actually made to bona fide customers (existence).
2 Recorded sales are correctly billed for the amount of goods ordered (completeness and accuracy).
3 Cut-off is proper (completeness and existence).
4 All revenue from the sale of goods and performance of service are recorded accurately in the journal and ledger based on sales, credit authorization, and sales agreements (completeness, accuracy, measurement, and rights and obligations).
5 Trade accounts receivable represent uncollected sales or other charges to bona fide customers and are owned by the entity (existence, valuation and rights, and obligations).
6 All disclosures are in compliance with local and international standards (presentation and disclosure).

	Obj. #	Done by	Refer
1 Vouch sales from shipping records to sales journal, authorization, and sales invoices, including relevant data (e.g. party, price, description, quantity, and dates). Sample 100.			
2 Foot journals and trace to the general ledger and master file printout.			
3 Obtain a sample of shipping documents and compare dates on shipping documents to dates recorded in the journal.			
4 Select a sample of general ledger sales entries and trace them to the sales journals. Sample 200 throughout year.			
5 Observe if authorized price list is used to price the product.			
6 Sample sales invoices for agreement with price list.			
7 Confirm a sample of receivables and perform alternative procedures for non-responses.			
8 Vouch (match) a sample of recorded receivables to sales agreements.			
9 Trace a sample of credit sales invoices to accounts receivable billings.			
10 Compare a sample of shipping documents to related sales invoices.			
11 Investigate the credit ratings for delinquent and large receivables accounts.			
12 Obtain an aged trial balance of receivables, test its clerical accuracy and reconcile to the ledgers.			
13 Perform procedures to identify receivables from related parties.			

The greater the diversity between the audit procedures selected, the greater the combined assurance derived from them.

Audit Evidence

Audit evidence is available from a variety of different sources: procedures to obtain an understanding of the client's business and the internal controls, tests of controls, analytical procedures, and detailed substantive testing (either substantive tests of transactions or tests of details of balances). How much the auditor can rely on the first two will determine the extent of the rest. If the auditor determines from the understanding of the business that inherent risk is low and from the understanding of internal controls that control risk is low, then less evidence is required from the substantive tests, as can be derived from the audit assurance model.

Audit Procedures

In planning the timing of audit work, crucial procedures should be performed first. Whenever possible, tailored audit plans, showing procedures to be performed, should be prepared in chronological order of execution. The outcome of certain audit procedures can require significant modification of the planned approach, and such procedures should be performed at the earliest opportunity.

Tests of controls and substantive procedures should cover the whole of the accounting period. Where the auditor intends to carry out audit work in advance of the period end (e.g. during an interim audit visit), he should plan whatever additional procedures are required at the final audit stage to ensure that the whole period is covered.

Documentation

The auditor should document the overall audit strategy and the audit plan, including reasons for significant changes made during the audit engagement. The auditor's documentation of reasons for significant changes to the overall audit strategy and audit plan includes the auditor's response to the events, conditions, or results of audit procedures that resulted in such changes. The manner in which these matters are documented is for the auditor to determine based on professional judgment.

8.7 Tests of Controls

The auditor's assessment of the identified risks provides a basis for determining which is the appropriate audit approach for designing and performing audit procedures. In some cases, the auditor may determine that only tests of controls are appropriate, whereas in other cases, the auditor may determine that only substantive procedures are appropriate. Generally, some combination of the two is used. Substantive procedures will be discussed in Chapter 10 Substantive Testing and Evidence.

Tests of controls are audit procedures to test the effectiveness of control policies and procedures in support of a reduced control risk. Key internal controls must be supported by tests of controls. The extent to which the test of controls are applied depends on the assessed control risk. The lower the assessed control risk, the more extensive the tests should be in order to support the high degree of reliance upon internal control.

How much and what evidence is sufficient to support a specific assessed level of control risk is a matter of professional judgment depending on the auditor's decisions about the nature, timing, and extent of tests of controls.

Testing for Operating Effectiveness

If an auditor's low assessment of control risk is based on the expectation that controls are operating effectively, he must perform tests of controls to obtain evidence that the controls were operating effectively during the period. Testing for operating effectiveness is different from determining if controls have been implemented. The auditor determines that the relevant controls exist and that the company is using them to show implementation. When performing tests of the operating effectiveness of controls, the auditor obtains audit evidence about how controls were applied at relevant times during the audit period, the consistency with which they were applied, and by whom or by what means they were applied.

◼ Nature of Tests of Control and Types of Evidence-Gathering Techniques

The nature of tests of controls is that the tests generally consist of one (or a combination) of four types of evidence-gathering techniques:

1 inquiry of client personnel,
2 observation,
3 inspection (examination of documents),
4 reperformance (or recalculation).

Inquiries of appropriate entity personnel, which is also used in the procedures to obtain an understanding, is a frequently used, although not very conclusive, test. For controls that leave no documentary evidence, the auditor generally observes them being applied (e.g. segregation of duties). Inspection of documents and reports is a strong control procedure for control activities that leave a clear trail of documentary evidence (e.g. written authorization of a sale). Reperformance of the application of the policy or procedure by the auditor is important when you have controls with related documents, but the contents of the documents are insufficient to assess reliability.

Inquiry as a Test of Controls

Inquiry consists of seeking information of knowledgeable persons inside or outside the entity. Inquiry evidence is based on interviews concerning the effectiveness of controls. Inquiry may be either in a direct or an indirect form. Direct inquiry involves asking questions of the persons who perform control procedures or monitoring activities. Indirect inquiry involves asking questions of other persons who are in a position to know whether the control procedures are operating effectively even though they do not perform the procedures themselves. For example, the auditor may determine that unauthorized personnel are not allowed access to the computer files by asking the computer librarian or a user of the computer system.

Direct and indirect inquiries often overlap. For example, if a user of accounting information is also responsible for monitoring the control procedures used to prepare the information, inquiries directed to that user may be indirect with respect to the control procedures and direct with respect to the monitoring activities. The auditor might ask a user of a sales report, "How do you know invoices are correctly priced?"

Certification Exam Question 8.6

Which of the following procedures most likely would provide an auditor with evidence about whether an entity's internal control activities are suitably designed to prevent or detect material misstatements?

(A) Reperforming the activities for a sample of transactions.
(B) Performing analytical procedures using data aggregated at a high level.
(C) Vouching a sample of transactions directly related to the activities.
(D) Observing the entity's personnel applying the activities.

The auditor might corroborate the user's answers with more probing inquiries, such as:

■ What errors have you found in reviewing this report?
■ When did you last perform the review?
■ Can you show me an example of questions you raised?
■ What do you do when your staff person is ill or on vacation?

Observation as a Test of Controls

Observation consists of looking at a process or procedure being performed by others, for example, the observation of the performance of internal control procedures that leave no audit trail. Observing the performance of a control procedure or monitoring activity provides substantial evidence of its effectiveness. For example, one might be assured about the effectiveness of inventory counting control procedures by seeing that those performing the count follow management's written instructions.

Inspection as a Test of Controls

Inspection consists of examining records, documents, or tangible assets. Many control activities leave a clear trail of documentary evidence in the form of either written or computer records. If performance of a control or monitoring activity is documented, we may obtain evidence of its performance by examining the trail of documents (audit trail).

Some documentary evidence may be stronger than others. For example, if the control performance is documented by initials of the person performing the control, examination of the initials provides little evidence of the effectiveness of the control. On the other hand, documentation of reconciliations or the disposition of rejected items may provide sufficient evidence of the effectiveness of the control.

Documentation of operation may not exist for some factors in the control environment, such as assignment of authority and responsibility, or for some types of control procedures, such as control procedures performed by a computer. In such circumstances, audit evidence about operating effectiveness may be obtained through audit procedures such as observation, inquiry, or the use of **computer assisted audit techniques (CAATs)**.

Reperformance as a Test of Controls

Reperformance is to perform the task done by an employee to verify the result of the transaction. If content of documents and records is insufficient to assess whether controls

Concept and a Company 8.2

Regina Company – Sales Returns, Bad Computers and Closed Eyes (?)

Concept   The control environment is the key control. What is an auditor to do?

Story   Founded in Rahway, New Jersey, in 1892, Regina Company, Inc. had originally been a music box manufacturer before entering the floor-care industry. In 1985, one year after Donald Sheelen became Regina's CEO, he introduced a series of new Regina products. To promote the new Regina products, he poured millions of dollars into the company's advertising budget. Ultimately, Regina's annual advertising expenses would exceed 20 percent of its annual sales and surpass the combined advertising expenditures of Regina's major competitors, Hoover and Eureka. Regina became very successful and was listed on a national stock exchange in 1987.

After going public, Sheelen and several of his key associates cooked the sales and earnings figures released by Regina. Instead of an $11 million profit for the fiscal year that ended June 30, 1988, the company had actually realized a multimillion-dollar loss. (Knapp 2001)

High Returns Hurt Sales

Although Regina's gross sales were impressive, the net revenue was hurt due to high sales returns. Sheelen's failure to pay sufficient attention to quality control issues during the manufacturing of the new products was to blame. The new products were not reliable because they were rushed to the market without being adequately tested. Regina was getting back huge returns of vacuum cleaners from its distributors as some plastic cleaner parts were melting. The impressive sales figures were largely undercut by customer return rates that were several times greater than those experienced by Regina's competitors.

In order to maintain the confidence of the securities markets Sheelen instructed Vincent Golden, Regina's chief financial officer, not to record all of the company's product returns for second quarter 1988. According to the SEC (SEC 1989), the company understated its sales returns by at least $13 million during the 1988 fiscal year. Regina's employees altered the computer system so that products returned by certain large-volume customers could be processed through the customer service department, but wouldn't be recorded on the company's books.

Create Sales

During the fourth quarter of fiscal 1988, Sheelen realized that the understated sales return wouldn't be sufficient to reach the sales and earnings targets for that year. He then instructed Golden to record phony sales during the fourth quarter of fiscal 1988. So the computer system was used to create false invoices in amounts of prior orders from certain large-volume customers. Large-volume customers were used because such customers were less likely to respond to audit confirmations. With that scheme, 200 fake invoices were generated, representing more than $5 million in sales. (SEC 1989)

Sales and earnings targets were still out of reach for fiscal 1988, so Sheelen and Golden came up with the idea of "ship-in-place" sales. These were sales transactions that customers had ordered, but were not due to be shipped for several weeks. Golden recorded approximately $6 million in ship-in-place sales in the last few days of fiscal 1988. The SEC (SEC

▶

Regina Company – Sales Returns, Bad Computers and Closed Eyes (?) (continued)

1989) charged that the ship-in-place transactions didn't qualify for revenue recognition under GAAP because no exchange had taken place.

Red Flags?

When Regina issued its fiscal 1988 result, David Rocker, a Wall Street money manager, subtracted its nine-month figures and discovered that although indicated fourth-quarter sales rose 28 percent from a year earlier, receivables had soared 84 percent, total inventories 100 percent, and inventories of finished goods alone 74 percent. At the same time, fourth-quarter outlays for research and development fell 37 percent and depreciation 88 percent. "Goods were backing up in the pipeline, and the lower depreciation charges showed earnings weren't for real," Mr. Rocker says. "Obviously, the auditors weren't asking the right questions. Regina's report raised more red flags than I'd seen in a long time." (Berton 1989)

The Computer Malfunctioned

It was becoming increasingly difficult to come up with new revenue tricks as real sales declined, so Sheelen and Golden decided to disclose publicly that Regina's prior financial statements were materially misstated. However, instead of telling the truth, Sheelen and Golden decided to blame the errors on "computer malfunctions." Sheelen issued a press release that Regina's sales would be "substantially lower" than previously forecasted for the first quarter of fiscal 1989 and that the company would post a loss for that quarter. By the next day Regina's stock had dropped 60 percent. Over the next few days, Sheelen and Golden resigned their positions with Regina and their auditor Peat Marwick withdrew the unqualified audit opinion issued only a few weeks earlier on the company's fiscal 1988 financial statements. (Knapp 2001)

What Could the Auditors Do?

A Peat Marwick partner at the time was quoted as saying a company management bent on fraud can easily bamboozle the auditor. "We're only human and prefer to trust the people we're auditing." Edward Grossman, an attorney representing shareholders in class-action suits against Regina's former management and Peat Marwick, says, "Auditors can close their eyes to danger signs." (Berton 1989)

Discussion Questions
- What are the tests of control that might have shown where the problems were?
- When the control environment is corrupt, what problems would an auditor experience in uncovering fraud?

References Berton, Lee, 1989, "Battle of the Books: Audit Firms Are Hit By More Investor Suits For Not Finding Fraud – Is Their Opinion a Guarantee? Work on Regina's Report Is Haunting Peat Marwick – SEC May Tighten Its Rules," *Wall Street Journal*, January 24, p. 1.

Knapp, M.C., 2001, "Regina Company, Inc.," *Contemporary Auditing, Real Issues & Cases*, South-Western Publishing Company, pp. 135–139.

SEC, 1989, *Accounting and Auditing Enforcement Release No. 215*, "SEC Charges Former Regina CEO and CFO with Financial Fraud," Securities and Exchange Commission, February 8.

are operating effectively, the auditor reperforms the control activity to see if the proper results were obtained. For example, an auditor may trace the sales prices on a sales invoice to the authorized price list in effect at the date of operation.

Reperformance of a control activity sometimes provides evidence of its effectiveness, but this evidence is rarely persuasive by itself. The mere absence of errors in the items tested does not provide conclusive evidence that the control was performed effectively. Reperformance is most often effective for testing programmed control procedures and other computer controls. For example, a computer audit specialist may use the client's computer and attempt to enter transactions into the accounting system that have characteristics that should cause them to be rejected.

Evidence Obtained Directly vs. Inferred Evidence

Evidence from tests of controls obtained directly by the auditor, such as through observation, provides more assurance than evidence obtained indirectly or by inference, such as through inquiry. Observation of a control being applied, however, does not ordinarily, by itself, provide sufficient evidence of the effectiveness of the control throughout the whole accounting period. Furthermore, the auditor's observation may not be representative of the usual performance of a control because management and staff may perform their tasks more diligently under the auditor's gaze. Consequently, supplementary tests are usually required to conclude that the control is continuously effective.

■ One Type of Evidence Not Sufficient

One type of audit gathering technique may not be sufficient to properly test the effectiveness of controls. Inquiry alone will not provide sufficient appropriate audit evidence. Tests of controls ordinarily include those procedures used to evaluate the design of controls (see Chapter 7 Internal Control and Control Risk) and frequently include reperformance of the application of the control by the auditor. Often, the auditor uses a combination of audit procedures to obtain sufficient audit evidence. For example, an auditor may observe the procedures for opening the mail and processing cash receipts to test the operating effectiveness of controls over cash receipts. Because an observation is pertinent only at a point in time at which it is made, the auditor may supplement the observation with inquiries of entity personnel and inspection of documentation about the operation of such controls at other times during the audit period.

Substantive Tests and Control Tests

Sometimes substantive tests may be used as tests of controls. When responding to the risk assessment, the auditor may use **tests of details** of transactions as tests of controls. The objective of tests of details performed as tests of controls is to evaluate whether a control operated effectively. The objective of tests of details performed as substantive procedures is to detect material misstatements in the financial statements.

Although the objectives of tests of control and details are different, both may be accomplished concurrently through performance of a test of details on the same transaction, also known as a dual-purpose test. For example, the auditor may examine an invoice to determine whether it has been approved and to provide substantive audit evidence of a transaction. The auditor gives consideration to the design and evaluation of such tests to accomplish both objectives. The absence of misstatements detected by a substantive procedure does not imply that controls related to the assertion being tested are effective.

Certification Exam Question 8.7

In assessing control risk, an auditor ordinarily selects from a variety of techniques, including:

(A) Inquiry and analytical procedures.
(B) Reperformance and observation.
(C) Comparison and confirmation.
(D) Inspection and verification.

■ Timing of Tests of Controls

The timeliness of evidential matter is about when the evidence was obtained and the portion of the audit period to which it may be applied. If the auditor tests controls at a particular time, the auditor only obtains audit evidence that the controls operated effectively at that time. However, if the auditor tests controls throughout a period, he obtains audit evidence of the effectiveness of the operation of the controls during that period. Another important timing matter is how much to rely on tests of prior periods as evidence that controls are effectively designed and continue to operate effectively during the current audit period.

When considering timing in the current period we know that some tests of controls, such as observation, pertain only to the point in time at which the auditing procedure was applied, for example, when testing controls over the entity's physical inventory counting at the period end. If, on the other hand, the auditor requires audit evidence of the effectiveness of a control over a period, audit evidence pertaining only to a point in time may be insufficient. Therefore, the auditor performs other tests that are capable of providing audit evidence that the control operated effectively at relevant times during the audit period, such as tests of general controls pertaining to the modification and use of a computer program during the audit period.

Interim Period Tests

When the auditor obtains audit evidence about the operating effectiveness of controls during an interim period, he should also determine what additional audit evidence should be obtained for the remaining period. To determine what additional evidence is needed, the auditor considers a number of things including the audit evidence obtained during the interim period, the length of the remaining period, the additional audit evidence obtained from the substantive procedures performed in the remaining period, and the overall control environment. The auditor then obtains audit evidence about the nature and extent of any significant changes in internal control that occur subsequent to the interim period.

Prior Period Tests

If the auditor plans to use audit evidence about controls obtained in prior audits, he should determine whether changes in those controls have occurred since the prior audit.

For example, in the prior audit, the auditor may have determined that an automated control was functioning as intended. He obtains audit evidence to determine whether changes to the automated control have been made that affect its continued effective functioning, for example, through the inspection of logs to indicate what controls have been changed. In some cases, the controls have not changed.

"If the auditor plans to rely on controls that have not changed since they were last tested, the auditor should test the operating effectiveness of such controls at least once in every third audit."[21] The auditor is required to retest a control being relied on at least every third audit, because the longer the time elapsed since the testing of the control was performed, the less audit evidence it may provide about the effectiveness of the control.

Controls That Have Changed

Current audit evidence may show that the controls have changed between the prior audit and the current period. If the auditor plans to rely on controls that have changed since they were last tested, he should test these controls in the current audit. Changes may affect the relevance of the audit evidence obtained in prior periods so that there may no longer be a basis for continued reliance. For example, changes in a system that enable an entity to receive a new report from the system probably do not affect the relevance of prior period audit evidence; however, a change that causes data to be accumulated or calculated differently does affect it.

The auditor cannot rely on audit evidence obtained in a prior audit about the operating effectiveness of controls over a significant risk if he plans to rely on the operating effectiveness of controls intended to mitigate that significant risk. He should obtain all audit evidence about the operating effectiveness of those controls from tests of controls performed in the current period.

■ Extent of Tests of Control

The more reliance the auditor puts on controls in his audit, the greater the extent (amount) of the auditor's tests of controls. In addition, as the rate of expected variability of the control increases, the auditor increases the extent of testing of the control.

Use of IT processing decreases the extent of testing controls. A programmed general or application control should function consistently unless the tables, files, or other permanent data used by the program are changed. Once the auditor determines that an automated control is functioning as intended, the auditor may perform tests to determine if the control continues to function effectively. Control tests to measure continued functioning might include determining if changes to the program are not made without being subject to the appropriate program change controls, that the authorized version of the program is used for processing transactions, and that other relevant general controls are effective.

■ Effect of Control Assessment on Substantive Tests

The assessed level of control risk for an assertion has a direct effect on the design of substantive tests. The lower the assessed level of control risk, the less evidence the auditor needs from substantive tests. The auditor's control risk assessment influences the nature, timing, and extent of substantive procedures to be performed. Consequently, as the assessed level of control risk decreases, the auditor may modify substantive tests (see Chapter 10 Substantive Testing and Evidence) in the following ways:

- changing the nature of substantive tests (e.g. using analytical review rather than detailed substantive testing);
- changing the timing of substantive tests, such as performing them at an interim date rather than at year-end;
- changing the extent of substantive tests, such as selecting a smaller sample size.

Ordinarily, the assessed level of control risk cannot be sufficiently low to eliminate the need to perform any substantive tests for all of the financial statement assertions. Consequently, regardless of the assessed levels of control risk, the auditor should perform some substantive tests for significant account balances and transaction classes.

8.8   Evaluate Sufficiency and Appropriateness of Audit Evidence

"Based on the audit procedures performed and the audit evidence obtained, the auditor should evaluate whether the assessments of the risks of material misstatement at the assertion level remain appropriate."[22] The auditor's assessment of the **components of audit risk** may change during the course of an audit. The audit evidence obtained may cause the auditor to modify the nature, timing, or extent of other planned audit procedures. The auditor may conclude that evidence is likely to be available to support a further reduction in the assessed level of control risks for some assertions. In all such cases, the auditor should revise his assessment of control risk and should consider changing his audit strategy for the related financial statement assertion/audit objective.

As the auditor performs planned audit procedures, information may come to the auditor's attention that differs significantly from the information on which the risk assessments were based. For example, the extent of misstatements that the auditor detects by performing substantive procedures may alter his judgment about the risk assessments. In addition, analytical procedures performed at the overall review stage of the audit may indicate a previously unrecognized risk of material misstatement. In such circumstances, the auditor may need to re-evaluate the planned audit procedures.

The sufficiency and appropriateness of audit evidence to support the auditor's conclusions throughout the audit are a matter of professional judgment. The auditor's judgment as to what constitutes sufficient appropriate audit evidence is influenced by such factors as the:[23]

- significance of the potential misstatement in the assertion and the likelihood of its having a material effect, individually or aggregated with other potential misstatements, on the financial statements;
- effectiveness of management's responses and controls to address the risks;
- experience gained during previous audits with respect to similar potential misstatements;
- results of audit procedures performed, including whether such audit procedures identified specific instances of fraud or error;
- source and reliability of the available information;

■ persuasiveness of the audit evidence;
■ understanding of the entity and its environment, including its internal control.

■ Reevaluate Initial Assessment of Internal Control

Based on the results of the tests of control, the auditor should evaluate whether the internal controls are designed and operating as contemplated in the preliminary assessment of control risk and conclude whether sufficient appropriate audit evidence has been obtained to reduce risk of material misstatement in the financial statements. The lower the assessed level of control risk for an assertion, the more assurance is needed from control tests.

The evidence may support the assessed risk, requiring no revision of control risk assessment. If, on the other hand, the evidence from tests of controls does not support the planned assessed level of control risk, the auditor should assess control risk higher and revise the audit strategy to increase substantive tests.

If the auditor has not obtained sufficient appropriate audit evidence as to a material financial statement assertion, he should obtain more audit evidence. If he is unable to obtain sufficient appropriate audit evidence, the auditor should express a qualified opinion or a disclaimer of opinion (see Chapter 12 Completing the Audit).

Certification Exam Question 8.8[24]

After assessing control risk at below the maximum level, an auditor desires to seek a further reduction in the assessed level of control risk. At this time, the auditor would consider whether:

(A) It would be efficient to obtain an understanding of the entity's information system.
(B) The entity's controls have been placed in operation.
(C) The entity's controls pertain to any financial statement assertions.
(D) Additional evidential matter sufficient to support a further reduction is likely to be available.

8.9 Summary

The nature, extent and timing of the audit procedures take their most significant impetus from a thorough understanding of design and operating effectiveness of internal control. Assessment of control risk includes three steps:

1 obtaining an understanding of internal controls culminating in documentation of the controls;
2 an initial assessment and response to assessed risk based on the design of internal control culminating in an audit planning memorandum and audit plan (audit program);
3 a final assessment based upon **test of controls** of operating effectiveness.

Control risk may be defined as the risk that a misstatement that could occur in an account balance or class of transactions and that could be material, individually or when aggregated with misstatements in other balances or classes, will not be prevented or detected and corrected on a timely basis by the accounting and internal control systems.

The auditor first evaluates the internal control environment as well as the accounting and internal control systems because the audit approach relies heavily on internal control. Generally, if an auditor can rely on internal controls, he can reduce substantive tests. If internal controls are weak or non-existent, the auditor becomes dependent on substantive tests to provide audit evidence.

Procedures to obtain an understanding are procedures used by the auditor to gather evidence about the design and placement in operation of specific control policies and procedures. Procedures to obtain an understanding focus attention on both the design of relevant policies, procedures, and records, and whether they have been placed in operation by the entity. For example, an effective control environment enables the auditor to have more confidence in internal control and the reliability of audit evidence generated internally within the entity.

In ISA 315 documentation requirements are considered important as a means of ensuring that auditors comply with significant requirements of the standards. The following audit processes require documentation:

- the discussion among the engagement team regarding the susceptibility of the entity's financial statements to material misstatement due to error or fraud, and the significant decisions reached;
- the understanding obtained regarding each of the aspects of the entity and its environment, and each of the five internal control components in order to assess both the sources of information from which the understanding was obtained and several risks;
- the identified and assessed risks of material misstatement at the financial statement level and at the assertion level;
- the risks identified and related controls evaluated as a result of significant risks and risks for which it is not possible to reduce risks of material misstatement.

Common documentation techniques are narrative descriptions, questionnaires, checklists, and flow charts. An internal control narrative is a written description of a client's internal control structure. An internal control questionnaire asks a series of questions about the controls in each audit area as a means of indicating to the auditor aspects of the internal control structure that may be inadequate. In most instances, it is designed to require a "yes" or "no" response, with "no" responses indicating potential internal control difficulties. A checklist is a list of controls that should normally be in place. An internal control flow chart is a symbolic, diagrammatic representation of the client's documents and their sequential flow in the organization. For most users, flowcharting is superior to narratives.

Assessing control risk is the process of evaluating the design and operating effectiveness of a company's internal controls as to how it prevents or detects material misstatements in the financial statement assertions. The conclusion reached as a result of assessing control risk is referred to as the assessed level of control risk. The combined aspects of the five components of internal control are considered when assessing control risk.

Assessing control risks starts with the financial statement assertions about significant account balances and transactions. Based on the assertions, audit objectives are set. For each of these audit objectives, the auditor should determine whether he intends to rely on internal controls for achieving the desired level of acceptable audit risk. The auditor then decides whether to identify the relevant internal controls. He will identify controls for the most material financial statement assertions or audit objectives.

The auditor's selection of audit procedures is based upon the assessment of risk. The auditor should develop an overall audit strategy describing the scope and conduct of the audit in order to reduce audit risk to an acceptably low level. The auditor should design and perform further audit procedures whose nature, timing, and extent are responsive to the assessed risks. There should be a clear link between the nature, timing, and extent of the auditor's audit procedures and the risk assessments. If there are weaknesses in the control environment, the auditor may alter the timing of the procedures, increase the extent, and change the type of audit evidence.

The final step in the planning process is to prepare an audit planning memorandum and an audit plan (audit program). An audit planning memorandum is a memo detailing the planned audit approach and budget. The audit plan (audit program) sets out the nature, timing, and extent of planned audit procedures required to implement the overall audit strategy into a comprehensive description of the work to be performed. It serves as a set of instructions to staff involved in the audit and as a means to control and record the proper execution of the work.

Tests of controls are audit procedures to test the effectiveness of control policies and procedures in support of a reduced control risk. Key internal controls must be supported by tests of controls. The extent to which the tests of controls are applied depends on the assessed control risk. The lower the assessed control risk, the more extensive the tests should be in order to support the high degree of reliance upon internal control.

Auditors must determine the nature, timing, and extent of procedures to test controls. The nature of tests of controls is that they generally consist of a combination of inquiry of client personnel, observation of controls, examination of documents, and reperformance of control procedures. The timing of controls considers when the evidence was obtained and the portion of the audit period to which it may be applied. The extent of the tests of controls depends on the degree to which inquiry, observation, examination of documentation, and reperformance is carried out.

Based on the audit procedures performed and the audit evidence obtained, the auditor should evaluate whether the assessments of the risks of material misstatement at the assertion level remain appropriate. The auditor's assessment of the components of audit risk may change during the course of an audit. The audit evidence obtained may cause the auditor to modify the nature, timing, or extent of other planned audit procedures. The auditor may conclude that evidence is likely to be available to support a further reduction in the assessed level of control risks for some assertions. In all such cases, the auditor should revise his assessment of control risk and should consider changing his audit strategy for the related financial statement assertion/audit objective.

8.10 Answers to Certification Exam Questions

8.1 (A) The answer is the one that is **not** a component of internal control. The five components of internal control are control environment, risk assessment, control procedures (activities), information, and communication system and monitoring. Answers (B), (C), and (D) are all one of the five. The correct answer is (A) because it is not one of the five components of internal control.

8.2 (D) The requirement is to find which of the answers represents a question that the auditor would most likely use on an internal control questionnaire. Choice (D) is the best of the four because the board of directors ordinarily should authorize loans. Answer (A) is not good because whether assets collateralized are essential or not is related to internal control. Answer (B) is not good because, generally, payments for notes payable are a fixed amount, payable to a specific lender specified by contract and no controls such as dual signatures are necessary. Answer (C) is incorrect because whether the loan is used to pay for fixed assets, current assets, or any other purpose (other than illegal ones) is not a relevant consideration for internal control.

8.3 (C) The requirement is to determine the terms in which control risk is assessed. Answer (C) is the right one because the auditor makes a preliminary assessment of control risk, at the assertion level for each material account balance or transaction cycle (ISA 315). Control risk is the risk that a misstatement that could be material will not be prevented or detected and corrected. Control risk is assessed for the entity as a whole and not determined solely for individual controls (answer (A)) or the control environment (answer (D)). Types of fraud (B), again is not general enough for the entity as a whole.

8.4 (C) The requirement is to determine what conditions in the payroll department would lead the auditor to say controls could not be relied upon (control risk is assessed at a maximum). Choice (C) looks like the best because authorizing payroll rate changes and recording payroll is a violation of segregation of duties. Examining authorization forms (answer (A)) and comparing payroll registers to batch totals (B) are good controls that decrease risk of misstatement. Hiring all subordinate payroll departments (D) is a personnel function that does not violate controls.

8.5 (A) The requirement is to determine an inquiry test of controls to assess the existence and occurrence assertion. Answer (A) is correct because the existence assertion related to payroll would correspond to the audit objective of determining that all payroll checks were issued to valid employees for actual hours worked. Segregation of duties between personnel and payroll departments is an important control. Answer (B) does not make the grade because inspection of pre-numbered payroll checks is related to the completeness assertion. Choice (C) is also not an option in that re-computing payroll deductions is a substantive (not control) test stemming from a different assertion – valuation. Answer (D) verifying the preparation of the monthly payroll account bank reconciliation, provides evidence for a different assertion – valuation (not existence).

8.6 (D) This question requires picking the procedure that would most likely provide an auditor with evidence of whether controls are designed to prevent or detect material misstatements. Answer (D) is correct because observing the performance of a control procedure provides substantial evidence of its effectiveness. Choice (A) is incorrect because re-performing activities does not indicate that the control prevents material misstatement. Choice (B) is wrong because analytical procedures is a substantive test, not used in a test of controls. Choice (C) is wrong because vouching is a substantive test.

8.7 (B) You are asked to find the answer that represents a technique for doing tests of controls to assess control risk. Answer (B) is the only one where both techniques are used in test of controls. Answer (A) is wrong because analytical procedures are not used in a control test. Answers (C) and (D) are wrong – both give one of the pair that is not a technique for any tests (comparison, verification). Answer (C) lists a substantive test technique (confirmation) as the other term of the pair.

8.8 (D) We are to identify a situation in which an auditor may desire to seek a further reduction in the assessed level of control risk. Choice (D) is right because such a reduction is only possible when additional evidential matter, evaluated by performing additional tests of controls, is available. Choice (A) is wrong because auditors who have progressed this far in the audit will ordinarily already have obtained the understanding of the information system to plan the audit. An understanding of internal control is performed at the beginning of all audits. Choice (C) is off the mark because a significant number of controls always pertain to financial statement assertions.

8.11 Notes

1 IFAC, 2004, *Handbook of International Auditing, Assurance, and Ethics Pronouncements*, Glossary of Terms at December 2002, International Federation of Accountants, New York.

2 Based on AICPA, 1990, "Control Risk Audit Guide Task Force", *Consideration of the Internal Control Structure in A Financial Statement Audit*, AICPA, New York, p. 60.

3 Ibid. p. 34–35.

4 IFAC, 2004, *Handbook of International Auditing, Assurance, and Ethics Pronouncements*, International Standard on Auditing 315 (ISA 315), "Understanding the Entity and Its Environment and Assessing the Risks of Material Misstatement," para. 81, International Federation of Accountants, New York.

5 Ibid. Para. 122.

6 Ibid. Each of the aspects of the entity and its environment are spelled out in para. 20.

7 Ibid. Para. 43.

8 Ibid. Para. 100.

9 Ibid. Para. 113.

10 Ibid. Para. 115.

11 Based on AICPA, 1990, "Control Risk Audit Guide Task Force", *Consideration of the Internal Control Structure in A Financial Statement Audit*, AICPA, New York, p. 117–118.

12 Internal Control components are: control environment, risk assessment, control procedures, information/communication, and monitoring. See Chapter 7 Internal Control and Control Risk.

13 IFAC, 2004, *Handbook of International Auditing, Assurance, and Ethics Pronouncements*, International Standards on Auditing 400 (ISA400), "Risk Assessments and Internal Control," para. 49, International Federation of Accountants, New York.

14 Arens, A.A., Elder, R.J., and Beasley, M.S., 2003, *Essentials of Auditing and Assurance Services An Integrated Approach*, Pearson Education/Prentice Hall, Upper Saddle River, New Jersey.

15 IAASB, 2004, IFAC *Handbook of International Auditing, Assurance, and Ethics Pronouncements* (ISA 300), "Planning the Audit," para. 8, International Federation of Accountants, New York, February.

16 IAASB, 2003, International Standard on Auditing 330 (ISA 330), "The Auditor's Procedures In Response to Assessed Risks," para. 4, International Federation of Accountants, New York.

17 Ibid. Para. 7.

18 Ibid. Para. 16.

19 Adapted and reprinted with permission from AICPA. Copyright © 2000 & 1985 by American Institute of Certified Public Accountants.

20 IFAC, 2004, *Handbook of International Auditing, Assurance, and Ethics Pronouncements*, International Standard on Auditing 300 (ISA 300), "Planning the Audit," International Federation of Accountants, New York.

21 IFAC, 2004, *Handbook of International Auditing, Assurance, and Ethics Pronouncements*, International Standard on Auditing 330 (ISA 330), "The Auditor's Procedures In Response to Assessed Risks," Para. 41, International Federation of Accountants, New York.

22 Ibid. Para. 66.

23 Ibid. Para. 71.

24 Adapted and reprinted with permission from AICPA. Copyright © 2000 & 1985 by American Institute of Certified Public Accountants.

8.12 Questions, Exercises and Cases

QUESTIONS

8.2 Understanding, Assessing and Testing Internal Controls

8.1 What are the three steps to assessing internal control risk?

8.3 Understanding of Internal Controls and Documentation

8.2 What are procedures to obtain an understanding? Give an example. According to ISA 315 what audit processes require documentation?

8.3 What are the four common techniques for documenting the internal control structure? Describe each.

8.4 Assessing Control Risk

8.4 What are reportable conditions? Give some examples.

8.5 When should control risk be set at a maximum?

8.5 Overall Responses to Assessed Risk

8.6 What is the purpose of the overall audit strategy? What are the considerations in an audit strategy?

8.7 What audit responses are included in overall responses to address the assessed risks of material misstatements?

8.6 Prepare Planning Memorandum and Audit Program

8.8 Define planning memorandum. What sections are typically contained in a planning memorandum?

8.9 Define audit plan (program). What is included in an audit program (plan)? What determines for each account balance and audit objective how much evidence should be gathered?

8.7 Tests of Controls

8.10 Define "test of controls." What is the difference between test of controls and procedures to obtain an understanding?

8.11 Tests of controls generally use what types of evidence-gathering procedures? Briefly describe each type.

8.12 If the auditor hopes to rely on prior audit evidence, evidence is needed in the current audit about what areas?

8.8 Evaluate Sufficiency and Appropriateness of Audit Evidence

8.13 What factors influence the auditor's judgment as to what constitutes sufficient appropriate audit evidence?

PROBLEMS AND EXERCISES

8.2 Understanding, Assessing and Testing Internal Controls

8.14 Understanding of Accounting and Internal Control. The auditor should obtain an understanding of the accounting and internal control systems sufficient to plan the audit and develop an effective audit approach.

Required:

From Illustration 8.1 and your understanding from prior chapters (especially Chapters 6 and 7):

A. Define accounting system and internal control.

B. What are the key elements of internal control evaluated in planning? Briefly discuss each one.

C. What procedures (in addition to previous experience with the client) are used to evaluate internal controls?

8.3 Understanding of Internal Controls and Documentation

8.15 Obtain Understanding of Internal Control. The auditor should obtain an understanding of the accounting and internal control systems sufficient to plan the audit and develop an effective audit approach.

Required:

A. The understanding must be good enough to adequately plan the audit in terms of what specific planning matters? Why are these matters important?

B. What factors affect the nature and extent of procedures? Give an example of each.

C. What component of internal control does the auditor typically review first to get an understanding? Why start there?

D. List two monitoring activities that the auditor would evaluate.

8.16 Documentation of the Internal Control System. The auditor's documentation of the internal control system should reflect an understanding sufficient to plan the audit. Rio Duro is a retail clothing business owned by Monica Luna and operated out of her home on a part-time basis. Her accounting system has as inputs a sales slip for all her sales (sold for cash with no accounts receivable), invoices for her purchases and expenses (she has no accounts payable). She enters the transactions in a general journal and posts once per month to a general ledger. She does all the accounting herself, holds the cash, orders, and sells the merchandise.

Required:

A. What characteristics should be described in the documentation of the internal control system?

B. What are the methods for documenting the internal control structure?

C. Using Rio Duro as an example, document the internal control based on the characteristics in A using each of the documentation methods in B.

8.4 Assessing Control Risk

8.17 Weaknesses in Internal Control. The Art Appreciation Society of Gateshead, UK, operates a museum for the benefit and enjoyment of the community. During hours when the museum is open to the public, two clerks who are positioned at the entrance collect a £5.00 admission fee from each non-member patron. Members of the Art Appreciation Society are permitted to enter free of charge upon presentation of their membership cards. At the end of each day, one of the clerks delivers the proceeds to the treasurer. The treasurer counts the cash in the presence of the clerk and places it in a safe. Each Friday afternoon the treasurer and one of the clerks deliver all cash held in the safe to the bank, and receive an authenticated deposit slip which provides the basis for the weekly entry in the cash receipts journal.

The Board of Directors of the Art Appreciation Society has identified a need to improve its control procedures for cash admission fees. The board has determined that the cost of installing turnstiles, sales booths, or otherwise altering the physical layout of the museum will greatly exceed any benefits which may be derived. However, the board has agreed that the sale of admission tickets must be an integral part of its improvement efforts.

Cold & Cough, CAs, have been asked by the Board of Directors of the Art Appreciation Society to review the internal control structure for cash admission fees and provide suggestions for improvement.

Required:

Indicate weaknesses in the existing procedures for cash admission fees, which Cold & Cough should identify, and recommend one improvement for each of the weaknesses identified. Organize the answer as in the following illustrative example:

Weakness	Recommendation
1 There is no basis for establishing the documentation of the number of paying patrons.	1 Prenumbered admission tickets should be issued upon payment of the admission the admission fee.

[Adapted and reprinted with permission from AICPA. Copyright © 2000 & 1985 by American Institute of Certified Public Accountants]

8.5 Overall Responses to Assessed Risk

8.18 Katmir is a manufacturer of mattresses in Kordofan Sudan. The company is 100 percent owned by the Alnashar family and all of the management are related to the founder, El Hussein Alnashar, who all employees refer to as "Honored Boss." Honored Boss does not trust accounting records and only has an outside accountant (who is his nephew) come to the factory for the last two weeks of every second month to do a physical inventory, put together financial statements, and do tax estimates.

For some time, Honored Boss has been looking for a buyer for his company because he wants to retire and he does not trust any of this children or relatives to run the company. Centaur Sleep Products of Cairo has shown an interest in purchasing the company. Centaur wishes to send an audit team to Katmir to do a physical inventory and review the books.

Required:

In determining what time the auditors should go to the Katmir factory to do their procedures, they consider such matters as: (1) the control environment; (2) when relevant information is available; (3) the nature of the risk; and (4) the period or date to which the audit evidence relates. Discuss what impact each of the four considerations mentioned above would have on setting the time to review Katmir's control procedures and to do substantive tests.

8.6 Prepare Planning Memorandum and Audit Program

8.19 **Audit Planning Memorandum**. Read the case of Constantijn & Nianias, Soma Orkaton Logistons (SOLs), audit of Eidola Company, below. Eidola has asked Constantijn & Nianias to do their income tax returns. The year end is December 31, 20X3 and inventory counts will be done at locations other than the main office at the end of September, October, and November. Internal controls should be tested by January 31, 20X4, tax and statutory filings will be finished March 1, and the audit report will be ready by February 15.

Constantijn & Nianias, Soma Orkaton Logistons (SOLs), have been hired to audit Eidola Company, a biochemical company listed on the Athens Stock Exchange. Constantijn & Nianias is auditing the client for the first time in the current year as a result of a dispute between Eidola and the previous auditor over the proper booking of sales and accounts receivable for sales of inventory that has not been delivered but has, for practical purposes, been completed and sold.

Eidola has been grown from a small start-up to a highly successful company in the industry in the past seven years, primarily as a result of many successful mergers negotiated by George Panis, the president and chairman of the board. Although other biotech firms have had difficulty in recent years, Eidola continues to prosper, as shown by its constantly increasing earnings and growth. Bayer, the large German chemical company, has a special discount contract with them and represents 15 percent of their sales. In the last year, however, the company's profits turned downward.

Panis is generally supported by his board of directors that include many of his old university classmates. The board, which meets twice annually, recently issued a policy on corporate ethics conduct. Panis says he owes much of his success to the hiring of aggressive young executives paid relatively low salaries combined with an unusually generous profit-sharing plan. The corporate structure is very informal as Panis does not believe than any employee should have a title or a specific job description as it "gives people airs". Panis's only corporate objective is "to make large profits so our stock price will increase and our shareholders will be happy".

The management information system at Eidola is very limited and they lack sophisticated accounting records for a company that size. The information system will be updated this year. The personnel in the accounting department are competent but somewhat overworked and underpaid relative to the other employees, and therefore turnover is high. The most comprehensive records are for production and marketing because Panis believes these areas are more essential to operations than accounting. There are only four internal auditors and they spend the majority of their time taking inventories, which is time consuming because inventories are located at 11 facilities in four countries.

The financial statements for the current year include a profit 20 percent less than the last year, but the auditors feel it should be a larger decrease because of the reduced volume and the disposal of a segment of the business, Kata-Karpos. The disposal of this segment was considered necessary because it had become increasingly unprofitable over the past three years. When it was acquired from Christopher Panis, George Panis's brother, it was considered profitable even though its largest customer was Kata-Klino, also owned by Christopher Panis.

Eidola is considered under-financed by market analysts. There is excessive current debt and management is reluctant to sell equity on the capital markets because increasing the number of shares will decrease share price. George Panis is now talking to several large companies in hopes of a merger.

Required:
Based on the information given, write a brief audit planning memorandum for Eidola Company.

8.20 Audit Program. The following are ten audit procedures taken from an audit program:
1 Review board of directors' minutes to verify approval of equipment purchases.
2 Discuss with the cash disbursements clerk his or her and duties and observe whether he or she has responsibility for handling cash or preparing the bank reconciliation.
3 Examine the accounting clerk's initials on monthly bank reconciliations as an indication

of whether they have been reviewed.

4   Review sales, cash receipts and sales returns cutoffs.

5   Examine the initials on vendors' invoices that indicate internal verification of pricing, extensions (price X units), and footing by a clerk.

6   Reconcile marketable security summary schedules to general ledger.

7   Compare the balance in payroll tax expense with previous years, taking into consideration any changes in payroll tax rates.

8   Count a sample of inventory and check against inventory sheets.

9   Account for a sequence of checks in the cash disbursements journal to determine whether any have been omitted.

10 Confirm accounts payable balances in writing with a sample of vendors.

Required:

A.   For each of the above audit procedures, give the audit area (accounts receivable, cash, etc.), and an example of an audit objective and a financial statement assertion.

B.   For each audit procedure, list a technique for gathering evidence used (inquiry of client personnel, inspection, observation, examination of documents, reperformance, confirmation, analytical procedures, and physical examination – see Chapter 10 for definitions of evidence-gathering techniques).

8.7 Tests of Controls

8.21 Tests of Controls. Auditors generally begin tests of controls by interviewing appropriate personnel who either perform or monitor control procedures. During these interviews, the auditors may also examine certain documents and reports used by persons in performing or monitoring control procedures as well as observe personnel performing their duties.

Basic Shoes, a shoe manufacturing company in Changchun, China, sells 95 percent of its product to companies outside China. They receive orders for shoes by fax and 20 percent advance payment of the order price. The sales department makes up a sales order and passes it to the manufacturing manager who verifies the order with the cashier's office which receives the advance money. If the cashier okays the order, the manufacturing manager then writes a manufacturing order to produce the goods and orders the necessary raw materials for the warehouse.

The shipping officer receives a copy of the sales order and matches it to the goods manufactured and then ships, forwarding the shipping documents to accounting. Accounting bills the customer after first matching shipping documents to the original sales order. The cashier's office receives the payment from the customer.

Required:

A.   List ten questions that you might ask Basic Shoe's personnel about the sales process.

B.   Discuss which person you would ask each of the questions and why you would ask them.

C.   What documents would you inspect for each question? Why?

D.   Which part of the sales process would you observe? Why?

E.   What control procedures do you believe they might add to ensure that customers do not order goods that they cannot pay for?

8.22 Tests of Controls. Explain what types of control tests an auditor should do in each of the following circumstances and why:

1   The auditor tests controls that contribute to the reliability of accounting systems and conclude they are effective.

2   There are control failures, but in identifying and testing alternative controls the auditor finds them to be effective and therefore concludes that the accounting systems are

reliable.

3   The auditor concludes that there are no effective alternative controls that address the transactions and potential errors to which failed controls relate.

4   The control failures and the absence of effective alternative controls causes the auditor to identify a specific risk.

CASES

8.23 Control Procedures and Audit Procedures for Computer Fraud.

Required:

For each of the following situations involving computer fraud, briefly describe:

A.   A control procedure that would have been effective in preventing or detecting the fraud.

B.   An audit procedure that would have detected the fraud.

Computer Frauds:

1   A computer programmer added a module to the payroll program that started with an "IF" statement to identify his employee number. If the payroll calculation applies to his record, the program was instructed to multiply computed pay by 1.5, thus increasing the programmer's pay by 50 percent.

2   A state health and social services department made support payments to needy residents. A resident could be input into the system only on the recommendation of a supervising caseworker. Some caseworkers entered fictitious residents on the system and had support payments sent to authorized addresses. The caseworkers then cashed the support payments and eventually transferred the cash to their own accounts.

3   A student posed as a newspaper reporter doing a story on a phone company's data processing center. After leaving the center, the student noticed a data processing manual that had been discarded. He took the manual home and learned the access code to the company's parts repair system. He could then log on and have repair parts delivered to a specific location. Later he picked up the parts, which he sold back to the company and to other customers.

4   A manufacturing company required all its hourly workers to sign in by passing their personal identification cards across an automated time clock that captured and trans-mitted data to the computer for subsequent processing. An employee who worked the first shift arranged with her brother who worked the second shift to use her card to sign out when her brother completed his work shift. The employee thus generated pay for 16 hours per day, one-half at overtime rates. The employee and her brother split the additional pay.

5   A disgruntled programmer often came to the office in the evenings to copy confidential client data such as customer lists, discounts, and so forth onto magnetic tapes, which he sold to competitors.

[Adapted from Rittenberg and Schweiger (1997) *Auditing Concepts for a Changing Environment*, 2nd edn, Dryden Press, Fort Worth, Texas.]

8.24 Control Procedures. Dreyfet department store maintains on-line prices on minicomputers in stores connected to the automatic cash registers For most products the product and price are read into the cash register by scanning devices that read the bar codes on the merchandise. The product name (abbreviated) and the prices are printed on the customer's cash receipt and are also captured internally as part of the sales recording process. The process also updates the perpetual inventory record at the store.

Prices for all products are set by the buyers and are entered on to the client's mainframe computer system and downloaded to the stores. Only the store manager can override the price on the store computer. All overrides are supposed to be reported to the buyer and the general merchandise manager for the department store division. The dollar amounts of sales of products for which price changes were made are used to develop a special report showing sales volume by product, average retail price, product cost, and loss (profit) per product.

Required:

A.   Identify the key control procedures the auditor would expect to find in the environment described.

B.   Develop an audit program to determine whether the control procedures are working as described.

C.   What are the implications to the audit if the control procedures are not working as described, especially if the store manager is making a wide variety of product price markdowns, but the price changes are not generating any exception reports?

D.   What are the implications to the audit if the auditor tests prices in six of 42 stores and finds that on 10 percent of the items tested, the price in the store's cash register differs from the price on the master sales file? Assume that most of the changes result in a lower price being charged.

[Adapted from Rittenberg & Schweiger (1997) *Auditing Concepts for a Changing Environment*, 2nd edn, Dryden Press, Fort Worth, Texas.]

Chapter 9

ANALYTICAL PROCEDURES

9.1 Learning Objectives

After studying this chapter you should be able to:

1 Understand the general nature of analytical procedures.

2 Describe four general analytical procedures.

3 Explain how expectations are developed and what sources are used.

4 Clarify how the effectiveness of an analytical procedure is a function of the nature of the account and the reliability and other characteristics of the data.

5 Calculate the customary ratios that are used during the planning phase to determine accounts that may represent significant risks to the entity of liquidity, solvency, profitability, and activity.

6 Understand some indications that the going concern assumption may be questioned.

7 Comprehend why and how analytical procedures may be used at each audit phase.

8 Grasp how analytical procedures are used in substantive procedures.

9 Describe some of the analytical procedures carried out by computer-aided audit techniques.

10 Illustrate data mining methods, techniques, and algorithms used to analyze client data.

11 Portray the auditor's procedures when analytical procedures identify significant fluctuations that deviate from predicted amounts.

9.2 Introduction

Analytical procedures consist of the analysis of significant ratios and trends including the resulting investigation of fluctuations and relationships that are inconsistent with other relevant information or deviate from predictable amounts.[1] Put another way, analytical procedures entail the use of comparisons and relationships to determine whether account balances or other data appear reasonable. Such procedures allow the auditor to look at things in overview and answer the question: Do the numbers make sense?

■ Relationships Among Data

A basic premise of using analytical procedures is that there exist plausible relationships among data and these relationships can reasonably be expected to continue. Analytical procedures include the comparison of the entity's financial statements with prior period information, anticipated results such as budgets, and similar industry information. For instance, an entity's **accounts receivable turnover** ratio may be compared to that ratio for the industry or for a similar company.

Analytical procedures are used to determine relationships among financial information that would be expected to conform to predictable patterns based on the entity's experience, such as gross margin percentages, and between financial and non-financial information such as the relationship between payroll costs and the number of employees.

■ Types of Analytical Procedures

General analytical procedures include trend analysis, ratio analysis, statistical and data mining analysis, and reasonableness tests. **Trend analysis** is the analysis of changes in an account balance over time. **Ratio analysis** is the comparison of relationships between financial statement accounts, the comparison of an account with non-financial data, or the comparison of relationships between firms in an industry. **Reasonableness testing** is the analysis of account balances or changes in account balances within an accounting period in terms of their "reasonableness" in light of expected relationships between accounts. **Data mining** is a set of computer-assisted techniques that use sophisticated statistical analysis, including artificial intelligence techniques, to examine large volumes of data with the objective of indicating hidden or unexpected information or patterns. For these tests auditors generally use computer-aided audit software (CAATs).

■ When to Use Analytical Procedures

"The auditor should apply analytical procedures at the planning and overall review stages of the audit."[2] Analytical procedures may also be applied to **substantive testing**. In the planning stage, the purpose of analytical procedures is to highlight risk areas to narrow the focus of planning the nature, timing, and extent of auditing procedures. In the overall review stage, the objective of analytical procedures is to assess the conclusions reached and evaluate the overall financial statement presentation. It may be used to detect material misstatements that other tests can overlook, such as fraud or understatement errors. In the substantive testing stage of the audit, analytical procedures are used to see "the big picture", i.e. obtain evidence to identify misstatements in account balances and thus to reduce the risk of misstatements.

■ Computer Assisted Audit Techniques (CAATs)

The use of **computer assisted audit techniques (CAATs)** may enable more extensive testing of electronic transactions and account files. CAATs can be used to select sample transactions from key electronic files, to sort transactions with specific characteristics, or to test an entire population instead of a sample. CAATs generally include data manipulation, calculation, data selection, data analysis, identification of exceptions and unusual transactions, regression analysis, and statistical analysis. CAATs are available on **generalized audit software** (GAS) which provides the auditors with the ability to access, manipulate, manage, analyze and report data in a variety of formats. **Data mining** software may also be used for analytical procedures.

When analytical procedures identify significant fluctuations or relationships that are inconsistent with other relevant information or that deviate from predicted amounts, the auditor should investigate and obtain adequate explanations and appropriate corroborative evidence. The investigation of unusual fluctuations and relationships ordinarily begins with inquiries of management followed by corroboration of management's responses and other audit procedures based on the results of these inquiries.

Certification Exam Question 9.1[3]

A basic premise underlying the application of analytical procedures is that:

(A) The study of financial ratios is an acceptable alternative to the investigation of unusual fluctuations.
(B) Statistical tests of financial information may lead to the discovery of material misstatements in the financial statements.
(C) Plausible relationships among data may reasonably be expected to exist and continue in the absence of known conditions to the contrary.
(D) These procedures cannot replace tests of balances and transactions.

9.3 The Analytical Review Process

The process of planning, executing, and drawing conclusions from analytical procedures is called **analytical review**. There are several views, theoretical and practical, of the sub-processes involved in analytical review.

The theoretical view[4] is that the review process consists of four diagnostic processes:

1 mental representation,
2 hypothesis generation,
3 information search,
4 hypothesis evaluation.

In particular, auditors hypothesize causes and related probabilities, gather evidence to test the hypotheses, and ultimately select which hypotheses are most likely to cause the fluctuation.[5]

Concept and a Company 9.1

"Crazy Eddie – His prices are insane!"

Concept	Analytical procedures to test inventory.
Story	In 1969, Eddie Antar, a 21-year-old high school dropout from Brooklyn, opened a consumer electronics store with 15 square meters of floor space in New York City. By 1987, Antar's firm. Crazy Eddie, Inc., had 43 retail outlets, sales exceeding $350 million, and outstanding common shares with a collective market value of $600 million.

Shortly after a hostile takeover of the company in November 1987, the firm's new owners discovered that Crazy Eddie's inventory was overstated by more than $65 million. Subsequent investigations by regulatory authorities would demonstrate that Crazy Eddie's profits had been intentionally overstated by Eddie Antar and several subordinates. (Belsky and Furman 1989)

Crazy Like a Fox

Antar acquired the nickname "Crazy Eddie" because of his unique sales tactic. Whenever a customer would attempt to leave his store without purchasing something, Eddie would block the store's exit, sometimes locking the door until the individual agreed to buy something – anything. To entice a reluctant customer to make a purchase, Antar would lower the price until the customer finally gave in. From 1972, Doctor Jerry was the spokesperson for Crazy Eddie. He made a series of ear-piercing television commercials that featured him screaming "Crazy Eddie – His prices are insane!" The company promised to refund the difference between the selling price of a product and any lower price for that same item that a customer found within 30 days of the purchase date. (Knapp 2001)

Inventory Overstated

Trouble was that in late 1986 the boom days had ended for the consumer electronics industry. To continue the growth of the company and keep the stock price up, Antar had to do something. Within the first six months after the company went public, Antar ordered a subordinate to overstate inventory by $2 million, resulting in the firm's gross profit being overstated by the same amount. The following year Antar ordered year-end inventory to be overstated by $9 million and accounts payable to be understated by $3 million. (Belsky and Furman 1989) Crazy Eddie employees overstated year-end inventory by preparing inventory count sheets for items that did not exist. To overstate accounts payable, bogus debit memos were prepared and entered in the company's accounting records.

The Audits

Crazy Eddie's auditor was Main Hurdman (later merged with Peat Marwick – now KPMG). Their audits were generally made difficult by management and employee collusion. There were several reported instances in which the auditors requested client documents, only to be told that those documents had been lost or inadvertently destroyed. Upon discovering which sites the auditors would be visiting to perform year-end inventory procedures, Antar would ship sufficient inventory to those stores or warehouses to conceal any shortages. Furthermore, personnel systematically destroyed incriminating documents to conceal inventory shortages from the auditors. (Weiss 1993)

Main Hurdman has been criticized for charging only $85,000 for a complete SEC audit, but millions to install a computerized inventory system. This is even more interesting because Antar ordered his employees to stop using the sophisticated, computer-based inventory system designed by Main Hurdman. Instead, the accounting personnel were required to return to a manual inventory system previously used by the company. The absence of a computer-based inventory system made it much more difficult for the auditors to determine exactly how much inventory the firm had at any point in time. (Weiss 1993)

Crazy Eddie Comparative Income Statements 1984–87

	31 March 87	31 March 86	31 March 85	31 March 84
Net sales	$352,523	$262,268	$136,319	$137,285
Cost of goods sold	−272,255	−194,371	−103,421	−106,934
Gross profit	80,268	67,897	32,898	30,351
Selling, G&A expense	−61,341	−42,975	−20,508	−22,560
Interest and other income	7,403	3,210	1,211	706
Interest expense	−5,233	−820	−438	−522
Income before taxes	$21,097	$27,312	$13,163	$7,975
Pension contribution	−500	−800	−600	−4,202
Income taxes	−10,001	−13,268	−6,734	
Net income	$10,596	$13,244	$5,829	$3,773
Net income per share	$0.34	$0.48	$0.24	$0.18

Crazy Eddie Comparative Balance Sheets 1984–87

	31 March 87	31 March 86	31 March 85	31 March 84
Current assets				
Cash	$9,347	$13,296	$22,273	$1,375
Short-term investments	121,957	26,840		
Receivables	10,846	2,246	2,740	2,604
Merchandise inventories	109,072	59,864	26,543	23,343
Prepaid expenses	10,639	2,363	645	514
Total current assets	261,861	104,609	52,201	27,836
Restricted cash		3,356	7,058	
Due from affiliates				5,739
Property, plant and equipment	26,401	7,172	3,696	1,845
Construction in process		6,253	1,154	
Other assets	6,596	5,560	1,419	1,149
Total assets	$294,858	$126,950	$65,528	$36,569
Current liabilities				
Accounts payable	$50,022	$51,723	$23,078	$20,106
Notes payable				2,900
Short-term debt	49,571	2,254	423	124
Unearned revenue	3,641	3,696	1,173	764
Accrued expenses	5,593	17,126	8,733	6,078
Total current liabilities	108,827	74,799	33,407	29,972

"Crazy Eddie – His prices are insane!" (continued)

Crazy Eddie Comparative Balance Sheets 1984–87 (continued)

	31 March 87	31 March 86	31 March 85	31 March 84
Long-term debt	8,459	7,701	7,625	46
Convertible subordinated debentures	80,975			
Unearned revenue	3,337	1,829	635	327
Stockholders' equity				
Common stock	313	280	134	50
Additional paid-in capital	57,678	17,668	12,298	574
Retained earnings	35,269	24,673	11,429	5,600
Total stockholders' equity	93,260	42,621	23,861	6,224
Total liabilities and stockholders'equity	$294,858	$126,950	$65,528	$36,569

Discussion Questions	Review the Crazy Eddie comparative financial statements and discuss:
	■ What analytical procedures can be performed to determine if inventory is misstated?
	■ What indicators other than financial hinted that there might be problems?

References	Belsky, G. and Furman, P., 1989, "Calculated Madness: The Rise and Fall of Crazy Eddie Antar," *Cram's New York Business,* June 5, pp. 21–33.
	Knapp, M., 2001, "Crazy Eddie, Inc," *Contemporary Auditing Real Issues & Cases,* South Western College Publishing, Cincinnati, Ohio, pp. 71–82.
	Weiss, M.I., 1993, "Auditors: Be Watchdogs, Not Just Bean Counters," *Accounting Today,* November 15, p. 41.

■ Four-Phase Process

Here we use a practitioner approach, the four-phase process most common in professional literature:[6]

- ■ phase one – formulate expectations (expectations);
- ■ phase two – compare the expected value to the recorded amount (identification);
- ■ phase three – investigate possible explanations for a difference between expected and recorded values (investigation);
- ■ phase four – evaluate the impact of the differences between expectation and recorded amounts on the audit and the financial statements (evaluation).

Illustration 9.1 shows the four-phase process and its inputs and outputs.

Phase One

In phase one of the analytical review process, the auditor develops expectations of what amounts should appear in financial statement account balances based on prior year financial statements, budgets, industry information and non-financial information. Expectations are the auditor's estimations of recorded accounts or ratios. The auditor develops his expectation in such a way that a significant difference between it and the recorded amount will indicate a misstatement.

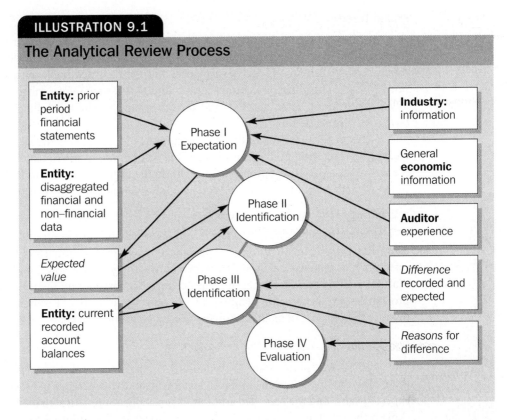

ILLUSTRATION 9.1

The Analytical Review Process

Forming an expectation is the most important phase of the analytical procedure process. The closer the auditor's expectation is to the correct balance or relationship, the more effective the procedure will be at identifying potential misstatements.

Expectations are formed from a variety of sources. Research[7] suggests that the use of industrial, economic, or environmental data can improve the predictive ability of analytical procedures. Other resources include industry data, data about similar businesses, and auditor experience. Expectations are also based on the entities prior financial statements, same store sales, non-financial data, budgets and public reports.

Phase Two

Phase two of the analytical review process (identification) is when the auditor compares his expected value with the recorded amount. Audit efficiency and effectiveness depend on competency in recognizing error patterns in financial data and in hypothesizing likely causes of those patterns to serve as a guide for further testing.

The auditor must consider how large a difference between expected value and recorded amount he will accept. In other words, at what point is the difference **material** (e.g. if the difference is 20 percent)? This point could be called a **materiality threshold**.

In substantive testing, an auditor testing for the possible **misstatement** of the book value of an account determines whether the audit difference was less than the auditor's materiality threshold. If the difference is less than the acceptable threshold, the auditor accepts the book value without further investigation. If the difference is greater, the next step is to investigate the difference.

Phase Three

In phase three of the analytical review process (investigation), the auditor undertakes an investigation of possible explanations for the expected/recorded amount difference. The difference between an auditor's expectation and the recorded book value of an account not subject to auditing procedures can be due to misstatements, inherent factors that affect the account being audited, and factors related to the reliability of data used to develop the expectation.

The greater the precision of the expectation, the more likely the difference between the auditor's expectation and the recorded value will be due to misstatements. Conversely, the less precise the expectation, the more likely the difference is due to factors related to inherent factors, and the reliability of data used to develop the expectation.

Inquiries and Corroboration of Differences

Where differences between expectation and recorded amounts are found, the first step is usually to ask management for an explanation. However, it is important that the auditor maintains his **professional skepticism** when considering these answers and it is suggested that the auditor conduct other audit procedures to corroborate them. When analytical procedures are used in the planning phase, corroboration is not immediately required because the purpose of analytical procedures in planning is to chart the work to follow.

Phase Four

The final phase (phase four – evaluation) of the analytical review process involves evaluating the impact on the financial statements of the difference between the auditor's expected value and the recorded amount. It is usually not practical to identify factors that explain the exact amount of a difference investigated. The auditor attempts to quantify that portion of the difference for which plausible explanations can be obtained and, where appropriate, corroborated. If the amount that cannot be explained is sufficiently small, the auditor may conclude there is no material misstatement.

9.4 Formulating Expectations

Expectations are developed by identifying plausible relationships that are reasonably expected to exist based on the auditor's understanding of the client and of his industry. These relationships may be determined by comparisons with the following sources:

- comparable information for prior periods;
- anticipated results (such as budgets and forecasts, or auditor expectations);
- similar industry information;
- non-financial information.

The auditor can identify account balances that have changed significantly simply by comparing the current client data with prior period data. He may compare the current year's account balances with that of the preceding year; the current trial balance with similar detail for the preceding year; and ratios and percentage relationships between years. He compares current recorded account balances of the entity with results expected by the entity. For example, company budgets may be compared with actual results for indications of potential misstatements or the auditor calculates the expected balance for interest expense (notes payable monthly balance times average monthly interest rate) and compares this to recorded interest rates.

One of the standard bases of comparison is with like companies in the same industry. For example, the auditor compares the gross margin of the industry to the client's gross margin.

Analytical procedures may include consideration of relationships between financial information and relevant non-financial information, such as payroll costs to number of employees. Another example is the revenue of a hotel may be estimated by multiplying the average room rate times the number of rooms times the average occupancy percentage (e.g. $100 average rate × 20 rooms × 60 percent average occupancy). Similarly revenues may be calculated for school tuition (average number of students enrolled times the average tuition cost), payroll, and cost of materials sold using non-financial factors.

■ Sources of Information and Precision of Expectations

The source of information on which the expectations are based (e.g. prior period statements, forecasts, industry information) determines, in part, the precision with which the auditor predicts an account balance. For example, information from other, similar stores in the same retail chain is more precise than general industry information. Recent years' financial statements are more precise a predictor of this year's balance than older financial statements. The desired precision of the expectation varies according to the purpose of the analytical procedure. Precision is more important for analytical procedures used as substantive tests than for those used in planning.

Certification Exam Question 9.2[8]

Which of the following comparisons would an auditor most likely make in evaluating an entity's costs and expenses?

(A) The current year's accounts receivable with the prior year's accounts receivable.
(B) The current year's payroll expense with the prior year's payroll expense.
(C) The budgeted current year's sales with the prior year's sales.
(D) The budgeted current year's warranty expense with the current year's contingent liabilities.

■ Nature of Account and Characteristics of Data

The effectiveness of an analytical procedure is a function of the **nature of the account** and the reliability and other **characteristics of the data**. In determining the nature of the account the auditor considers whether the balance is based on estimates or accumulations of transactions, the number of transactions represented by the balance, and the control environment. Subjectively determined balances are more easily manipulated than accumulations of transactions. If the characteristic of the account is that it comprises millions of transactions (e.g. retail revenue), it should be more predictable than those comprising a few transactions (e.g. obsolete inventory). Fixed expenses (e.g. leases) are more predictable than variable expenses (e.g. shipping).

Other data characteristics such as the level of detail (aggregation) on which the auditor is able to base his expectation and the reliability of the data are key characteristics. In general, the more disaggregated the data, the more precise the expectation. For example, the use of monthly instead of annual data tends to improve the precision of the expectation. Preparing an expectation by division is also more precise than an expectation based on consolidated data. Accounting researchers[9] conclude that disaggregated monthly, segment, or product line balances are required to implement reliable attention-directing analytical procedures.

The more reliable the source of the data, the more precise the expectation will be. Reliability of data is determined based on the strength of the company's internal control, if the data source is objective or independent, and if data has been subject to auditing procedures or not. Stronger internal control over financial reporting and accounting systems produces more reliable data on the financial statements. The use of reliable non-financial data (e.g. store square footage or occupancy rates) and the use of data that has been subjected to auditing procedures improve the precision of the expectation based on that data.

9.5   General Analytical Procedures

The general analytical procedures are trend analysis, ratio analysis, statistical and data mining analysis, and reasonableness tests. Determining which type of analytical procedure is appropriate is a matter of professional judgment. A review of audit practice indicates that simple judgmental approaches (such as comparison and ratio analysis) are used more frequently than complex statistical approaches (such as time series modeling or regression analysis).[10] These tests are generally carried out using computer software (i.e. CAATs). Trend analysis, ratio analysis, and reasonableness tests are discussed in this section. Statistical and data mining analysis is discussed in the following section on CAATs.

■ Trend Analysis

Trend analysis is the analysis of changes in an account balance or ratio over time. Trend analysis could compare last year's account balance to the current unaudited balance or balances in many time periods. Trend analysis works best when the account or relationship is fairly predictable (e.g. rent expense in a stable environment). It is less effective when the audited entity has experienced significant operating or accounting changes. The number of years used in the trend analysis is a function of the stability of operations. The more stable the operations over time, the more predictable the relations and the more appropriate the use of multiple time periods. Trend analysis at an aggregate level (e.g. on a consolidated basis) is relatively imprecise because a material misstatement is often small relative to the aggregate account balance. The most precise trend analysis would be on disaggregated data (e.g. by segment, product, or location, and monthly or quarterly rather than on an annual basis).

■ Ratio Analysis

Ratio analysis is the comparison of relationships between financial statement accounts, the comparison of an account with non-financial data, or the comparison of relationships between firms in an industry. Another example of ratio analysis (which is sometimes referred to as common size analysis) is to set all the account balances as either a percentage of total assets or revenue.

Ratio analysis is most appropriate when the relationship between accounts is fairly predictable and stable (e.g. the relationship between sales and accounts receivable). Ratio analysis can be more effective than trend analysis because comparisons between the balance sheet and income statement can often reveal unusual fluctuations that an analysis of the individual accounts would not. Like trend analysis, ratio analysis at an aggregate level is relatively imprecise because a material misstatement is often small relative to the natural variations in the ratios.

Types of Ratio Analysis

There are five types of ratio analysis used in analytical procedures (See Illustration 9.2):

1 ratios that compare client and industry data;
2 ratios that compare client data with similar prior period data;
3 ratios that compare client data with client-determined expected results;
4 ratios that compare client data with auditor-determined expected results;
5 ratios that compare client data with expected results using non-financial data.

ILLUSTRATION 9.2

Five Types of Ratio Analysis

Procedures	Examples
Ratios that compare client data with industry.	Standard ratios published by the industry by the Risk Management Association, Standard & Poors, Dun & Bradstreet and others.
Ratios that compare client data with similar prior period data.	Auditor compares the current year's account balances with that for the preceding year; current trial balances with similar detail for the preceding year; and ratios and percentage relationships between years.
Ratios that compare client data with client-determined expected results.	Client budgets may be compared with actual results for indications of potential misstatements.
Ratios that compare client data with auditor-determined expected results.	Auditor calculates the expected balance for interest expense and compares to recorded interest.
Ratios that compare client data with expected results using non-financial data.	Non-financial data may serve as a basis for expected results and comparison, the revenue of a hotel may be estimated by multiplying average room rate times the number of rooms times the average occupancy percentage.

The Risk Management Association (RMA), Standard and Poors, Dun & Bradstreet and others publish standard ratios by industry.[11] Similar ratios for both industry and entity may be compared to indicate differences that might affect the auditor's judgment of the nature and extent of audit procedures. The ratios indicate entity liquidity, solvency, profitability, and activity. See Illustration 9.3 for some standard ratios often used and compared.

ILLUSTRATION 9.3

Standard Client and Industry Ratios

Client and industry standard ratios	Calculation
Liquidity: (1) Current ratio (2) Quick ratio	(1) Current assets/Current liabilities (2) (Cash + Short-term securities + Accounts receivable)/Current liabilities
Solvency: (1) Debt to equity (2) Times interest earned (3) Debt service coverage	(1) Long-term debt/Stockholders' equity (2) (Net income before interest and taxes)/Interest expense (3) (Net income before interest and depreciation)/Principal and interest payments
Profitability: (1) Net profit margin (2) Gross margin (3) Return on investment (4) Times interest earned	(1) Net profit/Revenue (2) (Revenue less cost of goods sold)/Revenue (3) Net income/Stockholders' equity (4) (Net income before interest and taxes)/Interest expense
Activity: (1) Receivable turnover (2) Inventory turnover (3) Asset turnover	(1) Revenue/Average accounts receivable (2) Cost of goods sold/Average inventory (3) Revenue/Total assets

■ Reasonableness Testing

Reasonableness testing is the analysis of account balances or changes in account balances within an accounting period in terms of their "reasonableness" in light of expected relationships between accounts. This involves the development of an expectation based on financial data, non-financial data, or both. For example, using the number of employees hired and terminated, the timing of pay changes, and the effect of vacation and sick days, the model could predict the change in payroll expense from the previous year to the current balance within a fairly narrow dollar range.

In contrast to both trend and ratio analyses (which implicitly assume stable relationships), reasonableness tests use information to develop an explicit prediction of the account balance. The auditor develops assumptions for each of the key factors (e.g. industry and economic factors) to estimate the account balance. Considering the number of units sold, the unit price by product line, different pricing structures, and an understanding of industry trends during the period could explicitly form a reasonableness test for sales. This is in contrast to an implicit trend expectation for sales based on last year's sales. The latter expectation is appropriate only if there were no other factors affecting sales during the current year, which is not the usual situation.

Certification Exam Question 9.3[12]

What type of analytical procedure would an auditor most likely use in developing relationships among balance sheet accounts when reviewing the financial statements of a nonpublic entity?

(A) Trend analysis.
(B) Regression analysis.
(C) Ratio analysis.
(D) Risk analysis.

■ Trend Analysis, Ratio Analysis, and Reasonableness Tests Compared

Trend analysis, ratio analysis, and reasonableness tests differ as to the number of independent predictive variables considered, use of external data, and statistical precision. Trend analysis is limited to a single predictor, that is, the prior periods' data for that account. Trend analysis, by relying on a single predictor, does not allow the use of potentially relevant operating data, as do the other types of procedures. Because ratio analysis employs two or more related financial or non-financial sources of information, the result is a more precise expectation. Reasonableness tests and regression analysis further improve the precision of the expectation by allowing potentially as many variables (financial and non-financial) as are relevant for forming the expectation. Reasonableness tests and regression analysis are able to use external data (e.g. general economic and industry data) directly in forming the expectation. The most statistically precise expectations are formed using statistical and data mining analysis.

■ Standard Client and Industry Ratios

At the planning stage of an audit, there are certain customary ratios that are always calculated to determine accounts that may represent significant risks to the entity of liquidity, solvency, profitability, and activity. These ratios help to answer some key questions:

- Is there a possible going concern problem (liquidity ratios)?
- Is the entity's capital structure sustainable (solvency ratios)?
- Is gross margin reasonable (profitability)?
- Could inventory be overstated (activity)?

Illustration 9.3 (earlier) gives a list of these ratios.

■ Liquidity and Going Concern

Auditors must determine the possibility that the company is having liquidity problems – that is, is there a possibility that the company may no longer be a **going concern**? ISA 570[13] specifies that when performing audit procedures the auditor should consider the appropriateness of the going concern assumption underlying the preparation of the financial statements.

Analytical procedures may point to indications of risk that the going concern assumption needs to be questioned. Illustration 9.4 shows the indications of risk that the going concern assumption may be questioned. The significance of the indications in Illustration 9.4 can often be mitigated by other factors. For example, the effect of an entity being unable to make its normal debt repayments may be counterbalanced by management's plans to maintain adequate cash flows by alternative means, such as disposal of assets.

ILLUSTRATION 9.4

Indications that the Going Concern Assumption Might be Questioned[14]

This listing of indications of risk that continuance as a going concern may be questionable is not all-inclusive nor does the existence of one or more always signify that the going concern assumption needs to be questioned.

Financial Indications

- Net liability or net current liability position.
- Fixed-term borrowings approaching maturity without realistic prospects of renewal or repayment, or excessive reliance on short-term borrowing to finance long-term assets.
- Adverse key financial ratios.
- Substantial operating losses.
- Arrears or discontinuance of dividends.
- Inability to pay creditors on due dates.
- Difficulty in complying with the terms of loan agreements.
- Change from credit to cash-on-delivery transactions with suppliers.
- Inability to obtain financing for essential new product development or other essential investments.

Operating Indications

- Loss of key management without replacement.
- Loss of major market, franchise, license or principal supplier.
- Labor difficulties or shortages of important supplies.

Other indications

- Non-compliance with capital or other statutory requirements.
- Pending legal proceedings against the entity that may, if successful, result in claims that are likely to be satisfied.
- Changes in legislation or government policy.

Concept and a Company 9.2

Peregrine Systems – The 37th of December

Concept	Analytical procedures for revenue tests.

Story	The accounting irregularities that brought down Peregrine Systems, a San Diego, California, maker of software that large companies use to manage their technology resources, included inflated revenues of more than 60 percent or some $509 million.

Peregrine had reported revenues of $1.34 billion for 2000 and 2001. Of that, $225 million was based on "non-substantiated transactions" as the company booked revenues when it transferred goods to a software reseller, even when there were no firm commitments in place. Another $70 million of the fictitious revenue was from swap transactions and $100 million came from the premature booking of revenues from long-term instalment contracts. Peregrine had reported another $80 million of revenues that, for a variety of reasons, should not have been recorded until future years and that $34 million of revenues had been based on "erroneous calculations or unsupported transactions." (Waters 2003)

An SEC complaint, settled by Peregrine, alleged that the company improperly booked millions of dollars of revenue for purported software license sales to resellers. These transactions were non-binding sales of Peregrine software with the understanding – reflected in secret side agreements – that the resellers were not obligated to pay Peregrine. Those involved in the scheme called this "parking" the transaction. Peregrine personnel parked transactions when Peregrine was unable to complete direct sales it was negotiating (or hoping to negotiate) with end-users, but needed revenue to achieve its forecasts. (SEC 2003a)

Peregrine engaged in other deceptive practices to inflate the company's revenue, including entering into reciprocal transactions in which Peregrine essentially paid for its customers' purchases of Peregrine software. Peregrine routinely kept its books open after fiscal quarters ended, and improperly recorded as revenue, for the prior quarter, software transactions that were not consummated until after quarter end. Certain Peregrine officers characterized these transactions as having been completed on "the 37th of December". (SEC 2003a)

To conceal the revenue recognition scheme, Peregrine abused the receivable financing process. When Peregrine booked the non-binding contracts, and the customers predictably did not pay, the receivables ballooned on Peregrine's balance sheet. To make it appear that Peregrine was collecting its receivables more quickly than it was, Peregrine "sold" receivables to banks and then removed them from the company's balance sheet. There were several problems with this. First, Peregrine had given the banks recourse and frequently paid or repurchased unpaid receivables from them. Peregrine should have accounted for the bank transactions as loans and left the receivables on its balance sheet. Secondly, the sold receivables were not valid because the customers were not obligated to pay. Thirdly, several of the sold invoices were fake, including one that purported to reflect a $19.58 million sale. (SEC 2003b)

The SEC complaint also alleged that, as part of the cover up, Peregrine personnel wrote off millions of dollars in uncollectible – primarily sham – receivables, to acquisition-related accounts in Peregrine's financial statements and books and records. These write-offs were improper because they had nothing to do with acquisitions. (SEC 2003a)

▶

Peregrine Systems – The 37th of December (continued)

Chief Executive Officer, Mathew C. Gless, alleged a SEC civil suit, signed false SEC filings and false management representation letters to Peregrine's outside auditors, and responded falsely to an SEC Division of Corporation Finance Comment Letter that inquired about Peregrine's revenue recognition practice. According to the complaint, while Gless was aware of the ongoing fraud, he illegally sold 68,625 shares of Peregrine stock for approximately $4 million, based on material non-public information he possessed about Peregrine's true financial condition. (SEC 2003b)

Peregrine Comparative Balance Sheet 2000–2001 (in 000)

	31 March 01	31 March 00
ASSETS		
Cash and cash equivalents	$286,658	$33,511
Accounts receivable, net of allowance for doubtful accounts of $11,511 and $2,179, respectively	180,372	69,940
Other current assets	62,811	22,826
Total current assets	529,841	126,277
Property and equipment, net	82,717	29,537
Goodwill, net of accumulated amortization of $334,178 and $54,406, respectively	1,192,855	233,504
Other intangible assets, investments and other, net of accumulated amortization of $24,015 and $1,398, respectively	198,353	134,112
	$2,003,766	$523,430
LIABILITIES AND STOCKHOLDERS' EQUITY		
Current liabilities:		
Accounts payable	$36,024	$19,850
Accrued expenses	200,886	49,064
Current portion of deferred revenue	86,653	36,779
Current portion of long-term debt	1,731	74
Total current liabilities	325,294	105,767
Deferred revenue, net of current portion	8,299	4,556
Other long-term liabilities	17,197	
Long-term debt, net of current portion	884	1,257
Convertible subordinated notes	262,327	
Total liabilities	614,001	111,580
Stockholders' equity:		
Preferred stock, $0.001 par value, 5,000 shares authorized, no shares issued or outstanding		
Common stock, $0.001 par value, 500,000 shares authorized, 160,359 and 109,501 shares issued and outstanding,respectively	160	110
Additional paid-in capital	2,342,235	480,957
Accumulated deficit	−917,104	−64,863
Unearned portion of deferred compensation	−22,151	−678
Cumulative translation adjustment	−3,950	−666
Treasury stock, at cost	−9,425	−3,010
Total stockholders' equity	1,389,765	411,850
	$2,003,766	$523,430

Peregrine Systems Comparative Income Statement 1999–2001 (in 000)

Revenues:	31 March 01	31 March 00	31 March 99
Licenses	$354,610	$168,467	$87,362
Services	210,073	84,833	50,701
Total revenues	564,683	253,300	138,063
Costs and expenses:			
Cost of licenses	2,582	1,426	1,020
Cost of services	111,165	51,441	31,561
Amortization of purchased technology	11,844	1,338	50
Sales and marketing	223,966	101,443	50,803
Research and development	61,957	28,517	13,919
General and administrative	48,420	19,871	10,482
Acquisition costs and other	918,156	57,920	43,967
Total costs and expenses	1,378,090	261,956	151,802
Loss from operations before interest (net) and income tax expense	−813,407	−8,656	−13,739
Interest income (expense), net	−538	38	664
Loss from operations before income tax expense	−813,945	−8,618	−13,075
Income tax expense	−38,296	−16,452	−10,295
Net loss	−$852,241	−$25,070	−$23,370
Net loss per share basic and diluted:			
Net loss per share	−$6.16	−$0.24	−$0.27
Shares used in computation	138,447	102,332	87,166

Source: US Securities and Exchange Commission, www.sec.gov.

Discussion Questions

■ Review the Peregrine financial statements and determine what analytical procedures could be used to predict the revenue recognition fraud. Are there other indicators that a revenue recognition fraud was under way?

References

SEC, 2003a, *Litigation Release No. 18205A, Accounting and Auditing Enforcement Release No. 1808A,* "SEC Charges Peregrine Systems, Inc. with Financial Fraud and Agrees to Partial Settlement," US Securities and Exchange Commission, June 30.

SEC, 2003b, *Litigation Release No. 18093, Accounting and Auditing Enforcement Release No. 1759,* "SEC Charges Former Peregrine CFO with Financial Fraud," US Securities and Exchange Commission, April 16.

Waters, R., 2003, "Irregularities at Peregrine lifted revenues 60 percent," *Financial Times,* March 3, p. 19.

9.6 Analytical Procedures During Different Phases In The Audit Process

Analytical procedures are used: (a) to assist the auditor in planning the nature, timing, and extent of audit procedures; (b) as substantive procedures; and (c) as an overall review of the financial statements in the final stage of the audit. The auditor is required to apply analytical procedures at the planning and overall review stages of the audit.

■ Planning

Analytical procedures performed in the planning stage (Stage II in the Audit Process Model, Illustration 5.1) are used to identify unusual changes in the financial statements, or the absence of expected changes, and specific risks. During the planning stage, analytical procedures are usually focussed on account balances aggregated at the financial statement level and relationships between account balances.

"The auditor should apply analytical procedures at the planning stage to assist in understanding the business and in identifying areas of potential risk."[15] Application of analytical procedures indicates aspects of the business of which the auditor was unaware and will assist in determining the nature, timing, and extent of other audit procedures. Surveys of auditors show that the most extensive use of analytical procedures has been in the planning and completion stages.[16]

■ Substantive Testing

During the substantive testing stage (Phase III of the Audit Process Model, Illustration 5.1), analytical procedures are performed to obtain assurance that financial statement account balances do not contain material misstatements. In substantive testing, analytical procedures focus on underlying factors that affect those account balances through the development of an expectation of how the recorded balance should look.

■ Overall Review

Analytical procedures performed during the overall review stage (Phase IV of the Audit Process Model, Illustration 5.1) are designed to assist the auditor in assessing that all significant fluctuations and other unusual items have been adequately explained and that the overall financial statement presentation makes sense based on the audit results and an understanding of the business.

"The auditor should apply analytical procedures at or near the end of the audit when forming an overall conclusion as to whether the financial statements as a whole are consistent with the auditor's knowledge of the business."[17] Analytical procedures at the review stage are intended to corroborate conclusions formed during the audit of individual components of the financial statements. Moreover, they assist in determining the reasonableness of the financial statements. They may also identify areas requiring further procedures.

■ Tests of Controls Over Information Used for Analytics

An important consideration in applying analytical procedures is tests of controls over the preparation of information used for analytics. When those controls are effective, the auditor will have more confidence in the reliability of the information and, therefore, in the results of analytical procedures.

The controls over non-financial information can often be tested in conjunction with tests of accounting-related controls. For example, a company's controls over the processing of sales invoices may include controls over the recording of unit sales; therefore an auditor could test the controls over the recording of unit sales in conjunction with tests of the controls over the processing of sales invoices.

Certification Exam Question 9.4

Which of the following would **not** be considered an analytical procedure?

(A) Estimating payroll expense by multiplying the number of employees by the average hourly wage rate and the total hours worked.
(B) Projecting an error rate by comparing the results of a statistical sample with the actual population characteristics.
(C) Computing accounts receivable turnover by dividing credit sales by the average net receivables.
(D) Developing the expected current year sales based on the sales trend of the prior five years.

9.7 Analytical Procedures As Substantive Tests

Substantive procedures in the audit are designed to reduce **detection risk** relating to specific financial statement **assertions**. Substantive tests include tests of details (either **of balances** or **of transactions**) and analytical procedures. Auditors use analytical procedures to identify situations that require increased use of other procedures (i.e. tests of control, substantive audit procedures), but seldom to reduce audit effort.[18]

■ Analytical Procedures Instead of Tests of Details

There are a number of advantages of performing substantive analytical procedures instead of tests of details. One advantage is that the auditor may use his understanding of the client's business obtained during planning procedures. The key factors affecting business may be expected to reflect underlying financial data. Substantive analytical procedures often enable auditors to focus on a few key factors that affect the account balance. Substantive analytical procedures may be more efficient in performing understatement tests. For example, in a test for unrecorded sales, it may be easier to develop an expectation of sales and investigate any significant differences between the expectation and the recorded amount, than to sample statistically a reciprocal population and then perform tests of details.

In planning an audit that uses analytical procedures as substantive procedures, the auditor will need to consider a number of factors such as the:[19]

- objectives of the analytical procedures and the extent to which their results can be relied upon;
- nature of the entity and the degree to which information can be disaggregated;
- availability of both financial and non-financial information;
- reliability of the information available;
- source of the information available (e.g. independent sources are ordinarily more reliable than internal ones);
- comparability of the information available;
- knowledge gained during previous audits.

■ Disadvantages of Analytical Procedures

Substantive analytical procedures have some disadvantages. They may be more time-consuming initially to design and might be less effective than performing tests of details of balances. Obtaining data used to develop an expectation and ensuring the reliability of that data at an appropriate level of disaggregation can account for a substantial amount of the time otherwise spent performing tests of details. Analytical procedures may be less effective when applied to the financial statements of the entity as a whole than when applied to financial information on individual sections of an operation or to financial statements of components of a diversified entity.

Substantive analytical procedures will not necessarily deliver the desired results every year. In periods of instability and rapid change, it may be difficult to develop a sufficiently precise expectation of the recorded amount, and it may be more appropriate to apply tests of details. For example, if an economy reaches hyperinflation, it is unlikely that we will be able to develop meaningful expectations efficiently, except in limited circumstances.

■ Corroboration

When analytical procedures serve as substantive tests, the auditor should corroborate explanations for significant differences by obtaining sufficient audit evidence. For example, re-calculation of invoice extensions (quantity times price) may be corroborated by interviewing a salesperson about how invoices are filled out. This evidence needs to be of the same quality, as the evidence the auditor would expect to obtain to support tests of details.

To corroborate an explanation, one or more of the following techniques may be used:

- inquiries of persons outside the client's organization including bankers, suppliers, customers, etc.;
- inquiries of independent persons inside the client's organization (e.g. an explanation received from the Chief Financial Officer for an increase in advertising expenditures might be corroborated with the marketing director: it is normally inappropriate to corroborate explanations only by discussion with other accounting department personnel);
- evidence obtained from other auditing procedures;
- examination of supporting evidence. The auditor may examine supporting documentary evidence of transactions to corroborate explanations. For example, if an increase in cost of sales in one month was attributed to an unusually large sales contract, the auditor might examine supporting documentation, such as the sales contract and delivery dockets.

■ Substantive Analytical Procedures Examples

Fraudulent payments are often in large amounts. An analytical procedure to detect this is the use of a CAATs program (discussed in the next section) to stratify the payments by size and then extract all large payments. The auditor may sort the records by type of purchase, since the size of an expenditure is related to the typical cost of the product or service.

By analyzing revenue over at least three years, the auditor can detect unexpected trends in revenues. Sales can also be analyzed by type, activity, salesperson, month, or customer.

The sales data can be stratified to determine if sales in a certain area or by a certain salesperson are made up of a few large or unusual transactions.

Benford's Law calculations may be done by a CAATs. Benford's Law determines the expected frequency for each digit in any position in a set of random numbers. This means that the chances of any number appearing in a given database are mathematically predictable. Since the expected frequency for each number in the set is known, every number that appears in the database in excess of the expected frequency requires further investigation. For instance, payment amounts authorized by a manager may be consistently just below the maximum allowed for that manager.

■ Payroll

If the auditor suspects fraud in the payroll area, he may do a number of substantive tests to detect a "ghost employee," an employee who still "works for the company" even though his employment has been terminated, or excessive overtime charges. Three types of analytical tests can be performed to help detect these kinds of irregularities: duplicate and validity tests, exception testing, and recalculations.

Duplicate and validity tests are used to detect a ghost or a terminated employee. A CAATs program can help the auditor check for duplicate social security numbers, names, or, if direct deposit is used, bank account numbers. To find ghost employees, an auditor can also identify employees who take no sick or annual leave, or those who do not have insurance or other deductions taken out of their pay. Additionally, a CAATs program can verify that each employee's salary or wage is within the ranges for his job description and that tax withholding amounts are reasonable.

Certification Exam Question 9.5[20]

Which of the following tends to be most predictable for purposes of analytical procedures applied as substantive tests?

(A) Relationships involving balance sheet accounts.
(B) Transactions subject to management discretion.
(C) Relationships involving income statement accounts.
(D) Data subject to audit testing in the prior year.

9.8 Computer Assisted Audit Techniques (CAATs) and Generalized Audit Software (GAS)

The use of computer assisted audit techniques (CAATs) may enable more extensive testing of electronic transactions and account files.[21] CAATs can be used to select sample transactions from key electronic files, to sort transactions with specific characteristics, or to test an entire population instead of a sample. CAATs generally include regression and statistical analysis as well as the more widely used **file interrogation** techniques using generalized audit software (GAS) such as data manipulation, calculation, data selection, data analysis, identification of exceptions and unusual transactions.

■ Regression Analysis

Complicated analytical procedures may use regression analysis. **Regression analysis** is the use of statistical models to quantify the auditor's expectation in financial (euro, dollar) terms, with measurable risk and precision levels. For example, an expectation for sales may be developed based on management's sales forecast, commission expense, and changes in advertising expenditures. Regression analysis provides a very high level of precision because an explicit expectation is formed in which the relevant data can be incorporated in a model to predict current year sales.

Regression analysis potentially can take into account all of the relevant operating data (sales volume by product), changes in operations (changes in advertising levels, changes in product lines or product mix), and changes in economic conditions. Regression analysis provides the benefits of statistical precision. The statistical model provides not only a "best" expectation given the data at hand, but also provides quantitative measures of the "fit" of the model.

■ Generalized Audit Software (GAS)

Generalized audit software (GAS) packages contain numerous computer-assisted audit techniques for both doing analytical procedures and statistical sampling bundled into one piece of software. There are widely used GAS packages such as ACL[22] and Idea, and the Big Four audit firms have their own software such as Deloitte and Touche's STAR and MINI MAX. GAS packages provide the auditors with the ability to access, manipulate, manage, analyze, and report data in a variety of formats. This software allows the auditor to move from analytical procedures to statistical sampling for analytical procedures fairly easily.

File Interrogation Procedures Using GAS

Using GAS in an audit requires converting client data into a common format and then analyzing the data. This is generally referred to as file interrogation. File interrogation is a CAAT that allows the auditor to perform automated audit routines on client computer data. It is a method of using a computer to capture accounting data and reports and test the information contained therein. Because the nature of audit evidence changes, audit techniques that take advantage of technology are often more appropriate than traditional auditing techniques. In sophisticated environments, file interrogation techniques can often create efficiency and improve the quality of audit work.

Extracting information that meets specific criteria, selecting information, and testing the accuracy of calculations can be done with file interrogation. CAATs used in GAS allows auditors to analyze and test every item on a report to determine whether it meets predefined criteria, identify significant differences, create an independent report of exceptions, select an audit sample, and export the results into audit software.

■ Audit Tasks

In general terms, file interrogation can accomplish the following six types of audit tasks:

1 convert client data into common format;
2 analyze data;
3 compare different sets of data;
4 confirm the accuracy of calculations and make computations;
5 sample statistically;
6 test for gaps or duplicates in a sequence.

We will discuss the first three audit tasks in this section. For a discussion of the last three items (confirm accuracy of the calculations, statistical sampling, and tests for gaps) see Appendix A to Chapter 10 Substantive Testing and Evidence.

Convert Data Into a Common Format

The auditor can use GAS (e.g. ACL)) to convert client data into a common format (e.g. files ending in the extension *.fil) that can be manipulated by the software. Audit work is more efficient since data does not have to be manually entered and the conversion is usually performed with 100 percent accuracy. The data can then be used by the GAS or exported as several formats such as plain text, comma delimited, XML, Microsoft Word, Excel, or Access.

Analyze Data

GAS can handle large volumes of data quickly. Often, file interrogation can be used to analyze an entire population in less time than it would take to test a sample of items manually. The auditor can identify all records in a data file that meet specified criteria or reformat and aggregate data in a variety of ways.

Audit tests that can be performed with GAS include the following:

- Identify all inventory items relating to products no longer sold.
- Select all inventory items with no recorded location.
- Summarize inventory items by location to facilitate physical observation.
- Review account receivable balances for amounts over credit limits or older than a specified period.
- Summarize accounts receivable by age for comparison to the client's schedules.
- Review inventory quantities and unit costs for negative or unusually large amounts.
- Isolate all inventory items that have not moved since a specified date.
- Review assets for negative net book values.
- Summarize inventory by age to assess the reasonableness of obsolescence provisions.

Compare Different Sets of Data

If records on separate files contain comparable data, GAS can be used to compare the different sets of data. For example, the auditor could compare the following:

- changes in accounts receivable balances between two dates **with** the details of sales and cash receipts on transaction files;
- payroll details **with** personnel records;

- current inventory files **with** prior period files to identify potentially obsolete or slow-moving items;
- portfolio positions recorded in the accounting records of an investment company **with** the records maintained by the custodian.

Structured Approach for GAS-Based Analytical Procedures

To use analytical procedures in testing an account balance with GAS, the auditor is likely to follow the basic four-phase audit review model already discussed in section 9.3. The four phases using GAS are shown in Illustration 9.5. When using GAS to conduct the four phase audit review process, the auditor must first format the data so that it might be read with the software.

ILLUSTRATION 9.5

The Four-Phase Analytical Review Process Using GAS

Phase one in performing analytical procedures – expectations

- Determine appropriate base data and an appropriate level of disaggregation.
- Use regression analysis techniques to develop from the base data a plausible relationship (a regression model) between the amounts to be tested (the test variable such as accounts receivable balance) and one or more independent sets of data (predicting variables such as revenue, volume of shipments, collection history, selling square footage, number of customers, etc.) that are expected to relate to the test variable.
- Based on this relationship, use GAS software to calculate the expectations (regression estimates) for the test variable based on the current-period values of the predicting variables.

Phase two in performing analytical procedures – identification

- Use GAS's statistical techniques to assist in identifying significant differences for investigation (i.e. differences exceeding the materiality thresholds) based on the regression model, audit judgments as to monetary precision (MP), required audit assurance (R factor), and the direction of the test.

Phase three in performing analytical procedures – investigation

- Investigate and corroborate explanations for significant differences between the expectations and the recorded amounts.

Phase four in performing analytical procedures – evaluation

- Evaluate findings and determine the level of assurance, if any, to be drawn from the analytical procedures.

Examples

To illustrate, assume that the test variable is *sales* and the predicting variable is *cost of sales*. In most cases, it is plausible that a relationship exists between these two components of the income statement. The GAS uses sales and cost of sales data from prior periods to determine the precise nature of the relationship and to develop a regression model. Then, based on audited current-period amounts for cost of sales, GAS will project the current-period expectations for sales. GAS will then compare the expectations for sales with the actual recorded amounts and calculate the differences. GAS identifies for investigation any statistically significant differences between the current-period projected amounts and the actual recorded amounts for sales.

A regression model might be constructed for a chain of retail outlets based on prior-year performance, in which annual sales per outlet are related to floor area and number of sales personnel (relationships that are expected to be reasonably constant over time). That model might then be used to develop sales expectations based on the corresponding current-year floor area and sales personnel data. The application would identify those outlets where sales results require further investigation, and may assist in selecting locations to visit.

9.9 Analytical Procedures Using Data Mining Techniques

Data mining is a set of computer-assisted techniques that use sophisticated statistical analysis, including artificial intelligence techniques, to examine large volumes of data with the objective of indicating hidden or unexpected information or patterns. In database terms, data mining is referred to as knowledge discovery in databases (KDD). Data mining can be used in all types of databases or other information repositories. Data to be mined can be numerical data, textual data or even graphics and audio.

Used most extensively in **customer relationship management** (CRM) and fraud detection, data mining is for both verification and discovery objectives. Data mining is used in a top-down approach to verify auditors' expectations or explain events or conditions observed. For example, merchandise order and delivery dates are examined to see if the delivery date falls after the order date. Discovery is a bottom-up approach that uses automated exploration of hitherto unknown patterns. For example, the auditor uses a **neural network** to sift through financial and non-financial revenue and accounts receivable data to discover unusual patterns.

■ GAS and Data Mining

GAS's capability to assist in the overall audit process while requiring little technical skill is a major reason for its success. However, GAS has been criticized because it makes some tasks easier but it cannot complete any data analysis by itself. Data mining, on the other hand, analyzes data automatically but is more difficult to employ.

Data mining tools remain promising in a variety of application areas. With the development of appropriate data mining tools for the auditing profession, it may be expected to replace some professional expertise required in certain auditing processes. For now, although data mining procedures are useful in almost all steps of the audit process, its most practical and useful applications are in analytical procedures.

Data mining may use many methods and techniques and algorithms to analyze client data. Data mining methods include data description, dependency analysis, classification and prediction, cluster analysis, outlier analysis and evolution analysis The most frequently used algorithms are decision trees, apriori algorithms, and neural networks.

The purpose of **dependency analysis** is to search for the most significant relationship across large number of variables or attributes. **Classification** is the process of finding models, also known as classifiers, or functions that map records into one of several discrete prescribed classes.

The objective of **data description** is to provide an overall description of data, either in itself or in each class or concept. There are two main approaches in obtaining data description – data characterization and data discrimination. Data characterization is summarizing general characteristics of data and data discrimination, also called data comparison, by comparing characters of data between contrasting groups or classes.

The objective of **evolution analysis** is to determine the most significant changes in data sets over time. In other words, it is other types of algorithm methods (i.e. data description, dependency analysis, classification or clustering) plus time-related and sequence-related characteristics.

The objective of **cluster analysis** is to separate data with similar characteristics from the dissimilar ones. The difference between clustering and classification is that while clustering does not require pre-identified class labels, classification does. Outliers are data items that are distinctly dissimilar to others and can be viewed as noises or errors. However, such noises can be useful in some cases, such as fraud detection, where unusual items or exceptions are major concerns.

An example of the use of the clustering method is when the auditor clusters accounting transactions in such categories as assets, liabilities, revenue, expenses, etc. This might reveal those small transactions that occur repeatedly in a certain period of the month or the same transactions recorded in different account numbers. The auditor might find that sales in some months or divisions are excessively higher or lower than the normal. Expenses that are highly variable during the year might be found. Clustering might show the repeated purchase of the same fixed asset. Loans that are transacted between related companies and subsidiaries may be uncovered.

■ Algorithms – Decision Tree, Apriori, Neural Network

Data mining most frequently uses three algorithms.

- A **decision tree** is a predictive model that classifies data with a hierarchical structure. It consists of nodes, which contain classification questions, and branches that are the result of the questions. (For example the question, "Does this item increase at the same rate as revenue?" may be answered yes – which leads to one branch "growth similar to revenue" or may be answered no – which leads to another branch.)
- The **apriori algorithm** attempts to discover frequent item sets using rules to find associations between the presence or absence of items (Boolean association rules). The group of item sets that most frequently come together is identified.
- A **neural network** is a computer model based on the architecture of the brain. It first detects a pattern from data sets then predicts the best classifiers of that pattern, and finally learns from the mistakes.

9.10 Follow-Up in Case of Unexpected Deviations

When analytical procedures identify significant fluctuations or relationships that are inconsistent with other relevant information or that deviate from predicted amounts, the auditor should investigate and obtain adequate explanations and appropriate corroborative evidence.[23] A comparison of actual results with expected should include a consideration of why there is a difference.

There are primarily two reasons for a significant fluctuation or inconsistency. One is that there is a genuine business reason that was not obvious during planning procedures. The second reason is that there is a misstatement. Work must be done to determine which reason.

■ Investigation

The investigation of unusual fluctuations and relationships ordinarily begins with inquiries of management, followed by corroboration of management responses and determination if additional audit procedures are needed. Management's responses may be corroborated by comparing them with the auditor's knowledge of the business and other evidence obtained during the course of the audit.

If a reasonable explanation cannot be obtained, the auditor aggregates misstatements that the entity has not corrected. The auditor would then consider whether, in relation to individual amounts, subtotals, or totals in the financial statements, they materially misstate the financial statements taken as a whole. If management cannot provide a satisfactory explanation and there is a possibility of material misstatement, other audit procedures should be determined.

9.11 Summary

Analytical procedures consist of the analysis of significant ratios and trends including the resulting investigation of fluctuations and relationships that are inconsistent with other relevant information or deviate from predictable amounts. That is, analytical procedures entail the use of comparisons and relationships to determine whether account balances or other data appear reasonable. A basic premise of using analytical procedures is that there exist plausible relationships among data and these relationships can reasonably be expected to continue.

The process of planning, executing and drawing conclusions from analytical procedures is called analytical review. The four-phase process consists of the following:

- phase one is to formulate expectations (expectations);
- phase two is the comparison of the expected value to the recorded amount (identification);
- phase three requires investigation of possible explanations for a difference between expected and recorded values (investigation);

■ phase four involves evaluation of the impact on the audit and the financial statements of the differences between expectation and recorded amounts (evaluation).

Expectations are developed by identifying plausible relationships that are reasonably expected to exist based on the auditor's understanding of the client and of his industry. These relationships may be determined by comparisons with the following sources:

■ comparable information for prior periods;
■ anticipated results (such as budgets and forecasts, or auditor expectations);
■ similar industry information;
■ non-financial information.

The general analytical procedures are trend analysis, ratio analysis, statistical and data mining analysis, and reasonableness tests. Trend analysis is the analysis of changes in an account balance over time. Ratio analysis is the comparison of relationships between financial statement accounts, the comparison of an account with non-financial data, or the comparison of relationships between firms in an industry. Reasonableness testing is the analysis of account balances or changes in account balances within an accounting period in terms of their "reasonableness" in light of expected relationships between accounts. Data mining is a set of computer-assisted techniques that use sophisticated statistical analysis, including artificial intelligence techniques, to examine large volumes of data with the objective of indicating hidden or unexpected information or patterns.

The auditor should apply analytical procedures at the planning and overall review stages of the audit. Analytical procedures may also be applied to substantive testing. In the planning stage, the purpose of analytical procedures is to assist in planning the nature, timing, and extent of auditing procedures. In the overall review stage, the objective of analytical procedures is to assess the conclusions reached and evaluate the overall financial statement presentation. In the substantive testing stage of the audit, analytical procedures are used to obtain evidence to identify misstatements in account balances and thus to reduce the risk of misstatements.

Substantive procedures in the audit are designed to reduce detection risk relating to specific financial statement assertions. Substantive tests include tests of details and analytical procedures. Auditors use analytical procedures to identify situations that require increased use of other procedures (i.e. tests of control, substantive audit procedures), but seldom to reduce audit effort. There are a number of advantages of performing substantive analytical procedures instead of tests of details. The key factors affecting business may be expected to reflect the underlying financial data. Substantive analytical procedures often enable auditors to focus on a few key factors that affect the account balance.

The use of computer-assisted audit techniques (CAATs) may enable more extensive testing of electronic transactions and account files. Computer-assisted audit techniques can be used to select sample transactions from key electronic files, to sort transactions with specific characteristics, or to test an entire population instead of a sample. CAATs generally include regression and statistical analysis as well as the more widely used file interrogation techniques using generalized audit software (GAS) such as data manipulation, calculation, data selection, data analysis, identification of exceptions, and unusual transactions.

Data mining is a set of computer-assisted techniques that use sophisticated statistical analysis, including artificial intelligence techniques, to examine large volumes of data with the objective of indicating hidden or unexpected information or patterns. Data mining is used for both verification and discovery objectives. It is used in a top-down approach to verify auditors' expectations or explain events or conditions observed. Discovery is a bottom-up approach that uses automated exploration of hitherto unknown patterns.

When analytical procedures identify significant fluctuations or relationships that are inconsistent with other relevant information or that deviate from predicted amounts, the auditor should investigate and obtain adequate explanations and appropriate corroborative evidence. A comparison of actual results with expected should include a consideration of why there is a difference. The investigation of unusual fluctuations and relationships ordinarily begins with inquiries of management followed by corroboration of management's responses and other audit procedures based on the results of these inquiries.

9.12 Answers to Certification Exam Questions

9.1 (C) The requirement is to recognize a basic premise on which the application of analytical procedures is based. Answer (C) is correct because when using analytical procedures one must assume the source references on which expectations are based are plausibly related to recorded data. That data may reasonably be expected to exist and continue in the absence of known conditions to the contrary. Answer (A) is wrong because the study of financial ratios identifies unusual fluctuations – it is not an alternative to investigating fluctuations. Answer (B) is incorrect because analytical procedures may be either statistical or non-statistical. Answer (D) is incorrect because analytical procedures may be used as substantive tests, and can result in modification of the scope of tests.

9.2 (B) We are required to identify what comparison an auditor most likely would make when evaluating an entity's costs and expenses. Answer (B) is correct because payroll expense is an income statement expense that most likely would relate to that of the prior year. Answer (A) is not good because the accounts receivable is an asset, not a cost or expense. Answer (C) is incorrect because comparing budgeted sales with actual sales of the current year is more likely to be performed than comparing budgeted sales with those of prior years. Answer (D) is incorrect because an auditor would more likely compare current year budgeted warranty expense with actual warranty expense than he would compare current year's budgeted warranty expense with the current year's contingent liabilities.

9.3 (C) We need to find the type of analytical procedure that an auditor would most likely use in developing relationships among balance sheet accounts when reviewing the financial statements of a non-public entity. Answer (C) is correct because balance sheet accounts may be analyzed through a number of ratios (e.g. liquidity ratios). Answer (A) is on the wrong track because although auditors may use trend analysis on balance sheet items like accounts receivable and inventory, they are more likely to use ratios such as inventory turnover or accounts receivable turnover, whereas trend analysis is more likely to be used for income statement items. Answer (B) is not likely because regression analysis, due to its complexity, is not used as frequently as ratio analysis. Answer (D) is incorrect because risk analysis is not a type of analytical procedure.

9.4 (B) The question wants us to pick the answer that would **not** be considered an analytical procedure that measures plausible relationships between data. Answer (B) is the right one because projecting an error rate from a statistical sample to an actual population is not a comparison of a plausible relationship. Answers (A), (C), and (D) are all incorrect because they **are** analyses of plausible relationships.

9.5 (C) We are to decide the most predictable relationship considering analytical procedures applied as substantive tests. Answer (C) is correct because relationships involving income statement accounts tend to be more predictable than relationships involving only balance sheet accounts. For example, cost of goods sold, fixed costs, etc. will give more predictable results when analyzed with ratios than balance sheet ratios such as debt to equity, current liabilities as a percentage of assets, etc. Answer (A) is not as good as (C) because relationships involving income statements are more predictable. Answer (B) is wrong because transactions that are subject to management discretion are typically less predictable because of the very fact that subjective judgment is a major component. Answer (D) is incorrect because prior year data is not always a solid predictor of data in subsequent years.

9.13 Notes

1 IFAC, 2004, *Handbook of International Auditing, Assurance, and Ethics Pronouncements*, International Standards on Auditing 520, "Analytical Procedures", para. 3, International Federation of Accountants, New York.
2 Ibid. Para 2. This is also required by US Statement of Auditing Standard No. 56.
3 Adapted and reprinted with permission from AICPA. Copyright © 2000 & 1985 by American Institute of Certified Public Accountants.
4 See Blocher, E. and Cooper, J., 1988, "A study of auditors' analytical review performance," *Auditing: A Journal of Practice & Theory*, Spring, pp. 1–28; and Koonce, L., 1993, "A cognitive characterization of audit analytical review," *Auditing: A Journal of Practice & Theory* 12 (Supplement), pp. 57–76.
5 Asare, S. and Wright, A., 1997, "Hypothesis revision strategies in conducting analytical procedures," *Accounting, Organizations and Society* 22, November, pp. 737–55.
6 AICPA, 2001, *Analytical Procedures – AICPA Audit Guide*, American Institute of Certified Public Accountants.
7 See: (1) Bell, T.B., Marrs, F.O., Solomon, I., and Thomas, H., 1997, *Auditing Organizations Through A Strategic-Systems Lens*, New York, NY: KPMG Peat Marwick LLP, (2) Loebbecke, J.K. and Steinbart, P.J., 1987, "An investigation of the use of preliminary analytical review to provide substantive audit evidence," *Auditing: A Journal of Practice & Theory*, Spring, pp. 74–89; (3) Wild, J.J., 1987, "The prediction performance of a structural model of accounting numbers," *Journal of Accounting Research*, Vol. 25, no. 1, pp. 139–60.
8 Adapted and reprinted with permission from AICPA. Copyright © 2000 & 1985 by American Institute of Certified Public Accountants.
9 See: (1) Allen, R.D., Beasley, M.S., and Branson, B.C., 1999, "Improving analytical procedures: A case of using disaggregate multi-location data," *Auditing: A Journal of Practice & Theory*, 18, Fall, pp. 128–42; (2) Cogger, K.O., 1981, "A time-series analytic approach to aggregation issues in accounting data," *Journal of Accounting Research*, 19, Autumn, pp. 285–98; (3) Dzeng, S.C., 1994, "A comparison of analytical procedure expectation models using both aggregate and disaggregate data," *Auditing: A Journal of Practice & Theory*, 13, Fall, pp. 1–24.
10 Biggs, S.F., Mock, T.J., and Simnett, R., 1999, "Analytical Procedures: Promise, Problems and Implications for Practice," *Australian Accounting Review*, Vol. 9, No. 1, pp. 42–52.
11 See RMA, 2003, *Annual Statement Studies: Financial Ratio Benchmarks*, Risk Management Association, Philadelphia.

12 Adapted and reprinted with permission from AICPA. Copyright © 2000 & 1985 by American Institute of Certified Public Accountants.

13 IFAC, 2004, *Handbook of International Auditing, Assurance, and Ethics Pronouncements*, International Standards on Auditing 570 (ISA 570), "Going Concern," para. 2, International Federation of Accountants, New York.

14 IFAC, 2003, *Handbook of International Auditing, Assurance, and Ethics Pronouncements*, International Standards on Auditing 570 (ISA 570), "Going Concern," International Federation of Accountants, New York.

15 IFAC, 2004, *Handbook of International Auditing, Assurance, and Ethics Pronouncements*, International Standards on Auditing 520 (ISA 520), "Going Concern," para. 8, International Federation of Accountants, New York.

16 See, for example, Booth, P. and Simnett, R., 1991, "Auditors' perception of analytical review procedures," *Accounting Research Journal*, Spring, pp. 5–10.

17 See note 1. Para. 13.

18 See, for example, Bedard, J., 1989, "An archival investigation of audit program planning," *Auditing: A Journal of Practice and Theory*, Fall, pp. 57–71.

19 See note 1. Para. 12.

20 Adapted and reprinted with permission from AICPA. Copyright © 2000 & 1985 by American Institute of Certified Public Accountants.

21 IFAC, 2004, *Handbook of International Auditing, Assurance, and Ethics Pronouncements*, International Standard on Auditing 330 (ISA 330), "The Auditor's Procedures In Response to Assessed Risks," para. 19, International Federation of Accountants, New York.

22 ACL software is developed by ACL Services, Ltd. (**www.acl.com**).

23 See note 1. Para. 17.

9.14 Questions, Exercises and Cases

QUESTIONS

9.2 Introduction

9.1 Define analytical procedures and give the basic premise of using them.

9.2 When should the auditor use analytical procedures? What ISA standard states when they should be used?

9.3 The Analytical Review Process

9.3 Describe the four-phase process for analytical review.

9.4 Formulating Expectations

9.4 On what sources does an auditor base his expectations? Give examples of how the auditor may use each source.

9.5 Give an example of the nature of an account. Give an example of other characteristics of the data.

9.5 General Analytical Procedures

9.6 What are the five types of analytical procedures? Briefly discuss each.

9.7 In assessing going concern, list three financial indicators, three operating indicators, and three other indicators.

9.6 Analytical Procedures During Different Phases In The Audit Process

9.8 Why are analytical procedures used in the planning stages? Why are they used again near the end of the audit?

9.9 Why is it useful to do analytical procedures during the completion of an audit?

9.7 Analytical Procedures As Substantive Tests

9.10 Give the advantages and disadvantages of analytical procedures used as substantive tests.

9.11 What techniques are used to corroborate an explanation?

9.8 Computer Assisted Audit Techniques (CAATs) and Generalized Audit Software (GAS)

9.12 What is GAS and how does an auditor use it?

9.13 What are the six audit tasks accomplished by file interrogation? Describe two in detail.

9.9 Analytical Procedures Using Data Mining Techniques

9.14 Define data mining. How is it used for verification and discovery in the audit process?

9.15 Describe two data mining methods.

9.10 Follow-Up of Unexpected Deviations

9.16 What should an auditor do if he finds significant fluctuations when performing analytical procedures?

9.17 What should an auditor do if analytical procedures show significant fluctuations?

PROBLEMS AND EXERCISES

9.3 The Analytical Review Process

9.18 Four Phase Analytical Review Process. Based on Concept and a Company 9.2 "Peregrine Systems – the 37th of December," discuss what you would imagine each phase of the four phase analytical review process would involve.

9.4 Formulating Expectations

9.19 Expectation Sources. Based on the comparison of last year's results from Wal-Mart, Costco, Target and the retail industry, what would your expectations be about Target's revenue growth, gross margin, operating margins, and number of employees this year?

	WMT	COST	TGT	Industry
Market Cap	248.07B	17.55B	36.03B	932.18M
Employees	1,400,000	61,800	306,000	10.30K
Rev. Growth	12.20%	9.80%	10.10%	4.50%
Revenue	255.08B	43.87B	46.65B	2.04B
Gross Margin	22.20%	12.45%	31.70%	27.80%
EBITDA	18.50B	1.58B	4.62B	115.53M
Operating Margins	5.35%	2.68%	5.86%	2.16%
Net Income	8.67B	735.45M	1.70B	31.56M
Earnings Per Share	1.972	1.557	1.853	0.82
Price/Earnings Ratio	29.07	24.61	21.33	24.25

Abbreviations:
WMT = WalMart Corp.
COST = Costco Wholesale Corp
TGT = Target Corp
Industry = Supermarkets, Drugstores, & Mass Merchandisers

9.5 General Analytical Procedures

9.20 Analytical Procedures. At the beginning of the annual audit of Porster, BV, wholesale distributor of Valkenburg, the Netherlands, Lynna Heijn, Registeraccountant, was given a copy of Porster's financial statements as prepared by the company's accountant. On reviewing these statements, Heijn noted the following abnormal conditions:

1 The accounts receivable outstanding at the year-end represent an unusually high number of average days' credit sales.
2 The inventories on hand at the year-end represent an unusually high proportion of the current assets.
3 The working capital ratio of the company is almost twice that of the previous year.
4 The percentage of gross profit on net sales is considerably in excess of that of previous years.
5 The rate of turnover of inventory is unusually low in comparison with previous years.

Required:
Taking all the above conditions together, what irregularities might Heijn suspect regarding sales and inventories?
[CICA adapted]

9.21 Ratio and Trend Analysis. When an auditor discovers a significant change in a ratio when compared with the prior year's ratio, the auditor considers the possible reasons for the change.

Required:

Give the possible reasons for the following significant changes in ratios:

A.   The rate of inventory turnover (ratio of cost of sales to average industry) has decreased from the prior year's rate.

B.   The number of days' sales in receivables (ratio of average of daily accounts receivable to sales) has increased over the prior year.

9.6 Analytical Procedures During Different Phases In The Audit Process

9.22 Analytical Procedures. Analytical procedures are typically done during the planning phase.

Required:

A.   Define analytical procedures.

B.   Other than during planning, when does an auditor do analytical procedures?

C.   Name five ratios that an auditor could use to do analytical review and briefly describe each.

9.7 Analytical Procedures As Substantive Tests

9.23 Analytical Procedures. Analytical procedures are extremely useful in the initial audit planning stage.

Required:

A.   Explain why analytical procedures are considered substantive tests.

B.   Explain how analytical procedures are useful in the initial audit planning stage.

C.   Should analytical procedures be applied at any other stages of the audit process? Explain.

D.   List several types of comparisons an auditor might make in performing analytical procedures.

9.8 Computer Assisted Audit Techniques (CAATs) and Generalized Audit Software (GAS)

9.24 Using ACL software* and the ACL practice project file "Workbook.acl" perform the following procedures:

Required:

A.   Open the Accounts Receivable file (Ar.fil), then (1) Determine the number (count) of customers. (2) Find the customers who owe more than $5,000. (3) Perform Benford analysis.

B.   Open the inventory file (inventory.fil), then (1) Count the number of inventory items. (2) Determine the most expensive and least expensive item. (3) Find which products have a sales price less than the unit price.

* A demo version is available at **http://www.acl.com/explore/**. If the address has changed, search the site for "download" or "trial."

9.9 Analytical Procedures Using Data Mining Techniques

9.25 Start Microsoft Access and open the Northwind Sample Database.

Required:

A.   Sort the Product table by unit price, reorder point, units in stock.

B.   Do a visual inspection and sort the other tables. Are there any commonalities?

C.   Discuss the associations that you can see in this data. What is the nature of the possible errors?

9.10 Follow-Up of Unexpected Deviations

9.26 Extent of Reliance on Analytical Procedures. The extent of reliance that the auditor places on the results of analytical procedures depend on the materiality of the items involved, other audit procedures performed by the auditor, the accuracy with which expected results can be predicted, and the assessments of inherent and control risks.

Required:

A. Give two examples of circumstances in which the auditor can rely on analytical procedures and two circumstances when reliance on analytical procedures would not be advisable.

B. Explain the relationship between company controls and reliance on analytical procedures.

CASES

9.27 Using the references in footnotes to this chapter as a beginning place and accessing journal databases such as ABI Inform, discuss the theoretical view that the review process consists of four diagnostic processes: (1) mental representation, (2) hypothesis generation, (3) information search, and (4) hypothesis evaluation.

9.28 Go to **http://ecampus.bentley.edu/dept/ac/norwood/** and click to download the following: Norwood Office Supplies Case, Appendix B Assignment #1, and Case Study Files. Start ACL* and prepare Assignment #1 in Appendix B.

* A demo version is available at **http://www.acl.com/explore/**. If the address has changed, search the site for "download" or "trial."

9.29 Request "Data Warehousing Practice Set DW Inc." from **rhayes@calstatela.edu** and do the exercises using Access and Microsoft Analysis Services.

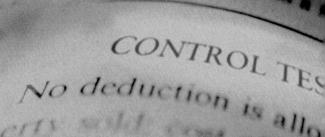

Chapter 10

SUBSTANTIVE TESTING AND EVIDENCE

10.1 Learning Objectives

After studying this chapter, you should be able to:

1 Understand the difference between legal evidence and audit evidence.

2 Discuss the systematic process of gathering evidence.

3 Define the management standard assertions: completeness, occurrence, accuracy, rights and obligations, valuation, existence, cutoff, classification, understanding, presentation and disclosure, and measurement.

4 Describe the components of and the meaning of "sufficient appropriate audit evidence."

5 Determine which evidence is relevant and which evidence is reliable.

6 Characterize a substantive procedure.

7 Explain what is meant by the nature, timing, and extent of substantive procedures.

8 Understand the seven evidence-gathering techniques: inquiry, observation, inspection, reperformance, recalculation, confirmation, and analytical procedures.

9 Discuss evidence-gathering procedures for physical inventory counting, confirmation of accounts receivable, and search for unrecorded liabilities.

10 Explain the circumstances in which substantive procedures are applied.

10.2 Introduction

Auditing is a systematic process of objectively obtaining and evaluating **evidence** regarding **assertions** about economic actions and events. It is the auditor's job to "obtain **sufficient appropriate audit evidence** to be able to draw reasonable conclusions on which to base the audit opinion."[1] Evidence is anything that can make a person believe that a fact, proposition, or assertion is true or false. **Audit evidence** is all of the information used by the auditor in arriving at the conclusions on which the audit opinion is based. It includes the accounting records and other information underlying the financial statements.

Audit evidence is different from the legal evidence required by **forensic accounting**. In a civil lawsuit, evidence must be strong enough to incline a person to believe one side or the other. In a criminal case, evidence must establish proof of a crime beyond a **reasonable doubt**. Audit evidence provides only **reasonable assurance**.

■ Accounting Records

Accounting records, the primary basis of audit evidence, generally include the records of initial entries and supporting records. Initial entries include point of sales transactions, **electronic data interchange (EDI)**, **electronic fund transfers (EFT)**, contracts, invoices, shipping notices, purchase orders, sales orders, the general and subsidiary ledgers, journal entries, and other adjustments to the financial statements. Supporting records examples are computer files, databases, worksheets, spreadsheets, computer and manual logs, computations, reconciliations, and disclosures.

Most accounting records are initiated, recorded, processed, and reported in electronic form such as a database. For the larger companies, accounting records are part of **enterprise resource planning (ERP)** which is a system that integrates all aspects of an organization's activities (such as database maintenance, financial reporting, operations and compliance) into one accounting information system.

■ Substantive Procedures

The main work of an auditor is to find evidence using test procedures. Substantive procedures are tests performed to obtain audit evidence to detect material misstatements in the financial statements and are of two types:

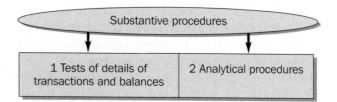

Audit evidence is the information used by the auditor in arriving at the conclusions on which the audit opinion is based. Audit evidence consists of source documents and accounting records underlying the financial statements and corroborating information from other sources.

This chapter provides guidance on the basis of evidence (**standards of proof** and documentation and financial statement assertions), what constitutes sufficient appropriate audit evidence (the quantity and quality of audit evidence) and the **substantive audit procedures** that auditors use for obtaining that audit evidence.[2]

Certification Exam Question 10.1[3]

The objective of tests of details of classes of transactions performed as substantive tests is to:

(A) Comply with International Financial Reporting Standards.
(B) Attain assurance about the reliability of the information system relevant to financial reporting.
(C) Detecting materials misstatement at the assertion level.
(D) Evaluate whether management's controls operated effectively.

10.3 The Basis of Evidence

Evidence for proof of audit assertions is different from evidence in a legal sense. Audit evidence needs only to prove reasonable assurance, whereas in a legal environment there is a more rigorous standard of proof and documentation. (See Illustration 10.1.)

■ Legal Evidence

Legal standards of proof are concepts that describe the quality of evidence for most legal systems. There are four standards of proof:

■ beyond a reasonable doubt;
■ preponderance of evidence;
■ clear and convincing evidence;
■ probable cause.

Reasonable doubt, the strongest of the standards, is applied in criminal cases. "A reasonable doubt is a doubt founded upon a consideration of all the evidence and must be based on reason."[4] In civil law, a **preponderance of evidence** is that upon listening to both sides, the weight of the evidence inclines a person with an impartial mind to one side rather than the other. **Clear and convincing evidence** is a proof that is stronger than a mere preponderance of evidence, but not convincing beyond a reasonable doubt. **Probable cause** serves as the basis for arrest and search warrants.

Evidence in the legal environment may be classified according to its proof results (direct or circumstantial) or according to its source (documentary, real, or testimonial). The results of the evidence may either directly or circumstantially support a standard of proof. **Direct evidence** comes from personal knowledge of the witnesses under oath as to

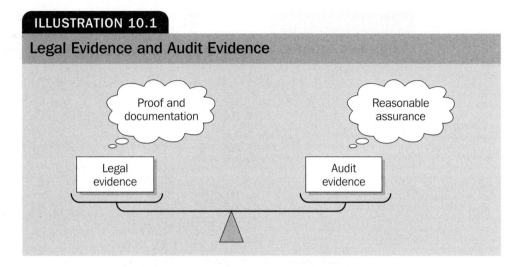

ILLUSTRATION 10.1

Legal Evidence and Audit Evidence

specific facts. **Circumstantial evidence** is based on facts and circumstances from which a court may infer that a factual matter has been proved. The source of the evidence may be *real,* i.e. it is tangible and can be presented to a court for inspection, or testimonial evidence which is evidence given by witnesses under oath. Financial facts are best proven by presentation of original documentary evidence backed by the testimony of a witness under oath.

■ Documentary Evidence

Documentary evidence is gathered from written, printed or electronic sources. Documentary evidence consists of computer files and records, e-mail, accounting records, paper (invoices, writings, pictures), documents (contracts, deed, reports), commercial records (e.g. from banks, brokerage, retailers, credit card) and government records (licenses, real estate, legal). The best proof of the contents of a document is the original document itself. However, if the original has been destroyed or is otherwise unavailable and the court accepts the explanation of its unavailability, secondary evidence may be used. Secondary evidence may be either the testimony of a witness or a copy of the evidence.

■ Financial Statement Assertions

Management is responsible for the fair presentation of financial statements so that they reflect the nature and operations of the company based on the applicable financial reporting framework (IAS, GAAP, etc.). Management prepares the financial statements based upon the accounting records and other information that the auditor may use as audit evidence such as minutes of meetings; confirmations from third parties; analysts' reports; comparable data about competitors (benchmarking); and controls manuals.

Management implicitly makes assertions that can be grouped into three substantive testing areas: **classes of transactions** and events, account balances at the period end, and disclosures. Illustration 10.2 makes a graphic presentation of the areas and assertions. The standard assertions are completeness, occurrence, accuracy, rights and obligations,

ILLUSTRATION 10.2

Financial Statement Assertions Grouped by Substantive Test Areas

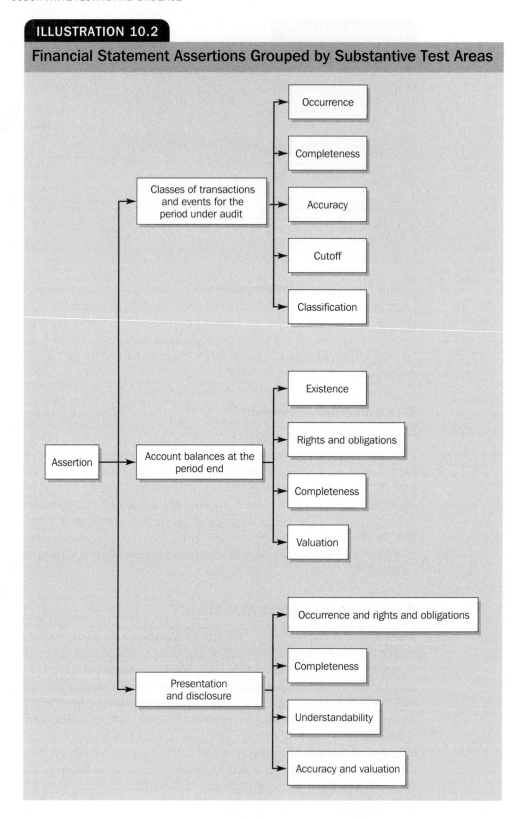

valuation, and existence. Other assertions are: cutoff, classification, transparency, presentation and disclosure, and measurement. The auditor assesses risks of potential misstatements based on these assertions and designs audit procedures to discover sufficient appropriate evidence.

Standard Assertions

Auditors have identified several assertions that management makes, directly or indirectly, relating to the financial statements. The standard assertions are **completeness, occurrence, accuracy, rights and obligations, valuation,** and **existence.** Completeness means that all transactions and events that should have been recorded have been recorded, i.e. there are no unrecorded assets, liabilities, transactions or events, or undisclosed items. The completeness assertion is important in all three substantive test areas. Occurrence is the assumption that transactions and events that have been recorded have occurred and pertain to the entity, that is, a transaction or event took place which pertains to the entity during the period. Rights and obligations means that at a given date the entity controls the rights to assets and that liabilities are the obligations of the entity. Valuation affirms that assets, liabilities and equity interests are included in the financial statements at appropriate amounts and any resulting valuation adjustments are appropriately recorded. Existence means that management maintains that all assets, liabilities, and equity interests exist at a given date.

Certification Exam Question 10.2[5]

An auditor most likely would make inquiries of production and sales personnel concerning possible obsolete or slow-moving inventory to support management's financial statement assertion of:

(A) Valuation.
(B) Rights and obligations.
(C) Existence.
(D) Completeness.

Certification Exam Question 10.3

In auditing intangible assets, an auditor most likely would review or recompute amortization and determine whether the amortization period is reasonable in support of management's financial statement assertion of:

(A) Valuation.
(B) Existence.
(C) Cutoff.
(D) Classification.

Other assertions are: *accuracy,* **cutoff, classification** and **understandability, presentation and disclosure,** and **measurement.** Accuracy means that amounts and other data relating to recorded transactions and events have been recorded accurately. Cutoff asserts that transactions and events have been recorded in the correct accounting period. Classification declares that transactions and events have been recorded in the proper accounts. Understandability holds that financial information is disclosed fairly.

Two assertions which are not mentioned in the IFAC standard, but are used in the field, are "presentation and disclosure" and "measurement." **Presentation and disclosure** asserts that an item is disclosed, classified, and described in accordance with the applicable financial reporting framework. **Measurement** is an assertion that a transaction or event is recorded at the proper amount and revenue or expense is allocated to the proper period.

■ Electronic Evidence

Some of the entity's accounting data and other information may be available only in electronic form. For example, entities may use electronic data interchange (EDI) or image processing systems. In EDI, the entity and its customers or suppliers use communication links to transact business electronically. Purchase, shipping, billing, cash receipt, and cash disbursement transactions are often consummated entirely by the exchange of electronic messages between the parties. In image processing systems, documents are scanned and converted into electronic images to facilitate storage and reference, and the source documents may not be retained after conversion. Certain electronic information may exist at a certain point in time, but may not be retrievable after a specified period of time if files are changed and if back-up files do not exist. The electronic nature of the accounting documentation usually requires that the auditor use computer-assisted audit techniques (CAATs).

Certification Exam Question 10.4

Cutoff tests designed to detect purchases made before the end of the year that have been recorded in the subsequent year most likely would provide assurance about management's assertion of:

(A) Valuation.
(B) Occurrence.
(C) Completeness.
(D) Classification and understandability.

10.4 Sufficient Appropriate Audit Evidence

The auditor should conclude whether sufficient appropriate audit evidence has been obtained to reduce to an acceptably low level the risk of material misstatements in the financial statements.[6] **Sufficiency** is the measure of the quantity (amount) of audit evidence. **Appropriateness** is the measure of the quality of audit evidence; that is, its relevance and its reliability in providing support for, or detecting misstatements in, the classes of transactions, account balances and disclosures, and related assertions.

Reliability is the quality of information when it is free from material error and bias and can be depended upon by users to represent faithfully that which it either purports to represent or could reasonably be expected to represent. **Relevance of evidence** is the appropriateness (pertinence) of the evidence to the audit objective being tested. The quantity (relevance and reliability) of audit evidence needed is affected by the risk of misstatement (the greater the risk, the more audit evidence is required) and also by the quality of the audit evidence (the higher the quality of evidence, the less is required). Therefore, the sufficiency and appropriateness of audit evidence are interrelated.[7] See Illustration 10.3.

ILLUSTRATION 10.3

The Quality of Audit Evidence

Relevance of evidence is the appropriateness (pertinence) of the evidence to the audit objective being tested

Reliability is the quality of information when it is free from material error and bias and can be depended upon by users to represent faithfully that which it either purports to represent or could reasonably be expected to represent.

The sufficiency and appropriateness of audit evidence to support the auditor's conclusions are a matter of professional judgment. The auditor's judgment as to what constitutes sufficient appropriate audit evidence is influenced by such factors as: [8]

■ the significance of the potential misstatement in the assertion and the likelihood of its having a material effect, individually or aggregated with other potential misstatements, on the financial statements: the more material the item, the greater the required sufficiency and appropriateness of evidence;

■ the effectiveness of management's responses and controls to address the risks: strong controls reduce evidence requirements;

■ the experience gained during previous audits with respect to similar potential misstatements: prior experience with the client will indicate how much evidence was taken before and if that was enough or appropriate;

■ results of audit procedures performed, including whether such audit procedures identified specific instances of fraud or error;

■ source and reliability of the available information;

■ persuasiveness of the audit evidence;

■ understanding of the entity and its environment, including its internal control.

Illustration 10.4 summarizes the considerations for determining whether audit evidence is "sufficient appropriate evidence."

ILLUSTRATION 10.4

Sufficient Appropriate Audit Evidence

Consideration	Sufficient and appropriate evidence
Materiality of the item being examined.	The more material the item the greater the amount of evidence required.
Effectiveness of management's responses to risk.	More effective management responses to risk and controls decreases quality and quantity of evidence required.
Prior audit experience with the client.	Prior audit experience with the client will indicate how much evidence was taken before and if that was enough.
Auditor's assessment of inherent and control risks.	The higher the inherent or control risk, the greater the amount of evidence required.
Reliability of the available information.	The less reliable the source of information, the greater the amount of evidence required.
Whether fraud or error is suspected.	If fraud is suspected, the amount of evidence required increases.

■ Reliable

The **reliability** of audit evidence is influenced by its source and its nature. (See Illustration 10.5.) The independence and qualification of the person providing evidence is important for reliability. Audit evidence is more reliable when it is obtained from independent sources outside the entity. The source of information may be internal – originating inside the client operation – or external, originating from a more objective party outside the organization. The source may be from an employee, third party or the auditor. Internal information that comes from a system with good internal controls is more reliable than information from a system where internal controls are not effective. The nature of the audit evidence may be visual, documentary, or oral.

ILLUSTRATION 10.5

Reliability of Evidence

	Least reliable	*Most reliable*
Source relative to entity	Internal (from inside entity)	External (from outside entity)
Source – person: employee or auditor	Employee of company	External auditor
Source – person: employee or third party	Employee of company	Third party
Source: independence of provider	Associated with company	Not associated with company
Source: qualification of provider	Little knowledge of subject	Expert in subject
Source: operation of internal controls	Not in operation	Effective operations

■ Persuasive

Unlike legal evidence, audit evidence does not have to be conclusive to be useful. Ordinarily, the auditor finds it necessary to rely on audit evidence that is persuasive rather than conclusive and will often seek audit evidence from different sources or of a different nature to support the same assertion. Not all the information available is examined. Conclusions can be reached about controls, transactions, or the account balance by using a sample of the available information that is analyzed by statistical sampling or judgment.

Audit evidence is more persuasive when there is consistency between items from different sources or of a different nature. Evidence is usually more persuasive for balance sheet accounts when it is obtained close to the balance sheet date. For income statements, evidence is more persuasive if it is a sample from the entire period. A random sample from the entire period is more persuasive than a sample from the first six months.

■ External/Internal

In general, audit evidence from external sources (e.g. **external confirmation** of cash account received from a bank) is more reliable than evidence generated internally. Internal information is made more reliable if the accounting and internal control systems are effective. Evidence obtained directly by the auditor is more reliable than that obtained from the client entity. Audit evidence obtained directly by the auditor (e.g. observation of the application of a control) is more reliable than audit evidence obtained indirectly or by inference (e.g. inquiry about the application of a control). Written documents are the second most reliable audit evidence. The least reliable audit evidence is oral representation of the client personnel. Oral interviews with third parties are more reliable than insider interviews, but less reliable than written documents.

■ Original Documentation

Audit evidence provided by original documents is more reliable than audit evidence provided by photocopies or facsimiles. Although forensic accounting frequently involves the authentication of documentation, financial statement audits rarely do, nor is the financial statement auditor expected to be an expert in such authentication. However, the financial statement auditor must consider the reliability of the information to be used as audit evidence, for example, how reliable are photocopies, facsimiles, or filmed, digitized or other electronic documents? An auditor may consider the relevance of controls over their preparation and maintenance of the documentation.

■ Cost/Benefit

The auditor also needs to think about the relationship between the cost of obtaining audit evidence and the usefulness of the information obtained. However, the matter of difficulty and expense involved is not in itself a valid basis for omitting a necessary procedure. If an auditor is unable to obtain sufficient appropriate audit evidence, he should express a qualified opinion or a disclaimer of opinion.

If the auditor has not obtained sufficient appropriate audit evidence as to a material financial statement assertion, he should attempt to obtain further audit evidence. If the auditor is unable to obtain sufficient appropriate audit evidence, he should express a qualified opinion or a disclaimer of opinion.

Concept and a Company 10.1
Mattel, Inc. Originators of "Bill and Hold" Toy with Accounting

Concept	Sufficient appropriate audit evidence. Mattel employs several accounting tricks that went unnoticed or were not investigated in the audit.
Story	Mattel, Inc. of El Segundo, California designs, manufactures and markets various toy products worldwide. Mattel brands include: Barbie dolls and accessories, Hot Wheels, Matchbox, Nickelodeon, Harry Potter, Yu-Gi-Oh!, He-Man and Masters of the Universe, Fisher-Price, Sesame Street, Winnie the Pooh, Blue's Clues, Barney, and View-Master, as well as games and puzzles.
	Almost from its founding in 1945, Mattel was very successful, but the company began experiencing serious problems in the early 1970s. Mattel tried several accounting schemes to keep their growth high including a "bill and hold" program, understatement of inventory

reserves, improper amortization of tooling costs, non-payment of royalties, and booking insurance recovery in the wrong period. (Knapp 2001)

Here we will address the sales and accounts receivable "bill and hold" issues.

Mattel Invents the Term

In order to inflate the company's reported earnings, top executives established the "bill and hold" program. This was the first instance of the term "bill and hold" for the practice of billing customers for future sales, recording the sales immediately, and holding on to the inventory – bill and hold. The SEC gave several reasons why the subject sales should not have been recorded in 1991 (SEC 1981):

- The merchandise was not shipped.
- The merchandise was not physically segregated from Mattel's inventory.
- The customer could cancel the order without penalty.
- Mattel retained the risks of ownership.
- In many instances, the invoices were prepared without knowledge of the customer.

Covering Their Tracks

To support the bill and hold sales, Mattel prepared bogus sales orders, sales invoices, and bills of lading. The bills of lading were signed by the same employees as both themselves and a common carrier and were stamped "bill and hold" on the face. When the goods were actually sold much later, Mattel's inventory records were full of errors. To resolve the problem, Mattel reversed the sales booked, but this created negative sales for the next period. To fix that problem, Mattel booked a fictitious $11 million sale in their general ledger, but not their accounts receivable subsidiary ledger, creating an unreconciled difference. They reversed another $7 million of the remaining bill and hold sales in fiscal 1992. (SEC 1981)

The Audit of Sales

Mattel's auditors, Arthur Andersen, sent accounts receivable confirmations. The confirmations were returned with discrepancies in what the customers claimed and what Mattel booked. To resolve the discrepancies, the auditors obtained copies of bills of lading to determine whether goods had actually been shipped. Even though the bills of lading were stamped "bill and hold," the auditors never asked Mattel to explain the phrase. Furthermore, the bills of lading lacked required routing or delivery instructions. The employee signatures as themselves and common carriers did not get noticed. (SEC 1981)

When the auditors looked at fiscal 1972 they found the $7 million reversing entry that caused that month's general ledger sales to be $7 million less than the sales figure in the corresponding sales invoice register. The staff auditor accepted the explanation of a Mattel employee that the offset to sales was due to "invoicing errors" uncovered by Mattel employees when comparing computer-prepared invoices to bills of lading. The Andersen senior reviewing the workpapers wrote the staff person, "Need a better explanation. This looks like a big problem," but the problem was investigated no further. (Knapp 2001)

Had Arthur Anderson utilized analytical procedures to evaluate the overall reasonableness of Mattel's monthly sales, they should have discovered that monthly sales varied dramatically from 1970 to 1972. This was a result of errors introduced by the bill and hold scheme and the subsequent reversals.

▶

Mattel, Inc. Originators of "Bill and Hold" Toy with Accounting (continued)

Discussion Questions	■ What alternative audit procedures could the Andersen auditors perform when (or if) they found the inconsistencies in conformations and bills of lading? ■ Why do you think the staff auditor accepted the explanation of the $7 million discrepancy by the Mattel employee? ■ Why was it not followed up?

References	Knapp, M., 2001, "Mattel, Inc," *Contemporary Auditing Real Issues & Cases*, South Western College Publishing, Cincinnati, Ohio. pp. 3–14. SEC, 1981, *Accounting Series Release No. 292*, "SEC Charges Mattel, Inc. with Financial Fraud," US Securities and Exchange Commission, June 22.

Certification Exam Question 10.5[9]

Auditors try to identify predictable relationships when using analytical procedures. Relationships involving transactions from which of the following accounts most likely would yield the most predictable evidence?

(A) Accounts receivable.
(B) Interest expense.
(C) Accounts payable.
(D) Travel and entertainment expense.

10.5 Substantive Audit Procedures

Substantive procedures are tests performed to obtain audit evidence to detect material misstatements in the financial statements. Substantive procedures are responses to the auditor's assessment of the risk of material misstatement. The higher the assessed risk, the more likely the extent of the substantive procedures will increase and the timing of procedures will be performed close to the period.

"Irrespective of the assessed risk of material misstatement, the auditor should plan and perform substantive procedures for each material class of transactions, account balance and disclosure."[10] Furthermore, if the auditor has determined that an assessed risk of material misstatement at the assertion level is a significant risk, the auditor should perform substantive procedures that are specifically responsive to that risk. For example, if there is a significant risk that management is inflating revenue to meet earnings expectations the auditor may design external confirmations (discussed in the next section) not only to confirm outstanding amounts, but also to confirm the details of the sales agreements, and then follow up those confirmations with inquiries regarding any changes in sales agreements and delivery terms.

The nature of the test is of two types: tests of details of transactions and balances; and analytical procedures (See Chapter 9 Analytical Procedures for a discussion of the subject). Tests of transactions are audit procedures related to examining the processing of particular classes of transactions through the accounting system and are usually performed for accounts such as property and equipment, long-term debt, and equity accounts. An example of a test of transactions is the search for unrecorded liabilities. Tests of balances are audit tests that substantiate the ending balance of a general ledger account or line item in a financial statement.

Substantive procedures, like tests of control and other audit procedures, may be described by their nature, timing and extent.

■ Nature of Substantive Procedures

The nature of substantive procedures includes tests of details (of transactions and of balances) and substantive analytical procedures. The auditor's substantive procedures include agreeing the financial statements to the accounting records, examining material adjustments made during the course of preparing the financial statements, and other procedures relating to the financial reporting closing process. Substantive analytical procedures, discussed in Chapter 9 Analytical Procedures, are generally more applicable to large volumes of transactions that tend to be predictable over time. Tests of details are ordinarily more appropriate to obtain audit evidence regarding certain financial statement assertions, including existence and valuation.

Tests of Balances

Tests of balances are substantive tests that provide either reasonable assurance of the validity of a general ledger balance or identify a misstatement in the account. When testing balances the auditor is concerned with overstatement or understatement of the line item in the financial statement. These tests are used to examine the actual details making up high turnover accounts such as cash, accounts receivable, accounts payable, etc. Tests of balances are important because the auditor's ultimate objective is to express an opinion on financial statements that are made up of account balances. In audits of small businesses, auditors may rely exclusively on tests of balances.

Illustration – Test of Accounts Receivable Balance

A test of balance may be illustrated as follows. If accounts receivable total €1,500,000 at the end of the year, tests of details may be made of the individual components of the total account. Assume that the accounts receivable control account balance of €1,500,000 is the total of 300 individual customer accounts. As a test of balances, an auditor might decide to confirm a sample of these 300 accounts. Based on an analysis of internal controls, the auditor may decide that the proper sample size should be 100 accounts that should be tested by confirmation. Thus the auditor tests the detail supporting the account to determine if the line item "Accounts Receivable" is overstated – i.e. the existence of the accounts has been confirmed. As an additional test, the auditor may examine cash receipts received after year-end, testing for understatement, which provides evidence as to both the existence and measurement of the accounts.

Concept and a Company 10.2

Kmart Executives Manipulate the Contract Process

Concept	Side agreements that materially impact a company may be concealed.
Story	Kmart Corporation is a US discount retailer and a general merchandise retailer. The company operates in the general merchandise retailing industry through 1,829 Kmart discount stores with locations in all 50 states, Puerto Rico, the United States Virgin Islands and Guam. On January 22, 2002, Kmart and 37 of its US subsidiaries filed voluntary petitions for reorganization under Chapter 11 of the federal bankruptcy laws.

Just prior to the bankruptcy, two executives lied to Kmart accounting personnel and concealed a side letter relating to the $42 million payment from one of Kmart's vendors in order to improperly recognize the entire amount in the quarter ended August 1, 2001. Those deceptions caused Kmart to understate losses by the material amount of $0.06 per share, or 32 percent. (Merrick 2003)

The Securities and Exchange Commission (SEC 2003) filed civil charges against the two men responsible for this misstatement – Joseph A. Hofmeister and Enio A. Montini Jr. Montini and Hofmeister negotiated a five-year contract for which American Greetings paid Kmart an "allowance" of $42,350,000 on June 20, 2001. The contract was for, among other things, exclusive rights to sell their product – greetings cards – in Kmart stores. American Greetings was to take over the 847 stores that were formerly supplied by Hallmark, the major competitor of American Greetings, at a rate of $50,000 per store. Under the terms of its 1997 contract with Hallmark, Kmart was obligated to repay a portion of certain prepaid allowances and other costs, and accordingly Kmart paid Hallmark $27,298,210 on or about June 4, 2001.

Accounting Makes a Difference in Bonus

Kmart classified these vendor allowances as a reduction in cost of goods sold in its statement of operations. One of the primary measures of performance for Montini and Hofmeister was contribution to gross margin. Because vendor allowances were generally accounted for as a reduction of cost of goods sold, this could help the two make their gross margin numbers and their bonuses. Montini also received an additional $750,000 forgivable cash loan after the deal was closed.

Secret Negotiations

Montini and Hofmeister conducted their negotiations with American Greetings in secret, excluding from the process key finance and accounting personnel. Since the accounting people had been frozen out of the negotiations, they depended on the two men to give them the details. Montini assured the Finance Divisional VP that there were "no strings attached" to the $42 million. In fact, American Greetings had insisted that any and all up front monies be covered by a payback provision. American Greetings worried that, given Kmart's shaky financial condition, the retailer might not survive the contract term. (SEC 2003)

Montini had made two agreement letters with American Greetings. One agreement letter appeared to exclude the $42,350,000 from any repayment obligation. A second letter (the side letter) obligated Kmart to pay American Greetings "liquidated damages" for early termination of the agreement. Montini and Hofmeister provided a copy of the signed "No

Strings Attached" letter, but not the "Liquidated Damages" letter, to the Finance DVP and Internal Audit.

GAAP, as well as the company's own accounting policies and practices, required that the $42 million be recognized over the term of the agreement. Instead, Kmart improperly recognized the entire $42 million allowance during the quarter ended August 1, 2001; $27 million as an "offset" to the payment to Hallmark and $15 million in "incremental" merchandise allowances.

Discussion Questions	■ What procedures can Kmart's independent auditor use to uncover the side agreement?
	■ What circumstances should have alerted Kmart's management and internal auditors to possible problems?

References	Merrick, A., 2003, "Leading the News: U.S Indicts 2 Ex-Executives of Kmart Corp," *Wall Street Journal*, February 27.
	SEC, 2003, *Litigation Release No. 18000*, "SEC Charges Two Former Kmart Executives with $42 Million Accounting Fraud," US Securities and Exchange Commission, February 26.

Test of Accounts Receivable = Test of Revenue

From this example we can see an interesting aspect of a test of balances which is that the test makes use of the inherent properties of double-entry accounting systems. Accounting transactions involve a double entry. From the auditor's perspective, this means that a test of one side of the transaction simultaneously tests the other side of the transaction.

Consider a credit sales transaction:

Debit Accounts Receivable	€1,000	
Credit Revenue		€1,000

If an auditor tests the debit side, accounts receivable, for overstatement, the auditor has simultaneously tested the credit side, revenue, for overstatement. That means that testing one asset for overstatement simultaneously indirectly tests another item.

Direction of Testing

Testing for overstatement or understatement is called the direction of testing. By coordinating the direction of testing each account balance is simultaneously tested for both overstatement and understatement. For instance, if all liability, equity, and revenue balances are tested for understatement and all asset and expense accounts are tested for overstatement, then all account balances in the balance sheet and the income statement will be tested, either directly or indirectly, for both overstatement and understatement.

■ The Timing and Extent of Substantive Procedures

There are several considerations in determining the timing of substantive procedures. In some instances, primarily as a practical matter, substantive procedures may be performed at an interim date. Only using interim testing procedures will increases the risk that misstatements existing at the period end will not be detected. That risk increases the longer the time between interim and period end. "When substantive procedures are performed at an interim date, the auditor should perform further substantive procedures or

367

substantive procedures combined with tests of controls to cover the remaining period that provide a reasonable basis for extending the audit conclusions from the interim date to the period end."[11]

Performing audit procedures at an interim date may assist the auditor in identifying and resolving issues at an early stage of the audit. Ordinarily, the auditor compares and reconciles information concerning the account balances at the period end with the comparable information at the interim date to identify amounts that appear unusual, investigates any such amounts, and performs substantive analytical procedures or tests of details to test the intervening period.

Extent of Substantive Procedures

The greater the risk of material misstatement, the greater the **extent** of substantive procedures. In planning tests of details of transactions or balances, the extent of testing is ordinarily thought of in terms of the sample size,[12] which is affected by the risk of material misstatement. The use of *CAATs*[13] may enable more extensive testing of electronic transactions and files. For example, in performing audit procedures, such techniques may be used to test an entire population instead of a sample. Because the risk of material misstatement takes account of internal control, the extent of substantive procedures may be reduced if tests of control show that controls are adequate.

10.6 Audit Procedures for Obtaining Audit Evidence

The auditor performs risk assessment procedures in order to provide a basis for the assessment of risks (discussed in Chapter 6). Risk assessment procedures by themselves do not provide sufficient appropriate audit evidence on which to base the audit opinion, however. Risk assessment procedures must be supplemented by further audit procedures in the form of tests of controls and substantive procedures.

We discussed tests of controls in Chapter 7. Even if the auditor tests controls, there are inherent limitations to internal control including the risk of management override, the possibility of human error, and the effect of systems changes. Therefore, substantive procedures for material classes of transactions, account balances, and disclosures are always required to obtain sufficient appropriate audit evidence.

■ Evidence Gathering Techniques

An auditor obtains audit evidence by one or more of the following evidence gathering techniques:

- inquiry;
- observation;
- inspection (of tangible assets, records, or documents);
- recalculation;
- reperformance;
- confirmation;
- analytical procedures.

See Illustration 10.6 for a list, definition and examples of evidence-gathering techniques.

ILLUSTRATION 10.6

Audit Procedures (Evidence Gathering Techniques)

Technique	Definition	Examples
Inquiry	Consists of seeking information of knowledgeable persons inside or outside the entity.	Obtaining written or oral information from the client in response to specific questions during the audit.
Observation	Consists of looking at a process or procedure being performed by others.	Observation by the auditor of the counting of inventories by entity's personnel, site visit at the client's facilities.
Inspection	Consists of examining records, documents, or tangible assets.	Reviewing sales orders, sales invoices, shipping documents, bank statements, customer return documents, customer complaint letters, etc.
Recalculation	Consists of checking the arithmetical accuracy of source documents and accounting records or performing independent calculations.	Extending sales invoices and inventory, adding journals and subsidiary records, checking the calculation of depreciation expense and prepaid expense.
Reperformance	Consists of independent execution of procedures or controls that were originally performed as part of the entity's internal control.	Use CAATs to check controls recorded in the database. Reperform aging of accounts receivable.
Confirmation	Consists of response to an inquiry to corroborate information contained in the accounting records.	Used to confirm the existence of accounts receivable and accounts payable, verify bank balances with banks, cash surrender value of life insurance, notes payable with lenders or bondholders.
Analytical procedures	Consist of the analysis of significant ratios and trends including the resulting investigation of fluctuations and relationships that are inconsistent with other relevant information or that deviate from predictable amounts.	Calculating trends in sales over the past few years, comparing net profit as a percentage of sales in current year with the percentage of the preceding year, comparing client current ratio to the industry current ratio, and comparing budgets to actual results.

■ Inquiry

The most frequently used technique for evidence gathering is inquiry. **Inquiry** consists of seeking information of knowledgeable persons inside or outside the entity. Inquiry of the client is the obtaining of written or oral information from the client in response to specific questions during the audit. Inquiries may range from formal written inquiries, addressed to third parties, to informal oral inquiries, addressed to persons inside the entity. Responses to these inquiries provide the auditor with information not previously possessed.

Responses to inquiries may provide the auditor with information not previously possessed or with corroborative audit evidence. Alternatively, responses might provide information that differs significantly from other information that the auditor has obtained, for example, information regarding the possibility of management override of controls. In some cases, responses to inquiries provide a basis for the auditor to modify or perform additional audit procedures.

Corroboration

In a typical audit, the largest amount of audit evidence is obtained from client inquiry, but it cannot be regarded as conclusive because it is not from an independent source and might be biased in the client's favor. Therefore, the auditor must gather evidence to corroborate inquiry evidence by doing other alternative procedures. For example, the auditor generally makes inquiries about internal control, accounting entries, and procedures. Later, for corroboration, the auditor may observe the control procedures (observation) or review related documentation (inspection).

Corroborative evidence for inquiry evidence is very important. In a famous US court case, *Escott et al.* v *Bar Chris Corporation* (1968), the court ruled against the auditor because he did not follow up on management answers to inquiries. The court opinion said in part:

> Most important of all, he (the auditor) was too easily satisfied with glib answers (by management) to his inquiries. This is not to say that he should have made a complete audit. But there were enough danger signals in the materials which he did examine to require some further investigation on his part ... It is not always sufficient merely to ask questions. [14]

■ Observation

Observation consists of looking at a process or procedure being performed by others, for example, the observation by the auditor of the counting of inventories by the entity's personnel or observation of internal control procedures that leave no audit trail. Observation provides audit evidence about the performance of a process or procedure, but is limited to the point in time at which the observation takes place and by the fact that the act of being observed may affect how the process or procedure is performed.

Observation is mostly visual, but also involves all the other senses. Hearing, touch, and smell may also be used in gathering evidence. For example, it is typical for the auditor to do a site visit at the client's facilities. On site visits the auditor can get an idea of the implementation of internal controls, notice what equipment is utilized and what equipment may be collecting dust – or rusting. An auditor with a good knowledge of the industry can tell what equipment and methods are obsolete by observing.

Sufficient evidence is rarely obtained through observation alone. Observation techniques should be followed up by other types of evidence gathering procedures. For example, observation evidence such as a quick visual inspection of a printing press may be corroborated by either a thorough and detailed inspection of the printing press by a mechanic or specialist, or inspection of documents and records relating to the equipment, both of which are evidence gathered by inspection techniques.

Observation of Physical Inventory Procedures

A good example of an observation audit procedure is count of physical inventory. ISA 501 discusses the inspection evidence gathering technique for physical inventory counting. It states: "When inventory is material to the financial statements, the auditor should obtain sufficient appropriate audit evidence regarding its existence and condition by attendance at physical inventory counting." [15]

The attendance by the auditor will enable him to inspect the inventory, to observe compliance with the operation of management's procedures for recording and controlling the results of the count, and to provide evidence as to the reliability of management's procedures.

Alternative Inventory Procedures

If unable to attend the physical inventory count on the date planned due to unforeseen circumstances, the auditor should take or observe some physical counts on an alternative date and, when necessary, perform tests of controls of intervening transactions. Where attendance is impractical, due to factors such as the nature and location of the inventory, the auditor should consider whether alternative procedures provide sufficient appropriate audit evidence of existence and condition to conclude that he need not make reference to a scope limitation. For example, documentation of the subsequent sale of specific inventory items acquired or purchased prior to the physical inventory count may provide sufficient evidence.

Planning Attendance at Inventory Count

In planning attendance at the physical inventory count or the alternative procedures, the auditor would consider:

- the nature of the accounting and internal control systems used regarding inventory;
- inherent, control and detection risks, and materiality related to inventory;
- whether adequate procedures are expected to be established and proper instructions issued for physical inventory counting;
- the timing of the count;
- the locations at which inventory is held; (When inventory is located at several locations, the auditor should determine at which locations attendance is appropriate, taking into account the materiality of the inventory and the assessment of inherent and control risk at different locations.)
- whether an expert's assistance is needed.

The auditor would review management's instructions regarding:

- the application of control procedures (e.g. collection of used stock sheets, accounting for unissued stock sheets and count and re-count procedures);

- accurate identification of the stage of completion of work in progress, of slow-moving, obsolete, or damaged items and items on **consignment;**[16]
- whether appropriate arrangements are made regarding the movement of inventory between areas and the shipping and receipt of inventory before and after the cutoff date.

Inventory Procedures in Addition to Observation

Inventory counts involve other procedures in addition to observing the inventory take. The auditor will perform test counts. When performing counts, he would test both the completeness and the accuracy of the count records by tracing items selected from those records to the physical inventory and items selected from the physical inventory to the count records. The auditor would also review cutoff procedures including details of the movement of inventory just prior to, during, and after the count so that the accounting for such movements can be checked at a later date. The auditor would test the final inventory listing to assess whether it accurately reflects actual inventory counts. When there is a perpetual inventory system and it is used to determine the period end balance, the auditor would assess the reasons for any significant differences between the physical count and the perpetual inventory records.

Inventory Not on Company Premises

When inventory is under the custody and control of a third party, or consignee, the auditor would ordinarily obtain direct confirmation from the third party as to the quantities and condition of inventory held on behalf of the entity. Depending on how material the inventory is the entity's operations, the auditor may also consider:

- the integrity and independence of the third party;
- observing, or arranging for another auditor to observe, the physical inventory count;
- obtaining another auditor's report on the adequacy of the third party's accounting and internal control systems for ensuring that inventory is correctly counted and adequately safeguarded;
- inspecting documentation regarding inventory held by third parties, for example, warehouse receipts, or obtaining confirmation from other parties when such inventory has been pledged as collateral.

■ Inspection (of Tangible Assets, Records or Documents)

Inspection consists of examining records, documents or tangible assets. Inspection is the auditor's examination of the client's documents and records to substantiate the information that is or should be included in the financial statements. Examples of evidence gathering by inspection techniques is the review by an auditor of sales orders, sales invoices, shipping documents, bank statements, customer return documents, customer complaint letters, etc. Other examples are the conduct of a thorough mechanical inspection of cash registers and point-of-sales devices and review of electronic records via CAATs.

Inspection of tangible assets consists of physical examination of the assets. Inspection of tangible assets may provide reliable audit evidence with respect to their existence, but not necessarily as to the entity's rights and obligations or the valuation of the assets.

Inspection of individual inventory items ordinarily accompanies the observation of inventory counting.

Inspection of Documents

Inspection of records and documents provides audit evidence of varying degrees of reliability depending on their nature, source, and the effectiveness of internal controls over their processing:

- The nature of documents include quantity of information contained, the difficulty of access to them, and who has custody.
- The source of the documents may be from inside or outside the firm.
- The source outside the firm may or may not be independent of the client.
- The source may be competent or incompetent.
- The controls over the recording process may be effective or ineffective.

Some documents represent direct audit evidence of the existence of an asset, for example, a document constituting a financial instrument such as a stock or bond. Very importantly, inspecting an executed contract may provide audit evidence relevant to the entity's application of accounting principles, such as revenue recognition.

External and Internal Documents

A document's source may be internal or external to the organization. An internal document is one that has been prepared and used within the client's organization and is retained without ever going to an outside party. An external document is one that has been in the hands of someone outside the client's organization who is a party to the transaction being documented. External documents may originate outside the entity and end up in their hands such as insurance policies, vendor's invoices (bills), bank statements, and cancelled notes payable. Other external documents originate inside the entity, go to a third party and are then returned to the entity. Cancelled cheques are an example of client to third party and then to client documents.

Internal documents are less reliable than external documents. Internal documents processed under good internal controls are more reliable than those processed under weak controls. External documents may be processed by both internal and external parties and, therefore, represent agreement over information contained in the document. Some external documents such as title papers to property, insurance policies, and contracts are very reliable evidence because they are prepared with considerable care and probably have been reviewed by lawyers.

Vouching

The use of documentation to support recorded transactions or amounts is called "vouching." **Vouching** is an audit process whereby the auditor selects sample items from an account and goes backwards through the accounting system to find the source documentation that supports the item selected (e.g. a sales invoice). For example, to vouch the existence of recorded acquisition transactions, the audit procedure would be to trace from the acquisitions journal to supporting vendor's invoices, cancelled checks or receiving reports.

■ Recalculation and Reperformance

Recalculation consists of checking the arithmetical accuracy of source documents and accounting records or of performing independent calculations. Some common recalculation audit procedures are extending sales invoices and inventory, adding journals and subsidiary records, and checking the calculation of depreciation expense and prepaid expense. Audit procedures to check the mechanical accuracy of recording include reviews to determine if the same information is entered correctly in point-of-sales records, receiving reports, journals, subsidiary ledgers and summarized in the general ledger. Computation evidence is relatively reliable because the auditor performs it. Recalculation may be performed through the use of CAATs, for instance to check the accuracy of totals in a file.

Certification Exam Question 10.6[17]

When control risk is assessed as low for assertions related to payroll, substantive tests of payroll balances most likely would be limited to applying analytical procedures and:

(A) Observing the distribution of paychecks.
(B) Footing and cross-footing the payroll register.
(C) Inspecting payroll tax returns.
(D) Recalculating payroll accruals.

Reperformance is the auditor's independent execution of procedures or controls that were originally performed as part of the entity's internal control, either manually or through the use of CAATs, for example, reperforming the aging of accounts receivable.

■ Confirmation

Confirmation consists of the response to an inquiry of a third party to corroborate information contained in the accounting records. For example, the auditor ordinarily seeks direct confirmation of receivables by communication with debtors. Confirmation is the auditor's receipt of a written or oral response from an independent third party verifying the accuracy of information requested. It is the act of obtaining audit evidence from a third party in support of a fact or condition. Illustration 10.7 gives a summary of the characteristics of confirmation as an evidence-gathering technique.

Confirmation procedures are typically used to confirm the existence of accounts receivable and accounts payable, but they may be used to confirm existence, quantity and condition of inventory held by third parties (e.g. public warehouse consignee) on behalf of the entity. They may be used to verify bank balances with banks; cash surrender value of life insurance or insurance coverage with insurers; notes payable with lenders or bondholders; shares outstanding with stock transfer agents; liabilities with creditors; and contracts terms with customers, suppliers, and creditors.

Because confirmations from independent third parties are usually in writing, and are requested directly by the auditor, they are highly persuasive evidence. The main disadvantage of confirmations is that they are costly, time-consuming, and an inconvenience to those asked to supply them.

ILLUSTRATION 10.7

Confirmation

Confirmation is the auditor's receipt of a written or oral response from an independent third party verifying the accuracy or information requested.

Advantage: Highly persuasive evidence.

Disadvantage: Costly and time-consuming and an inconvenience to those asked to supply them.

Four key characteristics of confirmations
1 Information requested is by the client auditor.
2 Request and response is in writing, sent to the auditor.
3 Response comes from an independent third party.
4 Positive confirmation involves a receipt of information.

Two types of positive confirmations
1 Positive confirmation with the request for information to be supplied by the recipient.
2 Positive confirmation with the information to be confirmed included on the form.

Certification Exam Question 10.7

Which of the following strategies most likely could improve the response rate of the confirmation of accounts receivable?

(A) Including a list of items or invoices that constitute the account balance.
(B) Restricting the selection of accounts to be confirmed to those customers with relatively large balances.
(C) Requesting customers to respond to the confirmation requests directly to the auditor by fax or e-mail.
(D) Notifying the recipients that second requests will be mailed if they fail to respond in a timely manner.

Confirmation of Management Assertions

As we discussed earlier in this chapter, audit evidence is collected to verify management assertions. External confirmation of an account receivable provides strong evidence regarding the existence of the account as at a certain date. Confirmation also provides evidence regarding the operation of cutoff procedures. Similarly, in the case of goods held on consignment, external confirmation is likely to provide strong evidence to support the existence and the rights and obligations assertions. When auditing the completeness assertion for accounts payable, the auditor needs to obtain evidence that there is no material unrecorded liability. Therefore, sending confirmation requests to an entity's principal suppliers asking them to provide copies of their statements of account directly to the auditor, even if the records show no amount currently owing to them, will usually be effective in detecting unrecorded liabilities.

Concept and a Company 10.3

Parmalat – Milk Spills After Sour Confirmation

Concept	Importance of confirmations. Responsibility of primary auditor.
Story	Parmalat Finanziaria SpA is a Parma, Italy-based company, whose main operating subsidiary, Parmalat SpA sells dairy products around the world, employs 36,000 people, and has world-wide operations in 30 countries, including the USA. It was Italy's biggest food maker and Italy's eighth largest industrial group with market capitalization of €1.8 billion. On December 24, 2003, Parmalat SpA filed for bankruptcy protection with a court in Parma, Italy, and on December 27, 2003, the court declared Parmalat SpA insolvent. (SEC 2003)

The problems at Parmalat first became apparent in mid-December 2003 when Parmalat failed to meet a €150 million ($184 million) payment to bondholders. This seemed odd because the company showed €4.2 billion in cash on their September 30 balance sheet. Parmalat had raised $8 billion in bonds between 1993 and 2003. Why did they need to keep raising money with their mountain of cash? Their standard reply was that the company was on an acquisition spree and needed cash – and the liquid funds were earning good returns. (Edmonson and Cohen 2004) Now the reckoning had come.

The following week in December, Parmalat executives admitted to their auditor Deloitte that they could not liquidate the €515 million Parmalat claimed it held in Epicurum, a Cayman Islands fund. When Enrico Bondi, an advisor, suggested liquidating the €3.95 billion held by a Cayman Islands subsidiary called Bonlat, the rabbit popped out of the hat. Italian prosecutors say that they discovered that managers simply invented assets to offset as much as €13 billion in liabilities and falsified accounts over a 15-year period. (Edmonson and Cohen 2004)

Bonlat

Parmalat purportedly held the €3.95 billion worth of cash and marketable securities in an account at Bank of America in New York City in the name of Bonlat Financing Corporation ("Bonlat"), a wholly-owned subsidiary incorporated in the Cayman Islands. Bonlat's auditors certified its 2002 financial statements based upon a confirmation that Bonlat held these assets at Bank of America. (SEC 2003)

Confirmation Letter

Grant Thornton, auditor for the Bonlat subsidiary, sent a letter to confirm the balance in the Bonlat account to Bank of America in December 2002. On March 6, 2003, three months later, the auditors received a letter on Bank of America stationary and signed by a senior officer confirming the existence of the account with a balance of €3.95 billion. The letter was mailed, not faxed, to Grant Thornton's offices in Milan. (Rigby and Michaels 2003)

Bank of America Says Letter is a Forgery

On December 19, 2003 the letter certifying that Bank of America held €3.95 billion for Parmalat's offshore unit Bonlat was declared false by the bank in a statement to the US SEC and in a press release. The bank account and the assets did not exist and the purported confirmation had been forged. Agnes Belgrave, the signatory of the letter who worked in Bank of America's Manhattan offices, denied any involvement in Parmalat's affairs. (Betts and Barber 2004) Although documents concerning the Cayman Island subsidiary had been destroyed, Italian prosecutors found documents and a scanning machine used to forge the bank documents on Bank of America letterhead at DPA, a shell company near Parma.

Parmalat CEO Calisto Tanzi flew out of Italy the day Bank of America announced that the letter showing €3.95 billion was false. He went to Switzerland then Portugal, then an undisclosed country in central or south America, and finally back to Milan where he was detained by police. (Barber 2003)

The Auditors

In 1999, Parmalat was forced to change its auditor under Italian law, and it replaced Grant Thornton with the Italian unit of Deloitte Touche Tohmatsu. However, Grant Thornton's Italian arm continued to audit at least 20 of Parmalat's units, including Bonlat. Deloitte became increasingly reliant on Grant Thornton for scrutiny of Parmalat's accounts. During its work on the 1999 accounts, other auditors had examined subsidiaries representing 22 percent of Parmalat's consolidated assets. On the 2002 accounts, Deloitte said other auditors examined subsidiaries representing 49 percent of consolidated assets. (Parker and Betts 2004)

A suit filed by US shareholders contends that both Deloitte and Grant Thornton issued materially false reports on Parmalat's 1998–2002 year-end financial statements. Deloitte, which took over as Parmalat's primary auditor, deliberately failed to verify reports from Grant Thornton on assets held by a Parmalat subsidiary. The suit also asserts that on at least eight occasions, Grant Thornton failed to send third-party confirmation request letters in connection with its audits of Parmalat's subsidiaries. Further, it asserts, the firm failed to conduct independent audits on the 17 Parmalat subsidiaries that it was engaged to audit from 1999 to 2003, but rather participated in the falsification of audit confirmation documents. (*International Herald Tribune* 2004)

Italian authorities arrested Lorenzo Penca, chairman of Grant Thornton SpA and Maurizio Bianchi, a partner in the firm's Milan office, on charges that their actions contributed to Parmalat's bankruptcy. They claimed that two men suggested ways that Parmalat executives could "falsify the balance sheet" of a subsidiary and then "falsely certified" the financial statements. (Galloni *et al.* 2004) Prosecutors in Italy have said Penca and Bianchi were behind the plan to create Bonlat and they failed to disclose details of two other offshore Parmalat vehicles in the Netherlands Antilles, according to court documents. (US District Court, Southern New York, 2003)

Discussion Questions	■ What audit procedures should auditors use in confirming a very material cash balance?
	■ If a primary auditor is significantly dependent on the work of another auditor, what reviews and substantive tests should they conduct?

References

Barber, T., 2003, "Tanzi takes a mystery tour amid the Parmalat mayhem," *Financial Times*, December 30, p. 12.

Betts, P. and Barber, T., 2004, "Parmalat probe uncovers fresh evidence," *Financial Times*, January 2, p. 1.

Edmonson, G. and Cohn, L., 2004, "How Parmalat Went Sour," *Business Week*, January 12, pp. 46–48.

Galloni, A., Bryan-Low, C., and Ascarelli, S., 2004, "Top Executives Are Arrested at Parmalat Auditor," *Wall Street Journal*, January 2, A3.

International Herald Tribune, 2004, "Investors file lawsuit in Parmalat inquiry Officials, auditors and lawyers named," January 7.

Parker, A., Tessell, T., and Betts, P., 2004, "Auditors come under growing scrutiny," *Financial Times*, January 3, p. 9.

Rigby, E. and Michaels, A., 2003, "Parmalat's auditor 'a victim of fraud'," *Financial Times*, December 27, p. 8.

SEC, 2003, *Litigation Release No. 18527, Accounting and Auditing Enforcement Release No. 1936*, "SEC Charges Parmalat with Financial Fraud," US. Securities and Exchange Commission, December 30.

US District Court for the Southern District of New York, 2003, 03CU10266 (CPKC). *Securities and Exchange Commission* v *Parmalat Finanziaria, SpA*, December 29.

Confirmation in Response to a Significant Risk

An auditor may use a confirmation in response to a significant risk. For example, if the auditor determines that management is under pressure to meet earnings expectations, there may be a related risk that management is inflating sales by entering into sales agreements that include terms that preclude revenue recognition or by invoicing sales before delivery. In these circumstances, the auditor may design external confirmations not only to confirm outstanding amounts, but also to confirm the details of the sales agreements, including date, any rights of return and delivery terms.

Confirmation of Accounts Receivable

The confirmation of accounts receivable is typical of the confirmation process. First the auditor looks through accounts receivable subsidiary ledgers and picks out some customers based on his professional judgment. The auditor may take a random sample or list customers with very large balances or very small balances, customers that are slow in paying, and/or customers that buy erratically. The auditor then gives this list to the client to prepare a confirmation letter requesting that customers reply directly to the auditor. Then the auditor, not the client, mails these letters. The auditor should check randomly to see if the letters are addressed to the same customers the auditor chose and for the amounts shown on the books.

Positive and Negative Confirmations

ISA 505 identifies two forms of confirmations: positive and negative confirmation.[18] The request for **positive confirmation** asks the recipient (debtor, creditor, or other third party) to confirm agreement or by asking the respondent to fill in information. A response to a positive confirmation request is expected to provide reliable audit evidence. The auditor may reduce the risk that a respondent replies to the request without verifying the information by using positive confirmation requests that do not state the amount (or other information) on the confirmation request, but asks the respondent to fill in the amount. However, using this type of "blank" confirmation request may result in lower response rates because additional effort is required of the respondents. The positive form is preferred when inherent or control risk is assessed as high because with the negative form no reply may be due to causes other than agreement with the recorded balance.

A **negative confirmation** request asks the respondent to reply only in the event of disagreement with the information provided in the request. However, if there is no response to a negative confirmation request, the auditor cannot be sure that intended third parties have received the confirmation requests and verified that the information contained therein is correct. For this reason, negative confirmation requests ordinarily provides less reliable evidence than the use of positive confirmation requests, and the auditor may consider performing other substantive procedures to supplement the use of negative confirmations.

Negative confirmation requests may be used to reduce audit risk to an acceptable level when:[19]

- the assessed level of inherent and control risk is low;
- a large number of small balances is involved;
- a substantial number of errors is not expected;
- the auditor has no reason to believe that respondents will disregard these requests.

No Response to Confirmation Letter

In case the auditor does not receive a reply to a confirmation request, he sends out a second confirmation letter. Regarding those customers who did not reply to the two positive external confirmation requests the auditor should perform alternative procedures. The alternative audit procedures should be such as to provide the evidence about the financial statement assertions that the confirmation request was intended to provide.[20] In a negative form of confirmation letters the reply is requested only in the event of disagreement with the recorded balance or information.

If Audit Client Does Not Allow Confirmations

When the auditor seeks to confirm certain balances or other information, and management requests him not to do so, he should consider whether there are valid grounds for management's requests and if there is evidence to support the validity of the request. If the auditor agrees to management's request not to seek external confirmation regarding a particular matter, the auditor should apply alternative procedures to obtain sufficient appropriate evidence regarding that matter.[21] If the auditor does not accept the validity of management's request and is prevented from carrying out the confirmations, there has been a **limitation on the scope**[22] of the auditor's work and he should consider the impact of this limitation on the auditor's report.

■ Analytical Procedures: Search for Unrecorded Liabilities

A substantive test usually performed on accounts payable is a search for unrecorded liabilities. This test may be part of the closing procedures or done in concert with the confirmation of accounts payable. This test provides evidence as to completeness and some evidence as to valuation.

To search for unrecorded liabilities, the auditor reviews disbursements made by the client for a period after the balance sheet date, sometimes to the date of the completion of field work. Even though a client may not record accounts payable at year-end, vendors will probably pressure the client to pay the accounts payable within a reasonable period of time. Due to this pressure, most unrecorded accounts payable are paid within a reasonable time after the balance sheet date. By reviewing cash disbursements subsequent to the balance sheet date, the auditor has a good idea of the potential population of unrecorded accounts payable.

Procedures to find unrecorded liabilities start with a review of the cash disbursements journal for the period after the balance sheet date. The auditor then vouches a sample of invoices to determine to which period the payment relates. For example, vouching a January electricity payment to an unaccounted December bill will indicate that the payment relates to the period of December, prior to year-end. This would result in an unrecorded liability for which the auditor may propose an adjusting entry, if it is material.

Reliability and Cost of Substantive Audit Procedures

The most reliable evidence gathering techniques (audit procedures) should be used whenever they are cost effective. The quality of internal controls has a significant effect on reliability. Further more, a specific substantive audit procedure is rarely sufficient by itself to provide competent evidence to satisfy the audit objective. However, assuming good internal controls and the ability to choose a specific method, a list of the most reliable to the least reliable evidence-gathering techniques are in general:

- recalculation,
- inspection,
- reperformance,
- observation,
- confirmation,
- analytical procedures,
- inquiry.

The most expensive evidence gathering techniques are confirmation and inspection. Confirmation is costly because of the time and outlay required in preparation, mailing, receipt, and follow-up. Inspection procedures that require the presence of both the client and auditors, such as an inventory count, are very expensive. Confirmation of documents is moderately expensive if clients are organized and have documents easily available. The three least expensive evidence-gathering procedures are observation, analytical procedures, and inquiries. Observation is normally done concurrently with other audit procedures.

The evidence-gathering procedures in order of cost from most costly to least costly are in general:

- confirmation (most costly),
- inspection,
- recalculation,
- reperformance,
- observation,
- analytical procedures,
- inquiry (least costly).

10.7 Summary

Auditing is a systematic process of objectively obtaining and evaluating evidence regarding assertions about economic actions and events. The auditor should obtain sufficient appropriate audit evidence to be able to draw reasonable conclusions on which to base the audit opinion. Evidence is anything that can make a person believe that a fact, proposition, or assertion is true or false. Audit evidence is different from the legal evidence required by forensic accounting. In a civil lawsuit, evidence must be strong enough to incline a person to believe one side or the other. In a criminal case; evidence must establish proof of a crime beyond a reasonable doubt. Audit evidence provides only reasonable assurance.

The systematic process of gathering evidence starts with evaluating the client and culminates in the use of substantive procedures. Substantive procedures are tests performed to obtain audit evidence to detect material misstatements in the financial statements, and are of two types: tests of details of transactions and balances, and analytical procedures. This chapter provides guidance on the basis of evidence (standards of proof and documentation and financial statement assertions), what constitutes sufficient appropriate audit evidence (the quantity and quality of audit evidence) and the substantive audit procedures that auditors use for obtaining that audit evidence.

Evidence in the legal environment may be classified according to its proof results (direct or circumstantial) or according to its source (documentary, real, or testimonial). The results of the evidence may either directly or circumstantially support a standard of proof. Documentary evidence is gathered from written, printed, or electronic sources. Documentary evidence consists of computer files and records, e-mail, accounting records, paper (invoices, writings, pictures), documents (contracts, deed, reports), commercial records (e.g. from banks, brokerage, retailers, credit card) and government records (licenses, real estate, legal).

Management implicitly makes assertions that can be grouped into three substantive testing areas: classes of transactions and events, account balances at the period end, and disclosures. The standard assertions are completeness, occurrence, accuracy, rights and obligations, valuation, and existence. Other assertions are: cutoff, classification, understandability, presentation and disclosure, and measurement. The auditor assesses risks of potential misstatements based on these assertions and designs audit procedures to discover sufficient appropriate evidence.

The auditor should conclude whether sufficient appropriate audit evidence has been obtained to reduce to an acceptably low level the risk of material misstatement in the financial statements. Sufficiency is the measure of the quantity (amount) of audit evidence. Appropriateness is the measure of the quality of audit evidence; that is, its relevance and its reliability in providing support for, or detecting misstatements in, the classes of transactions, account balances, and disclosures and related assertions. Reliability is the quality of information when it is free from material error and bias and can be depended upon by users to represent faithfully that which it either purports to represent or could reasonably be expected to represent. Relevance of evidence is the appropriateness (pertinence) of the evidence to the audit objective being tested.

Substantive procedures are tests performed to obtain audit evidence to detect material misstatements in the financial statements. The nature of the test is of two types: tests of details of transactions and balances, and analytical procedures. Tests of transactions are audit procedures related to examining the processing of particular classes of transactions through the accounting system and are usually performed for accounts such as property and equipment, long-term debt and equity accounts. Tests of balances are audit tests that substantiate the ending balance of a general ledger account or line item in a financial statement.

Substantive procedures may be described by their nature, timing, and extent. The nature of substantive procedures includes tests of details (of transactions and of balances) and substantive analytical procedures. Tests of balances are substantive tests that provide either reasonable assurance of the validity of a general ledger balance or identify a misstatement in the account. There are several considerations in determining the timing of substantive procedures. When substantive procedures are performed at an interim date, the auditor should perform further substantive procedures or substantive procedures to cover the remaining period. In planning tests of details of transactions or balances, the extent of testing is ordinarily thought of in terms of the sample size, which is affected by the risk of material misstatement.

An auditor obtains audit evidence by one or more of the following evidence gathering techniques: inquiry, observation, inspection (of tangible assets, records or documents), reperformance, recalculation, confirmation, and analytical procedures. Inquiry consists of seeking information from knowledgeable persons inside or outside the entity. Observation consists of looking at a process or procedure being performed by others. Inspection consists of examining records, documents or tangible assets. Reperformance is the auditor's independent execution of procedures or controls that were originally performed as part of the entity's internal control. Recalculation consists of checking the arithmetical accuracy of source documents and accounting records or of performing independent calculations. Confirmation consists of the response to an inquiry to corroborate information contained in the accounting records. There are two forms of confirmations: positive and negative.

Three substantive tests usually performed are observation of inventory, confirmation of accounts receivable, and search for unrecorded liabilities. When inventory is material to the financial statements, the auditor should obtain sufficient appropriate audit evidence regarding its existence and condition by attendance at physical inventory counting. Confirmation of accounts receivable provides evidence of the existence of revenue and current assets. The search for unrecorded liabilities provides evidence as to completeness and some evidence as to valuation and may be part of the closing procedures or in concert with the confirmation of accounts payable.

10.8 Answers to Certification Exam Questions

10.1 (C) The requirement is to state the objective of tests of details of classes of transactions. Choice (C) is the one because substantive procedures are performed in order to detect material misstatements at the assertion level, and include tests of details of classes of transactions, account balances, and disclosures and substantive analytical procedures (ISA 330, para. 48). Choice (A) is incorrect because there is no compliance with IFRS for transactions. IFRS has to do with accounting methods and disclosure. Choices (B) and (D) are incorrect. Attaining assurance about the reliability of the information system relevant to financial reporting and valuation of operating effectiveness of management controls involve assessing control risk, which is an objective of tests of controls, not substantive tests.

10.2 (A) The question asks what financial statement assertion pertains to the procedure of making inquiries about slow-moving or obsolete inventory. Answer (A) is the choice because an audit objective for inventory valuation is to determine that slow-moving, excess, defective and obsolete items included in inventory are properly identified. These determinations show if inventory is included in the financial statements at appropriate amounts and any resulting valuation adjustments are appropriately recorded. Answer (B) is not correct. Assertions about rights and obligations deal with whether the entity holds or controls the rights to assets like inventory and whether liabilities are the obligations of the entity. Choice (C) is wrong. Assertions about existence deal with whether assets, liabilities, and equity interests exist Answer (D) is incorrect. Assertions about completeness deal with whether all assets, liabilities, and equity interests that should have been recorded have been recorded.

10.3 (A) The question is concerned with what assertion fits the audit procedure of recomputing amortization for intangible assets. Choice (A) is right because the assertion about valuation is that amortization is included in the financial statements at appropriate amounts and any resulting valuation adjustments to intangible assets are appropriately recorded. Recalculation of the amortization and review of the amortization period would test the valuation assertion. Choice (B) is incorrect. Assertions about existence deal with whether assets, liabilities, and equity interests exist, which is not directly related to amortization. Choice (C) does not hold true. An assertion about cutoff is concerned with whether transactions and events have been recorded in the correct accounting period. Choice (D) is incorrect. Assertions about classification show whether transactions and events have been recorded in the proper accounts.

10.4 (C) The requirement is to determine what assertion fits the procedure of cutoff tests of direct purchases at year-end. Answer (C) is right because the auditor uses cutoff test to determine that inventory quantities include all products, materials, and supplies owned by the company. This provides assurance about the completeness assertion. Answer (A) is off the mark because assertions about valuation show whether assets, liabilities, and equity interests are included in the financial statements at appropriate amounts and any resulting valuation adjustments are appropriately recorded. Cutoff tests do not provide evidence related to the valuation assertion for purchases. Answer (B) is incorrect. Assertions about occurrence deal with whether transactions and events that have been recorded have occurred and pertain to the entity. Answer (D) is not an option because an assertion about classification and understandability holds that financial information is appropriately presented and described, and disclosures are clearly expressed.

10.5 (B) The requirement is to find analysis of which account would yield the most predictable evidence. Answer (B) is the best choice because interest expense should be predicted from knowing the interest rate and amount of debt or reading loan contracts. Answer (A) is not good because credit (which may allow prediction of accounts receivable) and cash sales are rarely reported separately. Furthermore, a company may have collection experience that varies from period to period. Similarly, an accounts payable balance (answer (C)) may vary across periods and depends on ability to pay, discounts offered, and other circumstances that may vary. Travel and entertainment expenses are related to budget, distribution network, product growth and management discretion, which will tend to make the expense unpredictable.

10.6 (D) The requirement is to determine what substantive procedure, along with analytical review, would be used to test payroll balances considering that control risk is low. Choice (D) is correct because if the control risk is assessed as low, less substantive testing is necessary. If control risk is low, substantive testing would normally be limited to analytical procedures and recalculating year-end accruals. Choice (A) is a no-go because observing distribution of paychecks is typically performed only when control risk is assessed as high. Choice (B) is not correct. Although footing and crossfooting the payroll register is an important substantive test, it is of limited effectiveness. Even if control risk is assessed as low, more effective substantive procedures should be performed. Choice (C) misses the mark because inspection of payroll tax returns would be performed only when control risk is assessed as high.

10.7 (A) One must determine what strategy would improve the response rate in a confirmation of accounts receivable. Answer (A) is the best answer in light of the fact that many accounting systems facilitate the confirmation of single transactions rather than entire balances. In such cases, inclusion of statements of account showing details of the balances being confirmed makes it easier for the customers, and are likely to improve the overall response rate. Answer (B) is incorrect because selecting only accounts for confirmation that have large balances would not necessarily improve the response rate. Answer (C) is a no-go because requesting electronic responses would not necessarily improve the response rate and some clients may not be able to do that. Answer (D) is incorrect. Why should the customer respond sooner when the consequence of not responding (receiving a second request) is no big deal?

10.9 Notes

1 IFAC, 2004, *Handbook of International Auditing, Assurance, and Ethics Pronouncements,* International Standard on Auditing 500 (ISA 500), "Audit Evidence," para. 2, International Federation of Accountants, New York.

2 IFAC, 2004, *Handbook of International Auditing, Assurance, and Ethics Pronouncements*, International Standard on Auditing 500R (ISA 500), "Audit Evidence," International Federation of Accountants, New York, February.

3 Adapted and reprinted with permission from AICPA. Copyright © 2000 & 1985 by American Institute of Certified Public Accountants.

4 A US court decision (*US* v *Sunderland*).

5 Adapted and reprinted with permission from AICPA. Copyright © 2000 & 1985 by American Institute of Certified Public Accountants.

6 IFAC, 2004, *Handbook of International Auditing, Assurance, and Ethics Pronouncements*, International Standard on Auditing 330 (ISA 330), "The Auditor's Procedures In Response to Assessed Risks," para. 70, International Federation of Accountants, New York.

7 IFAC, 2004, *Handbook of International Auditing, Assurance, and Ethics Pronouncements*, International Standard on Auditing 500A (ISA 500), "Audit Evidence," Para. 7.

8 See note 5. Para. 71.

9 Adapted and reprinted with permission from AICPA. Copyright © 2000 & 1985 by American Institute of Certified Public Accountants.

10 See note 5. Para. 49.

11 See note 5. Para. 56.

12 *Audit sampling* (sampling) involves the application of audit procedures to less than 100 percent of items within an account balance or class of transactions such that all sampling units have a chance of selection. This will enable the auditor to obtain and evaluate audit evidence about some characteristic of the items selected in order to form or assist in forming a conclusion concerning the population from which the sample is drawn. Audit sampling can use either a statistical or a nonstatistical approach.

13 *Computer-assisted audit techniques* – applications of auditing procedures using the computer as an audit tool are known as computer assisted audit techniques (CAATs).

14 Arens, A.A. and Loebbecke, J.K., 2000, *Auditing: An Integrated Approach*, Prentice Hall, New Jersey, p. 122.

15 IFAC, 2003, *Handbook of International Auditing, Assurance, and Ethics Pronouncements*, International Standard on Auditing (ISA) 501, "Audit Evidence – Additional Considerations for Specific Items", para. 5, International Federation of Accountants, New York.

16 *Consignment* is a specialized way of marketing certain types of goods. The consignor delivers goods to the consignee who acts as the consignor's agent in selling the merchandise to a third party. The consignee accepts the goods without any liability except to reasonably protect them from damage. The consignee receives a commission when the merchandise is sold. Goods on consignment are included in the consignor's inventory and excluded from the consignee's inventory since the consignor has legal title.

17 Adapted and reprinted with permission from AICPA. Copyright © 2000 & 1985 by American Institute of Certified Public Accountants.

18 IFAC, 2003, *Handbook of International Auditing, Assurance, and Ethics Pronouncements*, International Standard on Auditing (ISA) 505, "External Confirmations," paras. 20–24, International Federation of Accountants, New York.

19 Ibid. Para. 23.

20 Ibid. Para. 31.

21 Ibid. Para. 25.

22 *Limitation on scope* – a limitation on the scope of the auditor's work may sometimes be imposed by the entity (e.g. when the terms of the engagement specify that the auditor will not carry out an audit procedure that the auditor believes is necessary). A scope limitation may be imposed by circumstances (e.g. when the timing of the auditor's appointment is such that the auditor is unable to observe the counting of physical inventories). It may also arise when, in the opinion of the auditor, the entity's accounting records are inadequate or when the auditor is unable to carry out an audit procedure believed desirable.

10.10 | Questions, Exercises and Cases

QUESTIONS

10.2 Introduction

10.1 What are substantive procedures? Describe the different types of substantive procedures.

10.3 The Basis of Evidence

10.2 Define the three major sources of documentary evidence. List them in the order of their reliability.

10.3 List the major financial statement assertions. Define the assertions about account balances at the period end.

10.4 Sufficient Appropriate Audit Evidence

10.4 Why does an auditor prefer persuasive evidence as opposed to conclusive evidence?

10.5 Differentiate between the most reliable evidence and the least reliable evidence.

10.5 Substantive Audit Procedures

10.6 Discuss what is meant by direction of testing.

10.7 What is the difference between test of transactions and test of balances?

10.6 Audit Procedures for Obtaining Audit Evidence

10.8 Why should an auditor corroborate evidence for inquiry? Name a famous court case and discuss.

10.9 What alternative procedures can an auditor do when he is unable to attend a physical inventory?

10.10 What are four key characteristics of confirmation?

10.11 If a confirmation is not returned to the auditor what alternative procedures can he perform?

10.12 List the six evidence gathering techniques in order of reliability. List the six evidence gathering techniques in order of cost from highest to lowest.

PROBLEMS AND EXERCISES

10.3 The Basis of Evidence

10.13 **Management Assertions and Audit Objectives.** The following are management assertions (1 through 9). and audit objectives applied to the audit of accounts payable ((a) through (h)).

Management Assertion
1 Existence
2 Rights and obligations
3 Occurrence
4 Completeness
5 Valuation
6 Accuracy
7 Cutoff
8 Understandability
9 Classification

Specific Audit Objective

(a) Existing accounts payable are included in the accounts payable balance on the balance sheet date.

(b) Accounts payable are properly classified.

(c) Acquisition transactions in the acquisition and payment cycle are recorded in the proper period.

(d) Accounts payable representing the accounts payable balance on the balance sheet date agree with related subsidiary ledger amounts, and the total is correctly added and agrees with the general ledger.

(e) Accounts in the acquisition and payment cycle are properly disclosed according to IASs.

(f) Accounts payable representing the accounts payable balance on the balance sheet date are valued at the correct amount.

(g) Accounts payable exist.

(h) Any allowances for accounts payable discounts is taken.

Required:

A. Explain the differences between management assertions, general audit objectives, and specific audit objectives, and their relationships to each other.

B. For each specific audit objective, identify the appropriate management assertion.

10.4 Sufficient Appropriate Audit Evidence

10.14 Sufficient Appropriate Audit Evidence. The auditor finds it necessary to rely on audit evidence that is persuasive rather than conclusive and will often seek audit evidence from different sources or of a different nature to support the same assertion. The reliability of audit evidence is not only important in determining sufficiency (quantity) of the information, but also the appropriateness (quality) of the information. Reliability of audit evidence is influenced by its source and its nature.

Required:

A. Define these terms: reliability of evidence, persuasiveness of evidence, and relevance of evidence.

B. Arrange the following people as sources of information from most reliable to least reliable and explain your reasoning:

  1 new company employee,
  2 company employee with five years' experience,
  3 company lawyer,
  4 internal auditor,
  5 external auditor,
  6 auditor's lawyer,
  7 banker,
  8 top management,
  9 board of directors,
  10 company supplier,
  11 company customer.

10.15 Reliability and Cost of Evidence Gathering Techniques. The financial statements of Utgard Company of Drammen, Norway, a new client, indicate that large amounts of notes payable to banks were paid off during the period under audit. The auditor, Kristinge Korsvold, Statautoriseret Revisor, also notices that one customer's account is much larger than the rest, and therefore decides to examine the evidence supporting this account.

Required:

Evaluate the reliability of each of the following types of evidence supporting these transactions for:

Notes Payable:

A. Debit entries in the Notes Payable account.
B. Entries in the check register.
C. Paid checks.
D. Notes payable bearing bank perforation stamp PAID and the date of payment.
E. Statement by client's treasurer that notes had been paid at maturity.
F. Letter received by auditors directly from bank stating that no indebtedness on part of client existed as of the balance sheet date.

Customer Account:

G. Computer printout from accounts receivable subsidiary ledger.
H. Copies of sales invoices in amount of the receivable.
I. Purchase order received from customer.
J. Shipping document describing the articles sold.
K. Letter received by client from customer acknowledging the correctness of the receivable in the amount shown on client's accounting records.
L. Letter received by auditors directly from customer acknowledging the correctness of the amount shown as receivable on client's accounting records.

10.5 Substantive Audit Procedures

10.16 Substantive Tests – Analytical Procedures, Balances and Transactions. Substantive tests include (1) tests of the details of transactions, (2) tests of the details of balances, and (3) analytical procedures. Listed below are several specific audit procedures. Identify the type of substantive test – 1, 2, or 3.

A. Compare recorded travel expense with the budget.
B. Vouch entries in the check register to paid checks.
C. Recompute accrued interest payable.
D. Calculate inventory turnover ratios by product and compare with prior periods.
E. Reconcile the year-end bank account.
F. Discuss uncollectible accounts with the credit manager.
G. Count office supplies on hand at year-end.
H. Vouch entries in the sales journal to sales invoices.
I. Comparison of recorded amount of major disbursements with appropriate invoices
J. Comparison of recorded amount of major disbursements with budgeted amounts
K. Comparison of returned confirmation forms with individual accounts

[Adapted from Carmichael *et al.*, 1996, *Auditing Concepts and Methods*, McGraw Hill, New York.]

10.17 Tests of Balances. Your client is the Nicholas van Myra Central, a shopping center with 30 store tenants. All leases with the store tenants provide for a fixed rent plus a percentage of sales, net of sales taxes, in excess of a fixed dollar amount computed on an annual basis. Each lease also provides that the landlord may engage a Registeraccountant or Accountant-Administratieconsulent to audit all records of the tenant for assurance that sales are being properly reported to the landlord.

You have been requested by your client to audit the records of the JaiLai Chinese Ind. Restaurant to determine that the sales, totaling €725,000 for the year ended December 31, 20X4, have been properly reported to the landlord. The restaurant and the shopping center entered into a five-year lease on January 1, 20X4. The JaiLai offers only table

387

service. No liquor is served. During meal times there are four or five waitresses in attendance, who prepare handwritten prenumbered restaurant checks for the customers. Payment is made at a cash register, staffed by the proprietor, as the customer leaves. All sales are for cash.

The proprietor also is the bookkeeper. Complete files are kept of restaurant checks and cash register tapes. A daily sales book and general ledger are also maintained.

Required:
List the auditing procedures that you would employ to test the annual sales of the JaiLai Chinese Ind. Restaurant. (Disregard vending machine sales and counter sales of chewing gum and candy, and concentrate on the overall checks that would be appropriate.)

10.6 Audit Procedures for Obtaining Audit Evidence

10.18 Evidence Gathering Techniques. An auditor obtains audit evidence by one or more of the following evidence gathering techniques: inquiry, observation, inspection, reperformance, recalculation, confirmation, and analytical procedures.

Required:
For each of the evidence gathering technique give an example of a substantive test procedure.

10.19 Inquiry, Analytical Procedures, and Observation. In the examination of financial statements, auditors must judge the validity of the audit evidence they obtain. For the following questions, assume that the auditors have considered internal control and found it satisfactory.

Required:
A. In the course of examination, the auditors ask many questions of client officers and employees.
    1 Describe the factors that the auditors should consider in evaluating oral evidence provided by client officers and employees.
    2 Discuss the validity and limitations of oral evidence.
B. Analytical procedures include the computation of various balance sheet and operating ratios for comparison to prior years and industry averages. Discuss the validity and limitations of ratio analysis as evidential matter.
C. In connection with an examination of the financial statements of a manufacturing company, the auditors are observing the physical inventory of finished goods, which consists of expensive, highly complex electronic equipment. Discuss the validity and limitations of the audit evidence provided by this procedure.

10.20 Inspection. Discuss what you would accept as satisfactory documentary evidence in support of entries in the following?
A. Sales journal.
B. Sales returns register.
C. Voucher or invoice register.
D. Payroll register.
E. Check register.

10.21 Accounts Receivable Confirmations – Positive and Negative. In work on accounts receivable, use of confirmations is of great importance.

Required:

A. What is an audit confirmation?

B. What characteristics should an audit confirmation possess if an auditor is to consider it as sufficient appropriate audit evidence?

C. Distinguish between a positive and a negative accounts receivable confirmation.

D. In confirming a client's accounts receivable, what characteristics should be present in the accounts if the auditor is to use negative confirmations?

10.22 **Attendance at Physical Inventory Counting.** A processor of frozen foods carries an inventory of finished products consisting of 50 different types of items valued at approximately $2,000,000. About $750,000 of this value represents stock produced by the company and billed to customers prior to the audit date. This stock is being held for the customers at a monthly rental charge until they request shipment and is not separate from the company's inventory.

The company maintains separate perpetual ledgers at the plant office for both stock owned and stock being held for customers. The cost department also maintains a perpetual record of stock owned. The above perpetual records reflect quantities only.

The company does not take a complete physical inventory at any time during the year, since the temperature in the cold storage facilities is too low to allow one to spend more than 15 minutes inside at a time. It is not considered practical to move items outside or to defreeze the cold storage facilities for the purpose of taking a physical inventory. Because of these circumstances, it is impractical to test count quantities to the extent of completely counting specific items. The company considers as its inventory valuation at year-end the aggregate of the quantities reflected by the perpetual record of stock owned, maintained at the plant office, priced at the lower of cost or market.

Required:

A. What are the two principal problems facing the auditor in the audit of the inventory? Discuss briefly.

B. Outline the audit steps that you would take to enable you to render an unqualified opinion with respect to the inventory. (You may omit consideration of tests of unit prices and clerical accuracy.)

CASES

10.23 **Audit Objectives and Financial Statement Accounts.** Look at the financial statements of a major public company. Pick three accounts and discuss the financial statement assertions that might be associated with those accounts. For example, the financial statement assertions might be associated with "Accrued Product Liability" are valuation, existence, completeness, and presentation and disclosure. Valuation relates to product liability because a judgment (estimate) must be made regarding the expected cost of defective products.

10.24 **Substantive Tests: Balances and Transactions.** As part of systematic process of gathering and evaluating evidence regarding assertions about economic actions and events, tests of balances and tests of transactions are essential in obtaining audit evidence to detect material misstatements in the financial statements. In the following case, assume that you are an auditor. Before you conduct the actual tests you are expected to understand the concepts and procedures of tests of balances and transactions.

Required:

A. There are two types of substantive procedures. Identify each.

B. Describe the difference between tests of balances and tests of transactions. Give an example for each test and illustrate them.

C. For tests of balances, what are the major account balances in the balance sheet need to be examined. Why are these tests important?

D. For tests of transactions, what are the major accounts that an auditor need to verify transaction amounts and trace transactions to accounts in the financial statements. Why are these tests important?

E. How do inherent properties of double-entry accounting systems relate to the tests of balances? Give examples of double-entries that show the simultaneous affect of one transaction has on another.

F. For certain account balances such as assets, auditors prefer to test asset accounts for overstatement. Explain why. Are there any similar preferences for understatement for other accounts? If any, explain why.

G. As an auditor, you are aware of the control risks when design tests of transactions. Explain how these risks might effect the way you design and carry out the procedures.

[Written by Maria Wise, Claudia De Santiago, Perla Barajas, and Cam Long]

10.25 Tests of Balances. Swartz Platten, BV, sells chemicals in large, costly returnable containers. Its procedures in accounting for the containers are as follows:

1 When containers are purchased, their cost is charged to "Inventory-containers on hand."

2 Containers are billed to customers at cost; full credit is allowed for all containers returned in usable condition. The containers remain the property of Swartz Platten., at all times.

3 The cost of containers billed to customers is debited to "Accounts receivable-containers" and credited to "Liability for containers billed." At the same time, the cost of the containers billed is transferred to "Inventory-containers out" from "Inventory-containers on hand." Subsidiary ledgers are maintained for "Accounts receivable-containers" and "Inventory-containers out."

4 When containers are returned in usable condition, the entries in 3 are reversed.

5 A physical inventory of containers on hand is taken at the fiscal year-end.

6 As a partial control over containers in the hands of customers, sales representatives are asked to estimate periodically the number of containers held by each customer. These estimates are checked for reasonableness against the amount shown for the customer in the "Inventory-containers out" subsidiary ledger.

7 Physical shortages, unusable returned containers, and other inventory adjustments are charged or credited to "Containers expense-net." The corresponding adjustments to "Liability for containers billed" are also charged or credited to "Containers expense-net."

8 Containers kept by customers for more than one year are deemed unusable Roger van Deelgaard had been the auditor of Swartz Platten. for many years. He issued an unqualified opinion on the financial statements for the previous fiscal year. Two months before the current year-end, Swartz Platten's accountant requested that van Deelgaard investigate a strange situation which had developed: the balance in the "Liability for containers billed" had been steadily increasing, to the point where it exceeded the combined balances in "Inventory-containers out" and "Inventory-containers on hand."

Required:

A. What might have caused the situation described by the company's accountant?

B. List the procedures van Deelgaard should employ to determine the nature and extent of the misstatement.

[CICA adapted]

Audit Sampling and Other Selective Testing Procedures

Lucas A. Hoogduin

10.A.1 Preface

This appendix gives practical guidance on ISA Standard 530, Audit Sampling and Other Testing Procedures. Although most of the standard is devoted to audit sampling, it also covers detail testing procedures on items that were not selected randomly, or on all items in a population.

> The Standard's official text is given in boxes, like this.

Wherever we deemed it appropriate, we have added comments and practical hints. Some of the paragraphs speak for themselves, and we did not feel compelled to make any comment at all.

The reader does not need a lot of statistical background to follow the discussions, but some mathematical skill is helpful. We have not tried to give the full mathematical derivation of formulae and results, as we believe there are some good textbooks on this matter available (for example, *Statistiek voor accountancy* by Paul Touw and Lucas Hoogduin, Academic Service, Schoonhoven, 2002, ISBN 90 395 1743 6, which is currently being translated into English).

For almost a decade, detail testing has not been very popular among auditors. However, book-keeping scandals around the turn of the century (see the Concept and a Company cases throughout this book) have changed the environment considerably. Auditors feel more secure if they can base their audit opinion more on the results of detail testing, and audit clients appreciate it more if the audits are not carried out with interviews only. With the pendulum swinging back to detail testing, ISA 530 will become more popular in the near future.

Lucas Hoogduin is Director of KPMG's Business Advisory Services at their world headquarters. He has had many years of statistical audit experience, authoring several books on statistics. He brings long experience and statistically correct thinking to the IFAC standard on statistical sampling.

The Standard is organized in different sections that will be described below:

Section	Paragraphs
Introduction	1–2
Definitions	3–12
Audit Evidence	13–17
Risk Considerations in Obtaining Evidence	18–20
Procedures for Obtaining Evidence	21
Selecting Items for Testing to Gather Audit Evidence	22–27
Statistical versus Non-Statistical Sampling Approaches	28–30
Design of the Sample	31–39
Sample Size	40–41
Selecting the Sample	42–43
Performing the Audit Procedure	44–46
Nature and Cause of Errors	47–50
Projecting Errors	51–53
Evaluating the Sample Results	54–56

10.A.2 Introduction

1. The purpose of this Standard is to establish standards and provide guidance on the use of audit sampling procedures and other means of selecting items for testing to gather audit evidence.

2. When designing audit procedures, the auditor should determine appropriate means for selecting items for testing so as to gather audit evidence to meet the objectives of audit tests.

We will deal with appropriate means for selecting items for testing. But when does this need to be done? "When designing audit procedures" is a half-hearted answer. For what parts of a set of financial statements does the auditor design audit procedures?

10.A.3 Definitions

The Standards start off with a series of definitions. We will provide some background information on the various terms, and cross-reference them to the paragraphs where they play a most prominent role.

3. "Audit sampling" (sampling) involves the application of audit procedures to less than 100% of items within an account balance or class of transactions such that all sampling units have a chance of selection. This will enable the auditor to obtain and evaluate audit evidence about some characteristic of the items selected in order to form or assist in forming a conclusion concerning the population from which the sample is drawn. Audit sampling can use either a statistical or a non-statistical approach.

In the statistical realm, a random sample is defined as a sample taken in such a way that all combinations of sampling units have the same chance of selection. The difference between these two definitions may seem academic. On closer examination, however, it will follow that a selection procedure commonly used by auditors, systematic selection also known as fixed interval selection, is considered to be audit sampling under the ISA definition, whereas for real statisticians it is not a random sample. Another difference is that the ISA standard mentions just *a* chance of selection, whereas statisticians would like to see that the combinations of sampling units have **the same** chance of selection.[1]

The second sentence of this paragraph explains why it is important that all sampling units have a chance of selection: the objective is to form a conclusion about the population from which the sample is drawn. Statistical sampling employs the knowledge about all possible samples that could be drawn from the population, to ensure that the sample result, such as an interval estimate, is correct in at least, say, 95 percent of the cases.

(See also our comments on paragraph 10, where statistical sampling is discussed.)

> 4. For purposes of this Standard, *"error"* means either control deviations, when performing tests of control, or misstatements, when performing substantive procedures. Similarly, total error is used to mean either the rate of deviation or total misstatement.

A misstatement is the difference of the book value, the recorded value in the client's accounts, and the audit value, the value that the auditor believes it to be. Control deviations imply weaknesses in design or operation of internal controls. Errors may be adjustable or non-adjustable. If an error is adjustable, the auditor may post an adjustment based on the errors found, or in some cases even on the extrapolation of these errors as an estimate of the total error in the population. In some cases, errors are not adjustable, for example, the lack of internal control on the delivery of goods at a warehouse.

> 5. *"Anomalous error"* means an error that arises from an isolated event that has not recurred other than on specifically identifiable occasions and is therefore not representative of errors in the population.

This is a concept that has to be applied carefully. A wrongful interpretation or application could easily lead to errors not being detected. We will get back to this in the discussion of paragraph 50 later.

> 6. *"Population"* means the entire set of data from which a sample is selected and about which the auditor wishes to draw conclusions. For example, all of the items in an account balance or a class of transactions constitute a population. A population may be divided into strata, or sub-populations, with each stratum being examined separately. The term population is used to include the term stratum.

See also paragraph 35 and our comments thereon. There the Standard also gives examples of populations that can be investigated to give audit evidence on a certain balance, where the population is not that balance.

7. "Sampling risk" arises from the possibility that the auditor's conclusion, based on a sample may be different from the conclusion reached if the entire population were subjected to the same audit procedure. There are two types of sampling risk:

    a. the risk the auditor will conclude, in the case of a test of control, that control risk is lower than it actually is, or in the case of a substantive test, that a material error does not exist when in fact it does. This type of risk affects audit effectiveness and is more likely to lead to an inappropriate audit opinion; and

    b. the risk the auditor will conclude, in the case of a test of control, that control risk is higher than it actually is, or in the case of a substantive test, that a material error exists when in fact it does not. This type of risk affects audit efficiency as it would usually lead to additional work to establish that initial conclusions were incorrect.

    The mathematical complements of these risks are termed confidence levels.

The terminology in this paragraph is a little careless. In statistics, we use two different methods, estimation and hypothesis testing. To add to the linguistic confusion, we can test a hypothesis with an interval estimate.

In classical hypothesis testing, there are two risks defined. If we conclude that control risk is lower than it actually is, or if we conclude that a material error does not exist when in fact it does, we commit a *Type I error*. The risk of committing this type of error is usually called alpha-risk, but unfortunately in most auditing literature it is referred to as beta-risk. The converse, the type of risk in the b-part of the paragraph, is called a *Type II error*. This error is related to the decision to reject a population that in fact does not contain a material error. Statisticians typically call the risk of committing this type of risk beta-risk, whereas auditors would call it alpha-risk.

The mathematical complement of the Type I error can be called a *confidence level*, because in most cases we use an interval estimate to test the hypothesis. The mathematical complement of the Type II error is called the *power of the test*. It is a measure of how effective the test employed is in discriminating between populations that contain material errors and populations that contain non-material errors.

Let us illustrate these concepts with a simple example. We have two populations, A and B, which contain 100 items. Population A contains 10 errors (10 percent of 100) and 90 non-errors, and population B contains 3 errors (3 percent of 100) and 97 non-errors. The "tolerable" error, which is subjectively determined by the auditor (see paragraph 12) for this test is 10 errors (10 percent). Since population A has an unacceptable 10 percent errors, population A should be rejected, whereas population B (with a more tolerable 3 percent errors) should be approved.

The auditor now will define a decision rule, and calculate a sample size that coincides with it. Without boring the reader with the calculations now, we state that the auditor chooses a sample size of 25. We will lift this veil in our discussion on paragraph 40. The auditor approves the population if no errors are found, and rejects the population if the sample reveals one or more errors.

We now compare the possible sampling outcomes (finding no errors or finding errors) for the two populations. The probability of finding no errors in a sample of 25 from population A is 4.8 percent.[2] That is how the auditor got the sample size of 25. He allows a risk of approximately 5 percent (closest equivalent is 4.8 percent) that a sample from a population will reveal no errors. If, unknown to the auditor, the population is an incorrect one, the auditor will

Certification Exam Question Appendix 10.1

Which of the following best illustrates the concept of sampling risk?

(A) A randomly chosen sample may not be representative of the population as a whole on the characteristic of interest.

(B) An auditor may select audit procedures that are not appropriate to achieve the specific objective.

(C) An auditor may fail to recognize errors in the documents examined for the chosen sample.

(D) The documents related to the chosen sample may not be available for inspection.

approve this population, and commit a Type I error. In terms of an interval estimate, we could say that the auditor is 95.2 percent confident that the true number of errors in population A is somewhere between 0 and 10. We see therefore that the confidence level of 95.2 percent (100 percent less 4.8 percent probability of errors) is the mathematical complement of the risk related to the Type I error.

The probability of finding no errors in a sample of 25 from population B is 41.8 percent.[3] This may be shatteringly low, if you understand the consequences. It means that there is a probability of less than 50 percent that the auditor will draw the correct conclusion if the population contains a 3 percent error rate. The probability of 41.8 percent is the power of the test. It tells us something about how good this test is in making a distinction between populations that contain a 10 percent error rate and populations that contain a 3 percent error rate. The mathematical complement of the power of the test is the chance of Type II error. This error is related to the decision to reject a population that in fact does not contain a material error.

If the auditor believes that a power of 41.8 percent is too low, he may change his decision rule. He could, for instance approve populations if the sample reveals only 0 or 1 error, and reject them otherwise. This will be at the expense of a larger sample size: a sample size of 39 will do the trick.[4]

8. "Non-sampling risk" arises from factors that cause the auditor to reach an erroneous conclusion for any reason not related to the size of the sample. For example, most audit evidence is persuasive rather than conclusive, the auditor might use inappropriate procedures, or the auditor might misinterpret evidence and fail to recognize an error.

Non-sampling risk is discussed in paragraph 20.

9. "Sampling unit" means the individual items constituting a population, for example checks listed on deposit slips, credit entries on bank statements, sales invoices or debtors' (customer's) balances, or a monetary unit.

Two different purposes are intertwined in this definition of the sampling unit. The statistical purpose of the sampling unit is to identify individual units that could be subject to investigation. The total set of sampling units is called a population. If we take a random sample, all possible combinations of sampling units have the same probability of selection. For *monetary unit sampling*, the sampling unit is the monetary unit. For variables estimation techniques, the sampling unit is the physical unit, for example an invoice or an inventory location.

The auditor's purpose of the sampling unit is to determine at what level of detail he wants to perform his audit procedures. It is often advised that the lower the detail, the more effective the audit procedure will be. Take for instance the test on existence of accounts receivable. The auditor will send out confirmation requests to gather audit evidence, but he will have to choose between the customer's (debtor's) balance, the outstanding invoice or even a line item on that invoice as the sampling unit.

If the auditor takes the line item as the sampling unit, the effort to obtain audit evidence is minimum: the customer (debtor) only has to confirm what he owes with regard to this line item, and if the customer fails to reply the auditor only has to perform alternative procedures to obtain the necessary audit evidence.[5]

> 10. "Statistical sampling" means any approach to sampling that has the following characteristics:
>
> a. random selection of a sample; and
>
> b. use of probability theory to evaluate sample results, including measurement of sampling risk.
>
> A sampling approach that does not have characteristics (a) and (b) is considered non-statistical sampling.

Here we should also comment on two other terms that often crop up in discussions on the use of sampling. The first one is *representativeness*, and the other is homogeneity. We draw a random sample in the hope that it is representative. This means that the sample reflects the attributes of the population on which we wish to form a conclusion. For instance, if 5 percent of the population items were in error, then a sample of 60 items would hopefully reveal three errors. Only if this sample result is obtained (and the probability of this result is only 23 percent[6]) can the sample be considered to be representative.

Now, based on only three errors from a 60 population with 23 percent probability, we are faced with two problems: what should we do with the 77 percent of results that are not representative, and how can we ever find out if the sample was representative? The first problem is easily solved. After finding three errors in a sample of 60, no rational being will claim that the population contains *exactly* 5 percent errors. With possible sample results of zero, one, two, etc. to 60 errors, this would infer that the population contains 0 percent, $1\frac{2}{3}$ percent, $3\frac{1}{3}$ percent, etc. or 100 percent errors. The consequence is that it is implied that any value between the respective point estimates cannot exist. This is, of course, not true.

A statistician is more careful in drawing conclusions about the population error rate. For instance, with three errors found in a sample of 60, he will not claim that the population error rate is exactly 5 percent, but state that he is, say, 95 percent confident that the population error rate is between 1.37 percent and 12.42 percent.[7] He can claim his confidence of 95 percent, because he knows that the procedure he uses for calculating the bounds of the interval estimate will yield a correct statement with at least the stated confidence.

The problem of representativeness cannot be solved. We could only know whether a sample is representative or not if we were to know the characteristics of the population. But that is exactly the reason for sampling: to find out about these characteristics. Still, even though this problem cannot be solved, it is important to realize the notion of representativeness. First, by random sampling we know that there is only a limited probability of non-representative samples that lead to an invalid conclusion. Secondly, careful scrutiny of the sample findings may inspire the auditor to investigate the problem at hand further, knowing that even random samples may lead to wrong conclusions.

Finally a word on *homogeneity*. If we sample from a population that contains two equal subpopulations A and B, and subpopulation A has no errors, whereas subpopulation B has a 10 percent error rate, then it is often felt that this will cause problems because the population is not homogeneous. This is only partly true. The problem only lies in the fact that there is extra information about the distribution of the error. If we do not take this extra information into account when planning the sample, then the sample results will be the same as if we would take a sample of 60 from the entire population. Taking the extra information into account will lead us to sample more items from part B and less items from part A. In fact, the best allocation would be to sample all 60 items from part B, but that is not quite fair because it assumes that we know that part A is flawless.

If the auditor fears that the population under review is heterogeneous, he may choose to stratify the population. As we will see later when we discuss *stratification*, there should be a significant difference in error rates between the subpopulations to make stratification worthwhile.

> 11. "Stratification" is the process of dividing a population into subpopulations, each of which is a group of sampling units which have similar characteristics (often monetary value).

Stratification is further discussed in paragraphs 36 to 38. Stratification by monetary value is only useful for variables estimation techniques, which will be shown to be much more ineffective than monetary unit sampling. Stratification for monetary unit sampling hardly occurs in practice, as it is only effective if the auditor can discern sub-populations that have significantly different error rates.

> 12. "Tolerable error" means the maximum error in a population that the auditor is willing to accept.

The concept of tolerable error is mainly devised as a means to establish the minimum work to be performed on a certain balance or class of transactions. It is derived from materiality. It is sad that the profession has embraced the adjective "tolerable." If you look at it from a clean perspective, for instance in terms of hypothesis testing, the error the auditor is testing for may not be as tolerable as it seems. In fact, the auditor tries his utmost to detect the error if it exists and is covered by professional standards if he is unlucky not to detect it. We would therefore prefer the term "important" error instead of "tolerable."

10.A.4 Audit Evidence

Most of the guidance in this section is self-explanatory. We will only provide an important comment on paragraph 17.

> 13. In accordance with Standard 500 "Audit Evidence", audit evidence is obtained from an appropriate mix of tests of control and substantive procedures. The type of test to be performed is important to an understanding of the application of audit procedures in gathering audit evidence.

■ Tests of Control

14. In accordance with Standard 400 "Risk Assessments and Internal Control" tests of control are performed if the auditor plans to assess control risk less than high for a particular assertion.

15. Based on the auditor's understanding of the accounting and internal control systems, the auditor identifies the characteristics or attributes that indicate performance of a control, as well as possible deviation conditions which indicate departures from adequate performance. The presence or absence of attributes can then be tested by the auditor.

16. Audit sampling for tests of control is generally appropriate when application of the control leaves evidence of performance (for example, initials of the credit manager on a sales invoice indicating credit approval, or evidence of authorization of data input to a microcomputer based data processing system).

■ Substantive Procedures

17. Substantive procedures are concerned with amounts and are of two types: analytical procedures and tests of details of transactions and balances. The purpose of substantive procedures is to obtain audit evidence to detect material misstatements in the financial statements. When performing substantive tests of details, audit sampling and other means of selecting items for testing and gathering audit evidence may be used to verify one or more assertions about a financial statement amount (for example, the existence of accounts receivable), or to make an independent estimate of some amount (for example, the value of obsolete inventories).

Highlight the second sentence in this paragraph: the auditor uses substantive procedures to detect material misstatements. **In the auditor toolbox there is a very ingenious statistical method to assist him.** But do not be fooled by the last sentence: it is not the auditor's primary duty to make precise estimates. The amount of work necessary to achieve this is much more than what is typically needed for the detection of material errors. It is the client's responsibility to make precise estimates, and the auditor's responsibility to assess the method employed or to test the estimate.

If the auditor finds evidence that the assertion under review may be materially misstated, he should think twice before he starts collecting sufficient data material for a precise estimate. Paragraph 34 leaves the door open to this endeavor. If everything else fails, and the client is willing to pay for it, the auditor may test a large proportion or even all items in the population to find and adjust the errors.

■ Risk Considerations in Obtaining Evidence

This section deals with the risk of an incorrect conclusion. It does not provide strict rules as to what the maximum allowable risk should be.

18. **In obtaining evidence, the auditor should use professional judgment to assess audit risk and design audit procedures to ensure this risk is reduced to an acceptably low level.** (Bold type in the IFAC standards means that it is required).

19. Audit risk is the risk that the auditor gives an inappropriate audit opinion when the financial statements are materially misstated. Audit risk consists of inherent risk – the susceptibility of an account balance to material misstatement, assuming there are no related internal controls; control risk – the risk that a material misstatement will not be prevented or detected and corrected on a timely basis by the accounting and internal control systems; and, detection risk – the risk that the material misstatements will not be detected by the auditor's substantive procedures. These three components of audit risk are considered during the planning process in the design of audit procedures in order to reduce audit risk to an acceptably low level.

Before we dig in to the mathematical calculation of sample sizes, first a word on the level of sampling risk that the auditor is willing to accept. As explained in this paragraph, the acceptable level of detection risk is determined by the assessments of inherent and control risk (see Chapter 8). Since detection risk covers all substantive procedures, the acceptable level of sampling risk is dependent on the amount of audit evidence obtained from substantive procedures as well as the assessments of inherent and control risk.

There is no clear-cut formula that determines an exact level of acceptable sampling risk based on the risk assessments. It is generally accepted that audit evidence obtained from other procedures will increase the acceptable level of sampling risk, but the extent to which this minimum level can be increased is mainly a matter of professional judgment.

20. Sampling risk and non-sampling risk can affect the components of audit risk. For example, when performing tests of control, the auditor may find no errors in a sample and conclude that control risk is low, when the rate of error in the population is, in fact, unacceptably high (sampling risk). Or there may be errors in the sample that the auditor fails to recognize (non-sampling risk). With respect to substantive procedures, the auditor may use a variety of methods to reduce detection risk to an acceptable level. Depending on their nature, these methods will be subject to sampling and/or non-sampling risks. For example, the auditor may choose an inappropriate analytical procedure (non-sampling risk) or may find only minor misstatements in a test of details when, in fact, the population misstatement is greater than the tolerable amount (sampling risk). For both tests of control and substantive tests, sampling risk can be reduced by increasing sample size, while non-sampling risk can be reduced by proper engagement planning, supervision, and review.

■ Procedures for Obtaining Evidence

21. Procedures for obtaining audit evidence include inspection, observation, inquiry and confirmation, computation and analytical procedures. The choice of appropriate procedures is a matter of professional judgment in the circumstances. Application of these procedures will often involve the selection of items for testing from a population.

Analytical procedures feel a bit out of place here, as a whole ISA Standard (520) is devoted to them. What is meant here are analytical procedures that can be applied on a detail level. (See Chapter 9 on analytical procedures.)

10.A.5 Selecting Items for Testing to Gather Audit Evidence

22. **When designing audit procedures, the auditor should determine appropriate means of selecting items for testing. The means available to the auditor are:**

    a. Selecting all items (100% examination);

    b. Selecting specific items; and

    c. Audit sampling.

Selecting all items will be further discussed in paragraph 24. Selecting specific items is explained in paragraphs 25 and 26. A round-up comment on audit sampling is given in paragraph 27, but it is the main subject of the remaining paragraphs of this Standard after a discourse on non-statistical sampling in paragraphs 28 to 30.

23. The decision as to which approach to use will depend on the circumstances, and the application of any one or combination of the above means may be appropriate in particular circumstances. While the decision as to which means, or combination of means, to use is made on the basis of audit risk and audit efficiency, the auditor needs to be satisfied that methods used are effective in providing sufficient appropriate audit evidence to meet the objectives of the test.

■ Selecting all items

24. The auditor may decide that it will be most appropriate to examine the entire population of items that make up an account balance or class of transactions (or a stratum within that population). 100% examination is unlikely in the case of tests of control; however, it is more common for substantive procedures. For example, 100% examination may be appropriate when the population constitutes a small number of large value items, when both inherent and control risks are high and other means do not provide sufficient appropriate audit evidence, or when the repetitive nature of a calculation or other process performed by a computer information system makes a 100% examination cost effective.

■ Selecting Specific Items

25. The auditor may decide to select specific items from a population based on such factors as knowledge of the client's business, preliminary assessments of inherent and control risks, and the characteristics of the population being tested. The judgmental selection of specific items is subject to non-sampling risk.

Specific items selected may include:

- *High value or key items*. The auditor may decide to select specific items within a population because they are of high value, or exhibit some other characteristic, for example items that are suspicious, unusual, particularly risk-prone or that have a history of error.
- *All items over a certain amount*. The auditor may decide to examine items whose values exceed a certain amount so as to verify a large proportion of the total amount of an account balance or class of transactions.
- *Items to obtain information*. The auditor may examine items to obtain information about matters such as the client's business, the nature of transactions, accounting and internal control systems.
- *Items to test procedures*. The auditor may use judgment to select and examine specific items to determine whether or not a particular procedure is being performed.

As we focus on sampling issues in this appendix the judgmental selection is not discussed further.

26. While selective examination of specific items from an account balance or class of transactions will often be an efficient means of gathering audit evidence, it does not constitute audit sampling. The results of procedures applied to items selected in this way cannot be projected to the entire population. The auditor considers the need to obtain appropriate evidence regarding the remainder of the population when that remainder is material.

◼ Audit Sampling

27. The auditor may decide to apply audit sampling to an account balance or class of transactions. Audit sampling can be applied using either non-statistical or statistical sampling methods. Audit sampling is discussed in detail in paragraphs 31 through 56.

Although the bulk of this Standard is devoted to audit sampling, the reader should not forget that any type of evidence gathering on the detail level is the objective of this Standard.

10.A.6 Statistical versus Non-Statistical Sampling Approaches

28. The decision whether to use a statistical or non-statistical sampling approach is a matter for the auditor's judgment regarding the most efficient manner to obtain sufficient appropriate audit evidence in the particular circumstances. For example, in the case of tests of control the auditor's analysis of the nature and cause of errors will often be more important than the statistical analysis of the mere presence or absence (that is, the count) of errors. In such a situation, non-statistical sampling may be most appropriate.

This paragraph gives one good example of when non-statistical sampling is to be preferred above statistical sampling. A second example lies in populations that are not available in machine-readable format.

> 29. When applying statistical sampling, the sample size can be determined using either probability theory or professional judgment. Moreover, sample size is not a valid criterion to distinguish between statistical and non-statistical approaches. Sample size is a function of factors such as those identified in Appendices 1 and 2. When circumstances are similar, the effect on sample size of factors such as those identified in Appendices 1 and 2 will be similar regardless of whether a statistical or non-statistical approach is chosen.

This is in line with the main differences between statistical and non-statistical sampling. Not a word on sample sizes. We believe, however, that for a non-statistical sample to be as effective as a statistical sample, the sample size needs to be nearly doubled.

> 30. Often, while the approach adopted does not meet the definition of statistical sampling, elements of a statistical approach are used, for example the use of random selection using computer generated random numbers. However, only when the approach adopted has the characteristics of statistical sampling are statistical measurements of sampling risk valid.

The example says that random numbers are used to select the sample items. A sad example. Why on earth would an auditor use a randomly generated sample, which is the most cumbersome part of statistical sampling, and then leave out the evaluation of the results using probability theory. How would that look in court, when the statistical evaluation would yield a different conclusion from the non-statistical conclusion the auditor has formed?[8]

Certification Exam Question Appendix 10.2

An advantage of using statistical over non-statistical sampling methods in tests of controls is that the statistical methods:

(A) Can more easily convert the sample into a dual-purpose test useful for substantive testing.
(B) Eliminate the need to use judgment in determining appropriate sample sizes.
(C) Afford greater assurance than a non-statistical sample of equal size.
(D) Provide an objective basis for quantitatively evaluating sample risk.

10.A.7 Design of the Sample

Sample design is very important. Sample design must consider the objectives to test, the definition of the population, the sampling method and sample size. Most of these choices cannot be reversed after the audit evidence has been obtained. We will explain these concepts with the aid of a simple example: an inventory count (stock-take).

■ Inventory Count Example

Assume that you are the auditor of a large company that operates a central warehouse supplying more than 100 shops in a certain region. Even though internal controls are considered to be good, it appears that at the end of every year all small deviations have added up to a material error.

> **31. When designing an audit sample, the auditor should consider the objectives of the test and the attributes of the population from which the sample will be drawn.**

The objective of the inventory count is to assess completeness, existence and accuracy of inventories. The attributes that you will test is the total inventory value in a given inventory location.

> 32. The auditor first considers the specific objectives to be achieved and the combination of audit procedures which is likely to best achieve those objectives. Consideration of the nature of the audit evidence sought and possible error conditions or other characteristics relating to that audit evidence will assist the auditor in defining what constitutes an error and what population to use for sampling.

Given the fact that you expect an overall error that is material, you cannot place any reliance on internal control, and inherent risk is set as high. You will use statistical sampling to estimate the total value of inventories within precision bounds that are less than tolerable error. You are aware that selected items may be in error because inventory items are stored at a different location than actually recorded. Because you are concerned that total inventory may be understated, you use the collection of all inventory locations as the population, and define the inventory location as the sampling unit.

> 33. The auditor considers what conditions constitute an error by reference to the objectives of the test. A clear understanding of what constitutes an error is important to ensure that all, and only, those conditions that are relevant to the test objectives are included in the projection of errors. For example, in a substantive procedure relating to the existence of accounts receivable, such as confirmation, payments made by the customer before the confirmation date but received shortly after that date by the client are not considered an error. Also, a misposting between customer accounts does not affect the total accounts receivable balance. Therefore, it is not appropriate to consider this an error in evaluating the sample results of this particular procedure, even though it may have an important effect on other areas of the audit, such as the assessment of the likelihood of fraud or the adequacy of the allowance for doubtful accounts.

We already mentioned that inventory could be stored in a different location than recorded. This could lead to errors when you select a location that is physically empty, for which the related inventory item is stored elsewhere in the warehouse. Conversely, you could select a location that is empty, and find misplaced goods there. Errors like these should level out in total, but as part of a sample they could lead to large extrapolated differences.

To avoid this problem, you may print out a listing of all empty locations, and check that they, indeed, are empty. If locations are found empty that are not on the list, these are reported. Likewise, if a location that is supposed to be empty actually holds any goods, the number of items and article number are written down. With this extremely useful routine a first stratification is made. All inventory locations that contain misplaced items, plus all empty locations are segregated and all of them are audited. The population subject to sampling now comprises of all inventory location in which some (positive) value is accounted.

Likewise, you could select all locations that hold negative values. In practice, negative values cannot exist, and the locations holding them are very likely in error.

> 34. When performing tests of control, the auditor generally makes a preliminary assessment of the rate of error the auditor expects to find in the population to be tested and the level of control risk. This assessment is based on the auditor's prior knowledge or the examination of a small number of items from the population. Similarly, for substantive tests, the auditor generally makes a preliminary assessment of the amount of error in the population. These preliminary assessments are useful for designing an audit sample and in determining sample size. For example, if the expected rate of error is unacceptably high, tests of control will normally not be performed. However, when performing substantive procedures, if the expected amount of error is high, 100% examination or the use of a large sample size may be appropriate.

For the population under review, you expect a large error. Still, this does not mean that we have to perform a 100 percent examination. The sample size is determined under the following observations:

- The expected error will be comparable to the error found in previous inventory counts.
- The maximum allowable sampling risk will be 5 percent.
- Tolerable error for inventories is known.
- You will stratify the population by book value per inventory location.
- The population size is large. After the preliminary stratification you have approximately 20,000 locations left that contain some positive value.

Certification Exam Question Appendix 10.3

Which of the following sample planning factors would influence the sample size for a substantive test of details for a specific account?

	Expected amount of misstatements	Measure of tolerable misstatement
(A)	No	No
(B)	Yes	Yes
(C)	No	Yes
(D)	Yes	No

Population

> 35. It is important for the auditor to ensure that the population is:
>
> a. Appropriate to the objective of the sampling procedure, which will include consideration of the direction of testing. For example, if the auditor's objective is to test for overstatement of accounts payable, the population could be defined as the accounts payable listing. On the other hand, when testing for understatement of accounts payable, the population is not the accounts payable listing but rather subsequent disbursements, unpaid invoices, suppliers' statements, unmatched receiving reports or other populations that provide audit evidence of understatement of accounts payable; and

b. Complete. For example, if the auditor intends to select payment vouchers from a file, conclusions cannot be drawn about all vouchers for the period unless the auditor is satisfied that all vouchers have in fact been filed. Similarly, if the auditor intends to use the sample to draw conclusions about the operation of an accounting and internal control system during the financial reporting period, the population needs to include all relevant items from throughout the entire period. A different approach may be to stratify the population and use sampling only to draw conclusions about the control during, say, the first 10 months of a year, and to use alternative procedures or a separate sample regarding the remaining two months.

In the example of the inventory count (stock-take), taking the listing of all stock would be appropriate for the test. However, the listing may not be complete. An alternative would be to use the inventory locations as the sampling unit. This could satisfy both the appropriateness and completeness conditions, unless the company stores part of its stock outside known locations.

Stratification

36. Audit efficiency may be improved if the auditor stratifies a population by dividing it into discrete sub-populations which have an identifying characteristic. The objective of stratification is to reduce the variability of items within each stratum and therefore allow sample size to be reduced without a proportional increase in sampling risk. Sub-populations need to be carefully defined such that any sampling unit can only belong to one stratum.

The most important feature mentioned in this paragraph is the variability of items. For the purpose of estimation or hypothesis testing, we can distinguish between two causes of variability, error rate and error value. In monetary unit sampling, the auditor only has to worry about the error rate as a source of sampling variability. This is because the sampling unit in the statistical definition is the monetary unit, and all monetary units are equal in size. There simply does not exist any variability in terms of error value.

37. When performing substantive procedures, an account balance or class of transactions is often stratified by monetary value. This allows greater audit effort to be directed to the larger value items which may contain the greatest potential monetary error in terms of overstatement. Similarly, a population may be stratified according to a particular characteristic that indicates a higher risk of error, for example, when testing the valuation of accounts receivable, balances may be stratified by age.

Let us get one thing straight. If the auditor is primarily concerned with overstatement, and he desires to direct his effort to the larger value items which may contain the greatest potential monetary error in terms of overstatement, the solution is not stratification but monetary unit sampling. True, a stratified variables estimation sample will yield more precise results than an unstratified sample of the same size, but both will be outperformed by a monetary unit sample of the same size.

38. The results of procedures applied to a sample of items within a stratum can only be projected to the items that make up that stratum. To draw a conclusion on the entire population, the auditor will need to consider risk and materiality in relation to whatever other strata make up the entire population. For example, 20% of the items in a population may make up 90% of the value of an account balance. The auditor may decide to examine a sample of these items. The auditor evaluates the results of this sample and reaches a conclusion on the 90% of value separately from the remaining 10% (on which a further sample or other means of gathering evidence will be used, or which may be considered immaterial).

Stratification in this paragraph is somewhat different from that in the previous paragraph. In this paragraph, guidance is given to situations where the auditor focuses his audit effort to the few largest items that make up most of the population. The auditor audits a sample of these and has to decide whether he has gathered sufficient audit evidence for the population as a whole. It goes without saying that this approach is non-statistical. A monetary unit sample would have selected a larger number of high-value items and a smaller number of low-value items, and the results could then be evaluated to form an opinion on the population as a whole.

Projection of results of a stratified sample will be further discussed in paragraph 52.

Value weighted selection

39. It will often be efficient in substantive testing, particularly when testing for over-statements, to identify the sampling unit as the individual monetary units (e.g. dollars) that make up an account balance or class of transactions. Having selected specific monetary units from within the population, for example, the accounts receivable balance, the auditor then examines the particular items, for example, individual balances, that contain those monetary units. This approach to defining the sampling unit ensures that audit effort is directed to the larger value items because they have a greater chance of selection, and can result in smaller sample sizes. This approach is ordinarily used in conjunction with the systematic method of sample selection (described in Appendix 3) and is most efficient when selecting from a computerized database.

Monetary unit sampling is the most efficient and effective sampling technique in the auditor's toolbox. It is particularly useful when testing for overstatements, and it is advisable to use it in cases where the population is available in machine-readable format.

The remark about the advantages of selecting larger value items is strange. Statistically speaking, we do not select larger or smaller items. We select individual monetary units, and the auditor only needs to know to which physical unit they belong to be able to pull the evidence material to ascertain whether the monetary unit is correct or incorrect. The efficiency and effectiveness of monetary unit sampling is not affected by the error distribution: it does not matter whether a few large items collectively contain a material error or that a large number of small errors in lower-value items constitute a material error. Monetary unit sampling only "looks at" individual monetary units, that may or may not be in error.

We will continue the discussion on how to select items in the discussion on paragraph 43.

■ Sample Size

40. **In determining the sample size, the auditor should consider whether sampling risk is reduced to an acceptably low level.** Sample size is affected by the level of sampling risk that the auditor is willing to accept. The lower the risk the auditor is willing to accept, the greater the sample size will need to be.

As discussed in paragraph 19, the sampling risk that the auditor is willing to accept is dependent on his assessments of inherent and control risk, and the amount of audit evidence obtained from substantive analysis and other substantive procedures other than sampling relating to the same audit objective.

Having said that, we can now concentrate on the mathematical side of the story. Let us first turn to the example mentioned in paragraph 7, where the auditor calculated a sample of 25. We will now explain where this number comes from and what factors influence sample sizes in general.

The decision rule is: approve the population if no errors are found and reject it if an error is found. There is a population of 100 items, of which ten were in error. The auditor has decided that he wants to run a risk of no more than 5 percent that he will not find any errors in his sample.

The auditor increases the sample size until the cumulative product is less than 5 percent. By calculating the hypergeometric distribution (using, for example, Microsoft Excel's HYPGEOMDIST function), the auditor can verify that the probability of finding 24 correct items out of a population of 100 that contains ten errors is approximately 5.5 percent, and for 25 items it is 4.8 percent. The conclusion is that a sample of 25 is sufficiently large.

Let us now have a look at the factors that affect the sample size. First, clearly, the acceptable sampling risk is a determining factor. If the sampling risk were 10 percent instead of 5 percent, the sample size would be only 20, and if sampling risk were 1 percent the sample size has to be at least 36. The lower the acceptable sampling detection risk, the higher the sample size.

Certification Exam Question Appendix 10.4

The tolerable error for a test of a control is generally:

(A) Lower than the expected rate of errors in the related accounting records.
(B) Higher than the expected rate of errors in the related accounting records.
(C) Identical to the expected rate of errors in related accounting records.
(D) Unrelated to the expected rate of errors in the related accounting records.

Secondly, the "tolerable error" is a strong influence. In the example above, tolerable error is supposed to be ten items out of 100. If the auditor wants to cover for not finding any errors from a population of 100 that contains five errors, then he should look harder for them. At 5 percent sampling risk, he should audit at least 45 items to be confident enough to find at least one error, or, in other words, if the sample of 45 does not reveal any errors, he will be (95 percent) confident that the population does not contain more than five errors. Alternatively, if the tolerable error is 20 items, then a sample size of 13 is sufficient. The lower the tolerable error, the higher the sample size.

Does the population size play a role in this? (See Illustration 10.A.1.) The question has two sides to it, depending whether the tolerable error is a constant, or is expressed as a percentage of the population. The first side is easily solved: if the tolerable error is a constant, then increasing the population will decrease the tolerable error. If the population size would be 200 and the tolerable error would remain at ten, then the sample size would be 51. This result also answers the second side of the question: a 5 percent error in a population of 200 calls for a sample of 51, whereas a sample of 45 was sufficient for a 5 percent error in a population of 100. The effect of the population size will wear off dramatically, though.

ILLUSTRATION 10.A.1

Minimum sample size to detect 5 percent error[9]

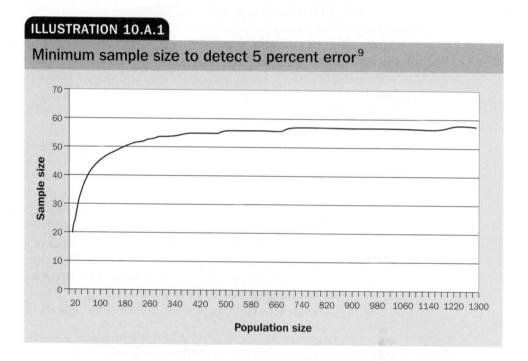

As a rule of thumb, we usually apply the hypergeometric distribution if the sample size is less than one-tenth of the population size, and use the binomial distribution in all other cases. If the population size for instance were 600, we would calculate the sample size at 59, which would be less than one-tenth of the population size. It would then not be necessary calculate the sample size with the hypergeometric distribution. If we did, the result would be 56.

As a conclusion, we may say that the population size does have an effect on the sample size, but that effect is dependent on whether the tolerable error is expressed as a percentage of the population or not, and the effect diminishes if the population becomes larger than 10 times the sample size as calculated using the binomial distribution.

Finally, the decision rule plays an important part. In the example that we introduced in the discussion on paragraph 7, we saw that if we wanted to reduce the risk of inadvertently rejecting a population that contains a not-so-material error, we could do this by changing the decision rule. More precisely, we increased the critical region, rejecting a population if the sample revealed two or more errors, and accepting a population if no more than one error was found. The minimum sample size would have to be increased from 25 to 39.

Illustration 10.A.2 shows what inputs are needed in the software package IDEA to calculate the required sample size:

ILLUSTRATION 10.A.2

IDEA Audit Software Screen to Determine Sample Size[9]

Illustration 10.A.2 shows that for a desired confidence of 90 percent, a population size of $118,498,593, a tolerable error of $10,000,000, and an expected error of $0, the sample size would be 27. IDEA uses fixed interval section for the selection process and therefore calculates the sampling interval at $118,498,593 divided by 27. It also shows that the total tainting of the sampled item has to be 0 for the population to be approved. (See also the various evaluation screens in our discussion on paragraph 54.)

41. The sample size can be determined by the application of a statistically-based formula or through the exercise of professional judgement objectively applied to the circumstances. Appendices 1 and 2 [of the Standard] indicate the influences that various factors typically have on the determination of sample size, and hence the level of sampling risk.

In the discussion to the previous paragraph, we have seen that the factors that determine the minimum sample size are:

- sampling risk,
- tolerable error,
- population size (Appendix 2 to the Standard calls the effect negligible),
- decision rule (referred to as the amount of error the auditor expects to find in the population.

The only other effect on the sample size is stratification, but as we have pointed out in our discussion on paragraph 36, stratification is only useful for variables estimation techniques: that is, all substantive sampling procedures other than monetary unit sampling.

The determination of the minimum sample size then boils down to the effects of sampling risk and tolerable error, if we can neglect the effect of population size and assume we only approve the population if no errors were found. The sample size required is found by dividing the logarithm of the sampling risk by the logarithm of $(1 - p)$, where p is the tolerable error expressed as a percentage of the total book value of the population.

Professional judgment objectively applied to the circumstances may produce a sample size that is different from the sample size obtained statistically. If the non-statistical sample size is lower, the auditor should have sound reasons to approve a population if errors were found in the sample. Moreover, even if he does not find any errors, he should document what supporting audit evidence allows him to use a lower non-statistical sample size.

■ Selecting the Sample

42. **The auditor should select items for the sample with the expectation that all sampling units in the population have a chance of selection**. Statistical sampling requires that sample items are selected at random so that each sampling unit has a known chance of being selected. The sampling units might be physical items (such as invoices) or monetary units. With non-statistical sampling, an auditor uses professional judgment to select the items for a sample. Because the purpose of sampling is to draw conclusions about the entire population, the auditor endeavors to select a representative sample by choosing sample items which have characteristics typical of the population, and the sample needs to be selected so that bias is avoided.

See our discussion on the definition of audit sampling in paragraph 3 and of statistical sampling in paragraph 10.

43. The principal methods of selecting samples are the use of random number tables or computer programs, systematic selection and haphazard selection. Each of these methods is discussed in Appendix 3 [of the Standard].

There are various ways to select individual monetary units. One method is systematic sampling, which is supported by generalized audit software such as IDEA or ACL. It is also referred to as fixed interval selection. The advantages of systematic sampling are that all items larger than the sampling interval have a 100 percent selection probability, and that it is available in the software packages mentioned. There are two disadvantages:

1 Strictly speaking systematic sampling does not agree with our definition of random sampling.

2 The method performs poorly if the error pattern in the population coincides with the sampling pattern.

It is very easy to obtain a monetary unit sample from a population that is available in a spreadsheet, such as Microsoft Excel. The auditor should perform the following steps to achieve this:

1. Calculate the sample size, and decide what the sampling interval would be if systematic sampling were deployed.
2. Select all items in the population that are larger than the sampling interval.
3. Recalculate the sample size based on the smaller population with the large items left out.
4. Calculate into a new cell the book value of the item divided by a random number (uniformly distributed between 0 and 1). The Excel formula =RAND() produces such random numbers.
5. Sort the file in descending order on the result from step 4. Select the desired number of items from the top.

■ Performing the Audit Procedure

> **44. The auditor should perform audit procedures appropriate to the particular test objective on each item selected.**

> 45. If a selected item is not appropriate for the application of the procedure, the procedure is ordinarily performed on a replacement item. For example, a voided check may be selected when testing for evidence of payment authorization. If the auditor is satisfied that the check had been properly voided such that it does not constitute an error, an appropriately chosen replacement is examined.

This is sound practice, because it actually means that the population was ill-defined, and the population that was sampled from actually contains items not of interest to the auditor.

> 46. Sometimes however, the auditor is unable to apply the planned audit procedures to a selected item because, for instance, documentation relating to that item has been lost. If suitable alternative procedures cannot be performed on that item, the auditor ordinarily considers that item to be in error. An example of a suitable alternative procedure might be the examination of subsequent receipts when no reply has been received in response to a positive confirmation request.

It may sound very strict to consider items on which no suitable substantive procedures can be performed as errors, but in doing so the auditor gains an idea on the worst-case situation. In practice, it may be advised to run two separate evaluations, one with the uncertain items evaluated as errors, and one with the uncertain items not evaluated as errors. The two evaluations then provide a bandwidth that more precisely describes the population.

■ Nature and Cause of Errors

This is a very important section from an auditing point of view. When following the guidance provided in these paragraphs, the auditor extends the knowledge about the errors from the simple occurrence to the cause, thus broadening his judgment necessary to arrive at the correct conclusion. A mere mathematical treatment of audit evidence is not sufficient.

> **47. The auditor should consider the sample results, the nature and cause of any errors identified, and their possible effect on the particular test objective and on other areas of the audit.**

48. When conducting tests of control, the auditor is primarily concerned with the design and operation of the controls themselves and the assessment of control risk. However, when errors are identified, the auditor also needs to consider matters such as:

   a. the direct effect of identified errors on the financial statements; and

   b. the effectiveness of the accounting and internal control systems and their effect on the audit approach when, for example, the errors result from management override of an internal control.

49. In analyzing the errors discovered, the auditor may observe that many have a common feature, for example, type of transaction, location, product line or period of time. In such circumstances, the auditor may decide to identify all items in the population that possess the common feature, and extend audit procedures in that stratum. In addition, such errors may be intentional, and may indicate the possibility of fraud.

Stratification may be done ex-post, that is, after the initial or pilot sample has revealed that errors may be concentrated in one or more sub-populations. Just stratifying the population is not sufficient. That is why this paragraph suggests that audit procedures be extended in the high-error strata. Only then will the overall estimate be more precise and will the auditor benefit from stratification.

50. Sometimes, the auditor may be able to establish that an error arises from an isolated event that has not recurred other than on specifically identifiable occasions and is therefore not representative of similar errors in the population (an anomalous error). To be considered an anomalous error, the auditor has to have a high degree of certainty that such error is not representative of the population. The auditor obtains this certainty by performing additional work. The additional work depends on the situation, but is adequate to provide the auditor with sufficient appropriate evidence that the error does not affect the remaining part of the population. One example is an error caused by a computer breakdown that is known to have occurred on only one day during the period. In that case, the auditor assesses the effect of the breakdown, for example by examining specific transactions processed on that day, and considers the effect of the cause of the breakdown on audit procedures and conclusions. Another example is an error that is found to be caused by use of an incorrect formula in calculating all inventory values at one particular branch. To establish that this is an anomalous error, the auditor needs to ensure the correct formula has been used at other branches.

As already mentioned, when the "anomalous error" was first introduced in the Definitions section, the concept was dangerous. This paragraph provides guidance on what to do when the auditor believes the errors found are of an anomalous nature. In any case, just labeling errors as anomalous should be avoided, and not taken into further consideration for the assessment of a material error in the population.

■ Projecting Errors

51. **For substantive procedures, the auditor should project monetary errors found in the sample to the population, and should consider the effect of the projected error on the particular test objective and on other areas of the audit**. The auditor projects the total error for the population to obtain a broad view of the scale of errors, and to compare this to the tolerable error. For substantive procedures, tolerable error is the tolerable misstatement, and will be an amount less than or equal to the auditor's preliminary estimate of materiality used for the individual account balances being audited.

This might be insufficient guidance and could lead to potential misappropriation of audit sampling. What does the auditor's decision process look like? How do errors need to be projected and what exactly is compared to the tolerable error? We can best explain what is needed when monetary unit sampling is used. After that, we can discuss how the same would apply for variables estimates, and finally for non-statistical samples.

In monetary unit sampling, for every single sampled item an audit value is established, and compared to the book value. Then a "tainting" (the difference between book and audit value) is calculated as a percentage of the book value. So if the book value equals the audit value, the tainting is zero, and if the audit value is zero (the item is entirely wrong) the tainting is 100 percent.

The results of the sample are then fed into a computer program, which calculates a point estimate of the error in the population, and a one-sided interval estimate of this error. The point estimate is the most likely estimate, and the upper limit of the interval estimate is the worst-case estimate. The auditor bases his decision on the position of both statistics relative to the tolerable error.

If the upper limit of the interval estimate is lower than the tolerable error, the auditor can conclude that the population does not contain a material error. If the upper limit of the interval estimate is higher than the tolerable error, and the point estimate is also higher, then the auditor has gathered convincing evidence that the population may contain a material error.

In all other cases, the risk of a material error is too large for the auditor to live with, but the evidence does not guarantee an error of this size. The auditor has to find out what is wrong, usually by investigating more items from the same population.

So far so good for monetary unit sampling. Let us now see what the differences are for variables estimates,[10] that is, all other forms of statistical sampling that are not value-weighted.

In variables estimation, the auditor obtains a point estimate on the error in the population, as well as a one-sided interval estimate. However, the calculations underlying these statistics assume that the data used are normally distributed, and in most cases they are not. The effect of this is that the upper limit on the interval estimate is treacherously underestimated. As a result, the upper limit will much more often be less than a tolerable error, which will make the auditor believe that he can approve the population.

Non-statistical sampling can only be evaluated as a variables estimation technique, and has haphazard selection as an additional disadvantage. This implies that the same decision rules

413

apply as for variables estimation, including the warning that upper limits tend to be dangerously understated.

> 52. [When an error has been established as an anomalous error, it may be excluded when projecting sample errors to the population. The effect of any such error, if uncorrected, still needs to be considered in addition to the projection of the non-anomalous errors.] If an account balance or class of transactions has been divided into strata, the error is projected for each stratum separately. Projected errors plus anomalous errors for each stratum are then combined when considering the possible effect of errors on the total account balance or class of transactions.

Let us have a look at an example. The population consists of 11,449 items with a total book value of $522,800. The population is split into two sub-populations, one containing 2,613 items with a higher than average value, the other containing the remaining 8,836 items with a value less than $46.

We sampled 171 items from the top stratum and 86 from the bottom stratum. The total error (book value minus audit value) in the top stratum sample was $429.24, that in the bottom stratum sample $33.13. Illustration 10.A.3 demonstrates the error projection using the ratio estimation method (Panel A) and difference method of projection (Panel B).

ILLUSTRATION 10.A.3

Error Projection

Panel A Ratio Estimation Method

Stratum	Error found (A)	Book value of sampled items (B)	Error ratio (C) = (A)/(B)	Total book value in stratum (D)	Projected error (C) × (D)
Lower	33.13	1,650.20	2.0076%	159,222.33	3,196.60
Upper	429.24	24,261.28	1.7692%	363,577.67	6,432.56
Total				522,800.00	9,629.16

Panel B Difference Method

Stratum	Error found (A)	Sample size (B)	Average error (C) = (A)/(B)	Total number of items in stratum (D)	Projected error (C) × (D)
Lower	33.13	86	0.38523	8,836	3,403.91
Upper	429.24	171	2.51018	2,613	6,559.09
Total				11,449	9,963.00

This example shows, as the Standard describes, that findings from a stratum should only be extrapolated over that stratum. Only then will the auditor benefit from the effort he has been through to stratify the population.

It may strike the reader as odd that the extrapolation methods generate two different estimates. Well, if they would generate the same result, there would not be a good reason for the existence of multiple methods. So two questions arise:

1 Is there a general condition under which they generate the same estimate?
2 Can we give any advice on when to use which method?

The answer to the first question is that the two estimators give the same result if the average book value in the sample equals the average book value in the population. The answer to the second question is determined by which statistics can be more easily obtained – the total book value per stratum or the number of items per stratum.

> 53. For tests of control, no explicit projection of errors is necessary since the sample error rate is also the projected rate of error for the population as a whole.

This is beside the point. The sample error rate is also the projected rate of error for the population as a whole for substantive tests.

Sometimes, tests of controls are set up in the form of a so-called sequential sampling procedure. In its practical form, the auditor samples 30 items. If no errors are revealed, the auditor places full reliance on controls. For every error found, an additional ten items are audited. The procedure should be stopped after having audited 60 items. If the total number of errors is more than six, then no reliance can be placed on controls. If the total number of errors is between three and six, the auditor assigns moderate reliance.

■ Evaluating the Sample Results

> 54. **The auditor should evaluate the sample results to determine whether the preliminary assessment of the relevant characteristic of the population is confirmed or needs to be revised.** In the case of a test of controls, an unexpectedly high sample error rate may lead to an increase in the assessed level of control risk, unless further evidence substantiating the initial assessment is obtained. In the case of a substantive procedure, an unexpectedly high error amount in a sample may cause the auditor to believe that an account balance or class of transactions is materially misstated, in the absence of further evidence that no material misstatement exists.

An example of the evaluation using IDEA is given in Illustration 10.A.4.

> 55. If the total amount of projected error [plus anomalous error] is less than but close to that which the auditor deems tolerable, the auditor considers the persuasiveness of the sample results in the light of other audit procedures, and may consider it appropriate to obtain additional audit evidence. The total of projected error plus anomalous error is the auditor's best estimate of error in the population. However, sampling results are affected by sampling risk. Thus when the best estimate of error is close to the tolerable error, the auditor recognizes the risk that a different sample would result in a different best estimate that could exceed the tolerable error. Considering the results of other audit procedures helps the auditor to assess this risk, while the risk is reduced if additional audit evidence is obtained.

ILLUSTRATION 10.A.4

IDEA Evaluation of Sample Results[11]

MUS – Low Error Rate

Summary

Confidence Level	90.00	Value of the sampled population excluding high values	7,091,439.04
High Value Amount	4,388,836.80	Total value of high value items	111,407,154.56
Sampling Interval	3,545,719.52	Value of the sampled population including high values	118,498,593.60
Basic Precision Pricing	100.00		

Results Excluding High Value Items	Overstatements	Understatements
Sample Size	2.00	2.00
Number of errors	1.00	1.00
Gross most likely error	67,713.47	1,290,074.80
Net most likely error	-1,222,361.33	1,222,361.33
Total Precision	4,848,928.34	4,848,928.34
Gross upper error limit	4,916,641.82	6,139,003.14
Net upper error limit	3,626,567.02	6,071,289.67
Results for High Value Items		
Number of high value items	8.00	8.00
Number of errors	0.00	0.00
Value of errors	0.00	0.00
Results Including High Value Items		
Total number of items examined	10.00	10.00
Number of errors	1.00	1.00
Gross most likely error	67,713.47	1,290,074.80
Net most likely error	-1,222,361.33	1,222,361.33

Conclusion:

Based on this sample, the most likely total overstatement in the population is 67,713.47, and the most likely total understatement is 1,290,074.80. You can infer with a confidence of 90.00% that the total overstatement in the population does not exceed 4,916,641.82, and that the total understatement in the population does not exceed 6,139,003.14

The guidance provided in this paragraph is mainly geared toward non-statistical sampling. As we have mentioned earlier in the discussion on paragraph 51, the evaluation of statistical samples uses the position of the upper limit of the interval estimate relative to tolerable error as the primary point of focus. As long as it is less than tolerable error, the auditor can approve the population. If it is larger, then the position of the point estimate will give a clue as to whether it is worthwhile continuing sampling items to gather evidence.

In non-statistical sampling we cannot obtain an upper limit of the interval estimate. That is why we have to choose a subjective boundary on the point estimate to decide whether the population can be approved or not. If the boundary is chosen too low, we would be better protected against inadvertently approving populations that contain material errors, but at the same time we would more often reject populations that have a smaller than material error. Conversely, if we take the boundary too high, then the probability of inadvertently approving populations that contain material errors further increases.

A minimal sample size is not sufficient to approve a population if the extrapolated error is less than one-third of tolerable error. The sample size must be nearly doubled to guard the auditor against the risk of inadvertently approving the population. As the sample size increases, the probability of inadvertent approval decreases. This is an indication that at higher sample sizes, say more than two times the minimum size necessary for a monetary unit sample, the decision point for non-statistical samples could be increased also.

56. If the evaluation of sample results indicates that the preliminary assessment of the relevant characteristic of the population needs to be revised, the auditor may:

a. request management to investigate identified errors and the potential for further errors, and to make any necessary adjustments; and/or

b. modify planned audit procedures. For example, in the case of a test of control, the auditor might extend the sample size, test an alternative control or modify related substantive procedures; and/or

c. consider the effect on the audit report.

This paragraph deals with the question: What do you have to do if you found (too many) errors? The first suggestion is to have the client sort out his problems and clean up the mess before you can sign off.

The second solution is to do the cleaning yourself. It means more audit work and probably an adjustment of the population under review on the basis of your sample findings. The adjustment can be made for the errors found or for the extrapolated error.

If both these solutions are not feasible, the ISA suggests that you do **not** issue an unqualified opinion. This requires some courage, because it jeopardizes the relationship with the client.

10.A.8 Answers to Certification Exam Questions

10A.1 (A) We are to find the answer that represents the concept of sampling risk. Sampling risk arises from the possibility that the auditor's conclusion, based on a sample, may be different from the conclusion reached if the entire population were subjected to the same audit procedure. Choices (B), (C), and (D) are all incorrect because they relate to errors which could occur even if 100 percent of the population were examined, in other words, non-sampling risk.

10A.2 (D) One must identify an advantage of statistical sampling over non-statistical sampling. Answer (D) is correct because statistical sampling means any approach to sampling that has the following characteristics: random selection of a sample; and use of probability theory to evaluate sample results, including measurement of sampling risk. These are objective characteristics and they are evaluated using a quantative method – statistical analysis. Choice (A) is incorrect because dual-purpose tests, which both test a control and serve as substantive test, can use either a statistical or a non-statistical sample. Choice (B) is not correct because both statistical and non-statistical sampling require the use of judgment. Choice (C) is wrong because assurance may be provided by either statistical or non-statistical sampling.

10A.3 (B) Does either the expected amount of misstatement or the measure of tolerable misstatement influence sample size for a substantive test of details? Check (B) as right because both the expected amount of misstatement and the tolerable misstatement affect sample size. Increases in the expected amount of misstatements increase sample size, while increases in the tolerable misstatement decrease sample size. Choices (A), (C) and (D) are incorrect because both expected amount of misstatements and measure of tolerable misstatement increase, not one or the other.

10A.4 (B) What is the relationship between the tolerable error and the expected rate of errors for a test of a control? Tolerable error means the maximum error in a population that the auditor is willing to accept. Choice (A) is bogus because if the tolerable error rate is less than the expected rate, the auditor would not plan to rely on internal control and would therefore omit tests of controls. Choice (C) is a loser because testing of controls is inappropriate if the expected rate of errors equals the tolerable error rate (mathematically, in this case, the sample size would equal the population size). Choice (D) is off the mark because to perform tests of controls one must assume that the tolerable rate of deviations is more than the expected error rate.

10.A.9 Notes

1 The slightly careless wording used in the ISA standard avoids discussions on monetary unit sampling, where the sampling unit statistically is the monetary unit, but physically is the item that contains the monetary unit that is selected. As a result, in monetary unit sampling the monetary units have the same selection probability, but the physical units have selection probabilities that are proportional to their size.

2 Calculated with the hypergeometric distribution. In Excel: =HYPGEOMDIST(0; 25; 10; 100).

3 Again, the hypergeometric distribution is employed. In Excel: =HYPGEOMDIST(0, 25, 3,100).

4 With a sample size of 39, the probability of finding 0 or 1 errors from a population of 100 that contains ten errors is 4.4 percent. The Excel equivalent is =HYPGEOMDIST(0, 39, 10,100) + HYPGEOMDIST(1, 39, 10, 100). The power of the test has now increased to 66.4 percent = HYPGEOMDIST(0, 39, 3,100) + HYPGEOMDIST(1, 39, 3, 100).

5 But there is a little catch to that. It occurs when monetary unit sampling is deployed, where negative (credit) items do not have a chance of selection and the sample size is directly proportional to the total balance of positive (debit) items. A balance that has a lot of unmatched credit items at a lower level may inflate when the sampling unit is chosen at that lower level. Moreover, the auditor then also has to devise an audit procedure on the completeness of credit items. If the sampling unit is chosen at the balance level, this will automatically provide information on the completeness of credit items.

6 Calculated with the binomial distribution, in Excel =BINOMDIST(3, 60, 0.05, 0).

7 Calculated with the exact upper and lower bounds for the binomial distributions.

8 Comment: More often we encounter situations, where the sample was drawn haphazardly and the sample results are evaluated as if they were produced by a statistical sample.

9 IDEA® is a registered trademark of CaseWare International Inc.

10 Sorry about the complexity. The notion is important though. This is the first time where it is claimed that variables estimation is a dangerous technique. Software like IDEA support it and suggest that it works better than MUS if the expected error is larger than 50 percent of tolerable error. This is not true. We have recently found proof that a value-weighted selection is the best possible approach, especially in cases where only overstatements are expected, but also in many other cases. Moreover, most auditors are not aware that the confidence intervals for variables estimation are underestimated. This means that they are led to believe that they have gained enough confidence whereas the true confidence is much lower.

11 IDEA® is a registered trademark of CaseWare International Inc.

10.A.10 Questions, Exercises and Cases

QUESTIONS

10A.1 Name the factors that an auditor typically takes into consideration when determining the necessary sample size.

10A.2 What is the difference between the significance level of a test and the power of a test?

10A.3 Is Type II error also part of the audit risk?

10A.4 When projecting errors for a non-statistical sampling method, the auditor can choose between extrapolating over the number of items in the population and extrapolating over the book value in the population. Typically, these methods will generate different results. Under which circumstances will the results be the same?

10A.5 Why is it difficult to determine the sample size for the estimate of the population error with a given confidence and pre-determined precision.

10A.6 To determine the completeness of accounts payable at year-end, the auditor decides to define the sampling population as the payments after year-end. Why does this test have limited value?

10A.7 What are the requirements for a representative sampling technique to qualify as a "statistical" sample?

10A.8 Appendices 1 and 2 to ISA 530 list a number of factors that influence sample size. Are these factors only relevant for statistical samples?

10A.9 Some people claim that an audit risk of 5 percent implies that 5 percent of financial statements with unqualified opinions contain material errors. What is your view on this?

EXERCISES

10A.10 Sampling for attributes is often used to allow an auditor to reach a conclusion concerning a rate of occurrence in a population. A common use in auditing is to test the rate of deviation from a prescribed internal control procedure to determine whether the planned assessed level of control risk is appropriate.

Required:
A. When an auditor samples for attributes, identify the factors that should influence the auditor's judgment concerning the determination of:
1 acceptable level of risk of assessing control risk too low,
2 tolerable deviation rate, and
3 expected population deviation rate.
B. State the effect on sample size of an increase in each of the following factors, assuming all other factors are held constant:
1 acceptable level of risk of assessing control risk too low,
2 tolerable deviation rate, and
3 expected population deviation rate.
C. Evaluate the sample results of a test for attributes if authorizations are found to be missing on seven check requests out of a sample of 100 tested. The population consists of 2,500 check requests, the tolerable deviation rate is 8 percent, and the acceptable level of risk of assessing control risk too low is considered to be low.
D. How may the use of statistical sampling assist the auditor in evaluating the sample results described in C above?

[Adapted and reprinted with permission from AICPA. Copyright © 2000 & 1985 by American Institute of Certified Public Accountants.]

10A.11 Rong & Wright, CA, of Hong Kong has decided to rely on an audit client's affecting receivables. Rong & Wright plans to use sampling to obtain substantive evidence concerning the reasonableness of the client's accounts receivable balances. Rong & Wright has identified the first few steps in an outline of the sampling plan as follows.

1 Determine the audit objectives of the test.
2 Define the population.
3 Define the sampling unit.
4 Consider the completeness of the population.
5 Identify individually significant items.

Required:

Identify the remaining steps which Rong & Wright should include in the outline of the sampling plan.

[Adapted and reprinted with permission from AICPA. Copyright © 2000 & 1985 by American Institute of Certified Public Accountants.]

Chapter 11

COMPLETING THE AUDIT

 11.1 Learning Objectives

After studying this chapter, you should be able to:

1 Reiterate the procedures for the audit completion stage.

2 State the elements of a system of quality control of an audit firm.

3 Give the implications of the Sarbanes-Oxley Act for quality control and audit review.

4 Understand why letters from client legal counsel are necessary and what they contain.

5 Obtain evidence that management acknowledges its responsibility for the fair representation of the financial statements in a management representation letter.

6 Conduct a review for contingent liabilities and commitments.

7 Explain what a related party transaction is and the procedures required to determine the completeness of information provided by management.

8 Conduct a review after the balance sheet date for subsequent events and understand what events cause financial statement adjustments.

9 Know the auditor's responsibilities when facts are discovered after the issuance of the audit report.

10 Explain the procedures involved in the review of financial statements including disclosures and other information presented with the audited financial statements.

11 Design and perform the wrap-up procedures.

12 Determine procedures to evaluate going concern issues.

13 Discuss the design and use of matters for the attention of partners.

ILLUSTRATION 11.1

Audit Process Model – Phase Flow Diagram

Phase I
Client Acceptance
Objective: Determine both acceptance of a client and acceptance by a client. Decide on acquiring a new client or continuation of relationship with an existing one and the type and amount of staff required.

Procedures:
(1) Evaluate the client's background andd reasons for the audit.
(2) Determine whether the auditor is able to meet the ethical requirements regarding the client.
(3) Determine need for other professionals.
(4) Communicate with predecesser auditor.
(5) Prepare client proposal.
(6) Select staff to perform the audit.
(7) Obtain an engagement letter.

Phase II
Planning the Audit
Objective: Determine the amount and type of evidence and review required to give the auditor assurance that there is no material missatement of the financial statements.

Procedures:
(1) Obtain industry, company, legal, related party and financial background information.
(2) Perform procedures to obtain an understanding of internal control.
(3) Assess the risks of material misstatements of the financial statements.
(4) Determine materiality.
(5) Prepare the planning memorandum and audit program (audit plan), which contains the auditor's response to the identified risk.

Phase III
Testing and Evidence
Objective: Test for evidence supporting internal controls and the fairness of the financial statements.

Procedures:
(1) Tests of controls.
(2) Substantive tests of transactions.
(3) Analytical procedures.
(4) Tests of details of balances.
(5) Search for unrecorded liabilities.

Phase IV
Evaluation and Reporting
Objective: Complete the audit procedures and issue an opinion.

Procedures:
(1) Evaluate governance evidence.
(2) Perform procedures to identify subsequent events.
(3) Review financial statement and other report material.
(4) Perform wrap–up procedures.
(5) Prepare Matters for Attention of Partners.
(6) Report to the board of directors.
(7) Prepare Audit report.

11.2 Introduction

The audit is not over until the audit report is signed. And even then it may not be over if facts are discovered after the balance sheet date and before the next report. After the fieldwork is almost complete, a series of procedures are generally carried out to "complete the audit." The intent of these procedures is to review the audit work, get certain assurances from the client, uncover any potential problems, check compliance with regulations, and check the consistency of the material that is to be presented to the users of financial statements.

In this text so far we have followed the standard audit process model (Illustration 11.1) through its phases – for client acceptance (Phase I), planning (Phase II), and elements of testing and evidence (Phase III). In this chapter, we will discuss the last phase, Phase IV, evaluation and reporting.

The procedures for completing this audit phase are: evaluate governance evidence; do procedures to identify **subsequent events**; review financial statements and other report material; do wrap-up procedures, prepare **Matters for Attention of Partners**; report to the board of directors and prepare audit report (which will be discussed in Chapter 12 Audit Reports and Communication). These procedures and the objective of the evaluation and reporting phase are shown in Illustration 11.2.

ILLUSTRATION 11.2

Audit Process Model – Phase IV Evaluation and Reporting

Objective: Complete the audit procedures and issue an opinion.

Procedures
1 Evaluate governance evidence.
2 Perform procedures to identify subsequent events.
3 Review financial statements and other report material.
4 Perform wrap-up procedures.
5 Prepare Matters for Attention of Partners.
6 Report to the board of directors.
7 Prepare Audit report.

The initial audit procedure in the closing cycle is usually to evaluate *governance* evidence, the evidence pertaining to the company and management. This means obtaining a **legal letter** and a **management representations letter**. Next in the governance evaluation is to look at **contingent liabilities** and **related parties**.

Discovery of subsequent facts and events may be essential to a correct opinion. The auditor must consider events up to the date of the auditor's report and between the balance sheet date and the issuance of the statements. Discovery of facts after the financial statements' issuance are not generally as crucial.

Of course, the auditors must review financial statements and financial statement disclosures, but they must also review other information contained in the annual report.

Other information that needs looking into is the board of directors' report, corporate governance disclosures (where applicable) and all other information in the annual report to shareholders.

The last work of the closing cycle is wrap-up procedures, matters for supervisors, report to the **audit committee**, and the audit report itself. Wrap-up procedures include:

- analytical procedures,
- review working papers,
- evaluation of going concern,
- client approval of adjusting entries.

Reporting and evaluation of matters for supervisory attention includes reports to managers and partners.

Prior to the final audit report the auditors will usually discuss their findings with the audit committee especially irregularities, illegal acts and **reportable conditions**. The final step in the closing cycle is the audit report, discussed in Chapter 12 Audit Reports and Communication.

Certification Exam Question 11.1

International Standards on Quality Control (ISQC) apply to:

(A) Auditing services only.
(B) Auditing and management advisory services.
(C) Auditing and tax services.
(D) Auditing and accounting and review services.

11.3   Quality Control

According to International Standard on Quality Control 1 (ISQC 1),[1] the **audit firm** should establish a system of quality control designed to provide it with reasonable assurance that the firm and its personnel comply with professional standards and regulatory and legal requirements, and that reports issued by the firm or **engagement partners** are appropriate in the circumstances.

■ Elements of a System of Quality Control

The elements of **quality control** policies adopted by an audit firm normally incorporate policies related to general firm activities and personnel. General firm activities for which quality control policies and procedures are required include leadership responsibilities for quality within the firm, acceptance and retention of clients, engagement performance, and **monitoring**. Quality controls applied to human resources include ethical requirements. The quality control policies and procedures should be documented and communicated to the firm's personnel.

■ Quality Control Leadership

The firm should establish policies and procedures designed to promote an internal culture based on the recognition that quality is essential in performing engagements. Such policies and procedures should require the firm's chief executive officer (or equivalent) or, if appropriate, the firm's managing board of partners (or equivalent), to assume ultimate responsibility for the firm's system of quality control. That person should have sufficient and appropriate experience and ability to assume the responsibility.

■ Ethical and Independence Requirements

The firm should establish policies and procedures designed to provide it with reasonable assurance that the firm and its personnel comply with relevant ethical requirements and maintain independence where required by the IFAC Code and national ethical requirements. The firm should establish policies to insure that it is notified of breaches of independence requirements, and to enable it to take appropriate actions to resolve such situations. At least annually, the firm should obtain written confirmation of compliance with its policies and procedures on independence from all applicable firm personnel.

The audit firm should establish policies and procedures:[2]

- setting out criteria for determining the need for safeguards to reduce the **familiarity threat** to an acceptable level when using the same senior personnel on an assurance engagement over a long period of time;
- for all audits of financial statements of listed entities, requiring the rotation of the engagement partner after a specified period in compliance with the IFAC Code and national ethical requirements that are more restrictive.

■ Acceptance and Continuance of Client Relationships and Specific Engagements

The firm should establish policies and procedures for the acceptance and continuance of client relationships and specific engagements, designed to provide it with reasonable assurance that it:

- has considered the integrity of the client and does not have information that would lead it to conclude that the client lacks integrity;
- is competent to perform the engagement and has the capabilities, time and resources to do so;
- can comply with ethical requirements.

When deciding to continue an existing engagement or accept a new engagement with an existing client, and where difficult issues have been identified, the firm should document how the issues were resolved. Where the firm obtains information that would have caused it to decline an engagement if that information had been available earlier, the firm should consider the professional and legal responsibilities that apply to the circumstances and the possibility of withdrawing from the engagement or from both the engagement and the client relationship.

An evaluation of prospective clients and a review, on an ongoing basis, of existing clients should be conducted. The continued adequacy and operational effectiveness of quality control policies and procedures require monitoring. The firm's general quality control policies and procedures should of course be communicated to its personnel.

■ Engagement Quality Control Review

The audit firm should establish policies and procedures for an engagement quality control review that provides an objective evaluation of the significant judgments made by the engagement team.[3] Firms should require an engagement quality control review for all audits of financial statements of listed entities. They should set policies for assurance and related services engagements, and all other audits and reviews of historical financial information.

The work performed by each person in the audit team may be reviewed by personnel of at least equal competence to consider whether:

- The work has been performed in accordance with the audit program.
- The work performed and the results obtained have been adequately documented.
- All significant audit matters have been resolved or are reflected in audit conclusions.
- The objectives of the audit procedures have been achieved.
- The conclusions expressed are consistent with the results of the work performed and support the audit opinion.

■ Monitoring

The firm should establish policies and procedures to see that quality control systems are relevant, adequate, operating effectively, and complied with in practice. Such policies and procedures should include ongoing evaluation and a periodic inspection of a selection of completed engagements.

At least annually, the firm should communicate the results of the monitoring of its quality control system to engagement partners and other appropriate individuals within the firm. Such communication should include the following:[4]

- a description of the monitoring procedures performed;
- the conclusions drawn from the monitoring procedures;
- where relevant, a description of systemic, repetitive or other significant deficiencies and of the actions taken to resolve or amend those deficiencies.

Supervisory personnel should:

1 Monitor the progress of the audit to consider whether:
   a   assistants have the necessary skills and competence to carry out their assigned tasks;
   b   assistants understand the audit directions;
   c   the work is being carried out in accordance with the overall audit plan and the audit program.
2 Become informed of and address significant accounting and auditing questions raised during the audit, by assessing their significance and modifying the overall audit plan and the audit program as appropriate.
3 Resolve any differences of professional judgment between personnel and consider the level of consultation that is appropriate.

■ Human Resources

The firm should establish policies and procedures to insure that it has sufficient personnel with the capabilities, competence, and ethical commitment to perform its engagements in line with professional standards and regulatory and legal requirements. The firm should assign responsibility for each engagement to an engagement partner with the appropriate capabilities, competence, authority, and time to perform the role. The firm should also assign appropriate staff with the necessary capabilities.

Presently two IAASB standards apply to audit quality: International Standards on Quality Control (ISQC) and ISA 220,[5] "Quality Control For Audit Work." IAASB issues International Standards on Quality Control (ISQCs) as the standards to be applied for all services falling under the Standards of the IAASB (i.e. ISAs, International Standards on Assurance Engagements (ISAEs), and International Standards on Related Services (ISRSs)).[6]

Certification Exam Question 11.2

One of a certified audit firm's basic objectives is to provide professional services that conform to professional standards. Reasonable assurance of achieving this basic objective is provided through:

(A) A system of quality control.
(B) A system of peer review.
(C) Continuing professional education.
(D) Compliance with International Financial Reporting Standards.

ISA 220 establishes standards and provides guidance on specific quality control procedures only for audit engagements. ISA 220 includes specific requirements for an engagement quality control reviewer to perform an objective evaluation of compliance with applicable **professional standards**. The responsibilities of the engagement partner under ISA 220 are shown in Illustration 11.3.

■ The Sarbanes-Oxley Act Quality Control and Audit Review

The Sarbanes-Oxley Act (SOX) addresses overall review procedures required of the auditor such as quality control, second partner review, and partner rotation. It also discusses the client's audit committee responsibilities and inspection by the **Public Company Accounting Oversight Board** (PCAOB).[7]

SOX applies not only to US audit firms, but also to audit firms throughout the world.[8] Any foreign public accounting firm that prepares or furnishes an audit report on a company publicly traded in the US is subject to SOX, in the same manner and to the same extent as a public accounting firm that is organized and operates under the laws of the USA or any state. The PCAOB may determine that a foreign public accounting firm, even though it does not issue audit reports, plays such a substantial role in the preparation and furnishing of such reports that it should be treated as a public accounting firm subject to SOX.[9]

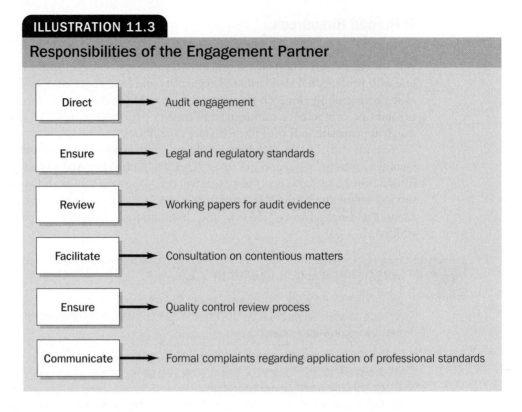

ILLUSTRATION 11.3

Responsibilities of the Engagement Partner

Direct	→ Audit engagement
Ensure	→ Legal and regulatory standards
Review	→ Working papers for audit evidence
Facilitate	→ Consultation on contentious matters
Ensure	→ Quality control review process
Communicate	→ Formal complaints regarding application of professional standards

Quality Control Policies

The Sarbanes-Oxley Act[10] (SOX) requires that every registered public accounting firm auditing publicly traded companies include in their quality control policies standards relating to:

- monitoring of professional ethics and independence from issuers on behalf of which the firm issues audit reports;
- consultation within such firm on accounting and auditing questions;
- supervision of audit work;
- hiring, professional development, and advancement of personnel;
- the acceptance and continuation of audit engagements;
- internal inspection;
- such other requirements as the **Public Company Accounting** Oversight Board (PCAOB) may prescribe.

PCAOB Inspections

In order to insure quality control, the PCAOB conducts a continuing program[11] of inspections[12] to assess the degree of compliance of the audit firm's performance of audits and issuance of audit reports with the rules of the PCAOB and professional standards. The PCAOB evaluates the sufficiency of the quality control system of the firm, and the manner of the documentation and communication of that system by the firm; and performs such testing as appropriate of the audit, supervisory, and quality control procedures of the firm.

The PCAOB is required to inspect a registered public accounting firm under SOX, section 104. The PCAOB will inspect and review selected audit and review engagements of the firm (which may include audit engagements that are the subject of ongoing litigation or other controversy between the firm and one or more third parties). A written report of the findings of the PCAOB is transmitted to the appropriate regulatory authorities. The report is made available in appropriate detail to the public, (except that the quality control portions of the report may not be made public under certain considerations).[13]

Certification Exam Question 11.3

The Sarbanes-Oxley Act requires that every registered public accounting firm auditing publicly traded companies include in their quality control policies standards relating to all of the following **except**:

(A) Consultation within such firm on accounting and auditing questions.
(B) Hiring, professional development, and advancement of personnel.
(C) Internal control policies.
(D) Internal inspection.

Ex-Employee Conflicts of Interest

In determining the acceptance and continuation of audit engagements the audit firm must consider ex-employee conflicts of interest and audit partner rotation. An accounting firm cannot perform any audit service for a firm if a chief executive officer, controller, chief financial officer, chief accounting officer, or equivalent position, was employed by that accounting firm and participated in any capacity in the audit of that issuer during the one-year period preceding the date of the initiation of the audit.[14] The audit partner must be rotated away from that client every five years.

Partnership Review and Rotation

Audits should be reviewed by partners in the accounting firm not connected with the audit and should rotate their audit partners every five years. Under SOX, section 103, auditors should provide a concurring or second partner review by a qualified person associated with the public accounting firm, other than the person in charge of the audit, or by an independent reviewer. SOX, section 303 makes it unlawful for a registered public accounting firm to provide audit services to an issuer if the lead audit partner having primary responsibility for the audit, or the audit partner responsible for reviewing the audit, has performed audit services for that issuer in each of the five previous fiscal years of that issuer. Section 103 also states the quality control standards that were discussed in 11.3 Quality Control, above.

Audit Committee Review of Auditors

Under SOX, section 301,[15] public company audit committees are directly responsible for the appointment, compensation, and oversight of the work of any registered public accounting firm employed by their company (including resolution of disagreements between management and the auditor regarding financial reporting). Each such registered public accounting firm reports directly to the audit committee. Auditors may also have to discuss accounting complaints with the audit committee. Each audit committee must have established procedures for the receipt, retention, and treatment of complaints regarding accounting, internal accounting controls, or auditing matters.

11.4 Evaluate Governance Evidence

There is important governance evidence that may be acquired any time during the audit, but definitely has to be done before the final judgment and evaluation phase (Phase IV of the Audit Process Model). The important governance information to be gathered from the client includes: a legal letter, a management representations letter, information about contingent liabilities and commitments, and identification of related parties. The auditor must review legal documents, contracts, board of directors meeting notes and management communication to determine if contingent liabilities exist. A search for unrecorded liabilities, discussed in Chapter 10 Substantive Testing and Evidence is also routine. Because of the numerous international (and generally local) standards requiring disclosure for related parties, evaluating the existence of related parties and transactions with related parties is an important part of the final review.

■ Obtain Evidence and Letters Concerning Litigation, Claims and Assessments

To discover litigation, claims and assessments that affect the client, the auditor relies on both his own field procedures and a letter from the client's legal counsel.

Field Procedures

The field procedures to discover claims against the client are:

- read the corporate meetings' minutes and notes of other appropriate meetings;
- read contracts, leases, correspondence, and other similar documents;
- review guarantees of indebtedness disclosed on bank confirmations;
- inspect other documents for possible client-made guarantees;
- determine if there are any **side letters**.

The auditor will ask management about the policies and procedures adopted for identifying, evaluating and accounting for contingencies; and obtain a description and evaluation of all pending contingencies (before or at balance sheet date). The auditor will obtain written assurance from the client that all **unasserted claims** that require disclosure are disclosed.

Legal Letter

The primary procedure that auditors rely on for discovering litigation, claims and assessments that affect the client is a letter from the client's legal counsel called a legal letter or **inquiry of client's attorneys**. Auditors analyze client legal expense for the present year and sometimes the prior years. The auditor requires that the client send a standard attorney letter to every legal adviser. The letter goes to both outside counsel (independent law firms) and inside general counsel (lawyers that are employees of the client). The standard

Certification Exam Question 11.4[16]

The primary reason an auditor requests letters of inquiry be sent to a client's attorneys is to provide the auditor with:

(A) The probable outcome of asserted claims and pending or threatened litigation.
(B) Corroboration of the information furnished by management about litigation, claims, and assessments.
(C) The attorneys' opinions of the client's historical experiences in recent similar litigation.
(D) A description and evaluation of litigation, claims, and assessments that existed at the balance sheet date.

letter from the client's attorney is prepared on the client's letterhead and signed by one of the client company's management. The desired date of the letter from the attorney is close to the date of the auditor's report.

A sample request for such a legal letter (or inquiry of client's attorneys letter) from the client is shown in Illustration 11.4.

For all litigation, claims and assessments, the inquiry of client's attorneys letter should request evidence relating to:

- existence of conditions or circumstances indicating a possible loss from litigation, claims or assessments;
- the period in which the underlying cause occurred;
- likelihood of an unfavorable outcome;
- amount of potential loss, including court costs.

Letter from Client's Legal Counsel

The letter from client's legal counsel informs the auditor of pending legislation and other information involving legal counsel that is relevant to the financial statements. It should include the following:

1 Identification of the client and the date of the audit.
2 A list, prepared by management, of material pending or threatened litigation, claims or assessments for which the lawyer has been engaged. The management may also request that its lawyer prepare this list.
3 A list, prepared by management, of unasserted claims and assessments which management considers probable of assertion, and that, if **asserted**,[17] would have a reasonable possibility of an unfavorable outcome. There should also be a request that the lawyer indicate any disagreements with the evaluation.
4 A request that the lawyer furnish information or comment about the nature and progress to date of each listed claim or assessment. If possible, the attorney would provide an evaluation of the likelihood and amount of potential losses.
5 A request for the identification of any unlisted pending or threatened legal actions, or a statement that the client's list is complete.
6 A statement by the client informing the lawyer of his responsibility to inform management whenever, in the lawyer's judgment, there is a legal matter requiring disclosure in the financial statements.

ILLUSTRATION 11.4

Legal Letter

Shoun Company
888 24th Street
Lubbock, Texas 79410-1894
January 26, 20x8

Duey Cheattham & Howe
69 Swindle Road
Bamboozle, Texas 78602–3847

Gentlemen:

Our auditors, Kusuda & Gasan, are now engaged in an audit of our financial statements as of December 31, 20X7 and for the year then ended. In connection with the audit, management has furnished Kusuda & Gasan with information concerning certain contingencies involving matters with respect to which you have been engaged and to which you have devoted substantive attention on behalf of the Company. These contingencies individually represent a maximum potential loss exposure in excess of $230,000.

Pending or Threatened Litigation, Claims, and Assessments

We have furnished our auditors with the following information relation to the only pending or threatened litigation, claim, or assessment your firm is handling on our behalf and to which you have devoted substantive attention in the form of legal consultation or representation:

1 Description of the nature of the case – Antitrust complaint filed against the company by the US Department of Justice for discriminatory pricing policies.

2 Process of case to date – Case is in the discovery phase.

3 Response to the case – Management intends to contest the case vigorously.

4 Evaluation of the likelihood of an unfavorable outcome and an estimate, if one can be made, of the amount or range of potential loss – Management believes that the probability of an unfavorable outcome is remote. No estimate of loss can be made.

Please furnish to Kusuda & Gasan such explanation, if any, that you consider necessary to supplement the foregoing information, including an explanation of those matters as to which your views may differ from those stated and an identification of the omission of any pending or threatened litigation, claim, or assessment, or a statement that the list of such matters is complete.

Unasserted Claims and Assessments

We understand that whenever, in the course of performing legal services for us with respect to a matter recognized to involve an unasserted possible claim or assessment that may call for financial statement disclosure, if you have formed a professional conclusion that we must disclose or consider disclosure concerning such possible claim or assessment, as a matter of professional responsibility to us, you will so advise us and will consult with us concerning the question of such disclosure and the applicable requirements of *International Financial Reporting Standard IAS 37*. Please specifically confirm to Kusuda & Gasan that our understanding is correct.

We will be representing to Kusuda & Gasan that there are no unasserted possible claims or assessments that you have advised are probable of assertion and must be disclosed in accordance with *International Financial Reporting Standard IAS 37* in the financial statements currently under audit.

Other Matters

Your response should include matters that existed at December 31, 20X7 and for the period from that date to the date of your response. Please make your response effective as of February 8 20X7, and specifically identify the nature of and reasons for any limitation on your response.

Also, please furnish Kusuda & Gasan with the amount of any unpaid fees due you as of December 31, 20X7 for services rendered through that date. Please mail your reply directly to Kusuda & Gasan, 3012 24th Street, Lubbock, Texas 79410-1894. A stamped, addressed envelope is enclosed for your convenience. Also, please furnish us a copy of your reply.

Sincerely,
Ken McPhail, President

7 A request that the lawyers identify and describe the nature of any reasons for any limitations on the response.

■ Obtain Management Representation Letter

During the course of an audit, management makes many representations to the auditor, either unsolicited or in response to specific inquiries. When these representations relate to matters that are material to the financial statements, the auditor must seek corroborative audit evidence, evaluate whether the representations made by management appear reasonable and consistent with other audit evidence, and consider whether the individuals making the representations are competent to do so. International Standard on Auditing 580[18] states: "The auditor should obtain evidence that management acknowledges its responsibility for the fair representation of the financial statements in accordance with the relevant financial reporting framework, and has approved the financial statements."

Certification Exam Question 11.5

Which of the following statements ordinarily is included among the written client representations obtained by the auditor?

(A) Compensating balances and other arrangements involving restrictions on cash balances have been disclosed.
(B) Management acknowledges responsibility for illegal actions committed by employees.
(C) Sufficient evidential matter has been made available to permit the issuance of an unqualified opinion.
(D) Management acknowledges that they have **not** contributed amounts to political campaigns in excess of that required by law.

The auditor can obtain this evidence from relevant minutes of meetings of board of directors, a signed copy of the financial statements, or by obtaining a written representation from management.

Written Representations from Management

In instances when other sufficient appropriate audit evidence cannot reasonably be expected to exist, "the auditor should obtain written representations from management on matters material to the financial statements."[19] The auditor may document in his working papers evidence of management's representations by summarizing oral discussions with management or by obtaining written representations from management. The possibility of misunderstandings between the auditor and management is reduced when oral representations are confirmed in writing by management.

Form and Content of Representations Letter

Written representations can take the form of a representation letter from management, or a letter from the auditor outlining his understanding of management's representation, duly acknowledged and confirmed by management.[20] The management representation letter should be addressed to the auditor or to the shareholders in an annual report. It should contain the information requested by the auditor, be appropriately dated with the same date as the auditor's report on the financial statements,[21] and signed. The members of management who have primary responsibility for the entity and its financial aspects, usually the senior executive officer and the chief financial officer, should sign the letter.

Matters that are ordinarily included in a management representation letter are:

- management's acknowledgement of its responsibility for the fair presentation of financial statements;
- availability of all financial records and related data;
- information regarding related party transactions;
- plans or intentions that may affect the carrying value or classification of assets;
- disclosure of compensating balances and other arrangements involving restrictions on cash balances.

A sample of a management representation letter to the auditor is shown in Illustration 11.5.

Concept and a Company 11.1

Universal Health Services and KPMG – "I am neither a certified public accountant nor a securities lawyer."

Concept   Management representation letter and responsibility for financial statements.

Story   Universal Health Services, Inc. (UHS) is a hospital company operating acute care and behavioral health hospitals, ambulatory surgery and radiation centers in the USA, Puerto Rico and France. UHS owns 25 acute-care and 39 behavioral health hospitals in these three countries.

In February 2003, UHS's CFO Kirk Gorman, a company veteran of 16 years, was asked to resign at the urging of its auditor, KPMG LLP. KPMG were doing their first audit for the company, having just replaced the prior auditor Arthur Andersen. According to UHS, there was a dispute related to Gorman's theoretical views about the split of duties and responsibilities between the CFO and the auditor. (Gallaro 2003)

Gorman wrote a letter to the Philadelphia office of KPMG explaining that, while he was willing to sign the management representation letter (attesting that the financial statements he submitted for audit were, to the best of his knowledge, accurate), he was relying on KPMG to ensure that the accounting treatment was in accordance with GAAP. (Leone 2003) He asked if KPMG would be willing to sign a similar statement vouching for the accuracy of its work. (*Corporate Finance* 2003) Furthermore, the letter released by UHS, stated that, "I do review and analyze the financial statements and disclosures in our 10-Q and 10-K filings, but I can't personally verify that all of our accounts are in accordance with GAAP." Because he was "neither a certified public accountant nor a securities lawyer" that lead him to "rely upon KPMG to ensure that our financial statements ... are in compliance with (generally accepted accounting principles) and securities regulations." (UHS 2002)

In a letter dated February 10 (UHS 2003), Gorman sought to clarify his position. He wrote that he had not intended to leave the impression that he doubted the veracity of the company's financial statements or that he wanted to shift responsibility for the statements' accuracy to KPMG. (Gallaro 2003)

Nevertheless, KPMG went to the UHS board and argued that it couldn't approve the company's financial statements as long as Gorman remained CFO. Due to "philosophical differences," the company asked Gorman to resign.

Discussion Questions	■ Who is responsible for the financial statements and why is that the case? ■ Should an auditor sign a statement vouching for the accuracy of his work? Why?

References	Corporate Finance, 2003, "Auditors turn up the heat on CFOs," *Corporate Finance*, London: March, p. 1. Gallaro, V., 2003, "Executive reservations," *Modern Healthcare*, Chicago: February 24, Vol. 33, Iss. 8, p. 12. Leone, M., 2003, "New certification and internal control requirements are heaping new hazards on finance chiefs. Here's how some are coping," *CFO.com*, Boston: May 9, p. 1. UHS, 2002, Letter to KPMG from Gorman, **www.uhs.com**, dated December 12.

If management refuses to provide representations that the auditor considers necessary, this will be considered a **limitation on scope** under international standards. It is also a limitation on scope if management has provided an oral representation but refuses to confirm it in writing. This scope limitation would mean that the auditor should express a qualified opinion or a disclaimer of opinion.

■ Review for Contingent Liabilities and Commitments

Contingent liability is a potential future obligation to an outside party for an unknown amount resulting from the outcome of a past event, for example an adverse tax court decision, lawsuit, and notes receivable discounted. Footnote disclosure is ordinarily required if there are probable losses.

Conditions for Existence of a Contingent Liability

Three conditions are required for a contingent liability to exist:

1 There is a potential future payment to an outside party or potential future assets impairment.
2 There is an uncertainty about the amount of payment or asset impairment.
3 The outcome will be resolved by some future event.

Procedures to Test for Contingencies

Audit procedures that test for contingencies are not just done in the last days of the audit, but from the beginning. Income tax disputes, investigations by government or industry authorities, and the amount of unused bank lines of credit are generally known from the start of the audit. Procedures such as reviews of contracts, correspondence, credit agreements and inquiries of management should point out possible contingencies.

One audit procedure for finding contingencies is the legal letter already discussed where the auditor analyzes legal expenses and statements from legal counsel and obtains a letter from each major lawyer as to the status of pending litigation. Three other common procedures are to: review working papers; examine letters of credit to confirm used and unused balances; and evaluation of known contingent liabilities.

ILLUSTRATION 11.5

Management Representation Letter[22]

The following letter is not intended to be a standard letter. Representations by management will vary from one entity to another and from one period to the next. Although seeking representations from management on a variety of matters may serve to focus management's attention on those matters, and thus cause management to specifically address those matters in more detail than would otherwise be the case, the auditor needs to be cognizant of the limitations of management representations as audit evidence as set out in this ISA.

Shoun Company
888 24th Street
Lubbock, Texas 79410-1894
January 26, 20x8

Kusuda & Gasan, CPAs
3012 24th Street
Lubbock, Texas 79410-1894.

Dear Ms. Kusuda,

This representation letter is provided in connection with your audit of the financial statements of ABC Company for the year ended December 31, 20X7 for the purpose of expressing an opinion as to whether the financial statements give a true and fair view of (present fairly, in all material respects,) the financial position of Shoun Company as of December 31, 20X7 and of the results of its operations and its cash flows for the year then ended in accordance with (indicate relevant financial reporting framework).

We acknowledge our responsibility for the fair presentation of the financial statements in accordance with (indicate relevant financial reporting framework). We confirm, to the best of our knowledge and belief, the following representations:

Include here representations relevant to the entity. Such representations may include:

- There have been no irregularities involving management or employees who have a significant role in the accounting and internal control systems or that could have a material effect on the financial statements.
- We have made available to you all books of account and supporting documentation and all minutes of meetings of shareholders and the board of directors (namely those held on March 15, 20X7 and September 30, 20X7, respectively).
- We confirm the completeness of the information provided regarding the identification of related parties.
- The financial statements are free of material misstatements, including omissions.
- The Company has complied with all aspects of contractual agreements that could have a material effect on the financial statements in the event of noncompliance.
- There has been no noncompliance with requirements of regulatory authorities that could have a material effect on the financial statements in the event of noncompliance.
- The following have been properly recorded and when appropriate, adequately disclosed in the financial statements:
    (a) The identity of, and balances and transactions with, related parties.
    (b) Losses arising from sale and purchase commitments.
    (c) Agreements and options to buy back assets previously sold.
    (d) Assets pledged as collateral.
- We have no plans or intentions that may materially alter the carrying value or classification of assets and liabilities reflected in the financial statements.
- We have no plans to abandon lines of product or other plans or intentions that will result in any excess or obsolete inventory, and no inventory is stated at an amount in excess of net realizable value.
- The Company has satisfactory title to all assets and there are no liens or encumbrances on the company's assets, except for those that are disclosed in Note X to the financial statements.

Illustration 11.5 (continued)

- We have recorded or disclosed, as appropriate, all liabilities, both actual and contingent, and have disclosed in Note X to the financial statements all guarantees that we have given to third parties.
- Other than ... described in Note X to the financial statements, there have been no events subsequent to period end which require adjustment of or disclosure in the financial statements or Notes thereto.
- The ... claim by XYZ Company has been settled for the total sum of XXX which has been properly accrued in the financial statements. No other claims in connection with litigation have been or are expected to be received.
- There are no formal or informal compensating balance arrangements with any of our cash and investment accounts. Except as disclosed in Note X to the financial statements, we have no other line of credit arrangements.
- We have properly recorded or disclosed in the financial statements the capital stock repurchase options and agreements, and capital stock reserved for options, warrants, conversions and other requirements.

Sincerely,
Ken McPhail, President
Kurt Hull, Controller

Contingencies that are of concern to the auditor, among others, are: pending litigation for patent infringement, product liability or other actions; guarantees of obligations of others; product warranties; income tax disputes; and notes receivable discounted.

Commitments

Similar to contingent liabilities are commitments. **Commitments** are agreements that the entity will hold to a fixed set of conditions, such as the purchase or sale of merchandise at a stated price, at a future date, regardless of what happens to profits or to the economy as a whole. Examples are commitments to purchase raw materials, lease premises, royalty agreements, licensing agreements and agreements to sell merchandise or services at a fixed price. There may be commitments to employees in the form of profit sharing, stock options, health benefits and pension plans.

All material commitments are ordinarily either described together in a separate footnote or combined in a footnote related to contingencies.

■ Related Parties

Parties are considered to be related if one party has the ability to control the other party or exercise significant influence over the other party in making financial and operation decisions. A **related party transaction** is a transfer of resources or obligations between related parties, regardless of whether a price is charged.

Two aspects of related party transactions of which an auditor must be aware is adequate disclosure of related party transactions and the possibility that the existence of related parties increases the risk of management fraud. International Financial Reporting Standards (IAS 24)[23] requires disclosure of the nature and volume of transactions with related parties. There are many legitimate reasons for significant transactions with related parties but the risk for an auditor is that management will conceal transactions between related parties causing the disclosures to be misstated, i.e. the related party disclosures are not complete.

Procedures to Discover Related Party Transactions

Because of the possibility of related party transactions, the auditor should perform audit procedures designed to obtain sufficient appropriate audit evidence regarding the identification and disclosure by management of related parties and the effect of related party transactions. However, an audit cannot be expected to detect all related party transactions.[24] Audit procedures must identify circumstances that increase the risk of misstatement or that indicate material misstatement regarding related parties has occurred. If these circumstances exist, the auditor should perform modified, extended, or additional procedures. Illustration 11.6 shows examples of circumstances and may indicate the existence of previously unidentified related parties.

Concept and a Company 11.2

Adelphia Communications

Concept	Related parties and unrecorded liabilities.
Story	Adelphia Communications, the sixth largest cable television provider in the USA was the subject of a Securities and Exchange Commission (SEC) and federal grand jury investigation into its finances as its accounting practices were questioned. The company was founded and managed by John Rigas and his family.

Adelphia had fraudulently excluded from the Company's annual and quarterly consolidated financial statements portions of its bank debt, totaling approximately $2.3 billion in undisclosed, off-balance-sheet bank debt as of December 31, 2001, by systematically recording those liabilities on the books of unconsolidated affiliates, which were controlled by the Rigas family (Rigas Entities). They included in those financial statements a footnote disclosure implicitly misrepresenting that such portions had been included on Adelphia's balance sheet (SEC 2002). Adelphia and its executives created sham transactions backed by fictitious documents to give the false appearance that Adelphia had actually repaid debts, when, in truth, it had simply shifted them to unconsolidated Rigas-controlled entities.

Since at least 1998, Adelphia used fraudulent misrepresentations and omissions of material fact to conceal rampant self-dealing by the Rigases, the family which founded and ran Adelphia, including use of Adelphia funds to: pay for vacation properties and New York City apartments; develop a golf course mostly owned by the Rigases; and purchase over $772 million of Adelphia shares of common stock and over $563 million of Adelphia notes for the Rigases' own benefit. (SEC 2002)

In addition to Adelphia's own business operations, it also managed and maintained virtually every aspect of the Rigas Entities that owned and operated cable television systems, including maintaining their books and records on a general ledger system shared with Adelphia and its subsidiaries. The Rigas Entities did not reimburse or otherwise compensate Adelphia for these services.

Adelphia and the Rigas Entities, including those that are in businesses unrelated to cable systems, participated jointly in a cash management system operated by Adelphia (the "Adelphia CMS"). Adelphia, its subsidiaries, and the Rigas Entities all deposited some or all of their cash generated or otherwise obtained from their operations, borrowings and other sources in the Adelphia CMS, withdrew cash from the Adelphia CMS to be used for their expenses, capital expenditures, repayments of debt and other uses, and engaged in transfers of funds with other participants in the Adelphia CMS. This resulted in the commingling of funds among the Adelphia CMS participants, including Adelphia subsidiaries and Rigas Entities, and created numerous related party payables and receivables among Adelphia, its subsidiaries, and the Rigas Entities. (SEC 2002)

To conceal that the Rigases were engaged in rampant self-dealing at Adelphia's expense, Adelphia misrepresented or concealed a number of significant transactions by which the Rigases used Adelphia resources with no reimbursement or other compensation to Adelphia. The defendants engaged in these practices to afford Adelphia continued access to commercial credit and the capital markets.

In November 2002, Adelphia Corporation filed suit against its former auditor, Deloitte & Touche, claiming the firm was partly responsible for the alleged fraud that cost company shareholders billions of dollars. "If Deloitte had acted consistently with its professional responsibilities as Adelphia's outside auditor, these losses could have been preventable," according to the complaint. The complaint alleges that some of the Rigas family's (which controlled Adelphia) acts of self-dealing were apparent to Deloitte on the books and records which Deloitte reviewed and that Deloitte knew or should have known of such acts! During its 2000 audit, for which an unqualified audit opinion was given, Deloitte asked the Rigases to disclose the full amount of the loans, which totaled $1.45 billion at the time but later amounted to more than $3 billion. The Rigases refused, and Deloitte never disclosed this issue or any disagreement to the audit committee. Adelphia's cash management system had a pool of corporate funds that the Rigases used as their personal bank account. The complaint alleges that Deloitte knew about the system and didn't report it to the audit committee. (Frank 2002)

Discussion Questions	■ What audit procedures could the auditor undertake to detect the Adelphia related-party transactions? ■ What kind of control environment encourages related-party transactions? ■ At what point would the auditor report related-party dealings to the board of directors?

References Frank, R., 2002, "The Economy: Adelphia Sues Deloitte & Touche, Accusing Former Auditor of Fraud," *Wall Street Journal* (Eastern edition), New York, NY, November 7, p. A.2.

SEC, 2002, *Litigation Release No. 17837 Accounting Auditing Enforcement Release No. 1664*, "Securities And Exchange Commission V. Adelphia Communications Corporation, John J. Rigas, Timothy J. Rigas, Michael J. Rigas, James P. Rigas, James R. Brown, and Michael C. Mulcahey," US Securities and Exchange Commission, November 14.

Certification Exam Question 11.6[25]

When auditing related-party transactions, an auditor places primary emphasis on:

(A) Ascertaining the rights and obligations of the related parties.
(B) Confirming the existence of the related parties.
(C) Verifying the valuation of the related-party transactions.
(D) Evaluating the disclosure of the related-party transactions.

ILLUSTRATION 11.6

Circumstances That May Indicate Unidentified Related Parties[26]

During the course of the audit, the auditor needs to be alert for transactions that appear unusual in the circumstances and may indicate the existence of previously unidentified related parties. Examples include:

■ Transactions which have abnormal terms of trade, such as unusual prices, interest rates, guarantees, and repayment terms.

■ Transactions which lack an apparent logical business reason for their occurrence.

■ Transactions in which substance differs from form.

■ Transactions processed in an unusual manner.

■ High-volume or significant transactions with certain customers or suppliers as compared with others.

■ Unrecorded transactions such as the receipt or provision of management services at no charge.

The auditor should review information provided by the directors and management identifying related party transactions and should be alert for other material related party transactions. He should review management information identifying the names of all known related parties.

The auditor is required under ISA 550 to perform the following procedures in respect of the completeness of this information:[27]

■ review prior year working papers for names of known related parties;
■ review the entity's procedures for identification of related parties;
■ inquire as to the affiliation of directors and officers with other entities;
■ review shareholder records to determine the names of principal shareholders or, if appropriate, obtain a listing of principal shareholders from the share register;
■ review minutes of the meetings of shareholders and the board of directors and other relevant statutory records such as the register of directors' interests;
■ inquire of other auditors currently involved in the audit, or predecessor auditors, as to their knowledge of additional related parties;
■ review the entity's income tax returns and other information supplied to the regulatory agencies.

The auditor should also carry out procedures which may identify related party transactions such as those shown in Illustration 11.7.

The auditor should obtain a written representation from management (as part of the management representation letter) concerning the completeness of information provided regarding the identification of related parties and the adequacy of related party disclosures in the financial statements.[28] If the auditor is unable to obtain sufficient audit evidence concerning related parties and transactions or concludes that their disclosures in the financial statements are not adequate, the auditor should modify the audit report.

ILLUSTRATION 11.7

Procedures to Identify Related Parties Transactions[29]

During the course of the audit, the auditor carries out procedures that may identify the existence of transactions with related parties. Examples include:

■ Performing detailed tests of transactions and balances.

■ Reviewing minutes of meetings of shareholders and directors.

■ Reviewing accounting records for large or unusual transactions or balances, paying particular attention to transactions recognized at or near the end of the reporting period.

■ Reviewing confirmations of loans receivable and payable and confirmations from banks. Such a review may indicate guarantor relationship and other related party transactions.

■ Reviewing investment transactions, for example, purchase or sale of an equity interest in a joint venture to another entity.

11.5 Review for Discovery of Subsequent Events

Review for subsequent events are the auditing procedures performed by auditors to identify and evaluate subsequent events. **Subsequent events** are transactions and other pertinent events that occurred after the balance sheet date and which affect the fair presentation or disclosure of the statements being audited. Under International Standard on Auditing (ISA) 560[30] the auditor should consider the effect of subsequent events on the financial statements and on the auditor's report.

Concept and a Company 11.3

Arabian American Development Company – the undisclosed event

Concept	Subsequent events and disclosure.
Story	Arabian, a Delaware corporation based in Dallas, Texas, is in the business of refining petrochemical products and developing mining operations in Saudi Arabia and the USA. Arabian maintains an office in Jeddah, Saudi Arabia, to manage its Saudi Arabian operations. Hatem El-Khalidi, age 78, a US citizen and resident of Jeddah, Saudi Arabia, helped found Arabian in 1967, and serves as the Chief Executive Officer, the President and a director of Arabian. Arabian and El-Khalidi, violated SEC rules which required Arabian to include in annual and quarterly reports any material information that might be necessary to make those reports not misleading. They failed to disclose a material lease that had a high probability of expiring, affecting severely the company's total assets. In 1993, Arabian obtained a 30-year lease from the Saudi Arabian government to mine zinc, lead and gold in the Al Masane area of Saudi Arabia. The Al Masane lease is Arabian's largest asset, accounting for approximately \$36 million (65 percent) of Arabian's \$56

▶

Arabian American Development Company – the undisclosed event (continued)

million in total assets. The lease agreement requires Arabian to build the mine, and begin mining operations, pursuant to a work schedule, and if Arabian fails to comply with the work schedule, the Saudi government may have the right to terminate the lease. (SEC 2003)

In the late 1990s the economic crisis in Southeast Asia caused a sharp drop in mineral prices, making it uneconomical for Arabian to comply with the work schedule required by the lease. In May 2000, the Ministry for Petroleum and Mineral Resources of Saudi Arabia, an agency of the Saudi Arabian government, notified Arabian, via correspondence sent to El-Khalidi in Saudi Arabia, that Arabian must implement the Al Masane Project, as required by the lease agreement. If Arabian failed to do so, the Ministry would begin procedures to terminate the lease. (SEC 2003)

Ignoring this correspondence, in April 2002, El-Khalidi signed a management representation letter with Grant Thornton, Arabian's outside auditor, representing, among other things: (1) that Arabian has complied with all aspects of contractual agreements that would have a material effect on the company's financial statements in the event of non-compliance; (2) that no events have occurred which would impair the company's ability to recover its investment in the Al Masane Project and other interests in Saudi Arabia; and (3) there is no impairment of the company's investment in the Al Masane Project. (SEC 2003)

In late November 2002, El-Khalidi disclosed to Arabian's Treasurer that the Saudi government was threatening to terminate the Al Masane lease. The Treasurer promptly informed Arabian's other officers and directors and, on December 23, 2002, Arabian filed a Form 8-K with the SEC that publicly disclosed for the first time that the Saudi government was threatening to terminate Arabian's lease. The Treasurer also informed Grant Thornton, which subsequently withdrew its audit reports for Arabian's 2000 and 2001 financial statements and resigned as Arabian's outside auditor. (SEC 2003)

Discussion Questions	<ul><li>Why should the problems with the mining lease be disclosed, even though it had no current impact on Arabian?</li><li>After Grant Thornton learned of the lease problem, what were their options in relation to their prior audit opinions?</li><li>Why do you think Grant Thornton resigned as auditor?</li></ul>
References	All material from SEC, 2003, Litigation Release No. 48638, Accounting and Auditing Enforcement Release No. 1898, "In the Matter of Arabian American Development Company and Hatem El-Khalidi," US Security and Exchange Commission, October 16.

■ Types of Events After the Balance Sheet Date

International Financial Reporting Standard IAS 10[31] deals with the treatment of financial statement of events, favorable and unfavorable, occurring after period end. It identifies two types of events:

1 those that provide further evidence of conditions that existed at period end;
2 those that are indicative of conditions that arose subsequent to period end.

The first type requires adjustment to the financial statements and the second type, if material, requires disclosure.

Events Relating to Conditions that Existed at Period End

Events relating to assets and liabilities conditions that existed at period end may require adjustment of the financial statements. For example, adjustments may be made for a loss on a trade receivable account that is confirmed by the bankruptcy of a customer that occurs after the balance sheet date. Other examples of these events that require adjustment of financial statements are:

■ settlement of litigation at an amount different from the amount recorded on the books;
■ disposal of equipment not being used in operations at a price below current book value;
■ sale of investments at a price below recorded cost.

Events Not Affecting Conditions at Period End

Events that fall into the second category, i.e. those that do not affect the condition of assets or liabilities at the balance sheet date, but are of such importance that non-disclosure would affect the ability of the users of the financial statements to make proper evaluations and decisions, should be disclosed. Examples of these types of events are:

■ a decline in the market value of securities held for temporary investment or resale;
■ issuance of bonds or equity securities;
■ a decline in the market value of inventory as a consequence of government action barring further sale of a product;
■ an uninsured loss of inventories as a result of fire.

■ Events Up to the Date of the Auditor's Report

The auditor should perform procedures designed to obtain sufficient appropriate audit evidence that all events up to the date of the auditor's report that may require adjustment of, or disclosure in, the financial statements have been identified. Some of these procedures are described in Illustration 11.8. When the auditor becomes aware of events which materially affect the financial statements, the auditor should consider whether such events are properly accounted for and adequately disclosed in the financial statements.

Certification Exam Question 11.[32]

After an audit report containing an unqualified opinion on a non-public client's financial statements was issued, the client decided to sell the shares of a subsidiary that accounts for 30 percent of its revenue and 25 percent of its net income. The auditor should:

(A) Determine whether the information is reliable and, if determined to be reliable, request that revised financial statements be issued.
(B) Notify the entity that the auditor's report may **no** longer be associated with the financial statements.
(C) Describe the effects of this subsequently discovered information in a communication with persons known to be relying on the financial statements.
(D) Take **no** action because the auditor has **no** obligation to make any further inquiries.

ILLUSTRATION 11.8

Procedures to Identify Events That May Require Adjustment of, or Disclosure in, the Financial Statements[33]

The procedures to identify events that may require adjustment of, or disclosure in, the financial statements would be performed as near as practicable to the date of the auditor's report and ordinarily include the following:

- Reviewing procedures management has established to ensure that subsequent events are identified.
- Reading minutes of the meetings of shareholders, the board of directors and audit and executive committees held after period end and inquiring about matters discussed at meetings for which minutes are not yet available.
- Reading the entity's latest available interim financial statements and, as considered necessary and appropriate, budgets, cash flow forecasts and other related management reports.
- Inquiring, or extending previous oral or written inquiries, of the entity's lawyers concerning litigation and claims.
- Inquiring of management as to whether any subsequent events have occurred which might affect the financial statements. Examples of inquiries of management on specific matters are:
  - the current status of items that were accounted for on the basis of preliminary or inconclusive data;
  - whether new commitments, borrowings or guarantees have been entered into;
  - whether sales of assets have occurred or are planned;
  - whether the issue of new shares or debentures or an agreement to merge or liquidate has been made or is planned;
  - whether any assets have been appropriated by government or destroyed, for example, by flood or fire;
  - whether there have been any developments regarding risk areas and contingencies;
  - whether any unusual accounting adjustments have been made or are contemplated;
  - whether any events have occurred or are likely to occur which will bring into question the appropriateness of accounting policies used in the financial statements as would be the case, for example, if such events call into question the validity of the going concern assumption.

■ Events Between the Balance Sheet Date and the Issuance of the Statements

The auditor does not have any responsibility to perform procedures or make any inquiry regarding the financial statements after the date of the auditor's report but before approval of the statements by shareholders. During this period it is the responsibility of management to inform the auditor of facts that may affect the financial statements. However, if the auditor becomes aware of a fact that may materially affect the financial statements during this period, he should discuss the matter with management and consider the possibility of amending the existing financial statements.

When Management Amends the Financial Statements

When management amends the financial statements, the auditor would carry out the procedures necessary in the circumstances and would provide management with a new report on the amended financial statements dated not earlier than the date the amended financial statements are signed or approved. The procedures outlined in Illustration 11.8 would be extended to the date of the new auditor's report.

When Management Does Not Amend the Financial Statements

When management does not amend the financial statements in circumstances where the auditor believes they need to be amended and the auditor's report has not been released, the auditor should express either a **qualified** or an **adverse** opinion. If the auditor's report has been released to the entity's governance body, the auditor would notify those persons not to issue financial statements and the auditor's report. If the financial statements are subsequently issued to the regulators or public, the auditor needs to take action to prevent reliance on that auditor's report.

■ Discovery of Facts After The Financial Statements Have Been Issued (After the Shareholders' Meeting)

After the financial statements have been issued the auditor has no obligation to make any inquiry regarding such financial statements. If, however, after the statements have been issued, the auditor becomes aware of a fact which existed at the date of the auditor's report and which, if known then, may have caused the auditor to issue a **modified auditor's report**, the auditor should discuss it with management and consider revision of the financial statements.

The new auditor's report should include an **emphasis of a matter paragraph** referring to a note to the financial statements that more extensively discusses the reason for the revision of the previously issued financial statements and to the earlier report issued by the auditor. The new auditor's report would be dated not earlier than the date the revised financial statements are approved. The procedures listed in Illustration 11.8 would ordinarily be extended to the date of the new auditor's report.

11.6 Review Financial Statements and Other Report Material

The final review of the financial statements involves procedures to determine if disclosures of financial statements and other required disclosures (for corporate governance, management reports, etc.) are adequate. The auditor is responsible for all information that appears with the audited financial statements, so therefore the auditor must also see if there are any inconsistencies between this other information and the financial statements.

■ Financial Statement Disclosures

An important consideration in completing the audit is determination of whether the disclosures in the financial statements are adequate. Adequate disclosure includes consideration of all the financial statements, including related footnotes.

Under the Sarbanes-Oxley Act (SOX) auditors have the responsibility of considering certain financial statement disclosures connected with the financial statements.[34] In Section 404,[35] SOX requires that each annual report of a publicly traded company contain an internal control report. The report should state the responsibility of management for establishing and maintaining an adequate internal control structure, and contain an assessment of the effectiveness of the internal control structure and the financial statement accounting procedures of company. Each public accounting firm that prepares or issues the audit report for these companies according to PCAOB Audit Standard #2 must attest to, and report on, the assessment made by the management. Companies must disclose all material correcting adjustments and off-balance sheet transactions. Pro-forma information included in any report must not contain an untrue statement of material fact, reconciled with the financial condition of the company.

Adequate Disclosure Ongoing

Review for adequate disclosure is an ongoing activity of the audit. For example, as part of the audit of accounts receivable, the auditor must be aware of the need to separate notes receivable and amounts due from affiliates and trade accounts due from customers because all of these may require different disclosure. Furthermore, there must be a segregation of current and non-current receivables and a disclosure of the factoring or discounting of notes receivable. An important part of verifying all account balances is determining whether financial accounting standards were applied on a basis consistent with that of the preceding year.

Financial Statement Disclosure Checklist

Many audit firms use a financial statement disclosure checklist. An independent partner or director designs these questionnaires to remind the auditor of common disclosure problems encountered on audits and also to facilitate the final review of the entire audit. Illustration 11.9 shows a partial financial statement disclosure checklist. Of course, in any given audit some aspects of the engagement require much greater expertise in accounting than can be obtained from such a checklist.

ILLUSTRATION 11.9

Financial Statement Disclosure Checklist: Inventory

1 Are the following disclosures included in the financial statements or notes?

  (a) The accounting policies adopted in measuring inventories, including the cost formula used.

  (b) The total carrying amount of inventories and the carrying amount in classifications.

  (c) The carrying amount of inventories carried at net realizable value.

  (d) The amount of any reversal of any write-down that is recognized as income in the period.

  (e) The circumstances or events that led to the reversal or write-down of inventories.

  (f) The carrying amount of inventories pledged as security for liabilities.

2 Do the financial statements disclose either:

  (a) the cost of inventories recognized as an expense during the period; or

  (b) the operating costs, applicable to revenues, recognized as an expense during the period, classified by their nature?

■ Corporate Governance Disclosures

Recently, there has been worldwide concern by shareholders that corporations should be governed in their best interests. This has led to a requirement on the London Stock Exchange for companies to report that they have followed a Code of Best Practice that was suggested by the Cadbury Committee.[36] The London Stock Exchange requires all listed companies registered in the UK, as a continuing obligation of listing, to state whether they are complying with the Code and to give reasons for any areas of non-compliance. The areas of greatest concern to auditors are the requirements that the directors report on internal control and going concern.

Certification Exam Question 11.8

When audited financial statements are presented in a client's document containing other information, the auditor should:

(A) Perform inquiry and analytical procedures to ascertain whether the other information is reasonable.
(B) Add an explanatory paragraph to the auditor's report without changing the opinion on the financial statements.
(C) Perform the appropriate substantive auditing procedures to corroborate the other information.
(D) Read the other information to determine that it is consistent with the audited financial statements.

The London Stock Exchange Code of Best Practice states that[37] the directors should report on the effectiveness of the company's system of internal control and that the business is a going concern, with supporting assumptions or qualifications as necessary.

SOX Governance Disclosures

Under the Sarbanes-Oxley Act (SOX) auditors have responsibility regarding certain governance disclosures connected with the financial statements.[38] The company must also disclose whether or not – and if not, the reason why – it has adopted a **code of ethics**[39] for senior financial officers, applicable to its principal financial officer and comptroller or principal accounting officer, or persons performing similar functions.[40] SOX section 407[41] requires company disclosure of whether or not – and if not, the reasons why – their audit committee is comprised of at least one member who is a financial expert.

In other countries similar developments took place. For example in France, the Netherlands, South Africa and Canada reports about corporate governance were published and broadly discussed. The expected roles of auditors vary between countries and, in most cases, they are less highly profiled than in the UK.

Governance Issues are discussed in Chapter 14 Corporate Governance.

■ Other Information in Annual Reports

ISA 720 states that the auditor should read the other information (in documents containing audited financial statements) to identify material inconsistencies with the audited financial statements.[42] "Other information," on which the auditor may have no obligation to report but which he must check for material inconsistencies, includes documents such as an **annual report**, a report by management or the board of directors on operations, financial summary or highlights, employment data, planned capital expenditures, financial ratios, names of officers and directors, selected quarterly data, and documents used in securities offerings.

Material Inconsistency

A material inconsistency exists when other information contradicts information contained in the audited financial statements. A material inconsistency may raise doubts about the audit conclusions drawn from audit evidence obtained and, possibly, about the basis for the auditor's opinion on the financial statements.

If the auditor identifies a material inconsistency on reading the other information, he should determine whether the audited financial statements or the other information needs to be amended. If an amendment is necessary in the other information and the entity refuses to make the amendment, the auditor should consider including in the auditor's report an **emphasis of matter paragraph** describing the material inconsistency or taking other action. If an amendment is necessary for the audited financial statements and the entity refuses to allow it, the auditor should express a qualified or adverse opinion.

Material Misstatement of Fact

If the auditor becomes aware that the other information appears to include a **material misstatement of fact** he should discuss the matter with the company's management. If the auditor still considers there is an apparent misstatement of fact, he should request that management consult with a qualified third party, such as the entity's legal counsel, and should consider the advice received. If management still refuses to correct the misstatement, the auditor should take appropriate action that might include notifying the board of directors.

11.7 Wrap-Up Procedures

Wrap-up procedures are those procedures done at the end of an audit that generally cannot be performed before the other audit work is complete. Wrap-up procedures include: supervisory review, final **analytical procedures** (discussed in Chapter 9 Analytical Procedures), working paper review, evaluating audit findings for material misstatements, client approval of adjusting entries, review of laws and regulation, and evaluation of the company as a going concern.

Illustration 11.10 summarizes the wrap-up procedures normally undertaken.

■ Supervisory Review

Wrap-up procedures start with the in-charge (senior) accountant reviewing the work of the staff accountant. In turn, the manager and partner in charge of the audit review the work submitted by the in-charge accountant. Often, for larger audits, an additional

ILLUSTRATION 11.10

Typical Wrap-up Procedures

Supervisory Review
- in charge reviews work of staff accountant
- manager reviews work of in charge
- partner reviews manager's work

Do analytical procedures
- review of trends and important ratios
- review of unexpected audit findings

Review working papers
- reviewed by an independent member of the audit firm
- reviewed for results of audit tests
- reviewed for sufficiency of evidence
- make a completing-the-engagement checklist
- make an unadjusted error worksheet

Evaluate audit findings for material misstatement
- sign off completion of steps in audit program
- identify monetary misstatements in financial statements
- propose adjustments to financial statements

Client approval of adjusting entries
- proposed the manager approves adjusting entries
- obtain client approval for all proposed adjusting and reclassification journal entries

Review laws and regulations
- Review recent changes in statutes and regulations
- Test compliance with regulations

Evaluate entity's continuance as a going concern
- review normal indications of risk
- do analytical procedures
- determine if going concern problems can be mitigated by other factors

review of the engagement is performed by a manager or partner not working on the engagement to provide an objective assessment of compliance with firm standards (and SOX where applicable). For auditing firms with multiple offices, it is common practice for review teams to visit the various offices periodically and review selected engagements.

Before signing off on the audit work, the in-charge or senior accountant must make sure that all phases of the work have been concluded in accordance with the audit planning memorandum, that applicable audit procedures have been satisfactorily completed, the audit objectives have been satisfied, that all is done in line with ISAs and that the working papers reflect conclusions supporting the audit opinion. Some audit firms, as we will see in Chapter 13 Overview of a Group Audit, draft an overall memorandum at the conclusion of the engagement commenting on the fairness of the presentation.

ILLUSTRATION 11.11

Review Checklist

Client _____ Closing Date _____	Yes	No	Comments
I. General Questions			
1 Have you reviewed work paper files?			
2 Are you satisfied that: (a) The judgments and conclusions reached are supported by documented evidence? (b) The work paper files contain no unresolved statements that are prejudicial to the interests of the firm? (c) Appropriate changes in the next examination, if any, have been summarized?			
3 Do the work papers include adequate documentation as to: (a) Changes in accounting policies? (b) Conformity with generally accepted accounting principles or another comprehensive basis of accounting, if appropriate? (c) Appropriate changes in the next examination, if any, have been summarized?			
4 Have you reviewed the audit conclusion on all material items in the financial statements?			
5 Based on your review and your knowledge of the client, do the financial statements fairly present the company's financial position, results of its operations and cash flow?			
6 Is the work performed consistent with the arrangements made with the client?			
7 Does the work performed comply with the firm's quality control policies in all material respects?			
8 Has the computer-assisted audit techniques-related documentation been reviewed by a qualified computer specialist?			
9 Have required job evaluation forms been completed?			
II. Financial Statements			
1 Is the name of the company exact?			
2 Are the dates of the balance sheet and period covered by statements of income, stockholders' equity, and cash flow exact?			
3 Are all material facts that are necessary to make the financial statements not misleading adequately disclosed?			
4 Have all material and/or extraordinary subsequent events been evaluated and properly treated and/or disclosed?			
5 Is there adequate footnote disclosure? Do the footnotes clearly communicate the facts?			
6 Do the financial statements maintain a uniform manner of format, capitalization, headings and appearance in general within itself?			

Illustration 11.11 (continued)

Client _____ Closing Date _____	Yes	No	Comments
7 Are you satisfied that other information contained agrees with the financial statements and auditor's report?			
III. The Audit Report			
1 Is the audit report addressed to the proper party?			
2 Is the audit report properly worded?			
3 Is an explanatory paragraph included in our opinion when the financial statements are inconsistent?			
4 Is the date of our report proper?			
5 Is any date in the footnotes that requires special mention, with respect to the date of our report, appropriately reflected in the date of our report (e.g. dual dating)?			
6 Is the option on the supplementary financial information proper and supported by auditor examination?			
7 Are disclosures in the opinion, financial statements, and notes to financial statements adequate?			
D. Client Relations			
1 Have we performed the engagement in accordance with the arrangement (including any request by the client for extra services)?			
2 Are you satisfied that the audit did not disclose any suspicions of irregularities or illegal acts?			
3 Are you satisfied that the client is a going concern?			
4 Have arrangements been made: (a) For the client's review and approval of the proposed adjustments? (b) For the client to review a draft of the report? (c) To communicate reportable conditions and material weaknesses in the internal control structure?			
5 Have suggestions been summarized for a management letter?			
6 Are we satisfied that no unusual client problem was noted during the audit?			
E. Report Production			
1 Are instructions as to processing specific, including the type of report, client number, numbers of copies required, due date, delivery instruction (when and how)?			
2 Does the report style and appearance conform appropriately with the standards we have established for all reports?			
3 Is the language of the report simple and concise?			

By (Audit Partner): _____
Date: _____

ILLUSTRATION 11.12

Independent Review Checklist

Client _____ Closing Date _____	Yes	No	Comments
1 In-charge engagement performance and administration review performed and the appropriate questionnaires completed and signed?			
2 Have all exceptions noted on the questionnaires discussed above been resolved?			
3 Have we obtained an appropriate engagement letter, legal representation letter, and client representation letter?			
4 Have you reviewed the vertical review for completeness and unusual problems?			
5 Were an audit program, time budget and time summary prepared, approved and properly utilized?			
6 Were all problem areas adequately reviewed and conclusions properly documented?			
7 Have you concurred with alternative procedures employed to satisfy us when such procedures deviate from our firm's basic audit policies?			
8 Are the financial statements free from material errors of omission?			
9 Are the engagement files, to the extent reviewed, free from any evidence of material non-compliance with auditing standards or firm policies?			
10 Is our audit report appropriate?			
11 Does our audit report comply with generally accepted auditing standards?			
12 Do the report style and appearance conform appropriately with the standards we have established for all reports?			
13 Is the language of the report simple and concise?			
14 Have identified reportable conditions in the internal control structure been appropriately communicated?			
15 Have all conditions, that you are aware of, that require reevaluation of our relationship with the client been appropriately considered?			
16 Have you reviewed the reference points raised in working paper review and noted the disposition thereof?			
17 Are you satisfied that there are no unresolved statements in the working paper files? If there are any, they must be properly and adequately explained.			
18 Have you removed all queries from working papers?			

By (Audit Partner): _____
Date: _____

Resolution of Review Questions

Resolution of review questions raised by the manager and partner will usually require more extensive documentation and explanation in the working papers. This phase of the review will usually involve a completion of a firm checklist to determine that all reporting standards have been complied with. Illustration 11.11 is a review checklist. Illustration 11.12 is a review checklist for use by those reviewers independent of the audit.

Certification Exam Question 11.9

An auditor's working papers serve mainly to:

(A) Provide the principal support for the auditor's report.
(B) Satisfy the auditor's responsibilities concerning the Code of Professional Conduct.
(C) Monitor the effectiveness of the audit firm's quality control procedures.
(D) Document the level of independence maintained by the auditor.

■ Working Paper Review

The "in-charge" or "senior" auditor will obtain the agreement of the manager that the fieldwork is complete before leaving the client's premises. This will usually involve the manager spending the last day or two of the fieldwork at the client's offices reviewing the working papers to determine that the audit programs are complete and that sufficient evidence has been obtained to support the opinion.

Working papers (or work papers) are a record of the auditor's planning; nature, timing and extent of the auditing procedures performed; results of such procedures; and the conclusions drawn from the evidence obtained. Working papers may be in the form of data stored on paper, film, electronic or other media. A detailed discussion of audit documentation and working papers appears in Appendix A to this chapter.

Aid in Supervision and Primary Support for Audit Opinion

Working papers serve two main functions: to aid in the conduct and supervision of the audit and as primary support for the auditor's opinion, especially the representation that the audit was conducted in accordance with ISAs.

Working papers are a physical aid in recording the results of audit tests. For example, when a sample is taken, the items sampled must be recorded and computations must be made. Since supervisors who perform few of the audit tests make final decisions concerning the audit opinion, the working papers serve as a basis for evaluating the evidence given. After the opinion has been given, working papers are the only physical proof that the auditor has that an adequate audit was conducted because original documents and accounting records remain with the client.

The working papers are reviewed for sufficiency of evidence. Evidence recorded in the working papers should be both relevant and valid. Relevance is largely a matter of the relationship between the evidential matter and the **financial statement assertion** involved. For example, if the assertion concerns existence of an asset, the reviewer should find that the auditor selected items included in the account balance and physically examined and confirmed those items.

Independent Review

Someone who did not take part in the audit reviews the working papers. This is called an independent review. At the completion of the audit, work papers may be reviewed by an independent member of the audit firm who has not participated in the audit for four basic reasons:

1 to evaluate the performance of inexperienced personnel;
2 to make sure that the audit meets the audit firm's standard of performance;
3 to counteract the bias that frequently enters the auditor's judgment;
4 to comply with audit regulation such as the Sarbanes-Oxley Act.

■ Evaluating Audit Findings for Material Misstatements

When the audit tests for each item in the financial statements are completed, the staff auditor doing the work will sign off completion of steps in the audit program, identify monetary misstatements in the financial statements, and propose adjustment to the financial statements. **Monetary misstatements** are misstatements that cause a distortion of the financial statements. Monetary misstatements may result from mistakes in processing transactions (such as mistakes in quantities, prices or computations), mistakes in the selection of accounting principles, and mistakes in facts or judgments about accounting estimates.

Misstatement Worksheet

The most practical way to consider whether the financial statements are materially misstated at the conclusion of the audit is to use a worksheet that determines the combined effect of uncorrected misstatements on important totals or subtotals in the financial statements. Known misstatement, likely misstatement, and allowance for undetected misstatement would be determined for each account balance included in the financial statements. **Known misstatement** is the amount of misstatement specifically identified by the auditor or as a result of applying audit procedures. **Likely misstatement** is the auditor's best estimate of misstatement based on an extrapolation or projection of misstatement detected in sampling applications. **Allowance for undetected misstatement** is the auditor's allowance for potential misstatement that remains undetected after applying audit procedures. In the combined effect worksheet procedure, a worksheet summarizing the results of sampling on each account balance is combined with a worksheet giving the results of audit tests that did not use sampling.

If the total misstatement for any account balance exceeds materiality by more than a small amount, the auditor must determine an effective method of resolving the problem. The auditor may persuade the client to correct more of the known misstatements in the financial statements. Additional procedures may be performed to reduce the basis allowance for undetected misstatements. The client may be asked to record projected misstatement for the applications.

■ Review Laws and Regulation

All countries have laws that apply to businesses operating there. The auditor should know the laws that apply to their client, review the criteria required to comply with that statute, and test for the client company's compliance.

Government Review of Publicly Traded Companies

The governing authorities may review publicly traded companies because they meet certain high-risk criteria. Therefore it is wise for the auditor to understand the criteria that will set the client apart for review and determine if any problems may occur. For example, the SEC reviews a publicly traded company if the following factors are evident:[43]

- companies that have issued material restatements of financial results;
- companies that experience significant volatility in their stock price as compared to other companies;
- companies with the largest market capitalization;
- emerging companies with disparities in price to earning ratios;
- companies whose operations significantly affect any material sector of the economy;
- any other factors that the Commission may consider relevant.

Certification Exam Question 11.10[44]

Which of the following conditions or events are most likely to cause an auditor to have substantial doubt about an entity's ability to continue as a going concern?

(A) Cash flows from operating activities are negative.
(B) Research and development projects are postponed.
(C) Significant related-party transactions are pervasive.
(D) Stock dividends replace annual cash dividends.

11.8 Going Concern Issues

Assessment of the **going concern assumption** is particularly important to the auditor. ISA 570[45] specifies that when performing audit procedures the auditor should consider the appropriateness of the going concern assumption underlying the preparation of the financial statements.

The going concern assumption is a fundamental principle in the preparation of financial statements. Under the going concern assumption, a company is viewed as continuing in business for the foreseeable future. As a result, assets and liabilities are recorded on the basis that the company will be able to realize its assets and discharge its liabilities in the normal course of business.

Most financial legislation, regulation, and accounting standards, including International Financial Reporting Standards, specifically require management to assess the entity's ability to continue as a going concern. IAS 1, "Presentation of Financial Statements," paragraphs 23 states: "When preparing financial statements, management should make an assessment of an entity's ability to continue as a going concern. Financial statements should be prepared on a going concern basis unless management intends to liquidate the entity or to cease trading, or has no realistic alternative but to do so."

Illustration 11.13 gives examples of events and conditions, which individually or collectively, may cast significant doubt about the going concern assumption. The significance of the indications in Illustration 11.13 can often be mitigated by other factors. For example, the effect of an entity being unable to make its normal debt repayments may be counterbalanced by management's plans to maintain adequate cash flows by alternative means, such as disposal of assets.

ILLUSTRATION 11.13

Indications that the Going Concern Assumption Might be Questioned[46]

This listing is not all-inclusive nor does the existence of one or more of the items always signify that a material uncertainty exists.

Financial Indications

- Net liability or net current liability position.
- Fixed-term borrowings approaching maturity without realistic prospects of renewal or repayment, or excessive reliance on short-term borrowing to finance long-term assets.
- Indications of withdrawal of financial support by debtors and other creditors.
- Negative operating cash flows indicated by historical or prospective financial statements.
- Adverse key financial ratios.
- Substantial operating losses or significant deterioration in the value of assets used to generate cash flows.
- Arrears or discontinuance of dividends.
- Inability to pay creditors on due dates.
- Difficulty in complying with the terms of loan agreements.
- Change from credit to cash-on-delivery transactions with suppliers.
- Inability to obtain financing for essential new product development or other essential investments.

Operating Indications

- Loss of key management without replacement.
- Loss of major market, franchise, license or principal supplier.
- Labor difficulties or shortages of important supplies.

Other indications

- Non-compliance with capital or other statutory requirements.
- Pending legal proceedings against the entity that may, if successful, result in judgments that could not be met.
- Changes in legislation or government policy expected to adversely affect the entity.

The auditor's responsibility is to consider the appropriateness of management's use of the going concern assumption in the preparation of the financial statements, and consider whether there are material uncertainties about the entity's ability to continue as a going concern that need to be disclosed in the financial statements.

■ Doubt Of Entity's Ability to Continue as a Going Concern

When events or conditions have been identified which may cast significant doubt on the entity's ability to continue as a going concern, the auditor should:[47]

- review management's plans for future actions based on its going concern assessment;
- seek written representations from management regarding its plans for future action;
- gather sufficient appropriate audit evidence to confirm or dispel whether or not a material uncertainty exists through carrying out procedures considered necessary.

■ Procedures to Gather Audit Evidence

Procedures to gather sufficient appropriate audit evidence may include:

- analyzing and discussing cash flow, profit and other relevant forecasts with management;
- analyzing and discussing the entity's latest available interim financial statements;
- reviewing the terms of debentures and loan agreements and determining whether any have been breached;
- reading minutes of the meetings of shareholders, the board of directors and important committees for reference to financing difficulties.
- asking the company's lawyer about the existence of litigation and claims and the reasonableness of management's assessments of their outcome and the estimate of their financial implications;
- confirming the existence, legality and enforceability of arrangements to provide or maintain financial support with related and third parties and assessing the financial ability of such parties to provide additional funds;
- considering the entity's plans to deal with unfilled customer orders;
- reviewing events after period end to identify those that either mitigate or otherwise affect the entity's ability to continue as a going concern.

If, based on the audit evidence obtained, the auditor determines a material uncertainty exists related to events or conditions that alone or in aggregate, may cast significant doubt on the entity's ability to continue as a going concern, disclosure and a possible modification of the audit opinion might occur. This will be discussed in Chapter 12 Audit Reports and Communication.

11.9 Matters for Attention of Partners (MAPs)

Matters for Attention of Partners (MAPs)[48] is a report by audit managers to the partner or director detailing the audit decisions reached and the reasons for those decisions.

There is not one standard type of MAP report because the way in which an auditing firm identifies and disposes of issues affecting the audit opinion will vary. In general the MAP (or an equivalent report referred to by a different name) documents significant matters on which an initial decision has been made by the audit manager or an audit partner and details of the eventual resolution of matters that the audit partner decided should be taken up with the client, including the reasoning involved in their resolution. Examples of decisions made and reported in MAP is whether an item is sufficiently material to require adjustment of or disclosure in the accounts. Typically the audit manager prepares the MAP and each item is read and commented on by the partner or director.

The areas discussed in the MAP relate to difficult questions of principle where there is a possibility that the auditor's judgment may subsequently be questioned, particularly by a third party. It is therefore important that the working papers record all those relevant facts available at the time the decision was made. This will allow determination at some future time of the reasonableness of the conclusion reached based on the facts.

■ Contents of MAP

The items included in the MAP are a cover page signed by audit manager and partners stating the basic conclusions of the audit; general matters; management comments; comments on results; discussions of accounts that required special consideration; compliance with statutory laws, ISAs and IASs; comments on accounting systems; comments on management letters; and discussion of any matters that were outstanding at that date.

Results of the audit and discussion of specific accounts may include explanation of findings about inadequate ratios, unusual trends, or decreases in sales or profits. For example, a matter discussed might be: "Decreases in gross margin are attributable to lower pricing necessitated by increased competition from Zego's Design Rite and General Software's Room Zoom and increased cost of producing CD ROMs." Major concerns about the accounts are mentioned. An example would be: "There have been large increases in research and development costs because of the company's policy of developing a major interactive design software product, code-named Walkabout."

The Matters for Attention should mention that the accounts have been prepared in accordance with the legal statutes (e.g. the Company Act in the UK). Matters for Attention might mention that all ISAs and IASs have been complied with. Any upgrade or additions to accounting systems (computerized accounting systems especially) would be mentioned for comment. Any matters involving management letters would be mentioned. Finally, any matters outstanding would be presented for comments.

11.10 Reports to The Board of Directors

The board of directors has significant influence over accounting and financial policies of the entity. The board also has the responsibility for hiring an independent auditor. The auditor must communicate important findings to the board.

■ Matters Discussed With the Board

Auditors may attend board of directors' meetings to discuss accounting and auditing matters. Some matters that might be discussed are the accounting system, internal controls, and impacts of changes in accounting standards, and disclosure. Discussion with the board is essential for matters that cannot be successfully resolved with the executive officers.

Auditors are required by the Security and Exchange Commission[49] to report to the audit committee of the publicly traded company:

- all critical accounting policies and practices to be used;
- all alternative treatments of financial information within generally accepted accounting principles that have been discussed with management officials of the issuer, ramifications of the use of such alternative disclosures and treatments, and the treatment preferred by the registered public accounting firm;
- other material written communications between the registered public accounting firm and the management of the issuer, such as any management letter or schedule of unadjusted differences.

■ Long-Form Audit Report

In some countries, such as Germany, the board of directors gets a special report that is longer and much more detailed than the audit opinion. It is called the long-form report to the board. It may include a number of items, as there is no standard form. Typical areas of discussion in the report are information that the client has omitted from its notes and the errors the auditor has found in performing his work. Chapter 12 Audit Reports and Communication will discuss the long-form audit report in more detail and also communications with the directors and audit committee.

Illustration 11.14 summarizes the documents to be obtained or reviewed by the auditor, and to be generated by the auditor and audit team, during the course of the audit.

ILLUSTRATION 11.14

Summary of Audit Process Documents

(a) **Documents to be obtained or reviewed by the auditor during the course of the audit:**

Predecessor auditor's working papers	Minutes of Board of Directors and Shareholders
Industry reports, trends, and information	Management Representations letter
Engagement letter	Legal letter – Letter of Inquiry from Client Counsel
Financial statements	Side letters, if any
Notes to financial statements	Related parties lists and relationship to firm
	Work of other auditors and experts, if any

(b) **Documents to be generated by the auditor and audit team during the course of the Audit:**

Client proposal	Completing-the-engagement checklist (optional)
Planning memorandum	Report to Audit Committee
Audit program plan	Report to Board of Directors
Working papers	Unadjusted error worksheet
Confirmation letters to lenders and creditors	Adjustments to Financial Statements
Matters for Attention of Partners (MAP)	Audit Report

11.11 Summary

This chapter describes the fourth and last phase of the audit. The procedures for completing this audit phase are:

- evaluate governance evidence;
- carry out procedures to identify subsequent events;
- review financial statements and other report material;
- carry out wrap-up procedures;
- prepare Matters for Attention of Partners;
- report to the board of directors and prepare audit report.

Presently two IAASB standards apply to audit quality: International Standards on Quality Control (ISQC) and ISA 220, "Quality Control For Audit Work." IAASB issues International Standards on Quality Control (ISQCs) as the standards to be applied for all services falling under the Standards of the IAASB (i.e. ISAs, International Standards on Assurance Engagements (ISAEs), and International Standards on Related Services (ISRSs)).

The elements of **quality control** policies adopted by an audit firm normally incorporate policies related to general firm activities and personnel. General firm activities for which quality control policies and procedures are required include leadership responsibilities for quality within the firm, acceptance and retention of clients, engagement performance, and **monitoring**. Quality controls applied to human resources include ethical requirements. The quality control policies and procedures should be documented and communicated to the firm's personnel.

The Sarbanes-Oxley Act, which applies to both US audit firms and audit firms throughout the world, addresses overall review procedures required of the auditor such as second partner review, partner rotation, and quality control. It also discusses the client's audit committee responsibilities and inspection by the Public Company Accounting Oversight Board.

There is important governance evidence that may be acquired any time during the audit, but definitely has to be acquired before the final reporting and evaluation phase (Phase IV of the Audit Process Model). The important governance information to be gathered from the client includes: a legal letter, a management representations letter, information about contingent liabilities and commitments, and identification of related parties.

Review for subsequent events are the auditing procedures performed by auditors to identify and evaluate subsequent events. Subsequent events are transactions and other pertinent events that occurred after the balance sheet date and which affect the fair presentation or disclosure of the statements being audited. Under International Standard on Auditing (ISA) 560, the auditor should consider the effect of subsequent events on the financial statements and on the auditor's report. There are two types of subsequent events:

1 those that provide further evidence of conditions that existed at period end;
2 those that are indicative of conditions that arose subsequent to period end.

The first type requires adjustment to the financial statements and the second type, if material, requires disclosure.

The final review of the financial statements involves procedures to determine if disclosures of financial statements and other required disclosures (for corporate governance, management reports, etc.) are adequate. The auditor is responsible for all information that appears with the audited financial statements, so therefore the auditor must also see if there are any inconsistencies between this other information and the financial statements.

Wrap-up procedures are those procedures done at the end of an audit that generally cannot be performed before the other audit work is complete. Wrap-up procedures include: supervisory review, final analytical procedures, working paper review, evaluating audit findings for material misstatements, client approval of adjusting entries, review of laws and regulation, and evaluation of the company as a going concern.

Assessment of the going concern assumption is particularly important to the auditor. ISA 570 specifies that when performing audit procedures the auditor should consider the appropriateness of the going concern assumption underlying the preparation of the financial statements. The auditor's responsibility is to consider the appropriateness of management's use of the going concern assumption in the preparation of the financial statements, and consider whether there are material uncertainties about the entity's ability to continue as a going concern that need to be disclosed in the financial statements.

Matters for Attention of Partners (MAPs) is a report by audit managers to the partner or director detailing the audit decisions reached and the reasons for those decisions. The areas discussed in the MAP relate to difficult questions of principle where there is a possibility that the auditor's judgment may subsequently be questioned, particularly by a third party. Typically the audit manager prepares the MAP and each item is read and commented on by the partner or director.

The board of directors has significant influence over accounting and financial policies of the entity. The board also has the responsibility for hiring an independent auditor. The auditor must communicate his important findings to the board.

11.12 Answers to Certification Exam Questions

11.1 (D) The requirement is to determine what auditor's services International Standards on Quality Control (ISQC) apply to. Answer (D) is the best answer because ISQC's apply across the board to all auditor's assurance and other related services. Answer (A) is not sufficient because ISQCs apply to more than auditing alone. Answers (B) and (C) are wrong because ISQCs do not apply to management advisory services or tax services.

11.2 (A) The requirement is to find the answer that gives a certified audit firm reasonable assurance of achieving their basic objective of providing professional services that conform with professional standards. Answer (A) fits the bill because according to International Standard on Quality Control 1 (ISQC 1), the audit firm should establish a system of quality control designed to provide it with reasonable assurance that the firm and its personnel comply with professional standards. Answers (B) peer review and (C) continuing professional education are not complete because they are sub-systems of quality control. Meeting IFRS (answer (D)) is the objective itself, not a means to achieve the objective.

11.3 (C) The requirement is find the answer that is the **exception** to quality control policies that the Sarbanes-Oxley Act requires of each registered public accounting firm auditing publicly traded companies. Answer (C) internal control policies is the only one not on the list of quality control polices required which includes monitoring of professional ethics and independence, consultation within the firm (answer (A)); supervision of audit work; hiring, professional development, and advancement of personnel (answer (B)); the acceptance and continuation of audit engagements; internal inspection (answer (D)); and other requirements as the Public Company Accounting Oversight Board (PCAOB) may prescribe.

11.4 (B) We need to identify the primary reason that an auditor requests a client send a letter of inquiry to its attorneys. Choice (B) is best because a legal letter is the auditor's primary means of obtaining corroboration of the information furnished by management concerning litigation, claims, and assessments. Choice (A) is wrong because it is often impossible to determine the probable outcome of legal claims. Choice (C) is unrealistic because no opinions on historical experiences are generally available. Choice (D) is off the mark because the client usually prepares the description of litigation, claims, and assessments.

11.5 (A) The need is to identify the information ordinarily included among the written client representations requested by the auditor. Answer (A) is correct because compensating balance as well as all assets that are pledged as collateral is required disclosure under IFRS. Answer (B) is faulty because management does not need to accept a responsibility for employee illegal actions. Answer (C) is mistaken because the auditor, not the client, determines whether sufficient evidential matter has been made available. Answer (D) is erroneous because management's political contributions are not of great importance to a financial statement audit.

11.6 (D) The requirement is to identify the correct statement concerning related-party transactions. Answer (D) is correct because International Financial Reporting Standards (IAS 24) requires disclosure of the nature and volume of transactions with related parties. ISA 550 says the auditor should perform audit procedures designed to obtain sufficient appropriate audit evidence regarding the identification and disclosure by management of related parties and the effect of related party transactions. Choice (A) is inaccurate because determining rights and obligations is a small part of the auditor's responsibility, not the primary emphasis. Choice (B) is false because while auditors carry out procedures to find related parties, this is not the primary emphasis. Answer (C) is untrue because verifying the valuation of related-party transactions is very difficult and sometimes impossible.

11.7 (D) What is an auditor's responsibility when after the issuance of an audit report a client sells the shares of a major subsidiary? Answer (D) is correct because the event arose after the issuance of the auditor's report, therefore no action is necessary. Answers (A), (B), and (C) are all inaccurate because they outline responsibilities which are not appropriate in this circumstance.

11.8 (D) What is an auditor's responsibility when audited financial statements are presented in a client's document containing other information? Choice (D) is the best because the auditor is required to read the other information to determine that it is consistent with the audited financial statements. Choices (A) and (C) are flawed because no such inquiry, analytical procedures, or other substantive auditing procedures are required. Choice (B) is imprecise because, unless the information seems incorrect or inconsistent with the audited financial statements, no explanatory paragraph needs to be added to the auditor's report.

11.9 (A) The requirement is to identify the main purpose of an auditor's working papers. Answer (A) is the best because, other than supervision, providing the principal support for the auditor's report is the main purpose. Answer (B) is incorrect because the Code of Professional Conduct does not require working papers. Answer (C) is incorrect because working papers monitor the audit, not the effectiveness of the audit firm's quality control procedures. Answer (D) is incorrect because working papers do not document the level of independence maintained by the auditor.

11.10 (A) The requirement is to find a condition or event among the answers that is most likely to cause an auditor to have substantial doubt about an entity's ability to continue as a going concern. Choice (A) is correct because negative cash flow over an extended period is likely to lead to liquidity problems. Choice (B) is inexact because although postponement of research and development projects may sometimes be due to extreme financial difficulties, there are often other reasons such as the change in the need to innovate. Answers (C) and (D) are inappropriate because neither significant related-party transactions nor stock dividends necessarily indicate substantial doubt about an entity's ability to continue as a going concern.

11.13 Notes

1 International Auditing and Assurance Standards Board (IAASB), 2004, *International Standard on Quality Control 1 (ISQC 1)*, "Quality Control for Firms That Perform Audits and Reviews of Historical Financial Information, and Other Assurance and Related Services Engagements," para. 3, International Federation of Accountants, New York, February.

2 Ibid. Para. 25.

3 Ibid. Para. 60.

4 Ibid. Para. 85.

5 IFAC, 2004, *Handbook of International Auditing, Assurance, and Ethics Pronouncements*, ISA 220, "Quality Control For Audit Work," International Federation of Accountants, New York.

6 International Auditing and Assurance Standards Board, 2003, *Interim Terms of Reference and Preface to the International Standards on Quality Control, Auditing, Assurance and Related Services*, International Federation of Accountants, New York, July.

7 The Public Company Accounting Oversight Board (PCAOB) was established under SOX section 101. It was established to oversee the audit of public companies that are subject to the securities laws of the USA in order to protect the interests of investors and the public in the preparation of informative, accurate, and independent audit reports.

8 107th US Congress, 2002, *Sarbanes-Oxley Act of 2002*, Public Law 107–204, section 106, "Foreign Public Accounting Firms," Senate and House of Representatives of the United States of America in Congress assembled, Washington, DC, July 30.

9 PCAOB, 2003, *PCAOB Release No. 2003-0204*, "Proposed Rules Relating To The Oversight Of Non-US Public Accounting Firms," Public Company Accounting Oversight Board, 10 December.

10 107th US Congress, 2002, *Sarbanes-Oxley Act of 2002*, Public Law 107–204, Section 103-a-2-B, Senate and House of Representatives of the United States of America in Congress assembled, Washington, DC, July 30.

11 Inspections are made annually with respect to each registered public accounting firm that regularly provides audit reports for more than 100 issuers (companies reporting to the US SEC); and not less frequently than once every three years with respect to each registered public accounting firm that regularly provides audit reports for 100 or fewer issuers.

12 PCAOB, 2003, *PCAOB Release No. 2003-019*, "Inspection Of Registered Public Accounting Firms," Public Company Accounting Oversight Board, 7 October. REQUIRED BY 107th US Congress, 2002, *Sarbanes-Oxley Act of 2002*, Public Law 107–204, SEC 104 (no-), "Inspections Of Registered Public Accounting Firms," Senate and House of Representatives of the United States of America in Congress assembled, Washington, DC, July 30.

13 No portions of the inspection report regarding quality control systems criticisms is made public if those criticisms or defects are being addressed by the public accounting firm inspected.

14 107th US Congress, 2002, *Sarbanes-Oxley Act of 2002*, Public Law 107–204, Section 206, "Conflicts Of Interest," Senate and House of Representatives of the United States of America in Congress assembled, Washington, DC, July 30.

15 107th US Congress, 2002, *Sarbanes-Oxley Act of 2002*, Public Law 107–204, TITLE III – Corporate Responsibility, Section 301, "Public Company Audit Committees," Senate and House of Representatives of the United States of America in Congress assembled, Washington, DC, July 30.

16 Adapted and reprinted with perimssion from AICPA. Copyright © 2000 & 1985 by American Institute of Certified Public Accountants.

17 Asserted claims are existing lawsuits.

18 IFAC, 2004, *Handbook of International Auditing, Assurance, and Ethics Pronouncements*, International Standards on Auditing 580 (ISA 580), Management Representations, para. 3, International Federation of Accountants, New York.

19 IFAC, 2004, *Handbook of International Auditing, Assurance, and Ethics Pronouncements*, International Standards on Auditing 580 (ISA 580), Management Representations (ISA 580), para. 4. International Federation of Accountants, New York.

20 Although not required by ISAs, a client representation letter documenting management's most important oral representations during the audit is required in the USA by SAS 19 (AU 333).

21 In certain circumstances, a separate representation letter regarding specific transactions or other events may also be obtained during the course of the audit or at a date after the date of the auditor's report, for example, on the date of a public offering.

22 Adapted from the 2004 IFAC, *Handbook of International Auditing, Assurance, and Ethics Pronouncements*, International Standards on Auditing 580 (ISA 580), "Management Representations," Appendix, International Federation of Accountants, New York.

23 International Accounting Standards Board (IASB), 2003, *International Financial Reporting Standards*, IAS 24, "Related Party Disclosures," IASB, London, 2003.

24 IFAC, 2004, *Handbook of International Auditing, Assurance, and Ethics Pronouncements*, International Standard on Auditing 550 (ISA 550), "Related Parties," para. 2, International Federation of Accountants, New York.

25 Adapted and reprinted with perimssion from AICPA. Copyright © 2000 & 1985 by American Institute of Certified Public Accountants.

26 IFAC, 2004, *Handbook of International Auditing, Assurance, and Ethics Pronouncements*, International Standard on Auditing 550 (ISA 550), "Related Parties," para. 11, International Federation of Accountants, New York.

27 Ibid. Para. 7.

28 Ibid. Para. 15.

29 Ibid. Para. 12.

30 IFAC, 2004, *Handbook of International Auditing, Assurance, and Ethics Pronouncements*, International Standard on Auditing 560 (ISA 560), "Subsequent Events," International Federation of Accountants, New York.

31 International Accounting Standards Board (IASB), 2003, *International Financial Reporting Standards* IAS 10, "Events After the Balance Sheet Date," IASB, London.

32 Adapted and reprinted with perimssion from AICPA. Copyright © 2000 & 1985 by American Institute of Certified Public Accountants.

33 IFAC, 2004, *Handbook of International Auditing, Assurance, and Ethics Pronouncements*, International Standard on Auditing 560 (ISA 560), "Subsequent Events," para. 5, International Federation of Accountants, New York.

34 107th US Congress, 2002, *Sarbanes-Oxley Act of 2002*, Public Law 107–204, section 501, "Disclosure in Periodic Reports," Senate and House of Representatives of the United States of America in Congress assembled, Washington, DC, July 30.

35 Ibid. Section 404.

36 Committee on the Financial Aspects of Corporate Governance, 1992, *Report of the Committee on the Financial Aspects of Corporate Governance* (The Cadbury Report), Gee and Co. Ltd, London, December.

37 Financial Reporting Council, 2003, *The Combined Code*, Financial Reporting Council, July.

38 107th US Congress, 2002, *Sarbanes-Oxley Act of 2002*, Public Law 107–204, section 501, "Disclosure in Periodic Reports," Senate and House of Representatives of the United States of America in Congress assembled, Washington, DC, July 30.

39 In SOX section 406, the term "code of ethics" means such standards as are reasonably necessary to promote:
   1 honest and ethical conduct, including the ethical handling of actual or apparent conflicts of interest between personal and professional relationships;
   2 full, fair, accurate, timely, and understandable disclosure in the periodic reports required to be filed by the issuer;
   3 compliance with applicable governmental rules and regulations.

40 107th US Congress, 2002, *Sarbanes-Oxley Act of 2002*, Public Law 107–204, section 406, "Code Of Ethics For Senior Financial Officers," Senate and House of Representatives of the United States of America in Congress assembled, Washington, DC, July 30.

41 Ibid. Section 407.

42 IFAC, 2004, *Handbook of International Auditing, Assurance, and Ethics Pronouncements*, International Standard on Auditing 720 (ISA 720), "Other Information in Documents Containing Audited Financial Statements," para. 2, International Federation of Accountants, New York.

43 107th US Congress, 2002, *Sarbanes-Oxley Act of 2002*, Public Law 107–204, section 408, "Enhanced Review Of Periodic Disclosures By Issuers," Senate and House of Representatives of the United States of America in Congress assembled, Washington, DC, July 30.

44 Adapted and reprinted with perimssion from AICPA. Copyright © 2000 & 1985 by American Institute of Certified Public Accountants.

45 IFAC, 2004, *Handbook of International Auditing, Assurance, and Ethics Pronouncements*, ISA 570, "Going Concern," para. 2, International Federation of Accountants, New York.

46 Ibid. Para. 8.

47 Ibid. Para. 26.

48 The term "Matters for the Attention of Partners" was once in widespread use, although there has been a trend away from its use. There is concern about use of the term because it implies that the partner is not part of the audit engagement team. The reality is that the partner is primarily responsible for the conduct of the audit. However, as there is not now a term to replace it in widespread use, we will use the term in this chapter.

49 107th US Congress, 2002, *Sarbanes-Oxley Act of 2002*, Public Law 107–204, section 204, "Auditor Reports To Audit Committees," Senate and House of Representatives of the United States of America in Congress assembled, Washington, DC, July 30.

11.14 Questions, Exercises and Cases

QUESTIONS

11.2 Introduction

11.1 What are the general procedures for completing the audit as shown in the standard Audit Process Model?

11.3 Quality Control

11.2 Describe the elements of quality control policies adopted by an audit firm.

11.3 Audit firms are expected to report on the monitoring of its quality control systems at least annually. What is included in that communication? What should supervisory personnel monitor and do in each audit?

11.4 Evaluation of Governance Evidence

11.4 What should be included in the letter from client's legal counsel?

11.5 What kind of evidence does ISA 580 suggest that the auditor get from management? Where might an auditor find evidence to fulfill this requirement?

11.6 What is a contingent liability? What three conditions must be met for a contingent liability to exist?

11.7 Name the procedures an auditor is required to perform under ISA 550 regarding completeness of related party information provided by management?

11.5 Review for Subsequent Events

11.8 What is a review for subsequent events? What should an auditor do if he becomes aware of facts that existed at the date of the auditor's report after the financial statements have been issued?

11.9 If the auditor becomes aware of a fact that may materially affect the financial statements after the date of the auditor's report but before the financial statements have been issued, what should an auditor do and how may this affect the financial statements? What if a material fact is discovered after the financial statements have been issued?

11.6 Review of Financial Statements and Other Report Material

11.10 When reviewing for adequate disclosure, what does an auditor look for? Give some examples.

11.11 When does a material inconsistency exist in information other than the financial statements? What other information must an auditor review for material inconsistencies? What should an auditor do if a material inconsistency is found?

11.7 Wrap-Up Procedures

11.12 What are wrap-up procedures? Give some examples.

11.13 What must the audit supervisor do before he can consider the audit work complete?

11.14 What are monetary misstatements? What mistakes can cause a monetary misstatement?

11.8 Going Concern Issues

11.15 What are some indications that the continuance of the company as a going concern may be questionable?

11.16 What should an auditor do if going concern is questionable? How may this affect the auditor's report?

11.9 Matters for the Attention of Partners

11.17 What is meant by MAP? What items are discussed in MAP and why are they important?

11.10 Reports to the Board of Directors

11.18 What are auditors required to discuss with the board of directors? The audit committee?

PROBLEMS AND EXERCISES

11.3 Quality Control

11.19 **Quality Review.** Charalambos Viachoutsicos is assigned the responsibility of setting up a quality review program at his St. Petersburg, Russia, audit firm, Levenchuk.

Required:
A.   What should the verification procedures include? Who should perform the procedures?
B.   What type of documentation is required?
C.   What should be covered in the report on the quality review program?
D.   What organizational authority is required for the personnel who carry out the quality audit?
E.   What qualifications should the personnel have?

11.4 Evaluation of Governance Evidence

11.20 **Inquiry of Client's Attorney.** Morgan LeFay, AS, of Horsens, Denmark, auditor Jan Ogier, Statsautoriseret Revisor, determines that LeFay has paid legal fees to four different law firms during the year under audit. Ogier requests standard attorney letters as of the balance sheet date from each of the four law firms.
Jan Ogier receives the following responses:
1   One attorney furnished the following opinion: "It is our opinion that, based on a complete investigation of the facts known to us, no liability will be established against LeFay in the suits referred to in your letter of inquiry."
2   Attorney number two states that there may be a potentially material lawsuit against the client but refuses to comment further to protect the legal rights of the client.
3   By the last day of field work, Ogier has not received any letter from the third attorney.
4   The letter from the fourth attorney writes that their firm deals exclusively in registering song copyrights and cannot comment on LeFay lawsuits or any other legal affairs.

Required:
A.   Discuss the adequacy of the attorney's response in each of the four cases. What procedures should Ogier take in response to each letter?
B.   What impact will each of these letters have on Ogier's audit report? Explain.
C.   Should you refer to the attorney's opinion in your audit report or disclosures?

11.21 **Representation Letter.** Robert Dingle, president of Alcmena Manufacturing, Ltd., of Perth, Australia, and the company external auditor Deny H. Lawrence, Chartered Accountant (CA), reviewed matters that were supposed to be included in a written representation letter. Upon receipt of the following client representation letter, Lawrence contacted Dingle to state that it was incomplete. The letter Lawrence received is given below.

> To D.H. Lawrence, CA
>
> In connection with your audit of the balance sheet of Alcmena Manufacturing as of December 31, 20X2, and the related statements of income, retained earnings, and cash flows for the year then ended, for the purpose of expressing an opinion as to whether the financial statements present fairly, in all material respects, the financial position, results of operations, and cash flows of Alcmena Manufacturing in conformity with generally accepted accounting principles, we confirm, to the best of our knowledge and belief, the following representations made to you during your audit. There were no:
>
> ■ Plans or intentions that may materially affect the carrying value or classification of assets and liabilities.
> ■ Communications from regulatory agencies concerning noncompliance with, or deficiencies in, financial reporting practices.
> ■ Agreements to repurchase assets previously sold.
> ■ Violations or possible violations of laws or regulations whose effects should be considered for disclosure in the financial statements or as a basis for recording a loss contingency.
> ■ Unasserted claims or assessments that our lawyer has advised are probable of assertion and must be disclosed in accordance with International Accounting Standards No. 10.
> ■ Capital stock repurchase options or agreements or capital stock reserved for options, warrants, conversions, or other requirements.
> ■ Compensating balance or other arrangements involving restrictions on cash balances.
>
> R. Dingle, President
> Alcmena Manufacturing Ltd.
> March 14, 20X3

Required:
Identify the other matters that Dingle's representation letter should specifically confirm.

11.22 **Related Parties.** D'orsay Dore, SA is being audited by Clement & Grandcourt, Expert Comptables. During the course of the audit Clement & Grandcourt discover D'orsay Dore sold inventory to Parisienne de Fedora for 90-day terms, three times the typical payment period required, and the payments went directly to the president of D'orsay Dore, not to the accounting department which was the usual practice. Industriel Cuir supplies over 40 percent of the raw materials D'orsay purchases whereas no other supplier provides more than 5 percent of raw materials. D'orsay management says that they do so much business with Industriel Cuir because they provide D'orsay management assistance at no charge.

D'orsay's business is greatest in the last month before the fiscal year end when they book 30 percent of their sales, some years in the last week before closing. D'orsay Dore has provided Clement & Grandcourt with a management representation letter that states that there are no related party transactions.

Required:

A. Should Clement & Grandcourt take D'orsay Dore's word when they say there are no related parties? Why?

B. List the circumstances at D'orsay Dore that may indicate the existence of unidentified related parties.

C. What audit procedures should Clement & Grandcourt perform to investigate the possibility of related parties?

11.5 Review for Subsequent Events

11.23 Subsequent Facts and Events. The following unrelated events occurred after the balance sheet date but before the audit report was prepared:

1   The granting of a retrospective pay increase to selected employees.
2   Receipt of a letter from the tax authorities stating that additional income tax is due for a prior year.
3   Filing of an antitrust suit by the federal government.
4   Declaration of a stock dividend.
5   Sale of a fixed asset at a substantial profit.

Required:

A. Define "review for subsequent events" and "subsequent events"

B. Identify what procedure to identify events the auditor might have used to bring each of these items to the auditor's attention. (Hint: See Illustration 11.8.)

C. Discuss the auditor's responsibility to recognize each of these in connection with the audit report.

[Adapted and reprinted with permission of AICPA. Copyright © 2000 & 1985 by American Institute of Certified Public Accountants.]

11.24 Subsequent Facts and Events. In connection with their audit of the financial statements of Swan Mfg. Corporation of Ayutthay, Thailand for the year ended December 31, 20X4, Virameteekul, Kanchana & Banharn, Chartered Accountants (CA) review of subsequent events disclosed the following items:

1   January 3, 20X5: The government approved a plan for the construction of an express highway. The plan will result in the expropriation of a portion of the land owned by Swan Mfg. Corporation. Construction will begin in late 20X5. No estimate of the condemnation award is available.

2   January 4, 20X5: The funds for Baht 1,000,000 loan to the corporation made by the company president, Somsak Na Lan, on July 15, 20X4, were obtained by him from a loan on his personal life insurance policy. The loan was recorded in the account "loan from officers." Mr. Somsak's source of the funds was not disclosed in the company records. The corporation pays the premiums on the life insurance policy, and Mrs. Somsak, wife of the president, is the beneficiary.

3   January 7, 20X5: The mineral content of a shipment of ore, en route on December 31, 20X4, was determined to be 72 percent. The shipment was recorded at year-end at an estimated content of 50 percent by a debit to raw material inventory and a credit to accounts payable in the amount of Baht 824,000. The final liability to the vendor is based on the actual mineral content of the shipment.

4   January 31, 20X5: As a result of reduced sales, production was curtailed in mid-January and some workers were laid off. On February 5, 20X5, all the remaining workers went on strike. To date the strike is unsettled.

Required:

Assume that the items described above came to your attention prior to completion of your audit work on February 15, 20X5. For each item:

A.   Give the audit procedures, if any, that would have brought the item to your attention. Indicate other sources of information that may have revealed the item.

B.   Discuss the disclosure that you would recommend for the item, listing all details that you would suggest should be disclosed. Indicate those items or details, if any, that should not be disclosed. Give your reasons for recommending or not recommending disclosure of the items or details.

11.6 Review of Financial Statement and Other Report Material

11.25 Board of Directors Disclosures. The board of directors of Celestial City Corporation of Taejon, Korea, is issuing a corporate governance report. In this audit year Celestial City lost 1,280,000,000 South Korean Won (won) due to a weakness in their internal controls in the treasury department which represents 11 percent of their current assets. The controller's assistant, Dongsung Young, who, a Certified Public Accountant (CPA), is asked to write the first draft of the internal control portion of the report.

Required:

Pretend that you are Mr Dongsung and write a draft of the internal controls portion of Celestial City Corporation's corporate governance report. Since Celestial City is publicly traded on the American Stock Exchange and a Depository Receipt use the Sarbanes-Oxley Act (SOX) section 404 requirements for the report. (See PCAOB, 2004, *PCAOB Release No. 2004-001*, 2004, "Proposed Auditing Standard – An Audit Of Internal Control Over Financial Reporting Performed In Conjunction With An Audit Of Financial Statements," Public Company Accounting Oversight Board, 9 March. At time of this writing, PCAOB website was at **www.pcaobus.org/rules/Release2004-001.pdf**)

11.7 Wrap-up Procedures

11.26 Independent Review Checklist. Compare the general checklist used by an audit firm to assure that the review of the audit work is thorough and complete (Illustration 11.11) with the checklist used by a person independent of the audit (Illustration 11.12).

Required:

A.   Which questionnaire is the longest?

B.   What questions does each questionnaire ask about the in-charge accountant? About the client?

C.   What questions does each checklist ask about the audit report?

D.   What is the primary difference between the review questionnaire and the independent review questionnaire? What are the similarities between the two?

11.27 Working Paper Review: Berins & Trichet, Reviseurs d'Entreprises, of Brussels, Belgium has a policy of having their audit papers reviewed by both the partner in charge and an independent reviewer.

Required:

A.   Define "working paper"

B.   Describe the difference between a regular working paper review and an independent review.

C.   What items does the regular reviewer examine? The independent reviewer?

11.8 Going Concern Issues

11.28 Going Concern. When an auditor finds the ability of a company to continue as a going concern is questionable, the auditor will use certain audit procedures to obtain further evidence. Jocques Entremont, Expert Comptable, the external auditor for Japonaiseries S.A., a company which retails Japanese art and woodcuts in Boulogne, France, suspects that there is a going concern problem.

Required:

A. List the procedures the auditor would perform.
B. Write the auditor's opinion if disclosure of the problem is considered adequate.
C. Write the auditor's opinion if adequate disclosure is not made.

11.9 Matters for the Attention of Partners

11.29 Matters for Attention of Partners. Mneme Monos, a Greek manufacturer of computer chip memories, is being audited by you and you are to make a report to the partner in charge, Abderus Calliope, Soma Orkoton Logiston (SOL). The chief executive officer, Zephyrus Briareus, is determined to make Mneme Monos the number one memory maker and has set up contracts with several distributors around the world, largely on his own initiative.

An analysis of financial statements shows that sales have increased 50 percent, but profits have dropped 13 percent. Cost of goods sold as a percentage of sales has increased although there have been only minor increases in inventory due to increase in the cost of silicon. Accounts receivable have increased 60 percent over last year. Expenses are up as a result of research and development expenditures.

Required:

Write a brief Matters for Attention of Partners memo about Mneme Monos to your managing partner, Abderus Calliope, including a cover page.

CASES

11.30 SEC Regulation, Tax, and Working Papers. Marshall and Wyatt, CPA, have been for several years the independent auditors of Interstate LDC Land Development Corporation of New Orleans, Louisiana. During these years, Interstate LDC prepared and filed its own annual income tax returns.

During 20X3, Interstate LDC requested Marshall and Wyatt to audit all the necessary financial statements of the corporation to be submitted to the US Securities and Exchange Commission (SEC) in connection with a multi-state public offering of one million shares of Interstate Land Development Corporation common stock. This public offering came under the provisions of the US Securities Act of 1933. The audit was performed carefully and the financial statements were fairly presented for the respective periods. These financial statements were included in the registration statement filed with the SEC.

While the registration statement was being processed by the SEC, but before the effective date, the US taxing authority, the Internal Revenue Service (IRS), obtained a federal court subpoena directing Marshall and Wyatt to turn over all of its working papers relating to Interstate LDC for the years 20X0–X2. Marshall and Wyatt initially refused to comply for two reasons. First, Marshall and Wyatt did not prepare Interstate LDC's tax returns. Second, Marshall and Wyatt claimed that the working papers were confidential matters subject to the privileged communications rule. Subsequently, however, Marshall and Wyatt did relinquish the subpoenaed working papers. Upon receiving the subpoena, Wyatt called Dan Dunkirk, the chairman of Interstate LDC's board of directors, and asked him about IRS investigation. Dunkirk responded, "I'm sure the IRS people are on a 'fishing expedition' and that they will not find any material deficiencies."

A few days later Chairman Dunkirk received a written memorandum from the IRS stating that Interstate LDC had underpaid its taxes during the period under review. The memorandum revealed that Interstate LDC was being assessed $800,000, including penalties and interest for the three years. Dunkirk forwarded a copy of this memorandum to Marshall and Wyatt.

This $800,000 assessment was material relative to the financial statements as of December 31, 20X3. The amount for each year individually, exclusive of penalty and interest, was not material relative to each respective year.

Required:

A. In general terms, discuss the extent to which a US CPA firm's potential liability to third parities is increased in an SEC registration audit.

B. Discuss the implications of the IRS investigation, if any, relative to Marshall and Wyatt's audit of Interstate LDC's 20X3 financial statements. Discuss any additional investigative procedures that the auditors should undertake or any audit judgments that should be made as result of this investigation.

C. Can Marshall and Wyatt validly refuse to surrender the subpoenaed working papers to the IRS? Explain.

Audit Documentation and Working Papers

11.A.1 Introduction

The standard on documentation, ISA 230,[1] provides foundation principles of documentation. It advises: "The auditor should document matters which are important in providing evidence to support the audit opinion and evidence that the audit was carried out in accordance with ISAs." The Audit Documentation standard from the US Public Company Accounting Oversight Board (PCAOB)[2] will also be considered in this appendix.[3]

Audit documentation is the principal record of the basis for the auditor's conclusions and provides the principal support for the representations in the auditor's report.[4] Audit documentation also facilitates the planning, performance, and supervision of the engagement and provides the basis for the review of the quality of the work by providing the reviewer with written documentation of the evidence supporting the auditor's significant conclusions. Audit documentation includes records on the planning and performance of the work, the procedures performed, evidence obtained, and conclusions reached by the auditor.

■ Working Papers

Audit documentation also may be referred to as **working papers** (or **work papers**). Working papers are a record of the auditor's planning; the nature, timing and extent of the auditing procedures performed; results of those procedures; and the conclusions drawn from the evidence obtained. Working papers may be in the form of data stored on paper, film, electronic media or other media. The terms working papers, work papers and documentation are often used inter-changeably in auditing.

Working papers:

■ Are a direct aid in the planning, performance, and supervision of the audit. If an auditor is to plan the audit adequately, the necessary reference information must be available in the working papers. The papers include a variety of planning information such as descriptive information about the internal control, background information about the client, a time budget for individual audit areas, the audit program, and the results of the preceding year's audit.

■ Record the audit evidence resulting from the audit work performed to provide support for the auditor's opinion including the representation that the audit was conducted in accordance with ISAs. Working papers are an important physical aid in recording the results of audit tests. For example, when a sample is taken, the items drawn must be recorded and computations must be made. Working papers are also necessary for co-ordination of the work leading to an opinion. Supervisors who perform few, if any, actual audit tests make final decisions concerning opinion given on the financial statements. The supervisors use the working papers as a basis for evaluating the evidence gathered.

■ Assist in review of the audit work. The working papers are used not only by supervisory personnel to evaluate whether sufficient competent evidence was accumulated, but also for other auditing and consulting work. Working papers are used by the consulting arm of accounting firms as a basis for income tax preparation, required government regulatory filings and other reports. They are a source of information for communications between auditors and boards of directors concerning internal control weaknesses. They are often used to train personnel.

■ Provide proof of the adequacy of the audit. After the opinion has been given, working papers are the main physical proof that an adequate audit was conducted. The auditor works with original documents and accounting records that must be left with the client when the audit has been completed, so the working papers act as an index to those documents. If the auditor is called upon to prove the adequacy of the audit in a court of law or to regulatory agencies, the working papers are his basis of proof.

ILLUSTRATION 11.A.1

Significant Findings or Issues Documented[8]

Significant findings or issues include, but are not limited to, the following:

■ Significant matters involving the selection, application, and consistency of accounting principles, including related disclosures. Such significant matters include accounting for complex or unusual transactions, accounting estimates, and uncertainties as well as related management assumptions.

■ Results of auditing procedures that indicate a need for significant modification of planned auditing procedures or the existence of material misstatements or omissions in the financial statements or the existence of significant deficiencies in internal control over financial reporting.

■ Audit adjustments and the ultimate resolution of these items. For purposes of this standard, an *audit adjustment* is a proposed correction of a misstatement of the financial statements that could, in the auditor's judgment, either individually or in the aggregate, have a material effect on the company's financial reporting process. Audit adjustments include corrections of misstatements, of which the auditor is aware, that were or should have been proposed based on the known audit evidence.

■ Disagreements among members of the engagement team or with others consulted on the engagement about conclusions reached on significant accounting or auditing matters.

■ Significant findings or issues identified during the review of quarterly financial information.

■ Circumstances that cause significant difficulty in applying auditing procedures.

■ Significant changes in the assessed level of audit risk for particular audit areas and the auditor's response to those changes.

■ Any other matters that could result in modification of the auditor's report.

■ Significant Matters (Findings or Issues)

ISA 230 states: "Working papers would include the auditor's reasoning on all significant matters which require the exercise of judgment, together with the auditor's conclusion thereon."[5] The guidance does not explain what a "significant matter" would be.

However, for a definition of significant matters, we may look to PCAOB's documentation standard that states: "The auditor must document significant findings or issues, actions taken to address them (including additional evidence obtained), and the basis for the conclusions reached."[6] See Illustration 11.A.1 for a list of significant findings or issues.

The auditor must identify all significant findings or issues in an engagement **completion memorandum**. This memorandum should be as specific as necessary in the circumstances for a reviewer to gain a thorough understanding of the significant findings or issues. This memorandum should include cross-references, as appropriate, to other supporting audit documentation.

11.A.2 Form and Content of the Working Papers

The content of the working papers should be "sufficiently complete and detailed to provide an overall understanding of the audit".[7] The working papers should contain information on planning the audit work; the **nature, timing**, and **extent** of the audit procedures performed; the results of the audit procedures; and the conclusions drawn leading to an opinion.[8]

PCAOB is more specific: "Audit documentation must contain sufficient information to enable an experienced auditor, having no previous connection with the engagement: (1) to understand the nature, timing, extent, and results of the procedures performed, evidence obtained, and conclusions reached, and (2) to determine who performed the work and the date such work was completed as well as the person who reviewed the work and the date of such review."[9]

The working papers should convey the auditor's reasoning on all matters, which require the exercise of judgment and the auditor's conclusions. Where the auditor encounters difficult questions of principle or judgment, working papers record the relevant facts that were known by the auditor at the time the conclusions were reached.

■ Extent of Contents

The extent of what is included in working papers is a matter of professional judgment. It is neither necessary nor practical to document every matter the auditor considers. In assessing the extent of working papers to be prepared and retained, the auditor should think about what would be necessary to provide another auditor, who has no previous experience, with an understanding of the audit work performed. The working papers should convey the basis of the principal decisions taken.

All auditing firms around the world have their own work paper formats, and these formats are modified from time to time. There is no one, standard, format. Format is influenced by audit requirements for direction, supervision and review of work performed by assistants as well as differences in audit firm methodology and technology.

Working papers are designed and organized to meet the circumstances and the auditor's needs for each individual audit. The use of standardized working papers (e.g. checklists, specimen letters, standard organization of working papers) may improve the efficiency with which such working papers are prepared and reviewed. They facilitate the delegation of work while providing a means to control its quality.

Concept and a Company 11.4

E&Y Partner Falsifies NextCard, Inc. Work papers

Concept	**Work papers.**
Story	In September 2003, former Ernst & Young partner Thomas C. Trauger was arrested for obstructing an examination into NextCard Inc. by federal-bank regulators by altering and deleting working papers from its year 2000 audit of the company. (Bryan-Low & Weil 2003)

On October 31, 2001, NextCard announced in a press release that the Office of the Comptroller of the Currency had asked the company to make certain changes regarding NextBank's accounting practices, including changes regarding the classification of losses on credit cards. NextBank, the bank subsidiary, was also asked to change the treatment of some allowances and securitizations of loans. In the summer of 2001, the Office of the Comptroller of the Currency asked Ernst & Young for a portion of its audit working papers regarding E&Y's audit of NextCard. (Bryan-Low & Weil 2003)

Trauger became concerned that E&Y's audit work would be examined. Along with the help of two senior managers, Trauger is alleged to have ordered the altering of audit documents and destroying documents that were inconsistent with the changes he was directing. These alterations consisted of both addition and deletions to the work papers. Specifically, the audit partner altered the summary review memorandum as well as memoranda regarding the audit of NextCard's allowance for loan and lease losses securitizations of receivables. (SEC 2003)

It is alleged that Trauger had his senior managers change the date on their laptop computers to make it seem like the work on the documents had been done during the time the original audit had actually occurred. The alterations and deletions made it appear as though E&Y had thoroughly considered all of the appropriate issues and available facts relating to NextCard's allowance for loan losses and NextCard's securitization of receivables. (SEC 2003) A SEC official said Trauger, who had approved an earlier "clean audit" of NextCard, was trying to downplay or eliminate evidence of problems that would have been red flags. (Iwata 2003)

Discussion Questions	■ How are work papers important to proving that the audit was done correctly? ■ What would an auditor accomplish by altering or destroying the work papers?
References	Bryan-Low, C. and Weil, J., 2003, "Former Partner at Ernst Is Arrested," *Wall Street Journal*, September 26. Iwata, E., 2003, "Accountant arrested under Sarbanes-Oxley; Harsher penalties possible for former E&Y senior partner,"[10] *USA Today*, September 26. SEC, 2003, *Litigation release 48543*, "Commission Issues Orders Alleging That Auditors Violated Rules of Practice By Altering and Deleting Audit Working Papers," US Securities and Exchange Commission, September 25.

11.A.3 Document Retention

ISA 230 states: "The auditor should adopt appropriate procedures for maintaining the confidentiality and safe custody of the working papers and for retaining them for a period sufficient to meet the needs of the practice and in accordance with legal and professional requirements of record retention."[11] The standard provides no further guidance on documentation retention.

By contrast, the proposed International Standard on Quality Control, ISQC 1, addresses the issue of document retention in the context of the firm's system of quality control. The high-level guidance in ISQC 1 states: "The firm retains this documentation for a period of time sufficient to permit those performing monitoring procedures to evaluate the firm's compliance with its system of quality control, or for a longer period if required by law or regulation."[12]

■ PCAOB and SOX Document Retention

The US SEC introduced detailed regulation (Rule 210.2-06)[13] on document retention as mandated by the Sarbanes-Oxley Act (SOX). The regulation specifies detailed requirements regarding the types of document (e.g. working papers, memos, correspondence, etc. that contain conclusions, opinions, analyses, etc.) that should be retained and the specific period of time they should be retained, regardless of whether such documents support, or are inconsistent with, the final audit conclusions.

Under SOX Section 103,[14] each registered public accounting firm is required to prepare and maintain audit working papers and other information related to any audit report for a period of not less than seven years.[15] PCAOB's Documentation standard states: "Audit documentation must be retained for seven years from the date of completion of the engagement, as indicated by the date of the auditor's report, unless a longer period of time is required by law."[16]

Under SOX Section 105,[17] the PCAOB may also:

- require the testimony of the firm or of any person associated with a registered public accounting firm;
- require the production of audit work papers and any other document or information in the possession of a registered public accounting firm or any associated, and may inspect the books and records of such firm or associated person to verify the accuracy of any documents or information supplied;
- request the testimony of, and production of any document in the possession of, any other person, including any client of a registered public accounting firm.

■ Adding To or Altering Documentation

Circumstances may require subsequent additions to the audit documentation, for example, if evidence is obtained after completion of the engagement, or if work performed before engagement was finished is documented after completion. When additions are made, according to PCAOB,[18] the documentation added must indicate the date the information was added, by whom it was added, and the reason for adding it.

Audit documentation must not be deleted or discarded. SOX describes criminal penalties for altering documents: "Whoever knowingly alters, destroys, mutilates, conceals, covers up, falsifies, or makes a false entry in any record, document, or tangible object with the intent to impede, obstruct, or influence the investigation or proper administration ... shall be fined under this title, imprisoned not more than 20 years, or both."[19]

Who Owns Working Papers?

ISA 230 states that working papers are generally considered to be the property of the auditor.[20] Although portions of or extracts from the working papers may be made available to the entity audited at the discretion of the auditor, they are not a substitute for the entity's accounting records. In international practice generally the only time anyone, including the client, has a legal right to examine the papers is when they are subpoenaed by a court as legal evidence.

During the audit a considerable amount of information of a confidential nature is gathered, including officer salaries, product cost and product plans. This information can be damaging to the client and useful to competitors if it gets out of the hands of the auditors. Therefore, auditors must take care to protect the working papers at all times.

11.A.4 Permanent and Current Files

There are two main divisions of audit working papers:

1 the permanent (or continuing) audit file;
2 the current audit file.

The **permanent file** is audit working papers containing all the data that are of continuing interest from year to year. The **current work paper file** contains all papers accumulated during the current year's audit.

Permanent File

The permanent file is intended to contain data of historical or continuing nature pertinent to the current audit. This file provides a convenient source of information about the audit that is of continuing interest. The permanent file of working papers ordinarily includes:[21]

- information concerning the legal and organizational structure of the entity such as copies or excerpts of company documents such as **corporate charter** or articles of association, **corporate bylaws**, plans, job manuals, and the corporate organizational chart;
- extracts or copies of important legal documents, agreements and minutes such as contracts, loan agreements, pension plans, agreements with **parent company** and **subsidiaries**, minutes of board of directors or executive committees, and profit-sharing documents.
- prior year analysis of fixed assets, long-term debt, terms of stock and bond issues, intangibles, allowances, and results of analytical procedures.
- information concerning the industry, economic environment and legislative environment within which the entity operates.

Illustration 11.A.2 is a sample listing of the contents of a permanent file. The illustration includes items not mentioned above.

ILLUSTRATION 11.A.2

Sample Work Papers – Permanent File Contents

Permanent File		Engagement Code: Client:
Index	# Pages	Description
I		**General Client and Engagement Information**
1		Engagement letter
2		Client information form
II		**Statutory and Legal Information**
1		Articles of association
2		Special legal, statutory or contractual definitions
3		Registrations, members register
4		Minutes of continuing relevance from management, directors and stockholder meetings
5		Insurance summary
6		Borrowing agreements, lease agreements
7		Title deeds
8		Details of any other important agreements
III		**Accounting System and Internal Control**
1		Documentation of accounting system and internal control
2		Chart of accounts
3		Authorization limits, initials and signature list
4		Accounting procedures instructions
IV		**Audit**
1		Correspondence of continuing relevance
2		Notes and minutes of continuing relevance
3		Documentation: computer applications
4		Registration: hardware and software
V		**Financial Statement Information**
1		Financial statement analysis/previous year's summary
2		Details: intangible fixed assets
3		Details: property, ships, airplanes
4		Details: other tangible fixed assets
5		Details: group companies and other participations
VI		**Personnel, employment conditions**
1		Previous year's summary, social reports
2		Overview of personnel
3		Collective bargaining agreements, standard employment contracts, salary scales
4		Employment conditions board of directors
5		Pension/early retirement rules and regulations
6		Sick pay rules and regulations
7		Expense allowance rules and regulations
8		Other employment conditions
VII		**Taxation**

■ Current File

Working papers for the current file include all documentation applicable to the year under audit. They ordinarily include client summary information such as a description of the client, client industry, client internal controls and the auditor's materials. Auditor's materials in the working papers include: [22]

- ■ evidence of the planning process including the **audit planning memorandum** (hereafter referred to as the audit plan) and the **audit program**; and any changes thereto;
- ■ evidence of the auditor's understanding of the accounting and internal control systems, for instance **internal control questionnaires, internal control flow charts, organization charts,** and a listing of controls and control weakness;
- ■ evidence of inherent and control risk assessments and any revisions;
- ■ evidence of the auditor's consideration of the work of internal auditing or another auditor and conclusions reached;
- ■ analyses of significant ratios and trends;
- ■ a record of the nature, timing and extent of audit procedures performed and the results of such procedures;
- ■ important current legal documents such as contracts and other agreements, leases, and minutes of high-level meetings;
- ■ evidence that the work performed by assistants was supervised and reviewed;
- ■ an indication as to who performed the audit procedures and when they were performed;
- ■ details of procedures applied regarding components whose financial statements are audited by another auditor;
- ■ copies of communications with other auditors, experts and other third parties such as **confirmation letters**;
- ■ copies of letters or notes concerning audit matters communicated to or discussed with the entity, including the terms of the engagement and material weaknesses in internal control;
- ■ letters of representation received from the entity such as the *engagement letter*, and **management representation letter**;
- ■ conclusions reached by the auditor concerning significant aspects of the audit, including how exceptions and unusual matters, if any, disclosed by the auditor's procedures were resolved or treated;
- ■ copies of the financial statements and auditor's report;
- ■ analyses of accounting transactions and balances such as transaction tracing, **trial balances, lead schedules,** and if necessary, recommend journal entries to correct the accounts (i.e. **adjusting** and reclassification **entries**) which are made when an auditor discovers material misstatements in the accounting records;
- ■ various supporting schedules (discussed below).

Illustration 11A.3 is an example of a list of the contents of a current file.

■ Lead Schedules

As early as possible after the balance sheet date, the auditor obtains a trial balance, a listing of the general ledger accounts and their year-end balances. Each line item in the trial balance is supported by a lead schedule, containing the detailed accounts from the general ledger making up the line item. Each detailed account on the lead schedule is, in turn, supported by audit

ILLUSTRATION 11.A.3

Sample Work Papers – Current File

Current File		*Engagement Code:* *Client:*
Index	*# Pages*	*Description*
I		**Reports**
1		Financial statements
2		Auditor's report/auditor's opinion
3		Consolidation package
4		Interoffice memorandum to group auditor
II		**Unconsolidated Financial Statements**
1		Trial balance
2		Reconciliation financial statements/consolidation package/trial balance
3		Adjusting and reclassifying entries
III		**Consolidated Financial Statements**
1		Consolidation schedules
2		Interoffice memoranda and reports from other offices
IV		**Engagement Planning**
1		Strategy document
2		Planning memorandum and audit plan
3		Instruction to/from other offices
4		Audit program
5		Audit progress reports
6		Budget
7		Detailed audit planning and work allocation
V		**Engagement Completion**
1		Completion memorandum
2		Accounting disclosure checklist
3		Subsequent events review
4		Notes for partner/manager
VI		**Engagement Administration**
1		Time sheets
2		Hours and fee-analysis
VII		**Control Overview Document**
VIII		**Representations**
1		Letter of representation
2		Major points discussed with management
3		Lawyer's letter
IX		**Planning Analysis**
1		Budget
2		Interim financial statements
X		**Correspondence in Respect of Current Year's Audit**
XI		**Obsolete Work Papers from Permanent file**

ILLUSTRATION 11.A.4

Sample Work Papers – Account Analysis Schedule

Financial Statement Specification File		*Engagement Code:* *Client:*
Index	*# Pages*	*Description*
A		Intangible fixed assets
B		Tangible fixed assets
C		Financial fixed assets
D		Inventory (Stocks)
E		Receivables
F		Securities
G		Cash
H		Share capital and reserves
I		Provisions
J		Long-term debt
K		Current liabilities
L		Lease commitments
M		Other commitments and contingent liabilities
N		Revenue
O		Expenses (by category)
P		Expenses (by function)
Q		Financial income and expenses
R		Taxation
S		Extraordinary items
T		Discontinued operations

work performed and the conclusions drawn. The largest portion of working papers includes the detailed schedules prepared by the client or the auditors in support of specific amounts on the financial statements.

The major types of supporting schedules are account analysis, list schedules, reconciliation of amounts, tests of reasonableness, procedures description, informational and outside documentation. An **account analysis schedule**, normally used for fixed assets, liabilities and equity accounts, shows the activity in a general ledger account during the entire period under audit, tying together the beginning and ending balances. The **list schedule** shows the detail of those items that make up an end-of-period balance in a general ledger account. A **reconciliation** relates a specific amount in the accounting records to another source of information, for example a reconciliation of accounts payable balances with vendor's statements. The **test of reasonableness schedule** contains information that enables the auditor to evaluate whether the client's balance appears to include a misstatement considering the circumstances. A **summary of procedures description schedule** summarizes the result of audit procedures performed. Information schedules contain non-audit information such as tax information, regulatory information and time budgets. Outside documentation includes confirmation replies, copies of client agreements, etc. Illustration 11.A.4 shows an account analysis schedule that might be used in the audit.

11.A.5 Preparation of Working Papers

The key concept in proper preparation of working papers is to structure the information so that it is easy to interpret and gives the extent of the work in a concise form. Although the design of working papers depends on the objectives involved, they would normally be properly identified, include the conclusions that were reached, would be indexed, and clearly indicate the audit work performed.

Every individual working paper should be properly identified with the client's name, the period covered, a description of contents of the working paper, the date of preparation and index code, and, most importantly, the initials of the person who prepared it. The conclusions reached about that segment of the audit should be stated plainly.

■ Tick Marks and Indexing

The preparation of working papers has strong traditional elements that indicate the audit work performed, cross-references, and suggested adjustments. These elements are tick marks, indexing, and adjusting journal entries.

Tick Marks

Tick marks are symbols used by the auditor to indicate the nature and extent of procedures applied in specific circumstances. Tick marks are notations directly on the working paper schedules. Tick marks are generally done by hand with a pen or pencil alongside a specific item. With the increased use of computers for auditing, tick marks may be input in a spreadsheet program.

Tick marks must be clearly explained at the bottom of the working paper in a legend. For example, the auditor indicates that he has examined supporting vouchers for items listed on a working paper by placing a tick mark or check mark (a symbol such as ✓) beside each item on which the procedures have been carried out. The legend at the bottom of the page will say something like "✓ = voucher and supporting documents examined." (See interest and long-term debt working papers in Illustration 11A.5.) The illustration is from a computer spreadsheet, with check marks (✓) added by hand later when the monthly balances were checked later against the trial balance.

Indexing

Working papers are indexed and cross-referenced to aid in the organizing and filing. Indexing work papers requires coding the individual sheets of paper so that necessary information may be found easily. The auditor prepares cross-references creating a trail through the working papers. A variety of indexing systems are in use. These systems include sequential numbering, combinations of letters and numbers, and digit-position index numbers. The working papers in Illustrations 11.A.2 and 11.A.3 use sequential numbering. Illustration 11.A.4 uses letters. Illustration 11.A.6 gives an example of the digit-position indexing system.

ILLUSTRATION 11.A.5

Sample Work Papers – Interest and Long-term Debt Work Paper

Interest and Long-term Debt Work Paper			
Client: Hu's Paradise Travel			
Topic: Overall test of interest expense			
Date: 31 December 20X5			
Index: Reasonableness schedule – 13			
Page: 1 of 1			
Prepared by: R. Mollie Hayes			
Review by _____			
Balance per General Ledger			€92,457
Short-term Loans			
Mo.	GL Bal. Mo. End	Agree Trial Balance	
Jan.	€218,316	✓	
Feb.	€214,983	✓	
Mar.	€210,459	✓	
Apr.	€315,000	✓	
May	€298,300	✓	
June	€200,000	✓	
July	€198,453	✓	
Aug.	€218,453	✓	
Sep.	€189,675	✓	
Oct.	€180,000	✓	
Nov.	€167,456	✓	
Dec.	€154,678	✓	
Total 12 Mo	€2,565,773	✓	
Ave. Bal (AB)	€213,814	✓	
AB @ 11.5%*			€24,589
Long-term Loans			
Beginning Balance	€896,897		
Ending Balance	€888,888		
Ave. Bal. (AB)	€892,893		
AB @ 7.5%**			€66,967
€			
Estimated Total Interest			€91,556
Difference from GL Balance			€900

Notes: * Based on examination of notes throughout year – 10.75% to 12.5%
** Agrees with permanent file LT debt schedule.
✓ Agree Trial Balance

ILLUSTRATION 11.A.6

Example of Digit-Position Indexing

1000 Draft of audit report
*

*

*

*

2000 Cash

2001 Count of petty cash

2002 Bank reconciliation

2100 Accounts receivable
*

*

*

*

3000 Fixed assets
*

*

3300 Review patents and copyrights
*

*

*

4000 Accounts payable

4002 Confirmation of Accounts payable
*

*

11.A.6 Adjusting Entry

An adjusting journal entry is the correcting entry required at the end of the reporting period due to a mistake made in the accounting records; also called **correcting entry**. The auditor does not make entries in the client's records. The auditor makes the entries on the work papers and reviews their recording by the client. The following adjusting journal entry is an example.

Repair is incorrectly debited to buildings by the following journal entry:

1/23/X1
Debit Buildings $2,000
   Credit Cash $2,000

To record expenditures for painting supervisor's office.

The adjusting journal entry necessary to correct this error is:

12/31/XI

Debit Buildings maintenance expense $2,000

    Credit Buildings $2,000

To correct expenditures for painting supervisor's office incorrectly debited to fixed assets.

11.A.7 Appendix Summary

The auditor should document matters that are important in providing both evidence to support the audit opinion and evidence that the audit was carried out in accordance with ISAs.

Audit documentation is the principal record of the basis for the auditor's conclusions and provides the principal support for the representations in the auditor's report. Audit documentation also facilitates the planning, performance, and supervision of the engagement, and provides the basis for the review of the quality of the work by providing the reviewer with written documentation of the evidence supporting the auditor's significant conclusions. Audit documentation includes records on the planning and performance of the work, the procedures performed, evidence obtained, and conclusions reached by the auditor.

Audit documentation also may be referred to as working papers or work papers. Working papers are a record of the auditor's planning; the nature, timing and extent of the auditing procedures performed; results of those procedures; and the conclusions drawn from the evidence obtained. Working papers may be in the form of data stored on paper, film, electronic media or other media. The terms working papers, work papers and documentation are often used inter-changeably in auditing.

The auditor should document matters that are important in providing evidence to support the audit opinion and evidence that the audit was carried out in accordance with International Standards on Auditing. Working papers:

- are a direct aid in the planning, performance, and supervision of the audit;
- record the audit evidence resulting from the audit work performed to provide support for the auditor's opinion including the representation that the audit was conducted in accordance with ISAs;
- assist in review of the audit work;
- provide proof of the adequacy of the audit.

The auditor must document significant findings or issues, actions taken to address them (including additional evidence obtained), and the basis for the conclusions reached in an engagement completion memorandum.

The content of the working papers should be sufficiently complete and detailed to provide an overall understanding of the audit. The working papers should contain information on planning the audit work; the nature, timing, and extent of the audit procedures performed; the results of the audit procedures; and the conclusions drawn leading to an opinion.

ISA 230 states: "The auditor should adopt appropriate procedures for maintaining the confidentiality and safe custody of the working papers and for retaining them for a period sufficient to meet the needs of the practice and in accordance with legal and professional requirements of record retention." The US SEC regulation on document retention as mandated by the Sarbanes-Oxley Act (SOX) specifies detailed requirements regarding the types of document, requires working papers be kept for not less than seven years, and describes criminal penalties for altering documents. ISA 230 states that working papers are generally considered to be the property of the auditor.

There are two main divisions of audit work papers:

1 the permanent (or continuing) audit file;
2 the current audit file.

The permanent file is audit working papers containing all the data that are of continuing interest from year to year. The current working paper file contains all papers accumulated during the current year's audit. The permanent file is intended to contain data of historical or continuing nature pertinent to the current audit. This file provides a convenient source of information about the audit that is of continuing interest.

The permanent file working papers ordinarily include:

- information concerning the legal and organizational structure of the entity;
- extracts or copies of important legal documents, agreements and minutes;
- prior year analysis of fixed assets, long-term debt, terms of stock and bond issues, intangibles, allowances, and results of analytical procedures;
- information concerning the industry, economic environment and legislative environment within which the entity operates.

Working papers for the current file include all documentation applicable to the year under audit. They ordinarily include client summary information such as a description of the client, client industry, client internal controls and the auditor's materials.

The key concept in proper preparation of working papers is to structure the information so that it is easy to interpret and gives the extent of the work in a concise form. Working papers include the conclusions that were reached; they should be indexed and clearly indicate the audit work performed. The preparation of working papers has strong traditional elements that indicate the audit work performed, cross-references, and suggested adjustments. These elements are tick marks, indexing, and adjusting journal entries.

11.A.8 Notes to Appendix

1 IFAC, 2004, *Handbook of International Auditing, Assurance, and Ethics Pronouncements*, International Standards on Auditing 230 (ISA 230), "Documentation," International Federation of Accountants, New York.
2 *Public Company Accounting Oversight Board* (PCAOB) was established under SOX, section 101. It was established to oversee the audit of public companies that are subject to the securities laws of the USA in order to protect the interests of investors and the public in the preparation of informative, accurate, and independent audit reports.
3 PCAOB, 2003, *PCAOB Release No. 2003-023*, "Proposed Auditing Standard On Audit Documentation," Public Company Accounting Oversight Board, November 21.
4 Ibid.
5 See note 1. Para. 6.
6 PCAOB, 2003, *PCAOB Release No. 2003-023*, "Proposed Auditing Standard On Audit Documentation," para. 9, Public Company Accounting Oversight Board, November 21.

7 IFAC, 2004, *Handbook of International Auditing, Assurance, and Ethics Pronouncements*, International Standards on Auditing 230 (ISA 230), "Documentation," para. 5, International Federation of Accountants, New York.

8 Ibid. Para. 6.

9 PCAOB, 2003, *PCAOB Release No. 2003-023*, "Proposed Auditing Standard On Audit Documentation," para. 5, Public Company Accounting Oversight Board, November 21.

10 PCAOB, 2003, *PCAOB Release No. 2003-023*, "Proposed Auditing Standard On Audit Documentation," para. 9, Public Company Accounting Oversight Board, November 21.

11 PCAOB, 2003, *PCAOB Release No. 2003-023*, "Proposed Auditing Standard On Audit Documentation", note 8, para. 13, Public Company Accounting Oversight Board, November 21.

12 International Auditing and Assurance Standards Board (IAASB), 2004, *International Standard on Quality Control 1 (ISQC 1)*, "Quality Control for Firms That Perform Audits and Reviews of Historical Financial Information, and Other Assurance and Related Services Engagements," para. 97, International Federation of Accountants, New York, February.

13 SEC, 2003, *Final Rule: Strengthening the Commission's Requirements Regarding Auditor Independence*, 17 CFR PARTS (Rules) 210, 240, 249 and 274, [RELEASE NO. 33-8183; 34-47265; 35-27642; IC-25915; IA-2103, FR-68, File No. S7-49-02], RIN 3235-AI73, US Securities and Exchange Commission, Washington, DC, March 27.

14 107th US Congress, 2002, *Sarbanes-Oxley Act of 2002*, Public Law 107–204, Section 103, "Auditing, Quality Control, And Independence Standards And Rules," Senate and House of Representatives of the United States of America in Congress assembled, Washington, DC, July 30.

15 This seven-year period becomes a little confusing because elsewhere in SOX, the period of five years for retention is cited. SOX Title VIII, SEC 801, amends Chapter 73, title 18, paragraph 1520 of the United States Code to say: "(a)(1) Any accountant who conducts an audit of an issuer of securities to which section 10A(a) of the Securities Exchange Act of 1934 (15 U.S.C. 78j–1(a)) applies, shall maintain all audit or review work papers for a period of five years from the end of the fiscal period in which the audit or review was concluded."

16 PCAOB, 2003, *PCAOB Release No. 2003-023*, "Proposed Auditing Standard On Audit Documentation," para. 13, Public Company Accounting Oversight Board, November 21.

17 107th US Congress, 2002, *Sarbanes-Oxley Act of 2002*, Public Law 107–204, Section 105, "Investigations And Disciplinary Proceedings," Senate and House of Representatives of the United States of America in Congress assembled, Washington, DC, July 30.

18 PCAOB, 2003, *PCAOB Release No. 2003-023*, "Proposed Auditing Standard On Audit Documentation," para. 15, Public Company Accounting Oversight Board, November 21.

19 107th US Congress, 2002, *Sarbanes-Oxley Act of 2002*, Public Law 107–204, Title Viii – "Corporate And Criminal Fraud Accountability," SEC. 801, Senate and House of Representatives of the United States of America in Congress assembled, Washington, DC, July 30.

20 IFAC, 2004, *Handbook of International Auditing, Assurance, and Ethics Pronouncements*, International Standards on Auditing 230 (ISA 230), "Documentation," para. 14, International Federation of Accountants, New York.

21 Most of the items listed are from IFAC, 2004, *Handbook of International Auditing, Assurance, and Ethics Pronouncements*, International Standards on Auditing 230 (ISA 230), "Documentation," para. 11, International Federation of Accountants, New York.

22 Most of the items listed below are from IFAC, 2004, *Handbook of International Auditing, Assurance, and Ethics Pronouncements*, International Standards on Auditing 230 (ISA 230), "Documentation," para. 11, International Federation of Accountants, New York.

11.A.9 Questions, Exercises and Cases

QUESTIONS

11A.1 Describe the difference between documentation, work papers, and working papers.

11A.2 Outside of documenting the audit, how else may working papers be used?

11A.3 What should working papers contain? How do working papers relate to auditor judgment?

11A.4 Define permanent file and current file and list the contents of each.

PROBLEMS AND EXERCISES

11A.5 **Legal Aspects of Working Papers.** Cisse and Kamotho, Kenya Certified Public Accountants (CPA(K)), were employed for several years by the Masama Balira Company of Kenya to make annual audits. As a result of a change in management, the corporation discontinued the engagement of Cisse and Kamotho and retained another firm of accountants. The Masama Balira Company thereupon demanded Cisse and Kamotho surrender all working papers prepared by the accounting firm in making audits for the corporation. Cisse and Kamotho refused on the grounds that the working papers were their property. Masama Balira Company brought legal action to recover the working papers. Should the legal action succeed? State briefly the standards, in general, as to ownership of accountants' working papers.

[Adapted and reprinted with permission from AICPA. Copyright © 2000 & 1985 by American Institute of Ceritified Accountants.]

11A.6 **Preparation of Work Papers.** You are instructing an inexperienced staff accountant on her first auditing assignment. She is to examine an account. An analysis of the account has been prepared by the client for inclusion in the audit working papers. Prepare a list of the comments and notations that the staff accountant should make on the account analysis to provide an adequate working paper as evidence of her examination. (Do not include a description of auditing procedures applicable to the account.)

[Adapted and reprinted with permission from AICPA. Copyright © 2000 & 1985 by American Institute of Ceritified Accountants.]

Chapter 12

AUDIT REPORTS AND COMMUNICATION

12.1 Learning Objectives

After studying this chapter, you should be able to:

1 Know the financial statement certification requirements of the chief executive officer and chief financial officer under the Sarbanes-Oxley Act.

2 Understand the basic elements of the auditor's report: contents and form.

3 Explain the contents and importance of the unqualified audit opinion.

4 Distinguish between the different types of opinions given in audit reports on financial statements.

5 Describe the circumstances that may result in modifications of an audit report on financial statements containing an unqualified opinion.

6 State the two circumstances that require an auditor's report containing an opinion other than an unqualified one.

7 Understand how some uncertainties lead to qualification of opinions in the audit report on financial statements.

8 Give the procedures required to finalize the audit.

9 Discuss the audit matters of governance interest arising from the audit of financial statements that the auditor must communicate to those charged with governance of an entity.

10 Give details contained in the long-form audit report.

11 Address the new developments in reporting brought about by XBRL and the possibility of continuous reporting.

12.2 Introduction

An audit report is very brief, occupying no more than a few lines. Because of its brevity those not knowledgeable in auditing may view it as constituting little more than a necessary legal formality, lacking in substance. This is a paradox because the audit report, although comprising only a few words, requires great care and is the consummation of a rigorous and lengthy audit process.

As an illustration of a long process being reduced to a few words, a study in the USA[1] found that in one given year a global audit firm's five largest clients required average audit work of 128,000 hours per client. This resulted in external reports of only 175 words or less. One might conclude that to get so many hours into so few words, accountants must be poets. More likely, this brevity is out of concern for the users of financial statements. The authors of that same study suggest that the anxious investor does not want to muddle through a lengthy catalog of work done and detailed findings (imagine how long that would be after 128,000 hours of work) when the final message is "it is OK."

However, in addition to this brief external audit report, the auditor is expected to address accounting and auditing issues more extensively in a long-form audit report (see Section 12.9).

■ Management Responsibility for Audit Report

Up until 2002, corporate officers of publicly traded companies in the USA were not held liable for misstated financial statements unless fraud could be proven. (In other words, the officers knew it was misstated and that was their intent.) All that changed with the Sarbanes-Oxley Act of 2002 (SOX) which now requires[2] that the principal executive officer or officers and the principal financial officer or officers, certify in each annual or quarterly report filed or submitted to the US Securities and Exchange Commission (SEC) the following:

- the signing officer has reviewed the report;
- the report does not contain any untrue statement of a material fact or omit to state a material fact;
- the financial statements, and other financial information, fairly present in all material respects the financial condition of the company;
- the signing officers:
  - are responsible for establishing and maintaining internal controls;
  - have evaluated the effectiveness of the company's internal controls;
  - have presented in the report their conclusions about the effectiveness of their internal controls based on their evaluation;
- the signing officers have disclosed to the company's auditors and the audit committee of the board of directors:
  - all significant deficiencies in the design or operation of internal controls which could adversely affect the company's ability to record, process, summarize, and report financial data, and have identified for the company's auditors any material weaknesses in internal controls;
  - any fraud, whether or not material, that involves management or other employees who have a significant role in the company's internal controls;

■ the signing officers have indicated in the report whether or not there were significant changes in internal controls or in other factors that could significantly affect internal controls subsequent to the date of their evaluation, including any corrective actions with regard to significant deficiencies and material weaknesses.

ILLUSTRATION 12.1

Certification of Schlumberger Financial Statements by Corporate Officers

---

Certification of Chief Executive Officer

I, Andrew Gould, certify that:

1. I have reviewed this annual report on Form 10-K of Schlumberger Limited;

2. Based on my knowledge, this report does not contain any untrue statement of a material fact or omit to state a material fact necessary to make the statements made, in light of the circumstances under which such statements were made, not misleading with respect to the period covered by this report;

3. Based on my knowledge, the financial statements, and other financial information included in this report, fairly present in all material respects the financial condition, results of operations and cash flows of the registrant as of, and for, the periods presented in this report;

4. The registrant's other certifying officer and I are responsible for establishing and maintaining disclosure controls and procedures (as defined in Exchange Act Rules 13a–15(e) and 15d–15(e)) for the registrant and have:

(a)　Designed such disclosure controls and procedures, or caused such disclosure controls and procedures to be designed under our supervision, to ensure that material information relating to the registrant, including its consolidated subsidiaries, is made known to us by others within those entities, particularly during the period in which this report is being prepared;

(b)　Evaluated the effectiveness of the registrant's disclosure controls and procedures and presented in this report our conclusions about the effectiveness of the disclosure controls and procedures, as of the end of the period covered by this report based on such evaluation; and

(c)　Disclosed in this report any change in the registrant's internal control over financial reporting that occurred during the registrant's most recent fiscal quarter (the registrant's fourth fiscal quarter in the case of an annual report) that has materially affected, or is reasonably likely to materially affect, the registrant's internal control over financial reporting; and

5. The registrant's other certifying officer and I have disclosed, based on our most recent evaluation of internal control over financial reporting, to the registrant's auditors and the audit committee of the registrant's board of directors (or persons fulfilling the equivalent functions);

(a)　All significant deficiencies and material weaknesses in the design or operation of internal control over financial reporting which are reasonably likely to adversely affect the registrant's ability to record, process, summarize and report financial information; and

(b)　Any fraud, whether or not material, that involves management or other employees who have a significant role in the registrant's internal control over financial reporting.

Date: March 3, 2004　　　/s/　Andrew Gould

　　　　　　　　　　　　　—————————————————

　　　　　　　　　　　　　Andrew Gould
　　　　　　　　　　　　　Chairman and Chief Executive Officer

Source: US Securities and Exchange Commission, www.sec.gov.

This applies also to officers of corporations headquartered outside the USA whose company's stock is traded on US stock exchanges.[3] This may prove in future to be a sticky point and already there is much international debate. In several European countries it is required by law that all members of the Board of Directors (or, in a two-tier system, the Executive Board and the Supervisory Board) sign the financial statements, thereby demonstrating that their responsibility for these statements is a joint one rather than only that of the CEO and CFO. However, this does not detract from the principle that the responsibility for the financial statements and the internal controls rests with those charged with governance, which is the key issue in SOX.

Illustration 12.1 is the certification of Schlumberger Limited's Chairman and Chief Executive Officer Andrew Gould that was submitted in the 10-K report to the SEC for

12.3 Basic Elements of the Auditor's Report

2003.

ISA 700, "The Auditor's Report on Financial Statements" states: "The auditor should review and assess the conclusions drawn from the audit evidence obtained as the basis for the expression of an opinion on the financial statements."[4] The auditor's report should contain a clear written expression of opinion on the financial statements taken as a whole.

■ Contents of the Auditor's Report

The auditor's report should include the following basic elements[5] that are discussed in more detail in the balance of this section:

- ■ title;
- ■ addressee;
- ■ opening or introductory paragraph:
  - – identification of the financial statements audited;
  - – a statement of the responsibility of the entity's management and the responsibility of the auditor;
- ■ **scope paragraph** (describing the nature of an audit):
  - – a reference to the ISAs or relevant national standards or practices;
  - – a description of the work the auditor performed;
- ■ opinion paragraph containing an expression of opinion on the financial statements;
- ■ the date of the report;
- ■ the auditor's address;
- ■ auditor's signature.

Title

The auditor's report should have an appropriate title that helps the reader to identify it and easily distinguish it from other reports, such as that of management. The most frequently used title is "Independent Auditor" or "Auditor's Report" in the title to distinguish the auditor's report from reports that might be issued by others.

Addressee

The report should be addressed as required by the circumstances of the engagement and the local regulations. The report is usually addressed either to the shareholders or supervisory board or the board of directors of the entity whose financial statements have been audited. In some countries, such as The Netherlands, auditor's reports are not addressed at all because the reports are meant to be used by (the anonymous) public at large.

Opening or Introductory Paragraph

The report should identify the financial statements that have been audited. This should include the name of the entity and the date and period covered by the financial statements. The report should include a statement that the financial statements are the responsibility of the entity's management.[6] The preparation of these statements requires management to make significant accounting estimates and judgments, as well as to determine the appropriate accounting principles and methods used when preparing the statements. The introductory paragraph should also have a statement that the responsibility of the auditor is to express an opinion on the financial statements based on the audit.

An illustration of an opening (introductory) paragraph is:

> "We have audited the accompanying balance sheet of the ABC Company as of December 31, 20X3, and the related statements of income and cash flows for the year then ended. These financial statements are the responsibility of the Company's management. Our responsibility is to express an opinion on these financial statements based on our audit."

Scope Paragraph

Scope refers to the auditor's ability to perform audit procedures deemed necessary in the circumstances. The scope paragraph is a factual statement of what the auditor did in the audit. This provides the reader assurance that the audit has been carried out in accordance with established standards or practices for such engagements.

The scope paragraph should include a statement that the audit was planned and performed to obtain reasonable assurance about whether the financial statements are free of material misstatement and that the audit provides a reasonable basis for the opinion. The use of these phrases, or similar wording, means that the audit provides a high level of assurance, but it is not a guarantee.

The report should indicate the auditing standards or practices followed in conducting the audit by reference to International Standards on Auditing (ISA) or to standards or practices established within a country. Unless otherwise stated, the auditing standards or practices followed are presumed to be those of the country indicated by the auditor's address.

If the company is traded on a US stock exchange, PCAOB's Auditing Standard No. 1[7] requires that in a report with respect to reference to generally accepted auditing standards, US generally accepted auditing standards, auditing standards generally accepted in the USA, or standards established by the AICPA, the auditor must instead refer to "the standards of the Public Company Accounting Oversight Board."

The auditor's report should describe the audit as examining, on a test basis, evidence to support the financial statements amounts and disclosures and assessing the accounting principles used in the preparation of those statements. The report should also describe the audit as evaluating the financial statements overall and assessing the significant estimates made by management in the preparation of those statements.

Certification Exam Question 12.1

Which of the following statements is a basic element of the auditor's standard report?

(A) The disclosures provide reasonable assurance that the financial statements are free of material misstatement.
(B) The auditor evaluated the overall internal control.
(C) An audit includes assessing significant estimates made by management.
(D) The financial statements are consistent with those of the prior period.

An illustration of a scope paragraph is:

"We conducted our audit in accordance with International Standards on Auditing (or refer to relevant national standards or practices). Those Standards require that we plan and perform the audit to obtain reasonable assurance about whether the financial statements are free of material misstatement. An audit includes examining, on a test basis, evidence supporting the amounts and disclosures in the financial statements. An audit also includes assessing the accounting principles used and significant estimates made by management, as well as evaluating the overall financial statement presentation. We believe that our audit provides a reasonable basis for our opinion."

Opinion Paragraph

The opinion paragraph of the auditor's report should clearly indicate the financial reporting framework used to prepare the financial statements (including identifying the country of origin of the financial reporting framework when the framework used is not International Financial Reporting Standards) and state the auditor's opinion as to whether the financial statements give a true and fair view (or are presented fairly, in all material respects) in accordance with that financial reporting framework and, where appropriate, whether the financial statements comply with statutory requirements.[8]

The terms used to express the auditor's opinion are "give a true and fair view" or "present fairly, in all material respects," and are equivalent. Both terms indicate, amongst other things, that the auditor considers only those matters that are material to the financial statements.

International Standard on Auditing (ISA) 200,[9] states that the objective of an audit of financial statements is to enable the auditor to express an opinion whether the financial statements are prepared, in all material respects, in accordance with an identified financial reporting framework. The financial reporting framework is determined by International Financial Reporting Standards (IFRSs), rules issued by professional bodies, and the development of general practice within the country, with the appropriate consideration of fairness and with due regard to local legislation.

To advise the reader of the context in which fairness is expressed, the auditor's opinion would indicate the framework upon which the financial statements are based by using words such as "... in accordance with International Accounting Standards (or [title of financial reporting framework with reference to the country of origin]) ..."

The reporting framework may be IFRSs or a national financial reporting framework. International Auditing Practice Statement (IAPS) 1014[10] provides guidance when the auditor expresses an opinion on financial statements that are prepared under IFRSs or both IFRSs and national financial reporting frameworks.

Sometimes the auditor may prepare the financial statements in accordance with both IFRSs and a national financial reporting framework. The financial statements must comply with both financial reporting frameworks simultaneously and without any need for reconciling statements if they are to be regarded as having been prepared in accordance with both. In practice, simultaneous compliance with both IFRSs and a national financial reporting framework is unlikely unless the country has adopted IFRSs as its national financial reporting framework or has eliminated all barriers for compliance with IFRSs.

The auditor considers each financial reporting framework separately. If a matter results in failure to comply with one of the frameworks, but does not cause a failure to comply with the other framework, then he expresses an unqualified opinion on compliance with that framework and a qualified opinion or an adverse opinion on compliance with the other framework. If the auditor is of the opinion that the failure to comply with one of the financial reporting frameworks causes the financial statements to fail to comply with the other financial reporting framework, he issues a qualified opinion or adverse opinion on compliance with both frameworks. As an illustration of an auditor's report where he is of the opinion that the financial statements comply with the national financial reporting framework, but a qualified opinion is appropriate for compliance with IFRSs, there is a sample report format given in IAPS 1014.[11]

An illustration of these matters in an opinion paragraph is:

"In our opinion, the financial statements give a true and fair view of (or 'present fairly, in all material respects') the financial position of the Company as of December 31, 20X3, and of the results of its operations and its cash flows for the year then ended in accordance with International Financial Reporting Standards (or [title of financial reporting framework with reference to the country of origin[12]]) (and comply with ...[13])."

Date of Report

The report must be dated. The auditor should date the report as the completion date of the audit (usually the last date of field work). This informs the reader that the auditor has considered the effect on the financial statements and on the report of events or transactions about which the auditor became aware and that occurred up to that date. Since the auditor's responsibility is to report on the financial statements as prepared and presented by management, the auditor should not date the report earlier than the date on which the financial statements are signed or approved by management.[14]

Auditor's Address

The report should name a specific location, which is usually the city in which the auditor maintains an office that serves the client audited. PCAOB's Auditing Standard No. 1[15] also requires that an auditor include the city and state (or city and country, in the case of non-US auditors) from which the auditor's report has been issued. Note: In some countries it is not required that the audit report give the specific address for the auditor.

Signature

The report should be signed in the name of the audit firm, or the personal name of the auditor, or both, as appropriate. The auditor's report is ordinarily signed in the name of the firm because the firm assumes responsibility for the audit. Note: In several countries (e.g. the USA, the UK, the Netherlands) it is currently not required that the personal name of the auditor be signed. Inclusion of the name in a reference is sufficient.

■ Form of an Auditor's Report

The most common type of audit report is the standard unqualified audit report. It is used for more than 90 percent of all audit reports.[16] Other audit reports are referred to as "other than unqualified reports". Other than unqualified reports include those reports that express: an adverse opinion, disclaimer of opinion, and qualified opinion (see Section 12.4).

The form of an auditor's report will generally be the form of the unqualified report consisting of three paragraphs: introduction, scope, and opinion (see above). Reports can also include a fourth paragraph (after the opinion paragraph) called "paragraph emphasizing an uncertainty" or "explanatory paragraph." In some countries a paragraph referring a qualification as a result of inadequate accounting procedures or disclosure may be inserted just before the opinion paragraph.

Illustration 12.2 shows the standard wording for an unqualified audit report.

ILLUSTRATION 12.2

Sample Wording – Auditor's Unqualified Report[17]

Auditor's Report

(Appropriate Addressee)

We have audited the accompanying* balance sheet of the ABC Company as of December 31 20X3, and the related statements of income, and cash flows for the year then ended. These financial statements are the responsibility of the Company's management. Our responsibility is to express an opinion on these financial statements based on our audit.

We conducted our audit in accordance with International Standards on Auditing (or refer to relevant national standards or practices). Those Standards require that we plan and perform the audit to obtain reasonable assurance about whether the financial statements are free of material misstatement. An audit includes examining, on a test basis, evidence supporting the amounts and disclosures in the financial statements. An audit also includes assessing the accounting principles used and significant estimates made by management as well as evaluating the overall financial statement presentation. We believe that our audit provides a reasonable basis for our opinion.

In our opinion, the financial statements give a true and fair view of (or "present fairly, in all material respects") the financial position of the Company as of December 31 20X3, and the results of its operations and its cash flows for the year then ended in accordance in accordance with International Financial Reporting Standards (or [title of financial reporting framework with reference to the country of origin]) (and comply with ...**).

Auditor
Date
Address

* The reference can be by page numbers.
**Refer to the relevant statutes or law.

The final paragraph in the standard unqualified report states the auditor's conclusion based on the results of the audit examination. This paragraph is so important that the entire audit report is frequently referred to as "the auditor's opinion." The opinion

ILLUSTRATION 12.3

Sample US Unqualified Report and Management's Report on Responsibility for Financial Reporting for Wm. Wrigley Jr. Company

Report Of Independent Auditors

To the Stockholders and Board of Directors of the Wm. Wrigley Jr. Company:

We have audited the accompanying consolidated balance sheets of the Wm. Wrigley Jr. Company and associated companies (the "Company") at December 31, 2003 and 2002 and the related consolidated statements of earnings, stockholders' equity and cash flows for each of the three years in the period ended December 31, 2003. These financial statements are the responsibility of the Company's management. Our responsibility is to express an opinion on these financial statements based on our audits.

We conducted our audits in accordance with auditing standards generally accepted in the United States. Those standards require that we plan and perform the audit to obtain reasonable assurance about whether the financial statements are free of material misstatement. An audit includes examining, on a test basis, evidence supporting the amounts and disclosures in the financial statements. An audit also includes assessing the accounting principles used and significant estimates made by management, as well as evaluating the overall financial statement presentation. We believe that our audits provide a reasonable basis for our opinion.

In our opinion, the financial statements referred to above present fairly, in all material respects, the consolidated financial position of the Company at December 31, 2003 and 2002, and the consolidated results of their operations and their cash flows for each of the three years in the period ended December 31, 2003, in conformity with accounting principles generally accepted in the United States.

Ernst & Young LLP
Chicago, Illinois
January 21, 2004

Management's Report
On Responsibility For Financial Reporting

Management of the Wm. Wrigley Jr. Company is responsible for the preparation and integrity of the financial statements and related information presented in this Annual Report. This responsibility is carried out through a system of internal controls to ensure that assets are safeguarded, transactions are properly authorized, and financial records are accurate.

These controls include a comprehensive internal audit program, written financial policies and procedures, appropriate division of responsibility, and careful selection and training of personnel. Written policies include a Code of Business Conduct prescribing that all employees maintain the highest ethical and business standards.

Ernst & Young LLP has conducted an independent audit of the financial statements, and its report appears below.

The Board of Directors exercises its control responsibility through an Audit Committee composed entirely of independent directors. The Audit Committee meets regularly to review accounting and control matters. Both Ernst & Young LLP and the internal auditors have direct access to the Audit Committee and periodically meet privately with them.

WM. WRIGLEY JR. COMPANY
Chicago, Illinois
January 21, 2004

Source: Wrigely Annual Report, www.wrigley.com.

paragraph is stated as an opinion rather than as statement of absolute fact or a guarantee. The intent is to indicate that the conclusions are based on professional judgment.

Generally accepted auditing standards in the USA (US GAAS) require the use of a three-paragraph report much like the international format. The scope paragraph is the second paragraph and the opinion paragraph is last. Illustration 12.3 is an unqualified report and management's report on Responsibility for Financial Reporting from the US company, Wm. Wrigley, Jr. Company, the maker of chewing gums such as Juicy Fruit, Doublemint, Spearmint, Big Red, etc.

■ Modified Opinion

An auditor's report is considered to be modified in the two different situations:

1 matters that do not affect the Auditor's Opinion (which would mean adding an **emphasis of matter paragraph**[18]);
2 matters that do affect the Auditor's Opinion (instances that call for either a (a) **qualified opinion**, (b) **disclaimer of opinion**, or (c) **adverse opinion**).

As the user's understanding will be better if the form and content of each type is uniform, ISA 700 includes suggested wording to express an unqualified opinion as well as examples of modifying phrases for use when issuing modified reports.

Certification Exam Question 12.2

Which paragraphs of an auditor's standard report on financial statements should refer to International Standards on Auditing (ISAs) and International Financial Reporting Standards (IFRS)?

	ISA	*IFRS*
(A)	Opening	Scope
(B)	Scope	Scope
(C)	Scope	Opinion
(D)	Opening	Opinion

12.4 Types of Reports Expressing Audit Opinions

The opinion expressed in the auditor's report may be one of four types: unqualified, qualified, adverse or disclaimer of opinion.

■ Standard Unqualified Opinion Auditor's Report

The auditor's unqualified report should be expressed when the auditor concludes that the financial statements give a true and fair view (or present fairly, in all material respects) in accordance with the identified financial reporting framework.[19] An auditor's report containing an unqualified opinion also indicates implicitly that any changes in accounting principles or in the method of their application, and their effects, have been properly determined and disclosed in the financial statements. Illustration 12.2 earlier shows sample wording for an auditor's unqualified report.

Requirements to Give Unqualified Opinion

In an auditor's report on financial statements an unqualified opinion is issued in a clear and affirmative manner when the auditor is satisfied in all material respects that:

- the financial information has been prepared using acceptable accounting policies, which have been consistently applied;
- the financial information complies with relevant regulations and statutory requirements;
- the view presented by the financial information as a whole is consistent with the auditor's knowledge of the business of the entity;
- there is adequate disclosure of all material matters relevant to the proper presentation of the financial information.

When Opinion Cannot be Unqualified

An auditor may not be able to express an unqualified opinion when either of the following circumstances exist and, in the auditor's judgment, they are material to the financial statements.

(a) there is a limitation on the scope of the auditor's work; or
(b) there is a disagreement with management regarding the acceptability of the accounting policies selected, the method of their application or the adequacy of financial statement disclosures.

(See Section 12.6 for further discussion.)

The circumstances described in (a), scope limitation, could lead to an auditor's report containing a qualified opinion or a disclaimer of opinion, or in some countries, even in a withdrawal from the engagement. The circumstances described in (b), disagreement with management, could lead to an auditor's report containing a qualified opinion or an adverse opinion.

Concept and a Company 12.1

Livent Produces An Accounting Theatrical

Concept	Impact of financial fraud on the auditors' opinion.
Story	Based out of Toronto, Livent was a company that produced live theatrical entertainment, such as *Ragtime, The Phantom of the Opera, Show Boat, Sunset Boulevard* and *Fosse*. It owned and operated theaters in Toronto, Vancouver, Chicago and New York in the 1990s. On May 1993, Livent became a public company in Canada, in May 1995 it began trading on the NASDAQ national stock market and on the Toronto Stock Exchange. (SEC January 13, 1999) An accounting fraud perpetrated by CEO Garth Drabinski, President Myron Gootlieb, and Tony Fiorino, CA, the Theater Controller, led to Livent declaring bankruptcy in the USA and Canada on November 18 and 19, 1998, respectively. (SEC 1999a)

In August 1998, a new management team at Livent discovered the vague, false and misleading financial statements and disclosures from former senior management. KPMG Peat Marwick conducted an independent investigation of the fraud. In November 1998, KPMG reported that Livent had submitted at least 17 false filings with the SEC which materially overstated income and operating cash flows throughout the relevant period. As a result of the scheme, Livent's restatements reported in a cumulative adverse effect on net income in excess of $98 million in Canadian dollars. (SEC 1999b)

The fraud included: a multi-million dollar kick-back scheme designed to misappropriate funds for management's own use; the improper shifting of preproduction costs, such as advertising for Ragtime, to fixed assets, such as the construction of theaters in Chicago and New York; and the improper recording of revenue for transactions that contained side agreements purposefully concealed from Livent's independent auditors. (SEC 1999a)

Livent's accounting staff used four basic forms of manipulation. First, the staff transferred preproduction costs for shows to fixed asset accounts such as the construction of theaters, in order to delay the amortization of those costs. Theater Controller Fiorino created dummy accounts for the amounts that were improperly transferred to fixed assets Second, the accounting staff, at the end of each quarter, simply removed certain expenses and the related liabilities from the general ledger. These items were literally erased from the company's books. Third, the accounting staff transferred costs from one show currently running to another show that had not yet been opened or that had a longer amortization period, again in order to delay the amortization of those costs.

Finally, senior management entered into various "revenue-producing" contracts containing purposefully concealed side agreements that, in effect, required Livent to pay back to the ticket buyers the amount originally advanced. From September 30, 1997 to December 31, 1997, the first vendor purchased tickets totaling $381,015 (US) from the box office at the Schubert Theater in Los Angeles. These purchases were made using the vendor's personal credit card or the vendor issued checks from one of his companies. Livent then reimbursed the vendor or his companies based on false invoices the vendor submitted for construction services to Livent. These transactions should have been booked as loans payable rather than as revenue. (SEC 1999a)

Livent's former senior officers directed that various improper adjustments be made to Livent's books, records, and accounts in order to manage income for each quarter to achieve a predetermined level. (SEC 1999b) Senior management instructed the accounting staff to regularly process the adjustments to the books, records and accounts in such a way as to conceal their existence from the auditors and then prepared financial statements incorporating the adjustments. Adjusting journal entries would have left a trail of "red flags" for the auditors, something Livent's senior management did not want to create. Consequently, starting in at least 1994, the manager of Livent's information services department wrote a program that would enable the accounting staff to override the accounting system without a paper or transaction trail. That manager then wrote programs to enable the accounting staff to execute changes on a batch, or volume, basis. This process had the effect of falsifying the books, records and accounts of the company so completely that the adjustments appeared as original transactions, and no trace of the actual original entries remained in the company's general ledger. (SEC 1999a)

As a result of the scheme, Livent's financial statements for fiscal years 1991 and 1992, prior to Livent becoming a US public company, were materially false and misleading in that Livent overstated pre-tax earnings, or understated pre-tax losses, in each of those years. For

Livent Produces An Accounting Theatrical (continued)

fiscal 1991, Livent reported a pre-tax loss of $1.2 million. In fact, Livent's loss in that year was approximately $4.6 million. For fiscal 1992, Livent reported pre-tax earnings of $2.9 million. In fact, the company's true earnings were approximately $100,000. (SEC 1999a)

As a further result of the scheme, Livent reported inflated pre-tax earnings, or understated pre-tax losses, for each of its fiscal years as a US public company, 1995 through 1997. For fiscal 1995, Livent reported pre-tax earnings of $18.2 million. In fact, the company's true earnings were approximately $15 million. For fiscal 1996, Livent reported pre-tax earnings of $14.2 million. In fact, the company incurred a loss of more than $20 million in that year. For fiscal 1997, Livent reported a pre-tax loss of $62.1 million. In fact, the company's true loss in fiscal 1997 was at least $83.6 million. (SEC 1999a)

Discussion Questions	■ How did each one of the four accounting fraud schemes impact Livent's financial statements? ■ What audit procedures might be used to discover these misstatements?
References	SEC, 1999a, *Accounting and Auditing Enforcement Release No. 1101. Administrative Proceeding No. 3-9814,* "In the Matter of Tony Fiorino, Chartered Accountant," Securities and Exchange Commission, January 21. SEC, 1999b, *Litigation Release No. 16033 Accounting and Auditing Enforcement Release No. 1102,* "Securities And Exchange Commission v. Garth H. Drabinsky, Myron I. Gottlieb, Robert Topol, Gordon C. Eckstein, Maria M. Messina, Diane J. Winkfein, D. Grant Malcolm And Tony Fiorino," Securities and Exchange Commission, January 21.

■ Auditor's Report Containing a Qualified Opinion

An auditor's report containing a qualified opinion is issued when the auditor concludes that an unqualified opinion cannot be expressed but that the effect of any disagreement with management, or limitation in scope, is not so material as to require an adverse opinion or a disclaimer of opinion. A qualified opinion should be expressed as fairly presenting the financial statements "except for" the effects of the matter to which the qualifications relates.

An example of the wording of a qualified report is given in Illustration 12.4. This illustration is a qualified opinion report based on limitation of scope. It should be noted that in some countries the auditor would not be allowed to accept an engagement with such a limitation of scope.

■ Auditor's Report Containing an Adverse Opinion

An adverse opinion is issued when the effect of a disagreement is so material and pervasive to the financial statements that the auditor concludes that a qualification of his report is not adequate to disclose the misleading or incomplete nature of the financial statements.

An example of the wording of an auditor's report containing an adverse opinion for inadequate disclosure is given in Illustration 12.5.

Notice that the adverse opinion report has a third paragraph, before the opinion paragraph, which is the paragraph discussing the disagreement. For example, in

ILLUSTRATION 12.4

Sample Wording – Limitation on Scope Qualified Opinion[20]

Auditor's Report

(Appropriate Addressee)

We have audited the accompanying* balance sheet of the ABC Company as of December 31, 20X5, and the related statements of income, and cash flows for the year then ended. These financial statements are the responsibility of the Company's management. Our responsibility is to express an opinion on these financial statements based on our audit.

Except as discussed in the following paragraph, we conducted our audit in accordance with International Standards on Auditing (or refer to relevant national standards or practices). Those Standards require that we plan and perform the audit to obtain reasonable assurance about whether the financial statements are free of material misstatement. An audit includes examining, on a test basis, evidence supporting the amounts and disclosures in the financial statements. An audit also includes assessing the accounting principles used and significant estimates made by management as well as evaluating the overall financial statement presentation. We believe that our audit provides a reasonable basis for our opinion.

We did not observe the counting of the physical inventories as of December 31, 20X4, since that date was prior to the time we were initially engaged as auditors for the Company. Owing to the nature of the Company's records, we were unable to satisfy ourselves as to inventory quantities by other audit procedures.

In our opinion, except for the effects of such adjustments, if any, as might have been determined to be necessary had we been able to satisfy ourselves as to physical inventory quantities, the financial statements give a true and fair view of (or "present fairly, in all material respects") the financial position of the Company as of December 31, 20X5, and the results of its operations and its cash flows for the year then ended in accordance with International Financial Reporting Standards (or [title of financial reporting framework with reference to the country of origin]) (and comply with …**).

Auditor
Date
Address

* The reference can be by page numbers.
** Refer to the relevant statutes or law.

Illustration 12.5, the auditor has a disagreement with management as to an allowance for non-performing loans.

It is obvious from reading the opinion paragraph that an adverse opinion report is likely to have a very negative effect on the readers of the report and the related financial statements; therefore, such reports are issued only after all attempts to persuade the client to adjust the financial statements have failed. The only other option available to the auditor in this situation is withdrawal from the engagement.

■ Auditor's Report Containing a Disclaimer of Opinion

An auditor's report containing a disclaimer of opinion should be expressed when the possible effect of a limitation on scope is so material and pervasive that the auditor has not been able to obtain sufficient appropriate audit evidence and therefore is unable to express an opinion on the financial statements.

ILLUSTRATION 12.5

Sample Wording – Inadequate Disclosure Adverse Opinion[21]

Auditor's Report

(Appropriate Addressee)

We have audited the accompanying* balance sheet of the ABC Company as of December 31, 20X3, and the related statements of income, and cash flows for the year then ended. These financial statements are the responsibility of the Company's management. Our responsibility is to express an opinion on these financial statements based on our audit.

We conducted our audit in accordance with International Standards on Auditing (or refer to relevant national standards or practices). Those Standards require that we plan and perform the audit to obtain reasonable assurance about whether the financial statements are free of material misstatement. An audit includes examining, on a test basis, evidence supporting the amounts and disclosures in the financial statements. An audit also includes assessing the accounting principles used and significant estimates made by management as well as evaluating the overall financial statement presentation. We believe that our audit provides a reasonable basis for our opinion.

As discussed in Note 12 management has valued its subsidiaries in countries A and B at their net equity value as of December 31, 20X2. Management has argued that there are no reliable and audited financial statements of these subsidiaries available for the year ended December 31, 20X3. However, management did not disclose that preliminary internal figures indicate severe losses at these subsidiaries at a level that is material to ABC Company's financial statements. Although we agree with management that the reliability of these figures is doubtful, we believe that the indications of substantial losses are such that a material decline in value of these subsidiaries' net equity as of December 31, 20X3, is probable. As a consequence, ABC Company's stockholders' equity as of December 31, 20X3 and its net result for the year 20X3 is likely to be overstated by €100,000,000.

In our opinion, because of the effects of the matters discussed in the preceding paragraph(s), the financial statements do not give a true and fair view of (or do not "present fairly") the financial position of the Company as of December 31, 20X3, and of the results of its operations and its cash flows for the year then ended in accordance with International Financial Reporting Standards (or [title of financial reporting framework with reference to the country of origin]) (and comply with ...**).

Auditor
Date
Address

---

* The reference can be by page numbers.
** Refer to the relevant statutes or law.

An example of the wording of a disclaimer of opinion report for limitation of scope is given in Illustration 12.6.

Whenever the auditor issues a report that is other than unqualified, he should include a clear description of all the substantive reasons that should be included in the report and a qualification of the possible effect(s) on the financial statements. This information should be set out in a separate paragraph, preceding the opinion or disclaimer of opinion and may include a reference to a more extensive discussion, if any, in a note to the financial statements.

ILLUSTRATION 12.6

Sample Wording – Limitation of Scope Disclaimer of Opinion[22]

Auditor's Report

(Appropriate Addressee)

We were engaged to audit the accompanying balance sheet of the ABC Company as of December 31, 20X3, and the related statements of income, and cash flows for the year then ended. These financial statements are the responsibility of the Company's management. (Omit the sentence stating the responsibility of the auditor.)

(The paragraph discussing the scope of the audit would either be omitted or amended according to the circumstances.)

(Add a paragraph discussing the scope limitation as follows:)

We were not able to observe all physical inventories and confirm accounts receivable due to limitations placed on the scope of our work by the Company. Because of the significance of the matters discussed in the preceding paragraph, we do not express an opinion on the financial statements.

Auditor
Date
Address

12.5 Matters that Do Not Affect the Auditor's Opinion (Modification of an Auditor's Report Containing an Unqualified Opinion)

In certain circumstances, an auditor's report may be modified by adding an emphasis of matter paragraph to highlight a matter affecting the financial statements. The addition of an emphasis of matter paragraph does not affect the auditor's opinion. The paragraph should follow the opinion paragraph and state that the auditor's opinion is not qualified by this.[23]

Ordinarily, an auditor might write an emphasis of a matter paragraph:

- if there is a significant **uncertainty** which may affect the financial statements, the resolution of which is dependent upon future events;
- to highlight a material matter regarding a going concern problem. (Illustration 12.8 shows emphasis of matter paragraph relating to going concern. Also see Chapter 11 Completing the Audit and ISA 570, "Going Concern.");
- other matters.

An illustration of an emphasis of matter paragraph for a significant uncertainty in an auditor's report follows:[24]

"Without qualifying our opinion we draw attention to Note X to the financial statements. The Company is the defendant in a lawsuit alleging infringement of certain patent rights and claiming royalties and punitive damages. The Company has filed a counter action, and preliminary hearings and discovery proceedings on both actions are in progress. The ultimate outcome of the matter cannot presently be determined, and no provision for any liability that may result has been made in the financial statements."

■ Uncertainties in the Emphasis of a Matter Paragraph

Examples of uncertainties that might be emphasized include the existence of related-party transactions, important accounting matters occurring subsequent to the balance sheet date (discussed in Chapter 11 Completing the Audit), and matters affecting the comparability of financial statements with those of previous years (e.g change in accounting methods). Illustrations 12.7 and 12.8 provide sample wording for uncertainty paragraphs.

ILLUSTRATION 12.7

Sample Wording – Auditor's Unqualified Report with Legal Uncertainty Emphasis of Matter Paragraph[25]

Auditor's Report

(Appropriate Addressee)

We have audited the accompanying* balance sheet of the ABC Company as of December 31, 20X3, and the related statements of income, and cash flows for the year then ended. These financial statements are the responsibility of the Company's management. Our responsibility is to express an opinion on these financial statements based on our audit.

We conducted our audit in accordance with International Standards on Auditing (or refer to relevant national standards or practices). Those Standards require that we plan and perform the audit to obtain reasonable assurance about whether the financial statements are free of material misstatement. An audit includes examining, on a test basis, evidence supporting the amounts and disclosures in the financial statements. An audit also includes assessing the accounting principles used and significant estimates made by management as well as evaluating the overall financial statement presentation. We believe that our audit provides a reasonable basis for our opinion.

In our opinion, the financial statements give a true and fair view of (or "present fairly, in all material respects") the financial position of the Company as of December 31, 20X3, and the results of its operations and its cash flows for the year then ended in accordance with International Financial Reporting Standards (or [title of financial reporting framework with reference to the country of origin]) (and comply with ...**).

Without qualifying our opinion we draw attention to Note X to the financial statements. The Company is the defendant in a lawsuit alleging infringement of certain patent rights and claiming royalties and punitive damages. The Company has filed a counter-action, and preliminary hearings and discovery proceedings on both actions are in progress. The ultimate outcome of the matter cannot presently be determined, and no provision for any liability that may result has been made in the financial statements.

Auditor
Date
Address

---

* The reference can be by page numbers.
** Refer to the relevant statutes or law.

ILLUSTRATION 12.8

Sample Wording – Auditor's Unqualified Report with Going Concern Emphasis of Matter Paragraph[26]

Auditor's Report

(Appropriate Addressee)

We have audited the accompanying* balance sheet of the ABC Company as of December 31, 20X3, and the related statements of income, and cash flows for the year then ended. These financial statements are the responsibility of the Company's management. Our responsibility is to express an opinion on these financial statements based on our audit.

We conducted our audit in accordance with International Standards on Auditing (or refer to relevant national standards or practices). Those Standards require that we plan and perform the audit to obtain reasonable assurance about whether the financial statements are free of material misstatement. An audit includes examining, on a test basis, evidence supporting the amounts and disclosures in the financial statements. An audit also includes assessing the accounting principles used and significant estimates made by management as well as evaluating the overall financial statement presentation. We believe that our audit provides a reasonable basis for our opinion.

In our opinion, the financial statements give a true and fair view of (or "present fairly, in all material respects") the financial position of the Company as of December 31, 20X3, and the results of its operations and its cash flows for the year then ended in accordance with International Financial Reporting Standards (or [title of financial reporting framework with reference to the country of origin]) (and comply with ...**).

Without qualifying our opinion, we draw attention to Note X in the financial statements which indicates that the Company incurred a net loss of ZZZ during the year ended December 31, 20X3 and, as of that date, the Company's current liabilities exceeded its total assets by ZZZ. These conditions, along with other matters as set forth in Note X, indicate the existence of a material uncertainty which may cast significant doubt about the Company's ability to continue as a going concern."

Auditor
Date
Address

* The reference can be by page numbers.
** Refer to the relevant statutes or law.

Other uncertainties, depending on their materiality and a country's laws, may lead to a modification of the unqualified report or a qualified report or disclaimer. Examples include: the outcome of major litigation and the outcome of long-term contracts, estimates of recoverability of asset values, and losses on discontinued operations. If an entity refuses to make a necessary amendment to information accompanying the financial statements, and when there are additional statutory reporting responsibilities, the report may also be qualified.

If the uncertainty is significant and material and not adequately disclosed in the notes, the auditor may wish to issue a qualified opinion or a disclaimer of opinion.

Illustrations 12.9 and 12.10 show unqualified reports of two large international companies, Intel and Dell, each requiring an emphasis of a matter paragraph.

ILLUSTRATION 12.9

Intel's 2002 Unqualified Audit Report with Change in Accounting Methods Emphasis of Matter Paragraph

---

REPORT OF ERNST & YOUNG LLP, INDEPENDENT AUDITORS

The Board of *Directors and Stockholders, Intel Corporation*
We have audited the accompanying consolidated balance sheets of Intel Corporation as of December 28, 2002 and December 29, 2001, and the related consolidated statements of income, stockholders' equity, and cash flows for each of the three years in the period ended December 28, 2002. Our audits also included the financial statement schedule listed in the Index at Item 15(a). These financial statements and schedule are the *responsibility of the* company's management. Our responsibility is to express an opinion on these *financial* statements and schedule based on our audits.

We conducted our audits in accordance with auditing standards generally accepted in the United States. Those standards require that we plan and perform the audit to obtain reasonable assurance about whether the financial statements are free of material misstatement. An audit includes examining, on a test basis, evidence supporting the amounts and disclosures in the financial statements. An audit also includes assessing the accounting principles used and significant estimates made by management, as well as evaluating the overall financial statement presentation. We believe that our audits provide a reasonable basis for our opinion.

In our opinion, the consolidated financial statements referred to above present fairly, in all material respects, the consolidated financial position of Intel Corporation at December 28, 2002 and December 29, 2001, and the consolidated results of its operations and its cash flows for each of the three years in the period ended December 28, 2002, in conformity with accounting principles generally accepted in the United States. Also, in our opinion, the related financial statement schedule, when considered in relation to the basic financial statements taken as a whole, presents fairly in all material respects the information set forth therein.

As discussed in Note 2 to the consolidated financial statements, effective December 30, 2001, the company adopted Statement of Financial Accounting Standards No. 142, "Goodwill and Other Intangible Assets."

Ernst & Young
San Jose, California
January 13, 2003

Source: US Securities and Exchange Commission, www.sec.gov.

■ Going Concern Emphasis of Matter

The **going concern assumption** is one of the fundamental assumptions underlying preparation of financial statements. An enterprise is normally viewed as a going concern, that is, as continuing in operation for the foreseeable future. ISA 570[27] establishes standards and provides guidance on the auditor's responsibilities regarding the appropriateness of the going concern assumption as a basis for preparing financial statements. When a question arises regarding the appropriateness of the going concern assumption, the auditor should gather sufficient appropriate audit evidence to attempt to resolve, to the auditor's satisfaction, the question regarding the entity's ability to continue in operation for the foreseeable future.

ILLUSTRATION 12.10

Dell's 2002 Unqualified Audit Report with Change in Revenue Recognition Emphasis of Matter Paragraph

REPORT OF INDEPENDENT ACCOUNTANTS

To the Board of Directors and Stockholders of
Dell Computer Corporation

In our opinion, the consolidated financial statements listed in the accompanying index present fairly, in all material respects, the financial position of Dell Computer Corporation and its subsidiaries at January 31, 2003 and February 1, 2002, and the results of their operations and their cash flows for each of the three fiscal years in the period ended January 31, 2003, in conformity with accounting principles generally accepted in the United States of America. In addition, in our opinion, the financial statement schedule listed in the accompanying index, presents fairly, in all material respects, the information set forth therein when read in conjunction with the related consolidated financial statements. These financial statements and financial statement schedule are the responsibility of the Company's management; our responsibility is to express an opinion on these financial statements and financial statement schedule based on our audits. We conducted our audits of these statements in accordance with auditing standards generally accepted in the United States of America, which require that we plan and perform the audit to obtain reasonable assurance about whether the financial statements are free of material misstatement. An audit includes examining, on a test basis, evidence supporting the amounts and disclosures in the financial statements, assessing the accounting principles used and significant estimates made by management, and evaluating the overall financial statement presentation. We believe that our audits provide a reasonable basis for our opinion.

As discussed in Note 1 to the consolidated financial statements, during fiscal 2001 the Company changed its revenue recognition for certain product shipments.

PRICEWATERHOUSECOOPERS LLP
Austin, Texas
February 13,
2003

Source: US Securities and Exchange Commission, www.sec.gov.

Certification Exam Question 12.3

When financial statements contain a departure from IFRS because, due to unusual circumstances, the statements would otherwise be misleading, the auditor should explain the unusual circumstances in a separate paragraph and express an opinion that is:

(A) Unqualified.
(B) Qualified.
(C) Adverse.
(D) Qualified or adverse, depending on materiality.

Illustration 11.13 in Chapter 11 Completing the Audit shows some of the indications that the company may have going concern problems. These indications may be mitigated by other factors. For instance delinquency in loan repayment may be countered by management plans to reschedule loans, sale of assets, etc.

■ Going Concern Disclosure

After the auditor has carried out the additional procedures deemed necessary, obtained all required information and considered the effect of management's plans, he should determine whether the questions raised regarding going concern have been satisfactorily resolved. If the going concern questions are not resolved, the auditor must adequately disclose in his report the principal conditions that raise doubt about the entity's ability to continue in operation in the foreseeable future. The disclosure should:

- describe the principal conditions that raise doubt;
- state that there are doubts about going concern, therefore the entity may be unable to realize its assets and discharge its liabilities in the normal course of business;

ILLUSTRATION 12.11

Sample Wording – Auditor's Qualified Report for Non-Disclosure of Going Concern Problem[29]

Auditor's Report

(Appropriate Addressee)

We have audited the accompanying* balance sheet of the ABC Company as of December 31, 20X3, and the related statements of income, and cash flows for the year then ended. These financial statements are the responsibility of the Company's management. Our responsibility is to express an opinion on these financial statements based on our audit.

We conducted our audit in accordance with International Standards on Auditing (or refer to relevant national standards or practices). Those Standards require that we plan and perform the audit to obtain reasonable assurance about whether the financial statements are free of material misstatement. An audit includes examining, on a test basis, evidence supporting the amounts and disclosures in the financial statements. An audit also includes assessing the accounting principles used and significant estimates made by management as well as evaluating the overall financial statement presentation. We believe that our audit provides a reasonable basis for our opinion.

The Company's financing arrangements expire and amounts outstanding are payable on March 19, 20X4. The Company has been unable to re-negotiate or obtain replacement financing. This situation indicates the existence of a material uncertainty which may cast significant doubt on the Company's ability to continue as a going concern and therefore it may be unable to realize its assets and discharge its liabilities in the normal course of business. The financial statements (and notes thereto) do not disclose this fact.

In our opinion, except for the omission of the information included in the preceding paragraph, the financial statements give a true and fair view of (present fairly, in all material respects) the financial position of the Company at December 31, 20X3 and the results of its operations and its cash flows for the year then ended in accordance with ...** (and comply with ...***).

Auditor
Date
Address

* The reference can be by page numbers.
** Indicate IFRSs or relevant national standards.
*** Refer to the relevant statutes or law.

■ state that the financial statements do not include any adjustments relating to the recoverability and classification of recorded asset amounts or to amounts and classification of liabilities that may be necessary should the entity be unable to continue as a going concern.

Illustration 12.8 earlier illustrates sample wording for a going concern if the problem is adequately disclosed.

If adequate disclosure is not made in the financial statements, the auditor should express a qualified or adverse opinion, as appropriate. Illustration 12.11 gives sample wording when an auditor's report containing a qualified opinion is called for because of non-disclosure of going concern.

12.6 Circumstances That May Result in Other Than an Unqualified Opinion

Based on ISA 700,[28] there are at least two circumstances where the auditor may not be able to express an unqualified opinion:

1 a limitation in scope;
2 a disagreement with management regarding the acceptability of the accounting policies selected, the method of their application or the adequacy of financial statement disclosures.

The circumstances described in 1 – scope limitation – could lead to a qualified opinion or a disclaimer of opinion. The circumstances described in 2 – disagreement with management – could lead to a qualified opinion or an adverse opinion.

In addition to scope limitation and disagreement with management, audit reports are often qualified if there are material uncertainties such as financial statements not in conformity with accounting standards and lack of independence.

Concept and a Company 12.2

Cendant Merger Goes Badly

Concept	Management representations as a basis for an unqualified opinion.
Story	Cendant Corporation was created through the 1997 merger of CUC, a company engaged in membership-based consumer services, such as auto, dining, shopping, and travel "clubs" and HFS international (franchiser of Avis, Ramada Inns, and Century 21). CUC's largest division, Comp-U-Card, marketed individual memberships in these clubs. Based in New York City, and with around 90,000 employees, Cendant today is a multi-billion dollar global franchiser and provider of consumer and business services in over 100 countries. Cendant Corporation's core operations today include franchising real estate (including Coldwell Banker, Century 21), hospitality (including Ramada, Howard Johnson, Days Inn, and Travelodge with over 6,400 hotels, around 540,000 rooms, and 5,200 lodging franchises),

▶

Cendant Merger Goes Badly (continued)

vehicle (Avis), financial (Jackson Hewitt (tax preparation)), and travel distribution services (cendant.com 2004).

On April 15, 1998, Cendant announced that it had uncovered accounting irregularities and would need to restate its financial statements. On September 29, 1998, Cendant filed restated financial statements reducing the Company's operating income for the years ending January 31, 1996, January 31, 1997 and December 31, 1997 by over $500 million. (SEC 2000)

From 1995 to 1998, CUC and Cendant's management engaged in various schemes to fraudulently inflate Cendant's reported income. These included manipulation of: (1) merger-related restructuring charges and reserves; (2) reported cash balances; (3) membership cancellation rates; and (4) intentional overstatement of income included in the 1997 financial statements. The first method became increasingly significant during the last years of the scheme, when the ever-larger adjustments were made in order to keep annual earnings to the levels expected by Wall Street analysts. (SEC 2000)

CUC and Cendant made false statements to their auditor, Ernst &Young, about financial results and accounting methods. False statements were made in management representation letters about, for instance, utilization of merger-related reserves, the adequacy of the reserve for membership cancellations, and the collectabilty of rejected credit card billings. (SEC 2003)

Some of the procedures that CUC and Cendant employed to conceal its fraudulent scheme from the auditors included: (1) backdating accounting entries; (2) making accounting entries in small amounts and/or in accounts or subsidiaries the company believed would receive less attention from the auditor; (3) in some instances ensuring that fraudulent accounting entries did not affect schedules already provided to the auditor; (4) withholding financial information and schedules to ensure that the auditor would not detect Cendant's accounting fraud; (5) ensuring that the company's financial results did not show unusual trends that might draw attention to its fraud; and (6) using senior management to instruct middle and lower level personnel to make fraudulent entries. (SEC 2003)

An SEC suit alleges that the two of the audit partners from E&Y were aware of numerous practices by CUC and Cendant. As a consequence, they had a duty to withhold their unqualified opinion and take appropriate additional steps. (SEC 2003)

E&Y provided accounting advice as well as audit services to CUC and Cendant in connection with the establishment and use of restructuring reserves. For example, they advised Cendant about cost categories that were typical components in corporate restructurings, including those cost categories that the audit partners knew were subjective in nature and for which audit evidence, other than management's representation, was difficult to obtain. For their opinion, the audit partners excessively relied on management representations concerning the appropriateness of the reserves and performed little substantive testing. (SEC 2003)

CUC and Cendant provided the audit partners with contradictory drafts of schedules when asked for support for the establishment of the Cendant Reserve. The schedules were inconsistent with regard to the nature and amount of the individual components of the reserve, i.e. component categories were added, deleted, and changed as the process progressed. While the component categories changed over time, the total amount of the reserve never changed materially. Despite this evidence, the audit partners did not obtain adequate analyses, documentation or support for changes they observed in the various revisions of the schedules submitted to support the establishment of the reserves. Instead, they relied excessively on frequently changing management representations. (SEC 2003)

Discussion Questions	■ To what extent is it possible for an auditor to rely on management claims in the management representations letter to determine the appropriateness of a material account balance? ■ If evidence is inconsistent with management representations what additional audit procedures should the auditor consider?
References	Cendant.com, 2003, "About Cendant; Franchising; Hotel Franchises," www.cendant.com. SEC, 2000, *Securities Exchange Act Of 1934 Release No. 42933/June 14, 2000. Accounting And Auditing Enforcement Release No. 1272,* "In the Matter of Cendant Corporation, Respondent," Securities and Exchange Commission, April 24/June 14. SEC, 2003, United States District Court, District of Columbia "SEC vs. Kenneth Wilchfort, CPA, and Marc Rabinowitz, CPA," Securities and Exchange Commission, April 24.

■ Limitation on Scope

Scope limitations arise when the auditors are unable for any reason to obtain the information and explanations considered necessary for the audit. Scope may be limited by the inability to carry out a procedure the auditors consider necessary and the absence of proper accounting records.

The client, for example, may sometimes impose a limitation on the scope of the auditor's work when the terms of the engagement specify that the auditor will not carry out an audit procedure that the auditor believes is necessary. Scope limitations may also be caused by circumstances beyond the control of either the client or the auditor. When restrictions are due to conditions beyond the client's control, a qualified opinion is more likely.

A scope limitation may be imposed by circumstances, for example, when the timing of the auditor's appointment makes it difficult to observe the counting of physical inventories. It may also arise when the accounting records are inadequate or when the auditor is unable to carry out a necessary audit procedure. In these circumstances, the auditor should attempt to carry out reasonable alternative procedures to obtain sufficient audit evidence to support an unqualified opinion.

Describe the Limitation

When there has been a limitation on the scope of the auditor's work that prevents him from issuing an auditor's report containing an unqualified opinion, the report should describe the limitation. The wording of the opinion should indicate that it is qualified as to the possible adjustments to the financial statements that might have been necessary had the limitation not existed.[30] In cases where the limitation is so significant that the auditor is unable to express an opinion, an auditor's report containing a disclaimer of opinion is called for.

Do Not Accept Engagement

ISA 700[31] states that when the limitation in terms of a proposed engagement is such that the auditor believes that he would need to issue an auditor's report containing a disclaimer of opinion, he would ordinarily not accept the audit engagement unless required to do so by statute or law. A statutory auditor should not accept an audit engagement when the limitation infringes on his statutory duties.

■ Disagreement with Management

The auditor may disagree with management regarding:

■ the acceptability of the accounting policies selected;

■ the method of policy application, including the adequacy of valuations and disclosures in the financial statements; or

---

ILLUSTRATION 12.12

Disagreement on Accounting Policies – Inappropriate Accounting Method Qualified Opinion[32]

Auditor's Report

(Appropriate Addressee)

We have audited the accompanying* balance sheet of the ABC Company as of December 31, 20X3, and the related statements of income, and cash flows for the year then ended. These financial statements are the responsibility of the Company's management. Our responsibility is to express an opinion on these financial statements based on our audit.

We conducted our audit in accordance with International Standards on Auditing (or refer to relevant national standards or practices). Those Standards require that we plan and perform the audit to obtain reasonable assurance about whether the financial statements are free of material misstatement. An audit includes examining, on a test basis, evidence supporting the amounts and disclosures in the financial statements. An audit also includes assessing the accounting principles used and significant estimates made by management as well as evaluating the overall financial statement presentation. We believe that our audit provides a reasonable basis for our opinion.

As discussed in Note X to the financial statements, no depreciation has been provided in the financial statements which practice, in our opinion, is not in accordance with International Accounting Standards. The provision for the year ended December 31, 20X3, should be XXX based on the straight-line method of depreciation using annual rates of 5 percent for the building and 20 percent for the equipment. Accordingly, the fixed assets should be reduced by accumulated depreciation of XXX and the loss for the year and accumulated deficit should be increased by XXX and XXX, respectively.

In our opinion, except for the effect on the financial statements of the matter referred to in the preceding paragraph, the financial statements give a true and fair view of (or "present fairly, in all material respects") the financial position of the Company as of December 31, 20X3, and the results of its operations and its cash flows for the year then ended in accordance with International Financial Reporting Standards (or [title of financial reporting framework with reference to the country of origin]) (and comply with ...**).

Auditor
Date
Address

---

* The reference can be by page numbers.
** Refer to the relevant statutes or law.

■ the compliance of the financial statements with relevant regulations and statutory requirements.

If any of these disagreements are material, the auditor should express a qualified opinion. If the effect of the disagreement is so material and pervasive to the financial statements that the auditor concludes that a qualification would not be adequate to disclose the misleading or incomplete nature of the financial statements, an adverse opinion should be expressed. Illustrations 12.12 and 12.13 give sample wording for an auditor's report containing a qualified opinion caused by disagreement with management for an inappropriate accounting method (Illustration 12.12) and inadequate disclosure (Illustration 12.13).

ILLUSTRATION 12.13

Disagreement on Accounting Policies – Inadequate Disclosure Qualified Opinion[33]

Auditor's Report

(Appropriate Addressee)

We have audited the accompanying* balance sheet of the ABC Company as of December 31, 20X3, and the related statements of income, and cash flows for the year then ended. These financial statements are the responsibility of the Company's management. Our responsibility is to express an opinion on these financial statements based on our audit.

We conducted our audit in accordance with International Standards on Auditing (or refer to relevant national standards or practices). Those Standards require that we plan and perform the audit to obtain reasonable assurance about whether the financial statements are free of material misstatement. An audit includes examining, on a test basis, evidence supporting the amounts and disclosures in the financial statements. An audit also includes assessing the accounting principles used and significant estimates made by management as well as evaluating the overall financial statement presentation. We believe that our audit provides a reasonable basis for our opinion.

On January 15, 20X4, the Company issued debentures in the amount of XXX for the purpose of financing plant expansion. The debenture agreement restricts the payment of future cash dividends to earnings after December 31, 19X3. In our opinion, disclosure of this information is required by with ...**

In our opinion, except for the omission of the information included in the preceding paragraph, the financial statements give a true and fair view of (or "present fairly, in all material respects") the financial position of the Company as of December 31, 20X3, and the results of its operations and its cash flows for the year then ended in accordance with International Financial Reporting Standards (or [title of financial reporting framework with reference to the country of origin]) (and comply with ...**).

Auditor
Date
Address

---

* The reference can be by page numbers.
** Refer to the relevant statutes or law.

Certification Exam Question 12.4[34]

An auditor concludes that a client's illegal act, which has a material effect on the financial statement, has not been properly accounted for or disclosed. Depending on the materiality of the effect on the financial statements, the auditor should express either:

(A) An adverse opinion or a disclaimer of opinion.
(B) A qualified opinion or an adverse opinion.
(C) A disclaimer of opinion or an unqualified opinion with a separate explanatory paragraph.
(D) An unqualified opinion with a separate explanatory paragraph or a qualified opinion.

12.7 Uncertainties Leading to Qualification of Opinions

The international standards of IFAC specify qualification of opinions based on limitation of scope and disagreement with management as conditions that lead to an auditor's report containing a qualified or adverse opinion. However, certain uncertainties may lead to an auditor's report containing a qualification of opinion in many countries. These uncertainties include: material uncertainties, lack of consistency, independence of auditor, reports in reference to an expert and fraud.

■ Materiality

Materiality is an essential consideration in determining the appropriate type of report for a given set of circumstances. An item is material if inclusion or exclusion of the item on the financial statements is sufficiently important to influence a decision made by a reasonable user of financial statements. If the amounts of a misstatement in the financial statements are so significant that the financial statements are materially affected as a whole, it is necessary to issue either a qualified or an adverse opinion, depending on the nature of the misstatement.

Lack of consistency in the application of accounting principles in the current period in relation to the preceding period may require a modification to an unqualified opinion based on standards in many countries. For instance, US GAAP requires that changes in accounting principles or their application be adequately disclosed and that the audit report be modified by adding an explanatory paragraph that describes the nature of the change. If the auditor does not concur with the appropriateness of the accounting principle change, in most countries, a qualified opinion is called for.

We discuss the modifications required by going concern problems, fraud, and non-compliance with laws elsewhere in this chapter. Going concern problems are discussed in Section 12.5 earlier. Fraud and non-compliance are discussed in Section 12.8.

■ Independence of Auditor

IFAC's Guideline on Ethics for Professional Accountants (see Chapter 3 Ethics for Professional Accountants) stresses the great importance of auditor independence both in fact and appearance. However, the ISA auditing standards do not require a qualified opinion or a disclaimer of opinion if the auditor is not independent, although this is the case in several countries. Some countries, such as the Netherlands, do not allow the auditor to accept the engagement in case he is not independent.

■ Reference to Expert

When expressing an unqualified opinion the auditor generally should not refer to the work of an expert in his report because such a reference might be misunderstood to be a qualification of the auditor's opinion or a division of responsibility. If the auditor, as a result of the other auditor's or expert's work, issues an opinion other than unqualified, he may in some circumstances describe the work of the expert.

Concept and a Company 12.3

Tyco International Ltd. – Management's Piggy Bank

Concept	Financial statement disclosure, corporate governance, and loans.
Story	Tyco is a US company that manufactures a wide variety of products, from electronic components to healthcare products. It operates in over 100 countries around the world and employs more than 240,000 people.

In 2002, three former top executives of Tyco (former CEOs Dennis Kozlowski, Mark Swartz, and the chief legal officer Mark Belnick) were sued by the SEC. Kozlowski and Swartz granted themselves hundreds of millions of dollars in secret low interest and interest-free loans from Tyco that they used for personal expenses. They later caused Tyco to forgive tens of millions of dollars they owed the company, without disclosure to investors as required by the federal securities laws. (SEC 2002) Kozlowski and Swartz engaged in numerous highly profitable related party transactions with Tyco and awarded themselves lavish perquisites – without disclosing either the transactions or perquisites to Tyco shareholders. (US District Court 2002)

"Messrs. Kozlowski and Swartz ... treated Tyco as their private bank, taking out hundreds of millions of dollars of loans in compensation without ever telling investors," said Stephen M. Cutler, the SEC's Director of Enforcement. (SEC 2002)

But Not What He Told Them

At the same time that Kozlowski and Swartz engaged in their massive covert fradulant use of corporate funds, Kozlowski regularly assured investors that at Tyco "nothing was hidden behind the scenes," that Tyco's disclosures were "exceptional" and that Tyco's management "prided itself on having sharp focus with creating shareholder value." Similarly, Swartz regularly assured investors that "Tyco's disclosure practice remains second to none." (US District Court 2002)

KELP and Relocation Loans

Most of Kozlowski's and Swartz's improper Tyco loans were taken through abuse of Tyco's Key Employee Corporate Loan Program (the "KELP"). A disclosure description of the plan as filed with the SEC, explicitly described its narrow purpose (US District Court 2002):

▶

Tyco International Ltd. – Management's Piggy Bank (continued)

> [U]nder the Program, loan proceeds may be used for the payment of federal income taxes due upon the vesting of Company common stock from time to time under the 1983 Restricted Stock Ownership Plans for Key Employees, and to refinance other existing outstanding loans for such purpose.

Kozlowski and Swartz bestowed upon themselves hundreds of millions of dollars in KELP loans which they used for purposes not legitimately authorized by the KELP. From 1997 to 2002, Kozlowski took an aggregate of approximately $270 million charged as KELP loans – even though he only used $29 million of that to cover taxes from the vesting of his Tyco stock. The rest was used for impermissible and unauthorized purposes. For example, with his KELP loans, Kozlowski amassed millions of dollars in fine art, yachts, and estate jewelry, as well as an apartment on Park Avenue and a palatial estate in Nantucket. He also used the KELP to fund his personal investments and business ventures. (US District Court 2002)

Kozlowski and Swartz also abused Tyco's relocation loan program to enrich themselves. When Tyco moved its corporate offices from New Hampshire to New York City, an interest-free loan program was established. It was designed to assist Tyco employees who were required to relocate from New Hampshire to New York. Kozlowski used approximately $21 million of "relocation" loans for various other purposes, including the purchase of prestigious properties in New Hampshire, Nantucket and Connecticut. Kozlowski even used approximately $7 million of Tyco's funds to purchase a Park Avenue apartment for his wife from whom he had been separated for many years and whom he subsequently divorced. (US District Court 2002)

Kozlowski and Swartz did not stop there. Instead, they oversaw and authorized transactions by which tens of millions of dollars of their KELP loans and relocation loans were forgiven and written off Tyco's books. They also directed the acceleration of the vesting of Tyco common stock for their benefit. (US District Court 2002)

They Deserve Bonuses

In December 2000, Kozlowski and Swartz engineered another program whereby Tyco paid them bonuses comprised of cash, Tyco common stock, and/or forgiveness of relocation loans. From that program, Kozlowski received 148,000 shares of Tyco common stock, a cash bonus of $700,000, and $16 million in relocation loan forgiveness. Swartz received 74,000 shares of Tyco common stock, a cash bonus of $350,000, and $8 million in relocation loan forgiveness. None of these payments were disclosed as part of Kozlowski's and Swartz's executive compensation in Tyco's annual reports. (US District Court 2002)

The Auditor

In 2003, the SEC sued Richard P. Scalzo, CPA, the PricewaterhouseCoopers LLP (PwC) audit engagement partner for Tyco from 1997 through 2001. (SEC 2003a)

The SEC alleged that Scalzo received "multiple and repeated facts" regarding the lack of integrity of Tyco's senior management, but he did not take appropriate audit steps in the face of this information. The SEC maintained that those facts were sufficient to obligate Scalzo to reevaluate the risk assessment of the Tyco audits and to perform additional audit procedures, including further audit testing of certain items (most notably, certain executive benefits, executive compensation, and related party transactions). He did not perform these procedures. (SEC 2003a)

Red Flags and Post Period Adjustments

In the September 30, 1997 audit, factual red flags appeared in the audit working papers. The working papers contained 26 pages of reports prepared by the company, listing the activity in the various KELP accounts of Tyco employees. Three of those 26 pages listed the KELP account activity for L. Dennis Kozlowski. Most of the line items for the Kozlowski account also include a brief description, and 18 carry descriptions that are immediately recognizable as not being for the payment of taxes on the vesting of restricted stock. For example, one item reads "WINE CELLAR," another reads "NEW ENG WINE," another "BMW REG/TAX," another "ANGIE KOZLOWS," and 13 read either "WALDORF," "WALDORF RENT," "WALDORF EXPEN," "WALDORF RENT A," or WALDORF RENT S." (SEC 2003b)

In the September 30, 1998 audit, the audit team noticed a series of transactions in which three Tyco executive exercised Tyco stock options, by borrowing from the KELP, and then sold the shares back to the company the next business day through an offshore Tyco subsidiary. Tyco then wrote a check to the executives, representing a net settlement of the transactions. After consulting with PwC national partners, the PwC audit team came to the conclusion that Tyco should include a compensation charge of approximately $40 million. (SEC 2003b)

Faced with the reality of having to book an unanticipated $40 million compensation charge, Tyco suddenly arrived at $40 million in additional, contemporaneous, post-period adjustments which had the effect of negating the impact of the $40 million charge. The $40 million in credits raise significant issues – $7.8 million resulted from Tyco reversing a previous "fourth quarter charge for restricted stock expense for certain executives no longer required." The rationale advanced for that reversal was that the executives had decided to forego the corresponding bonuses in the fourth quarter.

The company's treatment for certain executive bonuses provided evidence of problems. For example, Tyco made an initial public offering (IPO) of its previously wholly-owned subsidiary, TyCom Ltd. Because of the IPO's success, Kozlowski decided to grant $96 million in bonuses to Tyco officers and employees. Tyco accounted for the bonuses as: (1) a TyCom offering expense, (2) a credit for previous over-accruals of general and administrative expense, and (3) a contra-accrual for federal income taxes. None of it was booked as compensation expense.

Discussion Questions	▪ What tests should an auditor perform to find evidence concerning misstatement of executive compensation expense? ▪ Are public statements by the CEO to investors considered a disclosure that requires the attention of the auditor? ▪ If the Sarbanes-Oxley Act, Section 402 Enhanced Conflict Provisions was in effect in 2001, would that have made a difference to the disclosure requirements?
References	SEC, 2002, *Press Release 2002-135*, "SEC Sues Former Tyco CEO Kozlowski, two others for Fraud," Securities and Exchange Commission, September 12. SEC, 2003a, *Press Release 2003-95*, "Former Tyco Auditor Permanently Barred from Practicing before the Commission," Securities and Exchange Commission, August 13. SEC, 2003b, *Securities Exchange Act Of 1934 Release No. 48328. Accounting And Auditing Enforcement Release No. 1839*, "In the Matter of Richard P. Scalzo, CPA," Securities and Exchange Commission, August 13. United States District Court Southern District of New York, 2002, "Securities and Exchange Commission v. L. Dennis Kozlowski, Mark H. Swartz, And Mark A. Belnick," Securities and Exchange Commission, September 12.

Certification Exam Question 12.5

For which of the following events would an auditor issue a report that does not make any reference to consistency?

(A) A change in the method of accounting for inventories.
(B) A change from an accounting principle that is **not** generally accepted to one that is generally accepted.
(C) A change in the useful life used to calculate the provision for depreciation expense.
(D) Management's lack of reasonable justification for a change in accounting principle.

12.8 Communications with those Charged with Governance

The auditors are required to communicate their audit findings to the management and Board of Directors of a corporation. This is not only given in the ISA standards, but also required by law in some countries.[35] Audit matters of governance interest to be communicated by the auditor to the board or audit committee ordinarily include: material weaknesses in internal control, non-compliance with laws and regulations, fraud involving management, questions regarding management integrity, and other matters.

■ Communications with the Audit Committee

ISA 260 states: "The auditor should communicate **audit matters of governance interest** arising from the audit of financial statements with those charged with **governance** of an entity."[36] "Governance" is the term used to describe the role of persons entrusted with the supervision, control and direction of an entity. Those persons are the ones responsible for financial reporting and for ensuring that the company achieves its objectives. Those charged with corporate governance are usually the board of directors or supervisory board or the audit committee.

The audit committee is a body formed by a company's board of directors to allow the board to focus on issues affecting external reporting and, in some cases, internal control. In general, the board of directors is composed of **outside directors**. The audit committee selects and appraises the performance of the auditing firm. It develops a professional relationship with the external auditing firm to ensure that accounting and control matters are properly discussed. Besides evaluating external audit reports, the committee may evaluate internal audit reports, review management representations, and get involved with public disclosure of corporate activities. International Standards on Auditing 250, 260, and 300, all apply to communications between the external auditor and the audit committee.

■ Governance Structures

The structures of governance vary from country to country reflecting cultural and legal backgrounds. For example, in some countries, the supervision function, and the management function are legally separated into different bodies, such as a supervisory (wholly or mainly non-executive) board and a management (executive) board. In other countries, like the USA, both functions are the legal responsibility of a single, unitary board.

The requirements of national professional accountancy bodies, legislation, or regulation may impose obligations on the auditor to make communications on governance related matters. These additional communications requirements are not covered by International Standards on Auditing; however, they may affect the content, form and timing of communications with those charged with governance.

■ Audit Matters of Governance Interest

"Audit matters of governance interest" are those that arise from the audit of financial statements and are important for people in charge of governance. Audit matters of governance interest to be communicated by the auditor to the board or audit committee ordinarily include:[37]

- material weaknesses in internal control;
- non-compliance with laws and regulations;
- fraud involving management;
- questions regarding management integrity;
- the general approach and overall scope of the audit;
- the selection of, or changes in, significant accounting policies and practices that have a material effect on the financial statements;
- the potential effect on the financial statements of any significant risks and exposures, such as pending litigation, that requires disclosure in the financial statements;
- significant audit adjustments to the accounting records;
- material uncertainties related to the entity's ability to continue as a going concern;
- disagreements with management about matters that could be significant to the entity's financial statements or the auditor's report; (These communications include consideration of whether the matter has, or has not, been resolved and the significance of the matter.)
- expected modifications to the auditor's report.

■ Reportable Conditions

Major internal control problems (material weakness or **reportable conditions**) should be reported to management, and where necessary, the board of directors. In deciding whether a matter is a reportable condition, the auditor considers factors such as the size of the company and its ownership characteristics, the organizational structure, and the complexity and diversity of company activities. For example, an internal control structure deficiency that is a reportable condition for a large sophisticated financial institution may not be a reportable condition for a small manufacturing concern.

The reportable conditions are generally communicated in a separate letter, the so-called **management letter**. The management letter also includes suggestions for improvement of internal controls focused on financial, compliance and operational processes.

Certification Exam Question 12.6[38]

An auditor would **least** likely initiate a discussion with a client's audit committee concerning

(A) The methods used to account for significant unusual transactions.
(B) The maximum dollar amount of misstatements that could exist without causing the financial statements to be materially misstated.
(C) Indications of fraud and illegal acts committed by a corporate officer that were discovered by the auditor.
(D) Disagreements with management as to accounting principles that were resolved during the current year's audit.

■ Fraud and Non-Compliance with Laws

As required by ISA 240,[39] the auditor should communicate to management any material weaknesses in internal control related to the prevention or detection of fraud and error, which have come to the auditor's attention as a result of the performance of the audit. The auditor should also be satisfied that those charged with governance have been informed of any material weaknesses in internal control related to the prevention and detection of fraud that either have been brought to the auditor's attention by management or have been identified by the auditor during the audit.

Based on the risk assessment the auditor should design audit procedures to obtain reasonable assurance that misstatements arising from fraud and error that are material to the financial statements taken as a whole are detected. When the auditor encounters circumstances that may indicate that there is a material misstatement in the financial statements resulting from fraud or error, the auditor should perform procedures to determine whether the financial statements are materially misstated.[40]

Auditor Withdrawal

If the auditor concludes that it is not possible to continue performing the audit as a result of a misstatement resulting from fraud or suspected fraud, withdrawal from the engagement must then be seriously considered. If the auditor withdraws, he should:

■ discuss with those charged with governance the auditor's withdrawal from the engagement and the reasons for the withdrawal;
■ consider whether there is a professional or legal requirement to report to regulatory authorities, the auditor's withdrawal from the engagement and the reasons for the withdrawal.[41]

Matters Communicated to those Charged With Governance

The matters communicated by the auditor to those charged with governance is a matter of professional judgment but ordinarily would include:

■ questions regarding management competence and integrity;
■ fraud involving management;
■ other fraud that results in a material misstatement of the financial statements;
■ material misstatements resulting from error;

- misstatements that indicate material weaknesses in internal control, including the design or operation of the entity's financial reporting process;
- misstatements that may cause future financial statements to be materially misstated.

The auditor should communicate with the audit committee, the board of directors and senior management, each as appropriate in the circumstances, regarding noncompliance with applicable laws and regulations that comes to the auditor's attention. If the auditor suspects that members of senior management, including members of the board of directors, are involved in noncompliance, the auditor should report the matter to the next higher level of authority at the entity, if it exists, such as an audit committee or a supervisory board. [42]

Reporting Fraud or Error to A Third Party

The auditor's duty of confidentiality would ordinarily preclude reporting fraud or error to a third party. However, in certain circumstances, statute or law overrides this duty. For instance, in the USA, the auditor is required to report fraud or error by financial institutions to the supervisory authorities. In the Netherlands, if the directors do not take sufficiently corrective measures and the fraud is considered material, the auditors have to withdraw from the engagement. If such engagement is a statutory audit, the auditor must report the withdrawal to the Ministry of Justice. In France, auditors must report illegal acts and fraud. UK auditors are obligated to pursue matters of a suspicious nature and have a reporting duty similar to that in the USA.

German auditors have to report fraud to the boards of directors in their auditor's report; this is also indicated in the tax return of the company and, therefore indirectly, it is also a report to the authorities. In Mexico, auditors are liable for negligence if the auditor should have known of internal control failures, or if he was aware, and did not report them. Auditors may not be liable if they told management of shortcomings in internal control in the area in which a crime has been committed, did not tell because the area in which the crime was committed had no close relationship to financial statements, the crime occurred in collusion with others, or the criminal had "extraordinary ability."

12.9 Long-Form Audit Report

In many countries it is customary for the auditor to prepare a long-form report to the entity's board of directors in addition to the publicly published short-form report discussed in this chapter. The topics covered in the report may vary as there are no standards, but a typical long-form report will include:

- an overview of the audit engagement;
- an analysis of the financial statements;
- a discussion of risk management and internal control;
- various optional topics subject to the circumstances;
- auditor independence and quality control;
- fees.

In the overview, the long-form report will discuss nature, scope, organization, level of materiality, new audit work and work with other auditors and experts.

■ Discussion of Financial Issues

Highlights of the financial statements are discussed. Accounting issues need to be clarified. Several issues may require judgment in accounting such as provisions, accruals, and contingent liabilities. Changes in client, national, and international accounting policies are explained in terms of their impact on the financial statements. Acquisitions and divestments and their affect on the accounts should be covered. The financial position of the company for possible financing or refinancing and the related debt covenant ratios and defaults are gone into.

Other financial statement topics such as disagreement or discussion with management and future client developments are reviewed. Management and auditors may disagree on certain financial statement issues, so the long-form report must address these. Future client development affecting the annual report may include a discussion of future uncertainties and subsequent events.

■ Risk Discussion

Risk management and internal controls are ever more important to the board of directors. A discussion of risk in the long-form report may include:

- major operational and financial risks;
- effectiveness of the client's risk management;
- quality of internal reporting and management accounting;
- frauds and irregularities;
- ethics compliance and special areas such as treasury, new business and quality control.

Internal control topics unveiled might include: strengths and weaknesses of internal controls, recommendations for improving controls, information technology and internal audit department.

Risk management is an important topic for board members. Of course, the client is interested in major operational and financial risks so they are reviewed at least so far as they are related to the audit. The effectiveness of the client's risk management and quality of internal reporting and management accounting are meaningful to the board. Of crucial importance is the discussion of any frauds and irregularities suspected by the auditor or uncovered in the audit. Industry ethics affect the moral and legal position of the client so a discussion of compliance with ethics standards is very important. Popular areas for quality management are treasury effectiveness, new business development and quality control.

■ Internal Control Weaknesses

Auditors are required to report internal control weaknesses (reportable conditions) to management under ISA 400.[43] It states that the auditor should make management aware, at an appropriate level of responsibility, of material weaknesses in the design or operation of the accounting and internal control systems. It is important to indicate in the communication that only weaknesses which have come to the auditor's attention as a result of the audit have been reported and that the examination has not been designed to determine the adequacy of internal control for management purposes.[44]

As a matter of course, auditors report on the strengths and weaknesses of internal controls and recommendations for improving controls, especially technology, **computer information systems** (CIS), and internal control departments. Information technology is the platform for most controls of the accounting system and thus a discussion of new systems, new technology and CIS audit conclusions is of the utmost importance. Because the client is dependent on their internal audit department to set up and monitor internal controls, the spotlight of discussion often falls on this.

■ Other Topics Discussed

There may be topics not typically addressed that the auditor may feel warrant discussion because of the circumstances of the company, the economy, or the audit. These topics may include tax, pension, treasury function, and audit-related requirements.

Audit-related areas that might be discussed include special advisory projects on the financial statements, risk control, insurance coverage, and pension arrangements. Other areas related to the audit that may be reviewed are tax compliance work and constancy projects such as cost benchmarking, information technology, and logistics.

Furthermore, it becomes best practice or is already required by law in some countries, that the auditor describes how his independence has been warranted, and what quality control procedures he has applied to deliver a high-quality audit report. Also, an overview of audit fees compared to budget, and of other fees, might be presented.

12.10 XBRL and Continuous Reporting

New developments in technology have made it possible to track all accounting financial reporting information through the transaction process from initialization of the accounting entry to the final reports in whatever form. Developments have also made reporting and auditing on a real-time basis possible.

■ XBRL

XBRL (eXtensible Business Reporting Language) is an emerging technology standard that facilitates the business reporting process. An offshoot of XML (eXtensible Markup Language), XBRL is a freely licensed, open technology standard that makes it possible to store and/or transfer data along with the complex hierarchies, data-processing rules and descriptions.

XBRL also facilitates the analysis and distribution of data. It can determine how information is stored and how software presents, manipulates, and exchanges that information by using a set of standards and a family of taxonomies or "dictionaries" of terms. This is in part accomplished by attaching an XBRL word or "tag" to the corresponding piece of data in the report.

The XBRL US Adoption Committee of the American Institute of Certified Public Accountants (AICPA) studied XBRL use by computerized accounting software vendors.[45] The main objective of this study was to assess the current rate of XBRL enablement in certain software products. Two-thirds of the accounting software vendors (14 of 21) surveyed has already added XBRL facilities to one or more software products.

First, XBRL permits the automatic exchange and reliable extraction of financial information across all software formats and technologies, including the Internet. Secondly, it reduces the need to enter financial information more than one time, reducing the risk of data entry error and eliminating the need to manually key information for various formats (e.g. a printed financial statement, an **HTML** document for a company's website, an EDGAR filing document, a raw XML file or other specialized reporting formats such as credit reports and loan documents).

XBRL is not designed for financial transactions, but for business reporting. This includes annual reports, SEC filings, and a variety of other reports from companies to investors, regulators, and business analysts. XBRL is for performance data rather than market data, for entities rather than investment instruments, and reported data rather than document data.

◼ XML

XML,[46] or eXtensible markup language, upon which XBRL is based, is a universal way for both formatting and presenting data. XML is described as an extremely simple dialect [or "subset"] of SGML (standard generalized markup language, the language used to create both XML and HTML) the goal of which is to enable generic SGML to be served, received, and processed on the web in the way that is now possible with HTML.[47]

The way XML works is that programmers mark-up a text-based document with "words" or tags (similar to HTML tags) that tell what each word, number or group of words represent. For example, the tag <invoice number> might be used to describe the number of an invoice. Software can understand what <invoice number> means if it has access to the information's key, or schema.

ILLUSTRATION 12.14

Example of XBRL-Coded Data

```
<?xml version="1.0" encoding="utf-8"?>
<schema xmlns:xbrl="http://www.xbrl.org/core/metamodel"
 xmlns:html="http://www.w3.org/1999/xhtml"
  targetNamespace="http://www.xbrl.org/us/us-gaap-ci-2000-07-31.xsd">
. . .
<element name="salesRevenueGross.revenueFromAffiliates" type="monetary">
<annotation>
<appinfo>
<xbrl:rollup to="salesRevenueNet.salesRevenueGross" sense="add" order="3" />
<xbrl:label xml:lang="en">Revenue from Affiliates</xbrl:label>
</appinfo>
</annotation>
</element>
. . .
</schema>
```

XBRL is a fully compliant extension of the XML 1.0 recommendation. Registries for industry specific XML extensions can be found at rossettanet.org and xml.org. Illustration 12.14 is an example of XBRL-coded data.

■ Continuous Reporting and Auditing

There have been several dramatic changes in corporate accounting information systems in the last decade. Company information systems have interconnectivity of most processes. There has also been considerable development and widespread deployment of **enterprise resource planning** (ERP) systems. ERP is a customized packaged software system designed to facilitate an enterprise's transaction processing requirements across much of the information supply chain. ERP systems are based upon a common data foundation provided by large-scale **relational database** management systems (DBMS) such as Oracle's Oracle9i, Microsoft's SQL Server, IBM's DB2, etc. These innovations allow companies to report their financial statements on a semi-continuous basis.

Continuous reporting is the real-time disclosure of transaction data. Organizations keep real-time records for accounts such as cash, receivables, payables and inventories. The company treasurer may manage cash, investments and securities on a continuous basis.

At present there is no obstacle to disclose financial data on a real-time or short period basis, but corporations that have this ability, do not make it public. For example, US company Cisco has often publicly mentioned its "daily book close," but this information is not made public or posed on its website.[48]

The increased regulatory environment, complexity of modern corporations and the speed of business itself has created a need for continuous monitoring and assurance of the accounting information system, i.e. continuous auditing. There are many ways to monitor the accounting on a timely basis: viewing the records on a short periodic basis, performing audit procedures throughout the year, or using technology to monitor the system.

■ Embedded Audit Module

One much discussed method for using technology (ERP systems) to continuously audit is the embedded audit module (EAM).[49] Embedded audit modules (EAM) are database software routines that are placed at predetermined points to gather information about transactions or events within the system that auditors deem to be material. EAMs allow auditors to proactively monitor auditable conditions.

From a programming standpoint, EAMs are subroutines that are invoked whenever certain conditions of audit significance are met. The EAMs can be separated into triggers and stored procedures. Triggers are called automatically upon a change to a row or table in the database. Stored procedures however, can be called on a periodic basis by client applications or other stored procedures or triggers. An example of EAMs acting as stored procedures are those that perform checks on a batch of daily transactions after office hours so as not to disrupt normal business. If EAMs were operative continually throughout the accounting period, the auditor would have information about the operation of controls (i.e. EAMs as compliance-testing tools), as well as information about actual transaction errors (i.e. EAMS as substantive-testing tools).

Despite research on the EAMs dating back to the early 1980s,[50] EAMs still appear to be in the infant stages of practical development and deployment.

12.11 Summary

An audit report is very brief, occupying no more than a few lines.

The US Sarbanes-Oxley Act of 2002 requires that the principal executive officer or officers and the principal financial officer or officers of any firm, foreign or domestic, that is publicly traded, certify certain conditions in each annual or quarterly report filed or submitted to the US Securities and Exchange Commission (SEC). In Europe and other parts of the world, similar developments are observed. They may differ in practice due to national or regional legal and cultural differences, but in principle they have much in common.

The auditor's unqualified report, under ISA 700, should include the following basic elements: title, addressee, opening or introductory paragraph, scope paragraph (describing the nature of an audit), opinion paragraph containing an expression of opinion on the financial statements, the date of the report, the auditor's address and auditor's signature.

The most common type of audit report is the standard unqualified audit report. The form of the unqualified report consists of three, and sometimes four, paragraphs: an opening or introductory paragraph, scope paragraph, opinion paragraph, and, in certain circumstances, a fourth, emphasis paragraph. The opening or introductory paragraph contains an identification of the financial statements audited and a statement of the responsibility of the entity's management and the responsibility of the auditor. The scope paragraph includes a reference to the ISAs or relevant national standards or practices and a description of the work the auditor performed. The opinion paragraph contains an expression of opinion on the financial statements.

The opinion expressed in the auditor's report may be one of four types: unqualified, qualified, adverse or disclaimer of opinion. An auditor's report containing an unqualified opinion is issued in a clear and affirmative manner when the auditor is satisfied in all material respects that:

- the financial information has been prepared using acceptable accounting policies, consistently applied;
- the financial information complies with relevant regulations and statutory requirements;
- the view presented by the financial information as a whole is consistent with the auditor's knowledge of the business of the entity;
- there is adequate disclosure of all material matters relevant to the proper presentation of the financial information.

Audit reports that are not unqualified are referred to as "other than unqualified reports." An auditor's report containing a qualified opinion is issued when the auditor concludes that he cannot issue an unqualified opinion report but that the effect of any disagreement or limitation on scope is not so material as to require an auditor's report containing an adverse opinion or a disclaimer of opinion. An adverse opinion report is issued when the effect of a disagreement is so material and pervasive to the financial statements that the auditor concludes that a qualification of his report is not adequate to disclose the misleading or incomplete nature of the financial statements. A disclaimer of opinion report is issued when the possible effect of a limitation on scope or uncertainty resulting from the audit is so significant that the auditor is unable to express an opinion on the financial statements.

In certain circumstances, an auditor's report may be modified by adding an emphasis of matter paragraph to highlight a matter affecting the financial statements. The addition of an emphasis of matter paragraph does not affect the auditor's opinion. The paragraph should follow the opinion paragraph and state that the auditor's opinion is not qualified by this. Ordinarily, an auditor might write a emphasis of matter paragraph if there is a significant uncertainty that may affect the financial statements, the resolution of which is dependent upon future events and to highlight a material matter regarding a going concern problem.

Based on ISA 700, there are two circumstances that require an auditor's report containing an opinion other than an unqualified one: a limitation in scope and a disagreement with management. Scope limitations arise when the auditors are unable for any reason to obtain the information and explanations considered necessary for the audit. The auditor may disagree with management as to acceptability of the accounting policies selected; the method of policy application; or the compliance of the financial statements with relevant regulations and statutory requirements. Scope limitation could be lead to a qualified opinion or a disclaimer of opinion. Disagreement with management could lead to a qualified opinion or an adverse opinion. In addition to scope limitation and disagreement with management, some countries require qualified reports based on uncertainties arising from financial statements not in conformity with accounting standards and lack of independence.

The international standards of IFAC specify limitation of scope and disagreement with management as conditions that lead to an auditor's report containing a qualified or adverse opinion. However, certain uncertainties may lead to an auditor's report containing a qualification of opinion in many countries. These uncertainties include material uncertainties, substantial doubt about the going concern assumption, reports involving other auditors and fraud.

In order to minimize the auditor's liability related to events that occur after the balance sheet date, it is advantageous to issue the audit report as soon as possible after financial statements approval by the client. However, all audit procedures should be complete, approvals must be given by management, and the signatures must be collected to finalize the audit report.

The auditors are required to communicate their audit findings to the management or Board of Directors of a corporation. This is not only given in the ISA standards, but also required by law in some countries. The auditor should communicate audit matters of governance interest arising from the audit of financial statements with those charged with governance of an entity. "Governance" is the term used to describe the role of persons entrusted with the supervision, control and direction of an entity. Those persons are the ones responsible for financial reporting and for ensuring that the company achieves its objectives. Those charged with corporate governance are usually the board of directors or supervisory board or the audit committee.

The auditors are required to communicate their audit findings to the management and Board of Directors of a corporation. This is not only given in the ISA standards, but also required by law in some countries. Audit matters of governance interest to be communicated by the auditor to the board or audit committee ordinarily include: material weaknesses in internal control, non-compliance with laws and regulations, fraud involving management, questions regarding management integrity, and other matters.

In many countries it is customary for the auditor to prepare a long-form report to the entity's board of directors in addition to the publicly published short-form report discussed in this chapter. The topics covered in the report may vary as there are no standards, but a typical long-form report will include: an overview of the audit engagement, an analysis of the financial statements, a discussion of risk management and internal control, various optional topics subject to the circumstances, and fees.

New developments in technology have made it possible to track all accounting financial reporting information through the transaction process from initialization of the accounting entry to the final reports in whatever form (XBRL). Developments have also made reporting and auditing on a real-time basis possible.

12.12 Answers to Certification Exam Questions

12.1 (C) The requirement is one of the answers that would appear in the auditor's standard (unqualified) report. Choice (C) is correct because the auditor's standard report states that an audit includes assessing significant estimates made by management.

12.2 (C) Which paragraph of an auditor's standard audit report refers to International Standards on Auditing (ISAs) and which refers to International Financial Reporting Standards (IFRS)? Choice (C) is on target because the scope paragraph indicates that International Standards on Auditing (ISAs) have been followed, while the opinion paragraph indicates that the financial statements follow International Financial Reporting Standards (IFRS).

12.3 (A) The question is what type of opinion to be issued when financial statements depart from IFRS due to the existence of unusual circumstances which would cause the financial statements to be misleading had IFRS been followed? Answer (A) is accurate because the auditor should issue an unqualified opinion and should include a separate explanatory paragraph explaining the departure from IFRS. Answers (B), (C), and (D) are bogus because when the auditor feels that the departure is justified, neither an adverse nor qualified opinion is suitable.

12.4 (B) One needs to identify the proper type of audit reports when an illegal act having a material impact on the financial statements has not been adequately accounted for or disclosed. Choice (B) is on the mark because omission of required disclosures leads to either a qualified or an adverse opinion. Choice (A) is mistaken because a disclaimer of opinion is inappropriate when the auditor knows about an illegal act. Choices (C) and (D) are erroneous because neither a disclaimer of opinion nor an unqualified opinion with a separate explanatory paragraph is adequate for a material illegal act.

12.5 (C) The requirement is to identify the event when an auditor would issue a report that omits any reference to consistency. Answer (C) is correct because a change in the useful life of assets is a change in estimate, which would not require modification of the audit report. Estimates are generally not accurate because no one has perfect foresight, therefore, they are subject to change. Answers (A) and (B) are inaccurate because they both represent a change in accounting principle, and a change in accounting principle requires a consistency modification. Answer (D) is false because management's lack of reasonable justification for a change in accounting principle is a departure from IFRS, and the description of the departure will discuss the inconsistency.

12.6 (B) The requirement is to identify the discussion that an auditor is **least** likely to attempt with a client's audit committee. Answer (B) is most correct because auditors do not generally initiate a discussion on materiality, although they do occasionally respond to such questions. That said, even though one might interpret the standards to suggest that **all** disagreements with management as to accounting principles should be discussed with the board, for practical purposes, if a dispute is resolved during the current year's audit, it may be detrimental to management to bring it up with the board. Therefore, on a practical basis, (D) would be a good answer for something a real-world auditor would not feel necessary to bring up.

12.13 Notes

1 Quoted in Emile Woolf, 1997, *Auditing Today,* 6th Edition, Prentice Hall, Hertfordshire, UK.

2 107th US Congress, 2002, *Sarbanes-Oxley Act of 2002,* Public Law 107–204, Section 302, "Corporate Responsibility For Financial Reports," Senate and House of Representatives of the United States of America in Congress assembled, Washington, DC, July 30.

3 PCAOB, 2003, *PCAOB Release No. 2003–024,* "Proposed Rules Relating To The Oversight Of Non-U.S. Public," Public Company Accounting Oversight Board, 10 December.

4 IFAC, 2004, *Handbook of International Auditing, Assurance, and Ethics Pronouncements,* International Standard on Auditing 700 (ISA 700), "The Auditor's Report on Financial Statements," para. 2, International Federation of Accountants, New York.

5 Ibid. Paragraph 5-26.

6 The level of management responsibility for the financial statements will vary according to the legal situation in each country.

7 PCAOB, 2003, *PCAOB Release No. 2003-025,* "Auditing Standard No. 1 – References in Auditors' Reports to the Standards of the Public Company Accounting Oversight Board," para. 3, Public Company Accounting Oversight Board, 17 December.

8 IFAC, 2004, *Handbook of International Auditing, Assurance, and Ethics Pronouncements,* International Standard on Auditing 700 (ISA 700), "The Auditor's Report on Financial Statements," para. 17, International Federation of Accountants, New York.

9 IFAC, 2004, *Handbook of International Auditing, Assurance, and Ethics Pronouncements,* International Standard on Auditing 200 (ISA 200), "Objective and General Principles Governing an Audit of Financial Statements," para. 2, International Federation of Accountants, New York.

10 IFAC, 2004, *Handbook of International Auditing, Assurance, and Ethics Pronouncements,* International Auditing Practice Statement 1014 (IAPS 1014), "Reporting By Auditors On Compliance With International Financial Reporting Standards," International Federation of Accountants, New York, June.

11 Ibid. Paragraph 7.

12 In some circumstances it also may be necessary to refer to a particular jurisdiction within the country of origin to identify clearly the financial reporting framework used.

13 A reference to relevant statutes or law may be used here.

14 IFAC, 2004, *Handbook of International Auditing, Assurance, and Ethics Pronouncements,* International Standard on Auditing 700 (ISA 700), "The Auditor's Report on Financial Statements," para. 24, International Federation of Accountants, New York.

15 PCAOB, 2003, *PCAOB Release No. 2003-025,* "Auditing Standard No. 1 – References in Auditors' Reports to the Standards of the Public Company Accounting Oversight Board," para. 3, Public Company Accounting Oversight Board, 17 December.

16 Arens, A.A., Elder, R.J., and Beasley, M.S., 2003, *Essentials of Auditing and Assurance Services An Integrated Approach,* Pearson Education/Prentice Hall, Upper Saddle River, New Jersey.

17 IFAC, 2004, *Handbook of International Auditing, Assurance, and Ethics Pronouncements 2004*, International Standard on Auditing 700 (ISA 700), "The Auditor's Report on Financial Statements," para. 28, International Federation of Accountants, New York.

18 **Emphasis of matter paragraph(s)** – An auditor's report may be modified by adding an emphasis of matter paragraph(s) to highlight a matter affecting the financial statements which is included in a note to the financial statements that more extensively discusses the matter. The addition of such an emphasis of matter paragraph(s) does not affect the auditor's opinion. The auditor may also modify the auditor's report by using an emphasis of matter paragraph(s) to report matters other than those affecting the financial statements.

19 IFAC, 2004, *Handbook of International Auditing, Assurance, and Ethics Pronouncements*, International Standard on Auditing 700 (ISA 700), "The Auditor's Report on Financial Statements," para. 27, International Federation of Accountants, New York.

20 IFAC, 2004, *Handbook of International Auditing, Assurance, and Ethics Pronouncements*, International Standard on Auditing 700 (ISA 700), "The Auditor's Report on Financial Statements," para. 44, International Federation of Accountants. New York.

21 Wording by the authors, based on IFAC, 2004, *Handbook of International Auditing, Assurance, and Ethics Pronouncements*, International Standard on Auditing 700 (ISA 700), "The Auditor's Report on Financial Statements," para. 46, International Federation of Accountants, New York.

22 IFAC, 2004, *Handbook of International Auditing, Assurance, and Ethics Pronouncements*, International Standard on Auditing 700 (ISA 700), "The Auditor's Report on Financial Statements," para. 44, International Federation of Accountants, New York.

23 IFAC, 2004, *Handbook of International Auditing, Assurance, and Ethics Pronouncements*, International Standards on Auditing 700 (ISA 700), "The Auditor's Report on Financial Statements," para. 30, International Federation of Accountants, New York.

24 IFAC, 2004, *Handbook of International Auditing, Assurance, and Ethics Pronouncements*, International Standards on Auditing 700 (ISA 700), "The Auditor's Report on Financial Statements," para. 33, International Federation of Accountants, New York.

25 Ibid. Paragraph 33.

26 IFAC, 2004, *Handbook of International Auditing, Assurance, and Ethics Pronouncements*, International Standards on Auditing 570 (ISA 570), "Going Concern," para. 33, International Federation of Accountants, New York.

27 IFAC, 2004, *Handbook of International Auditing, Assurance, and Ethics Pronouncements*, International Standards on Auditing 570 (ISA 570), "Going Concern," International Federation of Accountants, New York.

28 IFAC, 2004, *Handbook of International Auditing, Assurance, and Ethics Pronouncements*, International Standards on Auditing 700 (ISA 700), "The Auditor's Report on Financial Statements," para. 36, International Federation of Accountants, New York.

29 IFAC, 2004, *Handbook of International Auditing, Assurance, and Ethics Pronouncements*, International Standards on Auditing 570 (ISA 570), "Going Concern," para. 34, International Federation of Accountants, New York.

30 IFAC, 2004, *Handbook of International Auditing, Assurance, and Ethics Pronouncements*, International Standard On Auditing 700 (ISA 700), "The Auditor's Report on Financial Statements," para. 43, International Federation of Accountants, New York.

31 Ibid. Para. 41.

32 Ibid. Para. 46.

33 Ibid. Para. 46.

34 Adapted and reprinted with permission from AICPA. Copyright © 2000 & 1985 by American Institute of Certified Accountants.

35 For instance, in the USA, the Sarbanes-Oxley Act requires auditors to report directly to the audit committee of the board of directors.

36 IFAC, 2004, *Handbook of International Auditing, Assurance, and Ethics Pronouncements*, International Standard On Auditing 260 (ISA 260), "Communication Of Audit Matters With Those Charged With Governance," para. 2, International Federation of Accountants, New York, June.

37 Ibid. Para. 11.

38 Adapted and reprinted with permission from AICPA. Copyright © 2000 & 1985 by American Institute of Certified Accountants.

39 IFAC, 2004, *Handbook of International Auditing, Assurance, and Ethics Pronouncements*, International Standards on Auditing 240 (ISA 240), "The Auditor's Responsibility to Consider Fraud and Error in an audit of financial statements," para. 65, International Federation of Accountants, New York.

40 Ibid. Para. 42.

41 Ibid. Para. 69.

42 IFAC, 2004, *Handbook of International Auditing, Assurance, and Ethics Pronouncements*, International Standards on Auditing No. 250 (ISA 250), "Consideration of Laws and Regulations in an Audit of Financial Statements," paras. 32 and 34, International Federation of Accountants, New York.

43 IFAC, 2004, *Handbook of International Auditing, Assurance, and Ethics Pronouncements*, International Standards on Auditing 400 (ISA 400), "Risk Assessment and Internal Control," para. 49, International Federation of Accountants, New York.

44 The US Standard SAS 60 (AU 325) also requires reporting "significant deficiencies in the design or operation of the internal control structure which would adversely affect the organization's ability to record, process, summarize and report financial data consistent with the assertions of management in the financial statements.

45 XBRL US Adoption Committee, 2003, *XBRL-Enabled Accounting Software Solutions: A Study Of Leading Vendors*, American Institute of Certified Public Accountants, August.

46 **XML** is a set of rules, guidelines, conventions, whatever you want to call them, for designing text formats for such data, in a way that produces files that are easy to generate and read (by a computer), that are unambiguous, and that avoid common pitfalls, such as lack of extensibility, lack of support for internationalization/localization, and platform-dependency. (Bos, Bert, 1999, *XML in 10 Points*, **www.w3.org/XML/1999/XML-in-10-points.**)

47 According to the World Wide Web Committee (W3C). The World Wide Web Committee, or W3C, is a world-wide consortium that establishes protocols or rules for the internet. Visit the W3C website at **www.w3c.org**.

48 Greenstein, M. and Vasarhelyi, M., 2002, *Electronic Commerce Security, risk Management, and Control*, 2nd edition, McGraw-Hill Irwin, Boston.

49 Nagel, K. and Gray, G.L., 2000, *Electronic Commerce Assurance Services*, 2nd edition, San Diego: Harcourt Professional Publishing.

50 Hansen, J.V. and Messier, W.F., 1983, "Scheduling the Monitoring of EDP Controls in Online Systems," *International Journal of Computer and Information Sciences*, 12(1): 35–49.

12.14 Questions, Exercises and Cases

QUESTIONS

12.2 Introduction

12.1 How long should an audit report be? Can all important information be conveyed in the standard length?

12.3 Basic Elements of the Auditor's Report

12.2 What elements make up an audit report? Briefly discuss each.

12.3 What are the phrases used to express the auditor's opinion that the financial statements have been prepared according to local legislation, rules issued by professional bodies, etc.?

12.4 Types of Reports Expressing Audit Opinions

12.4 What are the four different opinions an auditor can issue? Briefly discuss each.

12.5 When is an adverse opinion given? How is the wording of an adverse opinion different from that of an unqualified opinion?

12.6 When is a disclaimer opinion issued? How is the wording of a disclaimer opinion different from that of an unqualified opinion?

12.5 Matters that Do Not Affect the Auditor's Opinion (Modification of an Auditor's Report Containing an Unqualified Opinion)

12.7 Discuss the introductory paragraph, the scope paragraph, the opinion paragraph, and the explanatory paragraph. What is the difference between the four?

12.8 What circumstances might result in modifications to the wording of a standard unqualified opinion? What circumstances lead to adding an explanatory paragraph? What does this paragraph entail?

12.9 Give five indications that there are going concern problems. What are some procedures in connection with dispelling going concern questions?

12.6 Circumstances that May Result in Other than an Unqualified Opinion

12.10 How is the standard audit report different if the opinion is other than qualified? Discuss and contrast the qualified opinion and the unqualified opinion.

12.11 Define limitations of scope. Under what circumstances do scope limitations arise? Give some examples of scope limitations. What should an auditor do if a limitation on scope is imposed by circumstances beyond the client's control?

12.7 Uncertainties Leading to Qualification of Opinions

12.12 In what circumstances does materiality require a qualified opinion? An adverse opinion? A disclaimer of opinion?

12.13 When can an auditor make reference to an expert work in his audit report? When may he not make reference to an expert? Why? What is the international standard involved in this issue?

12.8 Communications with those Charged with Governance

12.14 When reporting fraud how would an auditor proceed if he were in France, the UK, Germany, or Mexico?

12.15 What steps should an auditor take if he becomes aware of a fact unknown to him at the statement date which materially affects the financial statements occurring after the financial statements are issued? In what circumstances are auditors allowed to communicate with shareholders?

12.9 Long-Form Audit Report

12.16 What topics are included in a typical "long-form" audit report? Briefly discuss each.

12.10 XBRL and Continuous Reporting

12.17 How can XBRL be used in an ERP system?

PROBLEMS AND EXERCISES

12.3 Basic Elements of the Auditor's Report

12.18 **Basic Elements of Audit Report.** When field work was finished on December 31, 20X0, the following standard unqualified auditor's report was given by Eldridge and Lloyd, Chartered Accountants (CAs), of Surrey, England:

> Auditor's Report
> We have audited the accompanying financial statements.
> In our opinion, the financial statements correctly show the account balances and comply with the Companies Acts 1948 to 1981.
>
> Eldridge and Lloyd, CAs

Required:
A. List the basic elements that should appear in an unqualified auditor's report.
B. List and explain the deficiencies and omissions in the Eldridge and Lloyd auditor's report.

12.19 **Form of the Audit Report.** The most common type of audit report is the standard unqualified report.

Required:
Review Illustration 12.2, the standard wording of the IAS audit report, and Illustration 12.3, the unqualified report of Wm. Wrigley Jr. Company.
A. List the differences, paragraph-by-paragraph, between the two reports.
B. List the similarities, paragraph-by-paragraph, between the two reports.

12.4 Types of Reports Expressing Audit Opinions

12.20 **Unqualified Audit Report.** Upon completion of all field work on September 23, 20X1, the following audit report was rendered by Alexander Dlouhy, Auditor, to the directors of Rabochaya Raum Company of Docesky, the Czech Republic.

> To the Directors of
> The Rabochaya Raum Company:
> We have examined the balance sheet and the related statement of income and retained earnings of The Rabochaya Raum Company as of July 31, 20X1. In accordance with your instructions, a complete audit was conducted.
> In many respects, this was an unusual year for The Rabochaya Raum Company. The weakening of the economy in the early part of the year and the strike of plant employees in the summer of 20X1 led to a decline in sales and net income. After making several tests of sales records, nothing came to our attention that would indicate that sales have not been properly recorded.

In our opinion, with the explanation given above, and with the exception of some minor errors that are considered immaterial the aforementioned financial statements present fairly the financial position of the Rabochaya Raum Company at July 31, 20X1, and the results of its operations for the year then ended, in conformity with pronouncements of International Accounting Standards Committee applied consistently throughout the period.
Alexander Dlouhy, Auditor
September 23, 20X1

Required:

List and explain the deficiencies and omissions in the auditor's report. Organize your answer sheet by paragraph (scope, explanatory, and opinion) of the auditor's report.

12.21 **Adverse Audit Opinion.** Bheda Bhasya, Ltd., a company from Ahmadabad, India, without consulting its Chartered Accountant (CA), has changed its accounting so that it is not in accordance with international accounting principles (IASs). During the regular audit engagement the CA discovers that the statements based on the accounts are so grossly misleading that they might be considered fraudulent.

Required:
A. Discuss the specific action to be taken by the CA.
B. What type of opinion would the CA issue? Why?
C. In this situation what obligation does the CA have to a new auditor if he is replaced? Discuss briefly.

12.5 Matters that Do Not Affect the Auditor's Opinion (Modification of an Auditor's Report Containing an Unqualified Opinion)

12.22 **Modification of Unqualified Opinion.** Jorge Leyva, *Licenciado en Contaduría Público*, has completed the examination of the financial statements of Medina Construcción of Caracas, Venezuela, for the year ended July 31, 20X4. Leyva also examined and reported on the Medina financial statements for the prior year. Leyva's report is as follows:

Auditor's report to Board of Directors of Medina Construcción.

We have audited the accompanying balance sheet of Medina Construcción as of December 31, 20X3, and the related statements of income and retained earnings for the year then ended. These financial statements are the responsibility of the Company's management. Our responsibility is to express an opinion on these financial statements based on our audit.

We conducted our audit in accordance with International Standards on Auditing and approved Auditing Standards of the *Federación de Collegios de Contadores Publicos*. Those standards require that we plan and perform the audit to obtain reasonable assurance about whether the financial statements are free of material misstatement. An audit includes examining, on a test basis, evidence supporting the amounts and disclosures in the financial statements. An audit also includes assessing the accounting principles used and significant estimates made by management, as well as evaluating the overall financial statement presentation. We believe that our audit provides a reasonable basis for our opinion.

In our opinion, the financial statements referred to above present fairly, in all material respects, the financial position of Medina Construcción as of December 31, 20X3, and the results of its operations for the year then ended in conformity with International Accounting Standards and comply with Venezuela's national law, applied on a basis consistent with that of the preceding year.

Jorge Leyva, LCP
November 13, 20X4
International Center
456 Alhambra
Calabozo, Venezuela

Other information:

1   Medina is presenting comparative financial statements

2   During 20X3, Medina changed its method of accounting for long-term construction contracts and properly reflected the effect of the change in the current year's financial statements and restated the prior year's financial statements. Leyva is satisfied with Medina's justification for making the change. The change is discussed in footnote number 8 to the report.

3   Leyva was unable to perform normal accounts receivable confirmation procedures, but alternate procedures were used to satisfy Leyva as to the validity of the receivables.

4   Medina Construcción is the defendant in a litigation, the outcome of which is highly uncertain. If the case is settled in favor of the plaintiff, Medina will be required to pay a substantial amount of cash, which might require the sale of certain fixed assets. The litigation and the possible effects have been properly disclosed in footnote number 11 to the report.

5   Medina issued debenture bonds payable on January 31, 20X6, in Venezuela Bolivars (VB) for the amount of VB1,000,000,000. The funds obtained from the issuance were used to finance the expansion of plant facilities. The debenture agreement restricts the payment of future cash dividends to earnings after December 31, 20X6. Medina declined to disclose this essential data in the footnotes to the financial statements.

Required:

A.   Consider all facts given and rewrite the auditor's report in acceptable and complete format incorporating any necessary departures form the standard unqualified report.

B.   Explain any items included in "Other Information" that need not be part of the auditor's report.

12.6 Circumstances that May Result in Other than an Unqualified Opinion

12.23   **Limitation on Scope.** Lorts Corporation of Maastricht, the Netherlands, (whose fiscal year will end December 31, 20X3) informs you on December 18, 20X3 that it has a serious shortage of working capital because of heavy operating losses incurred since October 1, 20X3. Application has been made to a bank for a loan, and the bank's loan officer has requested financial statements.

The management of Lorts Corporation requests a meeting with you. You try to imagine the following independent sets of circumstances.

1   Lorts asks that you save time by auditing the financial statements prepared by Lort's chief accountant as of September 30, 20X3. The scope of your audit would not be limited by Lorts in any way.

2   Lorts asks that you conduct an audit as of December 15, 20X3. The scope of your audit would not be limited by Lorts in any way.

3   Lorts asks that you conduct an audit as of December 31, 20X3 and render a report by January 16. To save time and reduce the cost of the audit, it is requested that your examination not include confirmation of accounts receivable or observation of the taking of inventory.

4   Lorts asks that you prepare financial statements as of December 15, 20X3 from the books and records of the company without audit. The statements are to be submitted on plain paper without your name being associated in any way with them. The reason for your preparing the statements is your familiarity with proper form for financial statements.

Required:

Indicate the type of opinion you would render under each of above set of circumstances. Give reasons for your decision.

12.24 Disagreement with Management. Emiko Iamiva, Certified Public Accountant (CPA), audited the Satsuma Company's earthquake insurance policies. All routine audit procedures with regard to the earthquake insurance register have been completed (i.e. vouching, footing, examination of canceled checks, computation of insurance expense and repayment, tracing of expense charges to appropriate expense accounts, etc.).

After the insurance review, Iamiva came to the conclusion that the insurance coverage against loss by earthquake is inadequate and that, if loss occurs, the company may have insufficient assets to liquidate its debts. After a discussion with Iamiva, management refuses to increase the amount of insurance coverage.

Required:

A. What mention will Iamiva make of this condition and contingency in his standard report? Why?

B. What effect will this condition and contingency have upon the audit opinion? Give reasons for your position.

12.7 Uncertainties Leading to Qualification of Opinions

12.25 Uncertainty Concerning Future Events. Vilma Castro, *Contador Público Autorizado*, has completed field work for her examination of the Wigwam Winche company of Panama City, Panama, for the year ended December 31, 20X1, and now is in the process of determining whether to modify her report. Presented below are two independent, unrelated situations which have arisen.

Situation 1

In September, 20X1, a lawsuit was filed against Wigwam to have the court order it to install pollution-control equipment in one of its older plants. Wigwam's legal counsel has informed Castro that it is not possible to forecast the outcome of this litigation. However, Wigwam's management has informed Castro that the cost of the pollution-control equipment is not economically feasible and that the plant will be closed if the case is lost. In addition, Castro has been told by management that the plant and its production equipment would have only minimal resale values and that the production that would be lost could not be recovered at other plants.

Situation 2

During 20X1, Wigwam purchased a franchise amounting to 20 percent of its assets for the exclusive right to produce and sell a newly patented product in the northeastern USA. There has been no production in marketable quantities of the product anywhere to date. Neither the franchiser nor any franchisee had conducted any market research with respect to the product.

In deciding the type of report or modification, if any, Castor will take into account such considerations as follows:

1 Uncertainty of outcome
2 Likelihood of error
3 Expertise of the auditor
4 Pervasive impact on the financial statements
5 Inherent importance of the item

Required:

Discuss Castro's type of report decision for each situation in terms of the above and other appropriate considerations. Assume each situation is adequately disclosed in the notes to the financial statements. Each situation should be considered independently. In discussing each situation, ignore the other.

12.26 Going Concern. In the audit of Cerberus, SA, of Bydgoszcz, Poland, Merek Olzewski, Certified Public Accountant (CPA), found indications that Cerberus may have going concern problems.

Required:
A. List three financial, two operating and two other indications that Olzewski might have found that show Cerberus may have going concern problems.
B. Because the going concern assumption is in question, what additional audit procedures would Olzewski undertake?

12.8 Communications with those Charged with Governance

12.27 Directors Report on Corporate Governance. Nordtek, A/S, a manufacturer of fine skiing equipment based in Skien, Norway, has manuals of policies and procedures for monitoring and reporting on internal controls. The board has distributed a code of business ethics to all employees. New employees must undergo extensive background checks and knowledge testing and are then trained thoroughly.

Eight of the ten members of the board of directors are independent of the company and all the audit committee members are independent (non-executive) directors. There are also board committees for executive remuneration, government relations and investment review.

Management uses comprehensive budgets, revised regularly, and requiring board approval. They have an internal audit department whose employees are regularly rotated on their tasks. The internal audit department tests the internal controls for effectiveness. This year they reported to the board of directors that there was a material weakness in Nordtek's safeguarding of inventory because the storerooms were unlocked and there were no checks on those who entered or left the premises.

Required:
Write a Director's Report on Corporate Governance Matters for Nordtek.

12.10 XBRL and Continuous Reporting

12.28 Embedded Audit Modules (EAM). EAM are database software routines that are placed at predetermined points to gather information about transactions or events within the system that auditors deem to be material. EAMs allow auditors to proactively monitor auditable conditions.

Required:
A. Explain triggers and stored procedures.
B. Give an example of an EAM that could be used to audit accounts receivable transactions. How would it work, and what data would be important to collect?

CASE

12.29 Material misstatements or omissions in Audit Reports: Auditors are required to report internal control weaknesses to management. The auditors however have no responsibility to report internal control weaknesses in the audit report and failing to do so does not constitute a material misstatement or omission.

Required:

A. Using the library, Lexis-Nexis, or internet find the case of *James G. Monroe and Penelope E. Monroe v. Gary C. Hughes: Thomas R. Hudson and Deloitte & Touche* (1994 U.S. App. LEXIS 18003). Summarize the case.

B. List the reasons why the auditing firm was not found guilty of issuing an audit report with a material misstatement or omission.

(Written by Gian Dang, Pratima V. Todd and Bonnie Williams)

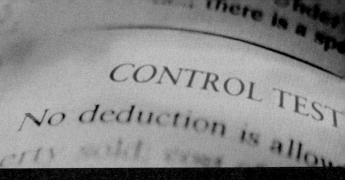

Chapter 13

OVERVIEW OF A GROUP AUDIT

13.1 Learning Objectives

After studying this chapter, you should be able to:

1 Understand the use of group audit instructions on international audits.

2 Discern the differences between the various documents used in planning an audit.

3 Describe the contents of group audit instructions.

4 Understand what is included in audit scope and coverage.

5 Discuss the meaning of critical and significant audit areas.

6 Discuss the issues involved in the audit planning memorandum.

7 Evaluate critical and significant audit areas in the audit planning process

8 Distinguish between an audit planning memorandum and an audit program.

9 Describe the components of the audit program.

10 Identify components of the completion memorandum.

11 Distinguish between how critical and significant audit areas are described in the completion memorandum and in the audit planning memorandum.

13.2 Introduction

This chapter takes you through the documents and procedures of an international audit, based on group audit instructions. The contents of this chapter are based on the working experience of the authors.[1] It should be noted that the hard paper audit documents referred to in this chapter are increasingly being replaced by electronic versions. Although all elements of a full audit will be briefly discussed, this chapter primarily focuses on substantive year-end procedures. A description of tests of control to be performed is not provided as this is dealt with in more detail in Chapter 8 Control Risk, Audit Planning and Test of Controls.

13.3 You are the Audit Manager

You are an audit manager at the Netherlands branch of Biggest International Group, Accountants (BIG for short), an international accounting firm. One Monday morning you receive a package you have been expecting. It includes several documents and a covering letter from a US office of your accounting firm. This US office wants you to audit some European subsidiaries of its client, Home Office Technology, Inc. (HOT), which is listed at the New York Stock Exchange. The company that will be your primary audit client is Local Office Technology (Local), a subsidiary of HOT.

The documents in the package are the **group audit instructions**. These documents are to familiarize you with what is expected by the BIG office, which is in charge of the HOT audit.[2] Based on these you and the partner in charge of the audit will put together an **audit planning memorandum** and an **audit program** (audit plan). A last document, a **completion memorandum**, will be required to summarize your audit findings.

The instructions from the US office are important to your understanding of the background of the client and the applicable accounting and auditing standards to be used in the audit. They point out some of the key audit objectives for this client. In this particular case, there have been several acquisitions by both HOT and Local, which will require increased substantive tests. There has also been a spin-off of a subsidiary independent distributor. Since HOT must account under US Securities Exchange Commission (SEC) GAAP standards and Local uses International Accounting Standards, you are required to reconcile Local's financial statements to US GAAP.

Your audit team will prepare an audit planning memorandum, the audit program and the completion memorandum. The audit-planning memorandum incorporates most of the important ideas of the audit. It is put together by your senior audit staff person and approved by you, the manager, and by the partner. It is also discussed with the client when in draft form. Discussion with the client rarely produces major changes. The audit program serves as a set of procedures to be performed by assistants involved in the audit and as a means to control proper execution of the work. It is prepared based on BIG's auditing software. The report on your auditing findings, the completion memorandum, describes critical and significant audit areas, accounting issues, and any matters that need to be highlighted.

■ Reviewing the Group Audit Instructions

As said, it is Monday morning and you have come to work at BIG loaded down with work that you took home for the weekend and did not finish. There is a package on your desk, delivered over the weekend, from BIG's US office. It is better to get straight to work on these projects, so you put everything else away, and pick up your yellow marker pen.

You first read the contents pages of the documents which are given in Illustration 13.1, then you read the documents and highlight certain important items with your yellow marker.

ILLUSTRATION 13.1

Contents of Group Audit Instructions

Sections

A. General

B. Specific procedures

C. Company

D. Audit scope, fees and coverage

E. Critical and significant audit concerns

F. Management letters

G. New accounting standards

H. Independence

■ Sections A (General) and B (Specific Procedures) of the Group Audit Instructions

The first two sections contain general information and specific procedures. The general information is about subsidiaries and audit standards required. Specific procedures include discussion on:

■ reporting package and deadline;
■ separate report information;
■ currency exchange considerations;
■ supplemental statements;
■ details about the completion memorandum;
■ potential material weakness in internal control;
■ *management letter* comments;
■ material differences;
■ specific details of the client audited.

Specific procedures listed in section B are numbered. You read the first procedure required which is to document planning policies in accordance with professional accounting literature and the audit service manual. You highlight the next section – the deadline for the reporting package – with your yellow marker. Other procedures such as identifying related parties, illegal or questionable acts (document who, where, results) and fraud are mentioned. You highlight legal and questionable acts because you know that this aspect is becoming more and more important to BIG and to national governments, especially under ISA 240 and 250 and the local laws.

The reporting package and deadline deals with audited financial statements, local currency and the national accounting principles applicable to HOT. The required supplemental schedules, completion memo, tax working papers and management letter comments (those that HOT management will see or those for BIG eyes only) are mentioned. You are asked to describe any unresolved issues or audit requirements not completed.

Financial Reporting Requirements

There is a fairly detailed discussion about compliance with the national accounting principles applicable to HOT. In Local's case, there is a separate financial report for statutory purposes issued by your office for Local. Differences between financial statements in local currency and in accordance with the national accounting principles applicable to HOT, and issued financial statements, should be detailed as a footnote. You highlight the last item because you know there are some differences.

Completion Memorandum

You highlight the next item about the completion memorandum because you know that it is the most important document sent back to BIG overseas. The completion memorandum should include a statement that the audit is in accordance with BIG's audit manual, working papers are prepared and reviewed, and that your working papers support the opinion. They also want to see a statement that you used a disclosure checklist and documentation of partner or senior inquiries of illegal or questionable acts with senior management, and discussion of any matters disclosed in the inquiries.

■ Section C of the Group Audit Instructions – Home Office Technology (HOT) – the Company

Section C opens with information about the main client Home Office Technology (HOT), the "Company." Details are given about the company including when it was organized, where, products, markets, service, sales force, type of customers and the industry's marketing strategy. You highlight the information about sales force, types of products, and industry's marketing strategy because you know this could be important in assessing inherent risk.

Organization Structure of HOT

The next piece of information is on the organization of HOT which lists all subsidiaries by location, principal activities, with any subsidiaries sold, acquired, spun-off or shutdown noted. You highlight the subsidiaries sold, acquired, etc. Where there is a change in ownership, there might be some accounting problems. The subsidiaries, which are important to your audit, are shown in Illustration 12.2.

You highlight "the industry," "rapid technological advances," and "competitors" because of possible inherent risk. Internal factors that are of importance are: product changes and customer reaction to those changes, acquisitions over the last ten years, and Local's overall strategy. You highlight "product changes" because this will increase control risk in that old control may not work for new products.

ILLUSTRATION 13.2

Subsidiaries Important to the Audit

Company	Structure	
Parent Company – Home Office Technology (HOT)	HOT Subsidiary – Local Office Technology (Local)	Local Subsidiary – Brother Office Technology (Brother)*
	Sister Information Systems (SIS)	Zap
	Brother Research Organization (BRO)	Design Info Planning and Programming Resources (DIPPER)
	Cousin Office Technology (Cousin)	Finance Investment National Enterprises (FINE)
	Uncle Office Technology (Uncle)	SIS subsidiary Newco

* Note: Brother owns Sister Information Systems (SIS), which owns Newco.

Questions About Local (HOT subsidiary)

General questions the auditor should ask are about Local's legal situation, industry, and products. Legal questions include:

- Is there an in-house legal department?
- Is there an in-charge manager?
- Who is Local's general counsel?

Regarding related parties, you must provide a list of: (a) directors (b) non-director officers (c) subsidiaries and (d) others. Also required is an analysis of the competition related to characteristics of the industry, evidence of rapid technological advances, and a list of competitors.

Certification Exam Question 13.1

An auditor obtains knowledge about a new client's business and its industry to:

(A) Make constructive suggestions concerning improvements to the client's internal control.
(B) Develop an attitude of professional skepticism concerning management's financial statement assertions.
(C) Evaluate whether the aggregation of known misstatements causes the financial statements taken as a whole to be materially misstated.
(D) Understand the events and transactions that may have an effect on the client's financial statements.

■ Section D of the Group Audit Instructions – Audit Scope, Fees and Coverage

Section D includes subsections on home office participation, audit fees, audit coverage, timing of certain audit procedures, computer assisted auditing techniques, the audit timetable and quarterly reviews.

The section begins with a list of names and telephone numbers of key personnel responsible for the Home Office Technology (HOT) audit: the partner, manager, and in-charge senior manager. There is also a list of key personnel names and telephone numbers, partner and manager at BIG's US office. The agreed audit scope and related amount of the audit fees are given.

Schedule of Planned Scope and Coverage

An audit coverage schedule of planned scope and coverage is detailed.[3,4] They give you a schedule of the percentage of estimated total consolidated amounts at December, 31 20XX for each company and the scope of the audit, for example, HOT's revenues represent 52 percent of the total consolidated revenues, and the audit. A partial schedule looks like Illustration 13.3.

ILLUSTRATION 13.3

HOT and Subsidiaries

Revenue, total assets, and accounts rec. as a percentage of Consolidated Values							
	Revenues		*Total Assets*		*Accounts Rec.*		*SCOPE*
	Total	*Audit*	*Total*	*Audit*	*Total*	*Audit*	*of Audit*
HOT	52	52	50	50	62	62	Full scope
Local	13	13	8	8	14	14	Full scope
Uncle	12	lr	8	lr	9	lr	Limited review
Others	5	dr	2	dr	–	na	Desk review

na = not audited dr = desk review lr = limited review

Timing of Audit Procedures

The timing of certain audit procedures is considered next. The general audit plan gives you a list of the audit area and a description of audit procedures, which you can perform prior to year-end. The schedule is as follows:

Audit area	*Discussion of audit procedures*
Accounts receivable	Confirm balances as of 30 November and *roll forward* to year-end
Research and development costs	Test of transactions for third quarter and roll forward to year-end
Investments	Test of balances as of 30 November and roll forward to year-end
Property plant and equipment	Test of balances as of 30 November and roll forward to year-end

Deadlines

The audit timetable calls for all working papers, reports and supporting schedules to be received by January 30, 20XX at BIG overseas. The audit-planning memorandum will be due December 12. You highlight that date because that is the most pressing one.

■ Section E of the Group Audit Instructions – Critical and Significant Audit Concerns

Section E is described as "Critical and Significant Audit Concerns." This is an important section that shows which items you will need to concentrate on during the audit. The specific areas of concern are revenue, research and development costs, third-party regulation, acquisitions, restructure accruals, management letters, benchmarking and new accounting standards that need to be applied.

Local Management's Revenue Recognition Policies

You must review if management's revenue recognition procedures are being followed. Management's procedure for revenue recognition is to record revenue only when four conditions are met. These four conditions are:

1. a signed purchase order is received;
2. credit worthiness of the customer is reviewed and the sale is documented;
3. the product has been shipped;
4. the product shipped is only the currently authorized product, not test products or samples.

Research and Development Costs

The final concerns for the audit are review of research and development costs, third-party royalties, acquisitions and restructuring accruals. Local pays royalties to third parties on some of their software, which will require review.

■ Sections F (Management Letters) and G (New Accounting Standards) of the Group Audit Instructions

Management letters are important to BIG. The instructions convey the suggestions for the management letter to be reviewed with Local managers. You also make sure that your comments are supported in the working papers and typed for inclusion in the consolidated management letter.

The final part of the group audit instructions discusses *benchmarking* and the new accounting standards that apply this year. Local is to be compared to benchmarks developed on several other companies and results are to be discussed with managers. New GAAP standards in the US include standards on financial instruments used as investments or hedging and certain internal controls.

■ Section H (Independence) of the Group Audit Instructions

It is requested that you and your audit team have a sufficient understanding of, and have complied with, the applicable independence requirements.[5]

You will write e-mails to your audit team members in order to determine and document their compliance with these rules.

Certification Exam Question 13.2

Which of the following is most likely to be unique to the audit work of certified accountants as compared to work performed by practitioners of other professions?

(A) Due professional care.
(B) Competence.
(C) Independence.
(D) Complex body of knowledge.

13.4 The Audit Planning Memorandum – Strategy Part

After reading the group audit instructions, the first order of business is to meet with the audit staff and discuss strategy for the audit. Based on the results of the meeting, your senior staff auditor will write up an audit planning memorandum that will be reviewed by senior team members. So, early on Friday morning, everyone meets at the office and discusses the BIG overseas materials and the audit plan.

Things get pretty well structured and the meeting is over by 11 o'clock, which is just as well because the partner has another meeting that day. You discuss some fine points with your audit senior who will have the memorandum for your review by Wednesday.

Wednesday afternoon your senior gives you the draft memorandum. He has split the audit-planning memorandum into a Strategy Part and a Plan Part.

An outline of the contents of the Strategy Part is shown in Illustration 13.4.

■ Section II and III of the Audit Planning Memorandum – Follow-up and Insights

Follow-up Section

Since Local is a continuing client, the audit should be started by following up on last year. The Follow-up from Last Year section discusses some questions:

- Has Local fixed the problems it had last year?
- How has the situation been improved?
- If they have improved, what tests will be done to ensure this conclusion?

Insights Section

The insights section gives some of the audit staff's insights into the company. One of Local's business activities, service contracts, has changed. Therefore, a change in controls is needed. Market position, new developments and problems involving revenue auditing are considered. Important customers and suppliers should be reviewed, especially big customers and new contracts. Confirmations of accounts receivable may prove difficult for Local because business custom in this country discourages sending confirmations to customers. The team will find another way to audit the revenue cycle.

ILLUSTRATION 13.4

Contents of Audit Planning Memorandum – Strategy Part

I.   Introduction

II. Follow-up from last year

III. Insights

    A. Critical success factors and key performance indicators

    B. Objectives and strategies

    C. Business activities and influence on controls

    D. Market position – position and competitors

    E. Important customer/suppliers

    F. New developments

    G. Changed business structure

    H. Financing and financial reporting environment

    I. Information system changes

IV. Initial risk analysis

V.   Internal controls and control procedures

VI. Identification of critical audit objectives

VII. Client service aspects item – action

    A. New structure of Internal Control due to new systems

    B. Functional currency charged to Home Office (HO)

    C. Proposed CIS review

VIII. Important contacts

    A. At Local

    B. Local professional advisers

IX. Service Audit Team

Some of the changes at Local may require more extensive audit procedures and investigation. Local has made some change in its business structure by taking over Newco and Design Information Planning & Programming Resources (DIPPER). This could cause control and accounting problems. Local has had information system changes, which may cause misstatement and control problems.

Concept and a Company 13.1

Ahold – Rapid Global Expansion and the Group Audit

Concept	Difficulties of a group audit.
Story	In 2003, Koninklijke Ahold N.V. (Royal Ahold), a 115-year-old Netherlands company, had 9,000 stores in 27 countries that served 40 million customers a week, and owned or had interest in about 9,000 supermarkets as well as discount and specialty stores in some 25 countries in Asia, Europe and the Americas. In February 2003, Ahold revealed improperly booked profit of approximately $1.12 billion. (Sams 2003)

549

Ahold – Rapid Global Expansion and the Group Audit (continued)

Ahold's auditor, Deloitte & Touche (DT), discovered the company's accounting irregularities as part of its 2002 year-end audit. As a result of the discovery, Ahold had to restate its audited financial statements for 2001 which had been given an unqualified audit opinion. (Weil 2003) Speaking at the company's annual meeting, Henny de Ruiter, in his last official engagement as Ahold chairman, said that Ahold's supervisory and executive boards felt responsible for the "horrendous" events. He added that Ahold would not replace DT, saying there was no evidence the auditor knew of the fraud prior to its discovery. (Bickerton & Watkins 2003)

Irregularities involving improper booking of vendor allowances were discovered in US subsidiaries US Foodservice and Tops Markets. The company's Disco subsidiary engaged transactions that were illegal and improperly accounted for. Unauthorized side letters (supplements to contracts) created errors of consolidation regarding joint ventures in Sweden/Norway, Brazil, Guatemala and Argentina. (Mirabella 2003)

Ahold's executive and supervisory boards ordered an investigation by a forensic team from PricewaterhouseCoopers (PwC). For the period April 1, 2000 (the effective date of Ahold's acquisition of US Foodservice) to December 28, 2002, (the end of Ahold's 2002 fiscal year), PwC has identified total overstatements of pre-tax earnings of approximately $880 million. Of this amount, approximately $110 million relates to fiscal year 2000, approximately $260 million relates to fiscal year 2001, and approximately $510 million relates to fiscal year 2002. In addition, PwC identified approximately $90 million of adjustments required to be made to the opening balances for US Foodservice at the date of its acquisition. This consists of a reclassification of such amount from current assets to goodwill primarily as a result of required write-offs of vendor receivables. (NACS 2003)

The forensic accounting work at Albert Heijn, Stop & Shop, Santa Isabel in Chile, Ahold's operations in Poland and the Czech Republic, and the ICA Ahold Scandinavian joint venture found no evidence of financial fraud. (NACS 2003)

The main problem in the US was improper booking of vendor allowances. The allowances are a broad industry term that covers everything from vendor payments for prime shelf space in a store, to rebates awarded to retailers who hit sales targets for suppliers' products. These payments were allegedly booked too high and were, in some cases, booked without the manufacturers' permission. Subsidiaries were also faulted for booking vendor allowances as revenue, when, in most cases, they should be booked as a reduction in the cost of sales. Ahold says that Tops was principally to blame for $29 million in overstated income. Another of its US subsidiaries, US Foodservice, overstated its pretax income by $880 million over three years. (Glenn 2003)

Cees van der Hoeven, Ahold's Chief Executive, took the retailer on a worldwide buying spree, from Chile to Thailand, running up net debts of around €13 billion. Ahold began its buying spree in 1976 when it acquired a Spanish supermarket and the Bi-Lo chain in the American South. In 1996, it bought Stop & Shop for $2.9 billion and added dozens of chains in Latin America, Europe and Asia. It tried to buy Pathmark Stores in 1999, but that deal was blocked by the US Federal Trade Commission. Ahold subsequently turned to food service for growth, acquiring US Foodservice for $3.6 billion in 2000 (**Knowledge@Wharton** 2004). Also, in 2000, Ahold acquired PYAO Monarch for $2.57 billion and paid $75 million for Peapod.

Ahold's broad strategy was to buy regional supermarket retailers and gain economies of scale and savings through consolidation of back-office and buying operations. Other chains sought to do the same thing, modeling themselves on the successful expansion of chain drugstores. However, grocery stores are more complicated than drugstores and depend to a greater extent on regional suppliers and marketing (**Knowledge@Wharton** 2004).

Discussion Questions	■ Discuss ways that a buying spree like that of Mr Van der Hoeven can create problems for the group auditor? ■ What pressures may be applied to the management of newly acquired divisions that would encourage misstatement of income? ■ What special audit procedures should be applied to an audit of an acquisitive company?

References	Bickerton, I. and Watkins, M., 2003, "Ahold says up to 10 people to blame for fraud," *Financial Times*, London, November 27, p. 15. Glynn, M., 2003, "Vendor Rebates To Retailers Are Under The Microscope," *Buffalo News*, Buffalo, NY, June 1, p. B.9. **Knowledge@Wharton**, 2004, "Royal Ahold's Royal Hold Up," **http://knowledge.wharton.upenn.edu/**, March 12. Mirabella, L., 2003, "Dutch grocery chain raided," *Cincinnati Post*, Cincinnati, Ohio, July 8, p. C.9.0. NACS 2003, "Ahold Releases Results of US Foodservice Forensic Accounting Investigation," *Daily News*, National Association of Convince Stores, May 9. Sams, R., 2003, "Ahold accounting probes reveal more irregularities," *Washington Business Journal*, July 1. Weil, J., 2003, "Deloitte's Work for Ahold Raises Questions on Auditing," *Wall Street Journal* (Eastern edition), New York, NY, February 25, p. A.10.

■ Section IV of the Audit Planning Memorandum – Initial Risk Analysis

Initial risk analysis must be conducted to determine main risks. You and the team made a schedule of risk arranged by process (sales, accounts receivable, and salary) and information source as follows (example):

Process	Information Source	Inherent Risk	Control Risk	Critical Audit Objective
Intangibles	Groot Warnsborn	High	High	Valuation
Sales of software	John Smith	High	High	Completeness
Accounts receivable	Patricia Hayward	High	Average	Valuation
Salary	Robert de Niro	Low	Low	None

■ Section V of the Audit Planning Memorandum – Internal Controls and Control Procedures

The team members noted that at Local no-one feels responsible for controls. That is not a good sign. A review of CIS showed that Local is highly dependent on *user controls*.[6] After the planned installation of new software this year, controls must be tested again. **Boundary testing** is audit testing of documentation at the lowest level of the information stream, for example, testing the first document (i.e. purchase order) that initiates an exchange.

Certification Exam Question 13.3

The element of the audit planning process most likely to be agreed upon with the client before implementation of the audit strategy is the determination of the:

(A) Evidence to be gathered to provide a sufficient basis for the auditor's opinion.
(B) Procedures to be undertaken to discover litigation, claims, and assessments.
(C) Pending legal matters to be included in the inquiry of the client's attorney.
(D) Timing of inventory observation procedures to be performed.

■ Section VI of the Audit Planning Memorandum – Identification of critical audit objectives

The strategy part identifies critical audit objectives. One of the critical audit objectives relates to the purchase of certain subsidiaries creating substantial goodwill. You feel that Local should speed up the recovery of the goodwill intangible fixed assets due to these recurring (substantial) operating losses. The team suggested to Local at the beginning of the year that they write off this goodwill immediately. No reaction from Local management has been received.

■ Section VII to IX of the Audit Planning Memorandum – Client Service, Important Contacts and Audit Team

Because auditing is a service and offered in a competitive business environment, a major concern of BIG is client service aspects of the audit. The team feels that changing the functional currency to US dollars, which is HOT's functional currency, may result in tax problems and proposes an EDP review because of the new finance system that has just been installed at Local. There is a note to contact BIG's tax office and BIG's CIS department.

List of Important Local Contacts

The team put together a list of Local's professional advisors and important contacts among Local employees. The list of important contacts at Local is categorized by name, quality (good/bad) of contact, frequency of contact and by whom the contact should be made (partner, manager or senior).

Audit Team

The final item in the strategy part of the audit planning memorandum is a schedule of the audit team. The schedule includes the audit team's names and experience at the client. Also listed will be other professionals at BIG who may be called for assistance, (e.g. tax personnel, CIS consultants and others).

Everyone on the team reviews the strategy part of the planning memorandum. It is now your job to combine their comments with the following discussion of the draft plan part of the audit planning memorandum. You call Local to set up interviews and a walk-through with some of the team for two days next week to develop a better understanding of Local and some of the areas that may require investigation.

Certification Exam Question 13.4

An auditor should design the written audit program so that:

(A) All material transactions will be selected for substantive testing.
(B) Substantive tests prior to the balance sheet date will be minimized.
(C) The audit procedures selected will achieve specific audit objectives.
(D) Each account balance will be tested under either tests of controls or tests of transactions.

ILLUSTRATION 13.5

Contents of Audit Planning Memorandum – Plan Part

I.   Introduction
   A. Client background
   B. Group structure
   C. Analytical review to assist in audit planning
II. Audit approach
   A. Scope
   B. Audit materiality (gauge)
   C. Assessment of inherent risk and preliminary assessments of control risk
III. Critical audit objectives
   A. Intangibles
   B. Sales of software
   C. Accounts receivable
IV. Significant audit areas and accounting issues
   A. Accounts receivable
   B. Accounts payable
   C. Inter-company receivables and payables
   D. Revenue recognition
   E. Unearned revenue
   F. Taxation
   G. Forward exchange contracts
   H. Related party
   I. Assets
   J. Statutory financial statements
V.   Fees
VI. Timetable
   A. Format financial statement and items requested
   B. Draft of management letter
VII. Client contacts
VIII. Local firm service team

13.5 The Audit Planning Memorandum – Plan Part

The strategy part of the audit planning memorandum sets the broad direction for the audit. The plan part of the audit planning memorandum summarizes technical matters, client service matters and logistical matters. Technical matters include further planning of our approach of critical audit objectives and internal control. It expands on the strategy part and provides, among other things, an overview of the client company, the industry environment, significant audit concerns, and areas of interest to the audit team. In other words, an audit has to be planned in greater detail using the strategy as a basis. An outline of this plan part appears in Illustration 13.5.

We will not discuss audit approach and critical audit objectives in greater detail, but we will sketch some considerations in audit planning to be made based upon risk analysis. We call these considerations "significant audit areas" and "accounting issues." These considerations (and, of course, the critical audit objectives) should be dealt with in the audit program (audit plan) that will be discussed below. Please note that the audit program primarily focuses on substantive year-end procedures to provide guidance for the audit work in a practical way. Of course, tests of control should be performed. However these have been described in more detail in Chapter 8 Control Risk, Audit Planning, and Test of Controls.

Concept and a Company 13.2

ZZZZ Best – How to Fool the Auditors

Concept   "I had to fool accountants and auditors into believing those numbers were real before I could perpetrate the fraud," Barry Minkow (ACFE 2002).

Story   ZZZZ Best began operations in the fall of 1982 as a door-to-door carpet cleaning business operating out of the Reseda, California, the garage of 16-year-old Barry Minkow. In the three-year period from 1984 to 1987, net income grew from less then $200,000 to more than $5 million on a revenue of $50. In the spring of 1987, ZZZZ Best had a market value of $200 million. By the end of 1987 the company was in bankruptcy and the assets were auctioned off for only $64,000 (Knapp 2004). The company for almost its entire history was a fraud.

ZZZZ Best had a legitimate carpet-cleaning business that accounted for 20 percent of reported revenue and a phony building restoration business which was 80 percent of revenue. To create loans for the company, ZZZZ Best management made fraudulent invoices, set up checking accounts for front companies, created fraudulent vendors, wrote checks for phony expenses, and kept the money circulating by check kiting at several banks. (Knapp 2004)

False Documents

Thousands of company checks in the company written by hand, in large numbers, and often payable to cash were made out to different people or firms but paid into the same account. The same money-obtained from ZZZZ Best investors and lenders kept going around and around from ZZZZ Best to phony vendors and customers and back to ZZZZ Best. The purpose of all these movement was to make ZZZZ Best look like a legitimate business. (Akst & Berton 1988)

"Accounts receivable are a wonderful thing," Barry Minkow said, "They are a tool used by a fraudster like me to ask to borrow money and to show earnings." (ACFE 2002) He would create an invoice from a phony customer, write a check to ZZZZ Best from the front company's checking account, and deposit it to the company account. "One way you cannot dispute a receivable is if it has been paid ... I was a paperwork manufacturing machine," he said. (ACFE 2002)

Convincing the Auditors

To avoid the auditors finding anything, Minkow employed a number of tricks besides false documentation. He steered the auditors to examine the legitimate carpet cleaning business instead of the non-existent building restoration business. "The restoration business was 80 percent of the revenue, but I made sure that the auditors did 80 percent of due diligence in the carpet cleaning business," he said. He also intimidated the auditors, ingratiated himself to the auditors, and in one instance created a completely false audit environment.

Auditing is a very competitive business. "Competition is what you leverage," Minkow said. "I can't remember how many times [I said] "Larry, I just know Coopers and Lybrand would love this account." Does he want to go back to his clients and managers and say that he lost the ZZZZ Best account because he wanted to be petty?" No, he does not want to lose the ZZZZ Best account, "and I leveraged that to the hilt, too." (ACFE 2002)

Minkow's charm and entrepreneurial spirit caused the media to tout him as an example of what America's youth could obtain if they applied themselves. As a guest on the *The Oprah Winfrey Show* on US network television in April 1987 he encouraged his peers to adopt his personal motto, "The sky is the limit." (Knapp 2004) He ingratiated himself by having dinner with the auditors and their wives. He felt that if the wives like him and the auditor wanted to be hard on Minkow, the wives would say, "but he is such a nice kid." Minkow said, "The final touch was 'Well, the kid is on Wall Street. If there was something wrong, someone would have found out by now.' " (ACFE 2002)

Classic Tricks

Minkow's tricks to mislead the accountants doing audit procedures are classic. They included phony confirmations, financial statements manipulated to reflect industry standards, false documentation and, in one instance, creation of an entire false audit environment.

Minkow paid an insurance claims adjuster from a legitimate company to confirm over the telephone to banks and any other interested third parties that ZZZZ Best was the recipient of insurance restoration contracts. ZZZZ Best's first external auditor, George Greenspan, maintained that he performed analytical procedures comparing the company to the industry, confirmed the existence of contracts, and obtained and reviewed copies of key documents. Greenspan, however, did not inspect any restoration sites. (US Congress 1988)

Ernst & Whinney (E&W) took over as ZZZZ Best's auditor in 1986. E&W repeatedly insisted on visiting several of the largest of the contract sites, so that finally Minkow agreed to a visit. E&W wanted to visit a large site in Sacramento, California for which ZZZZ Best claimed to have a multi-million dollar contract.

Minkow sent two associates to Sacramento to find a large building under construction or renovation that would be a plausible site for a restoration contract. Posing as leasing agents, they convinced the supervisor of the construction site to provide keys to the building one weekend on the pretext that a possible future tenant wanted to tour the building. Before

---

ZZZZ Best – How to Fool the Auditors (continued)

E&W visited the site, placards were placed on the walls indicating that ZZZZ Best was the contractor for building renovation. The building's security officer was paid to greet the visitors and demonstrate that he was aware in advance of the auditor's visit. (US Congress 1988)

Another site visit by E&W required that ZZZZ Best lease a partially completed building and hire subcontractors to do a large amount of work on the site. In total ZZZZ Best spent several million dollars just to deceive its auditors. (US Congress 1988)

ZZZZ Best required that E&W sign a confidentiality agreement before the visits were made on the pretext that that the insurance company required it. The agreement required that E&W not disclose the location of the building and not "make any follow-up telephone calls to any contractors, insurance companies, building owner or other individuals." (Knapp 2004)

Discussion Questions	■ What procedures should an auditor carry out to determine the validity of a significant source of company revenue? ■ What actions of Minkow and the company's audit history would have caused an auditor to become suspicious? ■ How does signing a confidentiality agreement affect auditor substantive procedures?
References	ACFE, 2002, "Cooking the Books" video, *Introduction to Higher Education*, Association of Certified Fraud Auditors, Austin, Texas, February 12. Akst, D. and Berton, L., 1988, "Accountants Who Specialize in Detecting Fraud Find Themselves in Great Demand," *The Wall Street Journal*, February 26. Knapp, M, 2004, "ZZZZ Best Company, Inc," *Contemporary Auditing Real Issues & Cases*, South-Western College Publishing, pp. 41–56. US Congress, House, Subcommittee on Oversight and Investigation of the Committee on Energy and Commerce, 1988, 100th Congress, *Hearing 100-115*, "Failure *of ZZZZ* Best Co," US Government Printing Office, Washington, DC, from January 27 to February 1.

■ Revenue Recognition Procedures Key

The group audit instructions from BIG Overseas stated that revenue recognition would be a key area. You plan to review revenue recognition policy by first testing cut-off procedures; then make a review of shipping documents as an alternative procedure to confirmation of accounts receivable, and boundary testing on the **revenue cycle**.

The almost continuous revision of International Financial Reporting Standard IAS 39[7] on financial instruments reinforces your feeling about being careful when financial instruments are a significant portion of the current assets. Local uses forward exchange contracts.

■ Fees, Timetable and Client Contacts

Fees and the timetable for the audit are important parts of the audit plan for obvious reasons. You calculate the budgeted hours and related fees for partner, manager, staff, and out-of-pocket expenses. The timetable for audit was given to you in the instructions as follows:

> (1) planning memo, time and fee estimate are due December 12, 20XX; (2) format financial statement and items requested by group audit instructions are due on January 23, 20XX and (3) a draft of management letter is due on January 30, 20XX.

You and the partner review and approve the plan and take it to the client for discussion. Local management and audit committee review the plan and meet with you. They recommend only a few changes in the plan based on timing. Now you are ready to finalize the audit planning memorandum and conduct the audit.

13.6 Audit Program (Audit Plan)

Using BIG's audit software, BIGdealer, you write the audit program. You use standardized audit procedures suggested by the software that are needed to substantially test the account balances and transactions outlined in the audit planning memorandum. Major steps that can be included are given (as example) in Illustration 13.6.

The audit program starts out with the basic data about value of assets and revenue, the basis on which the testing will be made and the gauge or monetary precision or materiality, the amount of maximum misstatements allowed. This data for the Local audit is shown on the first part of the audit program, Illustration 13.6.

ILLUSTRATION 13.6

Audit Program

Investments

Balances:	
Investments	25,000,000
Income or (losses)	200,000
Gain or (loss) on sales	300,000

OBJECTIVES:

I. All dividend, interest and other income is recorded; gains and losses on sales and other dispositions are recognized; premiums and discounts and related amortization are recorded. (Completeness and accuracy.)

II. Investments exist and are owned by the entity. (Existence and ownership.)

III. Valuation methods (e.g. equity, market, lower of cost or market) applied are in conformity with applicable accounting principles consistently applied, and write-down, or provision for write-down, is recorded, when appropriate. (Valuation, presentation and disclosures.)

	Obj. #	Done By	Refer.
1 Verify accuracy of relevant supporting schedules and agree to trial balance and subsidiary records. (a) Obtain and check mathematical accuracy of a detailed schedule of securities, including transactions for the year, classified as to (1) short-term investments, (2) long-term investments, (3) affiliated companies, and (4) other; agree beginning balances to the prior year's workpapers; and reconcile ending balances to the trial balance, general ledger, and subsidiary records, if any. Identify separately marketable equity securities.	I, II		

▶

Illustration 13.6 (continued)

	Obj. #	Done By	Refer.
2 Confirm investments held by third parties.	II		
3 For major acquisitions or dispositions of investments, agree to authorization in the minutes of the Board of Directors.	II		
4 *Vouch*[8] purchases of investments to supporting documentation.	I, II		
5 Vouch sales of investments to supporting documentation and recompute gain or loss on disposal. Trace collections to cash receipts.	I, II		
6 Examine latest financial statements of investees.	II, II, III		
7 Review disclosures (e.g. basis, assets pledged, related parties, equity method details interests, gross unrealized gain/losses). (a) Perform detail procedures as considered necessary.	I		
8 Determine the application of correct rates of exchange for amounts denominated in foreign currency	III		
9 Conclude (a) With respect to the set of assertions and related audit objective(s), the audit procedures applied were in accordance with firm and professional requirements; subject to any differences documented in the workpapers, the recorded amounts are materially correct and the accounting principles are proper and consistently applied; the information in the workpapers is sufficient to draw a conclusion as to proper disclosure.	II, II, III		

Expenses and Payables

Balances: Prepaid Expenses Trade Accounts Payables and Accruals	10,000,000 10,000,000

OBJECTIVES:

I. All unpaid amounts due to suppliers or others for goods and services received prior to year-end are included or otherwise accrued. (Completeness, existence, accuracy, and ownership.)

II. All cash disbursements are valid and properly recorded (i.e. they are for goods and services received by the entity; classification as asset expense, liability, and other accounts is appropriate). (Existence and accuracy.)

III. Accounting principles are appropriate and applied consistently (e.g. interest adjustments, if required, are recognized). (Valuation, presentation and disclosures.)

	Obj. #	Done By	Refer.
1 Compare amounts for trade payables, accruals, purchases, period expenses, and payments to prior periods and budgets.	I, II		
2 Verify the mathematical accuracy of relevant supporting schedules and agree to trial balance and subsidiary records.	I, II		
3 Review liabilities recorded after the end of the period and review subsequent cash payments. (a) Determine propriety of year-end accounts for both accounts payable and accrued liabilities by searching for unrecorded liabilities. Such review should encompass the period subsequent to the balance sheet date and include a review of unpaid vendor invoices, cash disbursements, unmatched receiving reports, significant liabilities recorded after year-end, and other relevant items.	I		

Illustration 13.6 (continued)

	Obj. #	Done By	Refer.
(b) Verify computation of period accruals. (c) Determine the extent to which it is necessary to examine documents supporting period-end accruals and check underlying mathematical calculations. Perform any necessary tests of details. (d) Verify *cut-off*[9] for: purchases, payments, supplier returns, and shipments direct to customer from suppliers. (e) For the period before and after the balance sheet date, check vendor invoices to and from receiving records to determine that a proper cutoff was made. (f) For the period before and after the balance sheet date. Check debit memos for purchase returns to and from shipping records to determine that a proper cutoff was made. (g) Request or confirm suppliers' statements. (h) Check suppliers' statements to recorded balances and investigate differences. (i) Send second requests where requested statements are not received or apply alternative auditing procedures (e.g. review subsequent payments, agree to receiving reports, purchase orders, correspondence files).			
4 Vouch purchases of inventory from perpetual records.	I		
5 Vouch claims for credit from suppliers (e.g. receivables from suppliers) to supporting documents.	I		
6 Vouch purchases and other disbursements from voucher register to supporting documents including relevant data.	II		
7 Vouch purchases of inventory to and from perpetual records.	II		
8 *Trace*[10] purchases from receiving reports to suppliers' invoices and voucher register including relevant data (e.g. party, price, description, quantity and date).	II		
9 Determine the application of correct rates of exchange for amounts expressed in foreign currency.	III		
10 Review classification and description of accounts (e.g. debit balance, current/non-current trade, related parties).	III		
11 Review accounting principles for appropriateness and consistency.	III		
12 Conclude (a) With respect to the set of assertions and related audit objective(s), the audit procedures applied were in accordance with firm and professional requirements; subject to any differences documented in the working papers, the recorded amounts are materially correct and the accounting principles are proper and consistently applied; the information in the working papers is sufficient to draw a conclusion as to proper disclosure.	II, II, III		

Revenue/Accounts Receivable

Balances: Revenue Accounts Receivable	35,000,000 35,000,000
OBJECTIVES:	
I. All revenue from the sale of goods and performance of service are recorded accurately. (Completeness and accuracy.)	
II. Recorded revenues are in conformity with proper revenue recognition methods consistently applied and adequately disclosed. (Valuation, presentation and disclosure.)	

▶

Illustration 13.6 (continued)

OBJECTIVES: (continued)			
III. Cut-off is proper. (Completeness and existence.)			
IV. Trade accounts receivable represent uncollected sales or other charges to *bona fide* customers and are owned by the entity. (Existence and ownership.)			
V. All cash collections are accurately recorded. (Completeness and accuracy.)			
VI. Non-cash credit to receivables (e.g. returns, allowances) are valid and accurate. (Existence and accuracy.)			
VII. Valuation of trade receivables is appropriate (i.e. provision is made for uncollectable amounts). (Valuation, presentation and disclosure.)			

		Obj. #	Done By	Refer.
1	Vouch sales from shipping records to sales authorization, sales invoices, and sales register, including relevant data (e.g. party, price, description, quantity, and dates).	I		
2	Test sales invoice price of items to authorized lists.	I, VII		
3	Test processing to general and subsidiary ledgers.	I		
4	Determine sequential numbering of sales invoices.	I		
5	Analyze the VAT-payable to total sales (Netherlands).	I		
6	Evaluate propriety and consistency of accounting principles. Consider: (a) Revenue recognition (current and deferred); Bill and hold transactions; Discontinued operations; Non-monetary exchanges; Warranties; Sales of receivables with or without recourse; Commissions; Special discounts and rebates; Consignment sales; Trade notes receivable; Troubled debt restructuring of customers; and Scrap sales.	II		
7	Verify cut-off for sales, cash receipts, returns, etc.	II, III		
8	Verify the mathematical accuracy of relevant supporting schedules and agree to trial balance and subsidiary records.	IV		
9	Confirm recorded receivables (amount, date, terms, interest rate, etc.). (a) Check replies to confirmations and investigate exceptions. (b) Send second requests where replies to positive requests are not received. (Exceptions to sending second requests for non-responding positive confirmations should be rare and the reasons for not sending them should be fully documented.) (c) Investigate undelivered requests returned by post office. If possible obtain better addresses and mail again. (d) Where replies are not received to positive requests for confirmation apply alternative audit procedures (e.g. check subsequent remittance advices, shipping documents, billing records, customer orders and correspondence files). (e) Summarize results of confirmation requests and all iterative procedures.	IV, V, VII		
10	Vouch recorded receivables to subsequent cash receipts.	IV, V VII		
11	Vouch sales from sales register to shipping records (including relevant data).	IV		
12	Vouch write-offs of uncollectable receivables to supporting documentation.	VI, VII		
13	Vouch aging details to supporting documents, discuss collectability of receivables with responsible officials, and review correspondence.	V, VI, VII		

Illustration 13.6 (continued)

	Obj. #	Done By	Refer.
14 Determine the extent to which it is necessary to perform the following tests of details: (a) Select credit memos, examine supporting documents and trace posting to the sales register. (b) Review credit memos issued after the balance sheet date and ascertain whether significant amounts relate to sales for the period under review. (c) Vouch returns to supporting documentation.	VI		
15 Verify the accuracy of client schedules supporting their analysis of the allowance for doubtful accounts. (a) Obtain an aged listing of trade receivables as of the balance sheet date. Reconcile the balance with the general ledger and trial balance, and compare a selected number of individual accounts of the listing with the detailed subsidiary trade receivable records. Verify the mathematical accuracy of any schedules.	V, VII		
16 Determine the application of correct rates of exchange for amounts expressed in foreign currency.	V		
17 Review disclosures (e.g. assets pledged, related parties, segments, significant customer data, economic dependency). (a) Perform additional procedures considered necessary.	V		
18 Conclude: (a) With respect to the set of assertions and related audit objective(s), the audit procedures applied were in accordance with BIG's and professional requirements; subject to any differences documented in the workpapers, the recorded amounts are materially correct and the accounting principles are proper and consistently applied; the information in the working papers is sufficient to draw a conclusion as to proper disclosure.	I, II, III, IV, V, VI		

Inventory/Cost of Sales

Balances: Inventories Cost of Sales	2,000,000 15,000,000

OBJECTIVES:

I. Inventory is accurately compiled and priced in conformity with acceptable methods (e.g. FIFO, LIFO) consistently applied. (Accuracy.)

II. Cut-off is proper. (Completeness and existence.)

III. Valuation of inventories is appropriate (e.g. write-down, or provision for write-down, is recorded when amounts otherwise exceed net realized values). (Valuation, presentation and disclosure.)

	Obj. #	Done By	Refer.
1 Verify accuracy of supporting schedules and agree to trial balance and subsidiary records.	I		
2 Test priced inventory listing. Obtain the client's final extended inventory listing and perform the following procedures: (a) Check the mathematical accuracy of the listing. (b) Agree test counts with recorded quantities. (c) Compare items on final inventory listing to physical inventory tags, sheets, or lists and vice versa. (d) Determine that unused, voided, and no-quantity tags are accounted for property.	I		

Illustration 13.6 (continued)

	Obj. #	Done By	Refer.
(e) Reconcile totals with general ledger control totals (f) Ascertain that corrections and adjustments to the final listing are proper. (g) Scan the inventory listing and investigate unusual quantities or amounts. (**Note:** The procedures enumerated below provide only general guidance for the examination of the three principal components of inventory costs and will require further modification. The cost methods and cost accumulation systems used to value inventories will vary from entity to entity. Also, depending upon the nature of the business, the components of inventory will vary. In some entities, material cost will represent a significant portion of the inventory's cost, while in others, labor costs represent the major component of cost. The audit procedures designed to test inventory costs should recognize the components of costs that are most significant and the appropriateness of the cost accumulation system.) (h) **Purchased Items (Materials)** Compare the unit cost of selected purchased items to vendor invoices. Consider the treatment of freight, duty, discounts, and so forth in arriving at unit cost. This test should encompass purchased items included in raw materials, work-in-process, and finished goods. (i) **Labor Costs** ■ Test direct and indirect labor costs included in inventory by tracing such costs to payroll registers, time cards, labor distribution reports, and so forth (This step should be co-ordinated with the work in the Payroll and Related Costs audit area.) ■ Compare direct and indirect labor application rates and individual direct and indirect labor accounts between periods and within periods and investigate reasons for unusual fluctuations. (j) **Overhead Costs** Determine the composition and allocation of factory overhead included in inventory. Evaluate the reasonableness of (a) the basis used to distribute overhead to departments, products, and so forth, and (b) expenses included in overhead. Investigate period-to-period fluctuations in overhead application rates and in individual overhead accounts. Review analysis of standard cost variance accounts to determine reasonableness of allocation to period costs and inventories. ■ If the physical inventory was not taken as of the balance sheet date, perform substantive analysis and other substantive procedures, as appropriate, during the roll-forward period.			
3 Vouch purchases of inventory to and from perpetual records.	I		
4 Vouch sales from perpetual inventory records.	I		

5 Ascertain that cut-off is proper.
■ Consider:
  – Sales/shipments to trade customers;
  – Purchases/receiving;
  – Intercompany activity;
  – Stage of production;
  – Customer returns;
  – Returns to suppliers;
  – Shipments direct to customers from suppliers.
    (Note: Care should be taken not to duplicate procedures performed in connection with the Accounts Payable and Trade Receivables cycles.)
	II		

Illustration 13.6 (continued)

	Obj. #	Done By	Refer.
■ Trace and test receiving reports noted during inventory observation to accounts payable or cash disbursements of the appropriate period. ■ For a period after inventory observation date, trace purchase invoices to and from receiving reports to test for inclusion in the proper period. Co-ordinate this procedure with similar procedures in the accounts payable area. ■ If inventory was in transit during the physical inventory, ascertain whether the cost of the items was accounted for properly. ■ Review open purchase orders and open receiving reports for possible unrecorded items. ■ Trace latest shipping reports noted during inventory observation to postings in the sales register of the appropriate period. Co-ordinate this work with work on the revenue cycle. ■ Ascertain that proper cut-off was obtained between classes of inventories (e.g. transfers of purchased items between raw materials and work-in-process and between work-in-process and finished goods).			
6 Determine the application of correct rates of exchange for amounts expressed in foreign currency.	III		
7 Review accounting principles for appropriateness and consistency. ■ For each major inventory classification, determine the basis of pricing (lower of cost or market, market, etc.), the method of determining cost (FIFO, LIFO, average, etc.), and the method of determining market (replacement, net realizable value, etc.). Verify that the basis of pricing and determination of cost of sales are in accordance with GAAP and consistent with the prior year.	III		
8 Review disclosures (e.g. valuation, liens, unusual market write downs) and perform additional procedures as necessary.	III		
9 Conclude: ■ With respect to the set of assertions and related audit objective(s), the audit procedures applied were in accordance with firm and professional requirements; subject to any differences documented in the workpapers, the recorded amounts are materially correct and the accounting principles are proper and consistently applied; the information in the working papers is sufficient to draw a conclusion as to proper disclosure.	I, II, III		

Asset Balances/Expense

Balances: Asset Balances	125,000,000
OBJECTIVES:	
I. Amounts prepaid, deferred, or capitalized are expected to provide future benefits for matching with expected future income; amounts and related amortization are calculated correctly; write-down or loss provision recorded, if appropriate. (Existence, Accuracy, Valuation, Ownership, Presentation and Disclosure.)	

	Obj. #	Done By	Refer.
1 Verify the mathematical accuracy of relevant supporting schedules and agree to trial balance and subsidiary records.	I		
2 Agree beginning balances in schedules to prior period's workpapers.	I		
3 Vouch significant additions during the period.	I		

▶

Illustration 13.6 (continued)

	Obj. #	Done By	Refer.
4 Ascertain that the amortization period is appropriate.	I		
5 Test calculations of amortization and unamortized balances.	I		
6 Test write-offs during the period.	I		
7 Review disclosures (e.g. valuation, liens, unusual write downs, amortization period) and perform additional procedures as necessary.	I		

Expense and Capitalized Balances

Balances: Expense Capitalized Balances	2,000,000 6,000,000

OBJECTIVES:

I. All capitalized leases are recorded at the appropriate amounts and operating base, rentals are appropriately charged to expense. (Completeness and accuracy).

	Obj. #	Done By	Refer.
1 Compare operating lease rent expense to prior periods and budgets.	I		
2 Consider performing substantive analysis procedures (as an alliterative or supplement to tests of details) for: ■ Operating lease expense; ■ Interest expense on obligation under capital leases; ■ Related rent and interest balance sheet accruals; and ■ Amortization expense.	I		
3 Verify classification and accounting treatment of leases accounted for as operating leases based on review and/or confirmation of lease terms.	I		
4 Recompute expense, accruals, and prepayments related to operating leases.	I		
5 Conclude: ■ With respect to the set of assertions and related audit objective(s), the audit procedures applied were in accordance with firm and professional requirements; subject to any differences documented in the workpapers, the recorded amounts are materially correct and the accounting principles are proper and consistently applied; the information in the working papers is sufficient to draw a conclusion as to proper disclosure.	I		

The rest of the audit program consists of objectives and procedures of each critical area tested. For example, the first area tested is investments. There is one audit objective and several audit procedures given for testing investments.

The remainder of this section will refer to the audit program (see Illustration 13.6). We will pick a few of the procedures and their related audit objectives to discuss in detail and explain how these procedures are carried out from your viewpoint as the audit manager.

■ Investments

For investments audit procedures there are three objectives:

I   All dividend, interest and other income is recorded; gains and losses on sales and other dispositions are recognized; premiums and discounts and related amortization are recorded. (The financial statement assertions of management are completeness and accuracy.)

II Investments exist and are owned by the entity. (The financial statement assertions of management are existence and ownership.)

III Valuation methods applied are in conformity with applicable accounting principles consistently applied, and write-down or provision for write-down is recorded when appropriate. (The financial statement assertions of management are valuation, presentation and disclosure.)

Procedure Number 3: Agree to Authorization in the Minutes of the Board of Directors

Looking at Illustration 13.6, you are responsible for procedure number 3, which is based on objective II: For major acquisitions or dispositions of investments, agree to authorization in the minutes of the board of directors.

Local this year bought controlling interest in Newco, Design Information Planning and Programming Resources (DIPPER), Financial Investment National Enterprises (FINE) and 15 percent of Zap. You check the minutes of the board of directors to see if the board of directors authorized the purchases.

Procedure Number 4: Vouch Purchases of Investments to Supporting Documentation (Based on Objectives I and II)

You need to verify the existence of the investments and the ownership. If the investment is a minority ownership (like the stock ownership of 15 percent of Zap), you need to check for the stock certificates. There are three ways this can be done. If they are bearer stock certificates in a third-party custodian vault you need to request a confirmation of custody by the custodian. If the certificates are in a Local's safe, you would just do a count and inspection of the stock certificates. It is also possible to request an up-to-date shareholder register from the company in which Local has invested.

A custodian, the stockbroker Smidt Barne, holds the stock certificates evidencing ownership of Zap. You send a confirmation request to Smidt Barne. You also send a request to Zap for a recent stockholder register.

Certification Exam Question 13.5

An auditor usually obtains evidence of stockholders' equity transactions by reviewing the entity's:

(A) Minutes of board of directors meetings.
(B) Transfer agent's records.
(C) Canceled stock certificates.
(D) Treasury stock certificate book.

Review Purchase Contracts, Due Diligence

If a company has a major, or controlling, interest (like the ownership in Newco, Design Information Planning and Programming Resources (DIPPER), and Financial Investment National Enterprises (FINE)) you need to review the purchase contracts, review the deeds of transfer, and check the bank statement to see if there was a cash outflow at the time of the purchase. If a **due diligence report** was carried out when Local was acquiring the company, you should see that, along with any other documentation that was done for the acquisition.

You ask management for purchase agreements for Newco, DIPPER and FINE. Your audit team reviews the purchase agreements for DIPPER and FINE to see that they were purchased and the time the purchase took place. Your team finds the amounts are appropriate. The team then traces the purchase amounts to the bank statement to verify the amount and payment. There is a due diligence report for the purchase of FINE, so you review that.

Oohh – Oh

You find that one purchase agreement shows Sister Information Systems (SIS), not Local, has entered into a share purchase agreement to purchase all shares of Newco for US$3,000,000 in six semi-annual payments. You find from your discussion with management that Newco is owned by SIS, which is owned by Brother, which is owned by Local. There is no documentation supporting ownership of Brother by Local. You make a note on your working papers and send out a confirmation request to Newco to verify that their shares are owned by SIS.

Review Accounting of Three Companies

Zap is carried on Local's books at cost. You think that accounting treatment is appropriate because the ownership of Zap by Local is only 15 percent, but you feel you can give no opinion on Zap unless you have their financial statements. You ask for financial statements, preferably audited.

You review the notes of the three controlled companies to see if there are any differences in accounting. This is important, because these companies will be consolidated and any differences in the financial statements must be adjusted on the consolidated statements.

Different auditors not from your own firm prepare two of the financial statements of the three controlled companies. Doiever, RA is the auditor of Financial Investment National Enterprises (FINE) and Lickanapromise, RA, audited Design Information Planning and Programming Resources (DIPPER). You know the firms' backgrounds and make a note of it in your working papers. You also send a questionnaire about the audit and a request for working papers to Doiever, RA and to Lickanapromise, RA. It is important to determine these auditors' reputations and that they took due care in the audit.

■ Expenses and Payables

Expenses and payables auditing have three audit objectives. For procedure number 3 which we will discuss, the audit objective is: All unpaid amounts due to suppliers or others for goods and services received prior to year-end are included or otherwise accrued. (Financial statement assertions are: completeness, existence, accuracy and ownership.) See Illustration 13.6.

Procedure Number 3: Review Liabilities Recorded After the End of the Period and Review Subsequent Cash Payments

You request that the client provide you with a list of all invoices for payment received after the balance sheet date. You pick invoices from the list on a random basis and see if they pertain to the period before or after the balance sheet date. If the invoice shows the payables are incurred before the balance sheet date, your team traces the invoices through the journals and ledgers to the balance sheet to see if they show up as accrued liabilities or accounts payable for that period.

You take the bank statements after the balance sheet date, pick out items randomly, and vouch them back to the corresponding payment invoice to see if they show up as accrued liabilities or accounts payable.

Procedure Number 5: Vouch Claims for Credit From Suppliers (e.g. Receivable from Suppliers) to Supporting Documents

First your team reviews any contracts Local has with their main suppliers. If Local has any credit with the suppliers you would check purchase administration to see what items were returned or what extra payments were made to create the credit. You determine whether Local's policy regarding credits has been followed. Finally, you vouch the credits back to the original documents.

Certification Exam Question 13.6

In auditing accounts payable, an auditor's procedures most likely would focus primarily on management's assertion of:

(A) Existence or occurrence.
(B) Presentation and disclosure.
(C) Completeness.
(D) Valuation or allocation.

■ Revenue and Accounts Receivables (Confirmations)

Auditing sales and receivables has seven audit objectives. Here are three of them, numbers IV, V, and VII:

IV Trade accounts receivable represent uncollected sales or other charges to bona fide customers and are owned by the entity. (Financial statement assertions are: existence and ownership.)

V   All cash collections are accurately recorded. (Financial statement assertions are: completeness and accuracy.)

VII Valuation of trade receivables is appropriate (i.e. provision is made for uncollectable amounts). (Financial statement assertions are: valuation, presentation and disclosure.)

Concept and a Company 13.3

ComROAD – From Whence Those Sales?

Concept	Revenue recognition audit.
Story	The Neuer Markt of the Frankfurt Stock exchange, Europe's version of Nasdaq-style capital raising and equity trading, closed its doors in late 2002. Deutsche Borse set up the Frankfurt-based Neuer in 1997 to latch onto the technology boom and provide a source of financing for German tech startups. In the first three years it brought nearly 350 companies public, peaking at above 8,500 in March 2000, a near-ten-fold increase. In the next two years, plagued by scandal and hurt by the global economic and technology downturn, the Neuer's main index plummeted more than 95 percent, wiping out more than $200 billion in market value. (Rombel 2002)

The most notorious scandal to hit the Neuer involved ComROAD Aktiengesellschaft, a German navigation-technology company that went public in 1999. It was delisted from the exchange in 2002 following the revelation that 97 percent of its claimed $94 million in revenue in 2001 was non-existent. Bodo Schnabel, the chief executive of ComROAD, was tried for insider trading and financial manipulation. (Ewing & Byrnes 2002)

ComROAD licensed technology it had developed to companies in the telecommunications, security and automotive markets (GTTS Partners). The GTTS Partner would pay a start-up fee of from €200,000 to €500,000 for ComROAD to deliver and install telematic service centers. The GTTS Partner then bought the car computer, StreetGuard software, StreetMachine software, and StreetPC, and marketed them through telecommunications, security, and automotive markets distribution channels. GTTS Partners generated monthly income from the use of their services and ComROAD would receive 10 percent of their gross profit. In early 2001, a reported 32 telematic service centers were installed. (ComROAD 2001)

ComROAD invented revenues from a non-existent client in Hong Kong, VT Electronics, which contributed between 63 percent and 97 percent of ComROAD's revenue between 1998 and 2000. (Smith 2002) It was a German journalist who discovered the fraud at ComROAD. She found it odd that almost all ComROAD's sales came from a company in Hong Kong. While on vacation, she went to Hong Kong at her own expense and tried to locate the company. She could find no record it existed. (Ewing 2003)

KPMG, ComROAD's external auditor, resigned in February 2002 after withdrawing its opinion on the accounts for 1998, 1999 and 2000. During those audit periods KPMG also assisted the company with its cash-flow statements. KPMG said it had helped compile the cash-flow statement, but that the cash flow statements had not been audited and were based on second-hand information from the company. (Smith 2002) |
| **Discussion Questions** | ■ What are the typical audit procedures to test for existence of revenue?
■ What additional procedures would an auditor perform if a majority of sales came from a single customer?
■ What aspect of ComROAD's business model made revenue recognition fraud relatively easy?
■ Did the existence of the Neuer reduce scrutiny of revenue? |
| **References** | ComROAD, 2001, "Shareholder Information" press release, ComROAD, August 13. |

Ewing, J. and Byrnes, N., 2002, "Continental Drift at KPMG: Already beset at home, the firm is reeling from scandal and stumbles in Germany," *Business Week*, New York: 27.

Ewing. J, 2003, "Business Investigations and Cooking the Books," presented at Investigative Journalism Summer School, London, 18–20 July. May. Issue 3784; p. 70.

Rombel, A, 2002, "Germany: Germany's symbol of dot-com excess heads for the scrap heap," *Global Finance*, New York, November, Vol. 16, Issue 11, p. 10.

Smith, P., 2002, "KPMG dragged into German fraud," **AccountancyAge.com**, April 25.

Procedure Number 9: Confirm Recorded Receivables

Audit procedure number 9, Confirm recorded receivable (amount, date, terms, interest rate, etc.), has several sub-procedures. Objectives IV and V apply.

(9a) Check Replies to Confirmations and Investigate Exceptions

First you look through the accounts receivable sub-ledgers and pick out some customers based on your professional judgment, referred to as a **scope sample**. You consider customers with very large balances or very small balances, customers that are slow in paying, and customers that buy erratically, i.e. a lot one week and nothing for several weeks.

Positive Confirmation

You give this list to Local to prepare a confirmation letter. It is a brief letter that says something to the effect, "We show that you owe us EURO ___ as of December 31, 20XX. Will you please confirm directly to our auditors that this figure is accurate?" Because you expect a reply, this is a **positive confirmation**. Then you, not the client, mail these letters, checking randomly to see if they are the customers you chose and for the amounts shown on the books.

Differences in Amounts

Some of the confirmation letters come back from customers stating that there are differences between the amount Local's books show they owe and the amount their books show they owe at December 31, 20XX. The customer may say, for instance, that they paid off the account balance on December 28. Your team checks the bank statements before and after December 31 to see when Local's customer's check was received. For most of these letters you find that the money was not received until after December 31 so Local's customer still owed the amounts on the balance sheet date and the balances are correct. In one case you find a minor, immaterial, error in recording that you nevertheless note in your working papers for later follow-up.

(9b) Send Second Requests Where Replies to Positive Requests are Not Received

Since the type of confirmation you are using as evidence is a positive confirmation, for those letters sent where you did not receive replies, you send out a second confirmation letter.

(9c) Investigate Undelivered Requests Returned by Post Office

Requests that are returned by the post office for incorrect addresses are investigated by asking the salesperson assigned to the customer the customer's correct address. Typically the salesperson has the current address if the customer has moved. For this audit there were only two returned letters and the salesperson quickly gave you the new, correct address.

However, if the problem continues, you would go to the last shipping invoice to see where the last order was sent. If you still cannot find a correct address, you may try telephoning the customer or re-sending to the same address. You may also apply alternative procedures.

(9d) Where Replies are Not Received to Positive Requests for Confirmation, Apply Alternative Audit Procedures

For those customers who did not reply to the two confirmation letters or as a result of lack of time, you may decide to perform alternative procedures. One procedure is to trace the accounts receivable to cash receipts to answer the question, "Has the money come in yet?" If money has not come in based on cash receipts, you look at the shipping records to see if the merchandise was shipped. You can also check the warehouse's order list to see if they prepared the order for pick up. Check that the transport agent signed for the item when it was picked up. Other procedures are checking customer correspondence files, customer orders and subsequent remittance advices.

Because of the lack of time, your team performs cash receipts and shipping traces on one third of the customers that had not replied by your deadline. Your team also checks customer orders. All are accurate. You also review customer correspondence files, which show no problems.

(9e) Summarize Results of Confirmation Requests and Alternative Procedures

Proper documentation always requires making extensive notes on accounts receivable audit activities.

Procedure Number 10, Based on Audit Objectives IV, V and VII: Vouch Recorded Receivables to Subsequent Cash Receipts.

You take a random sample of the accounts receivable sub-ledger customers who were not included in the scope sample who received confirmation letters and trace their payments to the cash receipts journal and the bank statement.

Procedure Number 11, Based on Audit Objective IV: Vouch Sales from Sales Register to Shipping Records

Your team takes a random sample of items from the sales register and vouches them to the shipping records. This determines if the items listed as sales were shipped. Your team finds that all amounts tested from the sales register equal amounts stated on the shipping document.

Certification Exam Question 13.7

Which of the following procedures would an auditor most likely perform for year-end accounts receivable confirmations when the auditor did **not** receive replies to second requests?

(A) Review the cash receipts journal for the month prior to the year-end.
(B) Intensify the study of internal control concerning the revenue cycle.
(C) Increase the assessed level of detection risk for the existence assertion.
(D) Inspect the shipping records documenting the merchandise sold to the debtors.

■ Inventory and Cost of Sales

Inventory audit has three audit objectives. We will discuss a procedure that concerns Objective I: Inventory is accurately compiled and priced in conformity with consistently applied acceptable methods. (The financial statement assertion related to this is accuracy.)

Procedure Number 2

Look at Illustration 13.6 for audit procedure number 2, which has several sub-procedures: Test priced inventory listing. Obtain the client's final extended inventory listing and perform the following procedures:

(2a) Check the Mathematical Accuracy of the Listing

You attend the physical count of the inventory. You read the count instructions. At the count you make sure:

■ all inventory locations get a "tag" (a description of the item and the quantity and perhaps the item number);
■ there are two people counting – one counting the items and the other verifying the count;
■ every count team has people from separate departments on the team (e.g. no two people on the same team are from accounting, no two persons on a team are from the warehouse, etc.);
■ there is a pre-numbered count list and that you get back all the copies of the list;
■ every location has a count sheet and you have all sheets returned;
■ you take a random sample of items and make sure they have been counted correctly.

(2b) Agree Test Counts with Recorded Quantities

You agree test counts with recorded quantities by taking a random sample of inventory items from the sub-ledgers and comparing the number of items recorded with the number of items counted. You then take a random sample of the inventory items counted and compare the number of items counted with the number of items recorded in the ledger.

To verify the price you take a sample of items from the inventory price list and compare that with shipping invoices. Determine if the pricing is FIFO, LIFO, etc. and verify the correct valuation formula was used.

(2c) Compare Items on Final Inventory Listing to Physical Inventory Tags, Sheets, or Lists and Vice Versa

You review the final inventory list and take a random sample of items and trace them to the inventory tags, sheets, etc.

(2d) Determine That Unused, Voided and No-quantity Tags are Accounted for Properly

If there are any unused, voided, and no-quantity tags, you must investigate. You find that there are a few of these tags, but it all checks out.

(2e) Reconcile Totals with General Ledger Control Totals

Counted inventory totals rarely agree with the totals in the inventory control account. The process of reconciliation is determining where the differences come from and making sure that the control account balance is adjusted to the counted amounts. You make adjusting entries in your working papers and suggest that Local's accounting department make these adjustments.

There is a difference between the counted inventory and the control totals. Tests of purchases and deliveries show that more raw material inventory was purchased and delivered than was counted. You are reasonably certain that the count is correct. The physical controls over inventory are fairly good; most of the valuable materials that were under lock and key in the storage room are still there. Other inventory sits on the shop floor, providing access to practically everyone. You suspect that the reduction in inventory was due to theft or wastage in the production process. You make a note for the management letter.

(2f) Ascertain that Corrections and Adjustments to the Final Listing are Proper

You need to find if obsolete inventory is written off, the lower of cost or market valuations are correct, work in process is accounted for correctly, and if there are any errors in overhead allocation to inventory.

Obsolete Inventory

To review if inventory is obsolete you talk to management and see if they have any products or product lines they plan to cancel in the future. You also take a look at the sales budget to see what products sales are based on. Based on this knowledge you choose three products that your professional judgment tells you may become obsolete: one product management is thinking of canceling and two products because sales projections include them in "misc. sales" and they are not detailed. You look at inventory turnover on a historical basis and determine that the product management intends to cancel is a very slow-moving product and should have increased allowances for obsolescence.

Cost Allocation for Inventory

You then take a look at the procedures for allocating labor and overhead to work-in-progress. First you review the written allocation procedures and then talk to the accountants who carry this allocation out. You must determine if the assumptions of inventory turnover are correct. That means finding if there are any cost, efficiency or utilization differences in actual inventory and standard costing. One machine has a maximum output of 100,000 units. The standard cost assumption is that the output hours less downtime would be 80,000 units. Machine costs are allocated to inventory based on this assumption. You discover the machine produces only 40,000 units. That utilization loss should be accounted for. You make a note on your working papers.

Based on the written allocation procedures and what management says they do, allocations seem reasonable. Furthermore, management updates standard costing every season and have recently experienced very few differences between actual and standard costs. Standard costing is periodically compared to, and revised, based on actual experience. The utilization of certain machines is less than expected, but these utilization differences have been accounted for. You recalculate month-end inventory allocations for two months to determine consistence of application of management's standard costing formula.

(2g) Scan the Inventory Listing and Investigate Unusual Quantities or Amounts

You review the inventory listing to see if there are any quantities that are in larger or smaller amounts than on previous inventory takes. There are two inventory items that did not appear on the last inventory take, one item that has increased 25 percent from last year and another item that has dropped 60 percent. The item that has dropped 60 percent is the item that the company plans to cancel and an allowance account has already been set up to write it off in the future. Management says the item that increased 25 percent is their hottest item this year and sales projections predict it will grow an additional 30 percent next year. The items that appeared this year for the first time are new items.

Procedure Number 3: Vouch Purchases of Inventory To and From Perpetual Records

It is important to test if cut-off was properly made. Did the count instructions have procedures for separating inventory into those items that were shipped and those that were stored? Did the procedures allow for goods that were going from one department to another? You review the count instructions to see if these separating procedures were requested. You supervise the count so that the inventory that needed to be separated was separated.

The warehouse department gives you their shipping and receiving log. You pick all items just before and after the balance sheet date and a random sample of other items. You see if any of these items are still in inventory based on the inventory count.

Certification Exam Question 13.8

When auditing inventories, an auditor would **least** likely verify that:

(A) The financial statement presentation of inventories is appropriate.
(B) Damaged goods and obsolete items have been properly accounted for.
(C) All inventory owned by the client is on hand at the time of the count.
(D) The client has used proper inventory pricing.

■ Asset Balances/Expense

Asset auditing has only one audit objective: amounts prepaid, deferred or capitalized are expected to provide future benefits for matching with expected future income; amounts and related amortization are calculated correctly; write-down or loss provision is recorded. The financial statement assertions are: existence, accuracy, valuation, ownership, presentation and disclosure.

Procedure Number 6: Test Write-offs During the Period

Audit procedure number 6: Test **write-offs** during the period. Write-offs are a valuation issue about the recoverability of long-lived assets. Many questions could be asked.

- Does the Board of Directors authorize assumptions by which the write-offs are calculated?
- Have these assumptions changed because of change in financial accounting standards?
- Are the projections management used to determine recoverability of assets reasonable and are they upgraded on a regular basis?
- Are the valuation methods used in the projections the same as those used in the financial statements?

■ Is the allocation of overheads properly and consistently done?

■ Is the recovery of goodwill amortized over a reasonable period of time?

■ A Look at Accounting Standards and Assumptions

You talk to management and read corporate minutes to see if the write-off assumptions are authorized. You find reference to update assumptions in an attachment to corporate minutes for the July meeting. The national accounting standards that apply to HOT require that research and development be charged to expenses in the year that it is paid. The national standards for accounting for Local allow you to capitalize and amortize certain research and development costs, but the GAAP standards used by HOT, which require charging to expenses all research and development, must be applied to Local, requiring that adjustments be made in the financial statements. You calculate these adjustments in your working papers and recommend Local book them.

You review the projections to see if they use the same assumptions on amortization as the financial statements and to see if the allocations are realistic. The same assumptions on amortization are used in both projections and financial statements. You see that raw materials are projected as increasing in cost by only 10 percent next year. You take a look at the financial statements and see that historically raw materials' cost has been increasing at close to 15 percent per year and this last year it increased by over 20 percent. You look at the basic profit drivers, sales income and service income and determine that projections are unrealistic.

Local management projects that goodwill paid for two subsidiaries three years ago should be amortized over another ten years. You note that the subsidiaries have lost money every year. You determine that the goodwill related to the purchase of these subsidiaries should be written off more quickly and you make a note in your working papers.

Certification Exam Question 13.9

In auditing intangible assets, an auditor most likely would review or recompute amortization and determine whether the amortization period is reasonable in support of management's financial statement assertion of:

(A) Valuation or allocation.
(B) Existence or occurrence.
(C) Completeness.
(D) Rights and obligations.

■ The End in Sight

You are sitting at your desk just staring out of the window. You look from the view of the motorway from your window back to the pile of work on your desk and then to the large picture on your office wall. Today is January 15. The audit is almost over. You sent copies of the audit plan and strategy memorandum to BIG's US branch just last week. Now you have to perform the last procedures and prepare the last documents – the completion memorandum and the management letter.

The sun is setting over the motorway. You have work to do before it rises again.

13.7 Completion Memorandum

Illustration 13.7 shows the outline of the Completion Memorandum.

ILLUSTRATION 13.7

Contents of Completion Memorandum

I. General
   A. Manager and partner review
   B. Schedules of Local and FS
   C. Going concern
   D. Opinion

II. Critical audit areas
   A. Inventories
   B. Accounts receivable
   C. Revenue Recognition
   D. Intercompany accounts
   E. Accounts Payable

III. Accounting issues
   A. Accounting for NEWCO
   B. Accounting for Design by Local
   C. Accounting for Finance Subsidiary (FS) by Local
   D. Accounting for ZAP
   E. Foreign Exchange
   F. Pension Plan
   G. Post-retirement benefits
   H. Group Structure

IV. Special audit problems
V. Other matters
   A. Illegal and questionable acts
   B. Management Letter
   C. Summary of Unadjusted Audit Differences
   D. Status of Statutory Financial Statements

VI. Outstanding matters
VII. Attached schedules

■ General

The first item in the completion memorandum is the statement that the engagement manager and partner have reviewed the audit papers related to critical areas. This is an essential procedure, because a review by the manager and the partner can uncover weak or incomplete areas of the audit which the audit staff might have overlooked or are not experienced enough to recognize as a problem.

The other important elements to discuss immediately are audit schedules, going concern considerations and your overall opinion on the work.[11] You state in the completion memo that schedules of Local and FINE are audited in accordance with BIG's manual. Local is a going concern, provided adjustments are made regarding recoverability of assets. Your audit opinion will be based upon the follow-up of subject matters like reorganization cost, taxation and inventory and follow-up of the outstanding matters. You are aware of the fact that your audit opinion is of much importance for the group auditor in order for him to sign off on the consolidated financial statements. The group auditor is responsible for expressing an audit opinion on whether the group financial statements give a true and fair view (or are presented fairly, in all material respects) in accordance with the applicable financial reporting framework.[12]

■ Critical Audit Areas

The areas you consider critical are discussed in the completion memorandum. Critical means with risk and significant areas.

Inventory and accounts receivable are reviewed. A full inventory take was done and the audit team was assured on test basis that the inventory was correctly counted. The team agreed the count sheets to the inventory sub-ledger and reconciled to the general ledger. The team used confirmation letters to test receivables. For outstanding invoices for non-respondents, they used alternative methods.

The collectability of the inter-company accounts was not tested for the audit for consolidation purposes. There were no confirmations by related parties. It is your opinion that further assurance from BIG's US branch is needed.

Accounts payable were tested with a confirmation process for main local suppliers. Other accounts payable procedures performed were cut-off test work, search for unrecorded liabilities on invoices and payments at year-end, test work on accrued expenses and analytical review on expenses. In your opinion accounts payable are understated by €300,000.

■ Accounting Issues

Accounting issues are broadly defined as accounting for Newco, for DIPPER by Local, for Financial Investment National Enterprises (FINE) by Local, and for ZAP. Other topics described in the completion memorandum are foreign exchange, pension plan and post-retirement benefits.

Sister Information Systems (SIS) entered into a share purchase and assignment agreement with Newco to purchase all existing shares of Newco. The purchase price of Newco was $6,000,000 payable in two semi-annual payments. Deferred payment for the purchase is $550,000. For Local accruals, neither the deferred purchase price nor related payables are recorded. Deferred payments are capitalized as an investment rather than loan or receivable from SIS.

Local's pension plan is a defined contribution plan. The enclosed statements disclose employees covered as a basis for contributions and the amount of cost recognized. The team reviewed the pension schedule.

■ Special Audit Problems: Financial Investment National Enterprises (FINE)

In this report, a special section is added on Financial Investment National Enterprises (FINE) because of audit problems with cash and cash equivalents, prepaid expenses and taxation.

Under a pledge agreement with the Oneandonly bank, HOT shall pledge to Oneandonly bank $3,530,000 in cash and securities. Forward Rate Notes (FRNs) of $1,700,000 with maturity dates over three months are classified as short-term investments. Disclosure is according to the GAAP applicable to HOT.

ILLUSTRATION 13.8

Outline of Management Letter to Local

I. Introduction

A Management Letter could have the following format:
- Finding
- Comment (e.g. short description of finding)
- Recommendation
- Management response
- Action (including timetable)

II. Material weaknesses in the design or operation of internal control

Typically BIG reports material weaknesses in writing, but an auditor may also report orally if they prepare minutes of the meetings. Material weaknesses is defined in laws and regulations as well as professional standards, therefore their condition may have regulatory implications.

For Local: No material weaknesses in internal control were found; therefore this part of the report reviews the auditor's reliance on internal controls.

III. Other reportable conditions relating to internal control

Deficiencies in internal control, although not sufficiently important to be classified as material weaknesses may be important. Management is informed of these deficiencies. For Local: No copy of a notarized deed of transfer was found for the transaction between HO, Cousin, and Local. There were no confirmations by related parties. These details are discussed. Tests of purchases and deliveries show that more raw material inventory was purchased and delivered than was counted. We are reasonably certain that the count is correct. We suspect that the reduction in inventory was due to theft or wastage in the production process. The standard cost assumption for one machine is that the output hours less downtime would be 80,000 units. Machine costs are allocated to inventory based on this assumption. The auditor discovers the machine produces only 40,000 units. That utilization loss should be expensed.

IV. Efficiency of internal control

Additional control activities can be recommended and the auditor may suggest that present control procedures are too complex. Improvements may be recommended through simplification and elimination of outdated policies and introduction of more cost effective procedures. For Local: Internal control procedures are not too complex. They are reasonable.

▶

Illustration 13.8 (continued)

V. Prior year's suggestions

The auditor may inquire about actions taken on suggestions made in BIG's previous reports to management. Matters of continuing significance may be reported. For Local had been audited in the prior year by BIG. The suggestions made at that time were carried out by Local during the past year.

VI. Accounting and auditing matters

The auditor may comment on the accounting treatment adopted for some of the items in the financial statements, on foreseeable accounting changes and the implications.

 For Local: In the auditor's opinion accounts payable are understated by €300,000. New reorganization announced after balance sheet date (a subsequent event). Based on discussion with management new reorganization was a post balance sheet event and as a consequence no opinion is given on provision. Taxation expense is €6,357,000. A provision for these taxes is not recorded in Local balance sheet because it applies to Sister company. We have no opinion on reasonableness of this change. There was no documentation on three payments to Newco of €117,000.

Local management projects that goodwill paid for two subsidiaries three years ago should be amortized over another ten years. We note that the subsidiaries have lost money every year. We determine that the goodwill related to the purchase of these subsidiaries should be written off more quickly and you make a note in your working papers.

VII. Other matters arising during the audit

The auditor may comment on changes in significant accounting policies, accounting estimates, audit adjustments, and disagreements with management.

For Local: Local considers HOT's national currency to be its functional currency in terms of values and size. Gains and losses on hedged contracts for foreign currencies are charged to current year income. The discount on contracts is amortized over the life of the contract. Gain from long-term intercompany loans translation was charged directly to stockholders equity because they hove a long term financing nature. Loans due are from Bro, Sis, and Cousin. Bro, Sis, & Cousin are subsidiaries of HO. There is no agreement with employees to pay post retirement benefits; therefore Local need not record a provision for post retirement benefits.

Different auditors than your own firm prepare two of the financial statements of the three controlled companies. Doiever, RA is the auditor of Finance Subsidiary and Lickanapromise audited Design. BIG sent a questionnaire about the audit and a request for working papers to Doiever, RA and to Lickanapromise.

Local uses forward exchange contracts. To audit them the auditor reviews to see if accounting treatment is in line with the new IAS 32 on financial instruments IAS and the national accounting standards of HO. The investments meet the conditions to be considered hedges. Several international accounting standards apply to related parties, however the Group Audit Instructions require that related parties be reported in accordance with HO national accounting standards.

VIII. Other services consistent with role as an auditor

Work that goes beyond the audit plan, such as tax or management consulting work. For Local: Local has permanent tax differences to be carried forward in accordance with a contract between Local and the national tax authorities. This requires disclosure and may lead to valuation problems. Our team consulted BIG's tax department and Local's tax advisers who review the agreement and found no problems. Our team proposed a CIS review by BIG's CIS department because of the new finance system that has just been installed at Local. It will be necessary to bring in CIS experts.

■ Other Matters

Other matters are a round-up of miscellaneous matters including illegal and questionable acts, management letter, summary of **unadjusted audit differences** and the status of statutory financial statements.

Possible occurrence of illegal and questionable acts and fraud was evaluated by making inquiries of management about occurrence of illegal and questionable acts and status of any investigations by regulatory agencies. Management is in a position to be aware of these activities and no illegal or questionable acts occurred and no investigations are underway.

Enclosed is a draft of the management letter (see outline in Illustration 13.8). The audit team noted no material weaknesses. Unadjusted audit differences are stated in Illustration 13.9. All differences were approved by the partner and discussed with management.

ILLUSTRATION 13.9

Summary of Unadjusted Audit Differences Found in the Audit

The following is a summary of unadjusted audit differences:

A. Cost assumption for machine 143 is that the output hours less downtime would be 80,000 units. Machine costs are allocated to inventory based on this assumption. The machine produces only 40,000 units. That utilization loss should be expensed.

| Dec 21 20XX | Utilization Loss | 120,000 | |
| | Inventory | | 120,000 |

To record allocation of 40,000 excessive units to inventory.

B. In the auditor's opinion accounts payable are understated by €300,000.

| Dec 21 20XX | Accounts Payable | 300,000 | |
| | Inventory | | 300,000 |

To reduce accounts payable by overstated amount.

C. Taxation expense, which has not been accrued is €6,357,000. A provision for these taxes is not recorded in Local balance sheet because it applies to Sister company

Dec 21 20XX	Taxation Expense – Local	5,000,000	
	Taxation Expense – Sister	1,357,000	
	Taxes Payable – Local		5,000,000
	Taxes Payable – Sister		1,357,000

To record tax expense for 20XX.

D. There was no documentation on three payments to Newco of €117,000 each.

| Dec 21 20XX | Interest Expense | 351,000 | |
| | Interest Payable | | 351,000 |

To record payments to Newco

A copy of the financial statements is enclosed. The issue of statement is awaiting classification of ownership of Newco and group structure.

■ Outstanding Matters

There may be some matters that are still pending because of time limitations or other complications during an audit. The Completion Memorandum lists the following items necessary before the audit can be considered closed.

1 Receipt of forecast to ensure the appropriateness of book value of intangible assets.
2 Receipt of confirmations that accounts receivables are collectable.
3 Receipt of certain bank confirmations.
4 Receipt of documents supporting ownership of subsidiaries.
5 Receipt of financial statement of ZAP.
6 Receipt of management representation letter.
7 Receipt of lawyers' letters.
8 Receipt of confirmation by HOT firm that HOT has pledged $12,000,000 under agreement with Oneandonly bank.

■ Attached Schedules

Attached to the memorandum are the following schedules:

1 Summary of audit difference. (See Illustration 13.9)
2 Elimination entries.
3 HOT balance sheet, income statement, other income (expense) schedule.
4 Financial statements in local currency (EURO) and HOT currency (USD).
5 Working papers.
6 Tax papers.

The completion memorandum is concluded with the signature of the auditor, the date and place of the signature.

The last sentence of the completion memorandum is finished. You put it in the out-basket for review by the partner. You look at the pile of papers on your desk, then at the view from the window. You see only a few sets of headlights going down the motorway this time of night. You drain the last drops of your cold coffee and put on your coat. It will be nice to get home.

13.8 Summary

The documents typically required in an audit of a subsidiary are a general audit plan with specific instructions and a general audit program guide from the primary auditor. Based on these documents and additional inquiry, the auditor will put together an audit planning memorandum, an audit program and a completion memorandum.

The parent company's auditors issue group audit instructions to participating offices. They may start with two opening sections – one with general information and one with specific procedures.

The strategy part of the audit planning memorandum may incorporate most of the important ideas of the audit. The whole audit team puts it together. The plan part of the audit planning memorandum will follow the concepts addressed in the strategy part and is a general outline of the auditors' approach to the audit.

The audit program (audit plan) serves as a set of instructions to assistants involved in the audit and as a means to control proper execution of the work. It is commonly prepared based on the auditing firm's audit program software.

The report on your auditing findings, the completion memorandum, describes critical and significant audit areas, accounting issues, and any matters that need to be highlighted. The completion memorandum, including the audit opinion, is the final document in the audit.

13.9 Answers to Certification Exam Questions

13.1 (D) Why does an auditor obtain knowledge about a new client's business and its industry? Choice (D) is proper because obtaining a level of knowledge of the client's business and industry enables the auditor to obtain an understanding of the events, transactions, and practices that may have a significant effect on the financial statements. Choice (A) is mistaken because although providing constructive suggestions in the management letter is important, but secondary, and reason for obtaining knowledge about a client's business and industry. Choice (B) is wrong because even though an auditor must keep an attitude of professional skepticism concerning the client, this attitude is a result of obtaining knowledge about the client's business and industry. Choice (C) is off the mark because information on the industry and business of a client will provide insufficient information in determining material misstatement in the financial statements.

13.2 (C) The requirement is to find what is unique to the audit work of certified accountants when compared to work of other professions. Answer (C) is exact because in no other profession is independence so important for the performance of professional work. Answers (A), (B), and (D) are false because, although it is true these characteristics are important for certified accountants, due professional care, competence, and a complex body of knowledge may be required for other professions.

13.3 (D) We need to recognize the element of the audit planning process most likely to be agreed between the client and auditor before implementation of the audit strategy. Choice (D) is right because the auditor should observe the counting of inventory and that requires coordination between auditor procedures and client count. Choice (A) is erroneous because it is not up to the audit client to determine what evidence is to be gathered. Choices (B) and (C) are mistaken because these procedures will be undertaken after implementation of the audit strategy begins.

13.4 (C) What is the best reason for an auditor to design a written audit program? Choice (C) is right on because an audit program gives in detail the audit procedures that will be necessary to accomplish the objectives of the audit. Choice (A) is erroneous because audit programs cover more than just selecting material transactions. Answer (B) is flawed because an audit plan will include numerous substantive tests that are performed prior to the balance sheet date. Answer (D) is mistaken because not all account balances are tested. For example, immaterial accounts often are not tested. Furthermore, account balances are not directly tested through tests of controls.

13.5 (A) What is a typical procedure to determine evidence of stockholders' equity transactions? Answer (A) is acceptable because the board of directors will, in general, authorize changes in stockholders' equity. Answer (B) is not always the case because small clients do not typically use a transfer agent. Besides, a transfer agent's job ordinarily has to do with transfers of outstanding stock. Answer (C) is erroneous because canceled stock certificates apply only for small clients. Answer (D) is invalid because "treasury stock certificate book" is a record that does not ordinarily exist.

13.6 (C) The requirement is to give the financial statement assertion that is most likely to be the focus of an auditor in his procedures when considering accounts payable. The simple net profit equation is revenue minus expense equals profit. Expenses are created when accounts payable are booked. If management wants to keep profit high they can either report higher sales or lower expense. Choice (C), completeness, is the one assertion that applies most to accounts payable because if accounts payable owed are omitted, net income is too high (i.e. overstated). Choice (A) is false because the existence assertion deals with whether recorded accounts payable are over-stated, understating net income, something management is unlikely to let happen. Choice (B) is mistaken because payables have few onerous disclosures. Choice (D) is not the case because there is usually no valuation questions regarding payables – they are valued at the cost of the related acquisition unless there is a chance of non-payment or reduced payments. See ISA 500 for more information on management's financial statement assertions.

13.7 (D) What is the most likely alternate procedure auditors will perform when replies have not been received on accounts receivable confirmation requests? Choice (D) is the best answer because inspection of shipping records provides evidence that the merchandise was in fact shipped to the customer. Choice (A) is incorrect because an auditor may look at the cash receipts journal after year end to see if the customer has paid the receivable, but reviews of the balance **prior** to year-end will not provide evidence on accounts unpaid as of year-end. Choice (B) is flawed because the lack of a reply to the confirmation can mean a lot of things, many beyond the control of the auditor, so it does not make sense to automatically assume that procedures should be modified. Choice (C) is mistaken because the lack of a reply does not necessarily mean the account is misstated.

13.8 (C) You need to find the answer which is **not** one of the auditor's objectives for inventory procedures. Answer (C) is right because verifying that all inventory owned by the client is on hand at the time of the count is not an objective. There are several reasons that not all the inventory owned would be at the premises. For example, some inventory should also be included in inventory that is out on consignment. Some inventory is in transit at year-end, and if the terms are FOB manufacturer, it should be included in inventory. Answer (A) is wrong because inventory has a lot of presentation and disclosure requirements to which the auditor must pay attention. Answers (B) and (D) are incorrect because proper accounting requires inventory be properly valued (valuation assertion) and damaged and obsolete items and proper inventory pricing pertain to the valuation.

13.9 (A) Do you know which financial statement assertion is most directly related to the proce-dure of reviewing or recomputing amortization of intangible assets? Answer (A) is correct because the amortization of intangible assets is based on the valuation assertion. The other assertions are less directly related. Answer (B) is mistaken because the existence or occurrence assertion answers the question of whether assets exist at a given date and whether transactions have occurred during a given period. Answer (C) is flawed because the completeness assertion is based on whether all transactions and accounts that should be presented in the financial statements are presented. Answer (D) is incorrect because the rights and obligations assertion deals with whether assets are the rights of the entity and liabilities are the obligations of the entity at a given date. Remember ISA 500 gives you the financial statement assertions.

13.10 Notes

1 The authors are grateful for the assistance of Herman Brons and Wendy Kotterer.

2 When an auditor, acting as group auditor, decides to use the work of a related auditor or other auditor, in the audit of group financial statements, the group auditor should communicate to the related auditors and other auditors to provide them with the group auditor's requirements. This communication is ordinarily in the form of Group Audit Instructions. More information on the requirements of the group auditor can be found in the Exposure Draft ISA 600 (Revised), "The Work of Related Auditors and Other Auditors in the Audit of Group Financial Statements" and the Proposed International Auditing Practice Statement: The Audit of Group Financial Statements.

3 IAASB, 2003, Proposed Revised International Standard on Auditing 600(Revised) (ISA 600), "The Work of Related Auditors and Other Auditors in the Audit of Group Financial Statements," para. 22, International Federation of Accountants, New York, December.

4 Ibid. Paragraphs 53–68.

5 Applicable independence requirements can be the IFAC *Code of Ethics for Professional Accountants*, or the Sarbanes-Oxley Act 2002.

6 **User control procedures** in audit testing of documentation represent manual checks of the completeness and accuracy of computer output against source documents and other input.

7 Although updates of IAS 39 were still being discussed by the IASC at their March 2004 meeting, the last update was IASB, 2003, *International Financial Reporting Standard IAS 39*, "Financial Instruments: Recognition and Measurement" International Accounting Standards Committee, London, December 19.

8 **Vouching** is the use of documentation to support recorded transactions or amounts. It is an audit process whereby the auditor starts with an account balance and goes backwards through the accounting system to the source document.

9 **Cutoff** – transactions and events have been recorded in the correct accounting period.

10 **Tracing** is an audit procedure whereby the auditor selects sample items from basic source documents and proceeds forward through the accounting system to find the final recording of the transaction (e.g. in the ledger).

11 The overall opinion on work performed relating to full scope audit, limited review or desk review will mostly be based on a reporting format provided by the group auditor. See also Exposure Draft ISA 600 (Revised), *The Work of Related Auditors and Other Auditors in the Audit of Group Financial Statements*, para. 22.

12 IAASB, 2003, Proposed Revised International Standard on Auditing 600 (ISA 600), "The Work of Related Auditors and Other Auditors in the Audit of Group Financial Statements.", para. 2, International Federation of Accountants, New York, December.

13.11 Questions, Exercises and Cases

QUESTIONS

13.2 You Are The Audit Manager

13.1 Name the sections of the "Group Audit Instructions" and describe each.

13.2 What kind of differences are there between the accounting for the main company (HO) and your local client (Local)?

13.3 What information are you required to provide about your client, Local, regarding their legal situation, related parties and industry?

13.4 What concerns are "Critical and Significant Audit Concerns" for the Local audit? Why are they significant?

13.3 The Audit Planning Memorandum – Strategy Part

13.5 What is the purpose of the strategy memorandum? What are the elements contained in this memorandum?

13.4 The Audit Planning Memorandum – Plan Part

13.6 What is the Plan Part of the Audit Planning Memorandum? What are the contents of the Plan Part?

13.5 Audit Program

13.7 What are the objectives for Local's investments audit procedures? Discuss the procedures used to test one of these objectives.

13.8 What may an auditor do if positive confirmations were not replied to on the second mailing?

13.9 When you as an auditor attend a physical count of inventory what things should you look for?

13.10 List the procedures for testing priced inventory listings.

13.11 What are the objectives when auditing an asset?

13.6 Completion Memorandum

13.12 What are the different areas in a completion memorandum? Briefly discuss each area.

13.13 What schedules do you attach to a completion memorandum?

PROBLEMS AND EXERCISES

13.3 The Audit Planning Memorandum – Strategy Part

13.14 **Audit Planning Memorandum-Strategy Part**. The following are three situations in which you are required to develop an audit strategy and prepare a partial strategy memorandum:

1 You are on the first year audit of Jaani, a medium-sized company of Parnu, Estonia, that is considering selling its business because of severe under-financing. A review of the acquisitions and payments indicates that controls over cash disbursements are excellent, but controls over acquisitions are not effective. The Jaani lacks shipping and receiving reports. They have no policy as to when to record acquisitions. When you review the general ledger, you observe that there are many large adjusting entries to correct accounts payable.

2   You are doing the audit of Lacplesis Bank, a small loan company in Latvia. It has extensive receivables from customers. Collections are an ongoing problem because many of the customers have severe financial problems resulting from adjustments to a capitalist economy. Because of these adverse economic conditions, loans receivable have significantly increased and collections are less than historical levels. Controls over granting loans, collections, and loans outstanding are considered effective. There is extensive follow-up weekly of all outstanding loans. In previous years, Lacplesis has had relatively few adjusting entries.

3   Cazadas Cooperative Vineyards with headquarters in Debreczen, Hungary, has inventory at approximately 40 locations in a two country region. The inventory can only be observed by traveling to the field locations by automobile. The internal controls over acquisitions, cash disbursements, and inventory perpetual records are considered effective. This is the sixth year that you have done the audit, and audit results in past years have always been excellent. The client is in excellent financial condition and is privately held.

Required:
For each of the three situations above:
A. Write a risk analysis of the main risks for the Strategy Memorandum.
B. Identify difficult questions you would address in the Strategy Memorandum.
C. List the techniques for gathering evidence (inquiry of client personnel, observation, examination of documents, reperformance, confirmation, analytical procedures and physical examination) you would use in the audit.

13.4 The Audit Planning Memorandum – Plan Part

13.15 Audit Planning Memorandum – Plan Part. Wigila Swaiaty, a for-profit cooperative, was organized in 1954 in Gdansk, Poland, to produce and distribute local crafts such as natural material Christmas decorations (82 percent of sales), wood work, folk art, sculpture and embroidery. Their sales by region are approximately 20 percent Poland, 45 percent Europe, 25 percent North America, and 10 percent the rest of the world. They sell directly to retailers in Poland and have a sales force of ten people. Outside of Poland they sell primarily to wholesalers of Christmas decorations. Their sales strategy is to increase sales of their non-Christmas decoration products overall and to increase sales to North America.

Wigila has one subsidiary company, Wigila BV (started in 1993) in Amsterdam, that is responsible for European sales. Wigila has a board of directors and an audit committee made up of outside directors. Both Gdansk and Amsterdam offices have the latest network hardware and software and Gdansk has a website. The computers run the most up-to-date versions of word processor, communications, accounting and financial software.

Wigila Swaiaty's Gadansk office has one employee who is responsible for legal matters and they use the services of a local solicitor firm Klodka & Waldemar. The company has six directors: Tom Miller, chairman and chief executive; Edward Miller, vice chairman; Doriusz Kaxzmarek and Marek Miller are directors who also work for Wigila as vice-president operations and chief executive officer of Wigila BV, respectively. Outside directors are Paul Pollorz and Gregorz Locoski.

The market for their main product line, natural material Christmas decorations, is worldwide. Wigila's main competitor in Poland is Gwiazdka who has 60 percent of the market versus Wigila's 30 percent. Wigila market share and main competitors in their other sales area are: 11 percent of North America, main competitor is You'lltyde with 26 percent; 26 percent of Europe, main competitor is Tauschung Tadesco with 14 percent; and the rest of the world share is less than 1 percent.

The industry has seen a rapid growth in computer usage to manage distribution and operations, but the manufacturing tools and techniques are hundreds of years old. Products are made by hand by individual craftsmen and collected by distributors such as Wigila. Unlike most distributors, Wigila is a cooperative. It is operated for profit and owned 50 percent by the craftsmen who provide the products. There is pressure on the management to increase sales and the compensation of all executives is tied to increases in sales.

The craftsmen-owners of Wigila receive their wages based on a per-piece basis. For artfully made "spheres" (the size of large apples and individually decorated) they may receive 10 percent of the wholesale price the company charges customers. For sculpture, on the other hand, they may receive up to 40 percent of the wholesale price. The craftsmen-owners wish the company to increase sales of non-Christmas decoration products as they have a higher profit margin for the craftsmen.

The auditor is Wieslaw Borowski, Auditor. The firm determines that one partner, one audit manager, three audit supervisors, and 10 audit staff will require 1,000 hours audit time at Polish Zloty (zloty) 600 for partner hours, 400 for audit manager, 250 for supervisors, and 150 for audit staff. Staff telephone and email numbers are provided in the Audit Plan.

A schedule of percentage of Revenues and Total Assets for Wigila Swaiaty and the subsidiary Wigila BV and the percentage of proposed audit scope is below.

Company	Revenues Total	Audit	Total Assets Total	Audit	Accts. Rec. Total	Audit	Scope of Audit
Wigila S.	55	55	85	100	45	70	Full scope
Wigila BV	45	45	15	0	55	30	Limited

Required:
A. As part of the General Audit Plan, describe five audit procedures that you believe Wieslaw Borowski can perform in the accounts receivable and sales audit areas.
B. Describe what you believe will be the critical and significant auditing concerns in Borowski's General Audit Plan.

13.5 Audit Program

13.16 **Audit Program**. The following are eight audit procedures taken from an audit program:
1 Review board of directors' minutes to verify approval of equipment purchases.
2 Review sales, cash receipts and sales returns cutoffs.
3 Examine the initials on vendors' invoices that indicate internal verification of pricing, extensions (price X units), and footing by a clerk.
4 Reconcile marketable security summary schedules to general ledger.
5 Compare the balance in payroll tax expense with previous years taking into consideration any changes in payroll tax rates.
6 Count a sample of inventory and check against inventory sheets.
7 Account for a sequence of checks in the cash disbursements journal to determine whether any have been omitted.
8 Confirm accounts payable balances in writing with a sample of vendors.

Required:
A. For each of the above audit procedures, give the audit area (accounts receivable, cash, etc.), and an example of an audit objective and a financial statement assertion.
B. For each audit procedure, list a technique for gathering evidence used (inquiry of client personnel, inspection, observation, examination of documents, reperformance, confirmation, analytical procedures and physical examination.)

13.17 Audit Program. A normal procedure in the audit of a corporate client consists of a careful reading of the minutes of meetings of the board of directors. One of the auditors' objectives in reading the minutes is to determine whether the transactions recorded in the accounting records are in agreement with actions approved by the board of directors.

Required:
A. What is the reasoning underlying this objective of reconciling transactions in the corporate accounting records with actions approved by the board of directors? Describe fully how the auditors achieve the stated objective after they have read the minutes of directors' meetings.
B. Discuss the effect that each of the following situations would have on specific audit steps in the auditors' examination and on the auditors' opinion:
1 The minutes book does not show approval for the sale of an important manufacturing division that was consummated during the year.
2 Some details of a contract negotiated during the year with the labor union are different from the outline of the contract included in the minutes of the board of directors.
3 The minutes of a meeting of directors held after the balance sheet date have not yet been written, but the corporation's secretary shows the auditors notes from which the minutes are to be prepared when the secretary has time.
C. What corporate actions should be approved by stockholders and recorded in the minutes of the stockholders' meetings?

13.18 Audit of Investments. In connection with an examination of the financial statements of Moravia of Prague (Praha), the Czech Republic, Libusa Stadic, Auditor, is considering the necessity of inspecting marketable securities on the balance sheet date, May 31, or at some other date. The marketable securities held by Moravia include negotiable bearer bonds, which are kept in a safe in the treasurer's office, and miscellaneous stocks and bonds kept in a safe-deposit box at Bohemia Bank. Both the negotiable bearer bonds and the miscellaneous stocks and bonds are material to proper presentation of Moravia's financial position.

Required:
A. What are the factors that Stadic should consider in determining the necessity for inspecting these securities on May 31, as opposed to other dates?
B. Assume that Stadic plans to send a member of her staff to Moravia's offices and Bohemia Bank on May 31 to make the security inspection. What instructions should she give to this staff member as to the conduct of the inspection and the evidence to be included in the audit working papers? (Note: Do not discuss the valuation of securities, the revenue from securities, or the examination of information contained in the accounting records of the company.)
C. Assume that Stadic finds it impracticable to send a member of her staff to Moravia's offices and Bohemia Bank on May 31. What alternative procedures may she employ to assure herself that the company had physical possession of its marketable securities on May 31, if the securities are inspected on (1) May 28? (2) June 5?

13.19 **Audit of Expense and Payables for Defalcations.** On January 11 at the beginning of Elijah Domacin's annual audit of the financial statements for the year ended December 31 of Zedruga Manufacturing Company of Skoplje, Serbia, the Company president confides in Domacin that an employee is living on a scale in excess of that which his salary would support.

The employee has been a buyer in the purchasing department for six years and has charge of purchasing all general materials and supplies. He is authorized to sign purchase orders for amounts up to Yugoslavian New Dinar (New Dinar) 1,000. Purchase orders in excess of New Dinar 1,000 require the countersignature of the general purchasing agent.

The president understands that the usual examination of financial statements is not designed, and cannot be relied upon, to disclose fraud or conflicts of interest, although their discovery may result. The president authorizes Domacin, however, to expand his regular audit procedures and to apply additional audit procedures to determine whether there is any evidence that the buyer has been misappropriating company funds or has been engaged in activities that involve a conflict of interests.

Required:
A. List the audit procedures that Domacin would apply to Zedruga's records and documents in an attempt to:
   1 Discover evidence within the purchasing department of defalcations being committed by the buyer. Give the purpose of each audit procedure.
   2 Provide leads as to possible collusion between the buyer and suppliers. Give the purpose of each audit procedure.
B. Assume that Domacin's investigation disclosed that some suppliers have been charging the Zedruga Manufacturing Company in excess of their usual prices and apparently have been making "kick-backs" to the buyer. The excess charges are material in amount. What effect, if any, would the defalcation have upon: 1 the financial statements that were prepared before the defalcation was uncovered; and 2 Domacin's auditor's report? Discuss.

13.20 **Confirmation of Accounts Receivables.** You have been assigned to the first audit of the accounts of the Super Blinchiki Company of St. Petersburg, Russia, for the year ending March 31, 20X8. The accounts receivable were confirmed December 31, 20X7, and at that date the receivables consisted of approximately 200 accounts with balances totaling Russian Roubles (Rouble) 956,750. Seventy-five of these accounts, with balances totaling Rouble 650,725, were selected for confirmation. All but 20 of the confirmation requests have been returned; 30 were signed without comments, 14 had minor differences that have been cleared satisfactorily, while 11 confirmations had the following comments:
   1 "We are sorry but we cannot answer your request for confirmation of our account as we use an accounts payable voucher system."
   2 "The balance of Roubles 1,050 was paid on December 23, 20X7."
   3 "The above balance of Roubles 7,750 was paid on January 5, 20X8."
   4 "The above balance has been paid."
   5 "We do not owe you anything at December 31, 20X7, as the goods, represented by your invoice dated December 30, 20X7, number 25,050, in the amount of Roubles 11,550, were received on January 5, 20X8, on FOB destination terms."
   6 "An advance payment of Roubles 2,500 made by us in November 20X7 should cover the two invoices totaling Roubles 1,350 shown on the statement attached."
   7 "We never received these goods."

8 "We are contesting the propriety of this Roubles 12,525 charge. We think the charge is excessive."

9 "Amount okay. As the goods have been shipped to us on consignment we will remit payment upon selling the goods."

10 "The Roubles 10,000 representing a deposit under a lease, will be applied against the rent due to us during 20X9, the last year of the lease."

11 "Your credit dated December 5, 20X7, in the amount of Roubles 440 cancels the above balance."

Required:

What steps would you take to clear satisfactorily each of the above 11 comments?

[Adapted and reprinted with permission from AICPA. Copyright © 2000 & 1985 by American Institute of Charterred Accountants.]

13.21 **Audit of Inventory**. Late in December, the Registeraccountant (RA) firm of Radbod & van Weg accepted an audit engagement at Brandewyn Juwelen, BV, a company that deals largely in diamonds. Brandewyn Juwelen has retail jewelry stores in several Netherlands cities and a diamond wholesale store in Amsterdam. The wholesale store also sets the diamonds in rings and other quality jewelry.

The retail stores place orders for diamond jewelry with the wholesale store in Amsterdam. A buyer employed by the wholesale store purchases diamonds in the Amsterdam diamond market; the wholesale store then fills orders from the retail stores and from independent customers and maintains a substantial inventory of diamonds. The corporation values its inventory by the specific identification cost method.

Required:

Assume that at the inventory date you are satisfied that Brandewyn Juwelen has no items left by customers for repair or sale on consignment and that no inventory owned by the corporation is in the possession of outsiders.

A. Discuss the problems the auditors should anticipate in planning for the observation of the physical inventory on this engagement because of the:

1 different locations of inventories;

2 nature of the inventory.

B. Assume that a shipment of diamond rings was in transit by corporation messenger from the wholesale store to a retail store on the inventory date. What additional audit steps would you take to satisfy yourself as to the gems that were in transit from the wholesale store on the inventory date?

[Adapted and reprinted with permission from AICPA. Copyright © 2000 & 1985 by American Institute of Charterred Accountants.]

13.22 **Audit of Assets**. Yarilo Company of Vinnista, Ukraine, owns and operates gas wells which are accounted for in three classifications:

1 *Producing* – for wells currently producing; there are engineers' estimates of the gas reserves. Each well is depleted on the basis of the gas produced as compared to its total reserve.

2 *Suspended* – although engineers' estimates indicate that these wells have considerable reserves of gas; they will not be operated until such time as additional production is required.

3 *Abandoned* – these wells either never produced commercially useful quantities of gas or the gas reserves have been used up.

The properties on which the wells are located are leased from the Russian and Ukraine governments at a specified annual rental, and payments are made until the well is abandoned. In addition, royalty payments are made at a specified rate, based on every 1,000 cubic feet of gas extracted from each well. The wells are recorded on the books at cost (including engineers' fees, materials and equipment purchased, labor, etc.), depleted only while producing, and written off when abandoned.

Required:

What procedures should the auditor follow to substantiate that all wells owned by the company are properly recorded, classified, and valued? What supporting evidence would the auditor examine in this connection?

[CICA adapted]

13.6 Completion Memorandum

13.23 Completion Memorandum. In the course of his initial examination of the financial statements of Yenitscheri Company, Omar Pishdadian, Sworn Financial Advisor (SFA), the auditor, obtained an understanding of the internal control structure relating to the purchasing, receiving, trade accounts payable, and cash disbursement cycles and has decided not to proceed with any tests of controls. Based upon analytical procedures, Pishdadian believes that the trade accounts payable balance on the balance sheet as of December 31, 20X2, may be understated.

Pishdadian requested and obtained a client-prepared trade accounts payable schedule listing the total amount owed to each vendor. Pishdadian ascertains that of the substantial amount of accounts payable outstanding at the close of the period, approximately 75 percent is owed to six creditors. Pishdadian has requested that he be permitted to confirm the balances owing to these six creditors by communicating with the creditors, but the president of the company is unwilling to approve Pishdadian's request on the grounds that correspondence in regard to the balances – all of which contain some overdue items – might give rise to demands on the part of the creditors for immediate payment of the overdue items and thereby embarrass Yenitscheri Company.

Accounts receivable represent a significant portion of the total assets of the company. At the beginning of the audit Pishdadian mailed out positive confirmations on a test basis. Included in his tests were confirmations requested from several Turkish government departments; the confirmation request for this one department was returned, along with the following notation: "The Pishdadian confirmation letter is returned herewith without action because the type of information requested cannot be compiled by the office with sufficient accuracy to be of any value."

Yenitscheri Company does not conduct a complete annual physical count of purchased parts and supplies in its principal warehouse, but uses statistical sampling instead to estimate the year-end inventory. Yenitscheri Company maintains a perpetual inventory record of parts and supplies and believes that statistical sampling is highly effective in determining inventory values and is sufficiently reliable to make a physical count of each item of inventory unnecessary.

Required:

When Pishdadian, SFA, writes up the Completion Memo:

A. What should he discuss in the "Critical audit areas" and "Significant Audit Areas" segments of the Memorandum?

B. You are Pishdadian's senior auditor. He is running short of time and wants you to write the "Accounting Issues" segment. Write the segment.

CASES

13.24 Audit of Investments. For several years you have made the annual audit for Sichou Jinhuangse Company of Nanjing, China. This company is not a dealer in securities. A list of presently held securities is kept, but an investment register is not maintained. During the audit, the following worksheet was prepared:

Columns 1–7

Description of security (name, maturity, rate, etc.)	Balance at beginning of year	Face value or number of shares	Cost or book value Additions during period	Date	Face value or number of shares	Cost Deductions during period

Columns 8–14

Date	Face value or number of shares	Cost or book value	Proceeds on disposals (net)	Profit or (loss) on disposals Balance at end of year	Face value or number of shares	Cost or book value

Columns 15–20

Market value Interest and dividends	Accrued at beginning of year	Purchased	Earned	Received	Accrued at end of year	

Required:
Draw a line down the middle of a lined sheet of paper.
A. On the left of the line, state the specific source(s) of information to be entered in each column and, where required, how the data of previous columns are combined.
B. On the right of the line, state the principal way(s) that such information would be tested.
[Adapted and reprinted with permission from AICPA. Copyright © 2000 & 1985 by American Institute of Certified Accountants.]

Chapter 14

CORPORATE GOVERNANCE

14.1 Learning Objectives

After studying this chapter, you should be able to:

1. Understand the concept of corporate governance.

2. Explain recent causes for corporate governance being in the spotlight.

3. Distinguish between different corporate governance structures.

4. Give examples of corporate governance codes.

5. Identify major elements of corporate governance.

6. Evaluate the role of the auditor in corporate governance.

7. List current developments in corporate governance.

14.2 Introduction

This chapter will discuss the concept of **corporate governance** and its different components. We also will sketch differences in corporate governance structures that exist all over the world. The distinction between a market-oriented versus network-oriented structure is central. The importance of the auditor in corporate governance will be described as well as some recent developments in corporate governance.

Topics covered in this chapter are: the nature of corporate governance, basis of current corporate governance discussions, corporate governance structures, corporate governance committees and reports (the Sarbanes-Oxley Act, European Union Laws Best Practice), and best practice (managing best practice, board responsibility, internal control, transparency). We will also discuss corporate governance and the role of the auditor including the audit profession and the short-term and medium-term EU priorities model.

14.3 The Nature of Corporate Governance

Corporate governance has been defined in many different ways by many different authors in many different countries. All aspects of corporate governance are subject to discussion in many parts of society, in both the private and the public sector.

We can liken "governance" to a game of darts.[1] The **Board of Directors** sets the mission, vision, objectives and strategy of the entity. (These are like the target in the game of darts.) Governance deals with **managing** as a key responsibility of the Board. (Managing is the aim, co-ordination and skill required to hit the bull's eye of the target.) It is also the Board's responsibility to design and monitor **controls** that reasonably assure that objectives are met (the darts player should ensure a good night's rest, make sure that windows are closed and that the audience is quiet). The third element of Governance is **supervision**. Independent supervision of management performance and remuneration is especially crucial (the umpire should supervise the darts game as cheating is not permitted). We all know that conflicts of interests between management and **stakeholders** do exist on a day-to-day basis, and can result in bankruptcies or major frauds. Governance also includes **transparency** to all stakeholders that can be recognized (principles and rules of the darts match should be disclosed). *INDEPENT SUPERVISORS*

Concept and a Company 14.1

Li & Fung Third Generation Corporate Governance

Concept	"The techniques are modern, but the culture is still Confucian," Victor Fung, Chairman. (*Economist* 2000)
Story	A 2001 study of 495 companies by CLSA Emerging Markets found a strong link between good corporate governance, earnings and stock values. According to the study, the

Li & Fung Third Generation Corporate Governance (continued)

correlation between good corporate governance and share performance for the largest companies is "a near perfect fit." In that study, Li & Fung were rated as one of the top companies. (Day 2001) A corporate governance poll conducted by *Euromoney* magazine rated Li & Fung fourth highest globally in corporate governance, and second highest in Asia. (*Euromoney* 2003)

Li & Fung, a family owned company founded in 1906 during the Ching Dynasty, acted as a trader – basically a broker, charging a fee to put buyers and sellers together. When they decided to make a public stock offering on the Hong Kong Stock Exchange in 1973, they had already begun changing their governance. William Fung, managing director of the company put it this way, "We typify the transition from a first-generation entrepreneurial firm to a company that is being made more professional to compete with Japan and the multinationals." (Kraar 1994)

In 1989, to pay relatives who wanted to cash out, William Fung and his elder brother Victor, who is chairman of both the family company and Prudential Asia, arranged an LBO with bank financing. After cleaning up the privatized company and selling off fringe businesses like chartered boats, the brothers took it public again in 1992. (Kraar 1994)

At Li & Fung, the Harvard-trained management has replaced family members in the company with professional managers, imported performance-related pay and instituted an open, western-style management regime. It accepts the need for stakeholding and transparent governance. (Caulkin 1996) Victor Fung explains, "You can run a large empire with very few people making few decisions. Now you need a large number of small decisions." (*Economist* 2000)

Li & Fung represent good corporate governance in several ways: leadership in outsourcing to customize customer products, leadership in employee management and fiscal controls, and encouraging best practices among its suppliers.

Distributed Manufacturing Around the Customer's Needs

Li & Fung performs the high-value-added tasks such as design and quality control in Hong Kong, and outsources the lower-value-added tasks to the best possible locations around the world. For example, to produce a garment the company might buy yarn from Korea have it woven and dyed in Taiwan, then shipped to Thailand for final assembly, using zippers from Japan. For every order, the goal is to customize the product to meet the customer's specific needs. They call this supply chain outsourcing "distributed manufacturing." (Magretta 1998)

Li & Fung is uniquely organized around the customer. They are divided into divisions and each division is structured around an individual customer or a group of customers with similar needs. Consider, for example, the Gymboree division where every one is focused solely on meeting Gymboree's needs. On every desk is a computer with direct software links to Gymboree. The staff is organized into specialized teams in such areas as technical support, merchandising, raw material purchasing, quality assurance, and shipping. (Magretta 1998)

People Management and Fiscal Controls

For the creative parts of the business, Li & Fung gives people considerable operating freedom. Substantial financial incentives tied directly to the unit's bottom line motivate the division leaders. There's no cap on bonuses. On the other hand, when it comes to financial controls and operating procedures, Li & Fung does not want creativity or entrepreneurial behavior. In these areas, Li & Fung centralizes and manages tightly. They have a fully computerized operating system for executing and tracking orders, and everyone in the company uses the system. (Magretta 1998)

Since 1993, Li & Fung have changed from a Hong Kong-based Chinese company that was 99.5 percent Chinese into a truly regional multinational with a workforce from at least 30 countries. Victor Fung says, "We are proud of our cultural heritage. But we don't want it to be an impediment to growth, and we want to make people comfortable that culturally we have a very open architecture." (Magretta 1998)

Best Practices at Suppliers

Wherever Li & Fung operates, they follow local rules and best practices. They make sure their suppliers are doing the right thing when it comes to issues such as child labor, environmental protection, and country-of-origin regulations. If they find factories that don't comply, they will not work with them. This generally does not happened because of the company's long relationship with the suppliers. (Magretta 1998)

Li & Fung, in the course of monitoring its supplier network, constantly compares the performance of hundreds of different companies. It then shares the information with all of them, giving them a detailed understanding of their performance gaps, ideas for addressing them, and strong incentives for taking action. Benchmarking, rather than being an occasional event, is an intrinsic part of process management. (Hagel 2002)

Discussion Questions	■ How might Li & Fung's reputation for good corporate governance impact its ongoing business? ■ As Li & Fung's auditor, which areas of the business would require the greatest test of controls? ■ Which are the most significant substantive tests?

References	Caulkin, S., 1996, "Chinese walls," *Management Today*, London, September, p. 62. Day, P., 2001, "Corporate Governance Can Be Strong Indicator Of Stock Performance Within Emerging Markets," *Wall Street Journal*, New York, May 1, p. C14. *Economist*, 2000, "The end of tycoons," April 29, Vol. 355, Issue 8168, p. 67. *Euromoney*, 2003, "Good practice boosts performance," September, Vol. 34, Issue 412, p. 222. Hagel III, J., 2002, "Leveraged Growth: Expanding Sales Without Sacrificing Profits," *Harvard Business Review*, October, Vol. 80, Issue 10, p. 68. Kraar, L., 1994, "The Overseas Chinese," *Fortune*, New York, October 31, Vol. 130, Issue 9, p. 91. Magretta, J., 1998, "Fast, Global, And Entrepreneurial: Supply Chain Management, Hong Kong Style. An interview with Victor Fung," *Harvard Business Review*, September/October, Vol. 76, Issue 5, p. 102.

■ Definitions of Corporate Governance

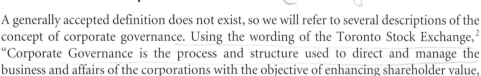

A generally accepted definition does not exist, so we will refer to several descriptions of the concept of corporate governance. Using the wording of the Toronto Stock Exchange,[2] "Corporate Governance is the process and structure used to direct and manage the business and affairs of the corporations with the objective of enhancing shareholder value, which includes ensuring the financial viability of the business. The process and structure define the division of power and establish mechanisms for achieving accountability among shareholders, the board and management." Corporate governance has been defined by the Cadbury Committee as "the system by which companies are directed and controlled."[3]

The Hampel Committee[4] made the point that this definition does not give sufficient recognition to other stakeholders groups who have legitimate interest in the organization. The Peters Committee[5] in the Netherlands noted that governance includes aspects like management and power, responsibility and influence and accountability and supervision, while integrity and transparency play an important part.

Certification Exam Question 14.1

Which of these is the most important responsibility of a board of directors?

(A) Setting corporate strategy, overall direction, mission, or vision.
(B) Caring for shareholder interest.
(C) Reviewing and approving the use of resources.
(D) Controlling top management.

The Organisation for Economic Co-operation and Development (OECD)[6] states: "Corporate governance comprehends that structure of relationships and corresponding responsibilities among a core group consisting of shareholders, board members and managers designed to best foster the competitive performance required to achieve the corporation's primary objective."

Summarizing, corporate governance essentially focusses on the dilemmas that result from the separation of ownership and control, and addresses, in particular, the principal-agent relationship between shareholders and directors on the one hand and the relationship between company agents and stakeholders on the other. Other parties are lenders to the corporation; its trading partners (workers, customers, and suppliers) as well as competitors and the general public. All of these parties have an interest in the success of corporation. All except competitors (and possibly the general public and analysts) stand to lose financially as a result of corporate failure. Each of the stakeholders has a different kind of relationship with the firm and specified rights to receive financial reports. These rights and relationships must be extensively described if we want to understand each claim and propose a reporting system that answers adequately this demand.

■ Stakeholders

In general, corporate governance (CG) is the process and structure used to manage and direct the business, with the objective of enhancing shareholder value. But it has been recognized that directors of the business should also take into account the impact of their decisions on other stakeholders.

Usually, a list of stakeholders would also include the community, the general public, consumer groups, etc. However, these groups have no legal rights and no legal power to enforce any contract. The stakeholder relationships include a relationship between the community and the firm, between governments and firms, and between community and governments. Through this legal network, members of the community can influence the firm and express their opinion.

By some opinions, members of the community are not direct stakeholders of the firm but mediated stakeholders through the government. However, in some cases, members of community may believe that the legal network does not provide them with adequate or sufficiently efficient means to be heard. They choose to bypass the legal system with legitimate actions like consumer boycotts or even illegitimate and illegal actions.

Certification Exam Question 14.2

The corporation is fundamentally governed by _____ overseeing _____ with the concurrence of _____.

(A) The shareholders; top management; the board of directors.
(B) Top management; the board of directors; the employees.
(C) The board of directors; top management; the shareholders.
(D) Top management; the shareholders; the board of directors.

■ Transparency

Transparency forms the backbone of good corporate governance. Transparency within governance is like a "lubricant" for an engine. Transparency includes concepts like openness, reporting, and disclosure.

In a business environment, transparency requires a sophisticated system of accounting. Such an accounting system should:

■ allow investors to assess the magnitude and timing of future cash flows to be generated by a business;
■ encourage efficient operations and maximization of results;
■ provide an early warning of problems in meeting objectives of the firm;
■ lead to quick corrective action whenever things go bad.

Let us now turn to some of the causes of the current global corporate governance discussion.

14.4 Causes of Current Corporate Governance Discussions

The current attention for corporate governance originated after the Watergate affair in the USA during the 1970s, gained steam based on the financial debacles in the US saving and loans industries in the early 1980s (See Chapter 3, Concept and a Company 3.2 on Lincoln Savings and Loan) and has come under the spotlight again after Enron, Parmalat, etc. Similar financial debacles and discussions about transparency of capital markets and shareholders activated the attention for corporate governance in the early nineties in countries like the UK, Australia, South Africa and New Zealand. Because of the internationalization and harmonization of capital markets, the discussions also arose in continental Europe and Asia.

Illustration 14.1 shows four causes of the current corporate governance discussion:

1 bankruptcies, fraud, and mismanagement;
2 the influence of public, customers and media;
3 globalization of capital markets;
4 developments in information technology (IT).

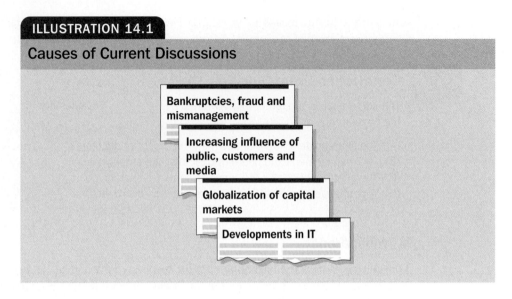

ILLUSTRATION 14.1

Causes of Current Discussions

- Bankruptcies, fraud and mismanagement
- Increasing influence of public, customers and media
- Globalization of capital markets
- Developments in IT

■ Bankruptcies, Fraud and Mismanagement

Major reasons for corporate governance being in the spotlight are unexpected bankruptcies, fraud and mismanagement. Some examples of notorious disasters are names like Barings, BCCI, Daiwa, Polly Peck, Orange County, Maxwell, Metallgesellschaft, Enron, Worldcom, Flowtex, Comroad, and Vivendi.

Concept and a Company 14.2

Vivendi – Increasing Company Value through "Operational Free Cash Flow"

Concept	Corporate disclosure and transparency.
Story	Vivendi Universal, SA is a media and telecommunications conglomerate with substantial holdings in the USA and Europe. Vivendi was formed in December 2000 as a result of a three-way merger of Vivendi's predecessor company with The Seagram Company Ltd ("Seagram") and French cable giant Canal Plus, SA ("Canal+"). Ordinary shares trade on the EuroNext Paris, SA (the Paris Bourse), and its American Depository Shares trade on the New York Stock Exchange and are registered with the SEC (US District Court 2003).
	Relevant subsidiaries include: Cegetel Group, based in France, a privately held telecommunications operator; Elektrim Telekomunikacja Sp.zoo (Telco), based in Poland, a holding company that owns various telecommunications assets; Maroc Telecom, based in Morocco, a telecommunications operator; Universal Music Group (UMG), based in the USA; and Houghton Mifflin Company, MP3.com, and USA Networks.
	The cost of the company's listed above and other acquisitions totaled more than $60 billion in cash, stock and assumed debt. In July 2002, Vivendi reported that it experienced a liquidity crisis and began selling many of its assets. Prior to this reported liquidity crisis, it is alleged that Vivendi, Jean-Marie Messier, former CEO, and Guillaume Hannezo, former CFO, committed multiple violations of the antifraud, books and records, internal controls and reporting provisions of the federal securities laws. (US District Court 2003)

SEC Complaint

Vivendi, under the direction of Messier and Hannezo, reported materially false and misleading information about growth and liquidity of its earnings before income taxes, depreciation, and amortization (EBITDA). (US District Court 2003) Specifically, the SEC's complaint includes the following allegations: (SEC 2003)

- During 2001 and the first half of 2002, Vivendi issued misleading press releases authorized by Messier, Hannezo, and other senior executives. The press releases falsely portrayed Vivendi's liquidity and cash flow as "excellent" or "strong" and as sufficient to meet Vivendi's future liquidity requirements.
- Vivendi failed to disclose future financial commitments regarding two of its subsidiaries. Vivendi failed to disclose the commitments in SEC filings and in meetings with analysts.
- Vivendi, at the direction of its senior executives, made improper adjustments that raised Vivendi's EBITDA.
- Vivendi and the other defendants failed to disclose all of the material facts about Vivendi's investment in a fund that purchased a two percent stake in Elektrim Telekomunikacja Sp. zoo (Telco), a Polish telecommunications company in which Vivendi already held a 49 percent stake.

Reports of Liquidity

Vivendi emphasized two non-US GAAP measurements when it announced its financial results to the public. First, Vivendi typically announced in press releases and other public statements its EBITDA. Second, Vivendi reported its "Operating Free Cash Flow" (also referred to as "Operational Free Cash Flow"), which Vivendi defined in its earnings releases as "EBITDA minus capital spending minus changes in working capital minus other expenses."

On June 26, 2002, Vivendi issued a press release in response to media speculation regarding the company's liquidity. In that press release, Vivendi claimed that it had "around 3.3 billion euro in unused credit lines to back up its commercial paper outstanding of nearly 1 billion euro. The cash situation has greatly improved since the beginning of the year." Vivendi's access to credit, however, was much worse than this press release indicated.

In reality, Vivendi's overall cash flow was "zero or negative," and Vivendi "produced negative cash flow from [its] core holdings" such as its entertainment businesses "that [was] barely offset by inaccessible cash flow from minority interests." (SEC 2003) Vivendi did not have the ability to unilaterally access the earnings and cash flow of two of its most profitable subsidiaries, Cegetel and Maroc Telecom. (US District Court 2003)

Financial Commitments With Subsidiaries

Vivendi owned the majority of Cegetel and Maroc Télécom, but due to legal restrictions, Vivendi (as a parent company) was not permitted unilaterally to access the cash flow of subsidiaries. In fact, during the relevant time period, Maroc Telecom did not transfer cash to Vivendi, and Vivendi only accessed Cegetel's cash through a short-term current account that Vivendi had to repay by July 31, 2002. During the relevant time period, over 30 percent of Vivendi's EBITDA and almost half of its cash flow were attributable to those two companies.

EBITDA

Concerned that Vivendi's EBITDA growth for the quarter ended June 30, 2001 might not meet or exceed market expectations, Vivendi personnel made various improper adjustments

Vivendi – Increasing Company Value through "Operational Free Cash Flow" (continued)

that raised Vivendi's EBITDA by almost 59 million euro (5 percent of the total EBITDA of 1.12 billion euro).

Vivendi's EBITDA was increased primarily by causing Cegetel to depart from its historical methodology for determining its reserve for bad debts (accounts receivable). This improper departure caused Cegetel's bad debts reserve for the second quarter of 2001 to be 45 million euro less than it should have been given historical methods. As a result, Vivendi's overall EBITDA for that period was increased by the same amount.

In order to reach an EBITDA figure of 250 million euro, UMG prematurely recognized just over 3 million euro in deferred revenue that it received in connection with a contract between UMG and other parties. This payment should not have been recognized because it would need to be refunded if Vivendi failed to meet certain conditions by mid-December 2001. (US District Court 2003)

Investment in Telco

Vivendi's did not disclose its investment in a fund that purchased a 2 percent stake in Telco, a Polish telecommunications holding company.

In June 2001, Vivendi, which owned 49 percent of Telco's equity, publicly announced its intention to purchase an additional 2 percent of Telco's shares (increasing Vivendi's ownership of Telco equity from 49 percent to 51 percent). After this announcement, Vivendi learned that Poland's antitrust authorities would have to approve the acquisition and that the credit rating agencies might react negatively to Vivendi's acquisition of additional Telco shares. As a result, rather than directly purchasing the 2 percent interest in Telco, Vivendi deposited $100 million into an investment fund administered by Société Générale Bank & Trust Luxembourg. That fund subsequently purchased a 2 percent stake in Telco in September 2001. (US District Court 2003)

Sarbanes-Oxley-based Settlements

Vivendi and its executives were one of the first cases where fines and repayment of salaries were required under the Sarbanes-Oxley Act of 2002. The settlements include Vivendi's consent to pay a $50 million civil money penalty. The settlements also include Messier's agreement to relinquish his claims to a 21 million euro severance package that he negotiated just before he resigned his positions at Vivendi, and payment of disgorgement and civil penalties by Messier and Hannezo that total over $1 million. (SEC 2003)

Discussion Questions	■ What audit procedures should have been undertaken at Vivendi to assure proper disclosures were made?
	■ Why is it not in the shareholders' best interest to use EBITDA reporting?
	■ Discuss if management-determined measurements like "Operational Free Cash Flow" should be allowed in reporting?
References	SEC, 2003, *Litigation Release No. 18523. Accounting and Auditing Enforcement Release No. 1935*, "SEC Files Settled Civil Fraud Action Against Vivendi Universal, SA, Its Former CEO, Jean-Marie Messier, and Its Former CFO, Guillaume Hannezo," US Security and Exchange Commission, December 24.
	US District Court, 2003, "*Securities and Exchange Commission v Vivendi Universal, S.A., Jean-Marie Messier, and Guillaume Hannezo*," United States District Court Southern District Of New York, December 23.

■ Influence of Shareholders and Public

A second development is the increasing demand for shareholder participation, and also the increasing influence of customers' and public opinion. Just think about the following dilemma. You are the director of Royal Shell and you have to decide to sink an outdated oil platform at sea or to dismantle it on land. Both options are legally acceptable. Also, assume that sinking the platform at sea is cheaper and will cause less environmental pollution than dismantling it on land. However, a well-known influential interest group kindly demands that the platform be dismantled on land. What do you decide to do?

This example is a complicated dilemma, because the interest group could influence public opinion, including your customers and suppliers! The worst-case scenario is that these important stakeholders decide to stop doing business with your company. It is not very difficult to calculate the financial burden should this scenario materialize. These new type of dilemmas are central to the current corporate governance discussions.

In the same context, several years ago, the Board of Renault in Paris decided to close their plant in Belgium after lots of financial calculations and considerations. They even included the financial burden of strikes. However, they did not expect that Belgian customers would decide not to buy anything from Renault for almost half a year. This is an interesting example of the congruency of long-term shareholders' interest, with both employees and consumers being very important stakeholders. But, one should admit, managing with hindsight is quite easy.

■ Globalization of Capital Markets

A third factor that places corporate governance in the spotlight is globalization of capital markets and businesses. Events like privatization in continental Europe, investments in Europe by Californian employee state pension fund Calpers, firms headquartered outside the USA getting listed on the NYSE (Daimler Benz), are just some examples. Globalization encourages harmonization of law and legislation. Examples are the EU guideline to apply **International Financial Reporting Standards** (IFRS) in all European Countries as of 2005 and the expected requirement of referring to ISA for **statutory audits.**

Empirical studies show that institutional investors are increasingly making investment decisions on the basis of whether an enterprise meets the demands of corporate governance. Fifty percent of international investors in the USA and Western Europe surveyed by McKinsey Consulting Group consider corporate governance at least as important as financial ratios when evaluating business. In Asia, Latin America, Africa and Eastern Europe the percentage is an even higher 80 percent.[7]

■ Information Technology

Finally, it should not be a surprise that Information Technology (IT) is a major enabler of the new economy and, consequently, of corporate governance developments and discussions. We just refer to phenomena like "the higher the losses and growth, the higher the market value." And what about considering the loss of market share of brick-and-mortar car dealers, security dealers and auction houses. IT introduces new **XML** languages like **XBRL** for business reporting. This may lead to fundamental changes in disclosure of information for decision making. And what to think of the political and fiscal consequences of loss of control over value added tax as transactions are being processed via the internet. These are all interesting IT-related issues that drive corporate governance developments.

Certification Exam Question 14.3

The role(s) of the Board of Directors in a company's strategy-making, strategy-implementing process include:

(A) Collaborating closely with senior management in crafting the company's strategic vision, business model, objectives, and strategy and then putting the Board's stamp of approval on how things are to be done to implement and execute the strategy successfully.

(B) Seeing that the overall task of strategy management is performed in a manner that benefits shareholders, critically appraising and ultimately approving strategic action plans, and evaluating the strategy-making and strategy-implementing skills of top management.

(C) Taking lead responsibility for the company's strategic vision and business model, but delegating responsibility for setting objectives, crafting strategy, and implementing and executing strategy to senior executives.

(D) Being heavily involved in long-term strategic planning but much less involved in the day-to-day aspects of strategy implementation and execution.

14.5 Corporate Governance Structures

To understand current developments, one should understand differences in national corporate governance structures as well. These differences are caused by factors like culture, history, legal systems, and so on. In other words, corporate behavior is influenced by history and culture of the country. Geert Hofstede, characterized the Anglo-Saxon culture as masculine and Continental culture as feminine.[8]

To illustrate, we briefly sketch some differences between the **market** corporate governance structure and **network** corporate governance structure (see Illustration 14.2). Examples of countries with a market-oriented corporate governance structure are countries like the USA and the Commonwealth countries. Examples of network-oriented corporate governance structure countries are those in continental Europe and some Asian countries. Market-oriented countries are more aggressive and confrontation-seeking, while "network cultures" seek consensus instead of conflict. Of course differences are not that black and white, but nevertheless, cultural distinction is a most powerful factor in explaining global differences in corporate governance (CG).[9]

Let us continue. In Anglo-Saxon countries, shares are widely distributed among individuals. In Continental countries, banks, insurance companies and other institutions mainly hold shares. As a consequence, stock exchanges play a more important role in market-oriented countries. At US high schools, share prices are a common basis for discussions among students. Because of this shareholder focus, directors often choose a short-term strategy to keep shareholders satisfied.

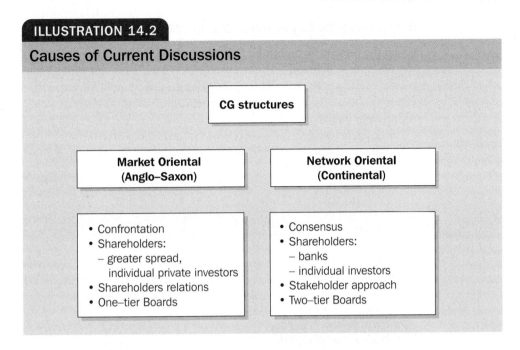

ILLUSTRATION 14.2

Causes of Current Discussions

CG structures

Market Oriental (Anglo–Saxon)	Network Oriental (Continental)

• Confrontation
• Shareholders:
  – greater spread,
    individual private investors
• Shareholders relations
• One–tier Boards
	• Consensus
	• Shareholders:
	  – banks
	  – individual investors
	• Stakeholder approach
	• Two–tier Boards

■ Network-Oriented Corporate Governance

In Germany and Japan, there is a culture of long-term support from shareholders because of influence from banks, which are equity providers as well as lenders. In France and Italy, there is a tradition of companies being family-oriented and, indeed, many companies still have a major shareholder. Such shareholders are usually represented on the board.

Because shareholder interests are not the only yardstick by which corporate perform-ance is measured, there is a greater expectation from shareholders that profits will be ploughed back into the organization. This, coupled with a lack of an aggressive takeover culture, helps to create a more long-term environment, without the fear of displacement engendered by the prospect of a hostile takeover.

■ Governance Boards Market vs. Network CG

Another major difference between the market-oriented and the network-oriented corpo-rate governance structures is the two-tier separation between the board of management and the supervisory board in the network structure. In the market-oriented, one-tier system, the complete board, that is: both executive and non-executive directors, is formally responsible for day-to-day operating activities. However, this responsibility is delegated to the executive members, while the non-executive board members have a supervisory role. This means that non-executives supervise **and**, at the same time, are jointly responsible for day-to-day operations. In the two-tier system, supervising and management are formally separated: the monitoring of executive board members is exclusively the responsibility of the supervisory board. Therefore supervisory board members seem to be more independent than their non-executive counterparts.

■ Demand for Supervision vs. Shareholder Rights

Given the previously mentioned fraud cases and bankruptcies, in Anglo-Saxon countries we observe a demand for stronger supervision and control. While in continental countries such as France and the Netherlands, the demand for more shareholder rights is apparent, because of the globalization of capital markets and a more active role for the supervisory board.

Given these worldwide developments, in several countries special corporate governance committees have been installed to prepare guidelines for good corporate governance.

14.6 Corporate Governance Committees and Reports

The most famous corporate governance codes are the Cadbury report in the UK (which focuses on the financial aspects of CG), the Dey Report[10] in Canada and the King Report[11] in South Africa. But there are others (shown in Illustration 14.3).

ILLUSTRATION 14.3

Corporate Governance Committees and Reports

- ■ VS – COSO Report [1992], Sarbanes-Oxley [2002]
- ■ UK – Cadbury [1992], Hampel [1998], Higgs [2003]
- ■ Canada – Dey: "Where were the directors?" [1994]
- ■ Germany – [1998] "Kontrag", Cromme Commission [2002]
- ■ France – [1995, 1999] Viénot Rapport, Bouton [2002]
- ■ Netherlands – Peters Committee [1997], Tabaksblat [2003]
- ■ South Africa – [1994] "The King Report"
- ■ Australia – [1994] "Bridging the Expectation Gap"
- ■ OECD – [1999] "Improving Competitiveness and Access to Capital in Global Markets"

In the Netherlands, the Peters Report[12] was published in 1997. As concluded by Peters[13] in 2002, the code was not applied by most public companies in the Netherlands. Therefore, a new committee chaired by Mr. Tabaksblat was installed. It presented a new code in December 2003. Like the French one, the Dutch capital market is increasingly influenced by Anglo-Saxon practice. As a consequence, the main CG guidelines focus on improving shareholders' rights and powerful supervision.

The interesting conclusion that can be derived from the different reports is the ongoing convergence of corporate governance structures. In other words, globalizing financial and investment markets seeks the best of both worlds in corporate practices and policies, and hence "best practice behavior."

■ Sarbanes-Oxley Act of 2002 [14]

After the financial failures in 2001 and 2002, the US Congress passed a new law to prevent future disasters like Enron, Global Crossing, Adelphia, Tyco, and WorldCom. On July 31, 2002 US president George W. Bush signed the law championed by Senators Sarbanes and Oxley. The rush to pass the law was driven by a sense of escalating financial failures, Congressional pressure, near-term congressional elections, and calls for oversight of public company auditors by the SEC.

The Sarbanes-Oxley Act consists of 11 "Sections":

I   Public Company Accounting Oversight Board
II   Auditor Independence
III   Corporate Responsibility
IV   Enhanced Financial Disclosures
V   Analyst Conflicts of Interest
VI   Commission Resources and Authority
VII   Studies and Reports
VIII   Corporate and Criminal Fraud Accountability Act of 2002
IX   White-Collar Crime Penalty Enhancements
X   Corporate Tax Returns
XI   Corporate Fraud and Accountability.

Most of the details of the law were not clearly worked out as it was written very rapidly. The SEC has since worked out further details. For example, a 93-page final rule [15] was written based on the two-paragraph Section 404 of the law. It is certain that the law will influence performance of the board of directors and auditors. The main characteristic is its legal force. Deviation from law leads to clear punishments. Company executives who fraudulently report financial statements are subject to criminal penalties if they "knowingly" violate the law ($1 million or ten year's imprisonment) or if they are "willful and knowing" in their violation ($5 million or 20 year's imprisonment).

Not Just US Companies

Another characteristic of the law is its scope. All US-listed companies (domestic and foreign registrants and auditors) have to comply with the Sarbanes-Oxley Act, despite the differences in culture and laws of foreign companies. Recognizing potential difficulties for foreign registrants, the SEC is not willing to provide exemptions to guarantee a level playing field. [16] The SEC ruled that exemptions to compliance with the Act will only be allowed in instances where the countries in which companies are domiciled have laws and regulations similar to that contained in the Sarbanes-Oxley Act.

■ European Union Laws

Partly in response to the Sarbanes-Oxley Act of 2002, the EU proposed to modernize company law and to enhance corporate governance in the European Union. [17] Good company law and good corporate governance practices throughout the EU will enhance the real economy. An effective approach would foster the global efficiency and competitiveness of business in the EU and help to strengthen shareholders' rights and third parties' protection.

EU Plan for Company Law

The EU Action Plan for Company Law,[18] including corporate governance, pays attention to the need for regulatory response at the European level amongst others respecting the subsidiary and proportionality principles of the EU Treaty. The Plan should be flexible in application, but firm in the principles. Finally, it should help shape international regulatory developments.

In 2001, a comparative study[19] concluded that the EU should not devote time and effort to the development of a European corporate governance code. This study identified more valuable areas for the European Commission to focus its efforts on; namely the reduction of legal and regulatory barriers to shareholder engagement in cross-border voting (participation barriers) as well as the reduction of barriers to shareholder's ability to evaluate the governance of companies (information barriers). Because of differences in European Law, a European Code would have to allow for many different options and, therefore, a common approach should be adopted with respect to a few essential rules and adequate coordination of corporate governance codes within Europe should be ensured.[20]

The EU intends to strengthen management of companies during the period 2003–09 along the following lines:

- modernizing the board of directors;
- board composition (independent non-executives or supervisory directors and creation of specific committees);
- director's remuneration (both ex ante and ex post);
- directors' responsibilities (special investigation right, wrongful trading rule, directors' disqualification).

Finally the Commission proposes to set up a European Corporate Governance Forum to co-ordinate corporate governance efforts of Member States.

14.7 Best Practice from a Global Perspective

Here we discuss some of the best practices that are on the worldwide agenda for modernization of governance related to the four elements of governance we mentioned: managing including board responsibility, supervision, internal control and transparency. We can only highlight some choice examples of what is currently seen as best practice from a global point of view. Among others, important sources are the OECD report entitled: "Corporate Governance, Improving Competitiveness and Access to Capital in Global Markets",[21] the Sarbanes-Oxley Act, the UK Combined Code, and the proposals reforming corporate governance in the EU.

■ Managing Best Practice

An important element of governance is "managing" which includes the concepts of mission, strategy, objectives, and compatibility with societal objectives.

Best practice requires that boards take leadership in defining corporate mission and strategy, as these issues are often seen as "corporate glue" and consequently are essential for the success and vitality of the company. To illustrate its importance, we refer to the Royal Dutch Shell Group. This company started to formulate and disclose its mission and principles way back in the seventies, because of the sharp attacks of pressure groups on the multinational's relationships with South Africa's apartheid regime. Nowadays – based upon years of experiences – Shell's board publicly discusses its mission and principles to provide cohesion, common purpose and shared values for a global and decentralized organization.

Closely related to mission and strategy, key objectives of the company are to engage profitably, efficiently and responsibly in selected businesses. These objectives lead us to another management best practice, namely "recognizing societal interest."

Certification Exam Question 14.4

Which of the following is **not** one of the matters auditors are expected to communicate about with the audit committee?

(A) Management's process of generating accounting estimates.
(B) Auditor's responsibility for other information in documents containing audited financial statements.
(C) The company's adoption of the new corporate governance principles issued by the OEDC.
(D) Auditor's view on accounting matters for which management received a legal opinion.

Recognizing Societal Interest

As companies do not act independently from the societies in which they operate, corporate actions must be compatible with societal objectives concerning social cohesion, individual welfare and equal opportunities for all. Attending to legitimate social concerns should benefit all parties in the long run, including shareholders. At times, however, there may be a trade off between short-term social costs and the long-term benefits to society of having a healthy, competitive private sector.

The current debate and search for **sustainability** is a very interesting example of societal interest. Sustainability is often indicated by the triple bottom-line reporting, about "economic, social and environmental issues." We quote Mark Moody Stuart[22] as Chair of Shell's Committee of Managing Directors: "My colleagues and I are totally committed to a business strategy that generates profits while contributing to the well-being of the planet and its people. We see no alternative."

Companies in the raw material industry, like Shell, are scared of losing reputation and consequently profit, and therefore want to control **reputational risk**. For that reason, best practice means that management has to focus on stakeholders' interest instead of having an exclusive focus on shareholders' interest.[23] The owner of the company should of course play an active role in corporate governance. According to the EU, institutional investors should provide information about the role they play as shareholders. Among others they should be obliged to disclose their investment policy and exercise of their voting rights. EU countries should consider strengthening shareholders' rights such as the right to ask questions, table resolutions, vote in absentia, etc.

Concept and a Company 14.3

Hollinger International – "Greed has been severely underestimated and denigrated, unfairly so, in my opinion" – Conrad Black, CEO (Newman 2004)

Concept	Board responsibility, executive control.

Story   Conrad Black (Lord Black of Crossharbour) was CEO of publicly traded Hollinger International (HI) and other related companies for 25 years. HI is a newspaper publisher with 270-odd publications, the most important being London's *Daily Telegraph*, the *Jerusalem Post*, London's *Spectator* magazine and the *Chicago Sun-Times*. The story of HI involves several other companies controlled by Lord Black, his wife, and his associate David Radler, former president of HI. These controlled companies include: holding companies Ravelston, Argus, and publicly traded Hollinger Inc. (H); Black's private management services firm, Ravelston Management Inc. (RMI); and newspaper companies Horizon and Bradford.

Hollinger International's board includes some well-known individuals. They included Margaret Thatcher, Henry Kissinger, his eminence Emmett Cardinal Carter, Chaim Herzog, a former president of Israel, James Thompson, a former governor of Illinois, Lord Carrington, the former secretary general of NATO, Richard Perle, one of the architects of George W. Bush's Iraq policy, as well as half a dozen other British lords, plus the Italian industrialist, Giovanni Agnelli. Not a single one of them (except Agnelli, who runs Fiat) was trained to read a balance sheet well enough to spot some of the irregularities taking place.

Unusual Governance Structure

HI corporate governance employed an unusual ownership model. HI was controlled by H through a device called "super voting shares," which allowed H to cast 72.6 percent of any vote while holding only 30.3 percent of the company's combined equity. H is, in turn, 77.8 percent owned by private companies Ravelston and Argus, which are owned primarily by Black, his wife and David Radler. (McDonald 2004) So the controlling interest in HI is held by Black via holding companies Ravelston, Argus and H.

Unusual Payments

Cash flows between the companies are even more complex. Argus depends on dividend payments from H. In turn, H depends on support payments from RMI, which depends on management fees from HI. RMI billed HI an annual average of US$28 million for its services between 1996 and 2004. The board waved through substantial fees going to Ravelston – about $24 million in 2002 – for what was vaguely defined as "advisory, consultative, procurement and administrative services," and a comparable payment in 2003. The companies also borrowed from each other – Ravelston owed $59.2 million to Argus as at September 2003. (*Wall Street Journal* 2004)

Whenever HI sold any assets (such as a newspaper), they paid H, Ravelston and Black, and his associates directly in "non-compete fees" – fees paid by the newspaper acquirer to prevent the seller from going into the same market with another newspaper. Of the US$73.7 million non-compete fees paid to Black and his associates, the Board of Directors did not approve $32 million. (*Wall Street Journal* 2004)

Events Leading to the Fall

Events that led to Conrad Black losing control of his media empire started March 10, 2003 when H issued US$120 million in debt at 11.875 percent, pledging most of its HI stock as collateral. A default on this loan would cause H to lose the HI controlling shares. One month later, H said it was uncertain if it could meet future financial obligations. In May, Standard & Poor's Rating Services downgraded H's credit rating to "selective default." In October, Moody's downgraded H because of "questionable corporate governance practices." (Newman 2004)

In November, HI stopped making payments to Ravelston, upon which H depends for cash flow. In January 2004, worried about loan default, thereby losing the HI shares pledged as collateral, Black and Ravelston agreed to sell its controlling interest in H and its newspaper assets to Press Holdings International Ltd for $605.5 million. (Newman 2004)

Shareholder reaction began May 19, 2003 when investment firm Tweedy Browne Co LLC, one of HI largest minority shareholders, filed its concerns about management with the US Securities and Exchange Commission. Among them were sales of HI assets to Horizon Publications Inc. (controlled by David Radler, HI's president, who also owns 14.2 percent of Ravelston). The complaint also questioned both "services agreements" in which HI paid US$203 million to Ravelston and affiliated firms from 1995 to 2002; and US$73.7 million in "non-compete payments" made directly to Black, other officers, and Ravelston, instead of to the company. Within one month, HI set up a special committee to investigate Tweedy Browne allegations. (Newman 2004)

The HI shareholder battles culminated on November 17, 2003 when HI announced the resignations of Black as CEO and Radler as president. One basis for dismissal is US$32 million in unauthorized non-compete payments made to Black. In January 2004, HI removed Black as chairman of the board. HI filed a lawsuit against Hollinger Inc., Ravelston, Black and Radler to recover "damages and disgorgement of more than US$200 million." (Newman 2004)

Black and Radler each agreed to repay US$7.2 million in unauthorized non-compete fees. In December, Black missed his first US$850,000 scheduled payment to H. Black told HI he would not repay "certain disputed non-compete payments" because he believed they were approved by independent directors.

At H's annual meeting, Black called the controversy over corporate governance a "sideshow." H announced all or part of the firm is up for sale. Four independent directors (friends of Black) who made up the H audit committee resigned after the company's board rejected their recommendations to keep Black.

In November, KPMG, H's outside auditor, received subpoenas from the SEC requesting documents. On November 20, Conrad Black resigned as CEO of H, two days earlier than expected, so he would not be required to sign the quarterly CEO certification of statements required by the SEC. (Heinzl 2003) In December, KPMG LLP quit as auditor of Hollinger Inc. after the company refused to make management changes.

H disclosed the possibility of conflicts of interest. In 2003's annual information form, H warned shareholders: "There may be a conflict between his [Black's] interests and interests of other shareholders." The same document pointed out that HI routinely did business with other companies controlled by Black. Those deals "may not be as favorable to the Company as those that could be negotiated with non-affiliated third parties," it stated. (McClearn 2004)

Concept and a Company 14.3 (continued)

Selling Out

Lord Black never disclosed his deal to sell control of H, and therefore the controlling interest in HI. HI learned of Black's clandestine dealings along with the rest of the world on January 18, 2004 when Black and Press Holdings International Ltd announced their agreement. To stop the HI board and special committee looking for a buyer for HI from interfering with the sale to Press Holdings, Ravelston filed action in Ontario court to preempt any effort by Hollinger International to halt the sale.

Court Judgment

The action to stop HI from interfering with Black's sale to Press Holdings, went to trial before Judge Leo Strine. Strine ruled against Conrad Black and said that Black's plan to sell control of his H newspaper empire to Press Holdings was about the legality of Black's business practices. Strine determined that Black had misled his former colleagues at HI, violated his fiduciary duties to its shareholders on numerous occasions and acted in bad faith on others. Strine even said the manner in which the board was led to "approve" one non-compete payment to Black was possibly "a fraud on the board." Ultimately, he didn't trust Black: "It became impossible for me to credit his word, after considering his trial testimony in light of the overwhelming evidence of his less-than-candid conduct towards his fellow directors," Strine wrote. "His explanations of key events and of his own motivations do not have the ring of truth." (McClern 2004)

Discussion Questions	■ What are the main problems with the corporate governance structure describe above?
	■ Given all the related party transactions, what audit procedures would you recommend?

References	Heinzl, M., 2003, "Hollinger Faces an SEC Inquiry; Unauthorized Payments Are the Apparent Subject; Colson Gets Broader Duties," *Wall Street Journal*, New York, November 20, p. B10.
	Newman, P.C., 2004, "Epitaph For A Heavyweight," *Mcclean's*, Toronto, February 2, Vol. 117, Issue 5, p. 44.
	McClearn, M., 2004, "The Verdict," *Canadian Business*, Toronto, March 1–14, Column 77, Issue 5, p. 22.
	McDonald, D., 2004, "The Man Who Wanted More," *Vanity Fair*, April, p. 148.
	Wall Street Journal, 2004, "Hollinger's Black Out," New York, January 20, p. A10.

■ Board Responsibility

The board defines the company's strategy, appoints the corporate officers responsible for managing the company and implementing this strategy, oversees management and ensures the quality of information provided to shareholders and to financial markets through the financial statements.[24]

Certification by Executives

Given fierce pressure caused by fraudulent financial reporting and bankruptcies, chief executive and financial officers of US-listed companies have to certify annual and quarterly reports filed with the SEC. Certification means that these executives reviewed the reports and based on their knowledge there are no untrue statements or omissions of material fact, and the statements fairly present the company's financial condition. Signing officers also sign for evaluating the effectiveness of disclosure controls and procedures as of a date within 90 days prior to the filing date of the report and for the fact that they presented their conclusions about effectiveness in the report. By signing they also confirm that disclosures have been made to auditors and the **audit committee** of all significant deficiencies in internal control or any fraud that involves employees with a significant role in internal control.

Penalties

Severe penalties are imposed for knowing that a report does not conform to requirements of the Act. The Sarbanes-Oxley Act forces responsibility on boards by forfeiture of certain bonuses and profits in case of fraudulent financial reporting. Also, board members can be barred from acting as a director in cases of non-compliance with the law. Another restrictive law to prevent board members from acting in a way that conflicts with the interest of the company is the prohibition of personal loans to executives. According to Sarbanes-Oxley, companies have to disclose whether a Code of Ethics for the CEO/CFO has been adopted, including contents, or if not, why not.

■ Supervising Best Practice

We now come to some best practices related to the "supervising" component of governance. Global debates lead to an agreed vision that good corporate governance requires a system of independent supervision and active oversight of management. The result today is a view of governance best practice that is largely designed to prevent directors being influenced too much by management.

Independent Directors

A director is independent when he has no relationship of any kind whatsoever with the corporation, its group or the management of either that is such as to color his judgment.[25] A reduction on management influence over boards is generally achieved by rules that ensure the independence of **non-executive members of the board** or, in continental European countries, supervisory board members. An important issue is the influence of shareholders, employees and other stakeholders on the appointment of supervisory board members.

Who the Board Represents

According to Anglo-Saxon best practice, the board represents the shareholders – not other constituencies. On the other hand, according to best practice in the Netherlands, the board should represent all stakeholders. Nowadays, shareholders and work councils elect supervisory members in Germany and in the Netherlands (where members are appointed by themselves, a so-called system of co-optation, creating a sphere of "old boys' network"). Here convergence to the Anglo-Saxon structure can be recognized, because of some hesitation of foreign investors like large pension funds (e.g. California employees' pension fund Calpers) to invest in Dutch-listed companies. As a result, a current debate in some network-oriented structures is focussing on how to increase the influence of shareholders and employees in the nomination process.

Appraisal of Directors

With respect to re-appointment of individual board members, appraisal of individual directors is a key element of corporate governance. Boards have a special responsibility for designing and approving appropriate remuneration schemes and this has been globally accepted as best practice. A special remuneration committee should therefore be installed and report to the shareholders each year on remuneration of both directors and management.

■ Audit Committee

A separate audit committee is another expression of best practice. Regulated corporate governance via audit committees began in the USA in 1978 with audit committee requirements by stock exchanges based on recommendations of the Cohen Commission.[26] Remarkably (at least to some of us today), audit committees were not required prior to 1978. The last round of changes in corporate governance in the USA were a result of former SEC Chairman Levitt's initiative[27] culminating in the NYSE/NASD Blue Ribbon Committee's recommendations of 2000.[28] Boards must be fully committed to building and maintaining effective audit committees.

As of 1978, the major American stock exchanges have required listed firms to have audit committees comprised of independent, outside, directors who own relatively little stock in a firm and who are not members of management. Over time and over various corporate failure eras, audit committees have been assigned increasing responsibilities for monitoring management, corporate reporting, and relations with the independent auditor. The audit committee acts on the behavior of stockholders in this regard.

The new proposed EU Directive on Statutory Audits[29] requires that audited companies will have to set up an audit committee, with independent members, which would oversee the audit process, communicating directly with the auditor without going through management. That committee would also select the auditor and propose the appointment to shareholders. In addition, if a company dismissed an auditor it would need to explain the reasons to the relevant authority in the Member State concerned.

Currently, the committees are charged with conducting meetings with the internal and external auditors, reviewing financial statements before they are issued to the public, and, in certain circumstances, taking action to control management. Audit committees are typically the primary locus for suggestions for improvement of the process and also focus of recent failures. These committees should focus on high quality financial reporting and risk management (including identification and control). Furthermore, audit committees should maintain a charter, and regularly assess the performance against this charter.

Independent Directors

Sarbanes-Oxley explicitly establishes an independence definition for audit committee members. An audit committee member should not receive fees other than for board service and should not be an "affiliated person" of the issuer (publicly listed company) or any subsidiary.

Financial Expert

Section 407 of the Sarbanes-Oxley Act states[30] that the SEC shall issue rules to require issuers to disclose whether at least one member of its audit committee is a "financial expert." The final SEC rules state[31] that the audit committee financial expert's expertise should be related to the body of generally accepted accounting principles used in the issuer's primary financial statements filed with the SEC. The company must disclose the name of the audit committee financial expert and whether that person is independent.

Auditor Oversight

As they are responsible for oversight of external reporting, internal controls and auditing, the audit committee should play a role in guarding independence of the auditor. In this respect, Sarbanes-Oxley and "best practice" teach that the audit committee is directly responsible for the appointment, compensation, and oversight of the auditor.

Auditor Reports to Audit Committee

To support the supervisory role of the audit committee, the Sarbanes-Oxley Act requires the auditor to report directly to the audit committee:[32]

- all critical accounting policies and practices in use by the publicly listed company;
- GAAP alternatives discussed with management and any alternative preferred by the audit firm;
- other material written communications such as **management letters** and **unadjusted audit differences**.

Whistle-Blower Communications

To be able to perform its tasks, Sarbanes-Oxley requires the audit committee to establish a protocol to address "whistle blower" communications.[33] This duty comprises:

- receipt, retention and treatment of complaints received by the company regarding accounting, internal controls, or auditing matters;
- confidential and anonymous submissions by employees.

Financial Expert On Audit Committee

A next interesting requirement in the USA's strive to have effective audit committees is the requirement to disclose in the annual report that the audit committee has at least one financial expert to be defined by the SEC.[34] The audit committee should consider "whether a person, through education and experience as a public accountant or auditor or a principal financial officer, comptroller, or principal accounting officer of an issuer, or from a position involving the performance of similar functions, has:

- an understanding of generally accepted accounting principles and financial statements;
- experience in:
  - the preparation or auditing of financial statements of generally comparable issuers; and
  - the application of such principles in connection with the accounting for estimates, accruals, and reserves;
- experience with internal accounting controls; and
- an understanding of audit committee functions."

To emphasize the importance of audit committees, Sarbanes-Oxley states that no compliance with audit committee requirements can lead to de-listing of US stock exchanges.

Board Training

Finally, according to "best practice" in the UK, France and the Netherlands, every new board member should follow appropriate training. Training should include general orientation for new supervisory board members, contact with the company's higher management officers and ongoing permanent education by means of external seminars and reading material. Once again, these requirements should be put onto the worldwide agenda for modernization of governance. In other words, best practice should recognize that supervising is a professional task, requiring specific expertise, experience and skills.

Internal Control Best Practice

The US Treadway Commission[35] recommended in 1978 that prevention and detection of fraud should be guaranteed through strong internal controls. Treadway also recommended that guidelines be developed on internal control to allow management to report against some framework. Such internal-control guidelines were published in 1992 and are known as the COSO Report.[36]

Cadbury Committee

The Cadbury Committee in the UK was also established in response to a concern about the reliability of financial reporting. The Code of Best Practice issued by Cadbury deals with internal controls as defined by COSO. The current UK Code[37] even requires that "the directors should, at least annually, conduct a review of the effectiveness of the group's system of internal controls and should report to shareholders that they have done so. This review should cover **all** controls, including financial, operational and compliance controls."

Since the publication of Cadbury's Code of Best Practice, several regulators and corporate governance committees followed in the footsteps of their UK trend-setting cousins and have also developed similar recommendations concerning internal control. European countries like Germany, France and the Netherlands adopted or are in the process of adopting this best practice.

SOX 404

Section 404 (SOX 404) of the Sarbanes-Oxley Act[38] requires the annual report of issuers to contain management reports which shall:

1 state management responsibility for internal control structure and procedures;
2 give an assessment of effectiveness.

To be able to perform such an assessment, management should select a set of criteria that are established like the COSO criteria. Management should document internal controls; perform a gap analyses and revise/redesign controls that seem to be inadequate; examine, monitor and evaluate the internal controls; and conclude on their design and operating effectiveness. Detailed standards for the report to comply with SOX 404 were discussed in Chapter 4 An Auditor's Framework.

Auditor Report on Management's Assertion About Internal Controls

Sarbanes-Oxley and PCAOB Audit Standard #2 require that the auditor report on management's assertion of the effectiveness of internal controls. The auditors' internal control attestation engagement is inseparable from the engagement to conduct an audit.

To be able to attest the auditor should:

- obtain understanding of internal control and management's evaluation;
- evaluate design effectiveness of controls;
- test and evaluate the operating effectiveness of controls;
- form an opinion.

Internal Audit Department

Referring to the COSO, internal control component "monitoring" includes the contribution of an internal audit department. The UK Code of Best Practice recommended that: "Companies which do not have an internal audit function should from time to time review the need for one." The Code also states that although internal audit should maintain independence from management, it can perform more than just a monitoring role. Internal audit arrangements naturally vary, but they have the potential to play a central role within the monitoring process.

■ Best Practice: Transparency

Finally, we discuss best practice transparency. Elements of transparency include timely disclosure of reliable, adequate and relevant information for decision making. Annual and consolidated financial statements should record the level of success that the executive board has enjoyed over the previous financial year. This helps to serve both the supervisory board and the capital market in their control and disciplining of management. Financial statements also contain information that can point to future corporate development, thus helping to create a basis for investment decisions. Investors want clear, reliable and internationally comparable information about enterprises. Available information should meet these needs.[39]

EU Corporate Governance Disclosure

Wall Street's pressure for profits can be great, with the potential risk that companies manage their earnings and disclosures. Stakeholders therefore call for reliable and relevant reporting of financial and non-financial information. Regulators and best practices are setting the tone. The EU intends to enhance corporate governance disclosure during the period 2003–09. The annual corporate governance statement should at least include the following six items:

1 operation of the shareholder meeting and its key powers and the description of shareholder rights and how they can be exercised;
2 the composition and operation of the board and its committees;
3 the shareholders holding major holdings and their voting and control rights as well as key agreements;
4 the other direct and indirect relationships between these major shareholders and the company;
5 any material transactions with other related parties;
6 the existence and nature of risk management systems.

Contrary to the legal enforcement of the Sarbanes-Oxley Act, the EU shows trust in the disciplinary force of the market. Companies are required to "comply or explain deviations of national code." The market should reward those who comply.

■ Introduction of a new Business Reporting Model

The modernization of current business reporting models is another best practice issue. Illustration 14.4 sketches some of the changes that closely follow changes in the corporate governance environment. The current model does serve as an effective foundation from which business reporting should start. However "real time" decisions are made by looking at both the lagging indicators (the historical financial statement) and leading indicators that enhance business reporting as the information is much closer to the event. The fact of the matter is that the one size fits all concept to financial reporting is over 20 years out of date. The loss of relevance, or at least the need for more information, can easily be identified.

ILLUSTRATION 14.4

Current and Future Business Reporting Models

Current Reporting Model	Future Reporting Model
Shareholder focus	Stakeholder focus (Shell, Ben and Jerry, Body Shop)
Paper-based reporting	Web-based reporting (Microsoft financial forum)
Standardized information	Customised information (relevant information for decision making)
Periodic reporting	Continuous (online, real-time)
Distribution of information	Dialog (i.e. a two-way communication)
Financial information	Broader indicator range (such as environment, health and safety)

The American Institute of Certified Public Accountants (AICPA) has established a Special Committee on Enhanced Business Reporting concurrently to:[40]

■ identify the migration path needed to get reporting done;
■ get companies to pilot ideas;
■ build consensus and support from users.

Implementation of enhanced business reporting could take place through collaboration with, commitment from, and support of:

■ the US Securities and Exchange Commission (SEC);
■ the US Financial Accounting Standards Board (FASB);
■ banks and other users;
■ the US Public Company Accounting Oversight Board (PCAOB);
■ large fund managers (e.g., Vanguard, TIAA-CREF);
■ the Council of Institutional Investors;
■ the Federation European (FEI) Think Tanks (e.g. Brookings).

Illustration 14.5 show the next steps expected for enhanced business reporting.

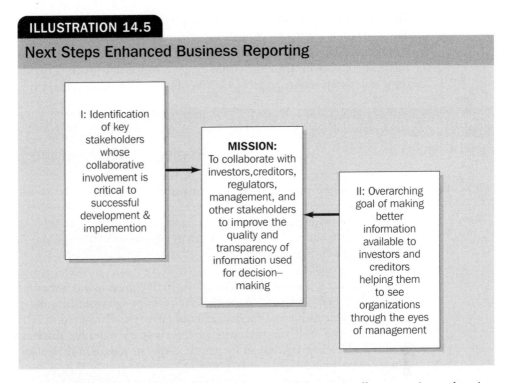

ILLUSTRATION 14.5

Next Steps Enhanced Business Reporting

In conclusion, we can simply say that the pace of change in all respects is accelerating in this global, online and inter-connected world. This acceleration is affecting all aspects of our business and industries, and involves all our various stakeholders' and interest groups. It must be accepted that while corporate governance is concerned with harnessing of energy and power, the ability of a company to create wealth for stakeholders should not be stifled by bureaucracy and over-regulation. Corporate governance is not an end in itself. However, the transparency of governance practices can help to play a role in maintaining public confidence. Dialogue on these practices can lead to informed reflection on the dynamic and inter-dependent relationships, which constitute the corporate environment and hopefully "best of both worlds."

How do we proceed? We agree with the OECD's view that public policy makers and regulators should encourage the development of improved governance practices, with strong emphasis on government enabling voluntary private sector development rather than attempting to regulate it.

14.8 Corporate Governance and the Role of the Auditor

The external auditor plays a central role in good corporate governance. Despite the fact that auditors are indirect[41] stakeholders, their core role is to:

- audit financial statements and other (financial) reporting;
- attest internal control statements;
- review or attest corporate governance statements.

The auditor's first role of auditing financial statements is discussed throughout this book. The attestation of internal control statements referred to in Section 14.6 has been elaborated on in Chapter 4 An Auditor's Services. That leaves the third important governance role – the review or attest of corporate governance statements. Providing assurance to these statements is only possible when verifiable and suitable criteria are available. [42]

Concept and a Company 14.4

HIH Insurance Board Failure to "See, Remedy and Report the Obvious"

Concept	Corporate culture, poor corporate governance model, the role of the auditor.
Story	HIH was one of Australia's biggest home-building market insurers selling home warranty insurance and builders' warranty insurance. Raymond Williams and Michael Payne established the business in 1968.

Despite Australian regulation designed to detect solvency problems at an early stage, "the corporate officers, auditors and regulators of HIH failed to see, remedy or report what should have been obvious." Poor leadership, inept management, and indifference to company problems marked the last years of HIH. Those involved in HIH management ignored or concealed the true state of the company's steadily deteriorating financial position, which lead by 2001 to the largest corporate failure in Australian history. (HIH Royal Commission 2003)

The problematic aspects of the corporate culture of HIH were caused by a number of factors. One was blind faith in a leadership that was ill-equipped for the task. Risks were not properly identified and managed. Unpleasant information was hidden, filtered or sanitized. Finally, there was no skeptical questioning and analysis.

Underwriting Losses

The main reason for HIH's financial decline was several billion dollars in underwriting losses based on claims arising from insured events in previous years. Past claims on policies that had not been properly priced had to be met out of present income, i.e. a deficiency resulted from "under-reserving" or "under-provisioning." The reserves were based on reports of independent actuaries and the assessment of those reports by the auditors. Actuaries were never called in before the Board of Directors to describe the report.

From as far back as 1997 their underwriting losses increased dramatically. In the year ending December 31, 1997 HIH made an underwriting loss of $33.8 million on net premium earned of $1,233.5 million. The comparative figures for the year ending June 30 2000 are $103.5 million and $1,995.4 million respectively. Between 1997 and 1999 the underwriting loss was up 206 percent while the net earned premium rose by only 25 percent. The reported underwriting losses were high, but without several one-off entries they would have been much worse. On September 12, 2000 Andersen, HIH's auditor, made a presentation to the HIH audit committee. They said that in the 12 months to December 1999, one-off adjustments reduced the underwriting loss by $157 million; and at June 30, 2000 they reduced the loss by $360 million.

Reliance on intangibles

Another feature of the financial trend was the increasing reliance on intangible assets to support shareholders' equity. In addition to goodwill and management rights, HIH had on its balance sheet future income tax benefits, deferred information technology costs, and deferred acquisition costs. Goodwill alone represented 50 percent of HIH's shareholders funds. By way of comparison, QBE and NRMA (two comparable Australian insurance companies) had a ratio of goodwill to shareholders funds of 4.9 percent and 0.4 percent respectively.

Acquisitions

At board level, there was little, if any, analysis of the future strategy of the company. Indeed, the company's strategy was not documented. As one director conceded, if he had been asked to commit to writing what the long-term strategy was he would have had difficulty doing so. Examples of this lack of strategy were the acquisition of a UK branch (where losses amounted to $1.7 billion), reacquisition of US operations (causing losses of $620 million), and a joint venture with Alliance Australia Limited.

The most disastrous business transaction involved joint venture arrangements agreed between HIH and Allianz which ultimately caused HIH to experience an insurmountable cash flow crisis in early 2001 and largely dictated the timing of HIH's collapse. In addition to the transfer of HIH's most profitable retail lines to the joint venture, HIH was required to contribute $200 million received for the retail lines plus an additional $300 in cash and assets to a trust to cover claims. All premium income (about $1 billion) was paid into the trust, and HIH was not allowed access to the funds until an actuarial assessment, about five months after the transfer.

The agreement to proceed with the Allianz proposal took a mere 75 minutes of the board of director's meeting. The trust provisions and their potential adverse effect on cash flow were either completely overlooked or not properly appreciated.

Corporate Governance Model

The corporate governance model at HIH was deficient in a number of ways. There was a dearth of clearly defined and recorded policies or guidelines. There were no clearly defined limits on the authority of the chief executive in areas such as investments, corporate donations, gifts, and staff emoluments. The board did not have a well-understood policy on matters that would be reserved to itself, but depended on the chief executive. In addition, it was heavily dependent on the advice of senior management. There were very few occasions when the board either rejected or materially changed a proposal put forward by management. The board was reluctant to disclose related-party transactions. The Chairman of the board gave board agendas to the CEO, but not to the board members, for comments.

Discussion Questions	■ What were the warning signs of financial decline that the auditors should have addressed in their procedures? ■ Describe why assessment of the corporate governance model is important to the audit? ■ What types of strategies and actions could the board of directors initiate which could have changed the outcome?
References	HIH Royal Commission, Justice Owen, R., 2003, *The Failure of HIH Insurance*, Commonwealth of Australia.

As "best practice" of the auditor's role of reviewing or auditing corporate governance statements, we refer to one of the more sophisticated corporate governance codes, the Cadbury report. According to Cadbury, the accountant has to be engaged to review correctness of management's statement regarding compliance with the code of best practice. Following the work of the Hampel Committee on Corporate Governance, in June 1998 the London Stock Exchange published a new listing rule together with related Principles of Good Governance and Code of Best Practice ("the Combined Code"). As before, a company's auditors are required to review such compliance statements (the second statement referred to above) before publication, but only in so far as it relates to certain Code provisions (See Appendix A of this chapter).[43] These are as follows:

- The board should have a formal schedule of matters specifically reserved to it for decision.
- There should be a procedure agreed by the board for directors in the furtherance of their duties to take independent professional advice if necessary, at the company's expense.
- Non-executive directors should be appointed for specified terms subject to re-election and to Companies Act provisions relating to the removal of a director, and reappointment should not be automatic.
- All directors should be subject to election by shareholders at the first opportunity after their appointment, and to re-election thereafter at intervals of no more than three years. The names of directors submitted for election or re-election should be accompanied by sufficient biographical details to enable shareholders to take an informed decision on their election.
- The directors should explain their responsibility for preparing the accounts and there should be a statement by the auditors about their reporting responsibilities.
- The directors should, at least annually, conduct a review of the effectiveness of the group's system of internal controls and should report to shareholders that they have done so. The review should cover all controls, including financial, operational and compliance controls, and risk management.
- The board should establish an audit committee of at least three directors, all non-executive, with written terms of reference which deal clearly with its authority and duties. The members of the committee, a majority of who should be independent non-executive directors, should be named in the report and accounts. Under Listing Rule 12.43(v), auditors are also required to review the directors' statement that the company is a going concern with supporting assumptions or qualifications as necessary.

In Appendix B to this chapter we provide an example of bank auditing and its relation to banking supervision as a best practice of governance and auditing in a public interest context.

■ The Audit Profession and Corporate Governance

The audit profession not only plays a significant role in corporate governance, but is also forced to look after its own corporate governance structure! Financial reporting scandals and the collapse of Arthur Andersen prompted several regulators and professional institutes to develop new legislation and best practices. We will first look into some important new developments hitting the profession as introduced by the Sarbanes-Oxley Act. Central in the Sarbanes-Oxley Act is the establishment of the Public Company

Accounting Oversight Board (PCAOB) with the objective of closely monitoring the audit profession to restore investor confidence. One of the consequences of this is the end of self-regulation by the US audit profession.

Duties of the PCAOB are:

- Register public accounting firms that prepare audit reports for issuers. Public accounting firms must register and disclose (1) names of public clients; (2) fees received for audit services, other accounting services and non-audit services; (3) statement of quality control policies; (4) list of all accountants; (5) any penalties pending against the firm or individuals; and (6) copies of client issuer disclosures of accounting disagreements.
- Establish or adopt rules on auditing, quality control, ethics, independence, as related to preparation of audit reports. Conduct investigations and disciplinary proceedings involving registered public accounting firms. Establish auditing standards.
- Establish quality control standards. Quality control standards could include rules to require monitoring professional ethics and independence.[44] Availability of a formal consultation process, supervision of audit work, client acceptance and continuation procedures and internal inspection policies are further examples.

Audit firms in the US and individuals associated with audit firms listed in the US are required to comply with requests for testimony and production of documents concerning their clients who have issued publicly traded equity or debt. This requirement applies to all audit firms of US registrants and implies that foreign auditors can be forced to testify in US courts.

The collapse of Enron and subsequent financial reporting scandals has prompted calls in the EU for further examination of statutory audits. Calls have been made to avoid knee-jerk regulatory reactions but instead to progress steadily in line with the overall objective of creating an efficient EU capital market by 2005.

EU Proposed Directive on Statutory Audit

In 2004, the Commission of the European Union proposed a major revision of the Eighth Company Law Directive, setting out a new structure for audit and corporate governance.[45] The proposal is the consequence of a reorientation of the EU policy on statutory audit that started in 1996 with a Green Paper on the role and responsibility of the statutory auditor in the EU.

The proposal will considerably broaden the scope of the existing Eighth Council Directive that basically deals with the approval of auditors. It clarifies the duties of statutory auditors, their independence and ethics, introduces a requirement for external quality assurance, and creates an audit regulatory committee to ensure public oversight over the audit profession.[46]

Whilst most of the Directive deals with enhancing audit quality within the EU, the proposal provides a basis for balanced and effective international regulatory co-operative approach with oversight bodies of third countries such as the US Public Company Accounting Oversight Board (PCAOB).

Mandate ISAs for EU

The proposal also foresees the use of international standards on auditing for all statutory audits conducted in the EU. Adoption of these standards, which at present are developed by the IAASB (the International Auditing and Assurance Standards Board), will be subject to strict conditions, such as the respect of proper due process. A final decision on whether and to what extent to endorse ISAs will depend largely on satisfactory governance arrangements relating to the operation of the IAASB being established.

According to the May 2003 Commission communication,[47] the Commission and the Audit Advisory Committee will work to prepare the implementation of ISAs from 2005. These will include: an analysis of EU and Member State audit requirements not covered by ISAs; the development of an endorsement procedure; a common audit report and high-quality translations. The Commission will work towards further improvements to the International Federation of Accountants (IFAC)/International Auditing and Assurance Standards Board (IAASC) audit standard-setting process, notably by ensuring that public interest is taken fully into account. Assuming satisfactory progress, the Commission will propose a binding legal instrument requiring the use of ISAs from 2005.

Oversight of Auditors

The proposed Directive would set out common criteria for public oversight systems, in particular that they should predominantly be led and staffed by non-practitioners, but including sufficient number with experience and/or expertise in audit. At EU level the proposed Directive would create an audit regulatory committee of Member State representatives, so that detailed measures implementing the Directive could be rapidly taken or modified and to allow for continuous monitoring of, and responses to, new developments.

Certification Exam Question 14.5

Under the Sarbanes-Oxley Act, which of the following companies is not subject to executive certification requirements?

(A) US publicly-traded company based outside the United States.
(B) Banks and savings associations.
(C) Unlisted company with public debt.
(D) Unlisted company with over $100,000,000 in sales.

The proposal lays out a concept for a model for co-operation between the relevant authorities of Member States, on the basis of "home country control," in other words regulators in the country where an audit firm is established would take full responsibility for supervising it, and on that basis it could work throughout the EU. However, individual audit staff would need to prove their aptitude and knowledge of the relevant country's legislation before they could undertake statutory audits in another Member State.

The proposed Directive would also establish procedures for the exchange of information between oversight bodies of Member States in investigations. In order to lay the foundations for better co-operation with foreign oversight bodies such as the US PCAOB, the proposed Directive would allow reciprocal co-operation with third countries, also based on the "home country control" principle.

Measures Applicable To All Statutory Auditors And Audit Firms

Some of the measures from the proposal that concern all statutory auditors and audit firms follow:[48]

- Audits must update their educational curriculum for auditors, which must now also include knowledge of international accounting standards (IAS) and international auditing standards (ISA).
- The ownership and the management of audit firms will be opened to statutory auditors of all Member States (not just the home country).
- Auditors and audit firms in all Member States will be registered with the EU.
- Basic principles of professional ethics and auditor independence are defined very closely to IFAC's ethics (see Chapter 3 Ethics for Professional Accountants).
- Member States will set rules for audit fees that ensure audit quality and prevent "low-balling" – in other words, preventing audit firms from offering the audit service for a marginal fee and compensating this with the fee income from other non-audit services.
- Auditors must use international auditing standards for all EU statutory audits once those standards have been endorsed under an EU procedure; Member States can only impose additional requirements in certain defined circumstances.
- Member States are obliged to introduce effective investigative and disciplinary systems.
- Common rules concerning the appointment and the resignation of statutory auditors and audit firms are adopted (e.g. statutory auditors to be dismissed only if there is a significant reason why they cannot finalize the audit). A requirement for companies to document their communication with the statutory auditor or audit firm is introduced.
- Companies must disclose in the notes to their financial statements the audit fee and other fees for non-audit services delivered by the auditor.

Measures applied to statutory auditors and audit firms of public interest companies

Provisions in the proposal applying specifically to auditors of **public interest companies** (defined broadly as listed companies, banks or insurance companies) are the introduction of an annual transparency report, auditor rotation, audit quality review every three years, a requirement that auditors to be selected by an audit committee, and mandated report of the auditor to the audit committee on audit key matters (especially material weaknesses of the internal control system), and discussion with the audit committee of any threats to the auditor's independence and confirmation in writing to the audit committee of his independence.

The transparency report and auditor rotation are important requirements. The annual transparency report for audit firms includes information on the governance of the audit firm, its international network, its quality assurance systems and the fees collected for audit and non-audit services (to demonstrate the relative importance of audit in the firm's overall business). Member States have the option of requiring either a change of the key audit partner dealing with an audited company every five years, if the same audit firm keeps the work, or a change of audit firm every seven years.

Certification Exam Question 14.6

Which of the following do Combined Code rules and SEC regulations require of the audit committee of a publicly traded corporation?

(A) Report by the auditor of all adjustments the auditor thinks proper under IFRS, but where the amounts are immaterial.

(B) Revenue recognition alternatives discussed with management, but then rejected.

(C) Report by the auditor of all adjustments the auditor proposed to management that management did not make.

(D) None of the above.

(E) All of the above.

 14.9 Summary

Corporate governance has been defined in many different ways, by many different authors, in many different countries. In general, corporate governance includes the process and structure used to manage and direct the business, with the objective of enhancing shareholder value. The Organisation for Economic Co-operation and Development (OECD) Corporate Governance Principles state: "Corporate governance involves a set of relationships between a company's management, its board, its shareholders and other stakeholders. Corporate governance also provides the structure through which the objectives of the company are set, and the means of attaining those objectives and monitoring performance are determined."

The Board of Directors sets the mission, vision, objectives and strategy of the entity. Governance deals with "managing" as a key responsibility of the Board. It is also the Board's responsibility to design and monitor controls that reasonably assure that objectives are met. The third element of governance is supervision. Independent supervision of management performance and remuneration is especially crucial. We all know that conflicts of interests between management and stakeholders do exist on a day-to-day basis, and can result in bankruptcies or major frauds. Governance also includes transparency to all stakeholders that can be recognized.

Corporate governance essentially focusses on the dilemma's that result from the separation of ownership and control, and addresses, in particular, the principal–agent relationship between shareholders and directors on the one hand and the relationship between company agents and stakeholders on the other. Other parties are lenders to the corporation; their trading partners (workers, customers, and suppliers); as well as competitors and the general public. All of these parties have an interest in the success of the corporation. Each of the stakeholders has a different kind of relationship with the company and specified rights to receive financial reports. These rights and relationships must be extensively described if we want to understand each claim and propose a reporting system that answers adequately this demand.

There are four causes of the current corporate governance discussion:

1 bankruptcies, fraud, and mismanagement;
2 the influence of public, customers and the media;
3 globalization of capital markets;
4 developments in information technology (IT).

Major reasons for corporate governance being in the spotlight are unexpected bankruptcies, fraud and mismanagement. A second development is the increasing demand for shareholder participation, and also the increasing influence of customers' and public opinion. Globalization supports striving for harmonization of law and legislation. IT is major enabler of the new economy and, consequently, of corporate governance developments and discussions.

To understand current developments, one should understand differences in national corporate governance structures. These differences are caused by factors like culture, history, legal systems, and so on. There are two basic systems of corporate governance: market and network corporate governance structures. Examples of countries with a market-oriented corporate governance structure are countries like the USA and the Commonwealth countries. Examples of network-oriented corporate governance structure countries are those in continental Europe and some Asian countries. Market-oriented countries are more aggressive and confrontation seeking, while "network cultures" seek consensus instead of conflict. Of course, differences are not that black and white, but nevertheless, cultural distinction is a most powerful factor in explaining global differences in corporate governance. The major difference between the market-oriented and the network-oriented corporate governance structures is the two-tier separation between the board of management and the supervisory board in the network structure. In the market-oriented, one-tier system, the complete board, that is both executive and non-executive directors, is formally responsible for day-to-day operating activities.

The most famous corporate governance codes are the Cadbury Report in the UK (which focuses on the financial aspects of corporate governance), the Dey Report in Canada and the King Report in South Africa. But there are others (shown in Illustration 14.3 earlier). In the Netherlands, the Peters Report was published in 1997. As concluded by Peters in 2002, the code was not applied by most public companies in the Netherlands; the Committee Tabaksblat presented a new code in December 2003.

The best practices that are on the worldwide agenda for modernization of governance are related to managing, board responsibility, supervision, internal control and transparency. Managing includes the concepts of mission, strategy, objectives, and compatibility with societal objectives. The board defines the company's strategy, appoints the corporate officers responsible for managing the company and implementing this strategy, oversees management and ensures the quality of information provided to shareholders and to financial markets through the financial statements. Global debates lead to an agreed vision that good corporate governance requires a system of independent supervision and active oversight of management. The US Treadway Commission recommended that prevention and detection of fraud should be guaranteed through strong internal controls. Treadway also recommended that guidelines be developed on internal control to allow management to report against some framework. Such internal-control guidelines were published in 1992 in what is known as the COSO Report. The Cadbury Committee in the UK was also established in response to a concern about the reliability of financial reporting. Section 404 of the Sarbanes-Oxley Act requires the annual report of issuers to contain a management report which: (1) states management's responsibility for internal control structures and procedures; and (2) give an assessment of effectiveness. Best practice transparency includes the elements of timely disclosure of reliable, adequate and relevant information for decision making. Transparency is another best practice issue, being the modernization of current business reporting models.

The external auditor plays a central role in good corporate governance. Despite the fact that auditors are indirect stakeholders, their core role is: (1) to audit financial statements and other (financial) reporting, (2) to attest internal control statements, and (3) to review or attest corporate governance statements.

Central in the Sarbanes-Oxley Act is the establishment of the Public Company Accounting Oversight Board (PCAOB) with the objective of closely monitoring the audit profession to restore investor confidence. One of the consequences of this is the end of self-regulation by the US audit profession. Duties of the PCAOB are: (1) to register public accounting firms that prepare audit reports for issuers; (2) to establish or adopt rules relating to auditing, quality control, ethics, independence, as related to the preparation of audit reports, (3) to conduct investigations and disciplinary proceedings involving registered public accounting firms, (4) to establish auditing standards, and (5) to establish quality control standards.

The European Commission has proposed a new revised Eighth Directive on statutory audit in the EU. The proposed Directive would clarify the duties of statutory auditors and set out certain ethical principles to ensure their objectivity and independence, for example, where audit firms are also providing their clients with other services. It would introduce a requirement for external quality assurance, ensure robust public oversight over the audit profession and improve co-operation between regulatory authorities in the EU. It would create an audit regulatory committee of Member State representatives. The proposal also foresees the use of international standards on auditing for all statutory audits conducted in the EU and provides a basis for balanced and effective international regulatory co-operation with third country regulators such as the US Public Company Accounting Oversight Board (PCAOB).

14.10 Answers to Certification Exam Questions

14.1 (A) The requirement is to determine the most important responsibility of the board of directors. Answer (A) is correct because the board must set the "tone at the top," setting a mission, a vision, and overall direction, and developing a corporate strategy. Answer (B) is incomplete because although the shareholder interest is very important, the board must consider other things such as those listed in (A). Answer (C) is wrong because the board will rarely have operations duties such as approving the use of resources. It is important the board control top management, answer (D), but their main function is not management.

14.2 (C) The requirement is to find the right answers in the blanks. Answer (C) gives the proper order – the board oversees management with the concurrence of shareholders. The other answers are wrong because shareholders do not oversee top management and top management does not oversee the board of directors or the shareholders.

14.3 (B) The requirement is to list the roles of the board of directors in company strategy. Answer (B) is the best one because it describes the board's process of overseeing management with the consent of the shareholders. Answer (A) is incorrect because the board does not get involved in the details of implementation. Answer (C) is inaccurate because the board does not delegate responsibility for setting objectives and crafting strategy. Answer (D) is not the best answer because sometimes the board does get involved in day-to-day strategy.

14.4 (C) The requirement is to find the one answer which is not a matter auditors would communicate to the audit committee. Answer (C) is the best answer, because it is not an auditor's duty to describe corporate governance principles to the committee. The other answers are things that are communicated between an auditor and audit committee including accounting estimates, auditor responsibility for documents associated with the financial statements, and accounting matters for which a legal opinion was received.

14.5 (D) The requirement is to give the company that would not be subject to executive certification requirements under the Sarbanes-Oxley Act. The companies that must certify are those that file reports with the SEC. Answer (D) is a company that would not need to certify because it is not publicly listed nor does it have any public financing which means it makes no reports to the SEC. Answer (C) is also an unlisted company, but it is financed by publicly-traded debt and must report to the SEC. All US publicly-traded companies (A) whether headquartered inside or outside the USA must certify. Banks and savings and loans companies must report to the US government.

14.6 (C) The requirement is to determine what the Combined Code requires of the audit committee. Answer (C) is right because it requires auditors to report all adjustments recommended but refused. Answer (A) is wrong because immaterial amounts are not ordinarily reported. Answer (B) is wrong because alternative revenue recognition policies that might be used are not as important as the ones that are used. It follows that (D) and (E) are both not applicable.

14.11 Notes

1 *Darts* is a game in which darts (slender, pointed missile with tail fins) are thrown by hand at a target of concentric circles.

2 Toronto Stock Exchange, 1994, *Where were the Directors?*, Toronto Stock Exchange. Note that the Toronto Stock Exchange issued *Request for Comments Corporate Governance Policy – Proposed New Disclosure Requirement and Amended Guidelines* on March 26, 2002. These new amendments did not offer a definition of corporate governance.

3 Committee on the Financial Aspects of Corporate Governance, 1992, *Report of the Committee on the Financial Aspects of Corporate Governance* (The Cadbury Report), Gee and Co., Ltd, London.

4 Hampel Committee, 1998, Committee on Corporate Governance, *Final Report*, Gee Publishing, London, January.

5 Peters Committee, 1997, *Corporate Governance in the Netherlands, Forty Recommendations*, Committee on Corporate Governance, Amsterdam, June.

6 Business Sector Advisory Group on Corporate Governance, 1998, *Corporate Governance, Improving Competitiveness and Access to Capital in Global Markets*, A Report to the OECD by the Business Sector Advisory Group on Corporate Governance, Ira M. Millstein (Chairman) et al. OECD. Also see OECD, 2004, *OECD Principles of Corporate Governance*. Draft Revised Text, Organisation for Economic Co-operation and Development, Paris, www.oecd.org/home/, January.

7 McKinsey & Company, 2002, *McKinsey Global Investor Opinion Survey on Corporate Governance*, London, July, www.mckinsey.com/practices/corporategovernance/PDF/GlobalInvestorOpinion Survey2002.pdf

8 Geert Hofstede, 1980, "International Differences in Work-Related Values," *Culture's Consequences*, Sage Publications, California, USA.

9 See, for example, International Capital Markets Group, 1995, *International Corporate Governance Who holds the reins?*, London.

10 Toronto Stock Exchange Committee on Corporate Governance (Dey Committee), 1994, *Where were the Directors? Guidelines for Improved Corporate Governance in Canada*, December.

11 Institute of Directors in Southern Africa, 1994, *King I Report on Corporate Governance*.

12 Committee on Corporate Governance (Peters Committee), 1997, *Corporate Governance in the Netherlands, Forty Recommendations*, Amsterdam, June.

13 De stand van zaken, 2002, *Corporate Governance in Nederland 2002, Een uitgave onder auspiciën van de Nederlandse Corporate Governance Stichting*, De stand van zaken, Amsterdam, 2002.

14 107th US Congress, 2002, *Sarbanes-Oxley Act of 2002*, Public Law 107–204, Senate and House of Representatives of the United States of America in Congress assembled, Washington, DC, July 30.

15 SEC, 2003, *Final Rule: Management's Reports on Internal Control Over Financial Reporting and Certification of Disclosure in Exchange Act Periodic Reports*, US Securities and Exchange Commission, June 11.

16 See PCAOB, 2003, *PCAOB Release No. 2003–024*, "Proposed Rules Relating To The Oversight Of Non-U.S. Public," Public Company Accounting Oversight Board, December 10.

17 Commission to the Council and the European Parliament, 2003, *Communication from the Commission to the Council and the European Parliament*, Brussels, May.

18 European Union, 2002, *The High Level Group of Company Law Experts on a modern regulatory framework for company law in Europe*, Brussels.

19 EU, 2002, *Comparative Study of Corporate Governance Codes relevant to the EU and its Member States*, European Union, Brussels, March.

20 In developing its approach, the Commission has paid attention to the following needs: considering where possible (a) the use of alternatives to legislation and (b) the preference to be given to disclosure requirements (because they are less intrusive in corporate life, and they can prove to be a highly effective market-led way of rapidly achieving results).

21 Business Sector Advisory Group on Corporate Governance, 1998, *Corporate Governance, Improving Competitiveness and Access to Capital in Global Markets*, A Report to the OECD by the Business Sector Advisory Group on Corporate Governance, Ira M. Millstein (Chairman), et al., OECD.

22 The Shell Report, 1999, **www.shell.com**.

23 Ibid. Triple Bottom Line.

24 Le conseil d'administration des sociétés côteés, 1995, *Vienot Report*, Le conseil d'administration des sociétés côteés, July.

25 Bouton, R., 2002, Pour un meilleur gouvernement des entreprises côteés, September.

26 Cohen Commission, 1978, *The Commission of Auditors' Responsibilities: Report, Conclusions and Recommendations*, American Institute of Certified Public Accountants, New York.

27 See Levitt, A. 1998, "The Numbers Game," *The CPA Journal*, 68 (12), 14–19; Levitt, A. and Dwyer, P., 2002, *Take on the Street*, New York: Random House.

28 NYSE/NASD Blue Ribbon Committee on Improving the Effectiveness of Corporate Audit Committees (BRC), 2000, *Recommendations*, New York Stock Exchange (NYSE) and the National Association of Securities Dealers (NASD), New York. See also SEC, 1999, "Audit Committee Disclosure," *Exchange Act Release No. 34-41987, 17 C.F.R. §§ 210, 228, 229 and 240*, Vol. 64, No. 198 (Oct. 14).

29 Commission of the European Communities, 2004, *Proposal for a Directive of the European Parliament and of the Council on Statutory Audit of Annual Accounts and Consolidated Accounts and Amending Council Directives 78/660/EEC and 83/349/EEC*, European Union, Brussels, March.

30 107th US Congress, 2002, *Sarbanes-Oxley Act of 2002*, Public Law 107–204, section 407, "Disclosure of Audit Committee Financial Expert," Senate and House of Representatives of the United States of America in Congress assembled, Washington, DC, July 30.

31 SEC, 2003, *Release No. 33-8220, File No. S7-02-03*, "Standards Relating To Listed Company Audit Committees," US Securities And Exchange Commission, April 10.

32 107th US Congress, 2002, SEC, 2004, "Auditor Reports To Audit Committees," *Sarbanes-Oxley Act of 2002*, Public Law 107–204, Senate and House of Representatives of the United States of America in Congress assembled, Washington, DC, July 30.

33 107th US Congress, 2002, SEC, 806, "Protection for Employees of Publicly Traded Companies Who Provide Evidence of Fraud," *Sarbanes-Oxley Act of 2002*, Public Law 107–204, Senate and House of Representatives of the United States of America in Congress assembled, Washington, DC, July 30.

34 107th US Congress, 2002, SEC, 103.4, "Auditing, Quality Control, And Independence Standards and Rules," *Sarbanes-Oxley Act of 2002*, Public Law 107–204, Senate and House of Representatives of the United States of America in Congress assembled, Washington, DC, July 30.

35 National Commission on Fraudulent Financial Reporting (Treadway Commission), 1987, *Report of the National Commission on Fraudulent Financial Reporting*, Washington, October.

36 Committee of Sponsoring Organizations of the Treadway Commission (COSO), 1992, *Internal Control – Integrated Framework*, American Institute of Certified Public Accountants, Jersey City, New Jersey.

37 The KPMG Review, 1999, *The Combined Code: A Practical Guide*, KPMG, United Kingdom, January.

38 107th US Congress, 2002, SEC, 404 "Management Assessment Of Internal Controls," *Sarbanes-Oxley Act of 2002*, Public Law 107–204, Senate and House of Representatives of the United States of America in Congress assembled, Washington, DC, July 30.

39 IDW, 2003, *Financial reporting, auditing and corporate governance*, IDW, Düsseldorf, April.

40 Anderson, Alan, vice president of AICPA, 2003, *Talk to 7th XBRL International Conference*, 7th XBRL International Conference, Amsterdam, May 2003.

41 Direct stakeholders are board members, employees, shareholders and other parties being owner or part of the company.

42 IFAC, 2004, *Handbook of International Auditing, Assurance, and Ethics Pronouncements*, International Standards on Auditing 200 (ISA 200), "Objective and General Principles Governing an Audit of Financial Statements", International Federation of Accountants, New York.

43 Hampel Committee, 1998, Committee on Corporate Governance, *Final Report (Hampel Report)*, Gee Publishing, London, January.

44 For further details about the independence requirements, refer to Chapter 3.

45 Commission Of The European Communities, 2004, *Proposal for a Directive of the European Parliament and of the Council on Statutory Audit of Annual Accounts and Consolidated Accounts and Amending Council Directives 78/660/EEC and 83/349/EEC*, European Union, Brussels, March.

46 Bolkestein, Frits, 2004, *Memorandum from Mr Bolkestein to the Commission on the proposal for a Directive of the European Parliament and of the Council on statutory audit in the EU*, European Union, Brussels, March.

47 Commission of the European Communities, 2003, *Modernising Company Law and Enhancing Corporate Governance in the EU – A Plan to Move Forward*, European Union, Brussels, 22 May.

48 Adapted from EU, 2004, *MEMO/04/60 European Commission Proposal for a Directive on Statutory Audit: Frequently Asked Questions*, Brussels, March 16.

14.12 Questions, Exercises and Cases

QUESTIONS

14.2 The Nature of Corporate Governance

14.1 Explain the concept of Corporate Governance.

14.2 Describe the difference between shareholders and stakeholders and discuss why differences play a central role in the corporate governance discussion.

14.3 Causes of Current Corporate Governance Discussions

14.3 Explain why the concept of corporate governance is being discussed all over the globe at the beginning of the twenty-first century.

14.4 Talk about why IFRS and XBRL could contribute to good corporate governance.

14.4 Corporate Governance Structures

14.5 Describe the differences between a market-oriented versus a network-oriented corporate governance structure.

14.6 What are advantages and disadvantages of a one-tier board structure.

14.5 Corporate Governance Committees and Reports

14.7 Should a corporate governance code be developed by governmental bodies and enforced by law or should a code be developed by private institutions as companies, shareholder representatives, lawyers and accountants and compliance be left to self-regulation?

14.6 Best Practice from a Global Perspective

14.8 Should auditors be appointed by management or the audit committee? Why?

14.9 According to Sarbanes-Oxley, at least one audit committee member should be a "financial expert." Discuss some criteria that should be met.

14.10 Should the audit committee review design and operating effectiveness of internal controls? Do you think the audit committee is part of "internal control?"

14.11 Describe the steps of the audit of internal controls over financial reporting.

14.12 Transparency is an important element of good corporate governance. Do you think a maximum level of transparency exists or should the company be able and willing to communicate all information at the request of stakeholders?

14.7 Corporate Governance And The Role Of The Auditor

14.13 List major differences between the internal and external audit.

14.14 What is meant by the statement: "Corporate governance is not an end in itself?"

14.15 Describe the role of the external auditor in corporate governance.

PROBLEMS AND EXERCISES

14.2 The Nature of Corporate Governance

14.16 Using the example of basketball, explain the nature of corporate governance in terms of a basketball team.

14.3 Causes of Current Corporate Governance Discussions

14.17 Bakka Bee, a construction firm in Toronto Canada. They are a firm with 200 employees in five countries. One of their divisions – in Peru – has encountered difficulties and may have to be liquidated. The company uses computers for everything from design of buildings to testing the quality of construction.

Required:
Discuss Bakka Bee in terms of the four causes of the current corporate governance discussion:
1 Bankruptcies, fraud, and mismanagement.
2 The influence of public, customers and media.
3 Globalization of capital markets.
4 Developments in information technology (IT).

14.4 Corporate Governance Structures

14.18 Pick one US-based company and one European company and compare and contrast their board of directors and other supervisory boards.

14.5 Corporate Governance Committees & Reports

14.19 According to the US Sarbanes-Oxley Act, auditors should audit the internal controls of financial reporting (SOX 404). However, from prior research it can be concluded that users of the auditor's opinion on financial statements assume an unqualified opinion implicates internal controls being adequately designed and operating. Explain why this expectation cannot be met by an audit of financial statements. Describe major differences in evaluating internal controls over financial reporting in a financial statements audit and auditing internal controls over financial reporting as a separate engagement.

14.6 Best Practice from a Global Perspective

14.20 Discuss the duties of the PCAOB.

14.21 Royal Shell publishes a "Triple Bottom Line Report" in which it reports about economic, social and environmental issues. This report (called *The Shell Report*) can be found on the internet (**www.shell.com**). Review *The Shell Report* and summarize potential stakeholders that could be interested in this report. For each potential stakeholder formulate a financial or non-financial performance indicator.

14.7 Corporate Governance And The Role Of The Auditor

14.22 Why is self-regulation by the audit profession in the US no longer in place? Find some arguments "pro and con" self-regulation?

CASES

14.23 Describe the system of oversight of the audit profession in your country. Compare this system with the PCAOB standards. Discuss differences. US students should analyze the oversight system in the UK and Europe as a whole, make a comparison and discuss differences.

The Combined Code (UK), July 2003: An Example of Auditors' Review of Corporate Governance Best Practice

■ Directors

Some key provisions

- The chairman should ensure that new directors receive a full, formal and tailored introduction on joining the board. (Code Provision A.5.1).
- The board should identify in the annual report each non-executive director it considers to be independent. The chairman should, on appointment, meet the independence criteria set out in A.3.1 (A.2.2).
- Except for smaller companies, at least half of the board, excluding the chairman, should comprise non-executive directors determined by the board to be independent (A.3.2).
- There should be a nomination committee which should lead the process for board appointments and make recommendations to the board. A majority of the members of the nomination committee should be independent non-executive directors (A.4.1).
- Nomination committees should evaluate the balance of skills, knowledge and experience on the board and, in the light of this evaluation prepare a description of the role and capabilities required for a particular appointment (A.4.2).
- All directors should be subject to election by shareholders at the first annual general meeting after their appointment, and to re-election thereafter at intervals of no more than three years. The names of directors submitted for election or re-election should be accompanied by sufficient biographical details to enable shareholders to take an informed decision on their election (A.7.1).
- Non-executive directors should be appointed for specified terms subject to re-election and to Companies Act provisions relating to the removal of a director, and re-appointment should not be automatic (A.7.2).

Example of audit implications

- The control environment could be considered weak if there are insufficient non-executive directors.

- If directors are not properly trained can they make strategic decisions about the company's operations?
- With more independent directors, the directors may not have the necessary understanding of the company's business and industry it operates in to make informed strategic decisions.
- With directors being up for re-election every three years there may be less continuity on the board.

According to the listing requirements of the London Stock Exchange, the company's auditors are required to review compliance statements relating to certain Code provisions (illustrative):

- The board should have a formal schedule of matters specifically reserved to it for decision (Code Provision A.1.1).
- The board should ensure that directors have access to independent professional advice at the company's expense where they judge it necessary to discharge their responsibilities as directors (A.5.2).
- Non-executive directors should be appointed for specified terms subject to re-election and to Companies Act provisions relating to the removal of a director. The board should set out to shareholders in the papers accompanying a resolution to elect a non-executive director why they believe an individual should be elected (A.7.2).
- All directors should be subject to election by shareholders at the first opportunity after their appointment, and to re-election thereafter at intervals of no more than three years. The names of directors submitted for election or re-election should be accompanied by sufficient biographical details to enable shareholders to take an informed decision on their election (A.7.1).

Audit procedures (illustrative)

- The board should have a formal schedule of matters specifically reserved to it for decision (Code Provision A.1.1).
  - inspect the schedule of specific matters noting when this was last updated;
  - inspect the board minutes recording adoption of the most recent schedule;
  - consider whether the contents of the schedule are likely to be adequate for the business taking into account its size, nature and complexity;
  - consider whether the schedule of matters appears to be followed by reference to board minutes throughout the period, and to any transactions, of which we are aware, that would appear to require board approval.
- The board should ensure that directors have access to independent professional advice at the company's expense where they judge it necessary to discharge their responsibilities as directors (A.5.2).
  - establish details of the agreed procedures;
  - inspect the board minutes recording adoption of these procedures, if these have been adopted this year;
  - if procedures are not formally laid down in writing, confirm their existence with directors and company secretary;
  - consider, by discussion with the directors and from our knowledge of the business, whether there was a need for independent advice during the period and, if so, whether procedures have been followed in practice.

■ Non-executive directors should be appointed for specified terms subject to re-election and to Companies Act provisions relating to the removal of a director. The board should set out to shareholders in the papers accompanying a resolution to elect a non-executive director why they believe an individual should be elected (A.7.2).

- inspect the service contracts/letter of appointment of all directors who were members of the board at any time during the period under review (see A.7.1 below).
- check whether the non-executive directors' contracts specify the terms of appointment;
- consider, for those non-executive directors who came to the end of their term during the period, whether there is evidence that their re-appointment was formally considered by the board and remuneration committee and in line with Companies Act provisions relating to the removal of a director.

■ All directors should be subject to election by shareholders at the first opportunity after their appointment, and to re-election thereafter at intervals of no more than three years. The names of directors submitted for election or re-election should be accompanied by sufficient biographical details to enable shareholders to take an informed decision on their election (A.7.1).

- ensure that all directors appointed during the year have been elected or will be elected by shareholders at the earliest opportunity;
- based on the inspection mentioned in A.7.2 above, determine whether any directors' service contract exceeds three years. If so, establish why this is the case;
- ensure that all directors submitted for election or re-election are accompanied by sufficient biographical details to enable shareholders to take an informed decision on their election.

14.A.1 Questions and Exercises

QUESTIONS

Appendix A to Chapter 14 – The Combined Code (UK) An Example of Auditors' Review of Corporate Governance Best Practice

14A.1 Choose one of the key provisions of the Combined Code and discuss what the impact of that provision on the company should be.

PROBLEMS AND EXERCISES

Appendix A to Chapter 14 – The Combined Code (UK) An Example of Auditors' Review of Corporate Governance Best Practice

14A.2 Appendix A lists audit procedures that the auditor must undertake to ensure that the board has a formal schedule of matters specifically reserved to it. For each audit procedure:
A. List the source of the evidence;
B. Describe how the evidence will be examined (a) by whom and (b) using what type of evidence gathering technique (inquiry, inspection, confirmation, etc.);
C. Give an example of the notation in the audit work papers; and
D. Describe the alternative procedures to be undertaken if a problem arises.

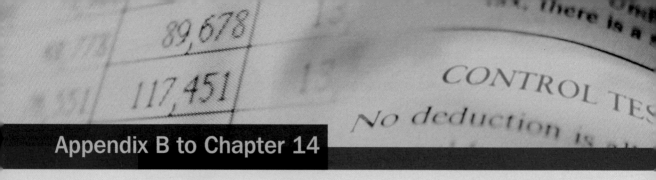

Governance and Auditing in a Public Interest Context

■ The Example of Bank Auditing and its Relation to Banking Supervision

In many commercial cases, the context of auditing is rather straightforward. Shareholders have appointed a board of directors who govern a company on their behalf. The board is responsible for arranging appropriate management of the company and faithfully reporting the results to the shareholders. This model is described as a principal–agent relationship in Chapter 2 The Audit Market.

Principal–Agent Relationship

Information asymmetry between principals and agents calls for the basic function of the auditor. Auditors reduce such asymmetry by independently verifying management's assertions to the board, and the board's assertions to the shareholders. Auditor independence, integrity and expertise are essential conditions for the principal's (shareholder) confidence in the effectiveness of the audit-function. If this confidence is shocked by an auditor's breach of these conditions, the audit function loses its value. Several financial scandals have demonstrated this, most notably in the complete disappearance of the Big Five firm Arthur Andersen after the Enron collapse.

However, in a public interest context the principal–agent relationships are more complex. We will use here the example of banks. Banks are commercial enterprises like many others, and they have basically a similar governance structure, and shareholders, as well. But there is another very important group of stakeholders, i.e. the creditors of the bank and more generally, all those who have an interest in the stability of the financial system as a whole. In essence, that includes every citizen, in other words, the public as a whole. This is meant by the expression "public interest."

Given the importance of the public interest in the better functioning of banks, the principal–agent model is applicable only in a comprehensive way. If virtually everybody is a principal to an interrelated complex of agents, it would overstretch the expectation that auditors could reduce the information asymmetry sufficiently. Moreover, the importance of stability of the financial system as a whole warrants the attention of public watchdogs on a more permanent basis.

Banking Supervision

Reducing information asymmetry with respect to financial reporting is not the only thing that matters to banks' principals. They need to be assured that they can rely on the financial system on an ongoing basis. This has called for a more permanent regulatory and supervisory function, hereafter called banking supervision. (Note that such function exists in more contexts, for example, insurance and securities supervision, and competition authorities). Banking supervision, often referred to as prudential supervision, serves the public interest by licensing banks; imposing on them regulations regarding corporate governance, capital adequacy, risk management and internal controls, and customer due diligence; and by on- and off-site supervision of banks' compliance.

In many of these areas, the work of banking supervisors interferes with that of internal and external auditors. Therefore, the **Basel Committee on Banking Supervision**[1] (the Basel Committee) and the International Auditing Practices Committee (IAPC) of the International Federation of Accountants (IFAC) have issued in 2001 an International Auditing Practice Statement (IAPS) 1004. (Note that the IAPC has been the predecessor of the International Auditing and Assurance Standards Board (IAASB).)

International Auditing Practice Statement 1004

IAPS 1004[2] describes the roles and responsibilities of a bank's board of directors and management, the bank's internal and external auditors, and the banking supervisors. It intends to provide an understanding of these roles and how they relate to each other. This should clarify each role, make the model as a whole more effective, and, as a result, strengthen the contribution of each participant to the public interest in financial stability.

IAPS 1004 is organised as follows. First, it sets out the primary responsibility of the board of directors and management. Then, it examines the essential features of the role of external auditors and of the role of banking supervisors. Finally, it reviews the relationship between the banking supervisor and the bank's external auditor, and describes additional ways in which external auditors and the accountancy profession can contribute to the supervisory process.

■ The Responsibilities of Bank's Board of Directors and Management[3]

From a corporate governance perspective, it is interesting to see that IAPS 1004 starts with the responsibility of those who are charged with the governance of the bank, its board of directors and its management. (This relates to the two decision-making functions within a bank and in many other institutions. In a number of countries these functions are formally separated in the previously described two tier-structure: a Supervisory Board and an Executive Board.) Indeed, it is important to have these key functions right. As financial scandals have demonstrated, without proper and fit directors to govern the control structures, the work of auditors and of supervisors becomes less effective.

IAPS 1004 then describes comprehensively what this responsibility includes.[4] It should ensure that:

■ those entrusted with banking tasks have sufficient expertise and integrity and that there are experienced staff in key positions;

- adequate policies, practices and procedures related to the different activities of the bank are established and complied with, including:
  - the promotion of high ethical and professional standards;
  - systems that accurately identify and measure all material risks and adequately monitor and control these risks;
  - the evaluation of the quality of assets and their proper recognition and measurement;
  - "know your customer" rules that prevent the bank being used, intentionally or unintentionally, by criminal elements;
  - the adoption of a suitable control environment, aimed at meeting the bank's prescribed performance, information and compliance objectives;
  - the testing of compliance and the evaluation of the effectiveness of internal controls by the internal audit function;
- appropriate management information systems are established;
- the bank has appropriate risk management policies and procedures;
- statutory and regulatory directives, including directives regarding solvency and liquidity, are observed;
- the interests not only of the shareholders but also of the depositors and other creditors are adequately protected.

If the whole of the long list is addressed appropriately, an important foundation of sound corporate governance is laid down in the controlling structure of this institution. Logically, IAPS 1004 then continues to deal with the role of audit committees and their reinforcement of the internal control system and the internal audit function. It, among other things, emphasizes the importance of: "regular meetings of the audit committee with the internal and external auditors. This should enhance the external auditors' independence and the credibility of the internal auditors, and assist the audit committee to perform its key role on strengthening corporate governance."

Regarding the establishment and effectiveness of the internal audit function, several best practice statements are made. These deal with the independence and competence of internal auditors, and the comprehensiveness of their function. Although this was written in a banking context, well before Enron, etc., this best practice is relevant for many non-financial institutions as well.

■ Role of the Bank's External Auditor and of the Banking Supervisor

Then the role of the bank's external auditor is described. So, in a nutshell, the full audit process is exemplarily pictured. This follows closely what this book is all about. The objective of an audit is to express an opinion on the financial statements. Consequently, it is important to take into account the country-specific financial reporting framework. To arrive at this opinion, the auditor designs audit procedures, assesses inherent and control risk and considers fraud risk factors. Several relevant ISAs are quoted.

Characteristics That Distinguish Banks

Next is an interesting section: a description of 14 characteristics of banks that distinguish them from most other commercial enterprises.[5] This analysis is again a best practice example of the need for auditors to carefully analyze and understand the audit object and its business environment. Without that, a professionally appropriate audit is hard to achieve. This has always been true, but in today's global and dynamic commercial context, it is imperative for each audit. Therefore, both audit committees and audit firms should warrant that this is adequately fulfilled.

The Statement continues with addressing issues such as testing of internal controls and substantive procedures, using the work of the internal auditor, the importance of judgment and materiality considerations, and communications with management.

Role of the Banking Supervisor

IAPS 1004 then deals with the role of the banking supervisor. It starts by explaining that the "key objective or prudential supervision is to maintain stability and confidence in the financial system, thereby reducing the risk of loss to depositors and other creditors." It then describes a key feature of banks, namely that "banking supervision is based on a system of licensing, which allows supervisors to identify the population to be supervised and to control entry into the banking system. In order to qualify for and retain a banking license, entities must observe certain prudential requirements."

Banking License

The following basic requirements for a banking license are ordinarily found in most systems of supervision:

- The bank must have suitable shareholders and members of the board (this notion includes integrity and standing in the business community as well as the financial strength of all major shareholders).
- The bank's management must be honest and trustworthy and must possess appropriate skills and experience to operate the bank in a sound and prudent manner.
- The bank's organization and internal control must be consistent with its business plans and strategies.
- The bank should have a legal structure in line with its operational structure.
- The bank must have adequate capital to withstand the risks inherent in the nature and size of its business.
- The bank must have sufficient liquidity to meet outflows of funds.

This licensing is a distinct feature of many financial institutions compared to commercial enterprises, which has all to do with the great public interest of a financially stable system. Therefore, although "ongoing banking supervision ordinarily is conducted on the basis of recommendations and guidance, banking supervisors have at their disposal recourse to legal powers to bring about timely corrective action when a bank fails to meet prudential requirements, when there are violations of laws or regulations, or when depositors are faced with a substantial risk of loss. In extreme circumstances, the supervisor may have the authority to revoke the bank's license."

Capital Base Accord

A key element for the solidity of banks is the requirement to maintain an adequate capital base. The Basel Committee of Banking Supervisors has agreed in 1988 the "Basel Accord" which defines the capital requirements for banks. A new and completely revised Accord is expected to become applicable from 2007. This "New Accord" will not only have modernized quantitative capital requirements ("Pillar I"), but will also explicitly state that supervisors have to assess this for each bank and eventually should intervene with the above-mentioned minimum capital requirements ("Pillar II"). Finally, the "Pillar III" requires a number of qualitative and quantitative disclosures in order to enhance market discipline.

Bank Risks

The Statement goes on to elaborate on a range of risks with which banks are faced, such as **credit risk, market risk, liquidity risk, operational risk, legal risk**, and **reputational risk**. Banks have to protect themselves against these risks by a sound risk management system and comprehensive internal controls. A well-known example is the credit risk, i.e. the risk that debtors do not repay their loans, resulting in loan losses.

There is an important lesson here for commercial enterprises as well. The above indicated risk analysis should take place in every company, supervised or not, adapted of course to the particular circumstances. Only on that basis can the directors and management establish solid controls and have those appropriately audited.

Supervisors' Efforts

Finally, this section of the Statement describes how supervisors make efforts to ensure the quality of management; collect, analyze and validate information through on-site inspections and the use of external auditors; and meet periodically with the audit committee or directors to enhance their understanding of a bank's corporate governance and system of operation. As the work of the external auditors is highly relevant to the supervisors, they pay full attention to the **independence**, competence, **objectivity** and quality assurance programs of the auditors. Supervisors seldom have the power to get the auditor removed from a bank's statutory audit if he is not performing the audit function efficiently.

Lesson for the Business Environment

Also, here a lesson which can be drawn from this banking example to the business environment at large. That is, business can learn how controls, audits and supervisory inspections come together to enhance the bank's corporate governance. Directors and management of non-supervised entities, as well as their auditors, may consider to what extent they should compensate for this non-supervision in order to achieve a high-level corporate governance system. Although the public interest in financial institutions may be somewhat larger than for commercial enterprises, the latter as well represents important investments from a rich variety of stakeholders, including employees, municipalities and creditors.

■ Relationship Between Banking Supervisor and External Auditor

It is obvious from our discussion that a good relationship between the banking supervisor and the external auditor effectively contributes to the corporate governance of a bank and to the efficiency of supervisory and auditing processes. This subject is dealt with in the last part of IAPS 1004. It states:[6]

> In many respects the banking supervisor and the external auditor have complementary concerns regarding the same matters though the focus of their concerns is different.
>
> ■ The banking supervisor is primarily concerned with maintaining the stability of the banking system and fostering the safety and soundness of individual banks in order to protect the interests of the depositors. Therefore, the supervisor monitors the present and future viability of banks and uses their financial statements in assessing their condition and performance.

The external auditor, on the other hand, is primarily concerned with reporting on the bank's financial statements ordinarily either to the bank's shareholders or board of directors. In doing so, the auditor considers the appropriateness of management's use of the going concern assumption. (...)

■ The banking supervisor is concerned with the maintenance of a sound system of internal control as a basis for safe and prudent management of the bank's business. The external auditor, in most situations, is concerned with the assessment of internal control to determine the degree of reliance to be placed on the system in planning and performing the audit.

■ The banking supervisor must be satisfied that each bank maintains adequate records prepared in accordance with consistent accounting policies and practices that enable the supervisor to appraise the financial conditions of the bank and the profitability of its business, and that the bank publishes or makes available on a regular basis financial statements that fairly reflect its condition. The external auditor is concerned with whether adequate and sufficiently reliable accounting records are maintained in order to enable the entity to prepare financial statements that do not contain material misstatements and thus enable the external auditor to express an opinion on those statements.

The Statement then poses some caveats, as objectives and scope of the work of the auditors and the supervisors, respectively, are not fully congruent or complementary to each other. Nevertheless, "there are many areas where the work of the banking supervisor and of the external auditor can be useful to each other. Communications from auditors to management and other reports submitted by auditors can provide supervisors with valuable insight into various aspects of the bank's operations. It is the practice in many countries for such reports to be made available to the supervisors.

Communications

"Similarly, external auditors may obtain helpful insights from information originating from the banking supervisor. When a supervisory inspection or a management interview takes place, the conclusions drawn from the inspection or interview are customarily communicated to the bank. These communications can be useful to auditors inasmuch as they provide an independent assessment in important areas such as the adequacy of the allowance for loan losses and focus attention on specific areas of supervisory concern."

But due care is important here; on one hand, to preserve the required professional confidentiality on both sides, on the other, to warrant that information that is known by one party and is vital to the other one, is communicated appropriately between them.

Governance Communications

This matter has been extensively discussed between IFAC and the Basel Committee. The consensus achieved appears from paragraph 52 of IAPS 1004: ISA 260, "Communications of Audit Matters With Those Charged With Governance," identifies matters of governance interest and requires auditors to communicate those matters on a timely basis to those charged with governance. Audit matters of governance interest include only those matters that have come to the attention of the auditor as a result of the performance of the audit. The auditor is not required, in an audit in accordance with ISAs, to design procedures for the specific purpose of identifying matters of governance interest.

Certain audit matters of governance interest are likely to be of interest to banking supervisors, particularly where those matters may require urgent action by the supervisor. When required by the supervisory, legal, or regulatory framework, or by a formal agreement or protocol, the auditor communicates such matters to the banking supervisor on a timely basis. In situations where there are no such requirements, agreements or protocols, the auditor encourages the bank's management or those charged with governance to communicate on a timely basis matters that, in the auditor's judgment, may be of urgent interest to the banking supervisor. Furthermore, even if there is no requirement to do so, the auditor considers communicating such matters to the banking supervisor when management or those charged with governance do not do so. In such circumstances, the auditor considers whether the law protects the auditor when such communications are made.

So the Statement summarizes[7] that "banking supervisors and internal and external auditors co-operate with each other to make their contributions to the supervisory process more efficient and effective. The co-operation optimizes supervision while allowing each party to concentrate on its own responsibilities."

Finally, IAPS 1004 deals with the possibility of additional requests for the external auditor to contribute to the supervisory process. Criteria are suggested to avoid, among otherthing, conflicts of interest and confusion about responsibilities and competence.

■ Summary

In this appendix the role of auditors has been discussed in the context of banks and in their relationship to banking supervisors. It appears that corporate governance is enhanced by the combined work of supervisors and auditors. The board of directors and management are the central parties in an appropriate corporate governance model. The quality of this governance should benefit from the professional contributions made by the internal and external auditors and by the supervisors. IAPS 1004 describes how to make best use of each role. A lesson for non-supervised entities may be that they should analyze what they miss as they are not supervised, and how to compensate for that in order to achieve a high quality of corporate governance. This is the more relevant as non-financial institutions are also seen as important from a public interest perspective.

B.1 Notes

1 The Basel Committee on Banking Supervision is a committee of banking supervisory authorities that was established by the central bank governors of the Group of Ten countries in 1975. It consists of senior representatives of banking supervisory authorities and central banks from Belgium, Canada, France, Germany, Italy, Japan, Luxembourg, the Netherlands, Spain, Sweden, Switzerland, the UK and the USA. It usually meets at the Bank for International Settlements in Basel, where its permanent Secretariat is located.

2 IFAC, 2004, *Handbook of International Auditing, Assurance, and Ethics Pronouncements*, International Auditing Practice Statement 1004 (IAPS 1004), "The Relationship Between Banking Supervisors and Banks' External Auditors," International Federation of Accountants, New York.

3 Ibid.

4 Ibid. Para. 8.

5 Ibid. Para. 18.

6 Ibid. Para. 46.

7 Ibid. Para. 55.

B.2 Questions and Exercises

QUESTIONS

Appendix B to Chapter 14 – Governance and Auditing in a Public Interest Context

14B.1 Explain how information asymmetry between principals and agents calls for the basic function of the auditor.

14B.2 What is the responsibility of a bank's board of directors and management?

PROBLEMS AND EXERCISES

Appendix B to Chapter 14 – Governance and Auditing in a Public Interest Context

14B.3 Read the following cases and describe how IAPS 1004 would apply to each:

1 Lincoln Savings and Loan (Chapter 3, Concept and Company 3.2).
2 Resona Bank (Chapter 5, Concept and Company 5.1).
3 Penn Square Bank (Chapter 5, Concept and Company 5.2).
4 CitiBank (Chapter 7, Concept and Company 7.3).

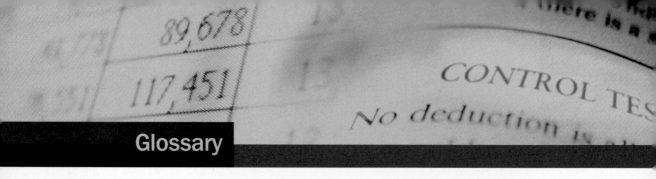

Remember: If you see a term in this glossary, then that term and its related process are discussed in the book. If you cannot find a term here, let the authors know at **rhayes@ calstatela.edu**.

Access controls – Procedures designed to restrict access to on-line terminal devices, programs and data. Access controls consist of "user authentication" and "user authorization." "User authentication" typically attempts to identify a user through unique logon identifications, passwords, access cards or biometric data. "User authorization" consists of access rules to determine the computer resources each user may access. Specifically, such procedures are designed to prevent or detect:

- unauthorized access to on-line terminal devices, programs and data;
- entry of unauthorized transactions;
- unauthorized changes to data files;
- the use of computer programs by unauthorized personnel; and
- the use of computer programs that have not been authorized.

Account analysis schedule – Normally used for fixed assets, liabilities and equity accounts, shows the activity in a general ledger account during the entire period under audit, tying together the beginning and ending balances.

Accounting estimate – An approximation of the amount of an item in the absence of a precise means of measurement.

Accounting system – The series of tasks and records of an entity by which transactions are processed as a means of maintaining financial records. Such systems identify, assemble, analyze, calculate, classify, record, summarize, and report transactions and other events.

Accounts receivable turnover – The ratio of operating revenues to accounts receivable; it measures a company's ability to convert revenues into cash.

Accuracy assertion – The assertion that amounts and other data relating to recorded transactions and events have been recorded accurately.

Adjusting journal entry – The correcting entry required at the end of the reporting period due to a mistake made in the accounting records; also called "correcting entry."

Adverse opinion – see **Modified auditor's report** and **Opinion**.

Advertising – The communication to the public of information as to the services or skills provided by professional accountants in public practice with a view to procuring professional business.

Advocacy threat – Occurs when a member of the assurance team promotes, or seems to promote, an assurance client's position or opinion.

Affiliate – A party that, directly or indirectly, controls, is controlled by, or is under common control with an enterprise.

Agency theory – A company is viewed as the result of more or less formal contracts, in which several groups make some kind of contribution to the company, given a certain price. A reputable auditor is appointed not only in the interest of third parties, but also in the interest of management. (See Watts, R.L., Zimmerman J.L., 1978, "Towards a positive theory of the determination of counting standards," *The Accounting Review*, (January): 112–134; and Watts, R.L., Zimmerman J.L., 1979, "The demand for and supply of accounting theories: The market for excuses," *The Accounting Review*, (April): 273–305.)

Agree – An audit procedure whereby the auditor takes one document or set of documents and compares it to another document or set which should contain the same information to determine if the two match (agree with each other).

Agreed-upon procedures – see **Agreed-upon procedures engagement**.

Agreed-upon procedures engagement – In an engagement to perform agreed-upon procedures, an auditor is engaged to carry out those procedures of an audit nature to which the auditor and the entity and any appropriate third parties have agreed and to report on factual findings. The recipients of the report must form their own conclusions from the report by the auditor. The report is restricted to those parties that have agreed to the procedures being performed since others, unaware of the reasons for the procedures, may misinterpret the results.

Analytical procedures – The analysis of significant ratios and trends including the resulting investigation of fluctuations and relationships that are inconsistent with other relevant information or deviate from predictable amounts.

Analytical review – The process of planning, executing, and drawing conclusions from analytical procedures.

Annual report – An entity ordinarily issues on an annual basis a document which includes its financial statements together with the audit report thereon. This document is frequently referred to as the "annual report."

Anomalous error – see **Audit sampling**.

Application controls in computer information systems – The specific controls over the relevant accounting applications maintained by the computer. The purpose of application controls is to establish specific control procedures over the accounting applications in order to provide reasonable assurance that all transactions are authorized and recorded, and are processed completely, accurately and on a timely basis.

Appropriateness – Appropriateness is the measure of the quality of audit evidence and its relevance to a particular assertion and its reliability.

ASCII (American Standard Code for Information Interchange) – A standard translation scheme used to translate computer bytes into readable characters; commonly used in micro-computers, minicomputers, and non-IBM mainframes.

Asserted claims – Existing law suits.

Assertions – Assertions are representations by management, explicit or otherwise, that are embodied in the financial statements. Sometimes called "financial statements assertions," they can be categorized as follows: *existence, rights and obligations, occurrence, completeness, valuation, accuracy cutoff, classification, understandability, measurement,* and *presentation and disclosure.*

Asset/Liability Management – A planning and control process, the key concept of which is matching the mix and maturities of assets and liabilities.

Assistants – Assistants are personnel involved in an individual audit other than the audit supervisor or manager.

Assurance – see **Reasonable assurance**.

Assurance client – An entity in respect of which a firm conducts an assurance engagement.

Assurance engagement – Means an engagement in which a practitioner expresses a conclusion that is designed to enhance the degree of confidence intended users can have about the evaluation or measurement of a subject matter, that is the responsibility of a party other than the intended users or the practitioner, against criteria.

Assurance team – (1) All professionals participating in the assurance engagement; (2) All others within a firm who can directly influence the outcome of the assurance engagement, including: (a) Those who recommend the compensation of, or who provide direct supervisory, management or other oversight of the assurance engagement partner in connection with the performance of the assurance engagement. (b) Those who provide consultation regarding technical or industry specific issues, transactions or events for the assurance engagement; and (c) Those who provide quality control for the assurance engagement; and (3) For the purposes of an audit client, all those within a network firm who can directly influence the outcome of the audit engagement.

Attendance – Attendance consists of being present during all or part of a process being performed by others; for example, attending physical inventory taking will enable the auditor to inspect inventory, to observe compliance of management's procedures to count quantities and record such counts and to test-count quantities.

Attestation – A professional opinion in report form on compliance of the responsible party with some specific criteria.

Audit – The objective of an audit of financial statements is to enable the auditor to express an opinion whether the financial statements are prepared, in all material respects, in accordance with an identified financial reporting framework. The phrases used to express the auditor's opinion are "give a true and fair view" or "present fairly, in all material respects," which are equivalent terms. A similar objective applies to the audit of financial or other information prepared in accordance with appropriate criteria.

Audit assurance – The expression of a conclusion by an auditor that is designed to enhance the degree of confidence intended users can have about the evaluation or measurement of historical financial statements that is the responsibility of the auditee against the criteria of International Financial Reporting Standards or other national accounting standards.

Audit client – An entity in respect of which a firm conducts an audit engagement. When the audit client is a listed entity, it will always include its related entities.

Audit committee – Selected members of a company's outside directors, who take an active role in overseeing the company's accounting and financial reporting policies and practices.

Audit documentation – The principal record of the basis for the auditor's conclusions and provides the principal support for the representations in the auditor's report.

Audit engagement – An assurance engagement to provide a high level of assurance that financial statements are free of material misstatement, such as an engagement in accordance with International Standards on Auditing. This includes a statutory audit which is an audit required by national legislation or other regulation.

Audit evidence – The information obtained by the auditor in arriving at the conclusions on which the audit opinion is based. Audit evidence will comprise source documents and accounting records underlying the financial statements and corroborating information from other sources.

Audit expectation gap – A gap that results from the fact that users of audit services have expectations regarding the duties of auditors that exceed the current practice in the profession.

Audit firm – Audit firm is either a firm or entity providing audit services, including where appropriate its partners, or a sole practitioner.

Audit matters of governance interest – Matters that arise from the audit of financial statements and, in the opinion of the auditor, are both important and relevant to those charged with governance in overseeing the financial reporting and disclosure process. Audit matters of governance interest include only those matters that have come to the attention of the auditor as a result of the performance of the audit.

Audit objective – The specific expression of a financial statement assertion or assertions for which evidence needs to be obtained. For example, the objective "Investments exist and are owned by the entity."

Audit of financial statements – see **Financial statement audit**.

Audit opinion – see **Opinion**.

Audit plan – A work plan that reflects the design and performance of all audit procedures, consisting of a detailed approach for the nature, timing and extent of audit procedures to be performed (including the performance of risk assessment procedures) and the rationale for their selection. The audit plan begins by planning risk assessment procedures and once these procedures have been performed it is updated and changed to reflect the further audit procedures needed to respond to the results of the risk assessments. Also called **audit program**.

Audit planning memorandum – A document prepared by the auditor which gives an overview of the client company, the industry environment, significant audit concerns, and areas of interest to the audit team. Furthermore, it details the planned audit approach and budget.

Audit program – An audit program sets out the nature, timing, and extent of planned audit procedures required to implement the overall audit plan. The audit program serves as a set of instructions to assistants involved in the audit and as a means to control the proper execution of the work. Also called **audit plan**.

Audit report – An **Audit report** in usually synonymous with an **Audit opinion**, but it may be a more comprehensive report. The comprehensive audit report contains all important administrative data related to the audit, including comments, results, and the corrective/ preventive actions that have been determined. The Audit report is an official document that is signed by the lead auditor and the head of the audited area.

Audit risk – Audit risk is the risk that the auditor gives an inappropriate audit opinion when the financial statements are materially misstated. Audit risk has three components: inherent risk, control risk and detection risk.

- **Control risk** – The risk that a misstatement that could occur in an account balance or class of transactions and that could be material, individually or when aggregated with misstatements in other balances or classes, will not be prevented or detected and corrected on a timely basis by the accounting and internal control systems.
- **Detection risk** – The risk that an auditor's substantive procedures will not detect a misstatement that exists in an account balance or class of transactions that could be material, individually or when aggregated with misstatements in other balances or classes.
- **Inherent risk** – A component of audit risk. It is the susceptibility of an account balance or class of transactions to misstatement that could be material, individually or when aggregated with misstatements in other balances of classes, assuming that there were no related internal controls.

Audit sampling – Audit sampling (sampling) involves the application of audit procedures to less than 100 percent of items within an account balance or class of transactions such that all sampling units have a chance of selection. This will enable the auditor to obtain and evaluate audit evidence about some characteristic of the items selected in order to form or assist in forming a conclusion concerning the population from which the sample is drawn. Audit sampling can use either a statistical or a non-statistical approach.

- **Anomalous error** – Anomalous error means an error that arises from an isolated event that has not recurred other than on specifically identifiable occasions and is therefore not representative of errors in the population.
- **Confidence level** – As used in sampling, the probability of being correct in assessing the level of control risk. The term is used interchangeably with *reliability*.
- **Error** – Either control deviations, when performing tests of control, or misstatements, when performing substantive procedures. Total error is either the rate of deviation or total misstatement.
- **Expected error** – The error that the auditor expects to be present in the population.
- **Homogeneity** – All items in the population have similar characteristics.
- **Monetary unit sampling** – A statistical sampling method that provides upper and lower misstatment bounds expressed in monetary amounts; also referred to as dollar unit sampling, cumulative monetary amount sampling, and sampling with probability proportional to size.
- **Non-sampling risk** – Non-sampling risk arises from factors that cause the auditor to reach an erroneous conclusion for any reason not related to the size of the sample. For example, most audit evidence is persuasive rather than conclusive, the auditor might use inappropriate procedures, or the auditor might misinterpret evidence and fail to recognize an error.
- **Population** – Population means the entire set of data from which a sample is selected and about which the auditor wishes to draw conclusions. A population may be divided into strata, or sub-populations, with each stratum being examined separately. The term population is used to include the term stratum.
- **Power of the test** – It is a measure of how effective the test employed is in discriminating between populations that contain material errors and populations that contain non-material errors.

■ **Representativeness** – A sample having-essentially the same characteristis as the population. Haphazard selection or a random-based selection method can be expected to produce a sample that is representative of the population.

■ **Sampling risk** – Sampling risk arises from the possibility that the auditor's conclusion, based on a sample, may be different from the conclusion reached if the entire population were subjected to the same audit procedure.

■ **Sampling unit** – Sampling unit means the individual items constituting a population, for example, checks listed on deposit slips, credit entries on bank statements, sales invoices or debtors' balances, or a monetary unit.

■ **Statistical sampling** – Statistical sampling means any approach to sampling that has the following characteristics:
  (a) random selection of a sample;
  (b) use of probability theory to evaluate sample results, including measurement of sampling risk.
  A sampling approach that does not have characteristics (a) and (b) is considered non-statistical sampling.

■ **Stratification** – Stratification is the process of dividing a population into subpopulations, each of which is a group of sampling units which have similar characteristics (often monetary value).

■ **Tolerable error** – Tolerable error means the maximum error in a population that the auditor is willing to accept.

■ **Type I error** – The auditor concludes, in the case of a test of control, that control risk is lower than it actually is, or in the case of a substantive test, that a material error does not exist when in fact it does. This type of risk affects audit effectiveness and is more likely to lead to an inappropriate audit opinion.

■ **Type II error** – The auditor concludes, in the case of a test of control, that control risk is higher than it actually is, or in the case of a substantive test, that a material error exists when in fact it does not. This type of risk affects audit efficiency as it would usually lead to additional work to establish that initial conclusions were incorrect.

Audit team – People who make up the group of auditors responsible for planning and executing an audit.

Audit trail – The information that is used to trace the status and contents of an individual transaction record backward or forward between output, processing, and source document.

Auditee – The entity which is audited.

Auditor – The person with final responsibility for the audit. This term is also used to refer to an audit firm. (For ease of reference, the term "auditor" is used throughout the ISAs when describing both auditing and related services which may be performed. Such reference is not intended to imply that a person performing related services need necessarily be the auditor of the entity's financial statements.)

■ **Continuing auditor** – The auditor who audited and reported on the prior period's financial statements and continues as the auditor for the current period.

■ **External auditor** – Where appropriate, the terms "external auditor" and "external audit" are used to distinguish the external auditor from an internal auditor and to distinguish the external audit from the activities of internal auditing.

■ **Existing auditor** – The auditor who is currently holding an audit or assurance services appointment with the prospective client.

■ **Incoming auditor** – The incoming auditor is a current period's auditor who did not audit the prior period's financial statements.

■ **Other auditor** – An independent auditor other than the group auditor or a related auditor.

■ **Personnel** – Personnel includes all partners and professional staff engaged in the audit practice of the firm.

■ **Predecessor auditor** – The auditor who was previously the auditor of an entity and who has been replaced by an incoming auditor.

■ **Proposed professional accountant** – A professional accountant in public practice who will act as the current financial statement period's auditor who did not audit the prior period's financial statements.

■ **Principal auditor** – The principal auditor is the auditor with responsibility for reporting on the financial statements of an entity when those financial statements include financial information of one or more components audited by another auditor.

■ **Related auditor** – An independent auditor from the group auditor's office, other office of the group auditor's firm, a network firm or another firm operating under common quality control policies and procedures as described in International Standard on Quality Control (ISQC) 1, "Quality Control for Audit, Assurance and Related Services Practices."

Auditor's association – An auditor is associated with financial information when the auditor attaches a report to that information or consents to the use of the auditor's name in a professional connection.

Authorization – The delegation of initiation of transactions and obligations on the company's behalf.

Bank reconciliation – A test of the agreement between a balance on the bank statement and the same balance on the company's books.

Basel Committee on Banking Supervision – A committee of banking supervisory authorities that was established by the central bank Governors of the Group of Ten countries in 1975. It consists of senior representatives of banking supervisory authorities and central banks from Belgium, Canada, France, Germany, Italy, Japan, Luxembourg, the Netherlands, Spain, Sweden, Switzerland, the UK and the USA. It usually meets at the Bank for International Settlements in Basel, where its permanent Secretariat is located.

Basis – The difference between the price of the hedged item and the price of the related hedging instrument.

Basis Risk – The risk that the basis will change while the hedging contract is open and, thus, the price correlation between the hedged item and hedging instrument will not be perfect.

Bearer securities – A document of title to stocks, bonds, shares, debentures, etc. transferable by hand, being made out to bearer (any person who has it in hand) and not a named person.

Benchmarking – The comparison of actual performance to a standard of typical competence developed by testing or a published standard.

Benford's Law – Provides the expected frequencies of the digits and digit combinations in tabulated data.

Board of Directors – Individuals responsible for overseeing the affairs of an entity, including the election of its officers. The board of a corporation that issues stock is elected by stockholders.

Bookkeeping services – Services including payroll services and the preparation of financial statements or financial information which forms the basis of the financial statements on which the audit report is provided for audit clients that are listed entities.

Boundary testing – Audit testing of documentation at the lowest level of the information stream; for example, testing the first document (i.e. purchase order) that initiates an exchange.

Breach of contract – A failure of one or both parties in a contract to fulfill the requirements of the contract.

Business operations – The ongoing activities of the business.

Business risks – Risks that result from significant conditions, events, circumstances, or actions that could adversely affect the entity's ability to achieve its objectives and execute its strategies.

Bylaws – Includes rules and procedures of the corporation including fiscal year, frequency of stockholder meetings, method of voting for board of directors, and the duties and powers of the corporate officer.

Cap – A series of call options based on a notional amount. The strike price of these options defines an upper limit to interest rates.

Capital structure – The proportions of capital of an entity that are derived from each source of financing, i.e. the proportion of debt versus equity.

Checklists – A list of considerations or procedures which are followed by the auditor.

Circumstantial evidence – Evidence based on facts and circumstances from which a court may infer that a factual matter has been proved.

Classes of transactions – Groups of accounting entries in an accounting cycle of transactions such as the revenue cycle, expenditure cycle, production cycle, or personnel cycle, or any sub-categories of those cycles.

Classification – The process of finding models, also known as classifiers, or functions that map records into one of several discrete prescribed classes.

Clear and convincing evidence – A proof that is stronger than a mere preponderance of evidence, but not convincing beyond a reasonable doubt.

Client account – Any bank account, which is used solely for the banking of clients' monies.

Clients' monies – Any monies, including documents of title to money (e.g. bills of exchange, promissory notes and documents of title) which can be converted into money (e.g. bearer bonds received by a professional accountant in public practice to be held or paid out on the instruction of the person from whom or on whose behalf they are received).

Close family – A parent, non-dependent child or sibling.

Close out – The consummation or settlement of a financial transaction.

Cluster Analysis – A technique that aggregates data based on certain specified common characteristics.

Collateral – Assets pledged by a borrower to secure a loan or other credit; these are subject to seizure in the event of default.

Collusion – The act of two or more employees to steal assets or misstate records.

Combined Code (of the Committee on Corporate Governance) – Represents the Code of Best Practice of the London Stock Exchange. (See the Committee on Corporate Governance. 1998, *The Combined Code*, London Stock Exchange, London, January; or KPMG Review, 1999, *The Combined Code: A Practical Guide*, KPMG, United Kingdom, January.)

Commitments – Agreements that the entity will hold to a fixed set of conditions, such as the purchase or sale of merchandise at a stated price, at a future date, regardless of what happens to profits or to the economy as a whole.

Commodity – A physical substance, such as food, grains, and metals that is interchangeable with other product of the same type.

Company bylaws – The rules and procedures adopted by a company's stockholders, including the company's fiscal year as well as duties and powers of the officers.

Comparatives – Comparatives in financial statements, may present amounts (such as financial position, results of operations, cash flows) and appropriate disclosures of an entity for more that one period, depending on the framework. The frameworks and methods of presentation are as follows:

- Corresponding figures where amounts and other disclosures for the preceding period are included as part of the current period financial statements, and are intended to be read in relation to the amounts and other disclosures relating to the current period (referred to as "current period figures"). These corresponding figures are not presented as complete financial statements capable of standing alone, but are an integral part of the current period financial statements intended to be read only in relationship to the current period figures.
- Comparative financial statements where amounts and other disclosures for the preceding period are included for comparison with the financial statements of the current period, but do not form part of the current period financial statements.

Competence – The knowledge and skills necessary to accomplish tasks that define the individual's job.

Compilation – see **Compilation engagement**.

Compilation engagement – In a compilation engagement, the accountant is engaged to use accounting expertise as opposed to auditing expertise to collect, classify and summarize financial information.

Completeness assertion – see **Financial statement assertions**.

Completion memorandum – A report on auditing findings at the completion of the audit that ordinarily describes critical and significant audit areas, accounting issues, and any matters that need to be highlighted.

Compliance auditing – Is a review of an organization's procedures to determine whether the organization is following a specific set of criteria (e.g. government regulation, commercial contract, lease).

Component – Component is a division, branch, subsidiary, joint venture, associated company, or other entity whose financial information is included in financial statements audited by the principal auditor.

Components of audit risk – There are three components of audit risk: inherent risk, control risk, and detection risk.

Components of financial statements – The auditor may be requested to express an opinion on one or more components of a financial statement, for example, accounts receivable, inventory, an employee's bonus calculation, or a provision for income taxes. This is described in ISA 800.

Components of internal control – There are five components of internal control: control environment, risk assessment, control procedures (activities), information and communication system, and monitoring.

Component management – Management responsible for the preparation and presentation of a component's financial information.

Comprehensive basis of accounting – A comprehensive basis of accounting comprises a set of criteria used in preparing financial statements which applies to all material items and which has substantial support.

Computation – Computation consists of checking the arithmetical accuracy of source documents and accounting records or of performing independent calculations.

Computer assisted audit techniques – Applications of auditing procedures using the computer as an audit tool are known as Computer Assisted Audit Techniques (CAATs).

Computer information systems – A computer information systems (CIS) environment exists when a computer of any type or size is involved in the processing by the entity of financial information of significance to the audit, whether that computer is operated by the entity or by a third party.

Confidence level – see **Audit sampling**.

Confirmation – Consists of the response to an inquiry of a third party to corroborate information contained in the accounting records – see **External confirmation**.

Confirmation letter – A letter sent to a third party to request information about, confirm, or corroborate a particular item affecting assertions made by management in the financial statements.

Consignment – A specialized way of marketing certain types of goods. The consignor delivers goods to the consignee who acts as the consignor's agent in selling the merchandise to a third party. The consignee accepts the goods without any liability except to reasonably protect them from damage. The consignee receives a commission when the merchandise is sold. Goods on consignment are included in the consignor's inventory and excluded from the consignee's inventory since the consignor has legal title.

Consulting services – Services that are designed to improve the effectiveness and efficiency of clients' operations, broadly defined as any services other than attestation and related services. Examples are executive search, legal services, financial services, strategic planning, and development of management information systems.

Contingency fee – An arrangement whereby no fee will be charged unless a specified finding or result is obtained or when the fee is otherwise contingent on the findings or results of these services.

Contingent fees – Fees calculated on a predetermined basis relating to the outcome or result of a transaction or the result of the work performed.

Contingent liability – A potential future obligation to an outside part for an unknown amount resulting from the outcome of a past event.

Continuing auditor – see **Auditor**.

Continuous reporting – The real-time disclosure of transaction data.

Contracts – Include long-term notes and payables, stock options, pension plans, contracts with vendors, government contracts, royalty agreements, union contracts, and leases.

Control environment – Comprises the overall attitude, awareness and actions of directors and management regarding the internal control system and its importance in the entity.

Control procedures – Those policies and procedures in addition to the control environment which management has established to achieve the entity's specific objectives.

Control risk – see **Audit risk**.

Controls – All the organizational activities aimed at having organizational members co-operate to reach the organizational goals.

Corporate bylaws – The rules and procedures adopted by a company's stockholders, including the company's fiscal year, as well as duties and powers of the officers.

Corporate charter – A legal document granted by the country, state or province in which a company is incorporated and recognizes a company as a separate legal entity. Included in the charter is the name of the company, date of incorporation, capital stock authorized, and the types of business activities the company may undertake.

Corporate finance and similar activities – Promoting, dealing in, or underwriting a client's share; committing the client to the terms of the transaction; and consummating a transaction on behalf of the client.

Corporate governance – see **Governance**.

Corporate minutes – Official record of the meetings of the board of directors and stockholders. Include authorization of compensation of officers, new contracts, acquisition of fixed assets, loans, and dividends payments.

Correcting entry – see **Adjusting journal entry**.

Correlation – The degree to which contract prices of hedging instruments reflect price movements in the cash-market position. The correlation factor represents the potential effectiveness of hedging a cash-market instrument with a contract where the deliverable financial instrument differs from the cash-market instrument. Generally, the correlation factor is determined by regression analysis or some other method of technical analysis of market behavior.

Corroborate – To attest the truth or accuracy of an inquiry.

Counterparty – The other party to a derivative transaction.

Credit risk – The risk that a customer or counterparty will not settle an obligation for full value, either when due or at any time thereafter.

Currency risk – The risk of loss arising from future movements in the exchange rates applicable to foreign currency assets, liabilities, rights, and obligations.

Custody – Physical control over assets or records.

Customer relationship management (CRM) – A software package that helps organize detailed data about customers so that the data can be used to facilitate better customer service.

Cutoff – Transactions and events have been recorded in the correct accounting period.

Cutoff procedures – Refers to recognizing assets and liabilities as of a proper date and accounting for revenue, expense and other transactions in the proper period.

Data description – A technique that provides an overall description of data, either in itself or in each class or concept, typically in summarized, concise, and precise form. It summarizes general characteristics of data and compares characteristics of data between contrasting groups or classes.

Data mining – A set of computer-assisted techniques that use sophisticated statistical analysis, including artificial intelligence techniques, to examine large volumes of data with the objective of indicating hidden or unexpected information or patterns.

Database – A collection of data that is shared and used by a number of different users for different purposes.

Dealer (for the purposes of IAPS 1012) – The person who commits the entity to a derivative transaction.

Defalcation – Theft of an entity's assets, also referred to as misappropriation of assets.

Dependency analysis – A technique that searches data for the most significant relationship across large number of variables or attributes. One use is to describe data items or events that frequently occur together or in sequence.

Derivative – A generic term used to categorize a wide variety of financial instruments whose value "depends on" or is "derived from" an underlying rate or price, such as interest rates, exchange rates, equity prices, or commodity prices. Many national financial reporting frameworks and the International Accounting Standards contain definitions of derivatives. For example, International Accounting Standard (IAS) 39, "Financial Instruments: Recognition and Measurement," defines a derivative as a financial instrument:

- whose value changes in response to the change in a specified interest rate, security price, commodity price, foreign exchange rate, index of prices or rates, a credit rating or credit index, or similar variable (sometimes called the "underlying");
- that requires no initial net investment or little initial net investment relative to other types of contracts that have a similar response to changes in market conditions; and
- that is settled at a future date.

Detection risk – see **Audit risk**.

Direct evidence – Comes from personal knowledge of the witnesses under oath as to specific facts.

Direct financial interest – A financial interest: (1) Owned directly by and under the control of an individual or entity (including those managed on a discretionary basis by others); or (2) Beneficially owned through a collective investment vehicle, estate, trust or other intermediary over which the individual or entity has control.

Directors and officers – Those charged with the governance of an entity, regardless of their title, which may vary from country to country.

Disclaimer of opinion – see **Modified auditor's report** and **Opinion**.

Disclosure – Typically required when accounts of interest (revenue, joint venture accounts) exceed certain amounts or have certain characteristics. (Revenue segments amounts are disclosed if they exceed 10 percent of total revenue and joint venture amounts, and consolidated if the company has effective control.)

Documentary evidence – Evidence gathered from written, printed or electronic sources.

Documentation – Documentation is the material (working papers) prepared by and for, or obtained and retained by the auditor in connection with the performance of, the audit.

Due diligence report – A report based on the analysis by an acquiring company's auditing firm of a company to be acquired.

Due professional care – The activities of a professional fulfilling his duties diligently and carefully. Due care for an auditor includes the completeness of the working papers, the sufficiency of the audit evidence, and the appropriateness of the audit report.

Edit check – An accuracy check performed by a computer accounting system edit program.

Electronic data interchange (EDI) – The electronic transmission of documents between organizations in a machine-readable form. EDI allows output of one system to be electronically transmitted and input into another system.

Electronic funds transfer (EFT) – A transfer of funds between two or more organizations or individuals using computer and network technology.

Embedded audit modules (EAM) – Database software routines that are placed at predetermined points to gather information about transactions or events within the system that auditors deem to be material. EAMs allow auditors to proactively monitor auditable conditions.

Embedded derivative instruments – Implicit or explicit terms in a contract or agreement that affect some or all of the cash flows or the value of other exchanges required by the contract in a manner similar to a derivative.

Emphasis of matter paragraph – The explanatory paragraph placed after the opinion paragraph in an unqualified auditor's opinion which emphasizes a matter related to the entity or its financial statements.

Employed professional accountant – A professional accountant employed in industry, commerce, the public sector, or education.

Encryption (cryptography) – The process of transforming programs and information into a form that cannot be understood without access to specific decoding algorithms (cryptographic keys). For example, the confidential personal data in a payroll system may be encrypted against unauthorized disclosure or modification. Encryption can provide an effective control for protecting confidential or sensitive programs and information from unauthorized access or modification. However, effective security depends upon proper controls over access to the cryptographic keys.

End user – An entity that enters into a financial transaction, either through an organized exchange or a broker, for the purpose of hedging, asset/liability management or speculating. End users consist primarily of corporations, government entities, institutional investors and financial institutions. The derivative activities of end users are often related the production or use of a commodity by the entity.

Engagement circumstances – The terms of the engagement, the characteristics of subject matter, the criteria to be used, the needs of the intended users, relevant characteristics of the responsible party, and its environment and other matters (e.g. events, transactions, conditions and practices) that may have a significant effect on the subject matter and the engagement.

Engagement letter – An engagement letter documents and confirms the auditor's acceptance of the appointment, the objective and scope of the audit, the extent of the auditor's responsibilities to the client and the form of any reports.

Engagement partner – The partner or other person with sufficient and appropriate experience and authority in the firm who has responsibility for the engagement and its performance, for issuing the report on the subject matter on behalf of the firm, and who is permitted by law, regulation or a professional body to act in the role in the relevant jurisdiction.

Engagement proposal – A written proposal from the auditor or audit firm to the proposed or existing client proposing that an audit or assurance engagement be undertaken.

Engagement quality control review – A process designed to provide an objective evaluation, before the report is issued, of the significant judgments the engagement team made and the conclusions they reached in formulating the report.

Engagement quality control reviewer – A partner, other person in the firm, suitably qualified external person, or a team made up of such individuals, with sufficient and appropriate experience and authority to objectively evaluate, before the report is issued, the significant judgments the engagement team made and the conclusions they reached in formulating the report.

Engagement team – The individuals involved in performing an engagement, including any experts employed or engaged by the firm in connection with that engagement.

Entity – A separate or self-contained existence that provides goods or services. For example, a company, organization, or agency.

Enterprise resource planning (ERP) – A system that integrates all aspects of an organization's activities (such as recording accounting transactions, database maintenance, financial reporting, operations and compliance) into one accounting information system.

Environmental matters – Environmental matters are defined as:

- initiatives to prevent, abate, or remedy damage to the environment, or to deal with conservation of renewable and non-renewable resources (such initiatives may be required by environmental laws and regulations or by contract, or they may be undertaken voluntarily);

- consequences of violating environmental laws and regulations;
- consequences of environmental damage done to others or to natural resources;
- consequences of vicarious liability imposed by law (e.g. liability for damages caused by previous owners).

Environmental performance report – An environmental performance report is a report, separate from the financial statements, in which an entity provides third parties with qualitative information on the entity's commitments towards the environmental aspects of the business, its policies and targets in that field, its achievement in managing the relationship between its business processes and environmental risk, and quantitative information on its environmental performance.

Environmental risk – In certain circumstances, factors relevant to the assessment of inherent risk for the development of the overall audit plan may include the risk of material misstatement of the financial statements due to environmental matters.

Error – An error is an unintentional mistake in financial statements. See also **Audit sampling**.

Evaluation assertion – Not an assertion given in the IFAC definitions (see **Financial statement assertions**). It is particular to specific firms. It means that the account balance has been evaluated for consistency.

Evidence – Anything that can make a person believe that a fact, proposition, or assertion is true or false.

Evidence-gathering techniques – Those techniques employed by an auditor to obtain evidence. There are six types of evidence-gathering techniques including inquiry, observation, inspection (physical evidence and examination of documents), computation (reperformance or mechanical accuracy), confirmation, and analytical procedures.

Evolution analysis – A technique that determines the most significant changes in data sets over time. It includes other types of algorithm methods (i.e. data description, dependency analysis, classification or clustering) plus time-related and sequence-related characteristics.

Exchange-traded derivatives – Derivatives traded under uniform rules through an organized exchange.

Existence – see **Financial statement assertion**.

Existing accountant – A professional accountant in public practice currently holding an audit appointment or carrying out accounting, taxation, consulting, or similar professional services for a client.

Existing auditor – The auditor who is currently holding an audit or assurance services appointment with the prospective client.

Expected error – see **Audit sampling**.

Expert – A person or firm possessing special skill, knowledge, and experience in a particular field other than accounting and auditing.

Extent of audit procedures – The size of the evidence sample audited.

External audit/auditor – see **Auditor**.

External confirmation – External confirmation is the process of obtaining and evaluating audit evidence through a direct communication from a third party in response to a request for information about a particular item affecting assertions made by management in the financial statements.

Fair value – The amount for which an asset could be exchanged, or a liability settled, between knowledgeable, willing parties in an arm's length transaction.

Familiarity threat – Occurs when, by virtue of a close relationship with an assurance client, its directors, officers or employees, an auditor becomes to sympathetic to the client's interests.

Fiduciary risk – The risk of loss arising from factors such as failure to maintain safe custody or negligence in the management of assets on behalf of other parties.

Fields – A group of bytes that make up a meaningful unit of information (e.g. account number, account balance, or account name).

File – Set of related data records.

File interrogation – A technique that performs automated routines on computer data.

File interrogation specifications – A document prepared by the engagement team that describes the file interrogation tests to be performed, documents any selection or calculation criteria, and documents control totals of one or more key fields.

File interrogation specialist – A professional in the firm who has appropriate training and experience in identifying, designing, and running file interrogation applications.

Financial instruments – Common stock, preferred stock, bonds, and other contracts or rights to assets, liabilities, or equity which convey financial interest to the holder.

Financial interest – An interest in an equity or other security, debenture, loan or other debt instrument of an entity, including rights and obligations to acquire such an interest and derivatives directly related to such interest.

Financial reporting policies – Company policies and accounting methods related to the reporting of accounting information.

Financial statement assertions – Financial statement assertions are assertions by management, explicit or otherwise, that are embodied in the financial statements and can be categorized as follows:

- **Accuracy** – Amounts and other data relating to recorded transactions and events have been recorded appropriately.
- **Classification** – Transactions and events have been recorded in the proper accounts.
- **Completeness** – All transactions, events, assets, liabilities, and equity interests that should have been recorded have been recorded.
- **Cutoff** – Transactions and events have been recorded in the correct accounting period.
- **Existence** – Assets, liabilities and equity interests exist.
- **Measurement** – A transaction or event is recorded at the proper amount and revenue or expense is allocated to the proper period.
- **Occurrence** – An assertion that a transaction or event took place which pertains to the entity during the period.
- **Presentation and disclosure** – An item is disclosed, classified, and described in accordance with the applicable financial reporting framework.
- **Rights and obligations** – An entity holds or controls the rights to assets, and liabilities are the obligations of the entity.

- **Transparency** – Financial information is appropriately classified and disclosures are understandable.
- **Valuation and allocation** – Assets, liabilities, and equity interests are included in the financial statements at appropriate amounts and any resulting valuation or allocation adjustments are appropriately recorded.

Financial statement audit – An audit of financial statements guided by ISAs 100–799 and IAPSs 1000–1100.

Financial statements – The balance sheets, income statements or profit and loss accounts, statements of changes in financial position (which may be presented in a variety of ways, for example, as a statement of cash flows or a statement of fund flows), notes, and other statements and explanatory material which are identified as being part of the financial statements.

Firewall – A combination of hardware and software that protects a WAN, LAN or PC from unauthorized access through the internet and from the introduction of unauthorized or harmful software, data or other material in electronic form.

Firm – (a) A sole practitioner, partnership or corporation of professional accountants; (b) An entity that controls such parties; and (c) An entity controlled by such parties.

Floor – A series of put options based on a notional amount. The strike price of these options defines a lower limit to the interest rate.

Forecast – A forecast is prospective financial information prepared on the basis of assumptions as to future events which management expects to take place and the actions management expects to take as of the date the information is prepared (best-estimate assumptions).

Foreign Exchange Contracts – Contracts that provide an option for, or require a future exchange of foreign currency assets or liabilities.

Foreign Exchange Risk – The risk of losses arising through repricing of foreign currency instruments because of exchange rate fluctuations.

Forensic accounting – The application of accounting methods and financial techniques to collect civil and criminal legal evidence.

Forward Contracts – A contract negotiated between two parties to purchase and sell a specified quantity of a financial instrument, foreign currency, or commodity at a price specified at the origination of the contract, with delivery and settlement at a specified future date.

Forward Rate Agreements – An agreement between two parties to exchange an amount determined by an interest rate differential at a given future date based on the difference between an agreed interest rate and a reference rate (LIBOR, Treasury bills, etc.) on a notional principal amount.

Fraud – Refers to an intentional act by one or more individuals among management, employees, or third parties, which results in a misrepresentation of financial statements.

Functional audit quality – The degree to which the process of carrying out the audit and communicating its results meets a consumer's expectations.

Futures contracts – Exchange-traded contracts to buy or sell a specified financial instrument, foreign currency or commodity at a specified future date or during a specified period at a specified price or yield.

General controls in computer information systems – The establishment of a framework of overall control over the computer information systems activities to provide a reasonable level of assurance that the overall objectives of internal control are achieved.

Generalized audit software (GAS) – A computer software package (e.g., ACL, Idea) that performs automated routines on electronic data files based on auditor expectations. GAS functions generally include reformatting, file manipulation, calculation, data selection, data analysis, file processing, statistics and reporting on the data. It may also include statistical sampling for detailed tests, generating confirmation letters.

Generally Accepted Auditing Standards (GAAS) – A set of auditing standards accepted by professional accountants.

Going concern assumption – Under the going concern assumption, an entity is ordinarily viewed as continuing in business for the foreseeable future with neither the intention nor the necessity of liquidation, ceasing trading, or seeking protection from creditors pursuant to laws or regulations. Accordingly, assets and liabilities are recorded on the basis that the entity will be able to realize its assets and discharge its liabilities in the normal course of business.

Governance – The term "governance" describes the role of persons entrusted with the supervision, control and direction of an entity. Those charged with governance ordinarily are accountable for ensuring that the entity achieves its objectives, financial reporting, and reporting to interested parties. Those charged with governance include management only when it performs such functions.

Government business enterprises – Government business enterprises are businesses which operate within the public sector ordinarily to meet a political or social interest objective. They are ordinarily required to operate commercially, that is, to make profits or to recoup, through user charges, a substantial proportion of their operating costs.

Group audit instructions – A communication from a group auditor to the related auditors and other auditors to provide them with the group auditor's requirements.

Group auditor – The independent auditor who signs the auditor's report on the group financial statements.

Group financial statements – Financial statements that include or should include financial information of more than one component by means of consolidation procedures or equity accounting methods. It may also mean a combination of components' financial information or an equivalent presentation.

Group management – Management responsible for the preparation and presentation of the group financial statements.

Gross negligence – see **Negligence of auditor**.

Hedge – A strategy that protects an entity against the risk of adverse price or interest rate movements on certain of its assets, liabilities or anticipated transactions. A hedge is used to avoid or reduce risks by creating a relationship by which losses on certain positions are expected to be counterbalanced, in whole or in part, by gains on separate positions in another market.

Hedge effectiveness – The degree to which offsetting changes in fair value or cash flows attributable to a hedged risk are achieved by the hedging instrument.

Hedged item – An asset, liability, firm commitment, or forecasted future transaction that
- exposes an entity to risk of changes in fair value or changes in future cash flows;
- for hedge accounting purposes, is designated as being hedged.

Hedging (for accounting purposes) – Designating one or more hedging instruments so that their change in fair value is an offset, completely or in part, to the change in fair value or cash flows of a hedged item.

Hedging instrument (for hedge accounting purposes) – A designated derivative or (in limited circumstances) another financial asset or liability whose value or cash flows are expected to offset changes in the fair value or cash flows of a designated hedged item.

Hidden reserves – Some financial reporting frameworks allow banks to manipulate their reported income by transferring amounts to non-disclosed reserves in years when they make large profits and transferring amounts from those reserves when they make losses or small profits. The reported income is the amount after such transfers. The practice served to make the entity appear more stable by reducing the volatility of its earnings, and would help to prevent a loss of confidence in the bank by reducing the occasions on which it would report low earnings.

Homogenity – see **Audit sampling**.

HTML (Hypertext Markup Language) – The language used to format web pages. Web browsers like Internet Explorer transmit information using the hypertext transport protocol (HTTP).

Illegal act – An act or omission that violates any law or any rule having the force of law.

Immediate family – A spouse (or equivalent) or dependant.

Incoming auditor – see **Auditor**.

Independence – (a) Independence of mind – the state of mind that permits the provision of an opinion without being affected by influences that compromise professional judgment, allowing an individual to act with integrity, and exercise objectivity and professional skepticism; and (b) Independence in appearance – the avoidance of facts and circumstances that are so significant a reasonable and informed third party, having knowledge of all relevant information, including any safeguards applied, would reasonably conclude a firm's, or a member of the assurance team's, integrity, objectivity or professional skepticism had been compromised.

Independent director – A director is independent when he has no relationship of any kind whatsoever with the corporation, its group, or the management of either that is such as to color his judgment. (Bouton, 2002)

Indirect financial interest – A financial interest beneficially owned through a collective investment vehicle, estate, trust or other intermediary over which the individual or entity has no control.

Information asymmetry – A condition in which at least some relevant information is known to some but not all parties involved. Information asymmetry causes markets to become inefficient, since all the market participants do not have access to the information they need for their decision making processes.

Information technology – The computing, communications and management information systems technology. This technology includes computer hardware and software systems such as operating systems, networks, databases and operating applications (word processing, presentation, monitoring and design systems), as well as communications.

Inherent limitations in an audit – Limitations that result from such factors as the use of testing, the inherent limitations of any accounting and internal control system, and the fact that most audit evidence is persuasive rather than conclusive. Furthermore, the work performed by an auditor to form an opinion is permeated by judgment.

Inherent risk – see **Audit risk**.

Inquiry – Consists of seeking information of knowledgeable persons inside or outside the entity.

Inspection – Inspection consists of examining records, documents, or tangible assets.

Inspection – In relation to completed engagements, procedures designed to provide evidence of compliance by engagement teams with the firm's quality control policies and procedures.

Inspired confidence, theory of – The demand for audit services is the direct consequence of the participation of outside stakeholders (*third parties*) in the company. These stakeholders demand accountability from the management, in return for their contribution to the company. Since information provided by management might be biased, because of a possible divergence between the interests of management and outside stakeholders, an audit of this information is required. (See Limperg, T.H., 1932, *Theory of Inspired Confidence*, University of Amsterdam, Amsterdam, 1932/1933.)

Intended users (for assurance services) – The class or classes of persons for whom the practitioner prepares the assurance report. It includes cases when there is only one intended user. The responsible party can be one of the intended users, but not the only one.

Interest rate risk – The risk that a movement in interest rates would have an adverse effect on the value of assets and liabilities or would affect interest cash flows.

Interest rate swap – A contract between two parties to exchange periodic interest payments on a notional amount (referred to as the notional principal) for a specified period. In the most common instance, an interest rate swap involves the exchange of streams of variable and fixed-rate interest payments.

Interim financial information or statements – Financial information (which may be less than full financial statements as defined above) issued at interim dates (usually half-yearly or quarterly) in respect of a financial period.

Internal auditing – An appraisal activity established within an entity as a service to the entity. Its functions include, amongst other things, examining, evaluating and monitoring the adequacy and effectiveness of the accounting and internal control systems.

Internal control – A process, effected by an entity's board of directors, management and other personnel, designed to provide reasonable assurance regarding the achievement of objectives in the following categories: effectiveness and efficiency of operations, reliability of financial reporting, and compliance with applicable laws and regulations. – Committee of Sponsoring Organizations of the Treadway Commission.

Internal control flow chart – A symbolic, diagrammatic representation of the client's documents and their sequential flow in the organization.

Internal control questionnaire – A series of questions about the controls in each audit area as a means of indicating to the auditor aspects of the internal control structure that may be inadequate.

Internal control narrative – A written description of a client's internal control structure.

Internal control structure – The set of policies and procedures designed to provide management with reasonable assurance that the goals and objectives it believes are important will be met.

Internal control system – An internal control system consists of all the policies and procedures (internal controls) adopted by the management of an entity to assist in achieving management's objective of ensuring, as far as practicable, the orderly and efficient conduct of its business, including adherence to management policies, the safeguarding of assets, the prevention and detection of fraud and error, the accuracy and completeness of the accounting records, and the timely preparation of reliable financial information. The internal control system extends beyond these matters which relate directly to the functions of the accounting system.

International Financial Reporting Standards (IFRS) – The international standards for financial statements developed by the International Accounting Standards Board (IASB). IFRS set out recognition, measurement, presentation and disclosure requirements dealing with transactions and events that are important in general purpose financial statements.

International Standards on Assurance Engagements (ISAEs) – Standards applied in assurance engagements dealing with *subject matters* other than historical financial information. Developed by IAASB.

International Standards on Auditing (ISAs) – Standards applied, as appropriate, in the *audit* or *review* of historical financial information. Developed by IAASB.

International Standards on Quality Control (ISQCs) – The standards relating to quality of audit applied to all services falling under the standards of the IAASB.

International Standards on Related Services (ISRSs) – Standards applied to *compilation engagements*, engagements to apply *agreed upon procedures* to information and other related services engagements as specified by the IAASB.

International Standards on Review Engagements (ISREs) – Standards applied to the *review* of historical financial information. Developed by IAASB.

Intimidation Threat – Occurs when a member of the assurance team may be deterred from acting objectively and exercising professional skepticism by threats, actual or perceived, from the directors, officers, or employees of an assurance client.

IT environment – The policies and procedures that the entity implements and the IT infrastructure (hardware, operating systems, etc.) and application software that it uses to support business operations and achieve business strategies.

Joint and several liability – All parties involved are liable for losses.

Key performance indicators (KPIs) – Quantitative measurements, both financial and non-financial, of the process's ability to meet its objectives and of the process performance. They are usually analyzed through trend analyses within a company, or benchmarking against a peer of the company or its industry. The KPIs that should be listed must be relevant to the critical success factors and/or the process objectives. The KPIs listed must have relevance to the organization. Taken together they should provide a key set of measures for measuring process performance and achieving process objectives.

Knowledge of the business – The auditor's general knowledge of the economy and the industry within which the entity operates and a more particular knowledge of how the entity operates.

Lead engagement partner – In connection with an audit, the partner responsible for signing the report on the consolidated financial statements of the audit client and, where relevant, the partner responsible for signing the report in respect of any entity whose financial statements form part of the consolidated financial statements and on which a separate stand-alone report is issued. When no consolidated financial statements are prepared, the lead engagement partner would be the partner responsible for signing the report on the financial statements.

Lead schedule – A listing of the detailed accounts which make up the line item total on a general ledger trial balance.

Legal letter (or *inquiry of client's attorneys*) – A letter from the client's legal counsel informing the auditor of pending litigation or other information involving legal counsel that is relevant to financial statement disclosure.

Legal and documentary risk – The risk that contracts are documented incorrectly or are not legally enforceable in the relevant jurisdiction in which the contracts are to be enforced or where the counterparties operate. This can include the risk that assets will turn out to be worthless or liabilities will turn out to be greater than expected because of inadequate or incorrect legal advice or documentation. In addition, existing laws may fail to resolve legal issues involving a bank; a court case involving a particular bank may have wider implications for the banking business and involve costs to it and many or all other banks; and laws affecting banks or other commercial enterprises may change. Banks are particularly susceptible to legal risks when entering into new types of transactions and when the legal right of a counterparty to enter into a transaction is not established.

Legal Risk – The risk that a legal or regulatory action could invalidate or otherwise preclude performance by the end user or its counterparty under the terms of the contract.

Lending Credibility Theory – Audited financial statements are used by management to enhance the stakeholders' faith in management's stewardship.

LIBOR (London Interbank Offered Rate) – An international interest rate benchmark. It is commonly used as a reprising benchmark for financial instruments such as adjustable rate mortgages, collateralized mortgage obligations, and interest rate swaps.

Limitation on scope – A limitation on the scope of the auditor's work may sometimes be imposed by the entity (e.g. when the terms of the engagement specify that the auditor will not carry out an audit procedure that the auditor believes is necessary). A scope limitation may be imposed by circumstances (e.g. when the timing of the auditor's appointment is such that the auditor is unable to observe the counting of physical inventories). It may also arise when, in the opinion of the auditor, the entity's accounting records are inadequate or when the auditor is unable to carry out an audit procedure believed desirable.

Linear contracts – Contracts that involve obligatory cash flows at a future date.

Liquidity – The capability of a financial instrument to be readily convertible into cash.

Liquidity risk – Changes in the ability to sell or dispose of the derivative. Derivatives bear the additional risk that a lack of sufficient contracts or willing counterparties may make it difficult to close out the derivative or enter into an offsetting contract.

List schedule – Shows the detail of those items that make up an end-of-period balance in a general ledger account.

Listed entity – An entity whose shares, stock or debt are quoted or listed on a recognized stock exchange, or are marketed under the regulations of a recognized stock exchange or other equivalent body.

Litigation support – The making of managerial decisions on behalf of an audit client or acting for an audit client in the resolution of a dispute or litigation when the amounts involved are material to the financial statements of the audit client.

Local area network (LAN) – A communications network that serves users within a confined geographical area. LANs were developed to facilitate the exchange and sharing of resources within an organization, including data, software, storage, printers, and telecommunications equipment. They allow for decentralized computing. The basic components of a LAN are transmission media and software, user terminals, and shared peripherals.

Management – Management comprises officers and others who also perform senior managerial functions. Management includes directors and the audit committee only in those instances when they perform such functions.

Management assertion – see **Financial statement assertions.**

Management letter – The auditor's written communications to management to point out weaknesses in the internal control, other reportable conditions, and possibilities for operational improvements.

Management report – A report that is needed for publicly traded companies in the US.

Management representations – Representations made by management to the auditor during the course of an audit, either unsolicited or in response to specific inquiries.

Management representations letter – A written communication from the client to the auditor formalizing representations made by management to the auditor about matters pertinent to the audit.

Margin – (1) The amount of deposit money a securities broker requires from an investor to purchase securities on behalf of the investor on credit. (2) An amount of money or securities deposited by both buyers and sellers of futures contracts and short options to ensure performance of the terms of the contract, i.e. the delivery or taking of delivery of the commodity, or the cancellation of the position by a subsequent offsetting trade. Margin in commodities is not a payment of equity or down payment on the commodity itself, but rather a performance bond or security deposit.

Margin call – A call from a broker to a customer (called a maintenance margin call) or from a clearinghouse to a clearing member (called a variation margin call) demanding the deposit of cash or marketable securities to maintain a requirement for the purchase or short sale of securities or to cover an adverse price movement.

Market risk – The risk of losses arising because of adverse changes in the value of derivatives due to changes in equity prices, interest rates, foreign exchange rates, commodity prices or other market factors. Interest rate risk and foreign exchange risk are sub-sets of market risk.

Material inconsistency – A material inconsistency exists when other information contradicts information contained in the audited financial statements. A material inconsistency may raise doubt about the audit conclusions drawn from audit evidence previously obtained and, possibly, about the basis for the auditor's opinion on the financial statements.

Material misstatement – A significant mistake in financial information which would arise from errors and fraud if it could influence the economic decisions of users taken on the basis of the financial statements.

Material misstatement of fact – A material misstatement of fact in other information exists when such information, not related to matters appearing in the audited financial statements, is incorrectly stated or presented.

Material weaknesses – The weaknesses in internal control that could have a material effect on the financial statements.

Materiality – Information is material if its omission or misstatement could influence the economic decisions of users taken on the basis of the financial statements. Materiality depends on the size of the item or error judged in the particular circumstances of its omission or misstatement. Thus, materiality provides a threshold or cutoff point rather than being a primary qualitative characteristic which information must have if it is to be useful.

Materiality threshold – In substantive testing, the amount of audited difference between the book value of an account and the tested value that an auditor will accept before he determines that an account is misstated.

Matters for Attention of Partners (MAP) – A report by audit managers to be reviewed by a partner or director detailing the audit decisions reached by managers or partners and the reasons for those decisions.

Measurement – see **Financial statement assertions.**

Minutes of the board of directors – The written notes of a meeting of the board of directors which lists the names of the attendees, summarizes the key topics discussed, and reports the results of any votes of the board.

Misappropriation – Employee theft of assets. Especially susceptible accounts are inventory and cash.

Misstatement – Incorrect information as a result of error, inappropriate application of standards, or fraud.

Modeling risk – The risk associated with the imperfections and subjectivity of valuation models used to determine the values of assets or liabilities.

Modified auditor's report – An auditor's report is considered to be modified if either an emphasis of matter paragraph(s) is added to the report or if the opinion is other than unqualified.

Monetary unit sampling – see **Audit sampling.**

Monitoring – For an audit firm a process comprising an ongoing consideration and evaluation of the firm's system of quality control, including a periodic inspection of a selection of completed engagements, designed to enable the firm to obtain reasonable assurance that its system of quality control is operating effectively.

National practices (auditing) – A set of auditing guidelines not having the authority of standards defined by an authoritative body at a country level and commonly applied by auditors in the conduct of an audit or related services.

National standards (auditing) – A set of auditing standards defined by law or regulations or an authoritative body at a country level, the application of which is mandatory in conducting an audit or related services and which should be complied with in the conduct of an audit or related services.

Nature of audit procedures – Primarily substantive (tests of transactions and tests of balances) tests, tests of controls, and analytical procedures.

Negative confirmation – A letter, addressed to the debtor, creditor, or third party, requesting a response only if the recipient disagrees with the amount of the stated account balance.

Negligence of auditor – An auditor in the performance of his duty may not use an appropriate level of care and therefore be legally liable.

- **Ordinary negligence** – The absence of reasonable care that can be expected in similar circumstances.
- **Gross negligence** is reckless behavior with not even slight care.

Network – A group of interconnected computers and terminals; a series of locations tied together by communications channels.

Network firm – An entity under common control, ownership, or management with the firm or any entity that a reasonable and informed third party having knowledge of all relevant information would reasonably conclude as being part of the firm nationally or internationally.

Neural network – A computer model based on the architecture of the brain. It first detects a pattern from data sets then predicts the best classifiers of that pattern, and finally learns from the mistakes.

Non-compliance – Used to refer to acts of omission or commission by the entity being audited, either intentional or unintentional, which are contrary to the prevailing laws or regulations.

Non-executive directors – A member of the board of directors who is not an executive of the entity supervised.

Non-linear contracts – Contracts that have option features where one party has the right, but not the obligation to demand that another party deliver the underlying item to it.

Non-sampling risk – see **Audit sampling**.

Nostros – Accounts held in the bank's name with a correspondent bank.

Notional amount – A number of currency units, shares, bushels, pounds or other units specified in a derivative instrument.

Object of an audit – see **Audit objective**.

Objectivity – A combination of impartiality, intellectual honesty and a freedom from conflicts of interest.

Observation – Observation consists of looking at a process or procedure being performed by others, for example, the observation by the auditor of the counting of inventories by the entity's personnel or the performance of internal control procedures that leave no audit trail.

Occurrence assertion – see **Financial statement assertions**.

Off-balance-sheet instrument – A derivative financial instrument that is not recorded on the balance sheet, although it may be disclosed.

Off-balance-sheet risk – The risk of loss to the entity in excess of the amount, if any, of the asset or liability that is recognized on the balance sheet.

Office – A distinct sub-group, whether organized on geographical or practice lines.

Opening balances – Opening balances are those account balances which exist at the beginning of the period. Opening balances are based upon the closing balances of the prior period and reflect the effects of transactions of prior periods and accounting policies applied in the prior period.

Operational auditing – A study of a specific unit of an organization for the purpose of measuring its performance.

Operational risk – The risk of direct or indirect loss resulting from inadequate or failed internal processes, people and systems, or from external events.

Opinion – The auditor's report contains a clear written expression of opinion on the financial statements as a whole.

- ■ **Adverse opinion** – An adverse opinion is expressed when the effect of a disagreement is so material and pervasive to the financial statements that the auditor concludes that a qualification of the report is not adequate to disclose the misleading or incomplete nature of the financial statements.
- ■ **Disclaimer of opinion** – A disclaimer of opinion is expressed when the possible effect of a limitation on scope is so material and pervasive that the auditor has not been able to obtain sufficient appropriate audit evidence and accordingly is unable to express an opinion on the financial statements.
- ■ **Qualified opinion** – A qualified opinion is expressed when the auditor concludes that an unqualified opinion cannot be expressed but that the effect of any disagreement with management, or limitation on scope, is not so material and pervasive as to require an adverse opinion or a disclaimer of opinion.
- ■ **Unqualified opinion** – An audit opinion expressed when the auditor concludes that the financial statements give a true and fair view (or are presented fairly, in all material respects) in accordance with the identified financial reporting framework. (See also **Modified auditor's report.**)

Option – A contract that gives the holder (or purchaser) the right, but not the obligation to buy (call) or sell (put) a specific or standard commodity, or financial instrument, at a specified price during a specified period (the American option) or at a specified date (the European option).

Ordinary negligence – see **Negligence of auditor**.

Other auditor – see **Auditor**.

Organization chart – A visual diagram of an organization's structure that depicts formal lines of reporting, communication, and responsibility among managers.

Organisation for Economic Co-operation and Development (OECD) – The OECD groups 30 member countries sharing a commitment to democratic government and market economy in a unique forum to discuss, develop and, refine economic and social policies. Countries compare experiences, seek answers to common problems and work to co-ordinate domestic and international policies to help members and non-members deal with an increasingly globalized world. Their exchanges may lead to agreements to act in a formal way, for example by establishing legally binding agreements to crack down on bribery, or codes for free flow of capital and services. Together, they produce around two-thirds of the world's goods and services.

Outcome of the audit process – The end results after planning and performing procedures on financial statements.

Outlier analysis – Analysis of data items (outliers) that are distinctly dissimilar to others, fall outside the standard distribution of data, and ordinarily are viewed as noises or errors in the data sets.

Outside directors – Directors on an entity's board of directors who are neither officers nor employees of the entity.

Parent – The entity in respect of which group financial statements are or should be prepared.

Parent company – The owner of a subsidiary company and this could be a holding company not engaged in a trade or business.

Partner – Any individual with authority, whether through office or otherwise, to bind the firm.

PCs or **personal computers** (also referred to as microcomputers) – Economical yet powerful self-contained general purpose computers consisting typically of a monitor (visual display unit), a case containing the computer electronics, and a keyboard (and mouse). These features may be combined in portable computers (laptops). Programs and data may be stored internally on a hard disk or on removable storage media such as CDs or floppy disks. PCs may be connected to online networks, printers and other devices such as scanners and modems.

Performance reviews – Independent checks on performance by a third party not directly involved in the activity.

Permanent audit file – A file of audit work papers containing all the data that is of continuing interest from year to year.

Personnel – Partners and staff (see **Auditor**).

Physical controls – Procedures to ensure the physical security of assets.

Planning – Planning involves developing a general strategy and a detailed approach for the expected nature, timing, and extent of the audit.

Planning memorandum – A written discussion of the audit strategy and audit plan which incorporates most of the important ideas of the audit.

Policy – Management's dictate of what should be done to effect control. A policy serves as the basis for procedures and their implementation.

Policeman theory – An auditor's job was to focus on arithmetical accuracy and on prevention and detection of fraud.

Population – see **Audit sampling.**

Position – The status of the net of claims and obligations in financial instruments of an entity.

Positive confirmation – The process of obtaining and evaluating audit evidence through a direct communication from a third party in response to a request for information about a particular item affecting assertions made by management in the financial statements. The request for *positive confirmation* asks the recipient (debtor, creditor, or other third party) to confirm agreement or by asking the respondent to fill in information.

Post balance sheet events – see **Subsequent events.**

Power of the test – see **Audit sampling.**

Practice – A sole practitioner, a partnership or a corporation of professional accountants which offers professional services to the public.

Practitioner – A professional accountant in public practice.

Predecessor auditor – The auditor who was previously the auditor of an entity and who has been replaced by an incoming auditor. (See also **Auditor.**)

Preformatting – An online data entry control in which the computer displays a form on the screen and the user fills in the blanks on the form.

Preponderance of evidence – Upon listening to both sides, the weight of the evidence inclines a person with an impartial mind to one side rather than the other.

Presentation and disclosure assertion – see **Financial statement assertions.**

Price risk – The risk of changes in the level of prices due to changes in interest rates, foreign exchange rates, or other factors that relate to market volatility of the underlying rate, index, or price.

Principal auditor – see **Auditor.**

Privity – A relationship that is established by contract between entities. There can be privity of contract without a written agreement under common law.

Probable cause – Serves as the basis for arrest and search warrants.

Procedures to obtain an understanding – Procedures used by the auditor to gather evidence about the design and placement in operation of specific control policies and procedures.

Professional accountant – That person, whether in public practice (including a sole practitioner, partnership or corporate body), industry, commerce, the public sector or education who is a member of an IFAC member body.

Professional accountant in public practice – Each partner or person occupying a position similar to that of a partner, and each employee in a practice providing professional services to a client irrespective of their functional classification (e.g. audit, tax, or consulting) and professional accountants in a practice having managerial responsibilities. This term is also used to refer to a firm of professional accountants in public practice.

Professional service – Any service requiring accountancy or related skills performed by a professional accountant including accounting, auditing, taxation, management consulting, and financial management services.

Professional skepticism – Having a questioning mind and performing a critical assessment of audit evidence through the audit process.

Professional standards – IAASB engagement standards and relevant ethical requirements, which ordinarily comprise Parts A and B of the IFAC Code of Ethics for Professional Accountants and national ethical requirements.

Programming controls – Procedures designed to prevent or detect improper changes to computer programs that are accessed through on-line terminal devices. Access may be restricted by controls such as the use of separate operational and program development libraries, and the use of specialized program library software. It is important for online changes to programs to be adequately documented, controlled and monitored.

Projection – A projection is prospective financial information prepared on the basis of: (a) Hypothetical assumptions about future events and management actions which are not necessarily expected to take place, such as when some entities are in a start-up phase or are considering a major change in the nature of operations; or (b) A mixture of best-estimate and hypothetical assumptions.

Proportionate liability – A defendant is not liable for the entire liability or loss incurred by plaintiffs, but only to the extent to which the loss is attributable to the defendant.

Proposed professional accountant – A professional accountant in public practice who will act as the current financial period's auditor (and who did not audit the prior period's financial statements).

Prospective financial information – Prospective financial information is financial information based on assumptions about events that may occur in the future and possible actions by an entity. Prospective financial information can be in the form of a forecast, a projection or a combination of both. (See also **Forecast** and **Projection**).

Provision – An adjustment to the carrying value of an asset to take account of factors that might reduce the asset's worth to the entity. Sometimes called an allowance.

Prudential ratios – Ratios used by regulators to determine the types and amounts of lending a bank can undertake.

Public Company Accounting Oversight Board (PCAOB) – An independent board established under the US Sarbanes-Oxley Act of 2002 to oversee the audit of public companies that are subject to the securities laws of the USA in order to protect the interests of investors and the public in the preparation of informative, accurate, and independent audit reports.

Public interest companies – Broadly defined by the EU 2004 proposal for statutory audits as listed (publicly-traded) companies, banks, or insurance companies.

Public sector – Refers to national governments, regional (e.g. state, provincial, territorial) governments, local (e.g. city, town) governments and related governmental entities (e.g. agencies, boards, commissions and enterprises).

Publicity – The communication to the public of facts about a professional accountant which are not designed for the deliberate promotion of that professional accountant.

Qualified opinion – see **Modified auditor's report** and **Opinion.**

Quality controls – The policies and procedures adopted by a firm to provide reasonable assurance that all audits done by the firm are being carried out in accordance with the Objective and General Principles Governing an Audit of Financial Statements, as set out in International Standard on Auditing 220 "Quality Control for Audit Work" and International Standard on Quality Control (ISQC).

Ratio analysis – The comparison of relationships between financial statement accounts, the comparison of an account with non-financial data, or the comparison of relationships between firms in an industry.

Reasonable assurance – In an audit engagement, the auditor provides a high, but not absolute, level of assurance, expressed positively in the audit report as reasonable assurance, that the information subject to audit is free of material misstatement.

Reasonable doubt – The degree of certainty a person has in accomplishing or transacting the more important concerns in everyday life.

Reasonableness testing – The analysis of account balances or changes in account balances within an accounting period in terms of their "reasonableness" in light of expected relationships between accounts.

Recalculation – Checking the arithmetical accuracy of source documents and accounting records or performing independent calculations.

Receiving accountant – A professional accountant in public practice to whom the existing accountant or client of the existing accountant has referred audit, accounting, taxation, consulting or similar appointments, or who is consulted in order to meet the needs of the client.

Reconciliation – Relates a specific amount in the accounting records to another source of information (e.g. a reconciliation of accounts payable balances with vendor's statements).

Recording – The creation of documentary evidence of a transaction and its entry into the accounting records.

Regression analysis – The use of statistical models to quantify the auditor's expectation in dollar terms, with measurable risk and precision levels.

Regulatory risk – The risk of loss arising from failure to comply with regulatory or legal requirements in the relevant jurisdiction in which the bank operates. It also includes any loss that could arise from changes in regulatory requirements.

Related auditor – An independent auditor from the group auditor's office, other office of the group auditor's firm, a network firm or another firm operating under common quality control policies and procedures as described in International Standard on Quality Control (ISQC) 1, "Quality Control for Audit, Assurance and Related Services Practices."

Related entity – An entity that has any of the following relationships with the client: (a) An entity that has direct or indirect control over the client provided the client is material to such entity; (b) An entity with a direct financial interest in the client provided that such entity has significant influence over the client and the interest in the client is material to such entity; (c) An entity over which the client has direct or indirect control; (d) An entity in which the client, or an entity related to the client under (c) above, has a direct financial interest that gives it significant influence over such entity and the interest is material to the client and its related entity in (c); and (e) An entity which is under common control with the client (hereinafter a "sister entity") provided the sister entity and the client are both material to the entity that controls both the client and sister entity.

Related party – Parties are considered to be related if one party has the ability to control the other party or exercise significant influence over the other party in making financial and operating decisions.

Related party transaction – A transfer of resources or obligations between related parties, regardless of whether a price is charged.

Related services – Related services comprise reviews, agreed-upon procedures and compilations.

Relational database – A database in which all data elements are logically viewed as being stored in the form of two-dimensional tables called "relations." Each column represents a field where the record's attributes are stored.

Relevance of evidence – The appropriateness (pertinence) of the evidence to the audit objective being tested.

Reliability – The quality of information when it is free from material error and bias and can be depended upon by users to represent faithfully that which it either purports to represent or could reasonably be expected to represent.

Reperformance – Performance of an auditor of a task done by an employee to verify the result of the transaction.

Replacement risk – (Sometimes called performance risk) the risk of failure of a customer or counterparty to perform the terms of a contract. This failure creates the need to replace the failed transaction with another at the current market price. This may result in a loss to the bank equivalent to the difference between the contract price and the current market price.

Reportable conditions – Significant deficiencies in the design or operation of the internal control structure which could adversely affect the organization's ability to record, process, summarize, and report financial data consistent with the assertions of management in the financial statements. (AICPA SAS 60 (AU 325).)

Representativeness – see **Audit sampling**.

Reputational risk – The risk of losing business because of negative public opinion and consequential damage to the entity's reputation arising from failure to properly manage some significant risks, or from involvement in improper or illegal activities by the entity or its senior management, such as money laundering or attempts to cover up losses.

Responsible party – Someone other than the intended user or the practitioner who is responsible for the subject matter (e.g. board of directors, management).

Revenue cycle – The recurring set of business activities and information-processing operations associated with providing goods and services to customers and collecting cash in payment for those sales.

Review – see **Review of financial statements**.

Review of financial statements – The objective of a review of financial statements engagement is to enable an auditor to state whether, on the basis of procedures which do not provide all the evidence that would be required in an audit, anything has come to the auditor's attention that causes the auditor to believe that the financial statements are not prepared, in all material respects, in accordance with an identified financial reporting framework.

Rights and obligations assertions – see **Financial statement assertions.**

Risk management – Using derivatives and other financial instruments to increase or decrease risks associated with existing or anticipated transactions.

Roll forward – An audit procedure whereby a month-end closing (handclose) is audited and then transactions in the intervening months, before the fiscal year-end closing (balance sheet date) are audited and combined with the results of the hand close.

Sales cycle – see **Revenue cycle.**

Sampling risk – see **Audit sampling.**

Sampling unit – see **Audit sampling.**

Sarbanes-Oxley Act of 2002 – This Act was passed by US Congress and signed into law by President W. Bush on July 30, 2002. The Act is intended to establish investor confidence by improving the quality of corporate disclosure and financial reporting, strengthen the independence of accounting firms, and increase the role and responsibility of corporate officers and directors in financial statements and corporate disclosures. It required the US Securities and Exchange Commission (SEC) to create a Public Company Accounting Oversight Board (PCAOB). The most famous sections are on internal control reporting in Section 404, "Management Assessment of Internal Controls." (107th US Congress, 2002, *Sarbanes-Oxley Act of 2002*, Public Law 107–204, Senate and House of Representatives of the United States of America in Congress assembled. Washington, DC, July 30.)

Scope limitation – see **Limitation on scope.**

Scope of an audit – The term "scope of an audit" refers to the audit procedures deemed necessary in the circumstances to achieve the objective of the audit.

Scope of a review – The term "scope of a review" refers to the review procedures deemed necessary in the circumstances to achieve the objective of the review.

Scope paragraph – The paragraph in an audit opinion that describes the nature of the audit and the standards by which it was carried out. It is the second paragraph in an unqualified and qualified audit opinion.

Scope sample – A sample of data from a subsidiary ledger or account classification (customer invoices, shipping documents) based on auditor judgment that represents a variety of types of information from that classification.

Second tier audit firm – An audit firm that is not one of the Big Four (first tier firms), but is one level below them in terms of revenue, assets, etc.

Segment information – Information in the financial statements regarding distinguishable components or industry and geographical aspects of an entity.

Segregation of duties – A segregation of the following activities in an organization: custody of assets, accounting (or recording), and authorization.

Self-interest threat – Occurs when an auditor could benefit from the financial interest in, or other self-interests conflict with, an assurance client.

Self-review threat – Occurs when (a) when any product or judgment of a previous assurance engagement or non-assurance engagement needs to be re-evaluated in reaching conclusions on the assurance engagement; or (b) when a member of the assurance team was previously a director or officer of the assurance client or was an employee in a position to exert direct and significant influence over the subject matter of the assurance engagement.

Sensitivity Analysis – A general class of models designed to assess the risk of loss in market-risk-sensitive instruments based upon hypothetical changes in market rates or prices.

Sequence check – An edit check that determines if a batch of input data is in the proper numerical or alphabetical sequence.

Service organization – A client may use a service organization such as one that executes transactions and maintains related accountability or records transactions and processes related data (e.g. a computer information systems service organization).

Settlement date – The date on which derivative transactions are to be settled by delivery or receipt of the underlying product or instrument in return for payment of cash.

Settlement risk – The risk that one side of a transaction will be settled without value being received from the customer or counterparty. This will generally result in the loss to the bank of the full principal amount.

Side agreements – see **Side letters**.

Side letters – Agreements made outside the standard company contracts. These otherwise undisclosed agreements may be signed by senior officers, but not approved by the board of directors.

Significance – Significance is related to materiality of the financial statement assertion affected.

Significant risk – A type of business risk that generally relates to judgmental matters and significant non-routine transactions requiring special audit consideration.

Small entity – A small entity is any entity in which:

(a) There is concentration of ownership and management in a small number of individuals (often a single individual); and

(b) One or more of the following are also found:
  (i) few sources of income;
  (ii) unsophisticated record-keeping;
  (iii) limited internal controls together with the potential for management override of controls.

Small entities will ordinarily display characteristic (a), and one or more of the characteristics included under (b).

Solicitation – An approach to a potential client for the purpose of offering professional services.

Solvency risk – The risk of loss arising from the possibility of the bank not having sufficient funds to meet its obligations, or from the bank's inability to access capital markets to raise required funds.

Special purpose auditor's report – A report issued in connection with the independent audit of financial information other than an auditor's report on financial statements, including:

(a) Financial statements prepared in accordance with a comprehensive basis of accounting other than International Accounting Standards or national standards;
(b) Specified accounts, elements of accounts, or items in a financial statement;
(c) Compliance with contractual agreements;
(d) Summarized financial statements.

Special purpose engagement – An independent audit of financial information other than financial statements in accordance with IFRS or the national financial reporting standards, including:

(a) Financial statements prepared in accordance with a comprehensive basis of accounting other than International Accounting Standards or national standards;
(b) Specified accounts, elements of accounts, or items in a financial statement;
(c) Compliance with contractual agreements;
(d) Summarized financial statements.

Special purpose entity (SPE) – Defined as an entity (e.g. corporation, partnership, trust, joint venture) created for a specific purpose or activity. SPEs may be used to transfer assets and liabilities from an entity; accounted for as a gain for that entity. Between 1993 and 2001, Enron created over 3,000 SPEs.

Speculation – Entering into an exposed position to maximize profits, that is, assuming risk in exchange for the opportunity to profit on anticipated market movements.

Staff – Individuals, other than the engagement partner, involved in performing engagements, including any experts employed or engaged by the firm in connection with that engagement.

Stakeholders – Individuals and entities who have a stake (claim, share, involvement, interest) in a company. Stakeholders may include shareholders, employees, government, banks, etc.

Standards of proof – Concepts that describe the quality of evidence for most legal systems. There are four standards of proof: (1) beyond a reasonable doubt, (2) preponderance of evidence, (3) clear and convincing evidence, and (4) probable cause.

Statistical sampling – see **Audit sampling**.

Statutory audit – Audits established by law.

Stratification – see **Audit sampling**.

Stress testing – Testing a valuation model by using assumptions and initial data outside normal market circumstances and assessing whether the model's predictions are still reliable.

Subject matter – In an assurance engagement, the topic about which the assurance is conducted. Subject matter could be financial statements, statistical information, non-financial performance indicators, capacity of a facility, etc.

Subsequent events – International Accounting Standard 10 identifies two types of events both favorable and unfavorable occurring after period end:

(a) Those that provide further evidence of conditions that existed at period end;
(b) Those that are indicative of conditions that arose subsequent to period end.

Subsidiary company – A firm in which a controlling interest is owned by another company, called a parent company.

Substantive procedures – Substantive procedures are tests performed to obtain audit evidence to detect material misstatements in the financial statements, and are of two types: (a) tests of details of transactions and balances; and (b) analytical procedures.

Substantive testing – see **Substantive procedures**.

Sufficiency – The measure of the quantity of audit evidence.

Sufficient appropriate audit evidence – *Sufficiency* is the measure of the quantity (amount) of audit evidence. *Appropriateness* is the measure of the quality of audit evidence and its relevance to a particular assertion and its reliability.

Suitably qualified external person – An individual outside the audit firm with the capabilities and competence to act as an engagement partner, for example, a partner of another firm or an employee (with appropriate experience) of either a professional accountancy body whose members may perform audits and reviews of historical financial information, or other assurance or related services engagements, or of an organization that provides relevant quality control services.

Summarized financial statements – An entity may prepare financial statements summarizing its annual audited financial statements for the purpose of informing user groups interested in the highlights only of the entity's financial performance and position.

Summary of procedures description schedule – A schedule which summarizes the result of audit procedures performed.

Supreme Audit Institution – The public body of a state which, however designated, constituted, or organized, exercises by virtue of law, the highest public auditing function of that state.

Suspense file – An account used to balance transactions when there is an error, the resolution of which is not possible at that time.

Sustainability – The set of perceptual and analytic abilities, ecological wisdom, and practical wherewithal essential to the meshing of human purposes with the larger patterns and flows of the natural world, and careful study of those patterns and flows to inform human purposes. As a value, it refers to giving equal weight in your decisions to the future as well as the present. Actions are sustainable if:

(a)   There is a balance between resources used and resources regenerated.
(b)   Resources are as clean or cleaner at end use as at beginning.
(c)   The viability, integrity, and diversity of natural systems are restored and maintained.
(d)   They lead to enhanced local and regional self-reliance.
(e)   They help create and maintain community and a culture of place.
(f)   Each generation preserves the legacies of future generations.

Swaption – A combination of a swap and an option.

Technical audit quality – The degree to which an audit meets a consumer's expectations with regard to the detection and reporting of errors and irregularities regarding the audited company and its financial statements.

Term structure of interest rates – The relationship between interest rates of different terms. When interest rates of bonds are plotted graphically according to their interest rate terms, this is called the "yield curve." Economists and investors believe that the shape of the yield curve reflects the market's future expectation for interest rates and thereby provide predictive information concerning the conditions for monetary policy.

Terms of the engagement – Agreed to conditions or terms to the employment of an auditing firm by a client to provide a specific service for a given period of time which is generally recorded in an engagement letter or other suitable form, such as a contract.

Test of reasonableness schedule – A schedule containing information that enables the auditor to evaluate whether the client's balance appears to include a misstatement considering the circumstances.

Tests of control – Tests of control are performed to obtain audit evidence about the effectiveness of the:

(a) Design of the accounting and internal control systems, that is, whether they are suitably designed to prevent or detect and correct material misstatements;

(b) Operation of the internal controls throughout the period.

Tests of details of balances – Audit tests that substantiate the ending balance of a general ledger or line item in a financial statement.

Tests of details of transactions – Audit procedures related to examining the processing of particular classes of transactions through the accounting system. Tests of transactions are usually performed for major classes of transactions.

Theory of Inspired Confidence – see **Inspired Confidence, theory of**.

Third parties – Someone other than the principals directly involved in a transaction or agreement.

Tick marks – Symbols used by the auditor to indicate the nature and extent of procedures applied in specific circumstances. Tick marks are notations directly on the working paper schedules. Tick marks are generally done by hand with a pen or pencil alongside a specific item.

Timing of audit procedures – Timing concerns the day on which audit proceedures occur and in what sequence. For example, are procedures planned at the end of the period or at an earlier (interim) date.

Tolerable error – see **Audit sampling**.

Tort – A wrongful act, damage or injury done willfully, negligently or in circumstances where liability is strictly applied.

Tracing – An audit procedure whereby the auditor selects sample items from basic source documents and proceeds forward through the accounting system to find the final recording of the transaction (e.g. in the ledger).

Trading – The buying and selling of financial instruments for short-term profit.

Transaction logs – Reports that are designed to create an audit trail for each on-line transaction. Such reports often document the source of a transaction (terminal, time and user) as well as the transaction's details.

Transfer risk – The risk of loss arising when counterparty's obligation is not denominated in the counterparty's home currency. The counterparty may be unable to obtain the currency of the obligation irrespective of the counterparty's particular financial condition.

Transparency – For corporations, practices that make rules, regulations, and accounting methods open and accessible to the public. Transparency includes concepts like openness, reporting and disclosure.

Trend analysis – The analysis of changes in an account balance over time.

Trial balance – A listing of the account balances from the general ledger, prepared at the end of the accounting period.

Triple bottom line – Sustainability reporting in terms of economic, environmental, and social performance based on Global Reporting Initiative.

Type I error – see **Audit sampling**.

Type II error – see **Audit sampling**.

Unadjusted audit differences – These are proposed adjusting entries with accompanying written justifications suggested by the auditor to bring the account balance on the company financial statements in line with the audited account balance.

Unasserted claim – A potential legal claim against a client where the condition for a claim exists but no claim has been filed.

Uncertainty – An uncertainty is a matter whose outcome depends on future actions or events not under the direct control of the entity but that may affect the financial statements.

Underlying – A specified interest rate, security price, commodity price, foreign exchange rate, index of prices or rates, or other variable. An underlying may be a price or rate of an asset or liability, but it is not the asset or liability itself.

Unqualified opinion – see **Opinion**.

User control procedures – Procedures in audit testing of documentation representing manual checks of the completeness and accuracy of computer output against source documents and other input.

Valuation assertion – see **Financial statement assertions**.

Valuation risk – The risk that the fair value of the derivative is determined incorrectly.

Valuation services – Involve the valuation of matters material to the financial statements and where the valuation involves a significant degree of subjectivity.

Value at risk (VAR) – A general class of models that provides a probabilistic assessment of the risk of loss in market-risk-sensitive instruments over a period of time, with a selected likelihood of occurrences based upon selected confidence intervals.

Volatility – A measure of the variability of the price of an asset or index.

Vostros – Accounts held by the bank in the name of a correspondent bank.

Vouching – The use of documentation to support recorded transactions or amounts. It is an audit process whereby the auditor starts with an account balance and goes backwards through the accounting system to the source document.

Walk-through test – Involves tracing a few transactions through the accounting system.

Weakness in internal control – The absence of adequate controls which increases the risk of misstatement in the financial statements.

Wide area network (WAN) – A communications network that transmits information across an expanded area such as between plant sites, cities, and nations. WANs allow for online access to applications from remote terminals. Several LANs can be interconnected in a WAN.

Working papers – Also known as *work papers* these are a record of the auditor's planning; nature, timing, and extent of the auditing procedures performed; and results of such procedures and the conclusions drawn from the evidence obtained. Working papers may be in the form of data stored on paper, film, electronic media, or other media.

Write-offs – Costs related to loss in value of an asset (non-collection of accounts receivable, loss in value of equipment, etc.) which are charged to expense or loss.

Written option – The writing, or sale, of an option contract that obligates the writer to fulfill the contract should the holder choose to exercise the option.

XBRL (Extensible Business Reporting Language) – Based on XML, this is a tagging system for financial data. It provides taxonomy for US Generally Accepted Accounting Principles and International Financial Reporting Standards, and can be used on a transactional basis. An offshoot of **XML**, XBRL is a freely licensed, open technology standard that makes it possible to store and/or transfer data along with the complex hierarchies, data-processing rules and descriptions.

XML (eXtensible Markup Language) – A set of rules, guidelines, or conventions for designing text formats for such data, in a way that produces files that are easy to generate and read (by a computer), that are unambiguous, and that avoid common pitfalls, such as lack of extensibility, lack of support for internationalization/localization, and platform-dependency. XML is an extension of the World Wide Web Consortium's (W3C) Standard Generalized Markup Language, SGML that allows creation of custom (extensible) data tags, provides a universal data format, allows data objects to be serialized into text streams, and can be parsed by all internet browsers.

Index